Cover:
STRIP MORPHOLOGIES AND HEALING ENVIRONMENTS by Daniel Coll I Capdevila

ISBN 978 1 902902 53 1

Printed by Cassochrome, Belgium.

© 2006 Architectural Association and the authors.
Reprinted 2008.
No part of this book may be reproduced in any manner whatsoever
without written permission from the publisher, except in the
context of reviews.

A catalogue of AA Publications is available from:
36 Bedford Square, London WC1B 3ES
T +44 (0)20 7887 4021 F +44 (0)20 7414 0782
publications@aaschool.ac.uk
aaschool.ac.uk/publications

MORPHO-ECOLOGIES

Edited by Michael Hensel and Achim Menges

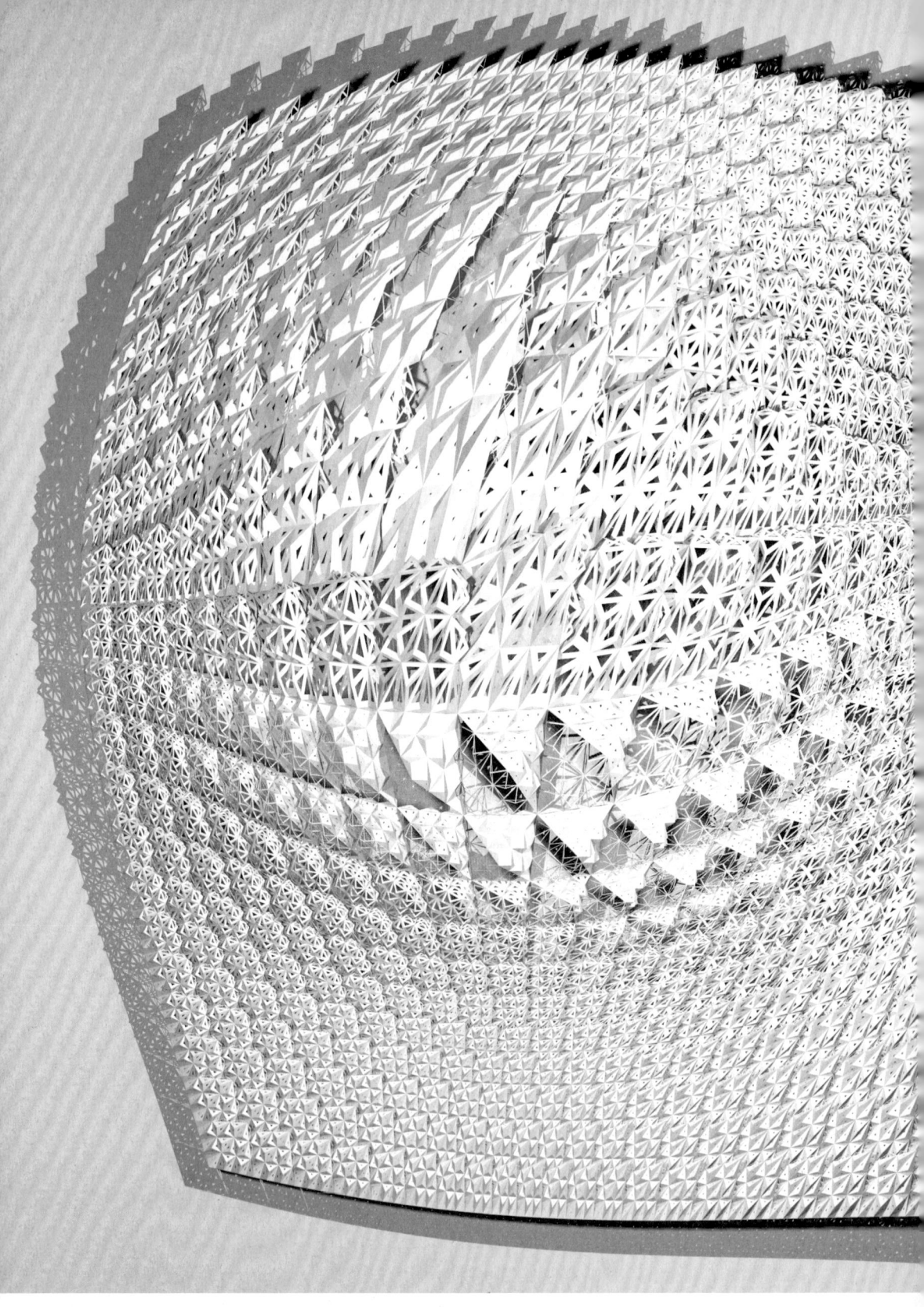
Transitional Morphologies by Dae Song Lee: bird's-eye view of a non-uniform wide-span spaceframe.

FOREWORD by Michael Hensel and Achim Menges	9
ACKNOWLEDGEMENTS	10
PREFACE by Brett Steele	11
INTRODUCTION by Michael Weinstock	12

PART 1

Morpho-Ecologies – Towards an Inclusive Discourse on Heterogeneous Architecture Michael Hensel and Achim Menges	16

PART 2

Material Systems – Proto-Architectures Introduction by Michael Hensel and Achim Menges	62
01 Spread Bundle Assembly by Judson Moore and Michael Robinson Comment by Wolf Mangelsdorf	68
02 Elastic Rod Assembly by Shireen Han Comment by Wolf Mangelsdorf	78
03 Complex Brick Assemblies by Defne Sunguroglu Comment by Wolf Mangelsdorf	86
04 Performative Morphologies – Vertical Helix by Neri Oxman	100
05 Discontinuous Strut Lattices by Jeremy Richey and Nathan Smith Comment by Christopher Hight	112
06 Fibrous Organisations by Cordula Stach Comment by Ludo Grooteman	122
07 Integral Envelope – Stick Morphology by Nazaneen Roxanne Shafaie Comment by Simon Beames	132
08 Photolepidote by Alexia Petridis Comment by Sean Lally	142
09 Strip Morphologies and Healing Environments by Daniel Coll I Capdevila Comment by Wolf Mangelsdorf	156
10 Continuous Laminae by Aleksandra Jaeschke Comment by Eva Scheffler	170
11 Meta-Patch by Joseph Kellner and Dave Newton Comments by Julian Vincent and Michael Weinstock	184

12 Transitional Morphologies by Dae Song Lee	196
13 Pleated Composites by Edouard Cabay	208
14 Membrane Organisation by Pavlos Sideris	218
15 Adaptive Pneumatic Shelters by Hani Fallaha Comment by Wolf Mangelsdorf	232
16 Integral Pneumatic Assembly by Mustasha Musa	244
17 Porous Mats by Gabriel Sanchiz Garin	250
18 Aggregates 01 by Eiichi Matsuda Comment by Theo Lorenz	262
19 Aggregates 02 by Anne Hawkins and Catie Newell Comment by Christopher Hight	274
20 Aggregates 03 by Gen Takahashi	286

PART 3

Differentiation in Nature and Design – Six Essays Introduction by Michael Hensel and Achim Menges	296
Differentiation, Hierarchy and Energy in Natural Systems Michael Weinstock	298
Imperfection as a Design Parameter Julian Vincent	308
Adaptable Equilibrium Wolf Mangelsdorf	322
Beyond the Algorithm – Seeking Differentiated Structures through Alternatives to Computational Design Processes Mark Burry	334
Architecture of the Many Peter Trummer	348
Moiré Affects – Epistemologies of Measure, Order and Differentiation in Modern Architecture Christopher Hight	354
BIBLIOGRAPHY	368
CONTRIBUTORS	370

Transitional Morphologies by Dae Song Lee: axonometric and close-up view of a non-uniform wide-span spaceframe.

Nothing happens in living Nature that does not bear some relation to the whole. The empirical evidence may seem quite isolated, we may view our experiments as mere isolated facts, but this is not to say that they are, in fact, isolated. The question is: how can we find the connection between these phenomena, these events? Johann Wolfgang von Goethe, 1792

Just a year after the launch of *Morpho-Ecologies* we have been both surprised and delighted by how well the book has sold. Such a positive response is truly overwhelming and we are greatly indebted to our readership for their interest and to Brett Steele, director of the Architectural Association, for having made the first book and now this reprint possible.

In the year since the publication of *Morpho-Ecologies* the impact of human intervention on global climate change has become increasingly evident. As the built environment plays a critical role in this development, architects face a serious challenge that entails questioning the way we think, practise and build. While the architectural community's fascination with the notion of morphogenesis continues undiminished, it seems that the *ecological* component of our approach is becoming increasingly relevant. This book, which at first glance may appear as merely documenting a disparate, experimental body of work, constitutes the beginning of a multifaceted long-term project that seeks to formulate a more sustainable, performance-oriented architecture. The thoughts and experiments presented here provide the means to question the preconceptions that are deeply entrenched in the conceptualisation of architecture as a material practice.

The continuing pursuit of this research is manifested in many new collaborations that have arisen out of *Morpho-Ecologies*. Our studios and activities have spread over the globe, from Norway to Chile, Germany and Australia, and an increasing number of research commissions have led to full-scale pilot projects. Through the dissemination of these activities, and this reprint of *Morpho-Ecologies*, we hope to convey the sincerity of our effort to set out a paradigm for design and sustainability that will invigorate our human environment while protecting our biosphere.

Michael Hensel and Achim Menges

London
January 2008

First of all we would like to thank Brett Steele, the Director of the AA School, for making this book possible and for supporting it generously.

We are extremely grateful to the students who participated in the AA's Dip 4 Morpho-Ecologies programme and in the Generative Proto-Architectures programmes at Rice School of Architecture and Rotterdam Academy of Architecture and Urban Design. Their work, shown in chapter 2, has inspired and carried forward the research we have undertaken together.

We would like to offer our gratitude to the speakers in the Differentiated Structures in Nature and Design Symposium held at the AA, and the other contributors whose papers are included in chapter 3, as well as the various authors of the comments that accompany many of the projects in chapter 2.

In particular we would like to thank George Jeronimidis for providing cutting-edge biomimetic engineering support; his work underlies central aspects of the research presented here. We would like to thank Frei Otto, Christina Kanstinger and Michael Weinstock for collaborating in the Maeda form-finding workshop at Hooke Park, as well as Buro Happold, and especially Michael Cook, Wolf Mangelsdorf and Nikolaos Stathopoulos, for their vital contributions to the research and the content of this book.

Many thanks to Bentley Systems, for most generously enabling us to work with the beta-version of the Generative Components software package, and in particular to Robert Aish, director of Research, for his unwavering help and support. Invaluable advice and teaching of GC in countless sessions was provided by the members and associates of the Smart Geometry Group, especially Hugh Whitehead, director of the Specialist Modelling Group at Foster and Partners, Chris Williams, Francis Aish and Roly Hudson.

Many thanks, too, to David Rutten for his most generous support with Rhino scripting.

We are indebted to Birger Sevaldson and Steinar Killi, of the Institute for Industrial Design at the Oslo School of Architecture, for their extensive collaboration in and sponsorship of rapid-prototyping, as well as to the University of Art and Design HfG Offenbach, for making possible and sponsoring the CAM production of full-scale prototypes.

Furthermore we would like to thank Simos Yannas, director of the AA's Environment and Energy programme, for his help and support with environmental analysis, and Mark Burry, for many vital discussions about morphology.

We are particularly grateful to Aleksandra Jaeschke from AION, for carrying out the graphic design of the book with great skill, dedication and patience.

For years of exciting collaboration, scholarly support and friendship, we would like to thank Michael Weinstock, Christopher Hight, Birger Sevaldson, Ludo Grooteman, Theo Lorenz and Pascal Schöning.

Finally, we would like to thank our families and friends, without whose loving support we would not have made it through the intense work, and who persistently reminded us that we too need to maintain our life functions while writing about a biological paradigm for architectural design.

Michael Hensel and Achim Menges

Architectural Association
June 2006

Morpho-Ecologies brings together twenty student projects undertaken over the past three years within the AA's Diploma Unit 4, led by Michael Hensel and Achim Menges. In significant ways, it can be seen to be a user's manual – which I take to be a refreshing format for contributing to today's most advanced computational approaches to questions of architectural form, structure and organisation. Taken together, the projects, commentaries and accompanying in-depth essays present the reader with a book literally for using – and not just contemplating – new design concepts, tools, techniques and organisational principles.

In an era increasingly defined by the demands of information exchange and communication, when fields like architecture are operating more and more like living, vital knowledge economies (or ecologies), learning structures demand the same kind of attention to inventive thinking, design and testing as any other kind of structure. That is what you will find on display here, in many exhilarating forms. We are presented with a book infused with the different kinds of learning of its different contributors: the students who have undertaken the projects, the tutors and critics who have shaped and reacted to their larger agenda, and the authors who have provided longer texts contemplating on the related theoretical background to the projects and their topics. Think of *Morpho-Ecologies* as a learning machine, in which each of the projects in turn is revealed on its own terms as part of this larger, focused effort towards architectural knowledge. It is a satisfying, engaging book that avoids the more familiar formats for this kind of contemporary architectural work: either the exceedingly dry academic papers of a purely technical kind, or (at the opposite end of the spectrum) glossy project photos dedicated to giving us the appearance of an architectural project or design experiment. By design, *Morpho-Ecologies* creates (or better yet, *differentiates*) a convincing space between these two extremes, and so offers us a format for architectural thinking that is at once technical and analytical, yet accessible and visual.

Thanks here must go to the many people that have played a vital role in achieving this book and the year-long student projects it contains: to our brilliant students for all their hard work and total dedication; to Aleksandra Jaeschke for the design of the book; to the many authors who have provided the valuable commentaries and essays that accompany the projects; and finally, to Michael Hensel and Achim Menges for their immense effort and energy in bringing together the entire undertaking, which opens up many paths for future architectural projects, investigation and thinking.

Brett Steele
Director, AA School

Architectural Association
September 2006

INTRODUCTION by Michael Weinstock

Our inheritance of the existing urban fabric of buildings and public spaces carries the implication of continuity and of a future existence – the continuing presence of the past posits the future. It is fruitless to emulate the past, and unnecessary to eradicate it, as the paradigmatic changes in the concepts and material practices of the contemporary world have produced a systemic change in the cultural, social and industrial context in which architecture is conceived and made. The material practice of architecture is at the beginning of a substantial reconfiguration, in which the convergence of fields of knowledge of biology, structures, engineering and computation has ignited an evolutionary process that is unclosed and not wholly reducible to a rigid set of prescribed forms and spaces.

The conceptual apparatus of architecture has always given a central role to the relations of mankind and nature. The human body has been a source of harmonious proportions and the shapes of many living organisms have been adapted for architectural use. Architecture's current fascination with nature is a reflection of the availability of new modes of imaging the interior structures of plants and animals, of electron microscopy of the intricate and very small, together with the mathematics of biological processes.

In the biological sciences the study of forms and their categorisation, or morphology, was the first instrumental set of zoology, predating evolutionary theory. More recently morphology has outstripped its historical confines, becoming morphogenesis, with an emphasis on the forces that generate living forms, on how forms and environments come into being. Biology has co-opted many formerly distinct disciplines in a series of exchanges between chemists, mathematicians and physicists. While the erosion of the rigid boundaries between the inherited taxonomy of 'pure' disciplines in the sciences has yet to find a full counterpart in the world of architecture, there are many examples in this book of such interdisciplinary work that sets out the parameters of future architectures.

It is logical to assume that future architectures cannot be entirely projected from the present. There has to be a dialogue between the new forms and spaces being designed and constructed today and their latent future. New modes of occupying urban and architectural space have emerged, with new rights of passage and a more complex relation to time – transit zones and interchange spaces, spaces of engagement with computers and media, temporary assemblies of consumption and solitude where communication is by codes and images as much as conversation. The boundaries between interior and exterior space, between public and private territories, are no longer unremittingly fixed. The increasing fluidity of these boundaries is accompanied by blurred and graduated territorial demarcations, allowing spaces to flow into one another, programmes to be unrestrained within building envelopes, and connectivity and integration to be enhanced. The experience of these spaces is central to contemporary existence, and we are bound to integrate them into our designs for future places. Designing and constructing adaptable structures and spaces requires us to recognise not only individual but also group dynamics, as well as the episodic, ephemeral nature of metropolitan experiences.

In order for architecture to become capable of accepting a diversity of uses and functions, there must be a critical revision of existing material and building systems. The search for new material systems begins with the articulation of boundaries as gradient thresholds between environmental conditions. Light conditions and acoustic or thermal gradients can be used to differentiate spaces, especially when aligned with topographical manipulations, and these fluid thresholds are intrinsically dynamic as the time of day or season varies. Environmental thresholds have yet another advantage over solid boundaries, in that they allow inhabitants to make choices from a range of conditions, to construct more individual spatial and programmatic experiences.

For the past 10 years Michael Hensel has been Master of Diploma Unit 4 at the Architectural Association. During this time there have been three distinct phases of research and exploration, each characterised by a clearly differentiated programme.

For the first three years, from 1996 to 1999, Michael taught with Ben van Berkel and Ludo Grooteman. The emphasis was on exploring new forms of urban space and built fabric; their design experiments attempted to rethink discrete building typologies and merge them into a continuous urban fabric. Organisational strategies and advanced digital modelling became their methodological toolset, supported and extended by operative diagramming techniques.

In the second phase, from 1999 to 2003 (with Ludo Grooteman), the research focus shifted to a more directly spatial agenda, in which the requirements for multiple programmes drove a search for spatial organisations combining landscape and urban forms. Temporal organisations for architectures were investigated through time-dependent programming and the material strategies became more complex. Differentiated material and construction systems began to appear in their design experiments, to facilitate more complex programmatic relations that combined urban activities with intense agricultural production. At the same time, the technical agenda of the design experiments developed, integrating material behaviour, system behaviour and manufacturing fabrication processes into the design strategies.

The third phase, the Morpho-Ecologies research agenda, commenced in 2003, with Achim Menges. The intricate relations of morphology and environment became the focus of exploration, with the development of form-found material systems coupled to environmental performance. A central part of this work is extensive physical modelling, from models to construction-scale prototypes, using simple as well as advanced CAD/CAM/CAE technologies. At the same time Michael and Achim have conducted studios at Rice School of Architecture and the Rotterdam Academy for Architecture and Urban Design, further investigating specific aspects of performative material systems.

The union of morphogenetic strategies for design, and the experimental development of material systems that can modulate and in turn be modulated by environmental conditions, challenges the traditional relations of space and material as well as the common processes of optimisation that emphasise the most efficient performance of a single function for the least amount of material. Natural systems provide a new conceptual model for these design experiments, as they are 'efficient' in a very different way to the traditional architectural and engineering understanding of efficiency. For example, in plant tissues the material organisation of the tubes that transport fluids and nutrients up and down the stem also provides structural support, and has a role in managing the changes in compressive or tension forces in neighbouring tissues that in turn produce changes in stem curvature and orientation. Multiple functions are integrated into natural material systems, which are complex hierarchical arrangements of material, and redundancy of material and capacity is an important strategy for efficient adaptability.

The work presented in this book brings together theoretical texts and an exemplary set of inventive material experiments that define a cartography of future architectures. It has been my pleasure and privilege to be part of a broad collaboration that is extending across geographical and disciplinary boundaries.

Michael Weinstock

Architectural Association
August 2006

MORPHO-ECOLOGIES

Above all we must remember that nothing that exists or comes into being, lasts or passes can be thought of as entirely isolated, entirely unadulterated. One thing is always permeated, accompanied, covered, or enveloped by another; it produces effects and endures them. And when so many things work through one another, where are we to find what governs and what serves, what leads the way and what follows? Johann Wolfgang von Goethe[1]

Biology is the science of life; it is concerned with the living. For this reason architectural design must go beyond using biology as merely a source of convenient metaphors or a superficial formal repertoire. Ecology is the study of the relationship between organisms and their environment. This definition also suits the discipline of architecture surprisingly well: in our view one of the central tasks of architecture is to provide opportunities for habitation through specific material and energetic interventions in the physical environment. Correlating morphogenesis and ecology, we have developed a new framework for architectural design that is firmly rooted within a biological paradigm and thus concerned with issues of higher-level functionality and performance capacity. We have named this approach Morpho-Ecology (ME).

SPATIAL STRATEGIES, SOCIAL FORMATIONS
AND PROGRAMMATIC RAMIFICATIONS

Over the course of history many different spatial strategies and arrangements have been deployed for the design of the human habitat, from universal to interstitial space, from stratified to entwined space, from the cellular room to *terrain vague*, and so forth. Today, however, the built environment is dominated by only two types of spatial organisation: the open plan and the corridor/cellular room arrangement. Both are defined by a specific attitude towards the boundary threshold. The open plan arrangement confines the boundary threshold to a perimeter condition that, at its most extreme, coincides with the building envelope, while the corridor and cellular room arrangement multiplies the internal boundary threshold in order to control circulation and achieve privacy.

In his seminal essay 'Figures, Doors and Passages'[2] Robin Evans describes how the 'medieval matrix of interconnected rooms' was supplanted, in seventeenth-century England, by the model of the corridor with rooms opening onto it. In this essay he connects social formation with spatial arrangement, discussing the medieval matrix in relation to the accidental social encounters between those who passed through these rooms and those who inhabited them. According to Evans, the matrix of interconnected rooms belongs to a culture of the carnal, of touch, immediacy and co-habitation. The shift towards the corridor model apparently originated from the need of the landed gentry to uncouple the space inhabited by their family from that of the servants. Social encounters became controlled, and proximity turned into social division, perhaps even exclusion. In his conclusion Evans asks why the corridor model still prevails as a predominant spatial organisation, when the social arrangement that brought it into being is no longer significant. He alerts the reader to the need to rethink spatial organisation via the arrangement of material boundary thresholds and its possible implications for social formation.

How did we arrive, then, at the current predominance of these spatial arrangements? The development of a spatial politic occurred alongside the development of industrial standards and fabrication, with the latter reinforcing the former. Modernist discourse postulated universal space as the key paradigm for democratic space. The open plan, ideally extended to an infinite grid, with the boundary threshold eventually condensed to immateriality, or at least to the thinness of a sheet of glass, was meant to deliver equal opportunities for inhabitation. Universal space was to be achieved through the modularisation and standardisation of building elements, with each element or system being required to perform one principal function (e.g. primary structure, secondary structure, sun-shading, rain-cover or climate envelope) to an optimum level. This single-objective approach to optimisation was based on an understanding of efficiency that entails using the minimum amount of material and energy to achieve projected structural capacity and performance. However, the desire to reduce the use of materials raised questions of liability and led to the addition of a required percentage of performance capacity to guarantee functionality and safety. Redundancy was, and still is, largely understood as an unfortunate necessity. A critical revision begs the question whether an alternative understanding of optimisation, efficiency and redundancy in relation to multi-performative material systems can open up a very different take on spatial organisation, environmental modulation and, ultimately, social formation.

The homogenisation of interior environments reached its first real peak in the late 1950s, with the development, by the 'Quickborner Team for Planning and Organisation',[3] of the Bürolandschaft – a vast open-plan office landscape in which clusters of workstations were arranged according to anticipated workflow. It was argued that a homogeneous interior environment minimised any visual, aural or tactile distractions, and a set of rules for environmental homogenisation was defined and applied accordingly. This form of spatial-environmental homogenisation was eventually applied to other building types as building standards were established ubiquitously.

In recent decades architectural discourse has largely moved away from universal space and declared a preference for heterogeneous space. This preference is evident in two distinct strategies. The first entails a two-step approach to varied space, commencing from generic shells that are subsequently tailored to the needs of their eventual inhabitants. The second strategy involves the design of exotically shaped buildings that from the outset are varied in expression and spatiality. The first strategy embraces modularised building systems, while the second operates on the differentiation of established building elements (individually articulated frame and tile components, for instance). Both strategies concur, however, in their embracing of standardised requirements for interiors and a limited range of building systems. The latter aspect is evident in some recently developed parametric modelling software that is specifically informed and constrained by established engineering and manufacturing protocols relative to material and machining technologies. Herein lies the problem. While plan organisation, envelope form, and fittings and finishes may have become more varied, material and building systems are not being critically reviewed; they are still geared towards established types and mono-functionality, while uniformity prevails in the interior climate and condition zoning. Architecture thus remains 'Neufertised' – as does our social environment.

Combining optimised mono-functional elements or sub-systems with homogenised comfort zones often requires an abundance of heating, cooling, air-conditioning, ventilation, lighting and servicing equipment. While capital energy, embodied in the materials and building processes, may be kept fairly low, the operational energy required to run a building can be extremely high. Moreover, a homogenised interior environment simply cannot satisfy multiple and conflicting habitation needs.

Rather than informing the design process from a very early stage, environmental design and engineering has tended to be a question of post-design optimisation. Some people may argue that architecture should not venture into the field of environmental engineering – that it should instead revel in the freedom of expression it has recently gained as a result of divorcing form even from material and manufacturing constraints. We argue that architects have always already 'engineered' environments. The question is whether this is to be done well and in an instrumental way, or whether architects will instead choose to remain ignorant, pursuing formal expression without regard for the environmental repercussions.

A first inroad into an alternative approach can be found in Reyner Banham's *The Architecture of the Well-tempered Environment*,[4] which is enjoying a revival among a new generation of architects.[5] Here Banham discusses the potential for learning from 'societies who do not build substantial structures [but instead] inhabit a space whose external boundaries are vague, adjustable and rarely regular'.[6] He distinguishes between two traditions: one that articulates the boundary threshold as a material condition, and another that operates through the opportunistic use of environmental gradient thresholds. According to Banham the latter establish environments, such as the campfire, that dynamically differentiate spaces by providing exposure to a spectrum of environmental conditions across a gradient. In contrast to the dichotomous tectonic divisions between inside and outside, private and public, warm and cold, these gradient and dynamic threshold conditions allow for differentiation and individual choice based on subjective needs and experiences. Banham posits that this understanding 'might prove to be of fundamental relevance for power-operated environments',[7] suggesting an alternative approach towards sustainability. This implies not only environmental sustainability, but also social sustainability relative to the conditions for collective inhabitation provided by heterogeneous and dynamic environments. The challenge is to formulate a synthesised approach based on a synergetic relation between material thresholds and environmental dynamics. The ME approach rejects the Newtonian conception of space as absolute, merely a container for the bodies contained within – a conception that gives absolute predominance to the material boundary threshold. Instead it is based on a relative notion of space, as championed by Leibniz and later Einstein, in which space is no longer just a given entity but is instead constructed through social operations and the local experience of space-time.[8]

The vast majority of the architecture designed and constructed today consists of substantial structures and hard environmental divisions packaged together with standardised building systems and statistically established homogeneous interior environments. This architecture takes no further account of individual or collective inhabitation, whether in the process of design, or by analysing emergent patterns of inhabitation and social formation once a project is built. Even the very notion of a project being 'finished' erodes the fact that performance unfolds in time and must therefore be analysed perpetually. The actual project, the evolving rather than the projected ecological dynamic inherent in the ME approach, only really begins with the inhabitation of the project in context.

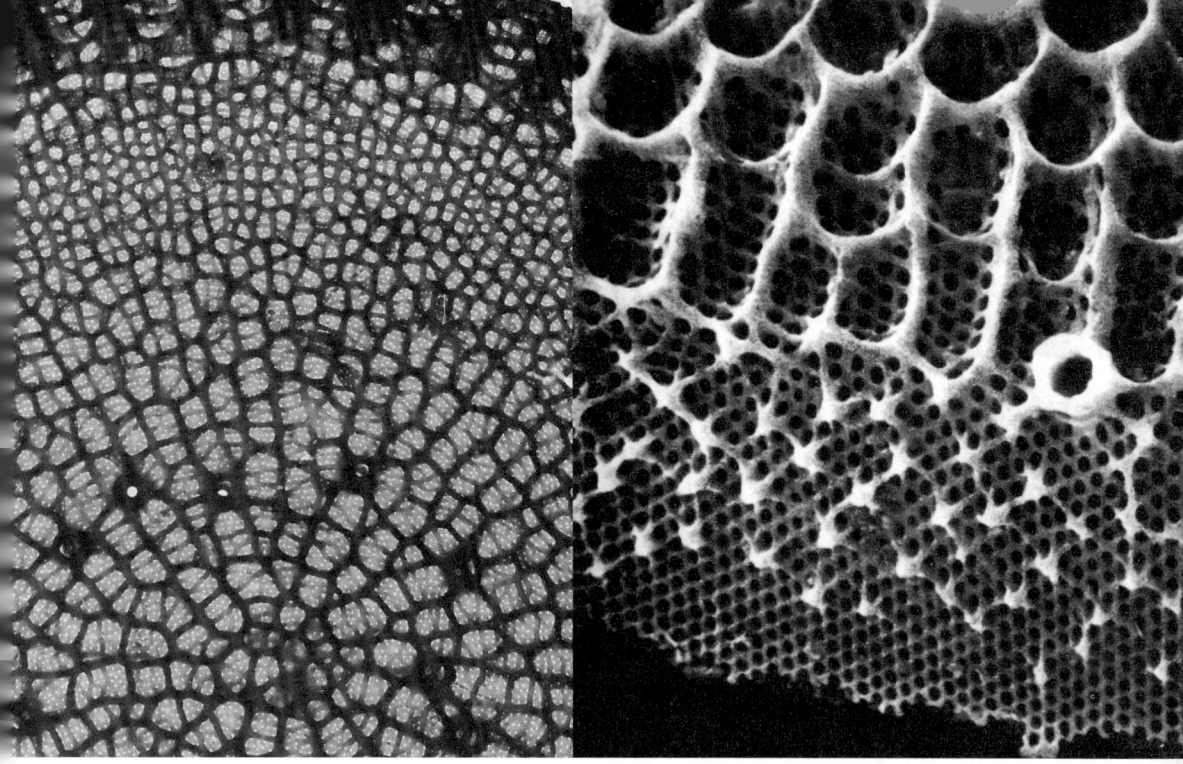

Diatomes or diatomophycea are unicellular or colonial algae. The cell is encased by a characteristic and highly differentiated cell wall, which is impregnated by silica. The images are part of the research into diatoms undertaken by Johann-Gerhard Helmcke in the context of the Sonderforschungsbereich SFB 230 'Natural Structures' . The images show two examples of highly differentiated diatom morphologies: [i] Thalassiosira fluviatis. Transmission Electron Mircoscope: 28,000:1 (left); [ii] Actinoptychus undulatus – Exterior surface of the shell. Scanning Electron Microscope: 10,000:1. (right).
© ILEK Institute for Lightweight Design and Construction, University of Stuttgart

It is an ongoing project that requires a critical rethinking of all central aspects of architectural practice today.

> *How does a surrounding element, with its various specific characteristics, affect the general form we have been studying? How does the form, both determined and a determinant, assert itself against these elements? What manner of hard parts, soft parts, interior parts, and exterior parts are created in the form by this effect? And what is wrought by the elements through all their diversity of height and depth, region and climate?* Johann Wolfgang von Goethe [9]

MORPHOLOGY AND MORPHOGENESIS

In the context of his studies in botany, Goethe defined *morphology* as the study of forms. In doing so, he laid the foundations for contemporary 'comparative morphology', the scientific method that delivers phylogenetic, ontogenetic and systematic knowledge of nature. Goethe posited a crucial distinction between *Gestalt*, or structured form, which refers to that which is already formed, and the process of *Bildung*, or formation, which changes structured form in an ongoing process. He stated 'when something has acquired a form it metamorphoses immediately into a new one'.[10] This raises questions as to how form emerges and how it continually differentiates, transforms and

View of the façade of the Merkur Department Store in Stuttgart (1959-61) by Egon Eiermann. The outer layer of the façade consisted of a uniform 60 x 60 cm ceramic block with two crossing curved surfaces that was designed to give the impression of a textile envelope and to modulate light conditions. Photo: Christian Heilmann (right) View of the space between the exterior wall of the Merkur Department Store in Stuttgart and the wall made from the moulded ceramic blocks. Light modulation and shadow cast pattern, which can be seen on the exterior wall, remains homogenous due to the uniformity of the ceramic block. (right) © saai – Südwestdeutsches Archiv für Architektur und Ingenieurbau, Universität Karlsruhe

performs in relation to its specific environment.

Developmental biology tackles some of these questions in three interrelated domains: morphogenesis, cell growth and cell differentiation. Cell growth encompasses increase in both cell numbers and cell size. Cellular differentiation describes the process by which cells acquire a type. Interestingly the morphology of cells may change dramatically during differentiation. Morphogenesis concerns the processes that control the organised spatial distribution of cells which arises during the embryonic development of an organism, producing the characteristic forms of tissues, organs and overall body anatomy. The ME approach takes up the concept of morphogenesis relating to the way the development of material systems is informed by inquiries into scale- and size-specific behaviour and related performance capacities. This involves exposure of the system at each stage of development to a series of extrinsic influences and stimuli provided by a given environment.

Natural morphogenesis, the process of evolutionary development and growth, generates polymorphic systems. These can be described as hierarchical arrangements of material that display both scale-dependent articulation and high-level integration across scales. In natural morphogenesis formation and materialisation processes are always inseparably related. By contrast, architecture is characterised by its prioritising of form-generation over inherent material logic. Materials are CNC-machined into the most hysterical shapes just because contemporary manufacturing makes it possible, with little regard for the inherent morphological and performative capacities of the employed materials and material systems. Means of materialisation, production and construction are pursued as top-down engineered material solutions after defining the shape of the building, its

View of an installation designed by Erwin Hauer for the showroom of Knoll Internacional de México, Mexico City, 1950. The screen modulates light, with its appearance changing considerably depending on the position of the light-source and the beholder. Light is modulated as a smooth gradient across each module and the screen at large.
© Erwin Hauer

structural system logic and the metric order by which standardised or non-standard elements can be described. These designs are then manufactured at the greatest expense of energy, with no particular gain in performance capacity.

The ME approach to architectural design aims instead to achieve morphological complexity and performative capacity in material constituents without separating formation from materialisation processes. The core of such an approach is an understanding of material systems as generative drivers in the design process – rather than derivatives of standardised building systems and elements facilitating the construction of predetermined design schemes. A design can thus be pursued through the material system's intrinsic performative capacities if the notion of the material system is extended to include its material characteristics, geometric behaviour, manufacturing constraints and assembly logics. This promotes an understanding of form, materials and structure not as separate elements, but as complex interrelations in polymorphic systems resulting from the response to varied input and feedback relations.

MATERIAL SYSTEMS

The ME approach to architectural design is based on the deliberate differentiation of material systems and assemblies beyond the established catalogue of types. By making the material systems dissimilar or distinct in degree and across ranges it provides for diverse spatial arrangements as well as climatic intensities. This process involves a deployment of inherent behavioural characteristics and modulation capacities of material elements and systems, rather than a retrospective optimisation of building systems towards mono-functional efficiency. It creates an understanding of efficiency as a

Close-up view of installation designed by Erwin Hauer for the showroom of Knoll Internacional de México. The screen consists of uniform 8-inch modules made of cast Hydrostone.
© Erwin Hauer

dynamic characteristic of the effective, based on utilising redundancy as latent performance capacity, rather than a safety measure.

To instrumentalise multiple-performance capacity it is necessary to understand material elements and systems in a synergetic and integral manner, in terms of their behavioural characteristics and capacities with respect to the purpose they serve both locally and within the behavioural economy of a larger system. Today's sustainable design claims to have this understanding, but implements it mainly as a question of energy-consumption, material life-cycles and waste production. If architects are to approach relational behavioural characteristics as a way of modulating space and environments, they need to combine generative methods and techniques with new methods, skills and tools for analysing the performative capacity of the overall system under investigation, as well as the narrower capacities of local elements that enable the global system to unfold.[11] Analysis is of central importance to the entire generative process, not only in revealing behavioural and self-organisational tendencies, but also in assessing and designing spatial-environmental modulation capacity. In this respect the feedback between stimuli and responses and the conditioning relation between constraint and capacity become the operative elements of heterogeneous spatial organisation. This suggests an architecture which modulates specified ranges and gradient conditions across space and over time, and is based on strategically nested capacities within the

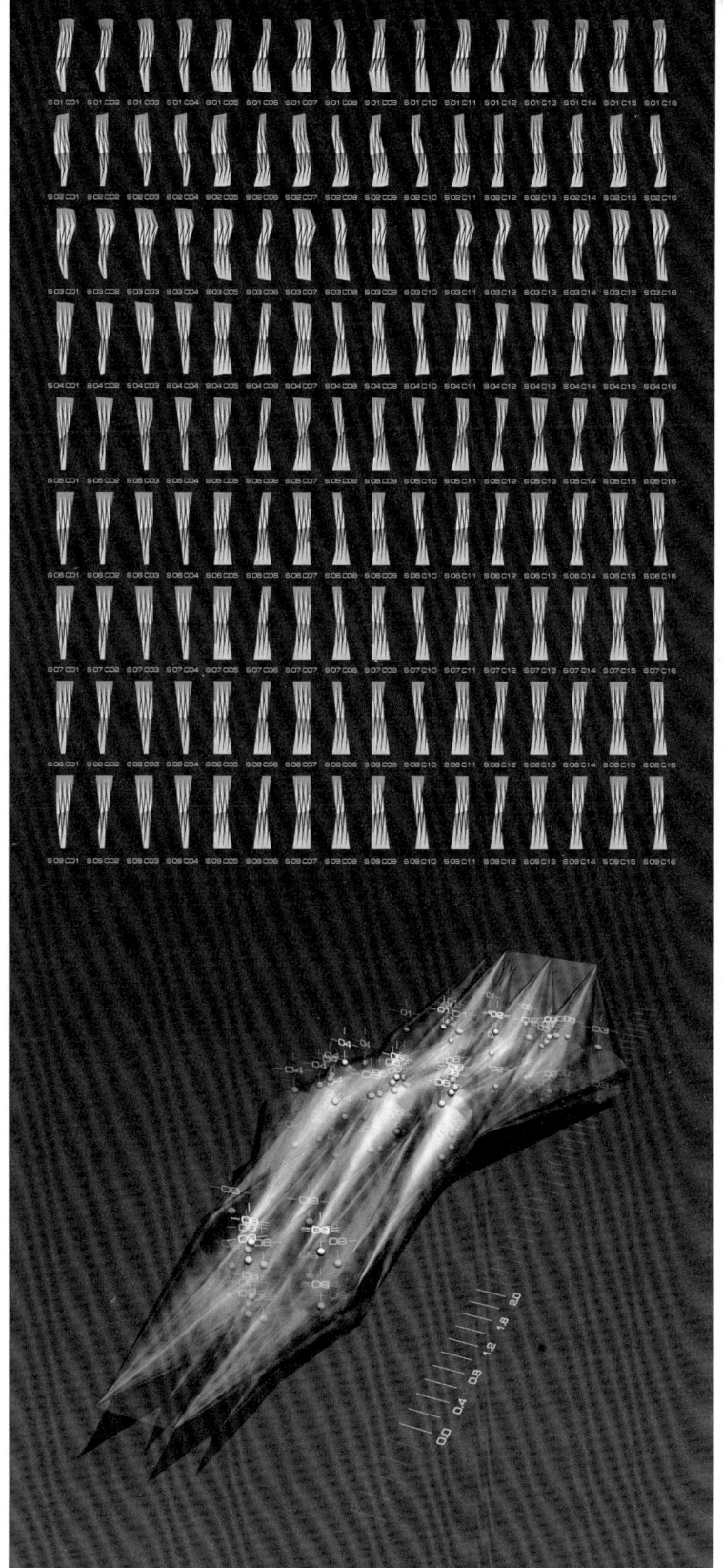

Achim Menges' design study for a pneumatic strawberry bar for the AA End of Year Party 2003 employed a process of computational morphogenesis to derive a pneumatic system with differentiated cushion geometry.

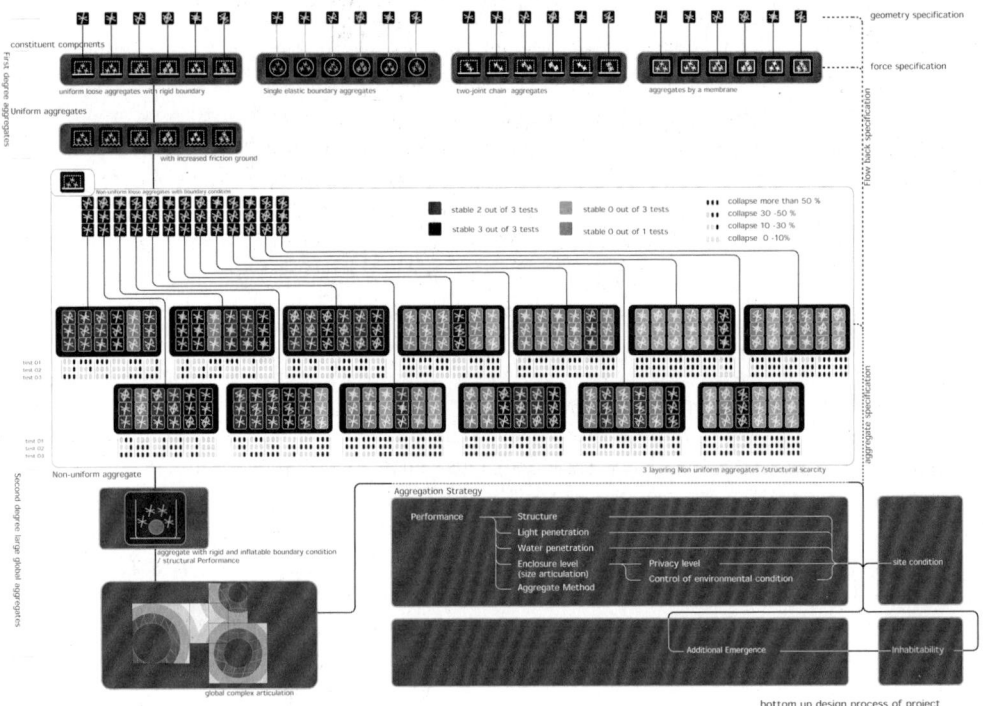

Data-structure that underlies the systematic deployment and analysis of specific element geometries of an aggregate system developed by Eiichi Matsuda.

material systems that make up the built environment.

Such an approach can learn from living nature. For example, most biological systems are articulated through higher-level, multi-functional integration across at least eight scales of magnitude: this allows scale-dependent and scale-interdependent hierarchical and multiple functionality. In addition, architects can learn from connections and transitions between systems and sub-systems of biological entities (such as the way tendons and bones connect, deploying the same fibre material across a smooth transition of mineralisation). In the building sector connections between parts and elements are almost always discontinuous, and are articulated as dividing seams instead of smoother transitions in materiality and thus functionality. Understanding and deploying gradient thresholds in materiality and environmental conditions can increase the potential for complex performance capacities of material systems. A first step towards this is a detailed understanding of the relation between material make-up and resultant behavioural characteristics. Collaborations with biomimetic engineers soon reveal the interrelation of scales, from the macro- down to the fibre-level. The projects based on the use of anisotropic materials, shown in part two of this book, highlight this. However, much of the functionality of materials is already determined on a molecular level and future research will have to take this into account.

One of the next fundamental contributions to architecture as a material practice is therefore likely to arrive from the discipline of biochemistry, which is concerned with the study of molecules and the chemical reactions that facilitate the processes that make living systems possible. If the biological paradigm for architectural design outlined here is expanded, the consequence may be a very literal understanding of the design product as synthetically alive and embedded within generative ecological relations. Including the molecular scale in the scope of architectural design would deliver advanced performativity and sustainability of a completely new magnitude.

Synthetic life research is increasing significantly. For instance Protocell Assembly, a project sponsored by the Los Alamos National Laboratory, is attempting 'to assemble a minimal self-replicating molecular machine', focusing on the conditions under which simple synthetic life-forms can be assembled. According to its mission statement the project 'seeks to develop the underpinning science for the assembly of functional proto-cells, i.e. simple self-reproducing nano-systems that can perform useful tasks'.[12] The Los Alamos team is currently attempting to achieve a synthetic life form nicknamed the 'Los Alamos Bug'. While some of the team is attempting to create synthetic life from existing biochemical structures that can be found in biological organisms, others are trying to create synthetic life from compounds that do not occur in living nature. Whatever their final approach may be, it has to be based on defining criteria to determine whether something is alive or not.

In 1971 the Hungarian chemical engineer and biologist Tibor Gánti laid the groundwork for this experiment by providing a detailed elaboration of the criteria for life in his book *The Principles of Life*.[13] He distinguished between two categories of life criteria: real or absolute, and potential. According to Gánti the former are necessary for an organism to be in a living state, while the latter are necessary for the organism's survival in the living world. In terms of real-life criteria, a living system must have [i] inherent unity; [ii] metabolism; [iii] inherent stability; [iv] an information-carrying sub-system (which is useful for the whole system); [v] programme control (processes in living systems must be regulated and controlled). Potential life criteria are [i] growth and reproduction; [ii] capacity for hereditary change and evolution; [iii] mortality. Synthetic-life research embraces a similar, if abbreviated, list of criteria, including containment (inherent unity), metabolism, heredity and evolution.[14]

Containment implies that a system must be an individual unit, a function provided by biological membranes. These are structures composed mostly of lipids and proteins that form the external boundary of cells and of major structures within cells. A lipid bi-layer membrane – composed only of lipids – is the foundation of all biological membranes, and a precondition of cell-based life. A lipid is an organic compound that is insoluble in a non-polar organic solvent. Lipids, together with carbohydrates and proteins, constitute the principal structural materials of living cells. The basic function of cell membranes is to provide integrity for the cell, that is, to separate the outside from the inside, as well as select and filter material through the membrane. As membranes form the boundary between the cytoplasm and the surrounding environment, they are affected by environmental stresses from the exterior as well as pathogenic processes from the interior of the cell. The continuous control of chemical processes in membranes typically involves three components: first, a sensor that will provide a response to the chemical; second, a controller that translates that response into a signal which is then transmitted to an actuator; and third, an actuator that drives the controlling mechanism. Systems combining all three components exist in living cells.

Scientists are conducting research into membrane materials that incorporate biological molecules capable of recognising a specific signal that will cause the membrane to respond by changing its porosity. This change enables other molecules to permeate the membrane. In doing so, the flux through the membrane will be controlled at a local level without the need for central control. While bio-membranes are not yet available on a scale relevant to the building industry, research is promising, and includes smart biological membranes that can interact with their environment based on self-assembling biological structures and polymers.[15] Current scales of applications are concerned mainly with micro-filtration and gaseous diffusion. Medical research focuses on coatings for therapeutic agents that can release drugs in response to the condition of the patients, or self-repairing coatings in replacement joints. With research progressing at a fast pace, biological membranes could deliver a completely new level of interaction and exchange between exterior and interior environments through programmable intelligent filtration and distribution on a molecular scale. In combination with metabolic processes, this might entail the removal of pollutants and the improvement of air and water quality in both exterior and interior environments.

Metabolism encompasses the physical and biochemical processes that occur within a living organism. The biological purpose of metabolism is the production and storing of usable energy. Organic molecules necessary for life are synthesised from simpler precursors, while other complex substances are broken down into simpler molecules to yield energy for vital processes. Photosynthesis is qualitatively and quantitatively the most important biochemical process on this planet. It converts the sun's energy into chemical forms of energy that can be used in biological systems; more specifically, it allows plants, algae and some bacteria to harness energy from light to produce food. Carbohydrates are synthesised from carbon dioxide and water using light as an energy source, and most forms of photosynthesis release oxygen as a by-product. The process has been studied in great detail and photosynthetic systems are frequently used in the development and application of advanced technologies. Artificial photosynthesis – which attempts to replicate the natural process – may eventually be harnessed to create self-sufficient and zero-pollution buildings that are independent from centralised energy-grids. Future applications of artificial photosynthesis may include solar energy, the production of enzymes and pharmaceuticals, bioremediation (the cleaning up of environmental pollutants) and the production of clean-burning fuels such as hydrogen. There are several lines of research under way whose main goal is to overcome the energy-consuming production and use of silicon-based photovoltaic cells. Light photosynthesis-capable membranes are one promising direction for further development. Others include the use of living organisms, such as algae and bacteria.[16] Synthetic metabolism thus has the potential to provide the energy needed for all significant synthetic life processes. Synthetic life architectures might generate their entire energy-requirement from artificial photosynthesis, providing a whole series of useful by-products and neutralising environmental pollutants.

Homeostasis is a property that regulates the internal environment of open systems, especially living organisms, for example by maintaining a stable body temperature; the technical equivalent is a thermostat. This commonly involves negative feedback, by which positive and negative control is exerted over the values of a variable or set of variables, and without which control of the system would cease to function. Like the previous criteria, homeostatic systems require sensors to measure parameters; signal transmission to a local or global control centre where deviations from desired values are measured; control centres to bring the values back to the required levels; and effectors capable of responding to a stimulus. The range of biological and available technical sensors, detectors, transducers and actuators is impressively broad.[17] Furthermore, technological set-ups that can facilitate conditions of homeostasis in a simple negative feedback are often so ubiquitous that one tends not to notice them. Overall there are two main issues to deal with: first, which stimulus or range of stimuli needs to be registered and transmitted to effectors or actuators to yield a desired response; and second, how can technologies be developed that operate more on biochemical principles than mechanical ones, so that the required functionality can be embedded into the material make-up of a synthetic-life architecture. In addition, it might be useful for architectural design to consider negative as well as positive feedback, beyond the criterion of homeostasis, to include responsiveness that can both stabilise or yield change in conditions and behaviours.

Heredity entails the conveyance of biological characteristics from a parent organism to offspring through genes. Evolution entails change in the genetic composition of a population across successive generations. This is posited as the result of natural selection acting on the genetic variation among individuals which, over time, results in the development of new species. The research team that is building the 'Los Alamos Bug' posits that if containment, metabolism and genome [heredity] fit together, they should provide the basis for evolution. Evolution is thus seen as an emergent process, the capacity that can be achieved by the correct functional relation and calibration between containment, metabolism and heredity, together with the necessary capability of reproduction. Growth and reproduction, the team argues, will yield natural selection, favouring for instance the individuals that can perform metabolic process most effectively. This argument suggests that evolution can be understood in some way as a process of optimisation of functionality and performance capacity. Biological systems are, however, so complex that it is often too difficult to deduce optimisation criteria and constraints in such a way that optimisation goals could be defined. Moreover, biological systems are characterised by multiple-performance capacities across ranges facilitated by the interaction of sub-systems across the minimum eight scales of magnitude. Disentangling this into single-objective optimisation goals is not only impossible, but also simply the wrong approach. Multiple sub-systems' functionality results in higher-level capacities. Once again, the whole is more than the sum of its parts.

Above and beyond the issue of methodological retooling there is the question of how to embed this capacity into materials and for what purpose. This brings us back to the criterion of heredity and how information can be embedded into material so that it can both be passed on and evolve. The Los Alamos team approached this challenge in an interesting manner. Their 'bug' features short strands of peptide nucleic acid that carry the genetic information. Like DNA, PNA is made of two strands. Due to their chemical characteristics and specific 'environmental' conditions these strands can combine or split into single strands. Single strands have the ability to attract fragments of matching PNA from their 'environment'. Doubling, splitting and attracting new fragments constitutes a very simple form of reproduction and heredity.

Other interesting work includes the Synthetic Biology Research at MIT, where currently a library of so called 'bio-bricks' are being developed.[18] These consist of short bits of DNA that control the activity of genes. From these, composite parts are formed that serve as genetic devices, with a genetic circuit functioning. Optimised is achieved through random mutation of the involved DNA and the selection of variants that can perform specified tasks better. One possible initial target is to produce devices that can make copies of themselves. Eminent analysts predict a technological revolution that may match and even surpass the electronic and computing revolution, by distilling the short bits of DNA into part-biological or full-biological devices with enormous performative capacity and re-programmability.

Returning to the question of evolution towards higher levels of performative capacity, it is interesting to consider the field of smart material research. According to one definition smart materials and structures are 'those objects that sense environmental events, process that sensory information, and then act on the environment'.[19] In stable environments this capacity would neither be of use, nor would it depend on evolution to adjust its response to changing stimuli. But life and its evolution depend on the exchange between organisms and a dynamic environment. For smart materials to make any real sense, they also need the capacity to evolve, so they are not immediately redundant when confronted with an environmental change which they cannot respond to in a manner beneficial for the overall system. Material research and bio-chemistry need to cross-inform one another to deliver smart materials that deserve this label. Obviously there is a lot of work to be done in this field before specific industrial applications can be delivered.

In general, there is of course the added difficulty, not only of meeting the life criteria introduced above, but also of linking them into an interdependent process that amounts to synthetic life. Moreover, the hierarchical functional organisation of biological organisms across a large range of scales of magnitude must be seen in relation to a specific context, in other words, to the numerous scalar interrelations within and between ecological systems. It is precisely this complex and dynamic exchange between organisms and their environment and the functionality that evolves from it that makes synthetic life interesting for architecture. A lot of research is necessary to tap into higher-level functionality in living nature, particularly on a molecular scale. It is therefore of great importance to keep an eye on the research in the field of synthetic life research and advances in related biochemical research. In the meantime the best we can do is address all scales all the way down to the fibre level

This study by Asif Amir Khan commenced from an analysis of pine cones and the way they open and close in relation to changes in the relative humidity level, which informed the design of a full-scale prototype of a screen that deploys the self-organisational capacity of thin timber sheets under changing humidity conditions. The photos are taken at 20-minute intervals showing the gradual opening of the apertures, each made from four timber elements.

in an interdependent manner. Here it is more important than ever before to harness the characteristic self-organisational behaviours and latent capacities of materials and material systems.

MATERIAL SELF-ORGANISATION

Self-organisation is a dynamic and adaptive process through which systems achieve and maintain structure without external control. Precluding external control does not however exclude the presence of extrinsic forces that act upon the system, since all physical systems exist within the context of physics. Self-organisational systems often display emergent properties or behaviours that arise out of the coherent interaction between lower-level entities, and the aim is to instrumentalise this behaviour as a response to stimuli towards performance-oriented designs.

Form-finding as a design method deploys the self-organisation of material systems under the influence of extrinsic forces to achieve optimisation towards a required range of performance capacity. In architectural design and engineering, form-finding is commonly used to develop

Multihalle in Mannheim by Mutschler and Frei Otto

optimised structural form, with the aim of reducing the amount of material and energy needed to resist gravitational forces and horizontal loads. In these cases one can speak of single-objective optimisation leading to lightweight structures. In developing these methods further the ME approach deploys form-finding towards multiple-objective optimisation. How can a material system fulfil spatial, structural and environmental requirements concurrently? What are the ramifications of negotiating requirements, particularly when they are conflicting?

    The two common tasks of form-finding are the generation of the form to be constructed, and the realisation of the building in the desired form. The design of the Multihalle in Mannheim by Mutschler and Frei Otto highlights this approach. The form of the gridshell is established in a tension-stressed model that is subsequently inverted to deliver a compression-stressed form, thus generating the form to be constructed. This model is made from rigid struts and loose joints, resulting in a net that in relation to the boundary perimeter and the established sag yields the optimal curvature to guarantee shell-action. The construction process is directly informed by this process, the timber lattice is laid out with the joints unfastened and propped up into the final shape. The perimeter is then fixed, the joints are fastened and the props removed. Now the gridshell can hold itself up, with its form being optimised for the structural behaviour of shells.

30 View of the cable-net roof of the Olympia Stadium in Munich by Behnisch and Partners and Frei Otto (1968-72).
Photo: Michael Hensel

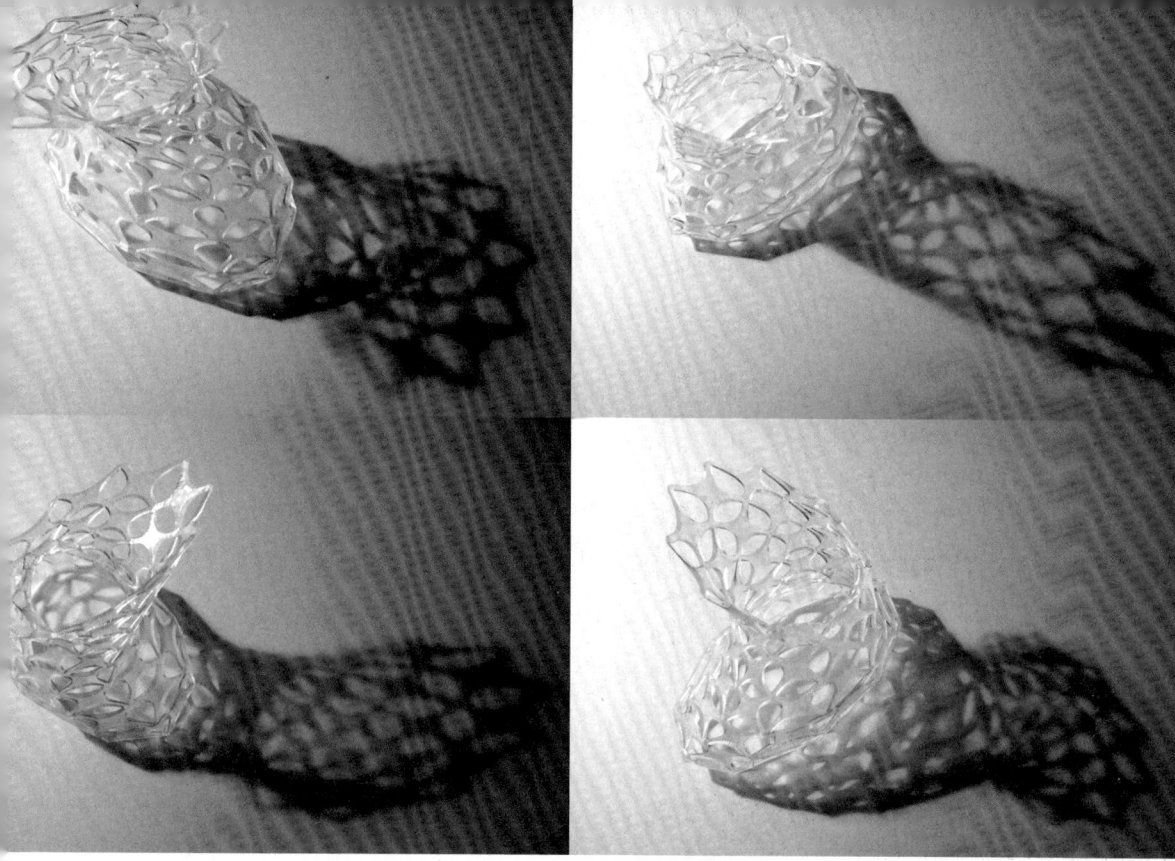

Rapid-prototype models, here a translucent stereo-lithography model, are used to investigate shadow cast pattern of particular instances of the material system. In this study by Caroline Grübel the material system is made from translucent cast rubber. When material characteristics are thus coordinated the rapid prototype can offer valuable insights in the specific performance of the system.

Multi-objective form-finding makes these tasks a great deal more complex and interesting. It is not always possible to deduce the construction logic in a simple way, since the resulting form may not be 100 per cent optimised for structural performance, that is, the material is not reduced to the minimum amount for the material system to hold itself up in relation to predefined loading scenarios.

Most current form-finding methods result in systems defined by curved geometries, whether minimal surfaces, pneumatic structures, tensile-stressed suspended forms (linear elements – catenaries; flat elements – suspended nets), compression-stressed inverted forms (linear elements – standing chains, thrust lines; flat elements – thrust surfaces, gridshells), this also applies for natural structures such as tensile-stressed (for membrane-forming materials) and compression-stressed material conglomerations (rubble heaps, drain funnels, caves, erosion formations), as well as structures in space and time (waves, systems subjected to vibrations, vortices and turbulence) whether in living or non-living nature. That is so because curvature entails structural capacity as well as orientation and exposure to an external input in a smoothly differentiated manner and also because living nature deploys fibrous material. The latter introduces directionality to material behaviour.

Form-finding, which takes place through physical and digital modelling, with physical models being at a reduced scale, introduces functional models to the toolset of architectural design. It is important not only to distinguish carefully between the different instrumental roles of physical and digital models, but also to define a series of sub-categories for each domain of modelling.

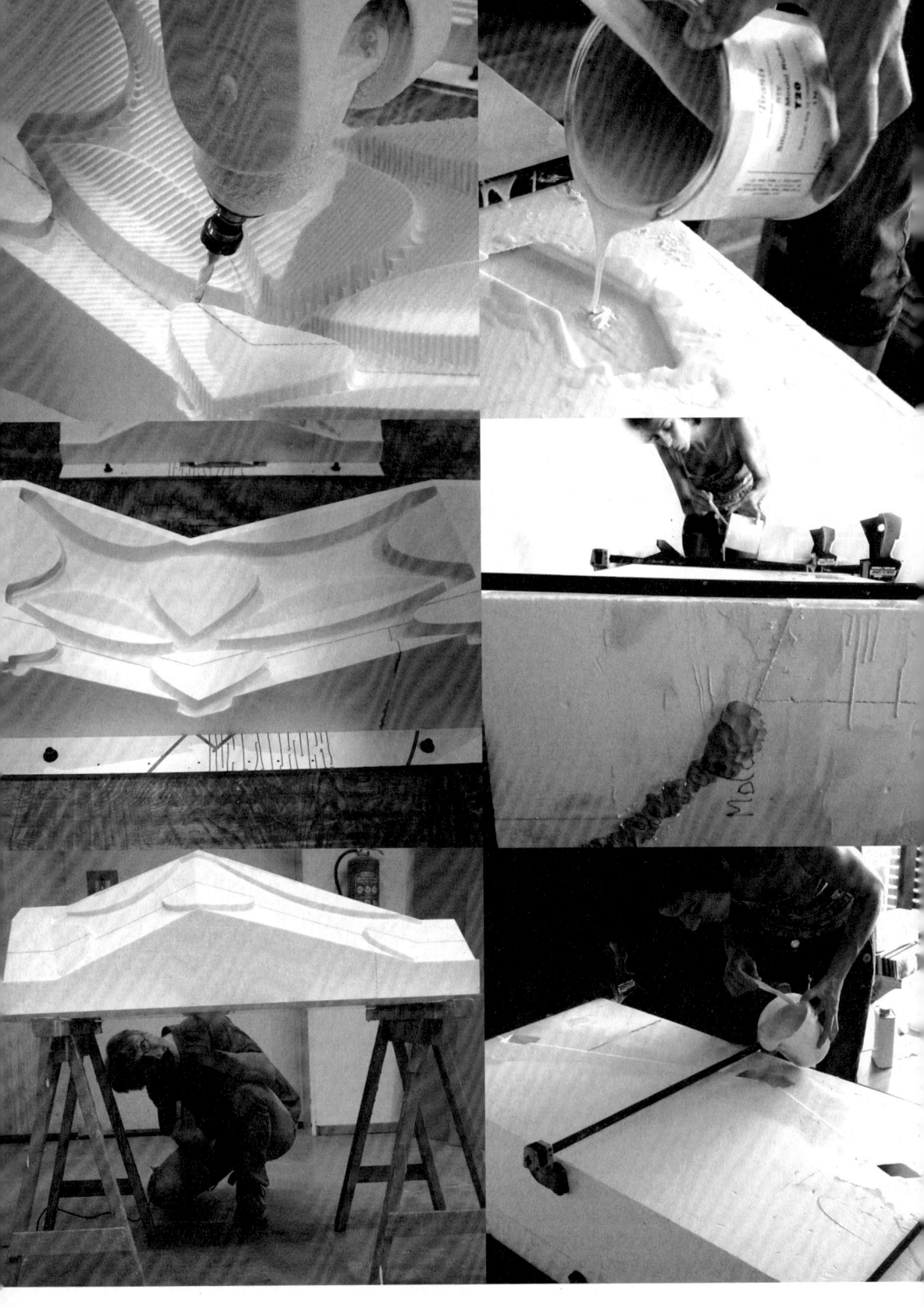

Various stages of the manufacturing sequence of a full-scale prototype for an elastic system by Caroline Grübel, including in columns from left to right: [i] CNC-milling of a mould, [ii] rubber casting, [iii] release of the cast from the mould, [iv] rubber cast with inserted rapid-prototyped aperture elements.

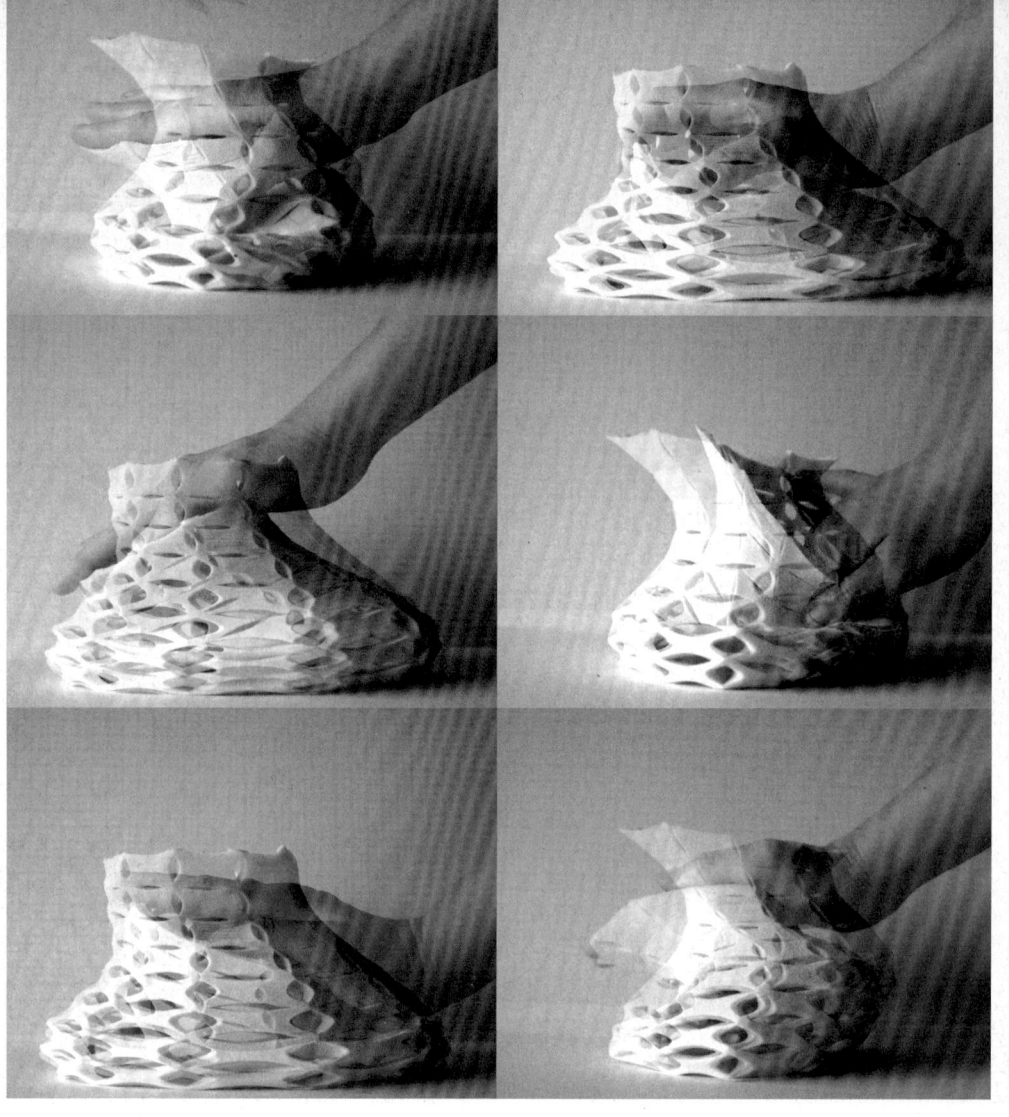

Rapid-prototyping is commonly used to fabricate representational models. Here selective laser-sintering is used to explore the possibilities of fabricating functional models. The sintered powder-mix shows the desired elastic behaviour of the intended construction-scale configuration. The eventual material system is made from a reinforced cast rubber to preserve a high elastic limit of the material throughout the assembly. In order to determine the non-uniform distribution of reinforcement different deformation pattern are studied. The models were part of a study by Caroline Grübel and produced at the Institute for Industrial Design at the Oslo School of Architecture under the guidance of Prof. Steinar Killi.

The instrumental set up of the ME approach requires physical models to shift away from being merely representational models, and become instead [i] scaled functional models that serve form-finding and performance capacity analysis functions; [ii] scaled rapid prototype models for checking geometric and topological coherency of larger assemblies of elements, while also serving form-finding purposes; and [iii] full-scale prototypes that serve to investigate manufacturing and assembly methods as well as performance capacities. Functional models will reveal some of the behavioural characteristics of the intended full-scale assembly. They can be load-tested, for instance, even though load-bearing behaviour does not scale linearly. Nevertheless, deformation can be registered and the scaling factor can to some extent be mathematically accounted for and corroborated in

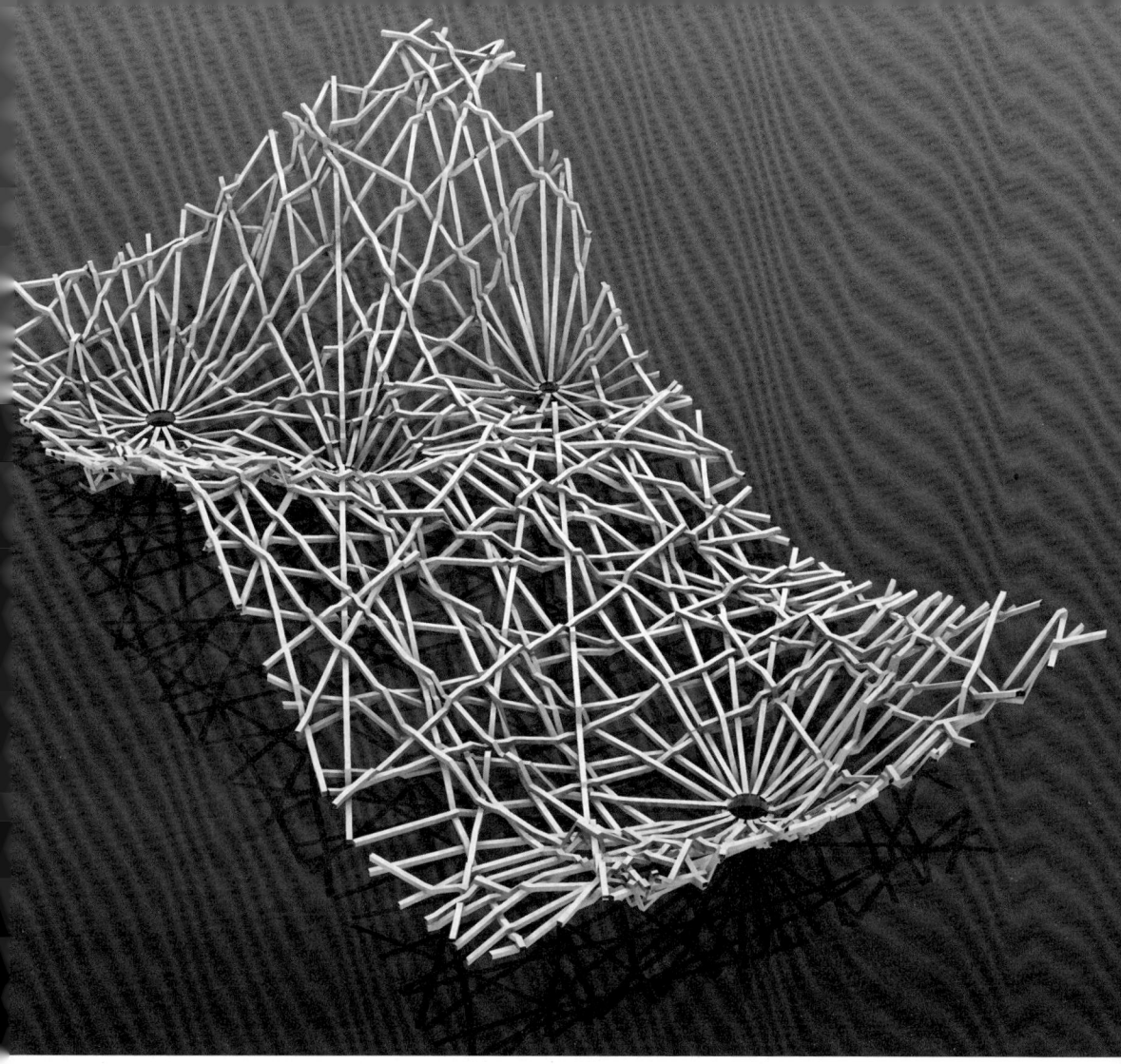

View of fibrous self-interlocking structure derived through digital growth and ontogenetic drifts. The 'Fibrous Surfaces' morphogenetic experiment was developed in 2004-05 by Achim Menges with Sylvia Felipe, Jordi Truco, Emmanuel Rufo and Udo Thoennissen.

full-scale prototypes. They can also be tested for their capacity to modulate micro-environments. The latter can be paralleled by digital analysis, as direct form-finding through, for example, dynamic relaxation tools, structural analysis through Finite Element method, airflow analysis through Fluid Dynamics analysis, and so on. This indicates the utilisation of tools which are traditionally seen as belonging to the engineering domain, but have now become central to performance-oriented design.

MANUFACTURING AND ASSEMBLY

In architecture computer-aided manufacturing (CAM) processes are playing a critical role in the shift from mass production, with its inherent standardisation, to the conception and production of

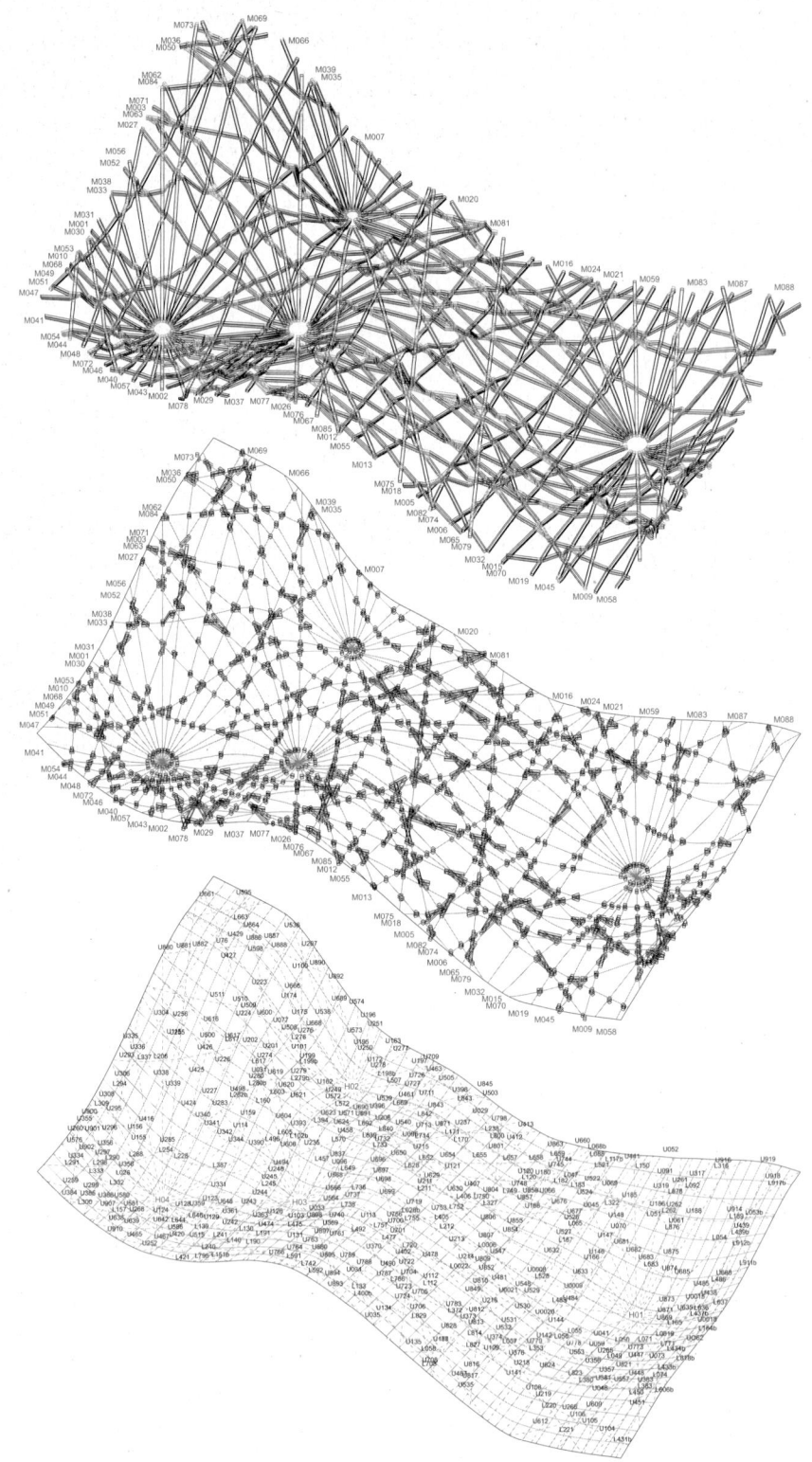

36   The surface geometry derived through a digital growth process based on extended Lindenmayer systems (bottom) provides the geometric data for an algorithmic distribution of parametric components (centre) which results in a complex network of self-interlocking straight members (top) that are immediately ready for production.

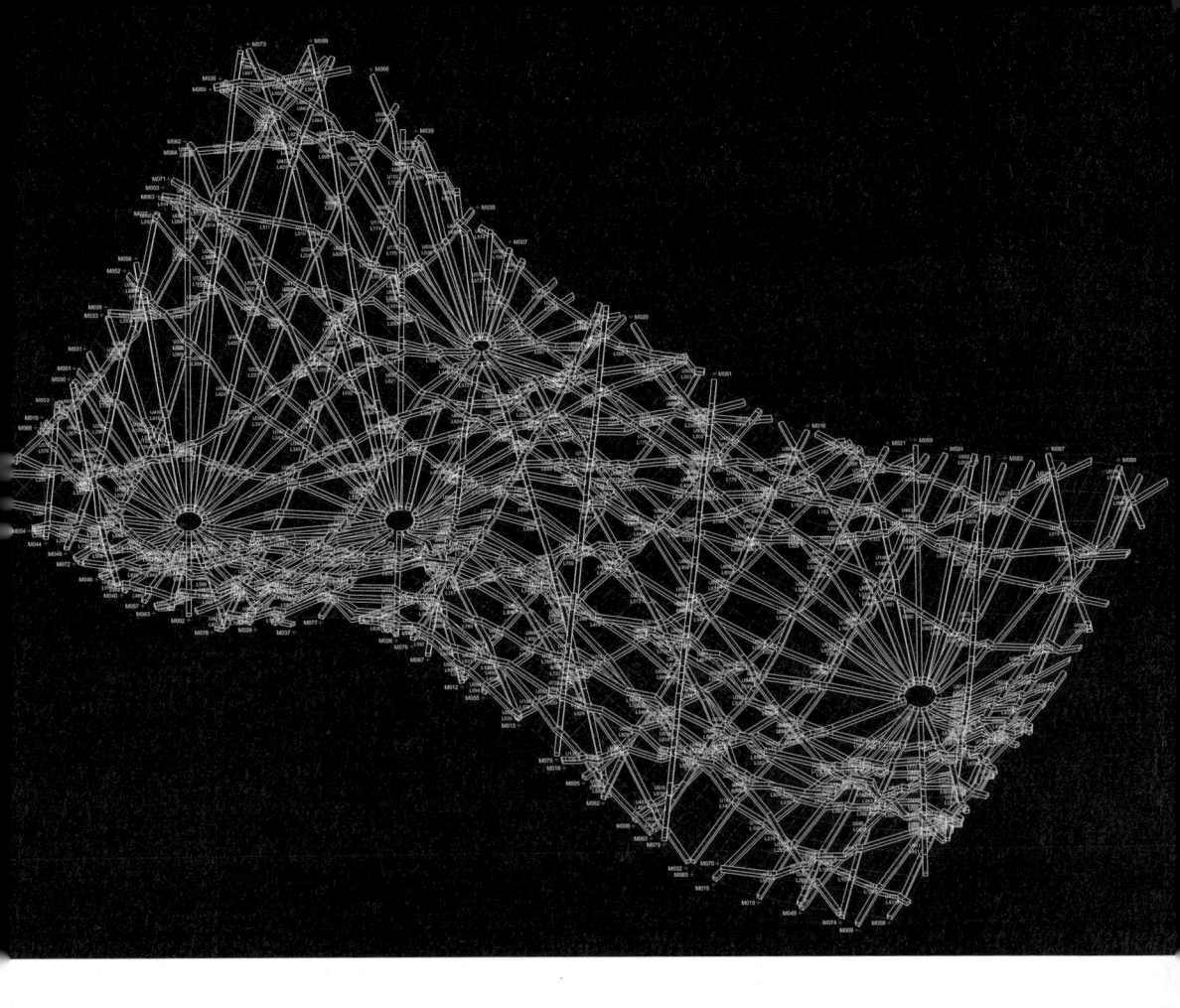

Integral parametric definition, assembly information and production data of a fibrous surface prototype structure consisting of 90 members and more than 900 joint points.

differentiated building elements. Material practice is changing rapidly through the introduction of concepts of variation or differentiation that embrace and exploit the possible geometric uniqueness of each produced part in digital fabrication. There is a move towards varied building elements and systems that are similar in degree, together with an increasingly integral relation between building systems and elements that are different in kind. While computer-aided manufacturing enables the production of differences, it still mainly serves to increase speed and precision, so preserving the facilitative character of the manufacturing process and the related protocols.

The term 'mass customisation' is symptomatic of design approaches that thrive on the recent reintroduction of affordable variation, yet remain extensions of long-established design processes based on the clear hierarchy of prioritised shape-definition and subsequent, merely facilitative production. It seems critical to understand that the achievement of variation and economy through processes of digital fabrication, by designers and manufacturers alike, does not in itself provide an inroad into strategies for exploiting the potential of differentiating material systems. The primarily facilitative nature and use of CAM becomes more obvious when it is considered in the context of its historical development. The US military supported the development of computer-controlled automation in the 1950s, introducing numerical control (NC) to machines for metalworking applications in order to surmount the limits of mass production. Over the following decades

Evolutionary computation is used to initiate a process that coevolves different generations of two interlocking surfaces articulated through perpendicular or tangential sections. The morphogenetic process yields an ever-increasing complexity of the two coevolved surfaces that nevertheless remains coherent with the logics of the material system and the manufacturing with the laser-cutter. The image shows two individual morphologies derived through this 'Morphogenetic Design Experiment' conducted by Achim Menges and Martin Hemberg (Software Development).

derivative computer numerical control (CNC) systems were introduced for a wide range of materials and scales of production, but computer-aided manufacturing only became widespread in the 1980s, with the arrival of personal computers and the increasing use of computer-aided design (CAD) applications. In the meantime, the predetermined and hierarchical phasing in the design process and the related preconceived manufacturing protocols have become deeply entrenched in the architectural profession, so that the link between the processes of designing and making, though direct, remains linear and facilitative, thus limiting the choice and development of new types of material assemblies. However, the far-reaching potential of computer numerically controlled fabrication becomes clear once it is understood as a key aspect of a design approach based on the synthesis of materialisation and form-generation processes. Here the fully defined limitations and possibilities of fabrication hardware and software become generative drivers in the set-up and development of material systems. Embedding the constraints of making in the underlying definition of the system allows for explorations of material self-organisation and assembly logics that remain coherent with the employed modes of manufacturing and production, thus offering the potential for genuine morphological differentiation.

GEOMETRY AND TOPOLOGY

A 'curve' is a geometric object that is one-dimensional and continuous. 'Curvature' is the amount by which a curve, surface, or other manifold deviates from a straight line or plane. There are two ways of describing a curve, by its parametrisation or by determining how much a curve bends at each point – its curvature. Calculus was invented concurrently by Sir Isaac Newton and Gottfried Wilhelm Leibniz between 1666 and 1680, and was further developed by Jacob and Johann Bernoulli. Differential and integral calculus delivered necessary tools for the problem of curvature and paved the way for works such as Alexis-Claude Clairaut's 'Curves of Double Curvature' – curves in three-dimensional space – which in turn opened up the study of the curvature of surfaces. Leonhard Euler's work on the parametrisation of curves became central to differential geometry. Karl Friedrich Gauss's major interest in differential geometry led to his paper 'Discourse on curved surfaces' (1827), recognised as one of the most important in the history of mathematics. The paper introduced a method for measuring precisely how curved a surface is at each of its points: the 'Gaussian curvature' of a surface at a point is the product of the principal curvatures at that point. Gauss's work on curvature eventually made possible the leap from curvature of one-dimensional curves to two-dimensional surfaces in three-dimensional space.

Curved surfaces yield great potential for architectural design. This potential is both geometrical and topological, with significant repercussions on the design, production, behaviour and effect of material form. One question, then, relates to how geometric, material and structural characteristics can be coherently developed in order to arrive at complex curved surfaces with high performative capacity. Curvature is interesting because it represents a first step towards synthesising geometry and topology with the logic of material systems through a process of form-finding based on the self-organisation of materials within a given context. Advances in digital software enable the modelling of higher-order surfaces constructed of curved primitives with complex mathematical descriptions, such as parametric polynomials [SPLINEs], non-uniform rational b-splines [NURBS], Beziers, parametric bi-cubic surfaces and n-patches. Moreover, software packages now also offer curvature analysis tools. The combination of digital modelling and analysis with physical form-finding allows for performance-driven parametric design of curved geometries. Most digital analysis, however, is still predicated on polygonal mesh models that evidently influence and deliver false results. To maintain rigour appropriate tools need to be selected or developed, and a lot of work still remains to be done.

Another critical aspect of modelling material systems is an understanding of the system's morphology beyond the metric, that is, its measurable, geometric characteristics. In order to instrumentalise material systems as spatial, structural and environmental modulators, the designer has to facilitate the set up of digital models not so much as a particular gestalt defined by a series of coordinates, but more as an envelope of possible formations with a potential for further differentiation that remains coherent with the processes of fabrication and assembly. Unlike conventional design and construction processes, the designer cannot rely entirely on Euclidean geometry but has to understand additional geometric concepts that define and differentiate a system.

The morphology of material systems is defined not only through a set of points but also through the relations of proximity and contiguity of these points. In Euclidean geometry the relation between points is expressed as fixed length and distances that stipulate how far apart points are in relation to one another. Euclidean geometry operates in 'metric spaces' based on concepts such as length, area and volume. However, there exist other geometric spaces, in which distances expressed in length cannot characterise proximity as the length does not remain fixed. One example is topological space, which can be stretched or scaled without changing the characteristics of its defining points.

Mathematicians have introduced various ways of describing geometric aspects that are not limited to metric concepts. In the nineteenth century most scientists still based their work on the assumption that the structure of physical space was captured in Euclidean geometry, but at the same time other kinds of geometry were being discovered. One example is the differential geometry of Gauss, others include projective geometry, affine geometry and topology. However, these non-metric concepts do not simply coexist with Euclidean geometry; they can be understood as

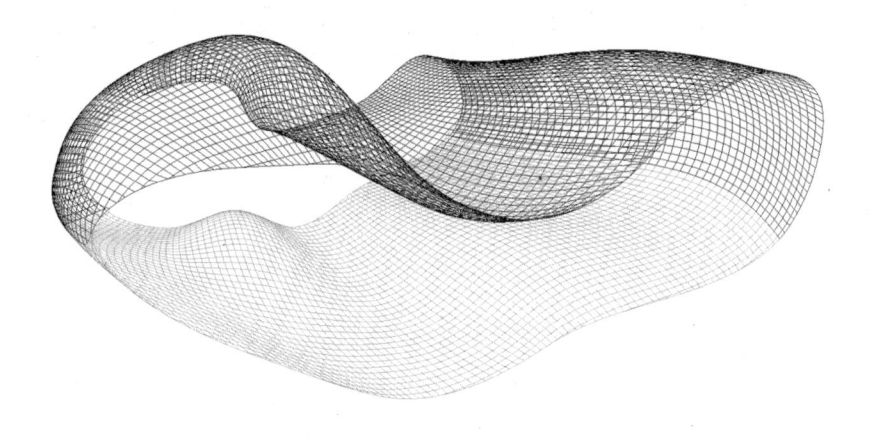

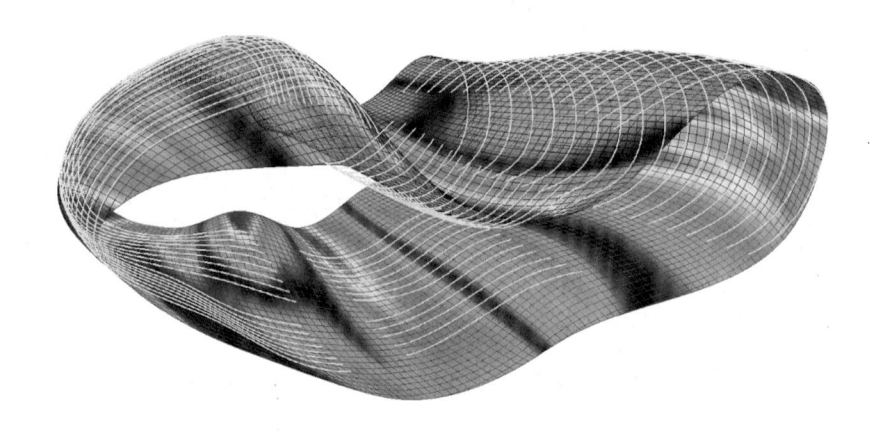

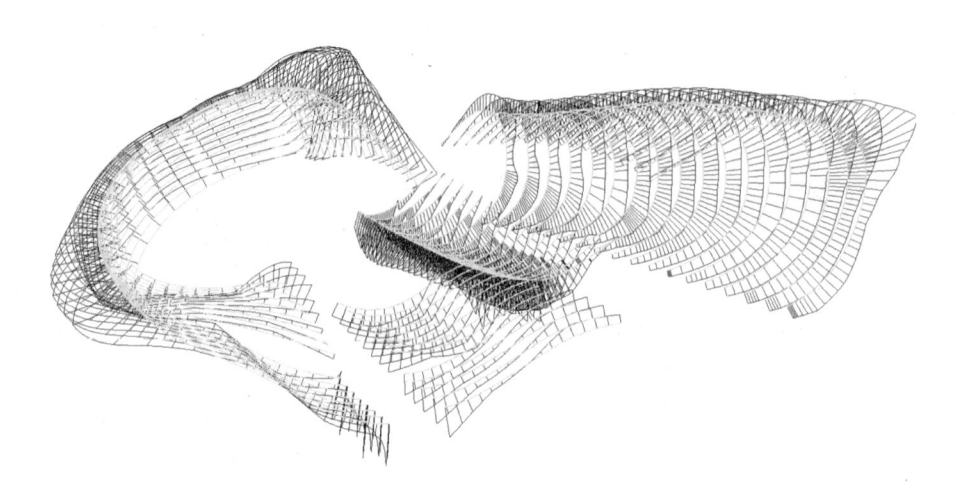

40 Tangential and perpendicular construction planes of the evolved Genr8 surfaces are derived by an analysis of geometric
interrelations (from top to bottom): The surface evolved in Genr8 is closed through geometric information of tangency alignments
in boundary points; perpendicular and tangential construction planes are distributed according to surface curvature; the position

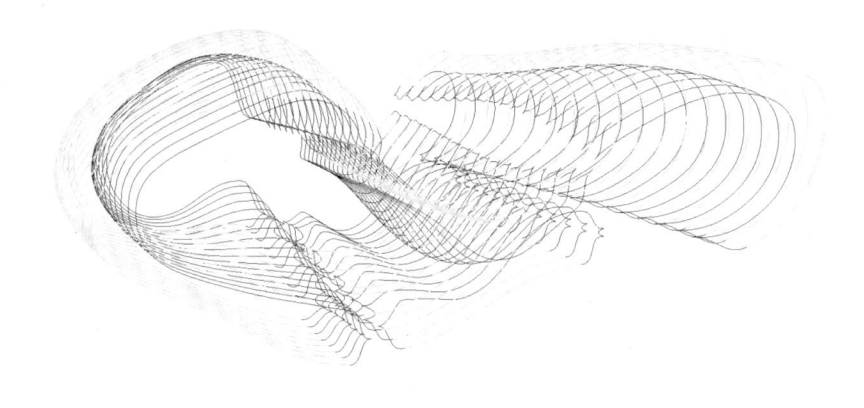

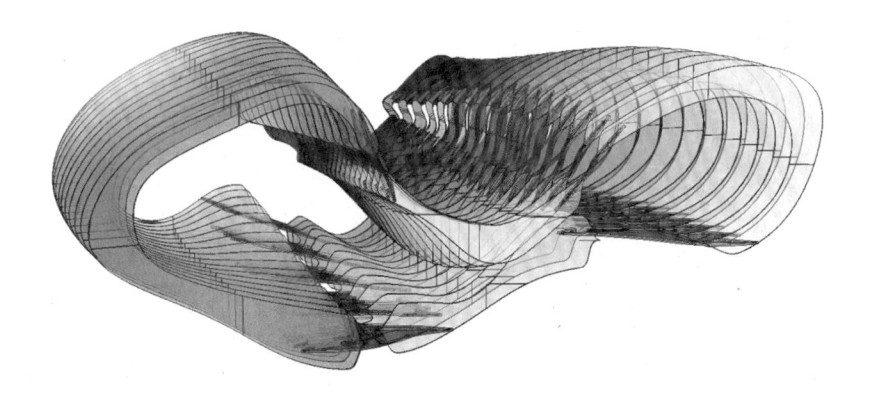

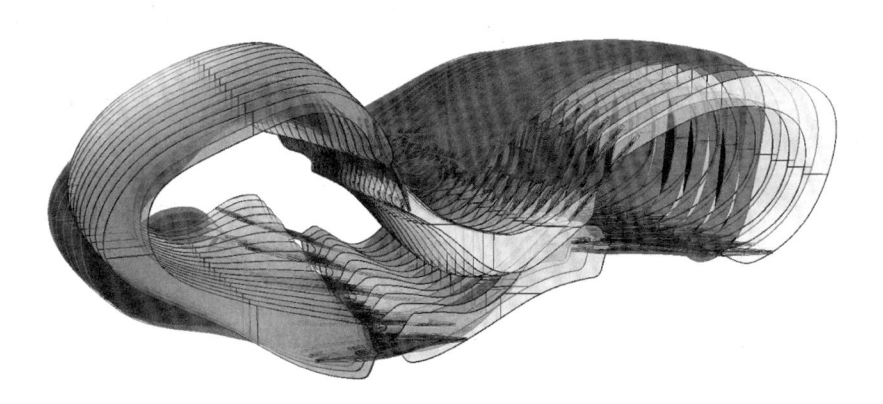

and offset of perpendicular sections is defined by surface directions and local curvature.
The rigorous geometric analysis of the evolved surface leads to a sectional articulation that organises the interrelation of multi-planar components and the co-evolved second system.

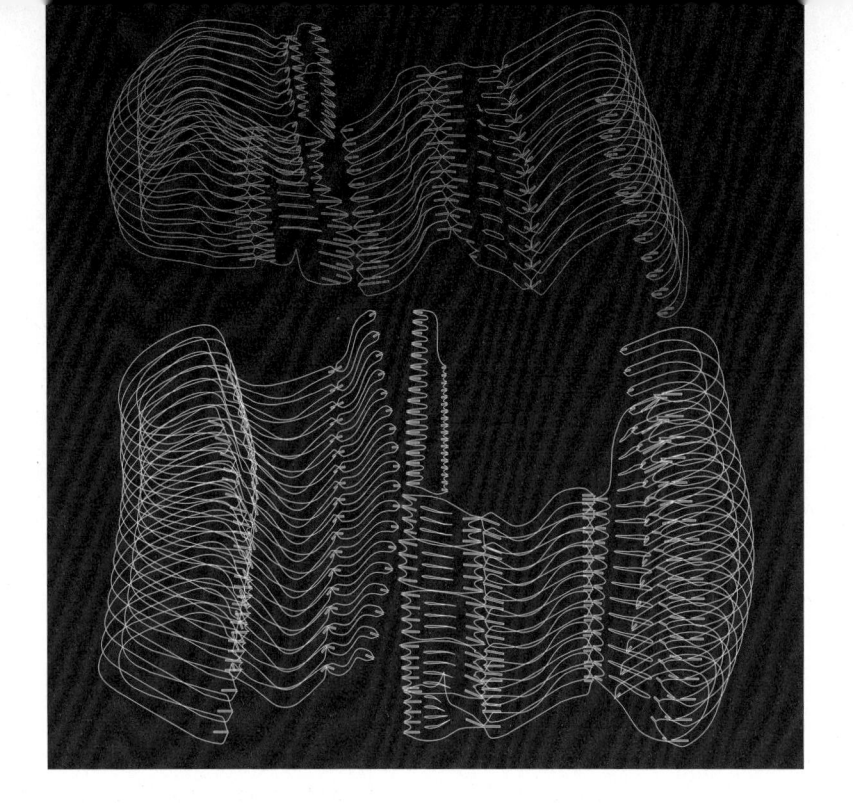

Co-planar arrangement of multi-planar sections prepared for laser cutting.

being related in a specific manner. In his highly influential 'Erlanger Programm'[20] the mathematician Felix Klein categorised all different known geometries according to their invariants under groups of transformations, based on the realisation that the different groups were embedded into one another. For example, the group of rigid transformations (including rotations, translations and reflections) does not alter geometric properties such as length, angles and shapes in Euclidean geometry. However, these metric properties change, that is they do not remain invariant under groups of transformations that characterise other geometries. For example, through affine geometry a new group of transformations called linear transformations is introduced, whereby the length of lines may be altered but other characteristics such as straightness or parallelism remain invariant. And in projective geometry the group of transformations called projectivities is adjoined to the aforementioned rigid and linear transformations. What is essential in Klein's work is the recognition of the interrelation of these geometries, which can be pictured as different levels of a hierarchy whereby each level and its related group of transformations embeds all transformations of the levels below it. The relation between different levels of this hierarchy can be explained by the typical example of conic sections, which is the geometric category of curves including circles, ellipses, parabolas and hyperbolas. In Euclidean geometry, two conic sections of the same type and with the same size, for example two circles with identical radii, are defined as being equivalent. To be equivalent in affine geometry they just have to be alike in type, for example they both need to be circles, regardless of their particular size. And in projective geometry all conic sections are the same. This demonstrates how more and more figures become progressively equivalent as one ascends from Euclidean geometry in the categorisation hierarchy, which can be further extended by the inclusion of differential geometry and topology. In topology, geometric figures are equivalent if they remain invariant under bending, stretching or other deforming transformations that do not add new or fuse existing points on the figure. This is of particular interest as many figures that are entirely distinct in Euclidean geometry such as circle, rectangle and triangle are equivalent in topology, as one can be deformed into another. They are homeomorph. Finally it becomes clear that by moving down the transformation-based hierarchy suggested by Felix Klein, one gains a more and more differentiated geometric space.

The outlined geometric understanding is of critical importance in the developmental process of a material system through differentiation and proliferation. Shifting the focus from a mere metric conception of the geometric relationships that define the system's morphology and behaviour towards an understanding that includes non-metric and topological aspects, provides the base for computational morphogenesis of material systems that enables the unfolding of differentiation which remains coherent with materialisation and fabrication logics. However, as most three-dimensional modelling applications are firmly based on the definition of geometry through fixed coordinates, alternative modelling techniques based on geometric/topological relationships and non-metric features need to be employed, with associative geometry and parametric modelling providing one inroad of particular interest.

ASSOCIATIVE GEOMETRY AND INTEGRAL DESIGN TECHNIQUES

In a parametric approach to digital design a model is defined as a set of geometric relationships or associations that are applied through parametric expressions and constraints. To understand the fundamental difference between an explicit geometric model and a parametric model, imagine a digital drawing of two circles with a line connecting their centre points. In an explicit geometric model, any change in the position of either circle will require the deletion and redrawing of the connecting line. In a parametric model, a relationship between the centres and the line can be established so that the line will follow any translation of either circle. Other relationships can also be prescribed, for example between the length of the line and the radius of one of the circles. This association can then be given a conditional statement, such as one preventing the two circles from intersecting. All predefined geometric relationships applied through parametric expressions and constraints remain consistent as the model is manipulated.

Most often the utilisation of parametric models in the field of digital architectural design reflects the fact that much of the architectural software in use today was originally developed for the aeronautical, naval, automobile and product-design industries. Due to an inherited emphasis on maintaining geometric control and workflow efficiency, the parametric models used in these programs are embedded with processes and constraints, which lend themselves to the post-rationalisation of complicated building geometries derived from other design processes. In architecture, deploying parametric control is primarily geared towards processes of rationalising complex geometries, the typical case being the doubly curved facades rationalised as a parametrically defined system, which can then be relatively quickly adapted to inevitable changes in the overall scheme. The geometric data relevant to manufacture and construction is contained within this parametric model and is therefore effortlessly recalculated and retrieved. Indeed, the skills for achieving the geometric complexity found in many recent 'iconic' buildings have long existed but are only now, through the process of parametric post-rationalisation, becoming affordable. However, in the context of the ME approach, the introduction of parametric design may have more profound repercussions. Not dissimilar to the alternative use of computer-aided manufacturing as a generative and integral driver in the design process, associative modelling can provide a critical cornerstone in the development of an integral design based on material systems rather than being a merely facilitative tool.

The underlying logic of parametric design can be instrumentalised here as an alternative design method, one in which the geometric rigour of parametric modelling can be deployed first to integrate manufacturing constraints, assembly logics and material characteristics in the definition of simple components, and then to proliferate the components into larger systems and assemblies. This

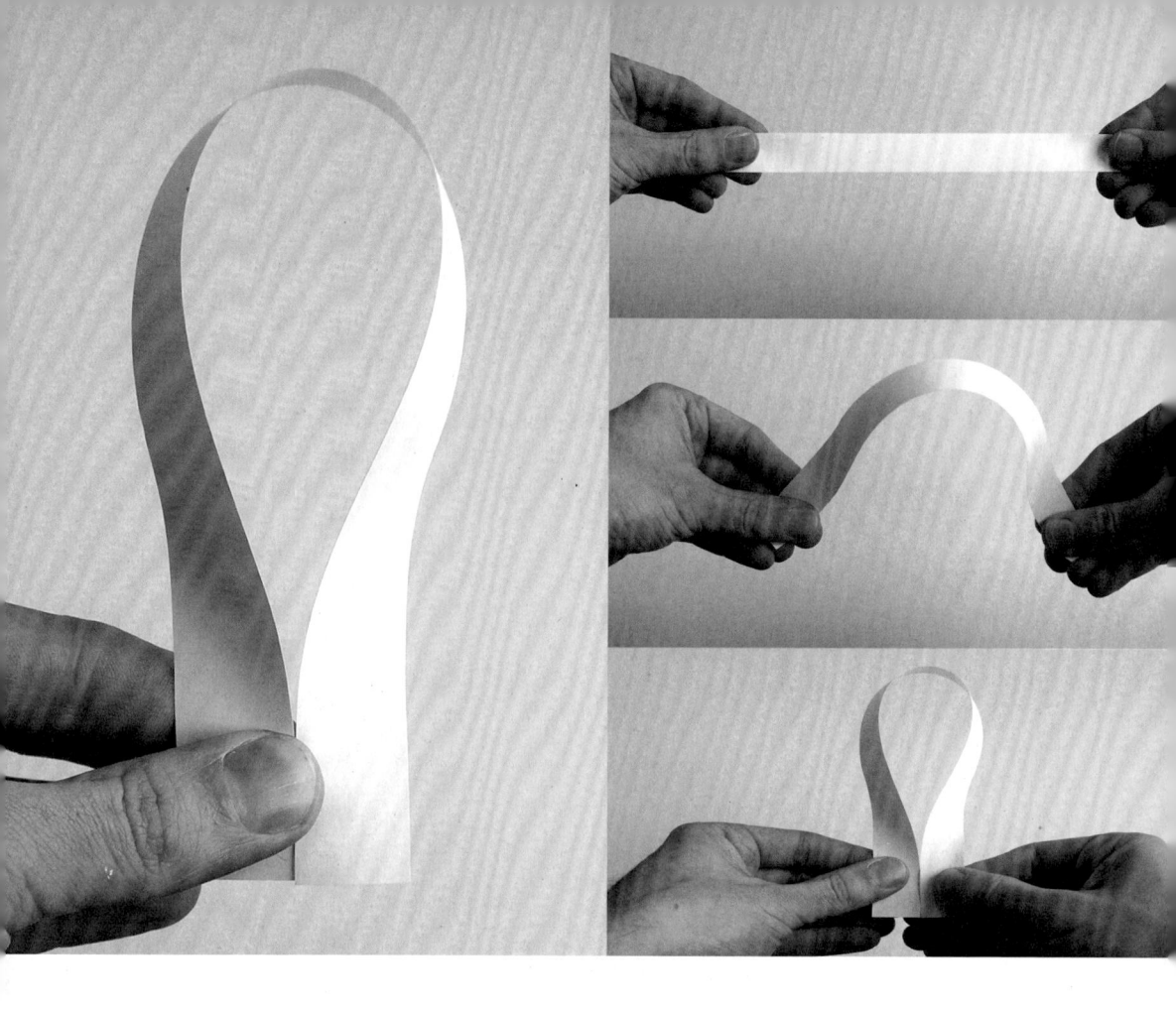

A paper strip element defined through a simple manipulation of aligning one strip end with the other provided the basic system component for the "Paperstrip Morphologies" conducted by Achim Menges with Andrew Kudless, Ranidia Leeman, Nikolaos Stathapoulos, Michuan Xu, 2004-05.

approach employs the exploration of parametric variables to understand the behaviour of such a system and then uses this understanding to strategise the system's response to environmental conditions and external forces.

How can one imagine such a process of integration, and what are the critical issues in this field of research? The aim is to understand processes that unfold morphological complexity and performative capacity from simple constituents without differentiating between formation and materialisation, and this is where concepts from developmental biology can play a role. One that is of particular interest here, and which can be instrumentalised in the realm of parametric design, is the inherently material, formative process of cellular differentiation and proliferation. Cellular differentiation, the process by which cells specialise in order to perform specific roles, operates on the principle of pluripotency – the capacity for morphological change in cells whose genetic material and underlying relationships remain, with very few exceptions, the same (pluripotent cells vary in number from as few as two in bacteria to 20 or 30 in jellyfish to 250 for such highly complex systems as human beings).[21] This striking concept suggests an application to parametric design in the identification of the constraints of materialisation as the potential for differentiation in a parametrically defined component. The understanding of such a pluripotent component would, however, be very

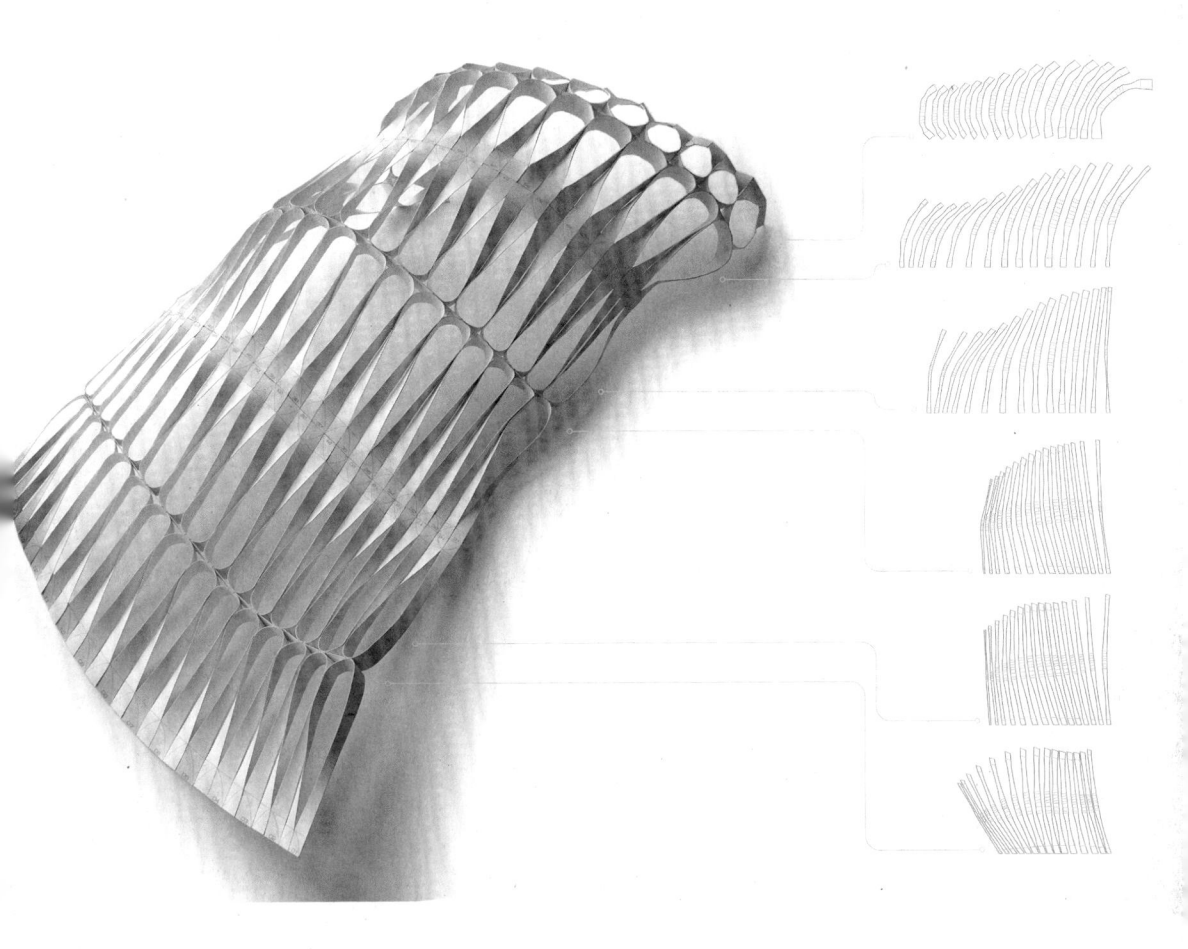

Physical test model of a population of 90 paper strip components and related strip cut patterns.

different from that of a repetitive module which facilitates the creation of a predetermined overall composition or construction.

The basic implications of such an understanding can be explained using the example of one of the most basic possible components: a strip of paper. Holding such a strip between left and right hand, aligning the short edges so that the paper forms a loop, then rotating one end around the axis of the long edges until the two short edges are again aligned, yields a particular strip morphology. In other words, with this simple manipulation – a displacement and rotation – of one strip end, it is possible to 'form-find' the specifically related bent and twisted shape.[22] This is the configuration that results from the geometry and internal resistance of the material system (the strip of paper) combined with the application of external forces (the displacement/rotation induced by the fingers during the manipulative process, and gravity). From experience we know that if one takes a couple of other strips and performs the same manipulation, they behave in a similar way: they display common geometric features (namely, two points of curvature change along each edge) and topological invariance (that is, they are still strips of paper). Nevertheless there are obvious limits to achieving these common characteristics in the specification of the strip. If the proportion of length to width of a strip or the ratio of this proportion to thickness exceeds a certain range, one will either be unable to perform the manipulation or the strip will kink or rip. It is also obvious that such limits exist if one changes to strips with different elastic properties. With these basic observations it is possible to

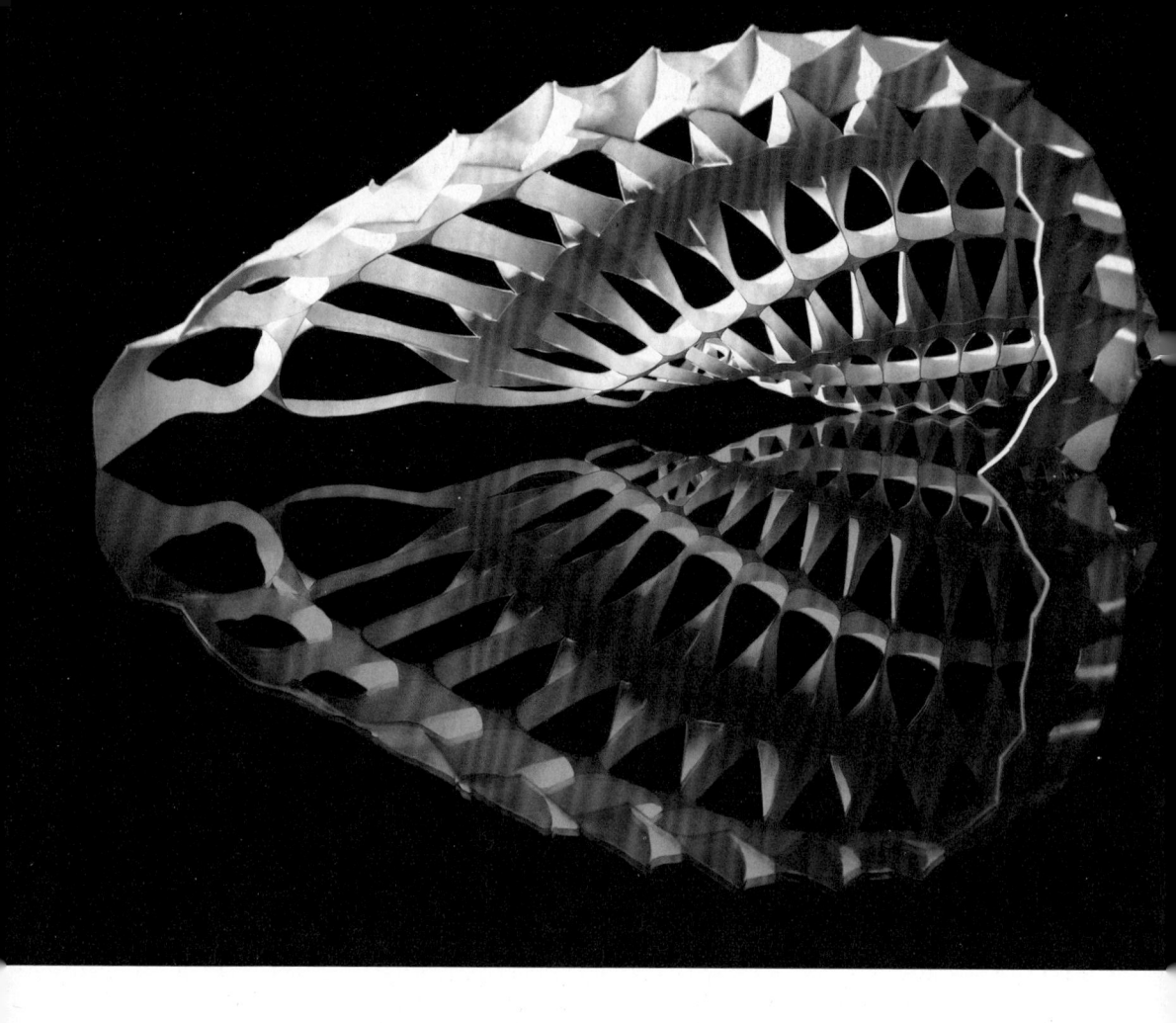

Physical test model of paper strip system derived through a parametric process embedding the material characteristics, manufacturing constraints and assembly logics observed in physical tests.

begin to think about a generic digital model that captures the common characteristics of the paper strip.

Initially one might be inclined to digitally replicate the manipulations executed in the physical realm. As the materials are known, the geometry of the bending and twisting manipulation could be computed and mathematically formulated as a function of the stiffness distributed over the length of the strip. This approach, however, would be limited to the initial geometry of the strip as an input for the simulation.[23] A very different approach would commence by defining a computational model which ensures that any morphology generated can be materialised as a paper strip. Such a model would require a holistic understanding not of paper strips but of the inherent 'logic' of the material system, which would allow for the establishment of a framework into which more specific data could be inserted. If we assume material properties as a constant for a moment, we can identify geometric relationships that capture the strip's manufacturing logics, self-formation tendencies and material constraints. The critical moment in establishing these relationships in a parametric model is the definition of their variant and invariant aspects, a calibration which needs to avoid over- or under-constraining the model and either drastically limiting or going beyond the envelope of possibilities for materialisation. The resulting parametric model would thus define the manipulated strip as a

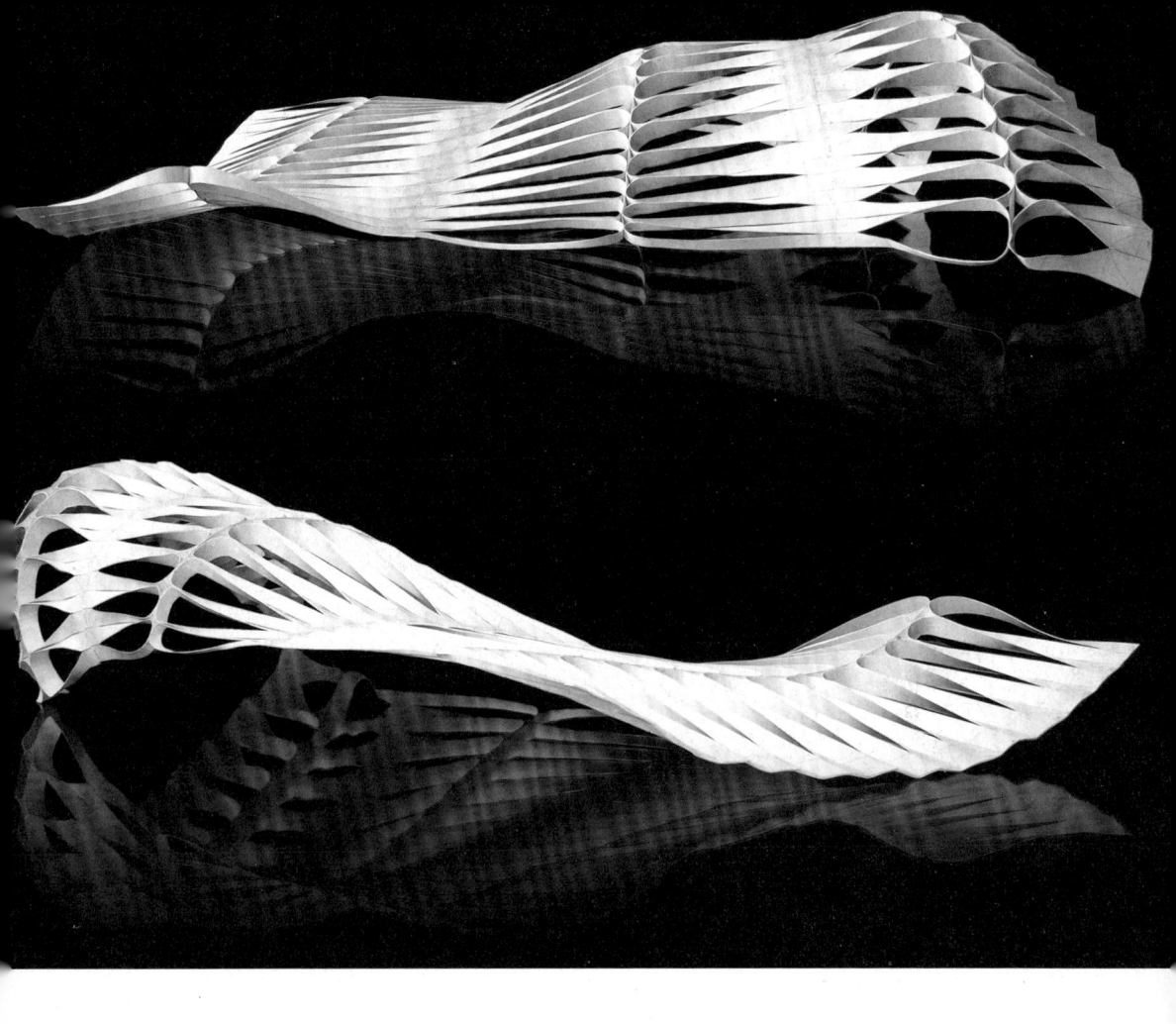

Physical test model of paper strip system derived through a parametric process embedding the material characteristics, manufacturing constraints and assembly logics observed in physical tests.

developable surface generated from two edge-curves that maintain characteristics of the formation process, such as points of curvature change and tangency alignments. In other words, whatever surface is developed can be unrolled onto a plane, thereby capturing the essential logics of the manufacturing process – the planar cutting of sheet material – but not, for example, limiting the outline of the unrolled strip to a rectangle. These material constraints would be embedded in the model through an expression that regulates the ratio of the length of the edge curves to the width and thickness of the strip. Furthermore, this parametric component would need to be defined by its relationship to adjacent components, both in terms of assembly logics and adaptation to variable neighbouring components. In the paper-strip example, attention would focus on attachment zones, defined as areas of tangency between neighbouring components. Finally, the parametric component would have to incorporate performative capacities: its possible behaviours and responses to an external environment. Considering, for example, the gap created by the loop in the paper strip, we can imagine these components comprising a larger system whose performative capacity would include visual permeability and the ability to modulate the transmission of light. To allow for this possibility, the designer might incorporate into the model external reference points that regulate the orientation and alignment of the strips as well as variables for altering structural capacity through,

Parametric outward proliferation of the paper strip system.

say, material thickness.

In this brief introduction to the creation of a simple parametric component, it is nonetheless possible to identify the key concepts and considerations of pluripotency in parametric design. First, the notion of 'component' has been expanded. Here a parametric component as the basic constituent of a material system is an open and extendable geometric framework of integration: it integrates the possibilities and limits of making, and the self-forming tendencies and constraints of materials. Furthermore, it anticipates the processes of assembly and is defined as part of a component collective, opening up the possibility for building up a larger system. Another key development is that this component's geometric aspects can be defined by the transformations under which they remain invariant, meaning that its possible geometric associations can be strategised according to characteristics of Euclidean geometry, affine geometry, projective geometry or topology. A critical task for the designer, then, is the negotiation between metric precision and topological exactitude.[24] Fundamental to the approach presented here, though, is the understanding of a component system as a population of individual components rather than as a finite number of variations on an archetype.[25] The transformative potential of the system is enabled by the differentiation of its sub-locations through the abilities of an open parametric component. Consequently such a system can be derived through a process of proliferating components into

Parametric inward proliferation of the paper strip system.

polymorphic populations. To initiate such a process of proliferation it is first necessary to define a 'proliferation environment' that provides both the constraints for the accretion of components as well as stimuli/inputs for their individual morphologies. Not to be confused with the external, physical or digital environment the system will be situated in, the proliferation environment is a geometric construct that lies within the domain of the designer. Thus it can also be parametrically described and thereby remain open to subsequent manipulations. The second aspect to be defined is the algorithm that drives the distribution of components in the proliferation environment. Here one can generally distinguish between three modes of proliferation: an outward proliferation of a component into a population that increases in number until the environment's boundaries are reached; an inward proliferation within the initial system's set up;[26] and a hierarchical proliferation based on environments/inputs for secondary, tertiary, etc., systems provided by the morphologically distinct but non-hierarchical populations derived from the first two modes of proliferation. Furthermore, these three modes can be deployed simultaneously or in combination, leading to nested populations of component systems.

In the simple case of the paper strip, we may define the proliferation environment as a parametrically controlled doubly curved surface populated with instances of the parametric component distributed along the virtual surface, according to a specific rule set by the designer. If

50 The parametric setup allows for manipulation on different scales: global manipulation of the system-proliferation rules and environment (top), regional geometric manipulation, for example from synclastic to anticlastic curvature (left) and local manipulations of individual components, such as proportional geometric relations or orientation (right).

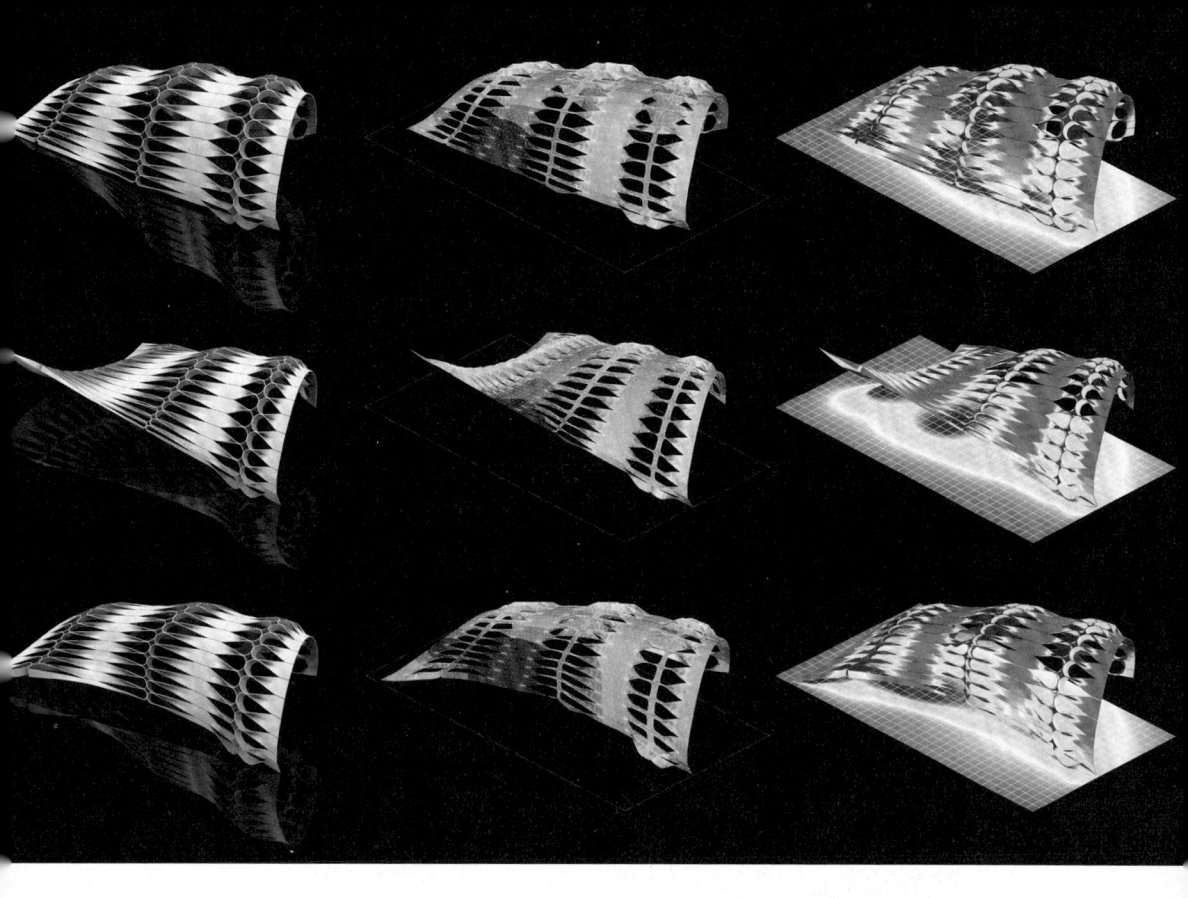

Geometric manipulations of the parametric strip system (left) and related patterns of structural behaviour (centre: contour plots of finite element analysis under gravity load) and modulation of light conditions (right: geographically specific illuminance analysis on the system and a register surface).

we now manipulate the geometry of the 'host surface' through changes to its parametric set up, we can observe how the individual component morphologies adapt. Similarly, if we change a variable of the basic outward proliferation, we may see an accompanying change in the number of components populating the surface. Indeed, as we introduce changes, we can identify results ranging from the 'local' manipulation of individual components to the 'regional' manipulation of component collectives to the 'global' manipulation of the component system. The parametric associations of and between components, collectives and the system allows the rapid implementation of these manipulations, leading to a multitude of self-updating system instances. It is essential to note, however, that the aim of these manipulations is not to derive variations of the system but to trace the behaviour of the system across various instances. If we then situate it in a simulated environment of external forces, the system's behavioural tendencies and performative capacity will be revealed.

For example, if we expose multiple instances of the proliferated component system to digitally simulated light flow, we can register the interrelations between parametric manipulations and the capacity for modulating light levels upon and beyond the surfaces that make up an assembly or larger system. An additional digital structural analysis of the same instances may reveal the related load-bearing behaviour of the system. The behavioural tendencies of the system interacting with external forces and modulating transmitted flows can be traced across various parametrically defined individual morphologies. The resulting patterns of force distribution and conditions of varying intensity can inform further cycles of local, regional and global parametric manipulations. This process of continually informing the open parametric framework of component definition and proliferation will yield an increasing differentiation with the capacity for negotiating multiple performance criteria within one system. The important point is that parametric design enables the recognition of patterns of geometric behaviour and related performative capacities and tendencies of the system. In continued feedback with the external environment, these behavioural tendencies can then inform the ontogenetic development of one specific system through the parametric differentiation of its sub-locations. These processes of differentiation remain consistent with the constraints of materialisation and equip the designer with strategies for unfolding the system's capacity to provide and organise a heterogeneous habitat for human activities within the built environment.

ECOLOGY

Ecological systems have at least five features that make them interesting. First, they are comprised of many parts; most contain hundreds of billions of individual organisms and tens of millions of species. Second, ecological systems are open systems that maintain themselves far from thermodynamic equilibrium by the uptake and transformation of energy and by the exchange of organisms and matter across their arbitrary boundaries. Third, ecological systems are adaptive, responding to changing environments both by behavioural adjustments of individuals and by Darwinian genetic changes in the attributes of populations. Fourth, ecological systems have irreversible histories, in part because all organisms are related to each other genetically in a hierarchic pattern of descent from a common ancestor. Fifth, ecological systems exhibit a rich variety of complex, non-linear dynamics. James H. Brown[27]

An environment consists of a complex of external factors that act upon a system and determine its articulation and development. Moreover, the environment of a given system must interact with that system in order for it to sustain itself and develop. In biology, environment is defined as the complex of climatic, biotic, social and edaphic factors that act upon an organism and determine its form and survival. It includes everything that directly affects the metabolism or behaviour of a living organism or species. Furthermore, it is the interaction between an organism and its environment that develops its functionality. In this respect the task of science is focused on defining the conditions that are objective and possible to generalise in such a way that they are applicable to overall species. This raises the question of whether environment can be described as a series of quantifiable conditions that are required by a given species.

The Estonian biologist Jakob von Uexküll formulated another approach, entitled *Umwelt*-theory, which examines how living organisms subjectively perceive and interpret their environments.[28] (*Umwelt* is the German word for environment.) Whilst ecologists assume that all organisms in the ecosystem share the same environment, Uexküll posited that organisms may have different perceptions of their environment even if they live in the same place. *Umwelt* is therefore not the same as an ecological niche, since niches are assumed to be measurable units of an ecosystem that can in some way be quantified. For Uexküll *Umwelt* is subjective, that is to say, organisms actively create their *Umwelt* through perpetual interaction with the world. *Umwelt* thus has a different functional importance, for an organism, than an ecological niche does. According to Uexküll, humans nevertheless share their *Umwelts* to a large extent through their exceptionally developed communication abilities.

The ME approach brings together Uexküll's *Umwelt*-theory and Banham's gradient threshold paradigm[29] in the relative notion of space – the idea that space is constructed through social operations and the local individual and collective experience of space-time conditions. Individuals actively create their *Umwelt* through perpetual interaction with the dynamics that unfold from the mutual modulation of the material and the energetic, the tectonic and the climatic. Thus individuals construct, as it were, a collective environment through social interaction and formation and real-time appropriation of heterogeneous space.

In terms of human creative production this relates in an interesting way to Umberto Eco's notion of *open works*,[30] which are characterised by a deliberate ambiguity of meaning. According to Eco, open works leave the arrangement of some of their constituents to the individual or to chance, which gives them a field of possible orders rather than a single definite one. The fact that the subject can move freely within this articulated yet ambiguous field of possibilities frees the works from conventional forms of expression and prescribed interpretations. However, as Eco points out, this requires a guiding directive from the designer to structure the field of possibilities for the beholder. The point here is not so much to rehearse or promote Uexküll's bio-semiotics or Eco's semiotic theory. The issue is not an emphasis on meaning as in contemporary semiotics, but rather its opposite: the direct experience and choice of context-specific conditions by the individual, which uncouples these conditions from meaning and thus from cultural exclusion. A freedom of movement and choice is provided by micro-climates and gradients. Hard control and soft modulation become consolidated in the provision of a carefully delinated field of possibilities.

The German philosopher Peter Sloterdijk has proposed that the dawn of climatic structures was the emergence, in early nineteenth-century England, of hothouses that provided a suitable environment for plants that were foreign to their host context.[31] According to Sloterdijk this development was made possible – as well as driven – by the invention of bent glass and the prefabrication of standardised glass and steel elements. He posits that one 'encounters the materialisation of a new view of building by virtue of which climatic factors were taken into account in the very structures made'. It is somewhat ironic, then, that the architecture of hothouses and their contemporary derivatives, greenhouses, has become standardised through the very same steel and glass elements that made this typology possible in the first place. Such standardisation reduces their performance capacity without increasing amounts of added on technological equipment for ventilation, heating or moisturising. A visit to any greenhouse immediately makes this evident.

Performance-oriented designs through differentiated material systems are a powerful means of providing desired micro-climates and gradients without having to resort to a plethora of equipment, that is, if we accept that air-conditioning is not the smartest solution we can possibly come up with. It is interesting to note that countries like Brazil had a broad range of building strategies that successfully provided comfortable (semi-)interior climates up to the 1970s. From the 1980s onwards, they began to decline, as electrical air-conditioning units became first a corporate and later a private status symbol. The ability to waste energy in this particular way became a sign of wealth, power and freedom, the compulsive extension of the 'American Dream' into the realm of energy consumption. We argue that the division between exterior and interior has become ever more dichotomous, to the detriment of freedom of choice and the creative articulation and utilisation of the built environment.

In order to overcome this condition, the architectural tool-set needs to be supplemented with techniques that register environmental dynamics. Mapping is a powerful technique that can serve both analytical and generative purposes. Maps have been important communication tools throughout history. Through maps and mapping a specific understanding of the world is constructed. Mapping unfolds potential by distributing a specific view or vision into the collective realm: individual experience culminates in collective understanding.

The ME approach relies on mapping in several ways: first, as a way to identify performance capacities of a material system; second, as a way to understand the range of environmental provision afforded by a material system through its specific degree of differentiation; and finally, as a way to uncover potential for inhabitation that can be instilled or heightened by the designer or freely utilised by the inhabitant. In other words: mapping reveals ecological potentials, if ecology is broadly understood as the study of the relation of organisms to their hosting environment.

Environmental mapping of Bairro do Recife notating temperature gradients (dot colour gradient), wind direction (vector direction) and wind speed (vector length) developed by Dae Song Lee, Gabriel Sanchiz and Defne Sunguroglu in the context of the 'Intense Space – Bairro do Recife Digital Port' workshop 2006 in collaboration with the Federal University of Pernambuco.
A spreadsheet lists the data of 20,000 measure points. The spreadsheet is linked with a map set up in an associative modelling software. Changes of the numerical values in the spreadsheet automatically update the map. The map serves as environmental input to the articulation of the geometry of a material system modelled in the same associative modelling software. With the updating of the map, the geometry of the material system is updated instantly.

Ecology can be studied at various levels ranging from the individual organism to populations, communities of species, ecosystems and the biosphere. Behavioural ecology, for instance, studies the ecological and evolutionary basis for behaviour and the role of behaviour in enabling adaptation to ecological niches. Behaviour is an observable action or response of an organism or a species to environmental factors. In other words, behavioural ecology concerns individual organisms and how these organisms are affected by and in turn affect their biotic and abiotic environment. This involves: first, a stimulus, in other words, an internal or external agent that produces a reaction or change in an organism; second, sensibility, which is the capacity to perceive a stimulus; and third, sensitivity, the capacity to respond to that stimulus. The latter (also called 'irritability') is regarded as a common property of all life forms. The related processes of sensing, growth and actuation are often embedded capacities within the material make-up of living nature.

Context-sensitive growth modelling can deliver a great method for architectural design, directly interrelating morphogenesis and environmental input. These tools are based on Lindenmayer or L-systems, a formal description of simple multi-cellular organisms developed from 1968 onwards by the Hungarian biologist Aristid Lindenmayer and subsequently by Professor Przemyslaw Prosinkiewic and his team at the University of Calgary.[32]

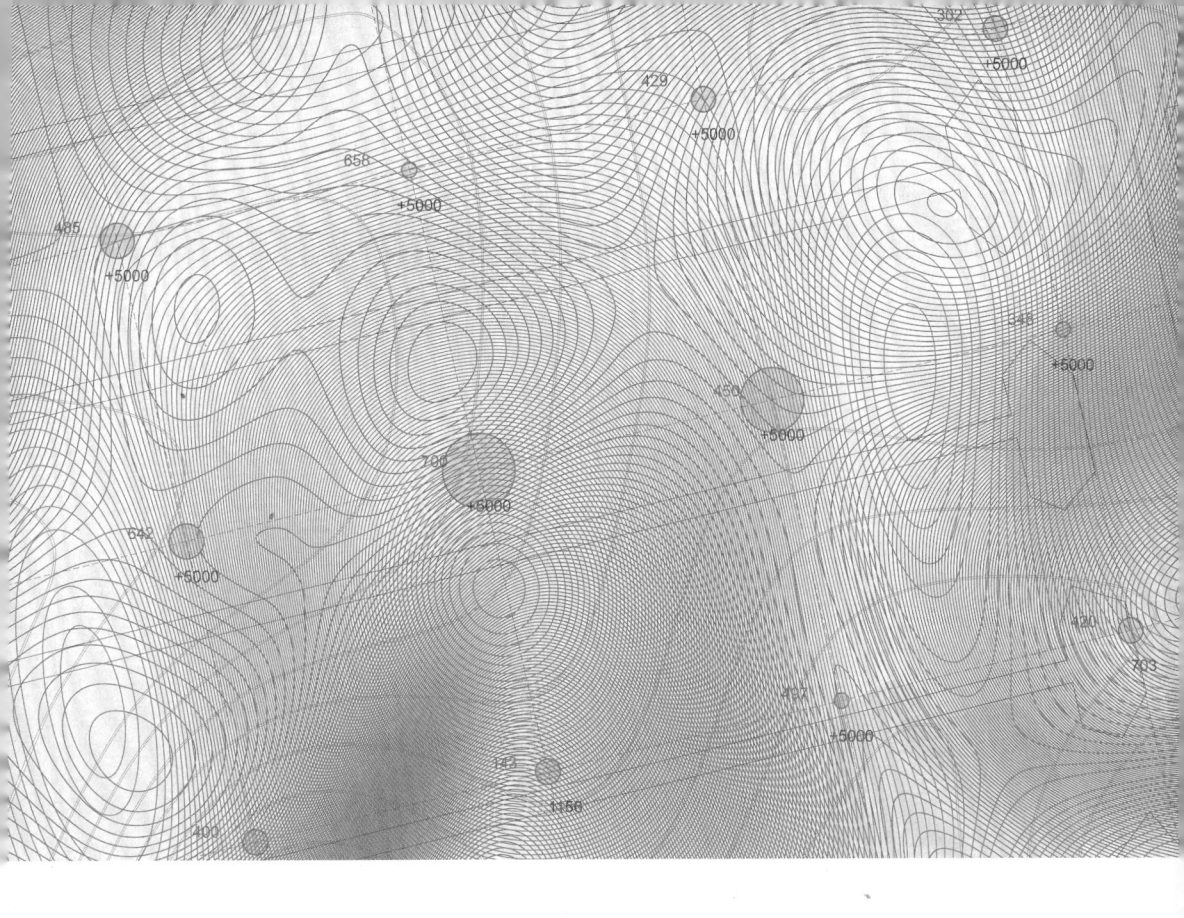

Mapping of the distribution and rate of change of luminous intensity over the course of one day on Bairro do Recife developed by Louis Gadd and Julia King in the context of the 'Intense Space – Bairro do Recife Digital Port' workshop 2006 in collaboration with the Federal University of Pernambuco.

One of the most interesting developments is the integration of biomechanics into plant development models, which allows plant growth to be informed with extrinsic physical, biological and environmental input. Advanced models incorporate the combined impact of gravity, tropism, contact between the various elements of a plant structure and contact with obstacles. The methodological set-up, the tool-set and the choice of determining variables are equally interesting for architectural design. Entire building systems and envelopes can thus be informed by multi-variable input and optimised to satisfy multiple performative objectives. Instead of a step-by-step optimisation at the end of the design process, response to extrinsic stimuli can now become an intrinsic part of the generative process.

A great deal of complexity is involved in the modelling of ecosystems, from the geometric and material characteristics of individuals and their particular features, all the way up to their position within the ecosystem and the multitude of feedback relations with their specific environment, including other individuals or species. Mapping – describing the multi-linear interrelations between material and environmental conditions and their impact on the way a certain habitat is populated and appropriated – can serve as an analytical inroad and generative underlay to the ME approach, and directly inform morphogenesis.

OUTLOOK

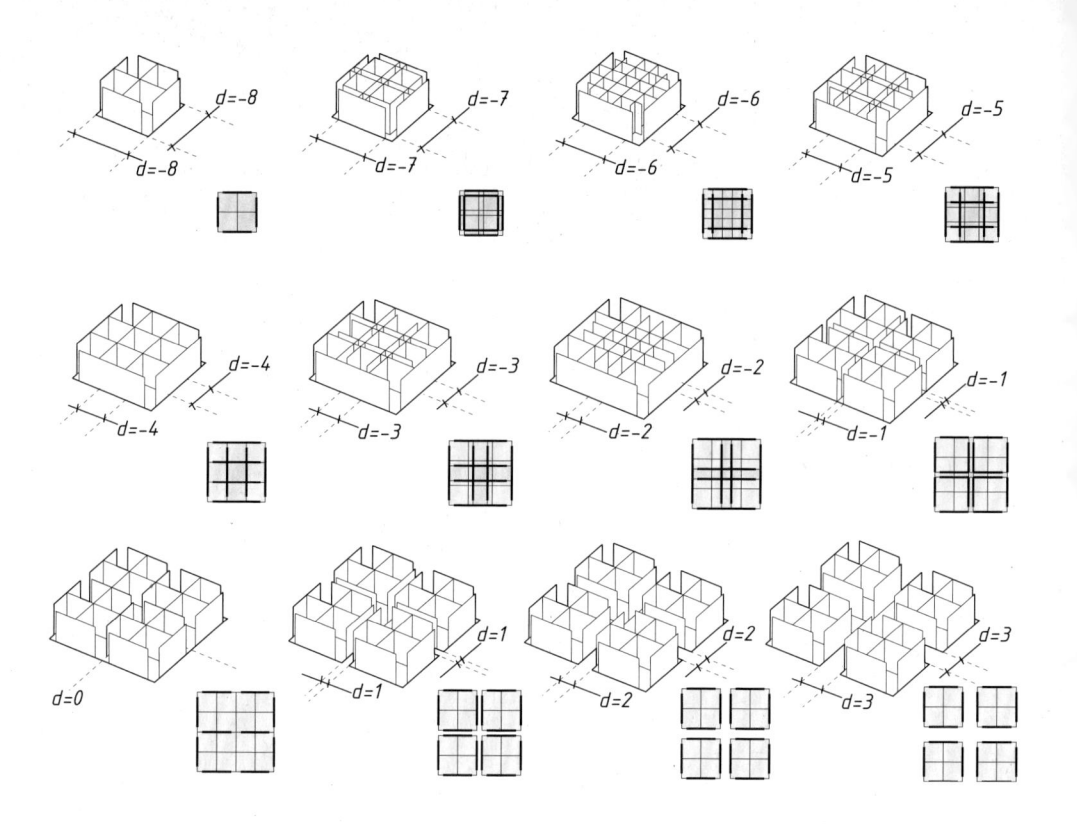

Parametric modelling of planar space organisation. Compacting of volumes in the horizontal plane.

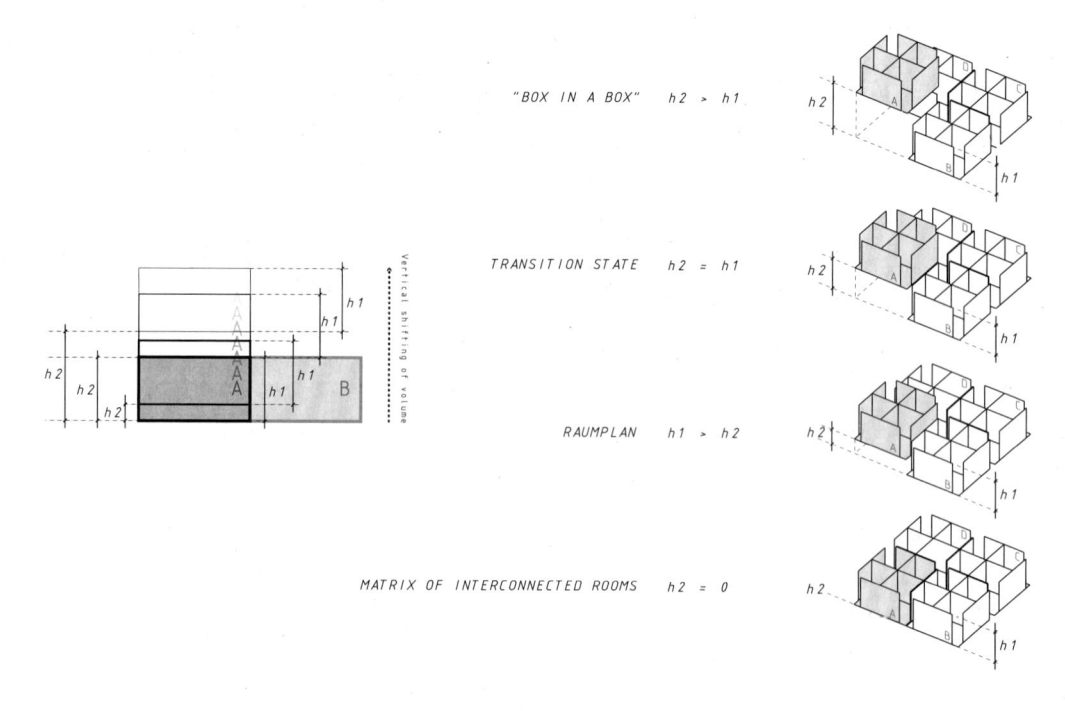

"BOX IN A BOX" $h2 > h1$

TRANSITION STATE $h2 = h1$

RAUMPLAN $h1 > h2$

MATRIX OF INTERCONNECTED ROOMS $h2 = 0$

Parametric modelling of sectional space organisation. Effects of vertical shifting.

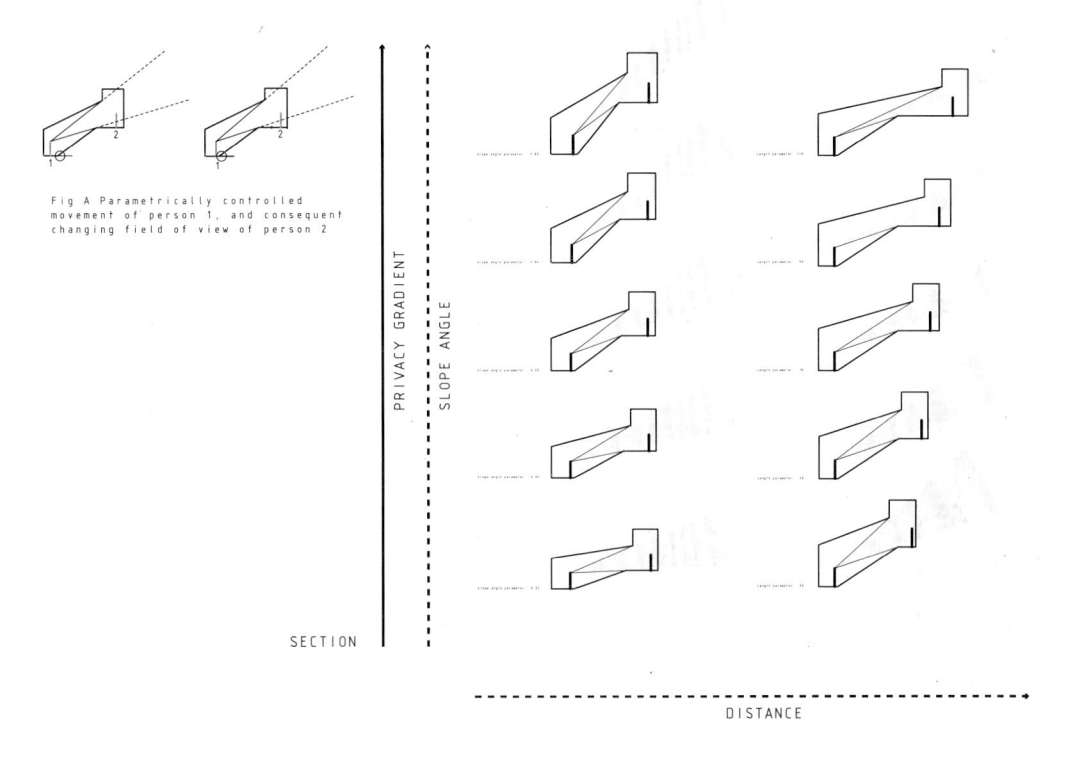

Fig A Parametrically controlled movement of person 1, and consequent changing field of view of person 2

PRIVACY GRADIENT
SLOPE ANGLE
SECTION
DISTANCE

Visual and spatial connectivity can be modelled using a parametrically defined sectional space organisation. This model then serves to be a framework component for the proliferation of multiple differentiated instances of the material system.

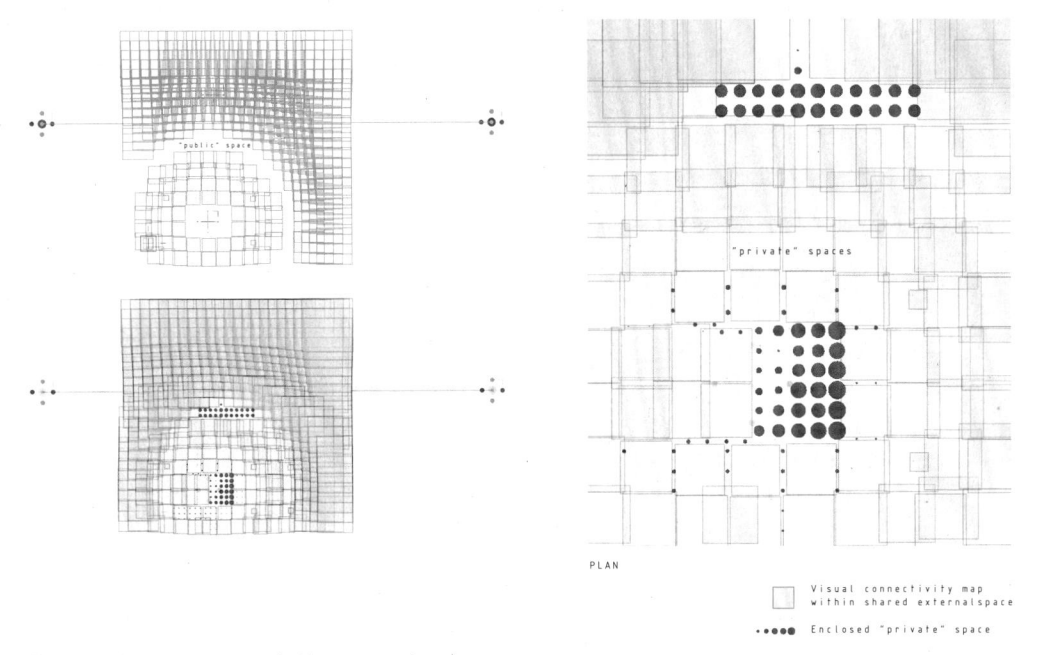

PLAN

Visual connectivity map within shared external space
Enclosed "private" space

Parametrically controlled private/public space gradation.

Parametric associative modelling is used not only for the articulation of material systems, but also for rigorously pursuing spatial organisation. In this study by Asif Amir Khan spatial connectivity is altered by shifting spatial units so as to change, for instance, a matrix of interconnected rooms into a raumplan or box-in-a-box sectional arrangement.

SPATIAL HETEROGENEITY AND EVOLVING ACTIVITIES

The increasing urbanisation of the human environment has accelerated the social, economic and environmental processes that shape it. This is evident, for instance, from the multiple space use research that is taking place in the Netherlands, as well as the increasing emphasis on urban metabolic studies worldwide. However, all of these studies still frame their research in terms of a division between programme and space relations or material and production and consumption processes. It is clear that there is an acute need for a more inclusive approach that architectonically correlates 'material' and 'programmatic' processes. The increasing complexity of space-use cycles and material life-cycles requires an understanding of the built environment as ecological, topological and structural provisions that facilitate an increasing, diversifying and intensifying amount of human activities, while remaining sustainable.

Ecology, as discussed above, refers here to the relationships between humans and their physical and social environments. Topology has been introduced as the connections between all the material elements in an environment, while structure refers to organisational capacities above and beyond load-bearing. The development and utilisation of topological analysis and optimisation methods is therefore of crucial importance, with differentiation and diversity becoming functional on a higher level through enhanced connectivity of open systems and thus facilitated feedback relations.
In this way ecology, topology and structure are inseparably intertwined. These interrelations become instrumental when the generative process is modified by positive feedback between linked properties and their reciprocal influences. The differentiation of a material system through a feedback process amplifies and modulates the dynamics of a hosting environment. Emergent organisational effects then facilitate the mutation and migration of human activities.

A crucial aspect of this approach is the emphasis on process and the acceleration of the evolution of an architectural environment, whereby the relation of form and space to programme acknowledges the dynamic patterns of human habitation. Environment is understood as a dynamic composite of habitat-specific conditions and habitant-specific itineraries, as a gradient field of performative micro- and macro-milieus.[33]

Together, these milieus produce an ecosystem, a dynamic relationship between material, structural and environmental intensities and human activities. Such an integral approach suggests that architectural design constitutes the modulation of micro-environmental conditions within an emergent macro-environmental context. It promotes modulations across entire ecosystems, so that the architectural environment yields diverse and intense social interactions, and mutable relations between habitat and inhabitants. This indicates a decisive shift away from a unit-based design approach towards condition-based design.

The implication is a simultaneous shift away from programme as design-defining towards design as programme-evolving. Programme should thus be understood, not as a pre-design list of requirements, but rather as a post-design opportunity for human activities to be time-, space- and environment-specific on the basis of individual and collective preferences. The consequences of this can hardly be discussed in great detail here, nor can many built examples and their effects be shown, although it may be implicit and latent in some of the works shown in this book.

If, however, one begins to observe exactly how people choose their place for certain activities in everyday life, it becomes clear that programme only maintains its hold through rigidly installed provisions (elevator shafts, toilet sinks, and so on) or through enforced policies. An everyday example can be found in the way people are constrained to work in a specific location because the workplace is allocated and the resources – for example, table and chair or assembly line – are in that space. Once choice is provided, patterns of inhabitation may well become far more erratic. Not everybody wants to read their newspaper in the same spot; it may be too dark, too bright, too exposed, too loud, too warm, too cold, too close to that person, or just (not) right. What is suitable for one person right now may not be so at a later point. Should we then declare a total programmatic laissez-faire, a return to a general non-plan paradigm, activity anarchy across space and time? Not necessarily so. It is feasible to provide areas that are quite controlled in terms of their provision of conditions in relation to the allocated activities while simultaneously instrumentalising the knowledge that people will choose, if given a choice. If architects aspire to a notion of democratic space they may well approach it in this way. They may recognise that hard control can co-exist and co-evolve together with a soft modulation and appropriation of micro-environments and that there can be a rigorous and instrumental approach to this dynamic that does not overconstrain it on the one hand or let it degenerate into short-term speculation and profit on the other.

The shift from programme as design-defining towards design as programme-evolving has deep implications across all levels of the deeply entrenched concepts and operations that characterise the vast majority of architecture and architectural practice today. One of the potentially most significant implications may well be the gradual erosion of the notion of building type. This is not to say that buildings may no longer serve defined purposes, but rather that building morphology may no longer indicate use at all. As exclusive programmatic and hard threshold alignments are gradually replaced with manifold spatial arrangements and environmental gradients, we may also witness the progressive decline of discrete building volumes and the emergence of new kinds of connective and performative urban fabrics. The latter may provide for diverse and intense human activities and inhabitation potential of a completely new level of magnitude.

Of all this we can offer here but the merest glimpse.

FOOTNOTES

[1] From 'Towards a Theory of Weather' [Versuch einer Witterungslehre, 1825]; in *Goethes Werke, Hamburger Ausgabe* vol. 13, 306-07; Ed. Erich Trunz, et al, Wegner; Hamburg, 1948-60; translation from *Goethe Scientific Studies*, 145-6; Miller, D., Suhrkamp; New York, 1988.

[2] Evans, Robin; 'Figures, Doors and Passages'; in *Translations from Drawings to Buildings and other Essays*; AA Documents 2, Architectural Association, London, 1997.

[3] See Pile, John; *Open Office Planning*, Architectural Press, London, 1978; also: Hookway, Brandon; *Pandemonium – The Rise of Predatory Locales in the Postwar World*, Princeton Architectural Press, 1999.

[4] Banham, Reyner; *The Architecture of the Well-tempered Environment*, University of Chicago Press, 1973.

[5] See for instance Lally, Sean and Young, Jessica eds.; *Softspace*; Routledge, 2006.

[6] Banham, op. cit.

[7] ibid.

[8] Thanks to Pascal Schöning for many insightful discussions.

[9] From 'Towards a General Comparative Theory' [Versuch einer allgemeinen Vergleichungslehre, probably dictated by Goethe in the early 1790s and published posthumously], in Goethe: *Die Schriften zur Naturwissenschaft*, I.10, 118-22; ed. G. Schmidt, et al; in Anfrage der Deutschen Akademie der Forschung, Leopoldina; Weimar; 1947; translation from *Goethe Scientific Studies*, op. cit. 54-6.

[10] From 'The Purpose is Set Forth' [Die Absicht ist eingeleitet, written 1807, published 1817]; in *Goethes Werke*,

Hamburger Ausgabe vol. 13, 54-6; Ed. Erich Trunz, et al; Wegner; Hamburg; 1948-60; translation from *Goethe Scientific Studies*, op. cit. 63-4.

[11] Evolutionary Biology can provide some useful analytical methods for this purpose. See Cummings, Robert, 'Functional Analysis', *Journal of Philosophy*, 72 (1975), 741-65.

[12] See http://www.protocell.org

[13] Gánti, Tibor; *The Principles of Life*, Oxford University Press, 2003; first published in Hungarian as *Az élet princípiuma*, Gondolat, 1971.

[14] *New Scientist*, 12 February 2005; 'Alive!'; Bob Holmes; 28-33.

[15] For further information see for instance Biochemical and Biomedical Engineering Research Group at Bath University http://www.bath.ac.uk/chem-eng/research/groups/babe.shtml

[16] For a detailed elaboration see Nachtigall, Werner; *Bionik – Grundlagen und Beispiele für Ingenieure und Naturwissenschafter*, 2nd edition, Springer Verlag, 2002, 318-36.

[17] See Addington, Michelle; Schodek, Daniel; 'Smart Materials and Technologies for the architecture and design professions'; *Elements and Control Systems*, Architectural Press, 2005, 109-37.

[18] For further information see Aldhous, Peter; 'Redesigning Life', in *New Scientist*, 20 May 2006, 43-7.

[19] *Encyclopaedia of Chemical Technology*; Ed. Kroschwitz, J., John Wiley & Sons, 1992.

[20] See *The History of Mathematics*; Ed. Fauvel, J. and Gray, J., Palgrave Macmillan, 1987, 534-37.

[21] The pluripotent stem cells in animals and meristematic cells in higher plants develop from initially totipotent cells. Totipotent cells are cells with the ability to differentiate into all cell types. In mammals, for example, only the zygote and early embryonic cells are totipotent.

[22] Frei Otto has been a pioneer in employing processes of form-finding. His work also includes experiments on 'bending lines', which are relevant to the paper strip example. See Otto, F. and Gass, S.; *Experiments: Form-Force-Mass*, Institute for Lightweight Structures, Stuttgart, 1990.

[23] This recognition does not rule out the possibility of using digital form-finding processes as a means for identifying a component's behavioural tendencies before parameterisation in a subsequent model.

[24] The biologist Arthur Winfree speaks of 'topological exactitude, indifferent to quantitative details' as one of the preconditions of complex biological structures and processes. See Winfree, A. T.; *When Time Breaks Down*; Princeton, 1987.

[25] '[For the typologist] there are a limited number of fixed, unchangeable 'ideas' underlying the observed variability, with the eidos (idea) being the only thing that is fixed and real.... The populationist stresses the uniqueness of everything in the organic world.... The ultimate conclusions of population thinker and typologists are exactly the opposite. For the typologist the type (eidos) is real and the variation an illusion, while for the populationist the type (the average) is an abstraction and only the variation is real.' Biologist Ernst Mayr, quoted in Sober, E.; *The Nature of Selection*, Cambridge MA, 1987.

[26] Inward proliferation would be comparable to the (linear) Sierpinski Carpet or Menger Sponge.

[27] Brown, James H., 'Complex Ecological Systems', in *Complexity – Metaphors, Models, and Reality*; Ed. Cowan, George A.; Pines, David; Meltzer, David; Santa Fe Institute; Perseus Books; Reading MA, 1994.

[28] See for instance Von Uexküll, Jacob, *Theoretical Biology*; translated by D. L. MacKinnon; International Library of Psychology, Philosophy and Scientific Method.; Kegan Paul, Trench, Trubner & Co., London, 1926.

[29] Banham, Reyner, *The Architecture of the well-tempered Environment*, University of Chicago Press, 1973.

[30] Umberto Eco, *The Open Work*, Harvard University Press, Cambridge MA, 1989.

[31] Sloterdijk, Peter; 'Atmospheric Politics'; in *Making Things Public – Atmospheres of Democracy*, 944-51; Ed. Latour, Bruno and Weibel, Peter; MIT Press, Cambridge MA, 2005.

[32] For further elaboration of L-systems and their application in plant modelling see Hensel, Michael; *Computing Self-organisation: Environmentally-sensitive Growth Modelling*; AD Wiley, London, 2006.

[33] See Albert Pope's argument in the essay 'The Primacy of Space', *Ladders*, Princeton Architectural Press, 1996.

MICHAEL HENSEL AND ACHIM MENGES

20 PROTO-ARCHITECTURES, RESEARCH AND DESIGN PROJECTS

The projects presented here are examples of research into heterogeneous architectures conducted in the AA's Diploma Unit 4 Morpho-Ecologies (ME) programme and in the Generative Proto-Architecture (GPA) visiting studios taught at the Rice School of Architecture and Rotterdam Academy of Architecture and Urban Design. Above all, the work aims at rethinking the discourse of heterogeneous space and architecture as a material practice through intensive research into differentiated material systems and their performative capacities.

In this context the GPA studios focused on basic research, exploring material systems in terms of their potential architectural capacities and applications. Dip4's ME programme went further, by conducting extensive research and producing pilot projects, and by bringing differentiated material systems into contact with specific environments in order to develop their performative capacities and explore the programmatic opportunities of the Morpho-Ecologies approach.

Understanding the importance of digital technology, not as a field of research per se, but rather as a vehicle for notating and instrumentalising the intricate relationship of form, material, structure and ultimately space, all projects commence from in-depth physical modelling experiments and proceed in a bottom-up manner from the development of basic material elements and their arrangement in space and time.

The starting-point for the development of material systems is form-finding, a design method that deploys the self-organisational capacities of materials in relation to extrinsic forces induced for example through the construction process, different loading scenarios or context-specific environmental conditions. At various critical stages the behaviour of the material system undergoes an essential change in response to the increasing size and differentiation of the system across various hierarchical levels of assemblies. At the same time the articulation of the system is informed by an expanding range of performance criteria. The focal point in such a design process is what we define as material systems. These are material assemblies that, in their articulation, embody a geometric and topological logic which is informed by the self-organisational tendencies of material elements, established through form-finding and an inherent logic of manufacturing and assembly, as well as their environmental modulation capacities. In order to become architecture, these material systems must be further informed by context-specific conditions, by strategies of spatial organisation and synthesised structural and environmental performance, and by speculations about emergent social formation and programmatic opportunities.

We have distinguished between three broad categories of material system, though the boundaries between them remain somewhat elusive. These categories are proliferated component systems, globally modulated systems, and aggregate systems.

[i] Proliferated component systems can be developed through Halbzeug (semi-finished product assemblies) or differentiated components. A Halbzeug is a semi-finished product lying between raw material and finished product. Semi-finished products are usually available in larger sizes, e.g. as sheets, rods, hollow rods, profiles, coils, etc., and need to be cut to the required size. The design process unfolds through a differentiation of the rules of assembly within narrow parameters that enable a rigorous proliferation and jointing process informed by internal and external constraints.

A component is a constituent part of a more complex assembly; unlike the Halbzeug, it is a fully defined, finished product. Components can be differentiated and assembled into larger systems in response to inherent material and geometric characteristics and extrinsic parameters.

[ii] A globally modulated system registers local manipulation throughout the entire system. Such a system acquires its articulation through the number and disposition of definition points, which together assert a gradient influence upon the entire system. Globally modulated systems exploit the capacity of materials to settle into a stable configuration resulting from their internal make-up and external forces, which include extrinsic loads as well as the critical location and bearing capacity of control points. They require a different design method than for differentiated assembly systems, since the focus is on a limited number of strategic control points rather than a comprehensive geometric description by a maximum number of points. Membranes are one example of such globally modulated systems.

[iii] An aggregate is formed by the loose combination of many separate units or items. An aggregate system is defined by the specification of the individual aggregate unit, the aggregation process and the external constraints. Aggregate systems are the opposite of assembly systems or composite systems, in that the units are not connected by joints or a binding matrix; nevertheless they are still systems as the interrelations of system constituents can be traced, defined and instrumentalised. Differentiation occurs through the manipulation of the individual aggregate, the aggregation process and external constraints.

The most obvious distinction between the proposed categories is between assemblies of components and aggregates. A system is said to be more than the sum of its parts. Kant's notion of a system demands a specific mode of connection between the system's parts, a linkage (Verknüpfung) that is more than just connection, enabling what Kant defines as 'the synthetic unity of the manifold'. Aggregates by definition do not display such linkages between parts, in fact parts are not connected at all. However, in a wider view aggregates can be understood as part of a larger formative system which can display linkages between causes and effects, between hierarchical multi-scalar feedback relations and hosting environment, much more directly than other material system categories. Extrinsic forces, such as gravity and airflow, shape natural aggregates into formations such as ripples, piles and dunes, which in turn modulate the same forces that have shaped them. Aggregates also interact in highly specific ways with other material assemblies. We have therefore included aggregates and the related formative processes within the scope of our material system research.

Our tentative taxonomy of material systems also takes into account the critical difference of elements or assemblies that are either elastically or plastically deformed. Elasticity refers to the ability of a body to resist a distorting influence or stress and then return to its initial size and shape once the stress is removed. All solids are elastic, but if the applied stress exceeds the elastic limit of a material element, a permanent or plastic deformation results. Both the resistance to stress and the elastic limit depend on the composition of the solid.

Elasticity implies that the elements that configure an assembly are bent, buckled or torqued into shape through the actual assembly procedure. The pre-stressed state of the resulting system can then become instrumental in exploiting the energy stored within the system. Since elastic deformation also remains reversible such systems retain to some extent the capacity for a range of stable states. However, it is important to carefully monitor and account for creep or plastic deformation, which arises as a result of long-term exposure to levels of applied load or stress below yield, that is structural collapse. The rate of plastic deformation is a function of the material properties, length of exposure to stress and also temperature. Creep is not necessarily a failure mode, but is instead a damage mechanism. The material strains over time until it finally fails or becomes permanently deformed, thus reducing the amount of energy stored within the system.

Material systems with a high elastic threshold can be conceived as bundles of slender rods that are nevertheless able to transmit load without catastrophic buckling. Elastic structures have been researched extensively by scientists and engineers and from the seventeenth century onwards, producing many useful theories with significant repercussions for civil and mechanical engineering applications. However, mathematical models and tools of sufficient complexity have only recently begun to emerge, informing and being informed by research in, for instance, the discipline of biomechanics. Frei Otto's research and projects have pursued research in this direction using timber in bending (e.g. the Mannheim Multihalle gridshell) or in tension (e.g. the refectory building at Hooke Park, Dorset). Despite their obvious potential, such elastically deformed systems have not found wide application: architects have tended to shy away, cowed by questions of liability and lack of experience. It is precisely for this reason that much of the work presented here investigates ways of better understanding and deploying the behaviour and capacities of such systems.

Membranes are form-active tension systems that also belong to the elastically deformed systems: their shape and extent must be determined as part of the solution through a form-finding process, like the configuration and arrangement of all other elastically deformed systems.

Plastically deformed or pre-shaped systems do not store energy in the way outlined above but often make construction easier by defining the specific morphology of all the constituent parts of the assembly – a process that is critical for the performance of the resultant overall system. This calls for a design process that enables constraints and possibilities of the relevant fabrication technologies to be embedded in the form-generation techniques that determine the particular geometry of all the parts.

Another important aspect is whether the internal make-up of the material at hand is invariant (that is, isotropic) or variant (anisotropic) with respect to direction. The former implies uniformity of physical properties in all directions within the material, for instance equal elasticity in all directions, while the latter implies directional differences and is characteristic of fibrous materials. These material properties determine the behaviour of both element and assembly in a fundamental way. The careful choice of material, with regard to its internal make-up and resultant behaviour, is therefore of central importance to the research presented here. In some cases this may lead to designing the actual makeup of a composite material according to required characteristics and properties. This is where knowledge of biomimetic engineering and material science becomes instrumental.

Overall, the categorisation introduced here may serve as an initial framework. Attempting a more systematic differentiation of the various material systems and pilot projects would do an injustice to their rich scope and their individual goals and focus. Moreover, establishing a unified taxonomy is a very difficult undertaking. Does one begin with the status of the initial element as a semi-finished product or an already defined component? When does the status of an element change from a semi-finished product to a component? Perhaps when the first functional assignment has informed its articulation? If so, this will happen at very different stages of development for each project. Should one organise the work in relation to existing types that the projects seem to adhere to, for example calling a design a proto-gridshell? Such an approach would prematurely channel the designs into particular directions and undermine the possibility of defining systems that are altogether different from those already established. Or should one consider the eventual performance profiles that arise for each project as the means of categorisation? Such an approach would run the risk of either being too general, thus failing to provide a useful taxonomy or, conversely, of leading to an overly specific catalogue of applications. We have therefore opted to outline some important differences and similarities between the systems and give them a loose order without forcing them into a taxonomic straitjacket that could distract from their potential. In doing so, we hope to satisfy the modality of systematic work while avoiding the pitfalls of defining the borders too narrowly.

One shared aspect of the different strands of this material system research is the way in which computer-aided design is instrumentalised. Rather than using representational tools intended for explicit scalar geometric descriptions, the projects employ parametric associative models and digital form-finding methods in a way that is far more immediate in its relation to materialisation, so enabling the designer to orchestrate the system's evolution and proliferation. The geometric rigour of such digital techniques is utilised to integrate manufacturing constraints, assembly logics and material characteristics in the definition of material components. Rather than designing a specific artefact, the focus is on defining, evolving and instrumentalising the behaviour of a material system that becomes increasingly refined and calibrated through the recognition of anticipated and emergent performative capacities across multiple instances of the system. This includes exploring parametric variables to understand the behaviour of a system and deploying this understanding to strategise the performance of the system interacting with context- and time-specific extrinsic influences, such as environmental conditions.

What ultimately binds this research together is the vision and belief of its authors in the potential of architecture as a material practice – a practice that is capable of evolving a heterogeneous, exciting and sustainable built environment with embedded higher-level functionality and higher-level integration between material system and environment.

The following section introduces 20 selected projects that indicate the scope of a much broader and ongoing research.

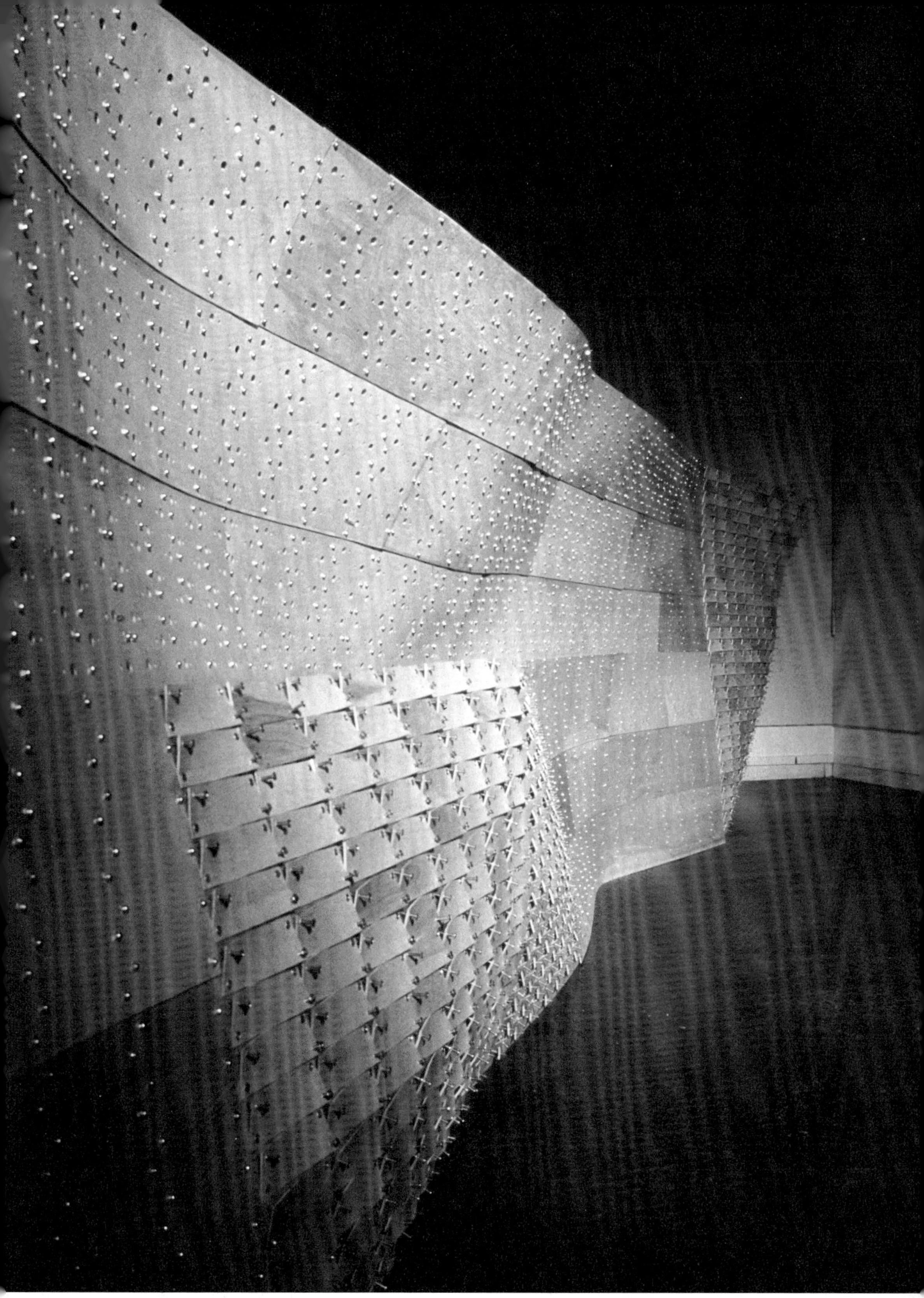

This research explores the potential of assemblies made from elastically deformed rods. Rods are slender elements with a longitudinal dimension that is much greater than the transverse dimension of the cross-section. Their elastic deformation can be induced through bending, buckling and torquing or torsional buckling. Overall, rods constitute simple but nontrivial elements through which elasticity can be utilised and straightforwardly experimentally verified.

The work of distinguished experts such as James Bernoulli, Leonhard Euler, Gustav Kirchhoff and John Henry Michell has made a significant contribution to the understanding of the behaviour of elastic rods. Euler, for instance, demonstrated that there is a critical load for buckling, which occurs when a compression member moves laterally and shortens under a load it can no longer support. With any load smaller than the critical one, a slender compression member would remain straight and support the load, while under any larger load it would bend sideways with a displacement of infinite size. Buckling is one of the most common and catastrophic causes of failure, which is perhaps the reason why the architectural profession has shied away from instrumentalising this mode of elastic deformation, even though it can rigorously pursue such systems with the mathematical models and tools available today.

After an initial study of elastically deformed single rods, in which the geometric logic of these manipulations was captured digitally, the research focused on assemblies known as spread bundles. These consist of a number of rods that are held at both ends and spread apart at a fixed distance between the constraints. This is done in order to reduce the amount of material required to deal with axial loading, compared to simple bundled poles made from parallel bundled rods, for instance. In this way buckling becomes instrumental as a way of pre-stressing in order to achieve effective performance in axial load-bearing.

Equipped with adjustable spacer elements, the bundles can be adapted to respond to different forces, which is essential for the assembly of larger structures consisting of multiple bundle components. A series of experiments were conducted to explore the behaviour of various multi-bundle configurations constructed from slender elements using different strategies of connection and spreading. The calibration of load-bearing capacity and parametric variables such as the local length of rod sections between support, connection or spread points, as well as the setting of the adjustable spacer units, were tested and digitally notated. This required the development of digital techniques that focus not on one particular bundle object but on the interdependency of geometric definition and system behaviour across a range of system configurations. By inputting the geometric data derived from the analysis of various test configurations, we extended the notational tool into an operational technique for establishing a parametric assembly and manipulation protocol. This led in turn to the development of a strategy of proliferating bundle components into a larger, vertical structure, based on the combined definition of the specification of system elements and relevant manipulation parameters. In order to corroborate and instrumentalise the anticipated behaviour we made a full-scale column spread bundles to monitor the behaviour of the assembly as it increased in size and self-weight. Three threaded steel rods with a cross-section of 6 mm were used to assemble each spread bundle. A minimal rotation of the rods from one end-constraint to the other induced a small amount of torsional buckling in each bundle. This had tremendous consequences as the assembly grew to become a larger vertical assembly.

Rods of stacked bundles were connected along their longitudinal axis so that tangency alignment was achieved in the point of connection. The separate rods that were connected at their end points began to behave as a single continuous rod, accumulating the rotational effect of the torsional buckling. Reaching an assembly height of 4 m, the self-weight and rotation of the assembly appeared to be well balanced. The overall assembly rotated under its own self-weight and settled into a stable configuration. As the assembly increased in size, the longitudinally connected bundle stacks began to buckle under the self-weight of the structure: to compensate a greater amount of cross-connection was inserted at smaller intervals into the cross-section of the overall assembly. This eventually made the overall assembly so slender again that it began to buckle at large, no longer able to rotate into a stable state. At a height of 7 m, the assembly had to be split into several arms of spread bundles, which were propped up against the surrounding walls to prevent too much rotation and buckling of the global assembly.

At this stage the assembly consisted of hundreds of rods and spacer elements, so the combined effects of increasing vertical loads and resulting rotational and buckling movements could be counterbalanced by geometric adjustments of the spacer elements. Incremental adjustment of local geometric settings of the spacer elements resulted in increased stability of the structure as a whole. After various cycles of adjustment according to the established parametric protocol the 7-m-tall column made entirely from elements with a maximum diameter of 6 mm reached a fully calibrated, stable configuration.

In terms of behaviour, the prototype structure can be understood as a macro-column consisting of various micro columns that are related through the materially discontinuous yet geometrically continuous rod elements. Further research might therefore investigate the possibility of more spatial distributions, orientations and connections, rather then bundling up all elements into a column type structure. In this way torsional buckling could be locally decelerated or accelerated in order to stabilise the structure and to store a beneficial amount of energy, while at the same time seeking to avoid creep – the slow plastic deformation of the slender rods and sub-assemblies, due to excessive buckling of the system.

regional assemblies

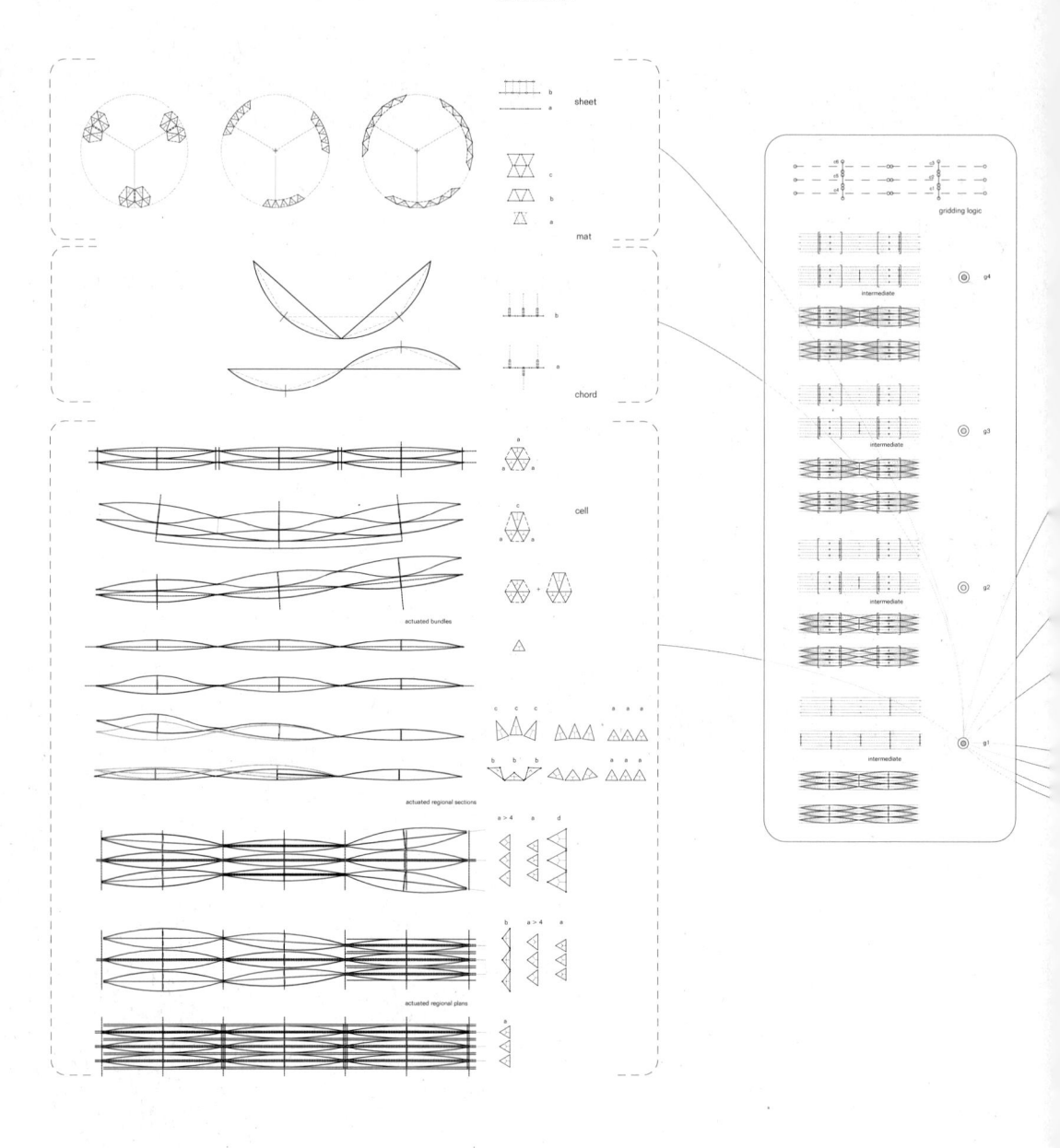

sheet

mat

chord

cell

actuated bundles

actuated regional sections

actuated regional plans

gridding logic

intermediate g4

intermediate g3

intermediate g2

intermediate g1

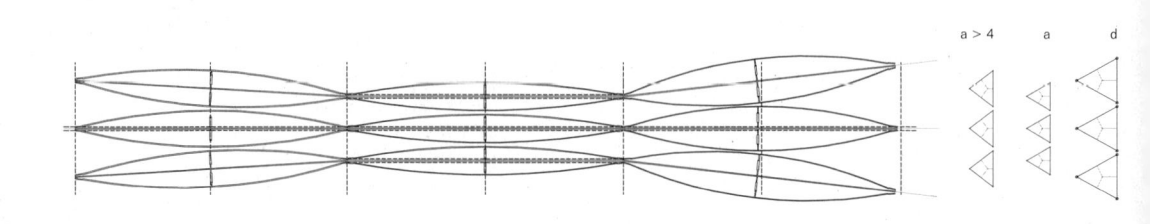

a > 4   a   d

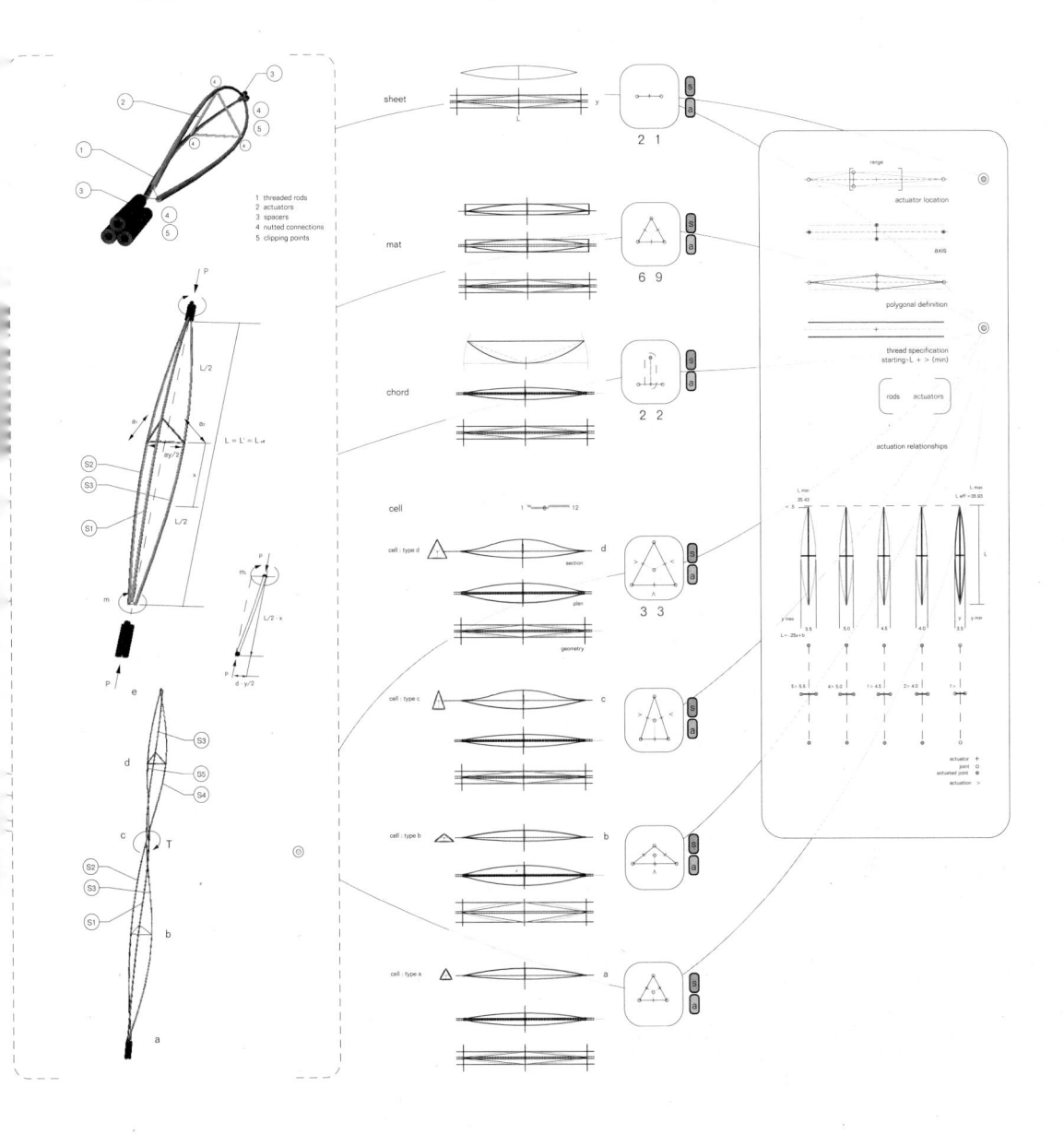

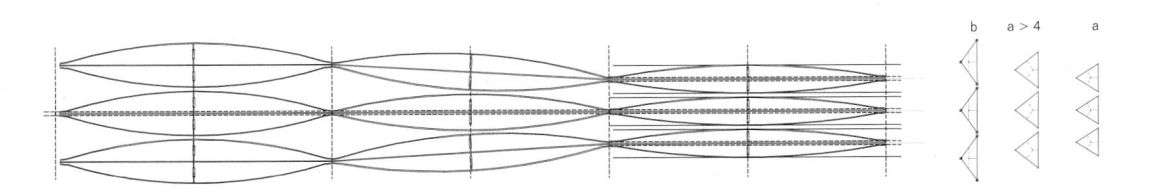

The manipulation chart of the spread bundle system shows local geometric parameters of component constituents, different component definitions and various regional bundle assemblies in relation to the resultant geometric behaviour of different system sub-assemblies.

72   The proliferation of bundle components is tested through the construction of a large prototype structure. Each bundle component is individually built from threaded rods and adjustable spacer elements. During assembly the system lies horizontal and is subsequently erected.

After the erection process the prototype structure is stabilised by the incremental adjustment of the spacer elements in order to counterbalance rotational and buckling movements resulting from the vertical loads.

74 In the construction process individually prepared spread bundle components are assembled such that tangency alignment is achieved in the point of connection. Thus the separate rods that are connected at their end points begin to behave as a single continuous rod, accumulating the rotational effect of the torsional buckling after erection.

The 7-metre tall prototype structure made entirely from elements with maximum diameter of 6 mm reached a fully calibrated, stable configuration after various cycles of adjustment according to the established parametric protocol.

Probably the most striking and fascinating aspect of this project is the great complexity of the macro-structure, created by the intelligent proliferation and addition of the most simple micro-structure components: three 6 mm steel rods connected at their ends and bent into a pre-stressed arrangement with three simple adjustable connectors.

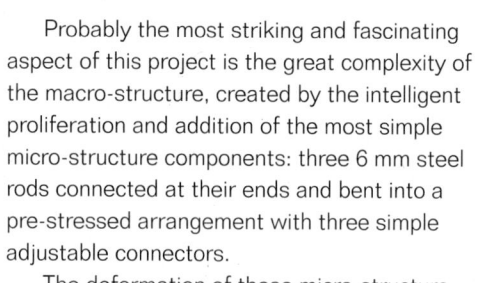

The deformation of these micro-structure elements achieves its key properties by playing an intelligent structural trick. The thin rods used as straight elements would be inherently unstable and prone to buckling failure under the smallest of compressive loads: spacing them apart with the adjustable spacers configures them into a more stable basic system, by pre-empting the failure mode and flexing them into a bent shape.

However this bent shape introduces a more elastic or flexible behaviour and deformations under changing load-paths become an important design feature. The project explores this quite unusual behaviour in an exemplary way by creating and studying a large-scale model. Along the way, a few discoveries are made that are characteristic of structural arrangements which depend to a large degree on geometry.

The first of these discoveries is the fact that the equilibrium that is required to arrive at a stable arrangement is not fixed and, due to the flexibility of the individual structural members, equilibrium requires constant adjustment both on the component level and in terms of macro-arrangement. The changing equilibrium is difficult to predict and is only reached through a number of iterations of adjustments.

At the same time, as the structure is modified by the addition of elements it has the tendency to find the nearest equilibrium state by itself, a process that again can be influenced by iterative adjustment. Due to the inherent flexibility of the structural elements the deformations are small and appear in a slow and controllable manner, avoiding the sudden failure one would experience if a compression element were to buckle.

Whilst this process of constant adjustment is necessary throughout the assembly process it becomes evident that the geometry of the global arrangement becomes the critical factor once the structure reaches a certain limit in size. Two distinctly different behaviours emerge: a converging and a non-converging self-adjustment of the structure due to its additive construction process and proliferation.

As the students discovered, up to a critical height of 4 metres the deformations that occur within the structure during the assembly process are predominantly self-stabilising. The critical size, or in this case height, will certainly vary depending on a few key parameters such as the width-to-height ratio, the bundling of the rod component, and the effects of cross-bracing, to mention only a few obvious aspects of the overall geometry.

Beyond the critical dimensions, the non-converging behaviour is the predominant feature. The adjustments of the global structural system result not only in larger deformations but in deformations that move away from the direction of proliferation and lead, albeit in a slow fashion, to what could be called a structural failure. The iterative local adjustments of the individual micro-structures, which make correction easy when the structure is converging towards a stable equilibrium state, are no longer sufficient for correction of the global arrangement.

Only the manipulation of the global system, the introduction of additional supports and/or the change of other geometrical key parameters are now able to generate a stable equilibrium. Here the very flexible assembly system allowed for further adjustments in the global geometrical arrangement to keep the structure from overturning. In summary: this behaviour shows clearly how the use of flexibility and elasticity provides adaptability whilst generating a dependence of the structure on its overall geometry.

The real benefit of carrying out the project in this way lies in its large scale, where the forces that act on the structure become of real significance while the material effects can be explored in an explicit and direct manner. A certain precision in the building elements as well as in the assembly process is required and achieved, making this a very valuable experiment. It shows clearly that elastic deformation can be introduced as a design feature allowing a degree of adaptation. The project explored this in a hands-on manner that shows a good understanding of the underlying principles.

As a further step it would now be interesting to go deeper into the individual constituents that characterise this adaptable structure, analysing and quantifying its principles. As discussed above, there are a number of influencing factors on a macro-level: height-to-width ratio, cross-bracing effects, stabilising and destabilising global arrangements, varying bundling arrangements.

Equally interesting and worth quantifying and analysing, though, are the transformations that happen in each of the components, such as the change of angle or direction of element curvature, or the varying degrees of pre-stress, which in turn influence the load-bearing capacity of the individual members and, bringing it back to a global context, the amounts of redundancy that are necessary to provide the desired adaptability.

This project is concerned with a largely neglected field of investigation – the strategic use of the bending of material elements to establish heterogeneous and partially reconfigurable spaces. The work focuses on utilising elastic rods comprised of anisotropic material, such as carbon-fibre, to configure larger, partially adaptive assemblies. Each rod is manipulated by bending and torquing (i.e. by displacing its two ends), so that energy can be stored within the system.

An initial set of experiments focused on bending single rods and comparing the different elastic limits of rods made from isotropic and anisotropic materials. The elastic limit is the point at which a material no longer undergoes a change in strain that is linearly proportional to the change in stress. When the material exceeds this limit, it undergoes plastic or permanent deformation. Materials with different elastic limits will manifest quite different self-organisational behaviour in reaction to forces, with beneficial or catastrophic consequences for an assembly such as the one developed here.

The second set of experiments looked at the make-up of an assembly of rods. An assembly consists of two types of elements, rods and connector plates. Each connector plate has a specific number of ways for the rod to be connected. Displacement of the rod from one connection point to another along an axis induces bending, while displacement along two axes induces torsional buckling. A number of experiments revealed that there are several stable states for an assembly that can be achieved by a rotation of a connector plate, which induces torsional buckling or a change in its direction of rotation, due to the tendency of rods to straighten out unless constrained. Some configurations self-stabilised in this way, by rotating into a stable state.

While the second set of experiments operated with parallel connector plates, subsequent experiments displaced the connector plates in space, increasing the elastic deformation of the rods step by step in order to investigate different spatial arrangements facilitated by these manipulations. The increase in elastic deformation results in more energy being stored locally within the system. For larger assemblies equilibrium can be found through careful placement of sub-assemblies of rod bundles that cancel each other out or accelerate movement until the next stable state is found. In this sense it is important to register, map and instrumentalise the possible and actual movement within the system, so that stable states can be reached even with complex assemblies that display multiple direction changes in the displacement of elements.

From an extensive series of tests of various system configurations, determined by different rod layouts and connector plate settings, a combined behavioural and morphological taxonomy of the system was established and digitally notated. In a large matrix, a range of parametric manipulations of the rod displacement and connector plate distribution are cross-related with the resulting self-organisational tendencies of the individual rods as well as the overall system. The inherent dependencies of form, material and behaviour in relation to the emerging performative capacities of various system configurations thus form the basis for further digital investigations and allow a comprehensive, parametric understanding of the system which facilitates the design process, with particular respect to more complex arrangements.

One important aspect of establishing a larger configuration is the strategic stabilisation of critical sub-locations of the system. In order to fix such crucial locations within the system, where the tendency of movement between stable states was undesirable, a further set of experiments was conducted and two options were tested. The first consisted of vacuum-forming plastic sheets around regions that needed to be stabilised, while the second achieved the same result by shrink-wrapping a plastic film around these regions. Shrink-wrapping originates from the packaging industry and consists of a plastic film that is wrapped around the articles and shrunk by heat to form a sealed, tight-fitting package. These two options differ mainly in terms of their ease of application, with the shrink-wrapped foil obviously being easier to remove and replace.

Applying both methods in tandem requires a careful consideration of how to bring about change between stable states in regions and sub-assemblies where this is most desirable – but also the least likely to occur. The embedded adaptability of the system to some extent facilitates the reconfiguration of spatial arrangements and constraints through the placing of structure in relation to the required spatial needs. Instrumentalising material and system behaviour through advanced digital modelling techniques then enables the unfolding of a spatial strategy through the combined consequences of the organisation, distribution and density of system elements, related structural performances and different degrees of spatial connectivity and enclosure. The overall system emerges as complex arrangements of rod and connector elements parametrically defined and manipulated through an open and extendible dataset with the ability to adjust to a range of spatial requirements.

The system was then implemented as a pilot project in Singapore City, in the design of an inhabitable pedestrian bridge that connects two neighbourhoods across a steep valley. In order to be more than just a connection between two locations, the bridge needs to be capable of providing for a range of activities from public assemblies to weekly markets. This design task required a careful study of possible movement patterns across the bridge for different projected activities. The densities of building elements were strategised as boundary thresholds for outdoor activities, while ensuring that the movement of pedestrians across the bridge remained unobstructed. Mapping of potential movement trajectories, placement of activities and hierarchical structuring of circulation space served this task. As a consequence the structural performance of the system, that is the stable state configurations of sub-assemblies and the overall system, needed to be coordinated with spatial requirements – an undertaking that required an extensive amount of corroboration through modelling and analysis.

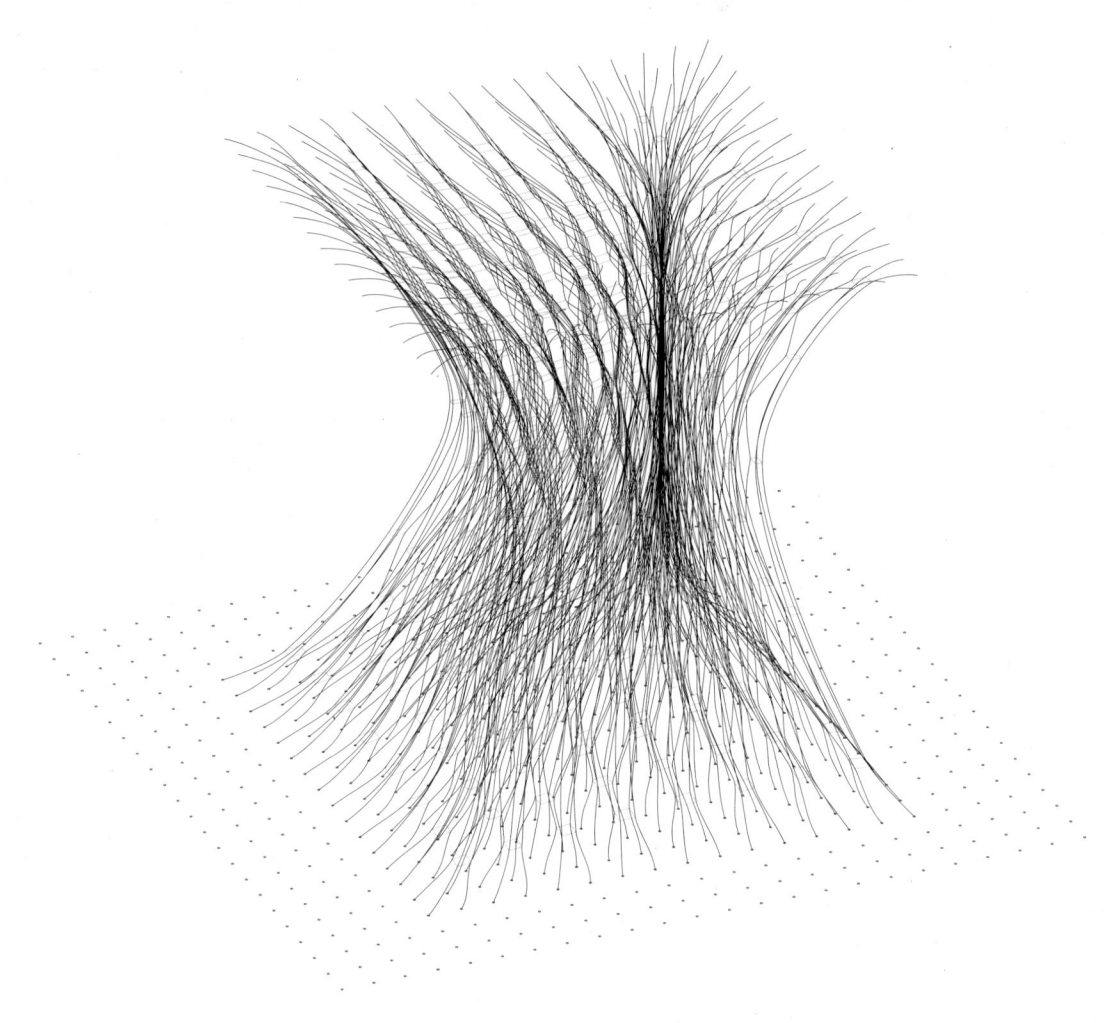

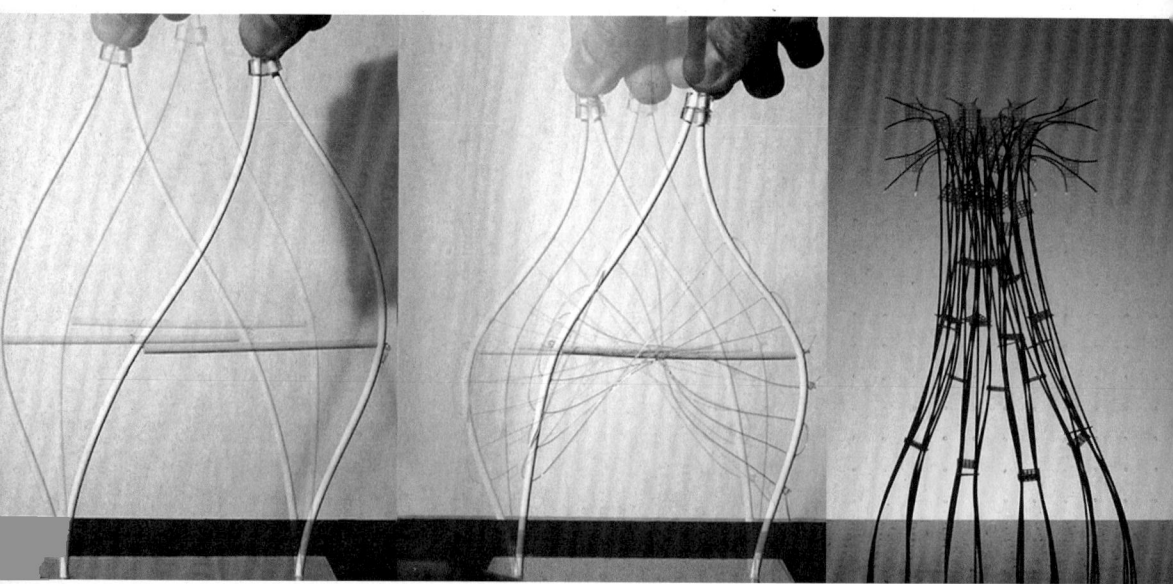

80 The system development is based on the bending behaviour of elastic rod elements (bottom). In a larger configuration of multiple bending rods the complex system behaviour can be digitally simulated and analysed (top).

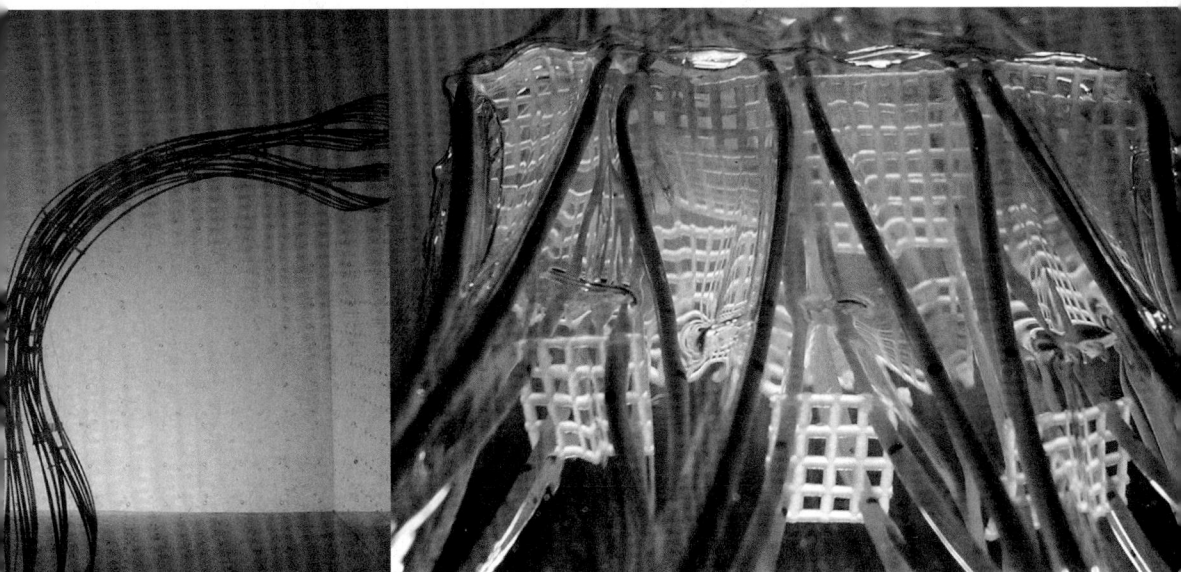

A combined behavioural and morphological taxonomy of elastic rod assemblies notates various system configurations determined by different rod layouts and connector plate settings (top). The resultant morphologies can be stabilized by the application of a thermoplastic skin (bottom).

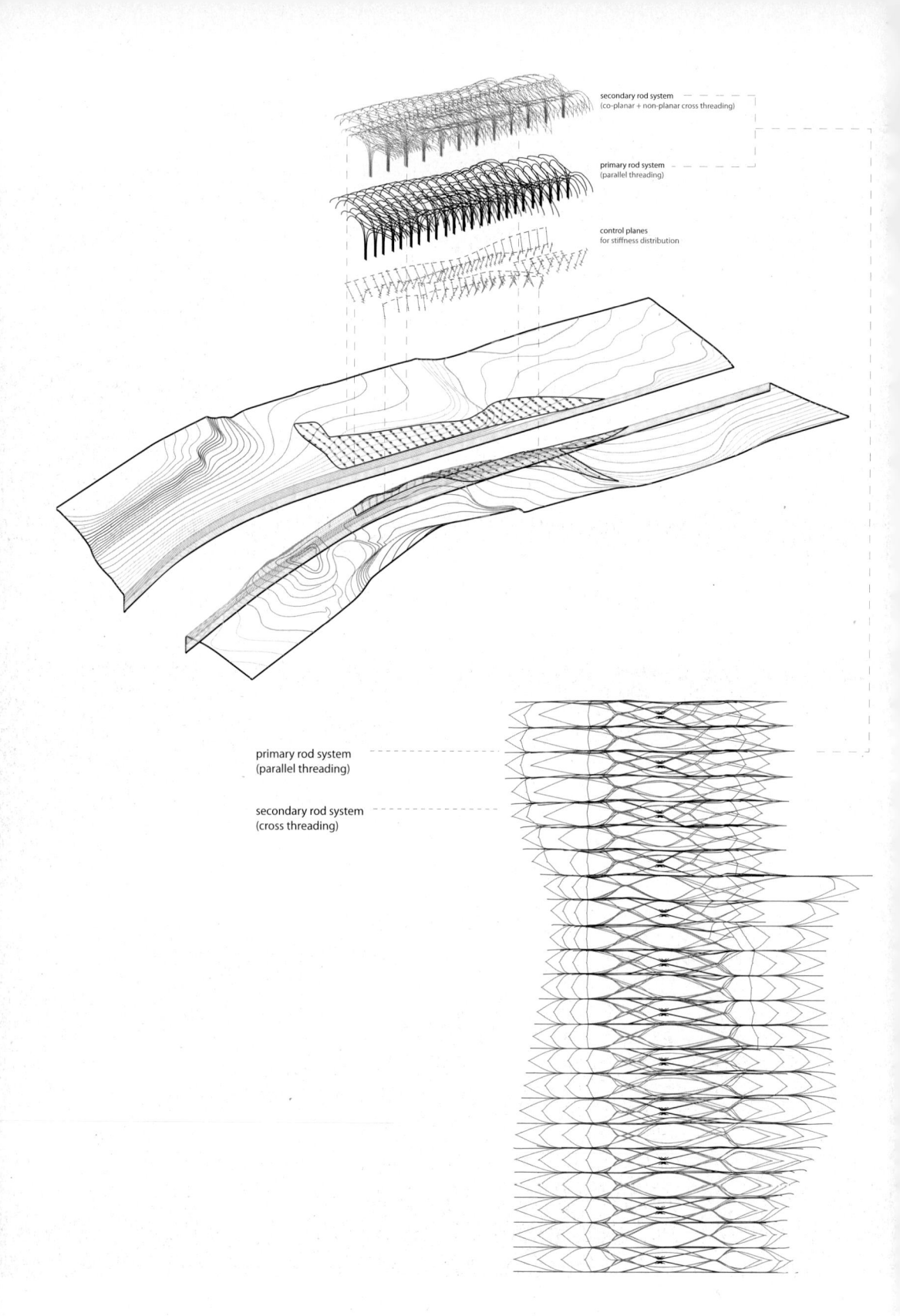

secondary rod system
(co-planar + non-planar cross threading)

primary rod system
(parallel threading)

control planes
for stiffness distribution

primary rod system
(parallel threading)

secondary rod system
(cross threading)

82   The pilot project design of an inhabitable bridge unfolds a spatial strategy from the combined material and system behaviour, related structural performances and different degrees of spatial connectivity and enclosure.

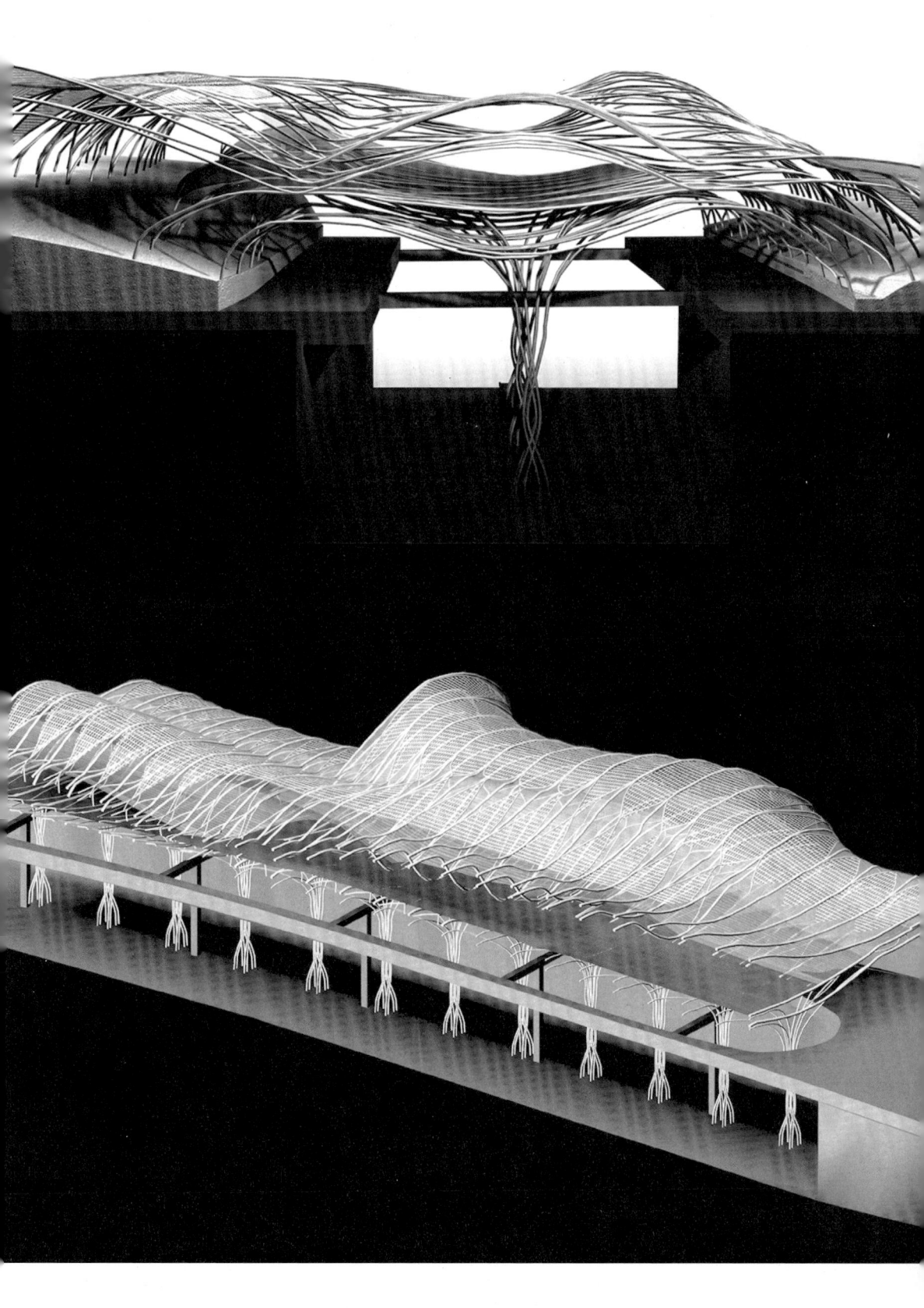

Responding to a range of structural and spatial criteria the pilot project consists of complex arrangements of rod and connector elements that are parametrically defined and manipulated through an open and extendable dataset.

COMMENTS

WOLF MANGELSDORF

To utilise the elasticity of individual rod elements in a larger structural assembly is a very interesting proposal. This approach, as explored in the research part of this project, could make adaptability and spatial adjustment of the structure through deformation a realistic prospect. The principle is explored on a model level with physical testing and the digital mapping of the geometries, and its application is investigated in a large-scale structural system for an adaptable accessible station roof.

These two parts of the project touch on two key points of the research into elastically adaptable structures, which are worth looking at in a little more depth: the influence of geometry and the importance of scale. Both relate to the behavioural studies of physical models and the deductions that can be made from them.

I will start with the first of these two aspects, the geometry, as the model exploration of the geometrical arrangements of structural elements is certainly simple to achieve and gives a good reflection of the behaviour of the individual structural elements, in this instance flexible rods, and their arrangement into larger systems, as rods interconnected with bundles.

This relates directly to the concepts regarding the influence of geometry on the structural action that I explore in my article on 'Adaptable Equilibrium'. With the efficient use of direct forces, that is tension and compression, bending stiffness becomes a secondary feature of the structure. This in turn allows structural elements to be more flexible and to utilise this flexibility for an – elastic – rearrangement of the overall system.

A number of important constraints apply when using this approach. Any transition state, movement or adjustment must be stable, both locally and globally. To achieve this it might be necessary to supplement geometrical stiffness locally with bending stiffness, either through the orientation of structural members or through a layering of structures and their interaction. Any deformation inevitably leads to a change in the amount of energy that is stored within the structure. This energy storage and, more importantly, the input and release of any energy stored, must be controlled at all times.

Here the first part of the project shows an interesting investigation into different geometrical arrangements, the bending and bundling of long rod elements and the composition of larger structures out of them. The research categorises the structural assemblies and maps out different configurations. Physical testing establishes rules that allow the model findings to be translated into the digital realm and subsequently used in the design. It becomes evident that the interconnection and the interdependence of the structural elements play an important role. Equally the geometry of the different configurations is explored, both on a component- and on a macro-level, showing how the geometrical arrangements of the different element combinations influence their overall behaviour and ability to act as a structure.

Interestingly, both bundling and branching appear to be the driving factors, a strategy that takes advantage of the disproportionally large stability of bundled rod elements in areas of force concentration whilst using individual elements where these larger forces split into smaller individual components – an approach that can be found in various natural structures. Even the reconfiguration and adjustment of the geometry, which eventually allows the structure to be adapted to different external or internal conditions, maintains this rule, so aiming to produce continuity in the geometrically achieved resistance in all transitory and final stages.

However the translation of the model findings, developed and deducted from small deformable physical models, leads to the rather more difficult aspect of scale and scalability. The scaling of bent structures is not linear, as the influence of member depth grows faster than that of member length. This relationship is a power-of-4 relationship when talking about stiffness. At the same time, the relation of axial stiffness to length scales is in square relationship. This makes it tricky to deduct results from the models, as we are intuitively expecting these to be linear as well as similar.

This is further complicated by the question of material. Whilst the plastic tubes utilised in the model tests are nicely flexible but also rather weak, the real structure is unlikely to be made from the same material. Aspects of stiffness, strength and continuity are of great importance, particularly as the deformation during the building process will potentially store large amounts of energy. This will be noticeable as the individual structure size goes up and with it, in the described power-of-4 relationship, its bending stiffness.

Looking at the two aspects – stiffness relationships and material requirements – together, one possible approach to achieving the desired deformability and flexible adaptability, as worked out in the models, whilst at the same time guaranteeing the controllability and stability of the building and deformation process, could be the further evolution of the geometrical arrangement on both micro- and macro-levels.

Whilst the models show a two-step micro-macro relationship, the concepts of addition and proliferation of individual elements could be introduced into the assembly process on a number of levels, making the relationship between micro and macro more complex but also allowing small size members to be used, so maintaining the flexibility that facilitates the desired features of the structure.

Two primary inspirations inform this project. The first is Eladio Dieste's brick structures, often double-curved surfaces with a non-symmetrical varied cross-section that is swept along a symmetrical longitudinal axis, producing unusual and beautiful spaces. Examples include the roofs of the Cítricos Caputto Fruit Packing Plant in Salto (1971-72, 1986-87), the Port Warehouse in Montevideo (1977-79), and the continuous double-curved vaults for the Cadyl Horizontal Silo in Young (1976-78). One could also mention the fabulous undulating walls and roofs of some of his churches, such as Christ the Worker in Atlántida (1958-60) or San Juan de Ávila in Madrid (1996).

The second inspiration is the traditional hilltop settlements of Turkey, built from stone in a dense accumulative fashion producing complex spatial arrangements in plan and in section. Embedded in these spatial arrangements is an underlying context-specific social arrangement of communities.

This project seeks to further develop the geometric repertoire made possible by the work of Dieste, working towards complex double-curved pre-stressed brick assemblies that do not rely on an additional concrete shell or even mortar to be structurally stable. In this context brick is initially referred to as a format of a material element, rather than a specific material choice.

At the same time the project attempts to strategise the spatial arrangements of Turkish hilltop settlements. It proposes a contemporary version, articulated as an amalgam of interconnected matrixes of rooms, raumplan and box-in-box arrangements that create different types of interstitial spaces. The relationship between spatial arrangement and social formation was discussed by Robin Evans in his essay 'Figures, Doors and Passages' (1978), in which he argued that the traditional matrix of connected rooms – an arrangement encouraging social encounters – could be revived as a viable and exciting model for public space.

An initial set of physical experiments examined the behaviour of slender rods under rotational displacement, inducing torsional buckling. The resulting surface curvatures determined possible ways of pre-stressing a brick assembly. Geometric variation and analysis facilitated the set-up of a first parametric definition of the sub-system of elastically deformed rods.

The next set of experiments aimed to stabilise particular geometric configurations by introducing bricks as compression elements traversed by rods in the longitudinal direction and by an additional set of perpendicular rods that fix the distance between the first set. Together with this, the shape of the brick was strategised in order to locate compression transmission and friction between adjacent bricks.

A 5-axis CNC-milling machine was used to produce a formwork for testing the structural behaviour and stability of different types and distributions of bricks. The formwork was given a complex shape, combining synclastic and anticlastic surface curvature with relatively tight radii, so that the most difficult instances could be investigated within a single model.

In parallel with this investigation the Finite Element method was used to digitally analyse the stress patterns occurring in the bricks upon pre-stressing and further loading, in order to ensure that the areas of compression transmission were correctly placed, shaped and sized.

Further analysis focused on the filtering of light and modulation of airflow resulting from the gaps between bricks, as well as the thermal mass, capacity and behaviour of the brick surface. With knowledge of the stress pattern of bricks in each region of the assembly, it is possible to reduce the brick-shape to the minimum necessary for transmitting load while allowing for a certain range of possible gap sizes, from zero to the maximum opening that still facilitates load transmission. Thermal mass and behaviour are directly related to this manipulation: presence or absence of material also implies presence or absence of thermal mass. However, two additional variables can be introduced here: the porosity of the material itself, and the amount of air trapped within the material. The former influences the thermal exchange between the two sides of the material, while the latter determines its insulation capacity or thermal energy transmission from one side of the material to the other. Recent developments of materials with 'tailored' porosity gradients may soon allow for carefully differentiated porosity, making the brick's specific material make-up and geometric articulation as crucial for an environmental input as its orientation.

The pilot project is located in Bairro de Recife in northeast Brazil. In this climate brick surfaces with gaps are a straightforward and common way of modulating the environment, as they offer shade while permitting airflow. The project adopts this familiar system but advances it, aiming not just to provide a sophisticated environmental screen but also to explore the system's capacity to define different spatial arrangements. The proposed pattern of spatial connectivity and sectional arrangements of spaces is developed in response to a harbour site divided by roads and high-security perimeter walls and fences. The harbour has some existing public spaces and attractions, such as a historical fortress, and is also a port-of-call for cruise liners. Its potential, however, has failed to unfold: its spaces lack visibility and connectivity, and there are too few shaded outdoor areas with attractive activities.

The project develops a public urban fabric that negotiates activities in such a way that important security perimeters can be maintained if and wherever necessary, making possible a great variety of public activities in a carefully modulated environment. In this way the brick wall has radically changed its role from a hard threshold to one that provides for filtering and modulation of gradient environmental conditions and for a much greater scope of connectivity and communication between adjacent and layered spaces. Far from being merely a canopy, screen or solid wall, brick assemblies assume a new manifestation as configurations made from simple elements with high-level architectural and environmental performance capacity. This is achieved by altering the material make-up of bricks, the way they are assembled into porous surfaces, and their spatial arrangement.

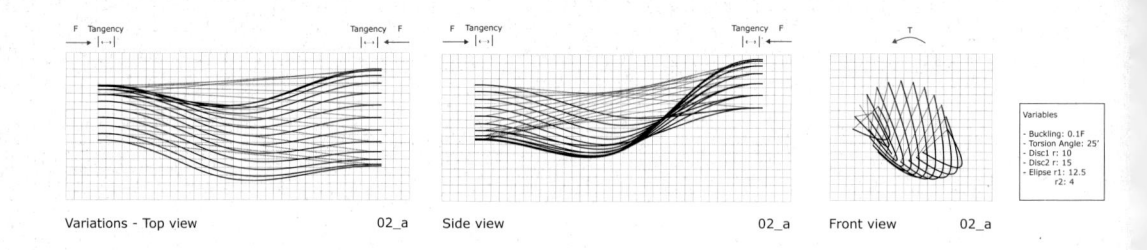

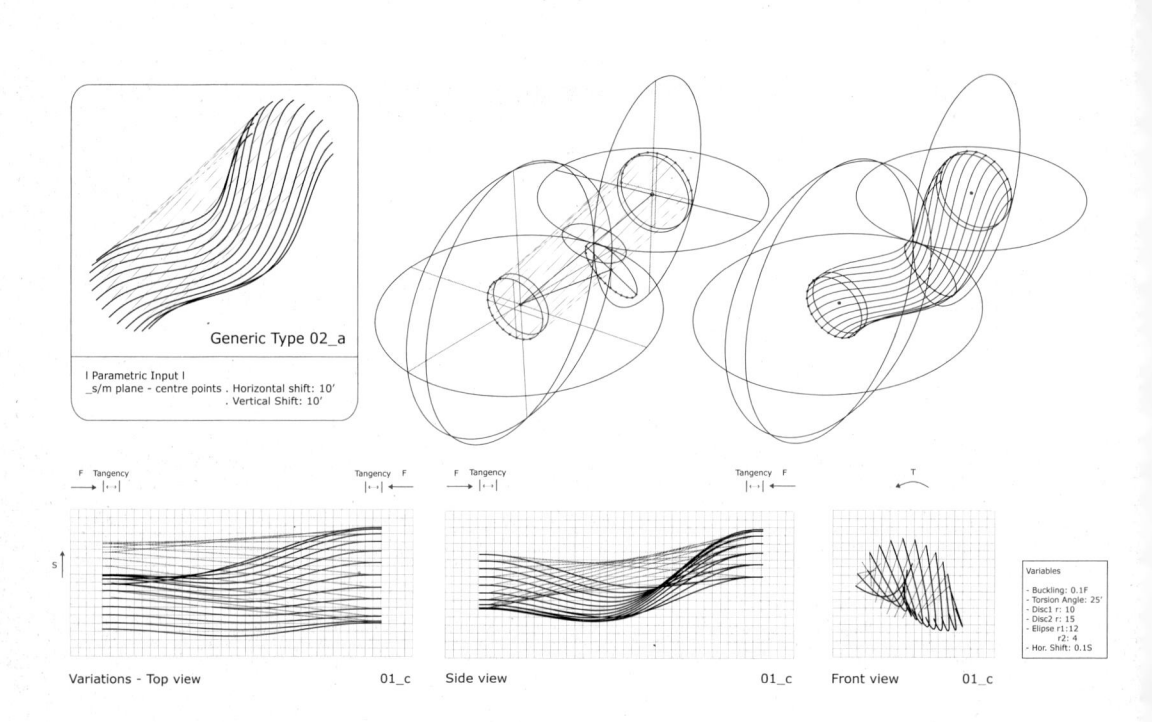

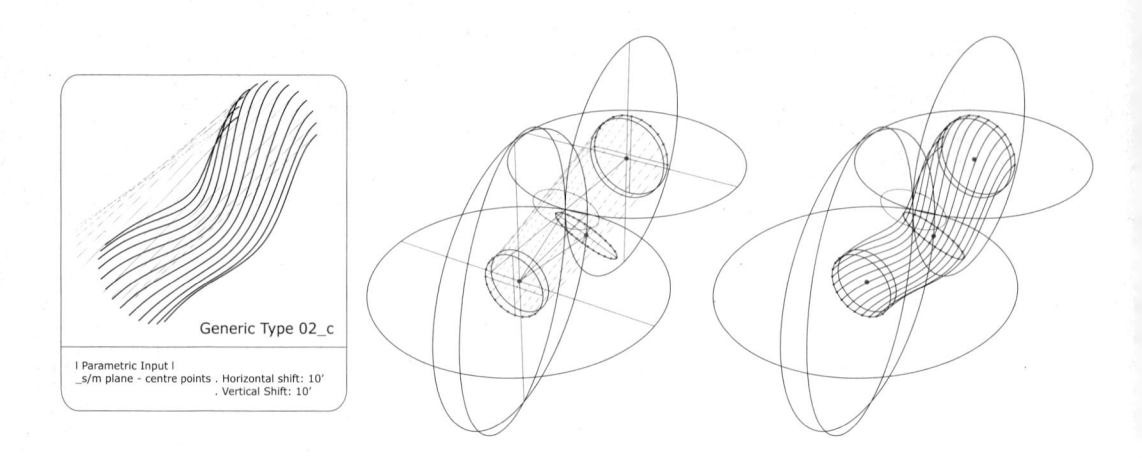

88 A first parametric definition of sub-systems of elastically deformed rods is based on the geometric variation and analysis of a series of physical form-finding experiments.

An initial set of physical tests examined the behaviour of slender rods under rotational displacement, inducing torsional buckling.
The resulting surface curvatures determine possible ways of pre-stressing brick assemblies in subsequent development phases.

Vertical Proliferation

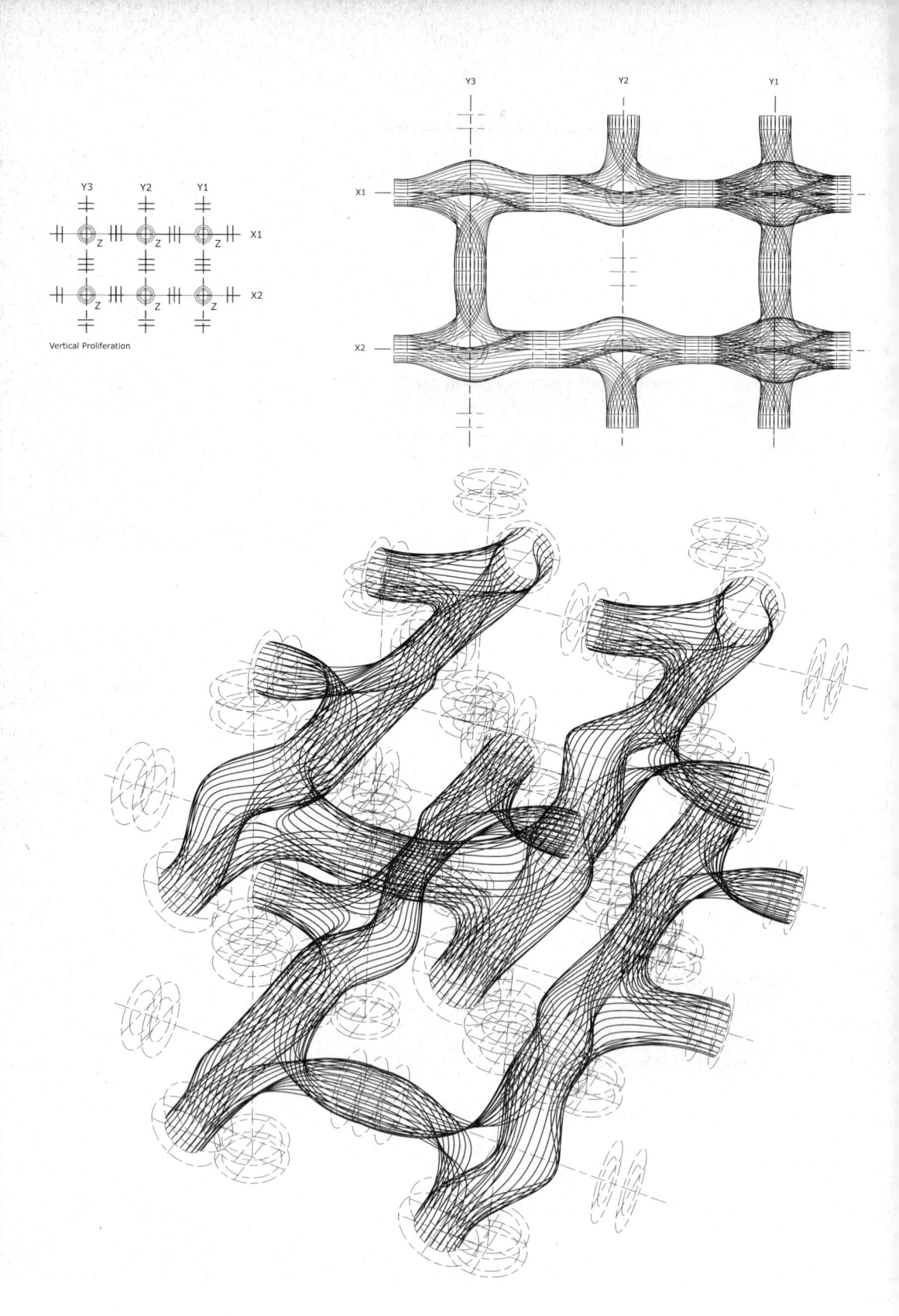

A generic parametric feature captures the behavioural tendencies of elastically deformed rod systems and allows for horizontal and vertical proliferation of the system.

Torsional buckling induced by the behaviour of slender rods under rotational displacement is used to pre-stress a brick assembly with varying structural behaviour across different sublocations (top). In relation to the structural behaviour the system's capacity to modulate light transmission is analysed (bottom).

91

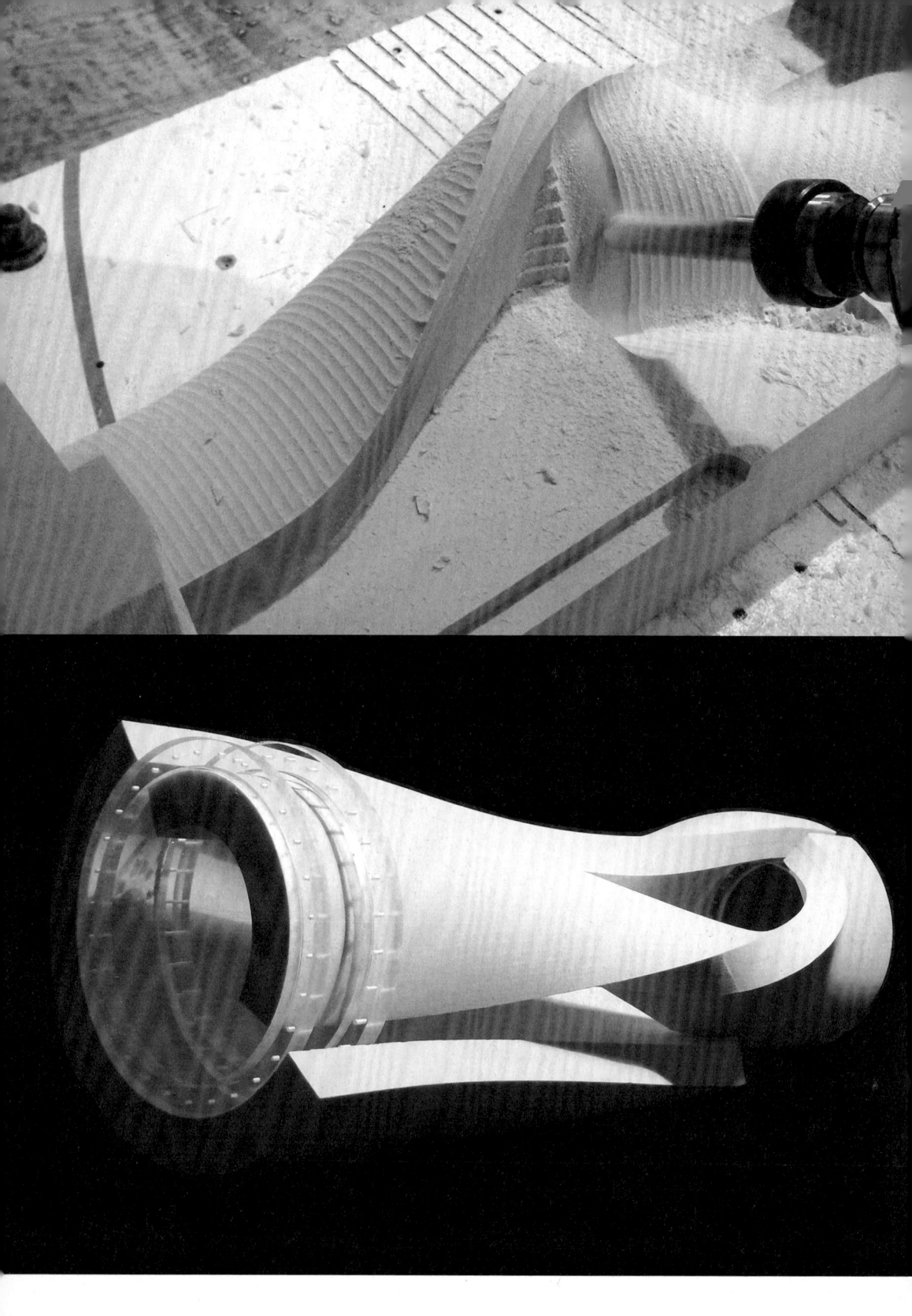

92 For testing the structural behaviour and stability of different types and distributions of brick elements of a larger assembly a specific formwork (bottom) was produced using a 5-axis CNC-milling machine (top).

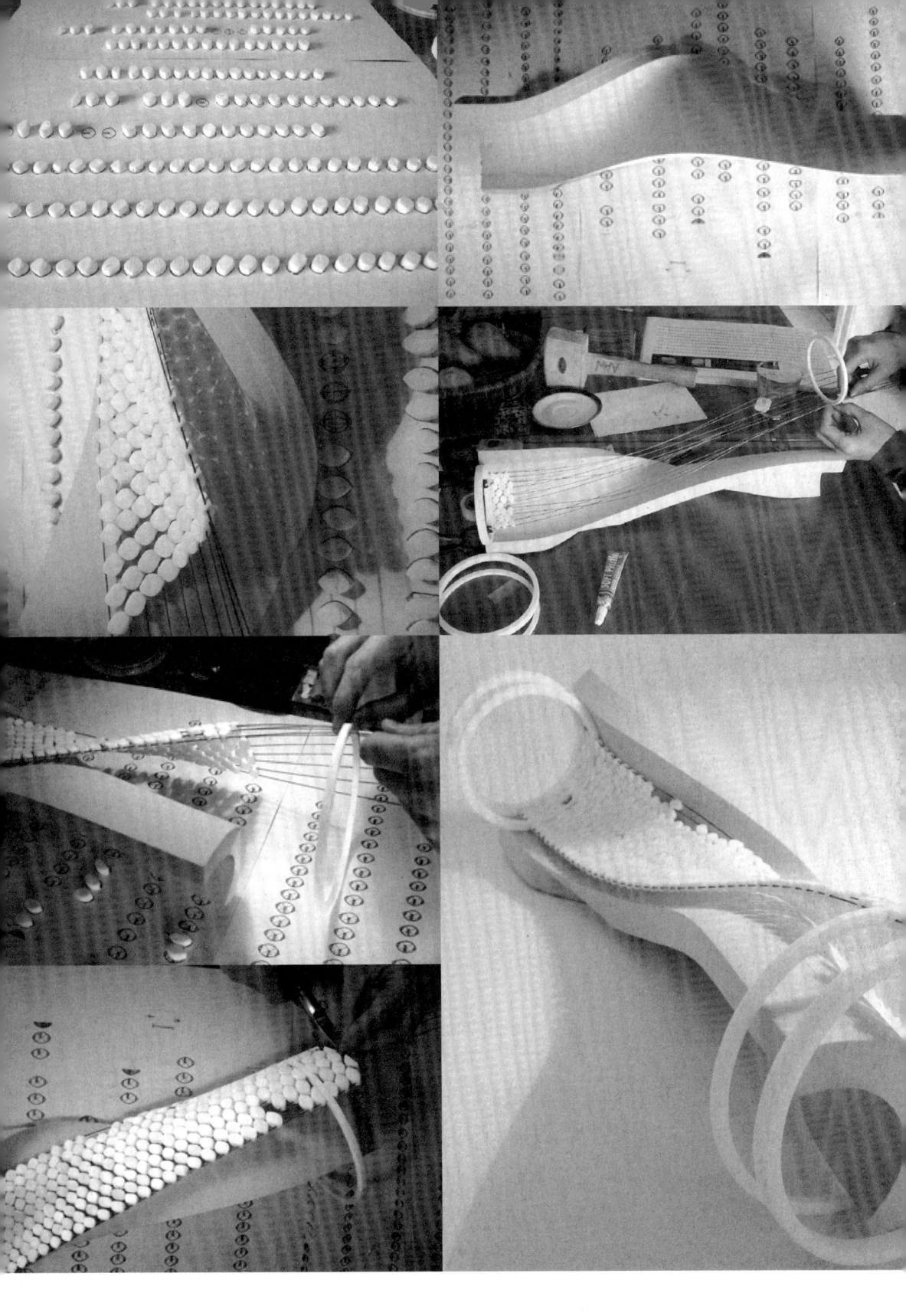

In order to test different pre tensioning strategies an assembly of 400 differentiated bricks produced through laser sintering were assembled on a specific formwork with different degrees of curvature.

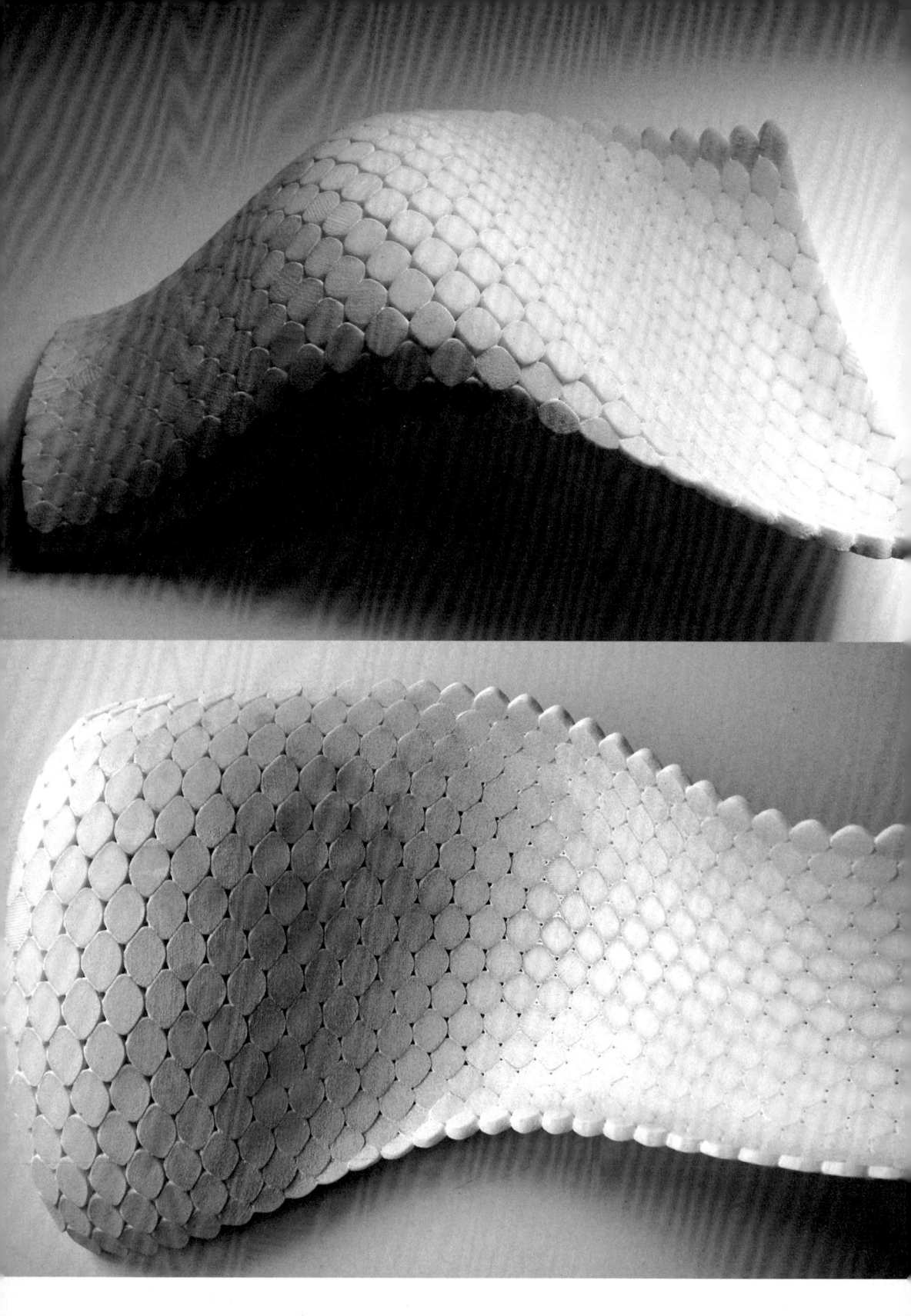

94　In order to investigate the system's behaviour in complex geometric regions a series of test models with complex morphologies combining synclastic and anticlastic surface curvature with relatively tight radii were rapid prototyped.

+02

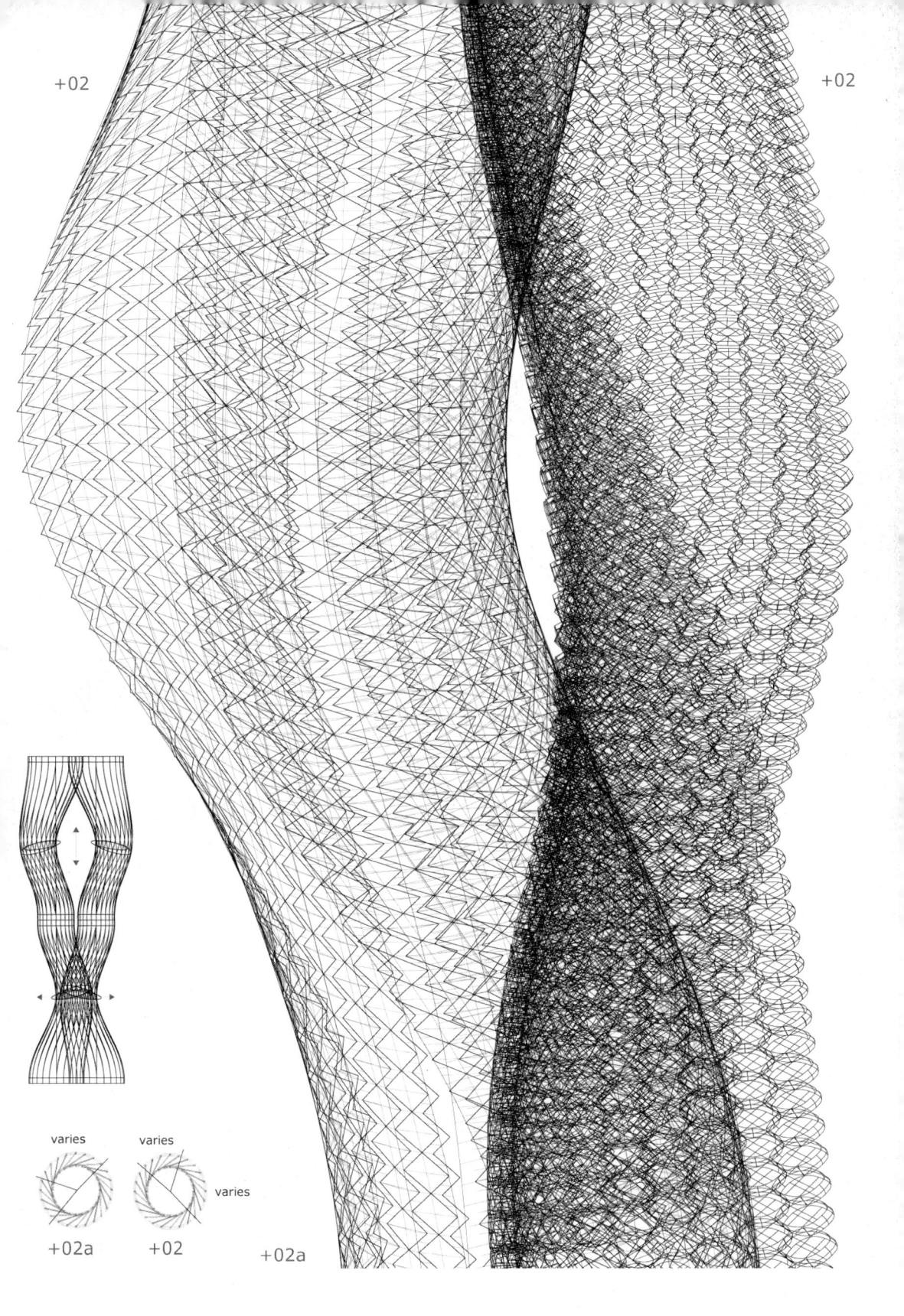

+02

varies

varies

varies

+02a

+02

+02a

The parametric definition of the system allows for an integral set up of the context specific system responding to a range of performance criteria. Within a performative context this section of a larger specific implementation of the system results from the negotiation of a series of structural, environmental and spatial parameters.

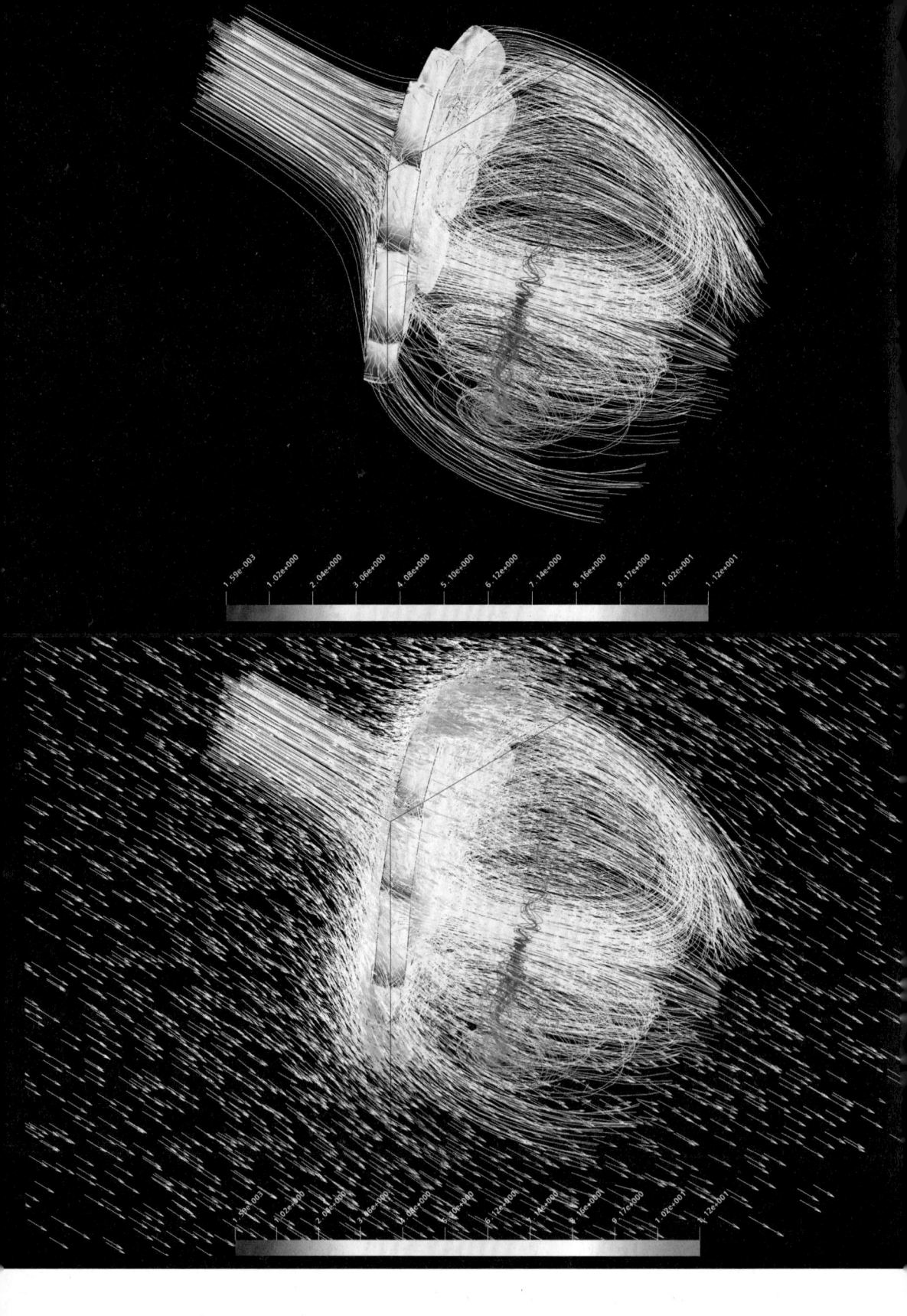

Using CFD (Computer Fluid Dynamics) modelling the system's performative capacity to modulate airflow through different degrees of local porosity was tested by airstream analysis (top) and vectorfields (bottom).

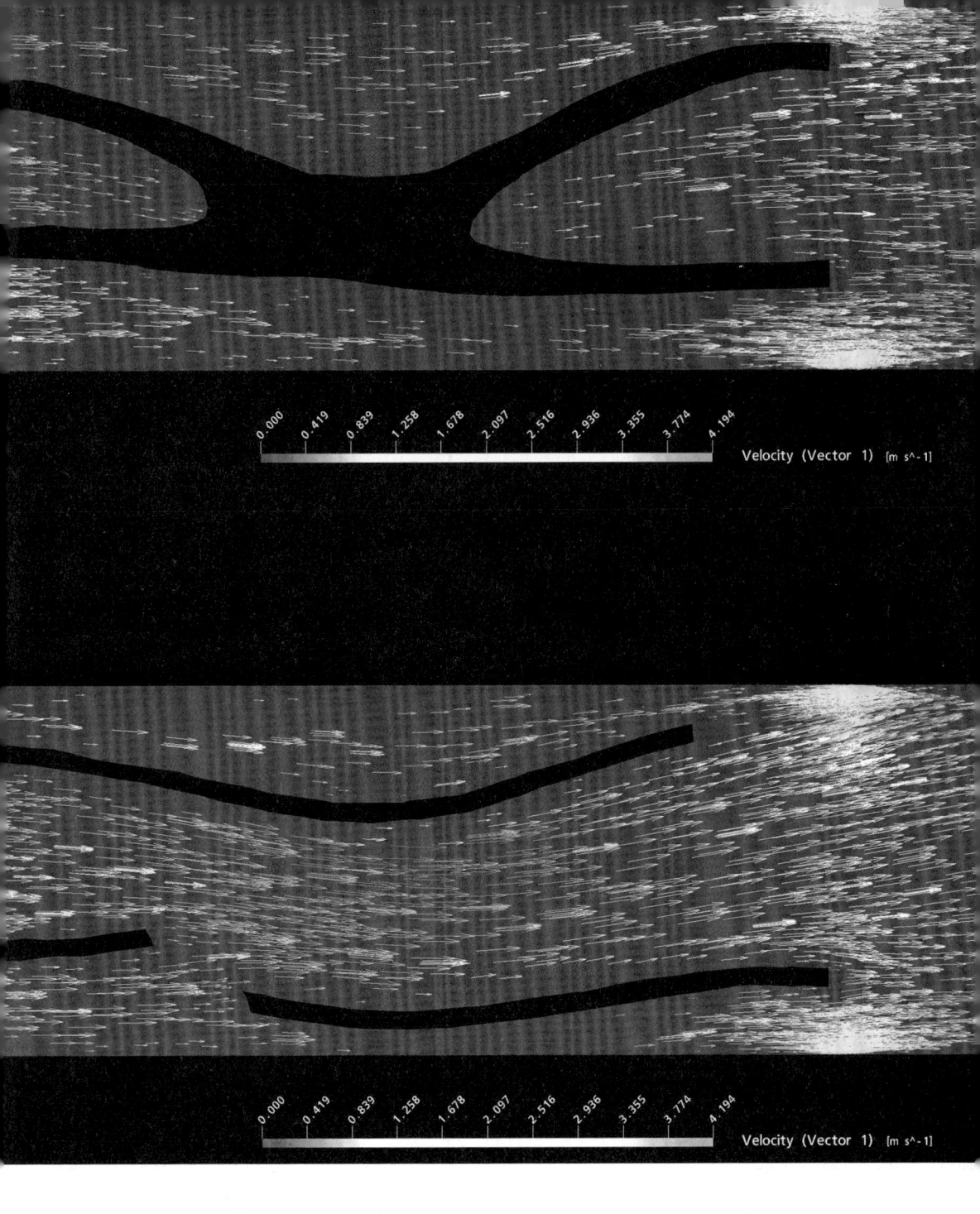

CFD tests of a larger geometric region show the system's capacity to strategically accelerate and decelerate airflow across a series of longitudinal sections.

97

COMMENTS

WOLF MANGELSDORF

The pre-stressing of brick structures, which is explored and applied in this project, is an intelligent concept that combines the advantages of the discontinuous material, brick, with those of surface structures, be they walls, vaults or other more complex surfaces. Simple pre-stressed walls are examples at the simple end of the scale; the fascinating structures by Eladio Dieste, from which this project takes its direct inspiration, mark the unrivalled and most complex end of the scale. I call them complex because of their structural action; they are actually very simple in their assembly.

All of these structures have as their starting point the brick surfaces, flat or curved, to which the pre-stress is applied in a post-tensioning process. The pre-stressing and the form-finding processes are separate. This project follows a different approach by investigating the formation and form-finding of surfaces through a controlled deformation process of what will eventually become the pre-stressing elements. In a sequence that at first seems to contradict the idea of pre-stressing, these rod elements are subjected to a twisting and buckling which determines the surfaces.

The twisting that is introduced into this process allows the deformation – which is effectively the buckling of the rods generating a series of lines that describe the surfaces – to be controlled rather than random. Through the twist in the cylindrical rod arrangements, the direction of movement and deflection when subjected to the buckling loads is pre-determined and in this way controlled.

The project investigates this phenomenon in some detail through controlled experiment set-ups that allow series of replicable and measurable results to be achieved, and ultimately lead to the development of a parametric digital model that is capable of generating these surfaces in an associative modelling environment. Through the parametric set-up, modulation of these line surfaces becomes possible without jeopardising the form-found geometric characteristics. At this point the brick is introduced and the process is reversed: whilst the twisting and compressing determined the geometry, the bricks are now able to act as compression elements and the rods can be brought back to their intended function of pre-stressing cables. The bricks (the project deliberately defines these not as material but as the elemental nature of the assembly) become the key players in locking the otherwise ephemeral geometry of the buckled rods.

Being tied into the main rods and with the help of additional perpendicular ties, the doubly curved surfaces are frozen with the application and introduction of simple single elements, though not without generating a particular challenge: all bricks are different, with their shape determined by their position within the pre-stressed system and the forces this pre-stressing puts into them. In this system it is important to see that all forces will need to remain axial and centred in the brick elements so as not to generate off-sets within the surface which could result in potentially damaging bending forces.

Here the design of the brick will need to be moved to the next level of detail, because a traditional brick design would not be able to accommodate these forces. Fortunately, the project recognises that the brick is to be seen as an element strategy rather than just fired clay. Material technology has moved on and a number of options can be explored.

These could be compounds that look at a set of standard base elements made from a simple material – potentially even the traditional brick – with a connector piece that is precision-cut and designed to facilitate the geometrical changes as well as the force transfer between the individual elements. Alternatively the bricks could be produced in their entirety as custom-made composite elements, where each of them has specially adapted boundaries that incorporate the design parameters of the global system into those of the individual component. A variety of options are possible and need to be explored, all of them will have their advantages and disadvantages. The challenge will lie in generating a complex element that is simple to produce and easy to control.

When looking at the performance specification of the material and the elements, the great advantage is that environmental criteria – the project emphasises this – can be integrated into their design. This allows a multitude of functions to be combined in simple elements. This may seem an ambitious approach, but by pushing the boundaries beyond the readily available it opens new avenues in material and geometrical design strategies.

2003 - 2004

NERI OXMAN

The predominant organisation of the vertical building type is the open, often deep-stacked plan that provides for programmatic flexibility by means of furnishing: the typical 'office landscapes' of the 60s still prevail. Moreover, modular building systems make a separation between structural and service core, floor plates and building envelope. This project investigates alternative design strategies, aiming for a differentiated and integrated organisation of spaces, circulation and structure, synthesised and organised by helical bodies which articulate intersecting 'skins' that make up the building volume and respond to the changing requirements of the different height zones of a tall building.

The notion of Performative Morphologies entails condition-based design processes in the sense that design is generated and modulated by condition statements, integrating system-intrinsic and extrinsic criteria and influences. This approach attempts to develop integrative methods which support design under conditions of multi-variant influences.

Initial studies focused on biomimetics, drawing design principles from living nature. A research into magnolia cones served to investigate spiral phyllotaxis. The cones display a symmetrical arrangement of clockwise and counterclockwise rotating helixes. The scales have the same form, but size varies according to location on the cone. Tessellation results in a low number of variations required to achieve the complex double-curved surfaces of cone and scales.

Various cones were 3d-scanned with the help of Professor Birger Sevaldson at the Institute for Industrial Design in Oslo. From the scans digital models were developed and analysed with respect to the surface curvature of the cone. Surface curvature was subsequently related to structural performance with the help of Professor George Jeronimidis at the Centre of Biomimetics at the University of Reading, and studies of the scales informed initial ideas for subdividing double-curved surfaces.

In the project vertical differentiation is manifested by the structural and geometrical characteristics of helical morphologies on both building and material scales. On the building scale the structure distributes static and dynamic loads over its entire surface. In addition, vertical circulation to the building's central core is not prohibited. On the material scale the project investigated the possibility for a combined component-composite approach which introduces a hybrid position between surface and structural member material logics.

In order to facilitate an instrumental approach to the design, a tool set was configured to generate helical morphologies through scripting and parametric applications. Digital tools were customised to fit the characteristics of helical arrangements in terms of geometric articulation. Modelling in Rhinoceros™ in combination with Excel™ scripting served to derive different instances of geometric articulations of the system. This approach is neither top-down, from an overall geometry to a detailed local articulation, nor bottom-up, from a defined component or local articulation to the overall system. The specific helical arrangement was developed in all relevant system scales simultaneously. In the process, Bentley System's Generative Components, among other software packages, was used to establish a relational geometric logic by which different instances of geometric articulation can more easily be derived through a parametric setup and modification. The evaluation of the structural performance of different geometric articulations integrated physical and digital methods. Scaled physical models were produced and evaluated by applying loads to register the resultant displacement on various system scales in order to examine deformation under loading. Digital analysis based on finite element method [FEM] enabled the determination of stresses and displacement, considering bending, buckling and torsional behaviour of the system. The results of the structural behaviour analysis informed each stage in the iterative design process.

The developed morphology distributes loads over its envelope, facilitated by a hybrid structure that combines the vectorial load-path of a linear component with the field distribution of a structural surface. The load-paths are treated differentially, with loads being bundled along vectors where necessary and distributed across surfaces wherever possible and useful, so embedding latent capacities that can compensate for local disruptions to the structural systems. Surfaces were configured from tubular elements that make up helical strands and tiles that close the envelope. Various relations between tubular strands and tiles were explored, ranging from component logic of connected parts to a composite logic of embedded elements.

An analytical method was developed which synthesised structural and geometrical data including local stress displacements, load application type and tile geometry. This involved creating an unrolled map of the strand and overlaying it with the result of the FEM-analysis to evaluate the local, regional and global load-distribution across the surface and to allocate the relevant connective relation between strands and tiles.

The distribution of circulation is not limited to service cores; instead, it is distributed across a multitude of helical paths, providing for different spatial experiences and evacuation routes.

Spatial arrangement and circulatory organisation was evaluated in parallel. Spatial pockets are formed by deriving intersecting surfaces in combination with the helical strands. Circulation paths follow the helical arrangement and interconnect spatial pockets. Parametric changes to the system affect the location, size and orientation of these spatial pockets towards environmental input, such as daylight and thermal exposure. This was analysed through digital simulation, and informed the iterative design process. In this way design generation and analysis went hand in hand, with each instance of the project development becoming increasingly informed by context-specific stimuli. Context-specific designs with highly specific spatial arrangements thus become feasible for a building type that up till now seemed diametrically opposed to such design solutions.

FEIDAD Design Merit Award 2005

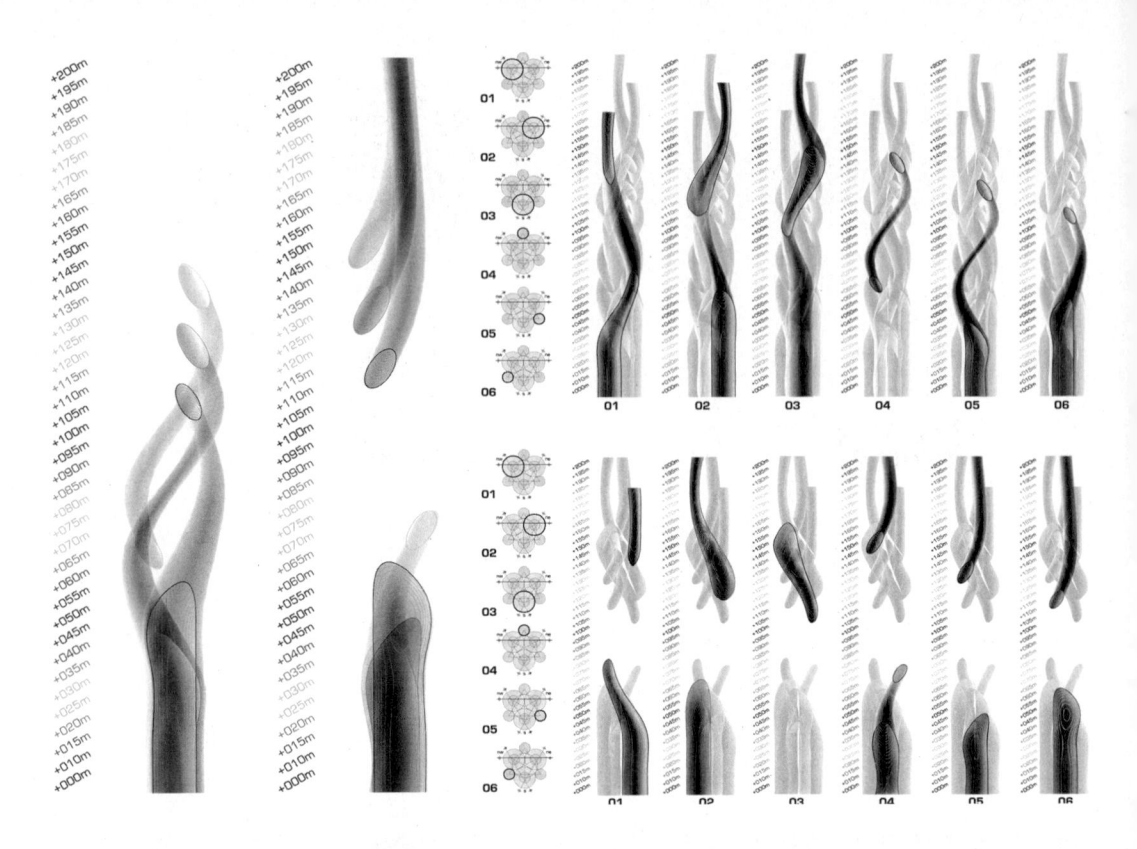

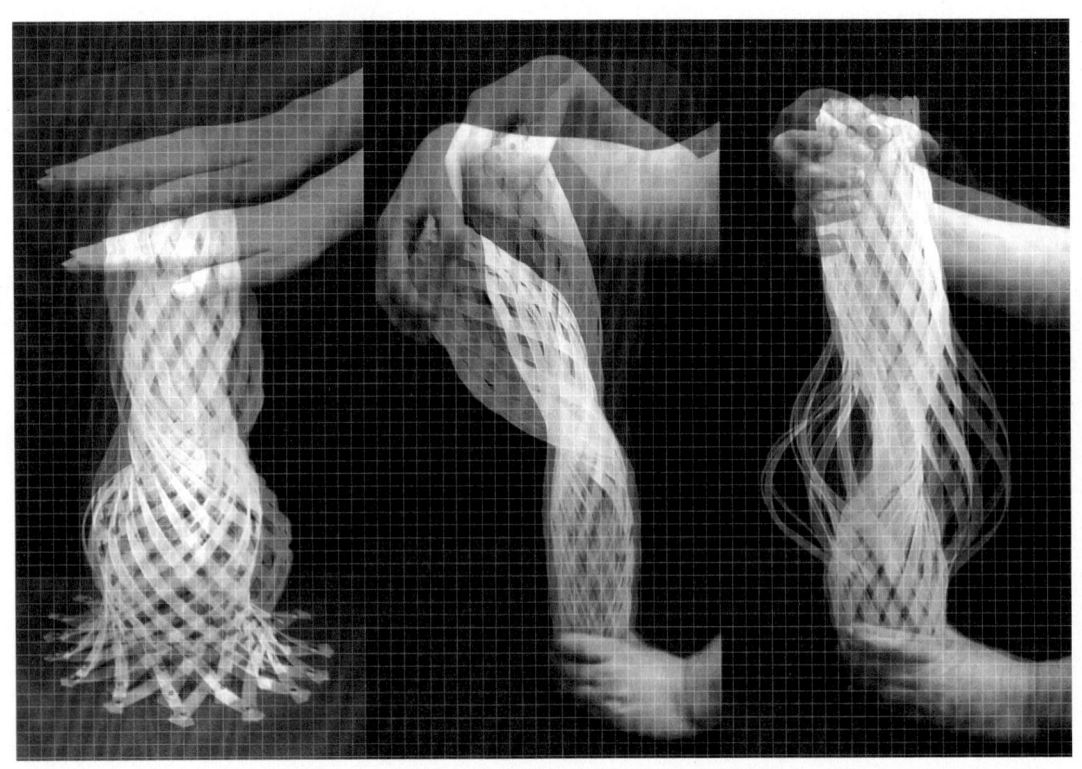

102 Bundling strategies for the arrangement of helical strands are informed by structural and circulatory requirements. Strands generally act as structural elements but also provide for circulatory paths when thickened locally. Physical model experiments are used to corroborate the behaviour of a double helix structure under axial compression, bending and torsional forces.

Type_02 model and scripting data

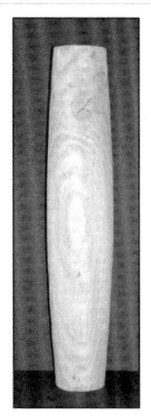

ser_01	ser_02	ser_03
0	0	6.5
0.469	0.328	6.432
1.66	1.124	6.186
3.27	2.087	5.686
5.025	2.982	4.993
6.588	3.63	4.272
8.259	4.172	3.433
10.075	4.556	2.47
11.747	4.739	1.571
13.615	4.756	0.59
15.357	4.602	-0.273
17.085	4.316	-1.057
18.857	3.902	-1.772
20.692	3.366	-2.395
22.487	2.764	-2.878
24.345	2.085	-3.244
26.169	1.389	-3.47
28.093	0.651	-3.562
29.861	-0.009	-3.524
31.726	-0.674	-3.375
33.768	-1.332	-3.08
35.512	-1.827	-2.737
37.335	-2.279	-2.313
39.427	-2.681	-1.744
41.162	-2.919	-1.225
42.994	-3.088	-0.651
45.083	-3.147	0.026
46.818	-3.092	0.588
48.647	-2.949	1.168
50.74	-2.653	1.791
52.457	-2.319	2.257
54.349	-1.868	2.711

DigitalModel (elevation)
GenericType_02 (bidirectional rotation)

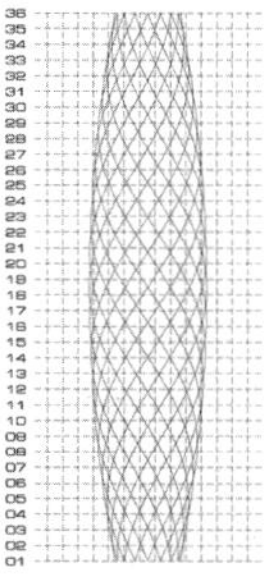

DigitalModel (elevation)
GenericType_02 (unidirectional rotation)

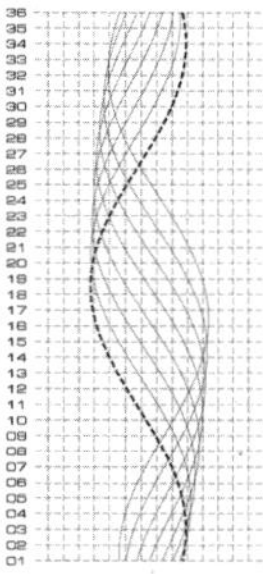

Type_01 model and scripting data

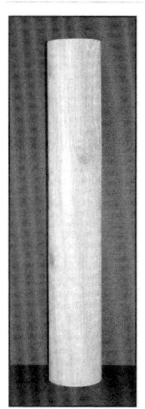

ser_01	ser_02	ser_03
0	0	6.5
0.469	0.328	6.432
1.66	1.124	6.186
3.27	2.087	5.686
5.025	2.982	4.993
6.588	3.63	4.272
8.259	4.172	3.433
10.075	4.556	2.47
11.747	4.739	1.571
13.615	4.756	0.59
15.357	4.602	-0.273
17.085	4.316	-1.057
18.857	3.902	-1.772
20.692	3.366	-2.395
22.487	2.764	-2.878
24.345	2.085	-3.244
26.169	1.389	-3.47
28.093	0.651	-3.562
29.861	-0.009	-3.524
31.726	-0.674	-3.375
33.768	-1.332	-3.08
35.512	-1.827	-2.737
37.335	-2.279	-2.313
39.427	-2.681	-1.744
41.162	-2.919	-1.225
42.994	-3.088	-0.651
45.083	-3.147	0.026
46.818	-3.092	0.588
48.647	-2.949	1.168
50.74	-2.653	1.791
52.457	-2.319	2.257
54.349	-1.868	2.711

DigitalModel (elevation)
GenericType_01 (bidirectional rotation)

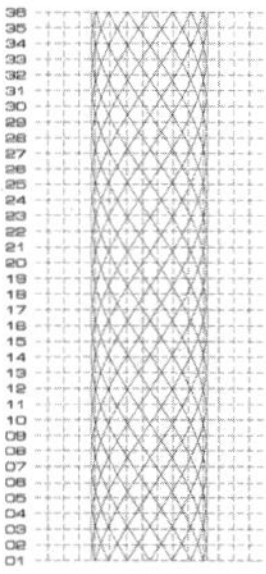

DigitalModel (elevation)
GenericType_01 (unidirectional rotation)

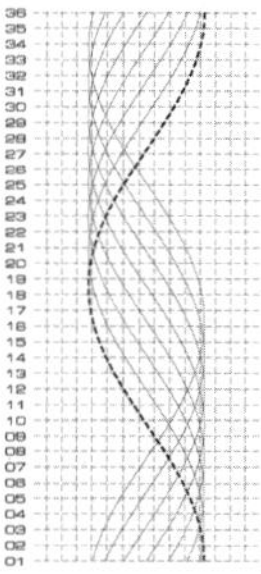

Type_04 model and scripting data

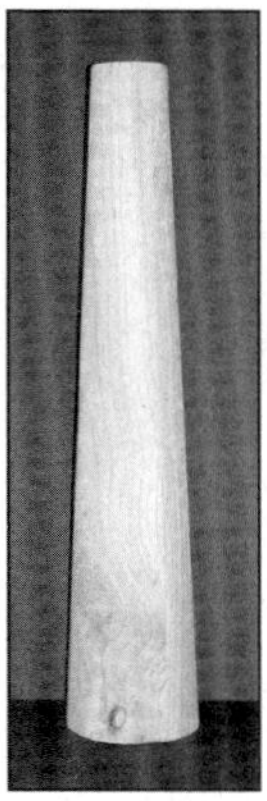

ser_01	ser_02	ser_03
0	0	6.5
0.469	0.328	6.432
1.66	1.124	6.186
3.27	2.087	5.686
5.025	2.982	4.993
6.588	3.63	4.272
8.259	4.172	3.433
10.075	4.556	2.47
11.747	4.739	1.571
13.615	4.756	0.59
15.357	4.602	-0.273
17.085	4.316	-1.057
18.857	3.902	-1.772
20.692	3.366	-2.395
22.487	2.764	-2.878
24.345	2.085	-3.244
26.169	1.389	-3.47
28.093	0.651	-3.562
29.861	-0.009	-3.524
31.726	-0.674	-3.375
33.768	-1.332	-3.08
35.512	-1.827	-2.737
37.335	-2.279	-2.313
39.427	-2.681	-1.744
41.162	-2.919	-1.225
42.994	-3.088	-0.651
45.083	-3.147	0.026
46.818	-3.092	0.588
48.647	-2.949	1.168
50.74	-2.653	1.791
52.457	-2.319	2.257
54.349	-1.868	2.711

DigitalModel (elevation)
GenericType_04 (bidirectional rotation)

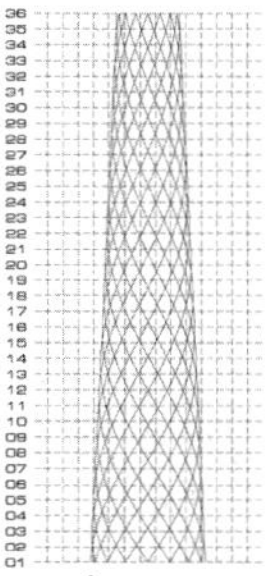

DigitalModel (elevation)
GenericType_04 (unidirectional rotation)

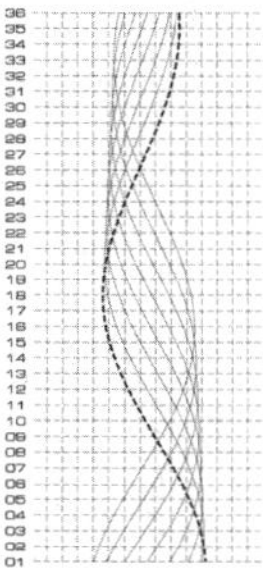

Type_03 model and scripting data

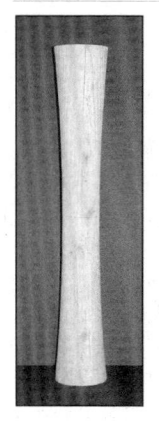

ser_01	ser_02	ser_03
0	0	6.5
0.469	0.328	6.432
1.66	1.124	6.186
3.27	2.087	5.686
5.025	2.982	4.993
6.588	3.63	4.272
8.259	4.172	3.433
10.075	4.556	2.47
11.747	4.739	1.571
13.615	4.756	0.59
15.357	4.602	-0.273
17.085	4.316	-1.057
18.857	3.902	-1.772
20.692	3.366	-2.395
22.487	2.764	-2.878
24.345	2.085	-3.244
26.169	1.389	-3.47
28.093	0.651	-3.562
29.861	-0.009	-3.524
31.726	-0.674	-3.375
33.768	-1.332	-3.08
35.512	-1.827	-2.737
37.335	-2.279	-2.313
39.427	-2.681	-1.744
41.162	-2.919	-1.225
42.994	-3.088	-0.651
45.083	-3.147	0.026
46.818	-3.092	0.588
48.647	-2.949	1.168
50.74	-2.653	1.791
52.457	-2.319	2.257
54.349	-1.868	2.711

DigitalModel (elevation)
GenericType_03 (bidirectional rotation)

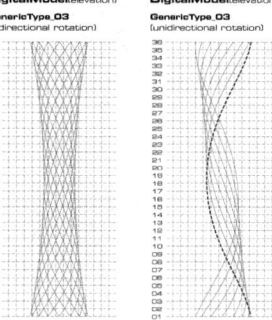

DigitalModel (elevation)
GenericType_03 (unidirectional rotation)

Various formers were made with a lathe in order to produce physical models for structural testing. The basic helical curves that underlie the geometry of the formers were also scripted in order to facilitate geometrical variation in digital modelling in a systematic manner.

104　　Two rendered elevational views of a digital model show the non-uniform articulation and arrangement of helical strands without the tile-fillings. Without the tiles, the helical system acts structurally as a vector-active system. With the tiles selected areas can act locally as a surface active system. The careful analysis and consideration of force distribution and flow in non-uniform arrangements is of fundamental importance in order to develop strategies towards an advanced structural performance.

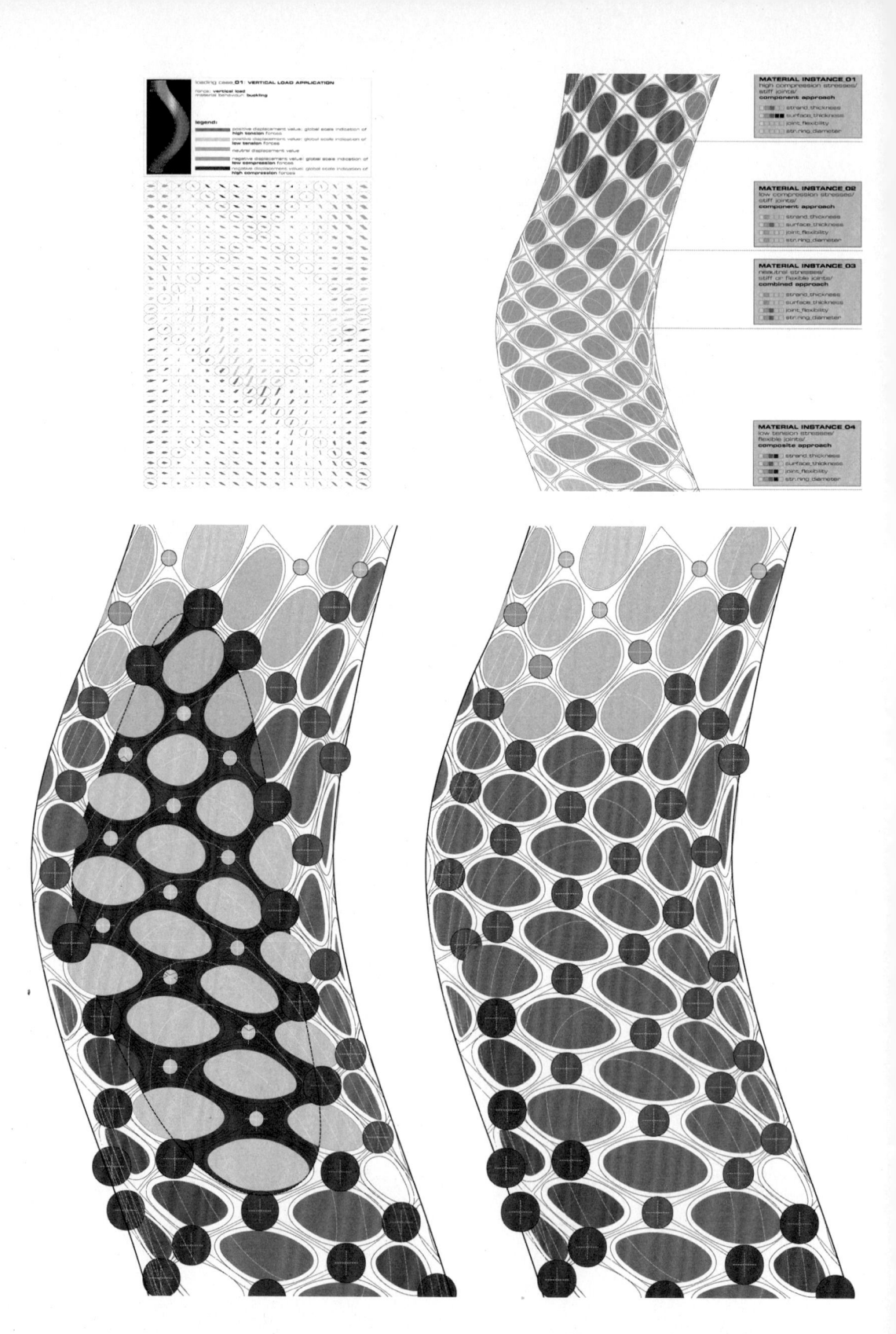

106 Three typical load cases were analysed by means of finite element method, superimposed and mapped onto a part of the global surface indicating the force distribution across different skin elements.

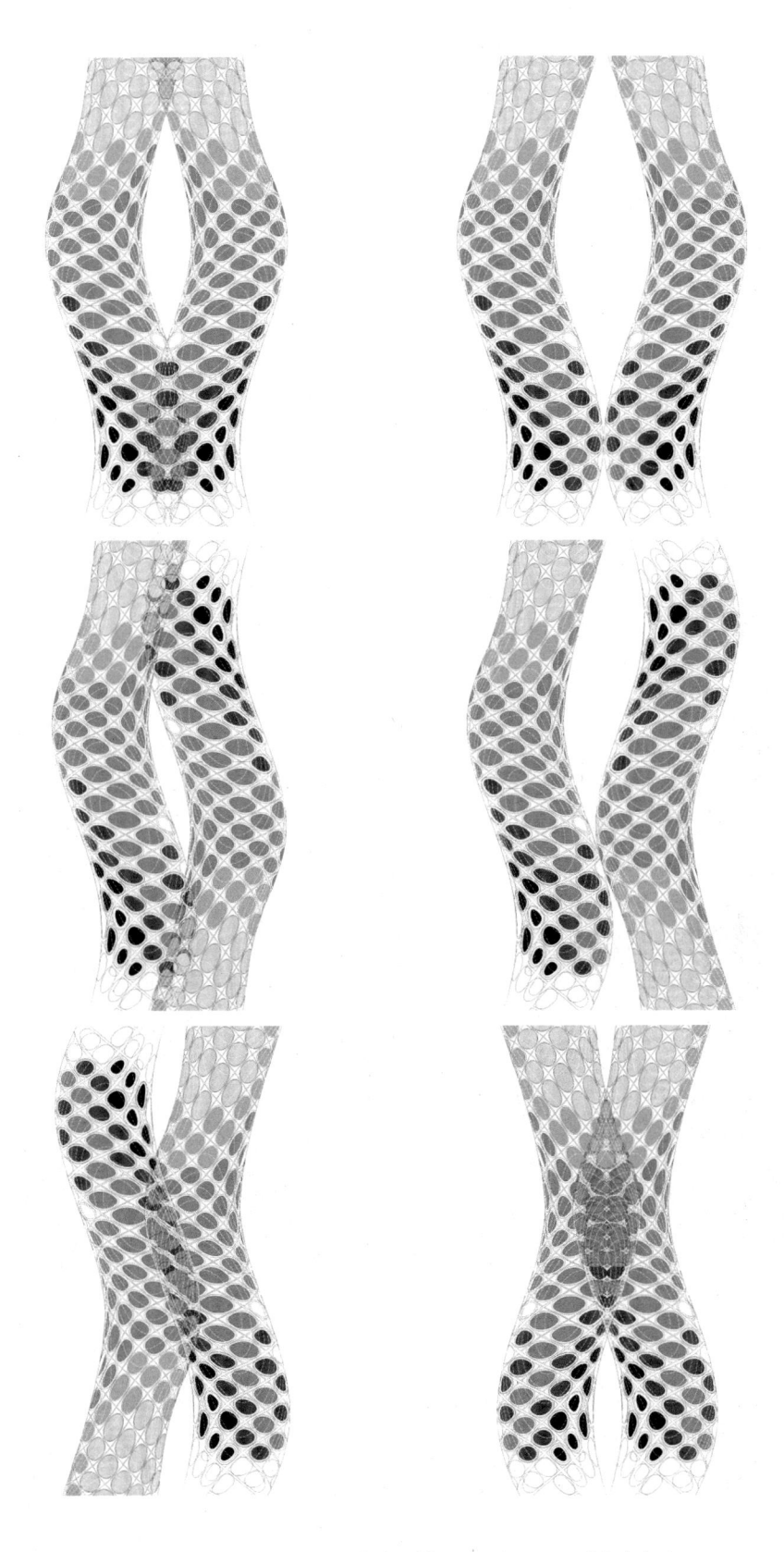

Stress pattern mapping in the non-uniform tiling system was applied to different configurations of the helical system.

projection_plane_02a | projection_plane_01 | projection_plane_02b

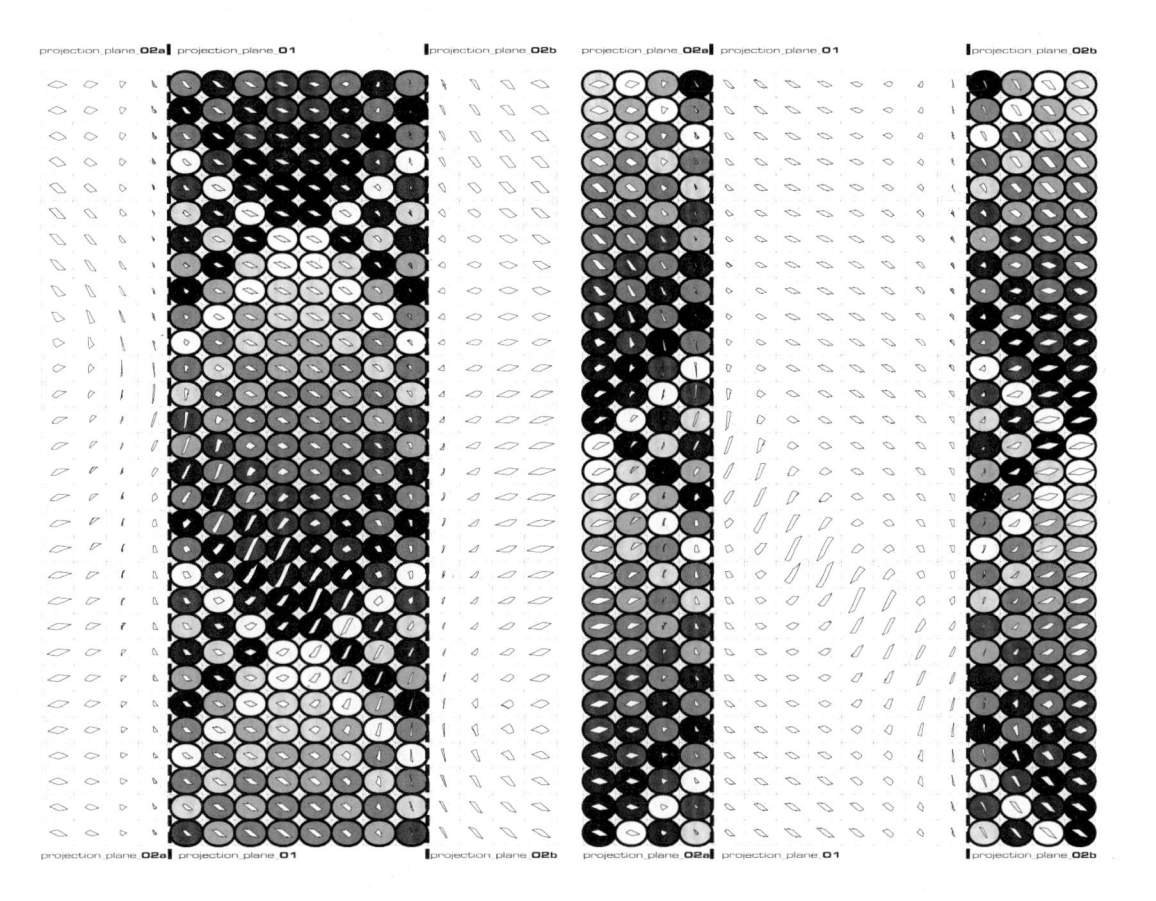

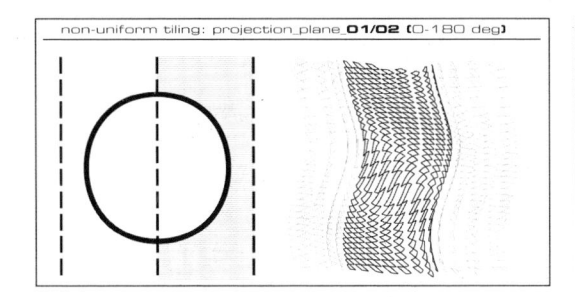

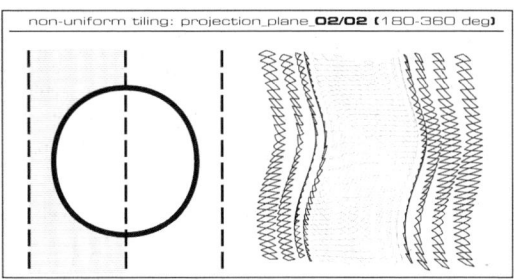

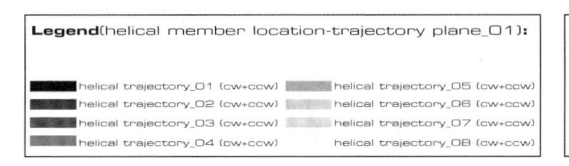

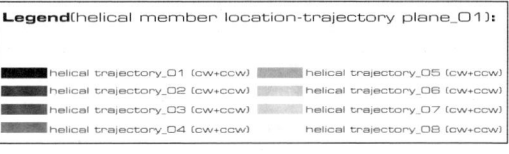

Each of the 480 registered tiles is defined by its geometry, surface area, and stress condition. The non-uniform tiling was applied to the skin by projecting uniform skin elements to the non-uniform global body. Shades of grey correspond to the relative location of each of the 16 strands comprising the entire volume.

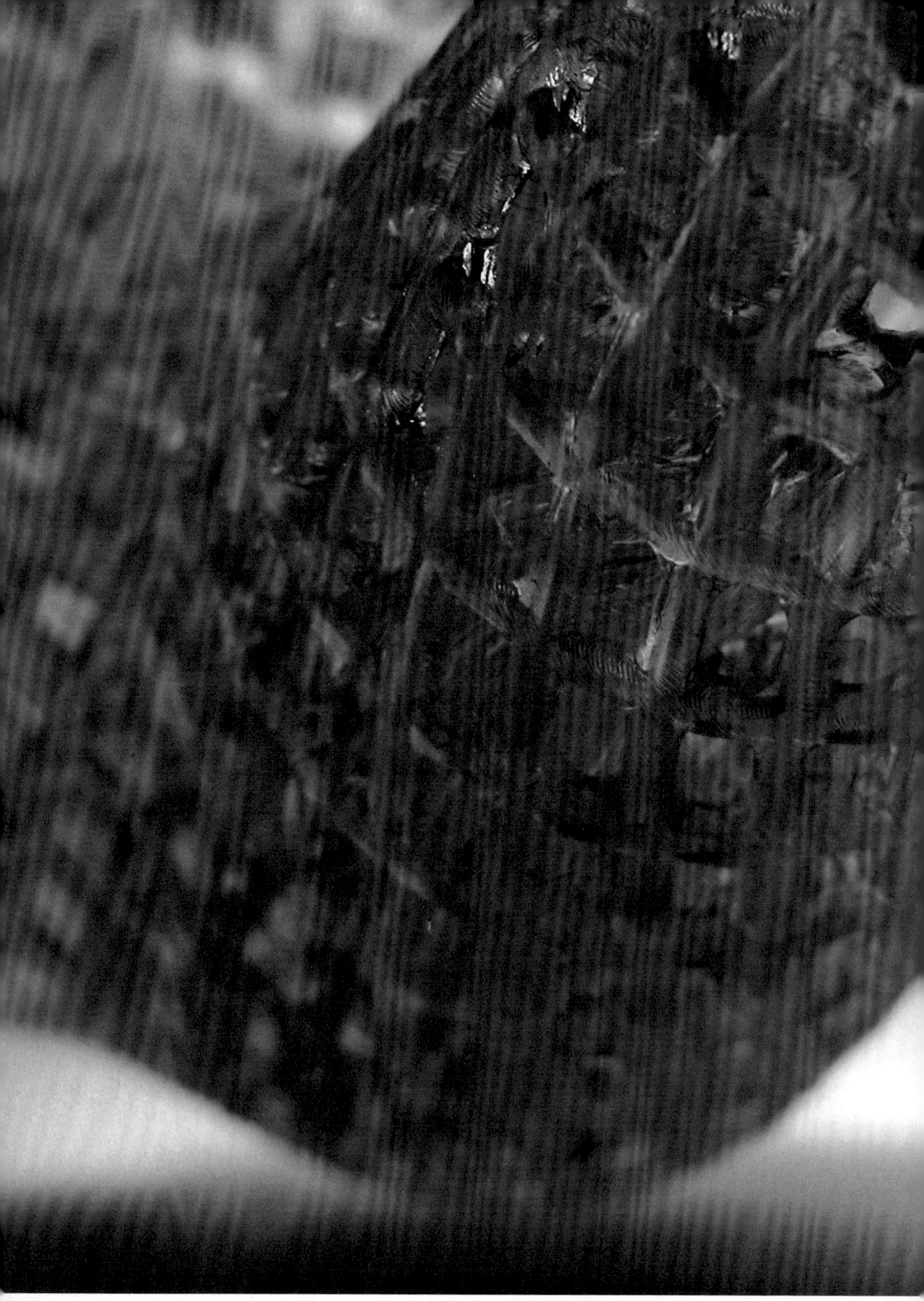

Based on digital models, various rapid-prototype models (selective laser-sintering and stereo-lithography) were made in order to study the non-uniform articulation of the helical system.

Complex morphologies are generally the result of an elaborate process of form-generation, with the consequence that all elements required for their assembly differ in shape and size. Although the differentiation of parts does not pose any fundamental problems in these days of digital fabrication, this project explores instead the limits of a material system consisting of uniform elements only. In doing so, it uses basic semi-finished products that exist in abundance in any DIY store: identical timber struts and cable-ties.

The starting-point of the research was recognition that, with all material elements being the same and only one joint type available, the way to create an irregular morphology from uniform elements is by altering the orientation of the sticks at each connection point within the system. The crucial parameters for connection were identified as the location of the connection point along the length of a strut, and the way struts were layered within a sub-assembly. Once we had established the logic of sub-assembly of eight struts, consisting of two attached layers of four struts, the possibilities embedded in these two parameters became apparent – altering the location of the struts either above or below each other and changing the distance between the connection points results in changing angles of the initially perpendicularly oriented sticks. This behaviour was carefully mapped and analysed in order to establish the range of curvature that could be induced between sub-assemblies. It became the key for the proliferation of the eight-strut sub-assembly into a larger and more varied system.

Further tests aimed at corroborating the relation between specific, digitally defined connection protocols, the anticipated system geometry and the resulting, physically modelled assemblies. Based on different connection protocols a series of systems were assembled, each consisting of 240 struts. Subsequently the location of all elements was measured in an analogue way from the physical model and analysed with particular regard to the transformation the system undergoes as the number of struts increases. This behaviour is due to the accumulative effect of connection locations and articulation relative to the layering of struts, as well as the increasing self-weight of the assembly. The data was then transferred to digital models in order to capture and articulate the parametric set-up of the system.

Through these tests six different assembly types were identified, each with a specific adjustment scope defined by parametric variables. Possible configurations included acutely curved, convex and concave-to-planar lattice articulations. Furthermore, the three critical parameters for a full-scale prototype could now be precisely described. The most important parameter still defines the connection points described in the object coordinate space that regulates the interaction of adjacent system elements and sub-systems. The second parameter is the overall number of system elements and their orientation in relation to gravity in the world-coordinate space that regulates the interaction of sub-assemblies with external forces. Thirdly, once the system passes a threshold of total element numbers, it gains the ability to curl back on itself, with the resulting layering becoming an additional means of altering the influence of the first two parameters. On the basis of these parameters, a connection protocol for a self-supporting, double-curved prototype was established.

Standard gridshells are form-found according to a pre-determined footprint and desired height. The curvature of the gridshell and length of continuous struts in bending are then determined through form-finding methods. Tension-stressed models are inverted into compression-stressed structures. This commonly delivers not only the form to be built, but also the construction method. Gridshells are laid out with the joints unfastened. They are then lifted or propped up into the pre-established shape and fixed along the perimeter. When all joints have been fastened the gridshell is structurally active. That is to say, the shape of the gridshell is pre-established and can only fit this configuration, unless the footprint is changed and the form-finding method repeated. Once form-found the gridshell can only be erected in this shape. The system developed here operates on an alternative logic. While typical gridshells are form-found top-down, the lattice morphology under investigation is form-found bottom-up, through a continuous alteration and growth of sub-assemblies, as well as changed connectivity between sub-assemblies and between layers of lattices the system. The possibility of the lattice curling back upon itself, to be layered and connected between layers, eliminates the requirement for a perimeter constraint.

There is no finite state of assembly as such: construction and alteration can always continue and the shape will adapt to the new configuration and location of joints and the changing self-weight of the assembly. It is therefore always important to establish for each configuration or state of assembly the orientation of the assembly to the axis of gravity. This implies that the point of equilibrium needs to be established for each state of assembly. Additional connections between layers of the lattice change the equilibrium state once again. Through this logic the lattice system acquires versatility through adaptability and the lack of a final state configuration.

A large prototype was built or, rather, a large prototypical assembly was taken through different stages of element addition and subtraction and different levels of connectivity between lattice layers. The alteration of connectivity showed that difference in curvature between connected layers can substantially increase the load-bearing capacity of the assembly by increasing stiffness, which makes it possible to change the orientation of the assembly relative to the axis of gravity without jeopardising its structural capacity.

The resultant, self-supporting, multi-layered and intricately curved material system assembled from thousands of identical timber sticks and cable-ties begins to reveal the geometric complexity and spatial opportunities afforded by this research. If design intelligence were invested in the bottom-up process driven by material experiments and digital modelling, mapping and analysis, a complex morphology could be developed, controlled and articulated by just two different, yet uniform, system constituents.

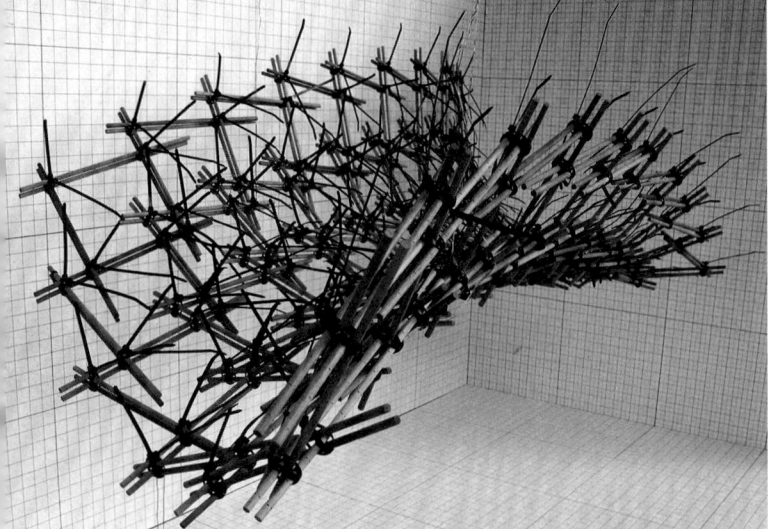

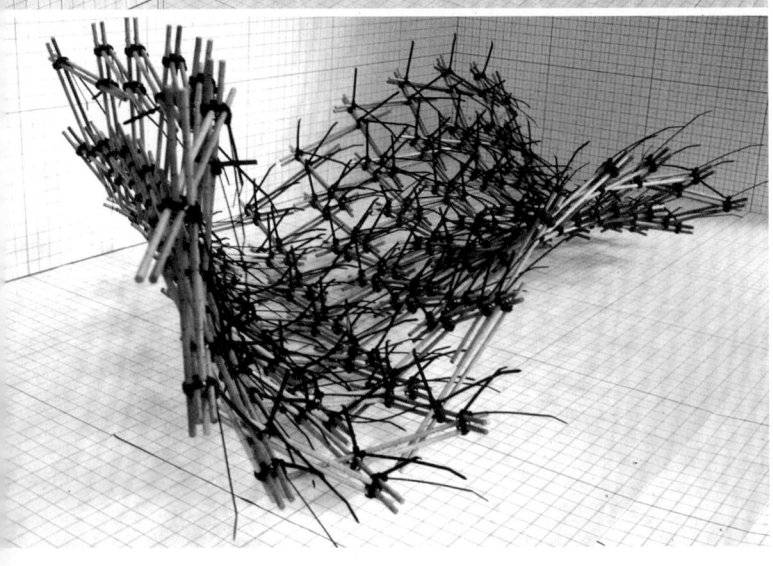

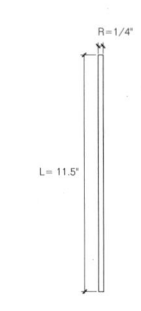

COMPONENT = C-1
C-1 = 1/4" (RADIUS) x 11.5" (LENGTH)
WOODEN DOWEL

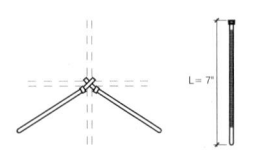

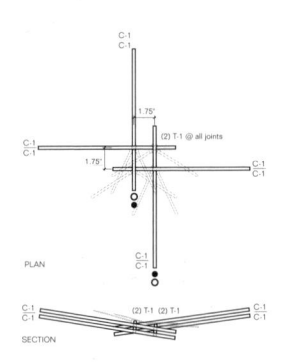

CABLE TIE = T-1
T-1 = 7" MULTI-PURPOSE TIE

MODULE TYPE #3 = M-3 VARIANT A
(FULL PINWHEEL JOINT CONFIGURATION A)

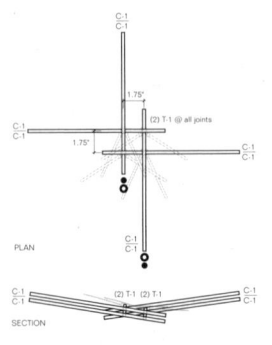

MODULE TYPE #3 = M-3 VARIANT B
(FULL PINWHEEL JOINT CONFIGURATION B)

114 Wooden dowels joined by cable ties are assembled to form basic double-layered elements. The geometry of these elements can be changed by altering the relative location of joints and dowels in the element (right). Through the assembly of strategically varied elements different lattice morphologies can be achieved and constructed (left).

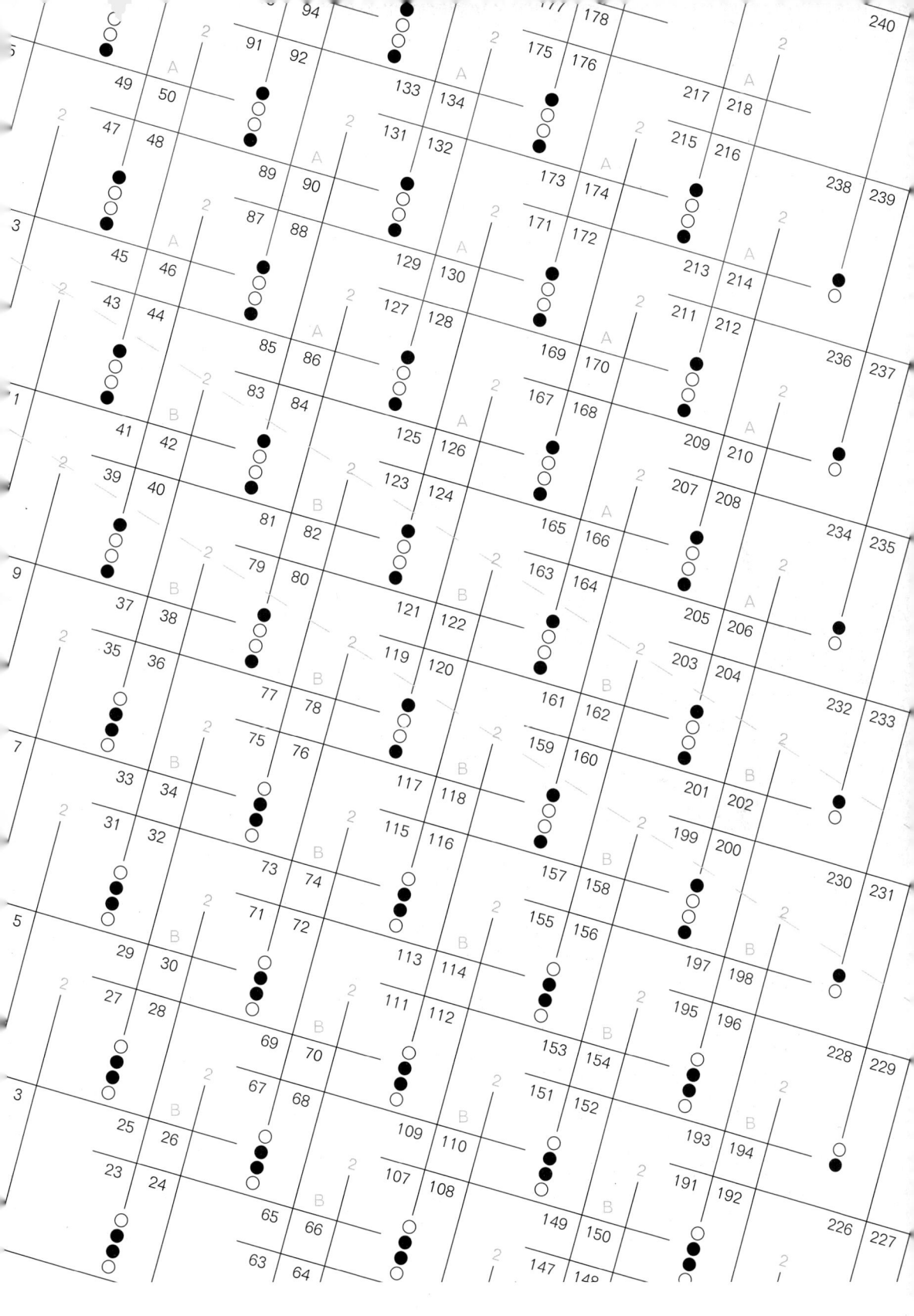

The information for the construction of a larger lattice with double-curvature is notated in an assembly protocol that defines all critical parameters for the assembly of the system from equal parts.

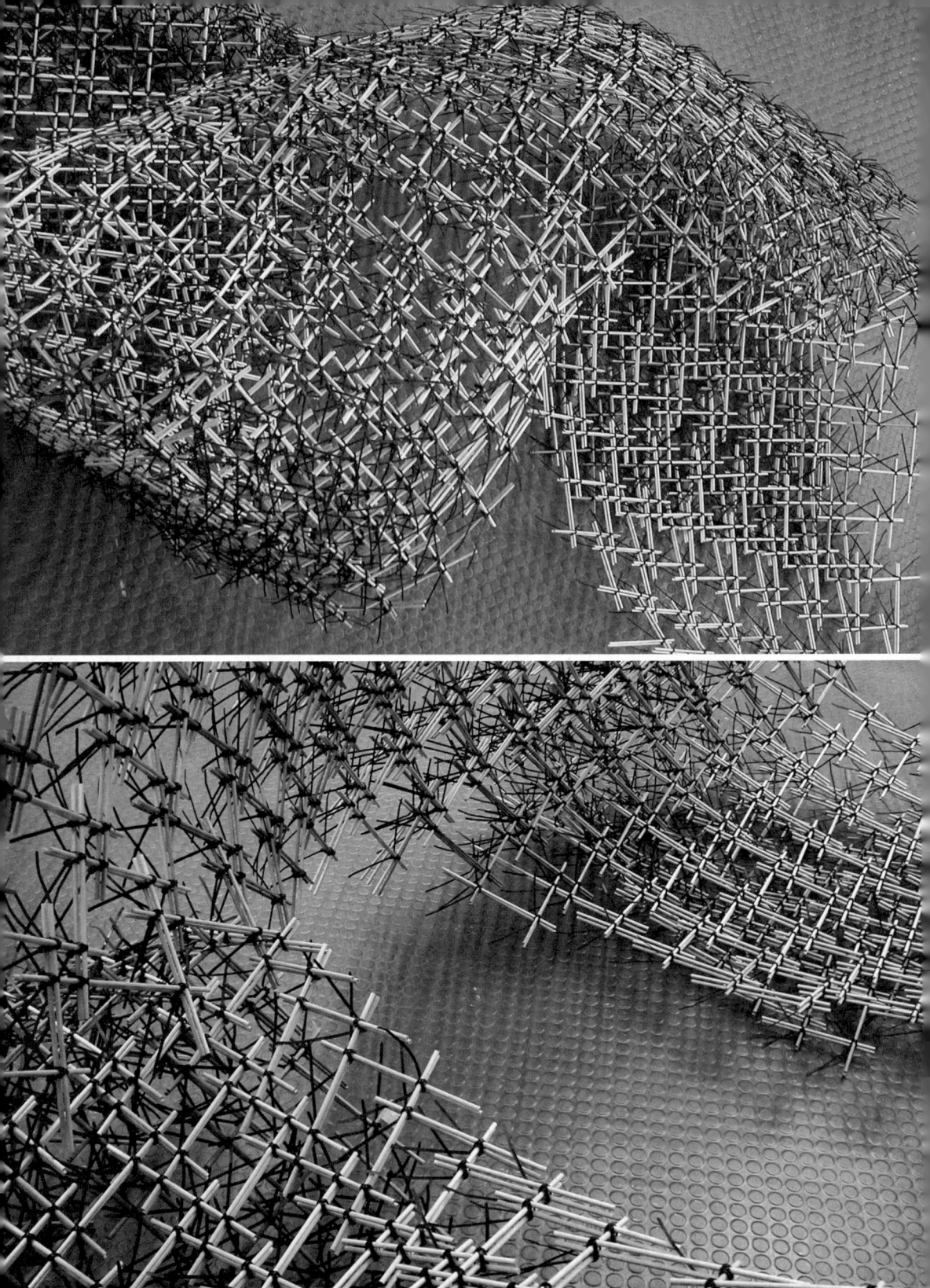

116 Detail views of a double-curved lattice system articulated through the strategic differentiation of the dowel-element's connections.

A self-supporting, double-curved full-scale lattice prototype, assembled from equal dowels and cable ties only, was constructed for the 'Modulations' exhibition at Rice School of Architecture, Houston.

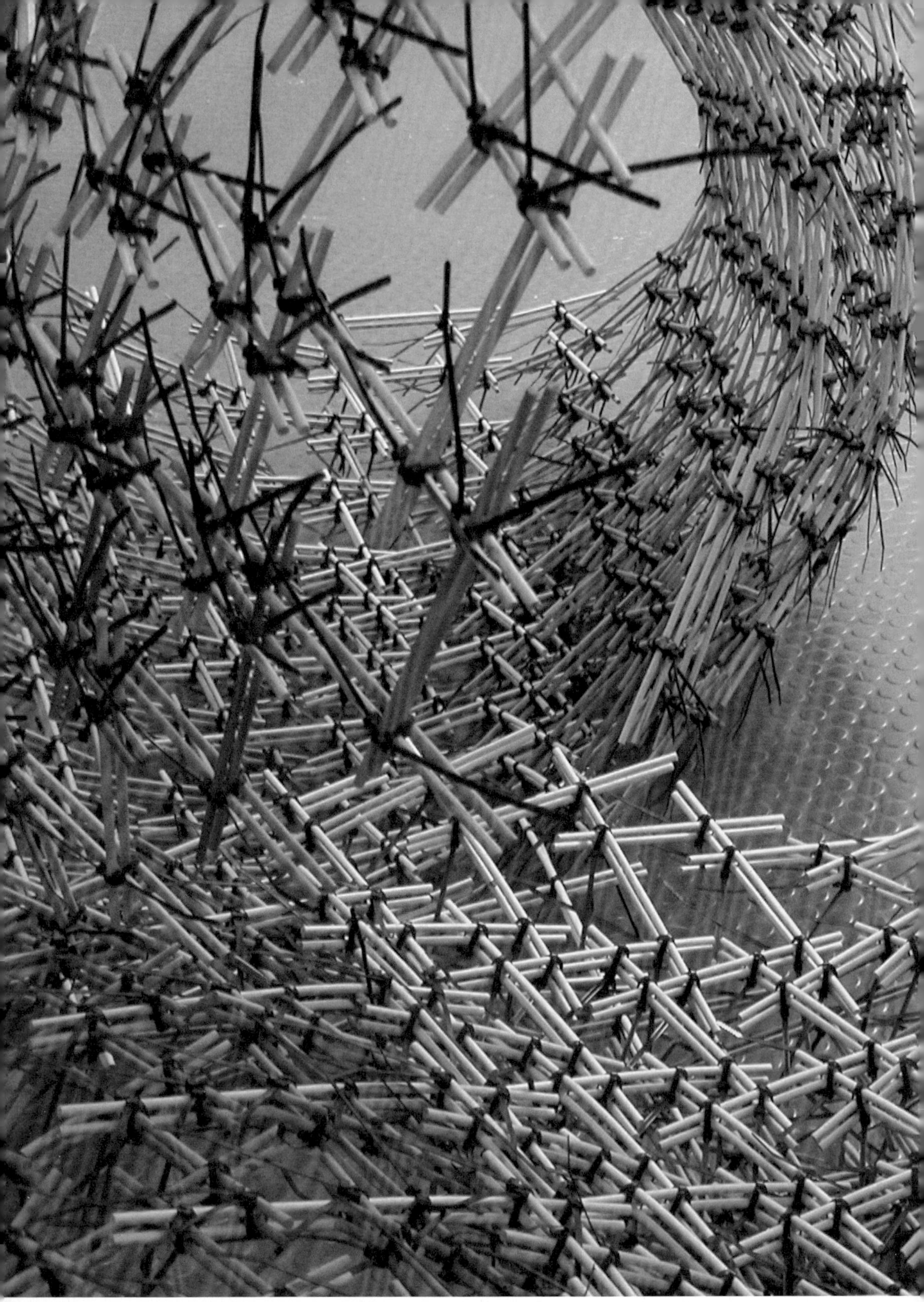

Close-up view of full-scale lattice prototype structure.

COMMENTS — CHRISTOPHER HIGHT

In her early book *Crystals, Fabrics and Fields* the cyborg godmother, Donna Haraway, detailed the debates between organicists and mechanists in early twentieth-century embryology. In part, the debates rotated around the mechanists' desire for a singular universal explanation versus the organicists' persistent claim for an irreducibility of biological forms and evolutionary processes. In these debates, metaphors of fields and lattices were crucial to understand the mysterious processes that guide the formation of life. The history of that most modern of architectural pursuits, the development of the lattice shell, has followed similarly diverging paths. The thin shell was quintessentially modern both because it depended on an ethics of structural expression and lightness made possible by industrialisation, and also because it evoked classical models (the dome) while at once deterritorialising the typologies and metaphysics associated with those historical precedents, promising instead a new conjunction of structure, space and social order. The lattice shell, even more than the concrete shell, embodies such ethics in its use of mass-produced repetitive components with (usually transparent) spanning panels. The two directions in which the lattice shell was developed as a techno-social diagram reveal how modern architecture paralleled the debates of the embryologists. The mechanist, represented here by Buckminster Fuller, developed the geodesic shell as a universal meniscus; his lattice could be deployed without differentiation or scale as a house or as a Manhattan-sized bubble. Like the Dymaxion map of the world (based on similar geometries), or his 'invention' of tensegrity, the geodesic was a global and total order, designed to reduce all of human habitation to a single overarching solution. The organicist Frei Otto, on the other hand, developed the gridshell as a programmatically specified envelope. Indeed, his structural solution depends on the absolute delineation of programme as the edge contour that allows the structure to work in the first place, melding form and function in a precise isomorphism. With Otto, function or programme could not be altered, enlarged or contracted without recalculating and rebuilding the entire shell; Fuller's solution responded to transformations of programme simply by increasing volume without altering the form, or by multiplying shells in potentially infinite arrays. Otto's material realism, which held that a real and necessary correspondence between programme and structure could create infinitely variable enclosures, was diametrically opposed to Fuller's geometric transcendentalism. Both privileged lattice-like constructions over continuous shells or post-and lintels, in part because they mimicked biological and mineral formations found in nature, but Otto saw the lattice as a form determined by the evolution of functional differentiation, and thus organicist, while Fuller treated the crystalline lattice as a universal principle under which all function and social differentiation could be subsumed.

Given this, it was perhaps inevitable that Fuller's geodesic sphere would be chosen by Disney as the logo of global ubiquity, where architecture becomes a simulation of the truly geodesic space of capital, while Otto has emerged as a godfather of sorts for architects committed to reasserting the presence of architecture through expert design of construction and form. Thus the gridshell today seems an architecture of refinement, esoteric rather than universal or organic.

For example, in Shigeru Ban's recent experiments the shell is a hat on an otherwise normative (orthographic) solution for the architectural containment of programme; it still requires the perimeter edge, but in contrast to Otto's shells the relationship between edge, programme and structure have become incidental. The shells are neither simple spheres nor parabolic ruled surfaces that speak of some abstract universal. Nor are Ban's pavilions specific to site or programme. Even their material lightness (physical and phenomenal) has become a spectacle (Wow, it's made of cardboard? How amazing! How ecological! – indeed, to multicultural consumers of global architecture – How very Japanese!). Venturi's decorated shed turned on its side as structure becomes a differentiation not of programme but of the brands that the pavilions house, with architecture being the design of elaborately signifying scaffolds.

The nascent potential of the Discontinuous Strut Lattice presented here lies in the possibility of an alternative that does not collapse back to modernist mechanism versus organicism but has a more disruptive or even productive relationship to the sorts of contemporary programmes which it houses. One can see it as blending Fuller's component logic with Otto's continuous bending element strategy, using differentiated units to create a mass-customised, differentiated continuity that suggests a post-Fordist performativity which is neither quite functionalist nor post-modern iconography. The most significant move in this regard is its removal of the need either for a perimeter contour defined by programmatic requirements or for some transcendent universal form to hold the form. Instead, as the shell is wrapped on itself to create resistances and rigidity, the differentiation of form and the programmatic effects of this form must be in continual negotiation. Similarly, the structures have orientation vis a vis gravity but are not deployed as concave shells over a specific delineated site-edge. Like tumbleweeds, their relationship to site and ground is mobile; but unlike Fuller, it is not neutral. Rather than represent lightness via a crystalline lattice, the fields of sticks and cable-ties create a fabric that sags under its dead weight, and must be laminated and folded to create structural performance, through which scale becomes important in a way heretofore unknown in gridshells. The meniscus of form that contains programme has become a fuzzy layering, in which the interior and exterior are no longer sharply delineated, just as the modern city is less delineation of public and private and more the gradation of overlapping networks of interiority. Pursuing the relationship of these impure 'prototypical' structures to programme would raise challenges to the genealogy of the shell as a prototypical architecture for a modern society, and may offer innovations in the relationship of architectural form to the cyborgs they house.

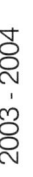

The project aimed at developing an understanding and instrumentalisation of the self-organisational tendencies of fibrous, particularly woven, materials with the goal of developing a related method of modelling for design and a pilot project to test the developed toolset.

The work commenced with the manipulation of single threads within a woven fabric and the registration of the resulting effect on a local, meso- and overall system scale relative to the area of manipulation. Threads were selectively pulled or displaced in order to affect a controlled contraction of the fabric into a series of emergent folds. The distribution and extent of the folds were carefully mapped over a large number of experiments. In order to register the geometric ramifications of the specific manipulations and derive a first set of digital models, each resulting deformation of the fabric was hardened with resin, measured, mapped and digitised. However, the physical models proved to be too fragile for the process of digitisation, with the mechanical arm of the digitiser affecting additional deformation. Instead the large number of measurements taken from the models served to deduce precisely the recurrent pattern of deformation, so that digital models based on the geometric logic that underlies this pattern formation could be constructed. Tangency alignments and curvature continuity became crucial features in the mapping and modelling. In addition the entire process of deformation of the fabric became of interest. Consequently it was important not only to digitally model the various resultant deformation states, but also the dynamics of the process itself.

The first series of tests were undertaken on a fabric with homogeneous fibre-layout, with fibres at uniform density and intervals. The next set of experiments focused on heterogeneous fibre-layouts, with fibres at non-uniform densities and irregular intervals, exposed to the same set of manipulations. The form-finding experiments provided a first set of information for a specific toolset that was developed concurrently.

Scaling a material system and its specific

behaviour for an architectural application is not a trivial task. In this specific project it involved careful consideration as to whether the entire woven organisation was to be scaled, or its behaviour retained but the system translated.

Here we decided to translate the system while trying to retain its overall malleability to some degree, and its local displacement within joints to a much greater extent.

A detailed study of gridshell systems, in particular Mutschler and Frei Otto's Mannheim Multihalle, delivered a first inroad into a promising translation of the system. Various materials and cross-sections of very thin rods were tested as replacements for the fabric threads, to understand better the necessary calibration between elasticity and stiffness of these elements. In addition lattice layout and joint articulation were of crucial importance for the investigation. Numerous different uniform and non-uniform lattice layouts were tested together with different types of sliding joints. The experiments showed that in order to cope with compressive and tensile forces effectively, the degree of malleability across an entire lattice needed to be varied. This could be achieved in three different ways: first, by articulating the rods differently in order to determine their stiffness and elasticity individually and by region; secondly, by changing joint types and thus the way movement is enabled or constrained locally and by region; thirdly, by non-uniform and irregular lattice layouts that stiffen or weaken lattice regions strategically. A fourth strategy was added: the layering of lattices becomes useful when a certain curvature needs to be retained between more malleable regions.

The pilot project envisaged a partly changeable office landscape made from the articulation of the 0-datum into an undulating terrain, enveloped and strategically partitioned by the lattice system. This office landscape, however, is organised not as a typical open-plan arrangement but as a matrix of interconnected rooms, with some visual aspects and connections similar to those of the raumplan, as a result of the undulating terrain and roof and the connections distributed in various sectional arrangements and heights. Circulation and visual connectivity were introduced as control parameters. Working relations between office users were analysed and led to a series of organisational diagrams. The design commenced by selecting anchor areas for particular office activities. In these strategic areas the material system needed to be tightly controlled, in the way it makes spatial provisions as a boundary threshold. Subsequently the primary circulation routes/visual connections between the anchor areas were defined to act as constraints on the system. Again this determined widths and heights of spaces. The lattice can be understood as draped over these defined spaces, with its perimeter locally fixed to retain them while at the same time form-finding itself in the areas between.

Methodologically, the initial design tool was applied to carefully developed connectivity diagrams, and new areas with varying degrees of visual and physical connectivity started to emerge around the tightly controlled areas. A further set of mappings then revealed the ability of the system as a whole to modulate visual and physical relationships, revealing unanticipated spatial conditions. The malleability of the lattice allows operational, circulation and visual connections (and thus workflow) to remain reconfigurable: activities can freely migrate to locations with sufficient space and connectivity. Freed from the need to establish and satisfy an exhaustive list of probable programmatic scenarios and configurations, the project develops as a hybrid between an open plan and a matrix of interconnected rooms; something more constricted than the former, but less constricted than the latter. The malleable lattice areas together with the articulated terrain can increase or decrease connectivity and available space and in doing so influence the migration of activities to other locations or their adaptation to new constraints.

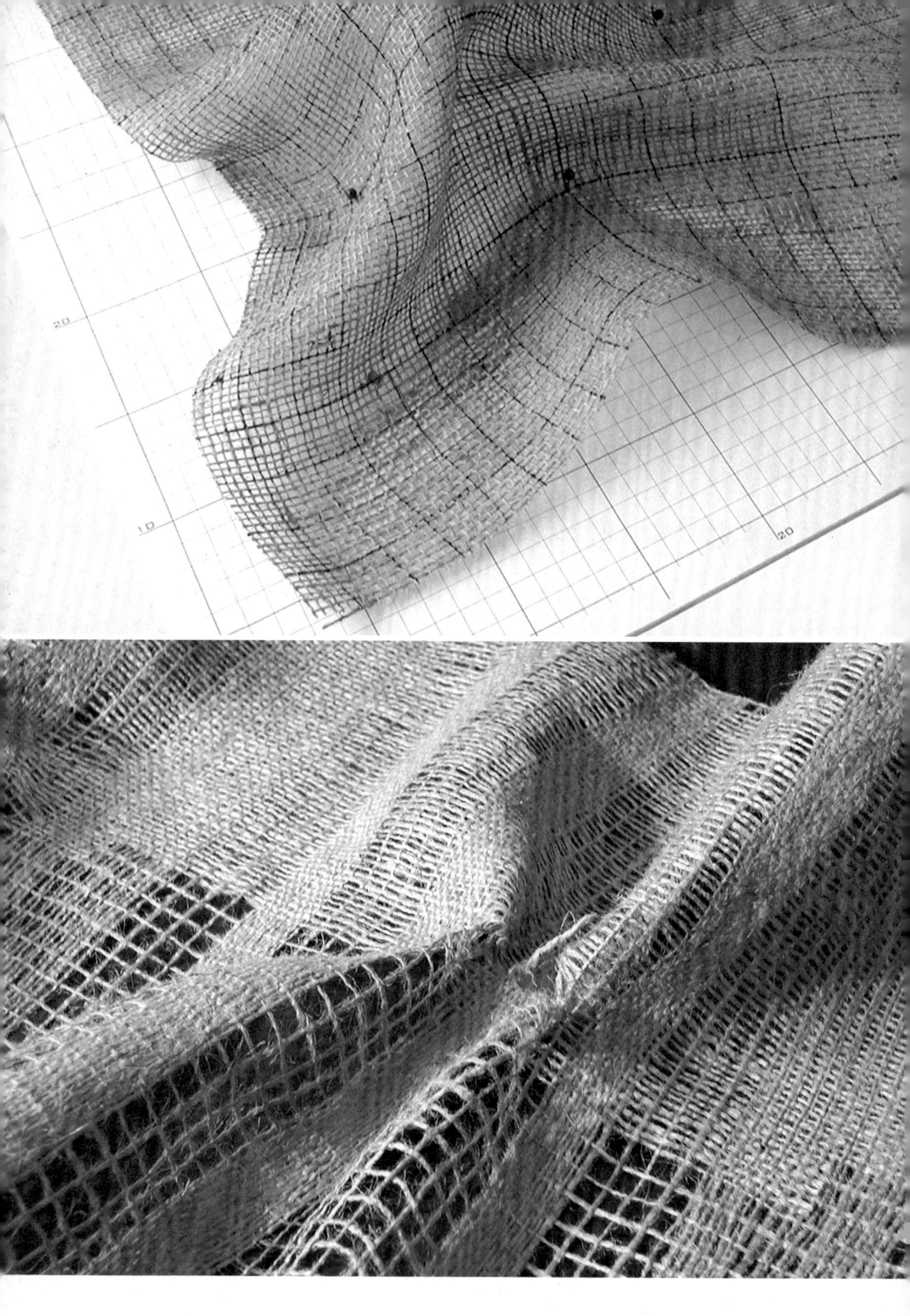

124 Experiments in manipulating woven fabric by displacing a number of attachment points (top) or pulling single threads (bottom) register the effect upon the fabric on a local, meso- and overall system scale relative to the area of influence.

The morphological changes in the overall geometry of the fabric resulting from local manipulations are analysed and subsequently articulated as a series of laser-cut models through the translation of surface isocurves.

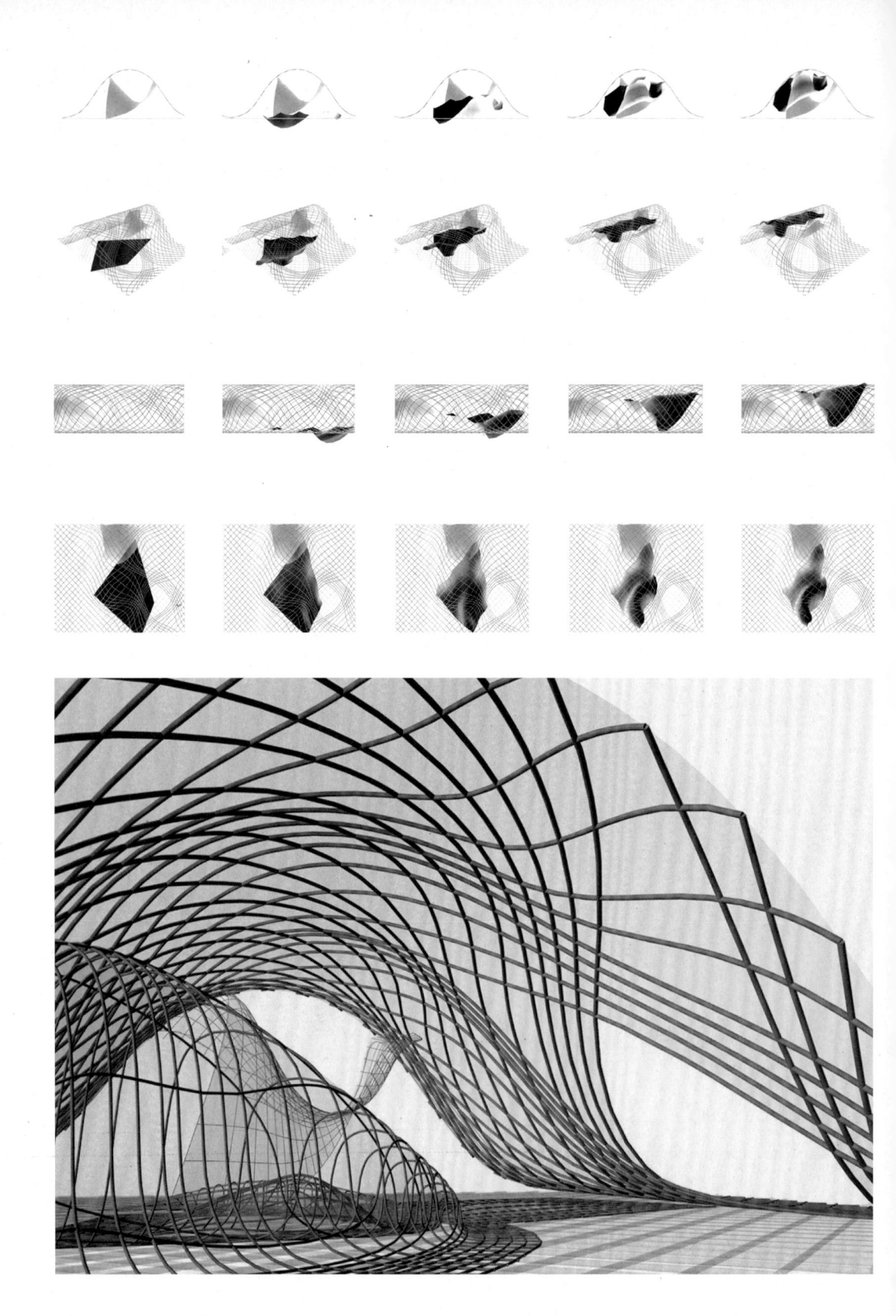

126 Digital form-finding processes are employed to investigate the behaviour of hanging fabric surfaces. In an iterative process based on the simulation of gravity and fabric properties the surface settles into a stable state of equilibrium of external forces and internal resistances (top). The resulting geometries are translated into lattice structures (bottom).

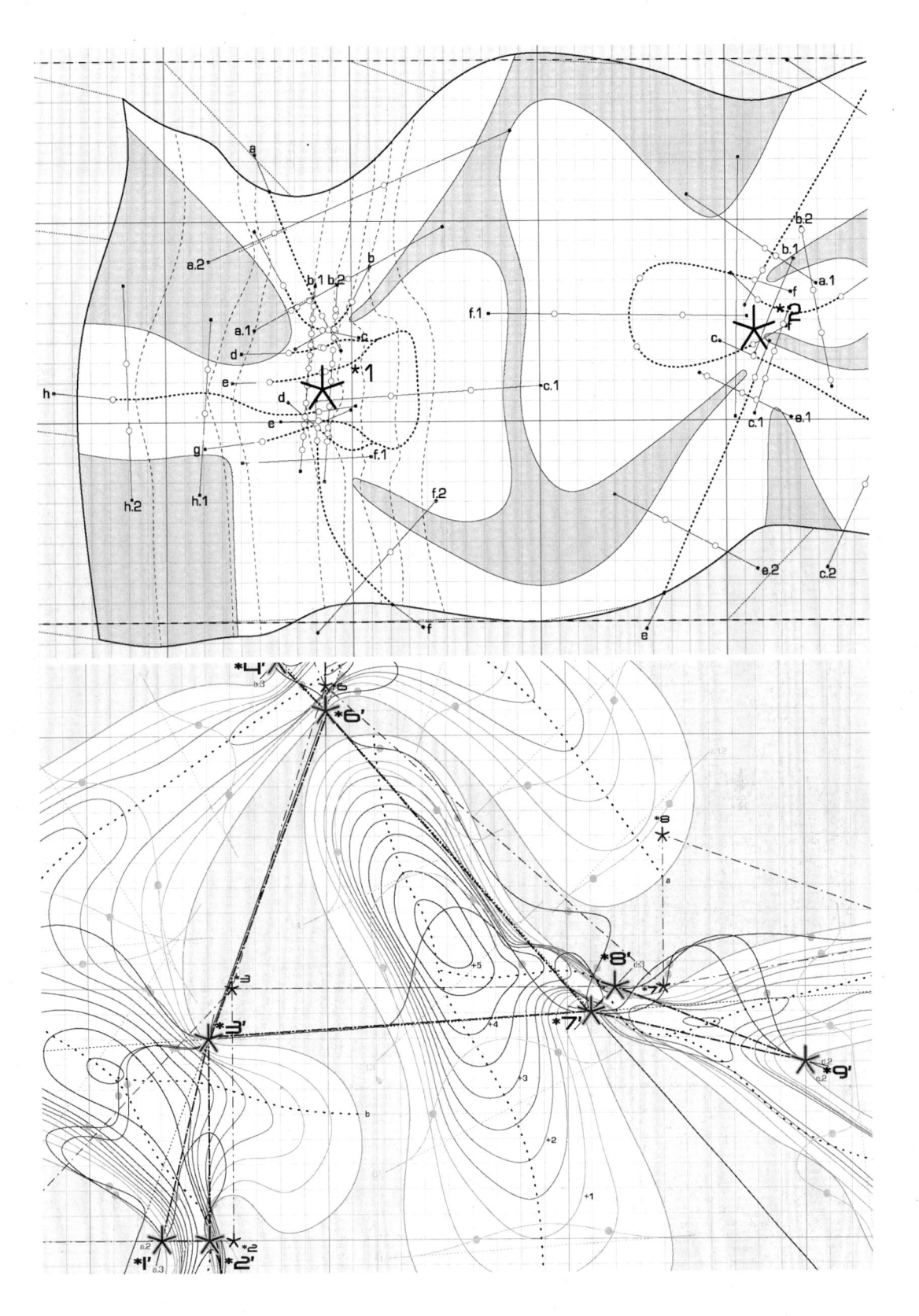

In order to register the effect of local geometric manipulations on the perimeter line (top) and topography (bottom) of the surface, a specific mapping technique is developed.

100m

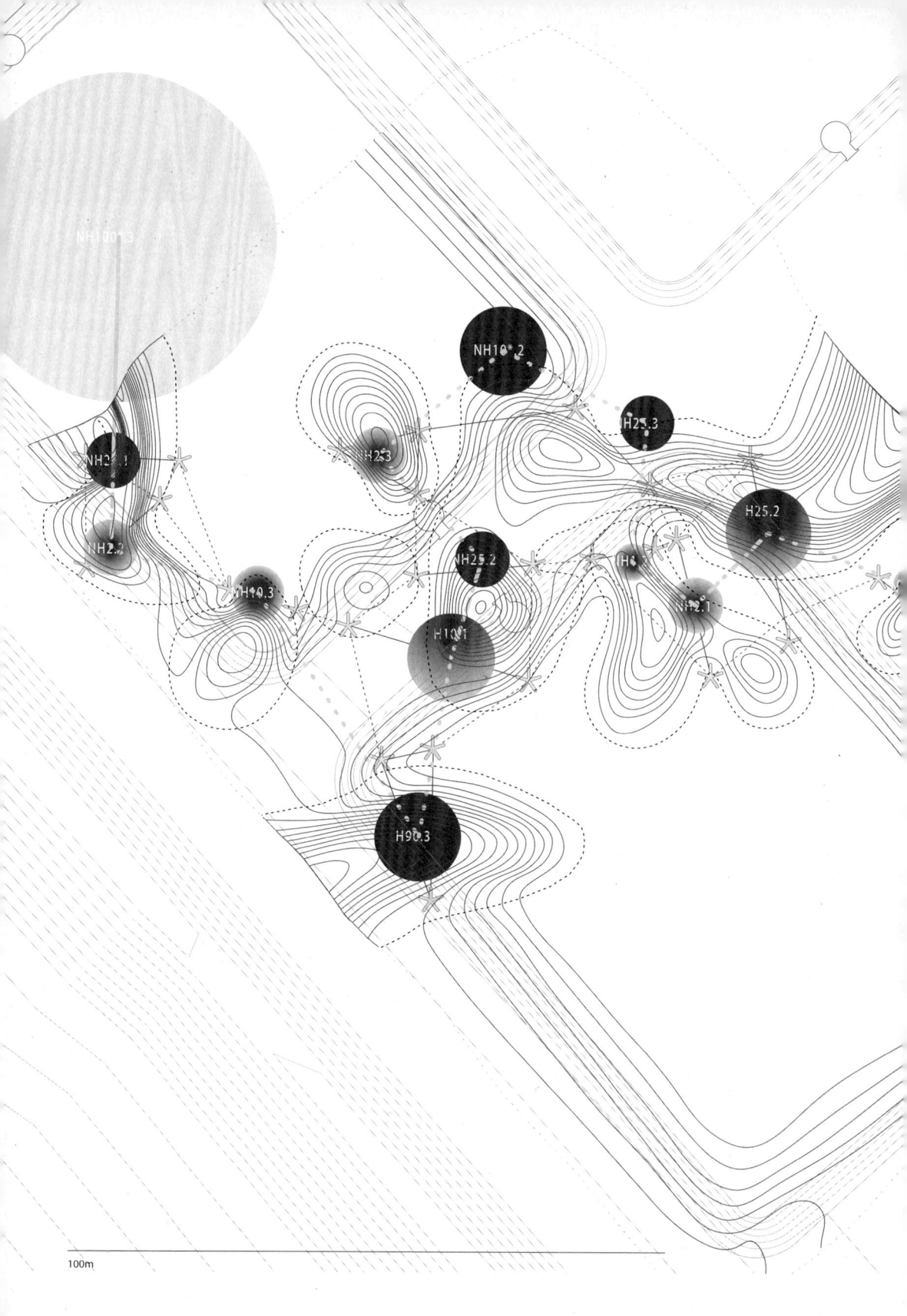

128 The initial mapping technique employed to register the geometric data of various physical tests is extended to become an operative, parametric design tool allowing for the exact specification of strategic surface manipulations and resultant overall geometry.

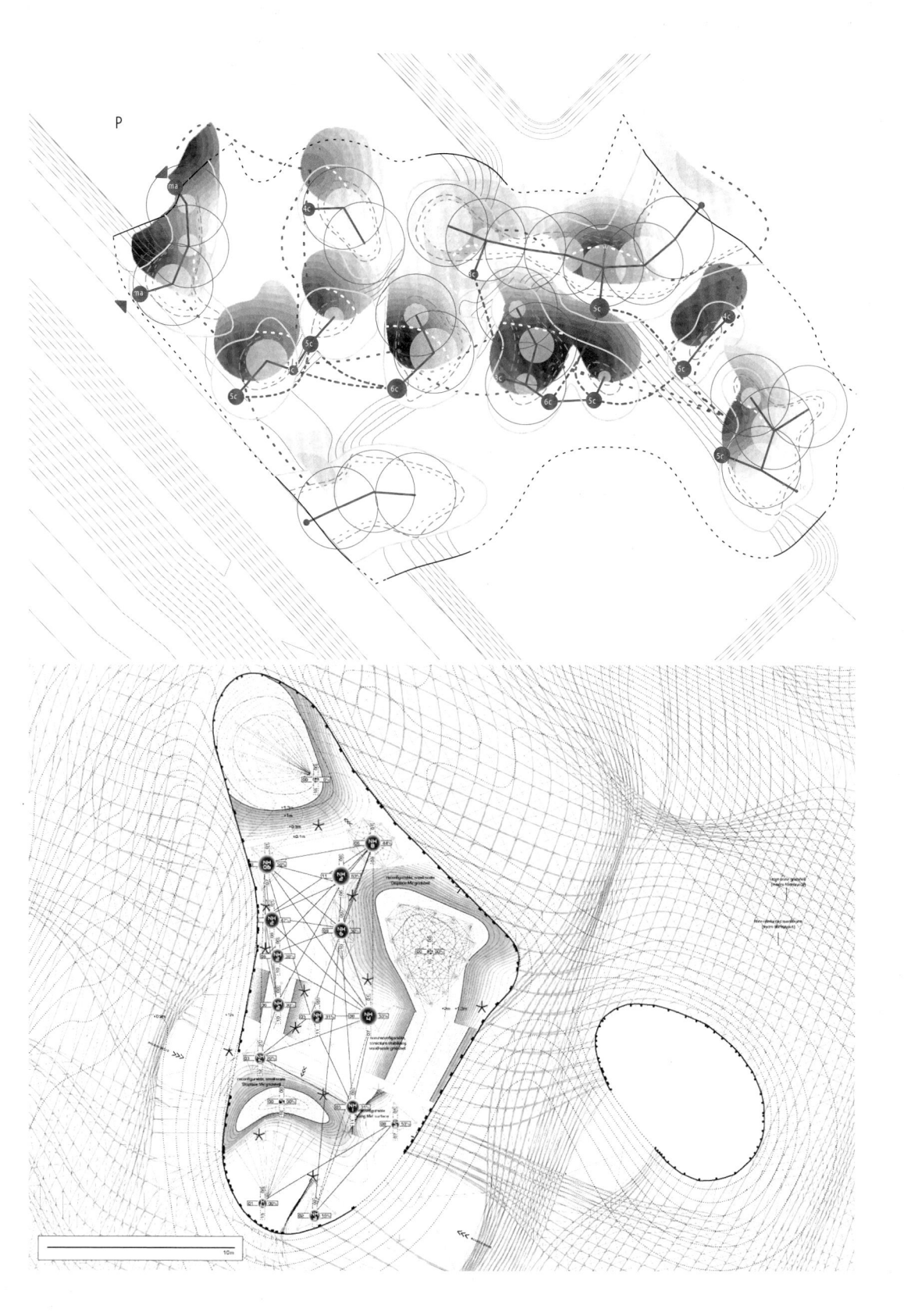

The articulation of the context-specific system is defined by the distribution of areas of varied degrees of visual and physical connectivity (top). The system is articulated according to these controlled areas but at the same time it provides a wide range of emerging visual and physical relationships (bottom).

129

COMMENTS

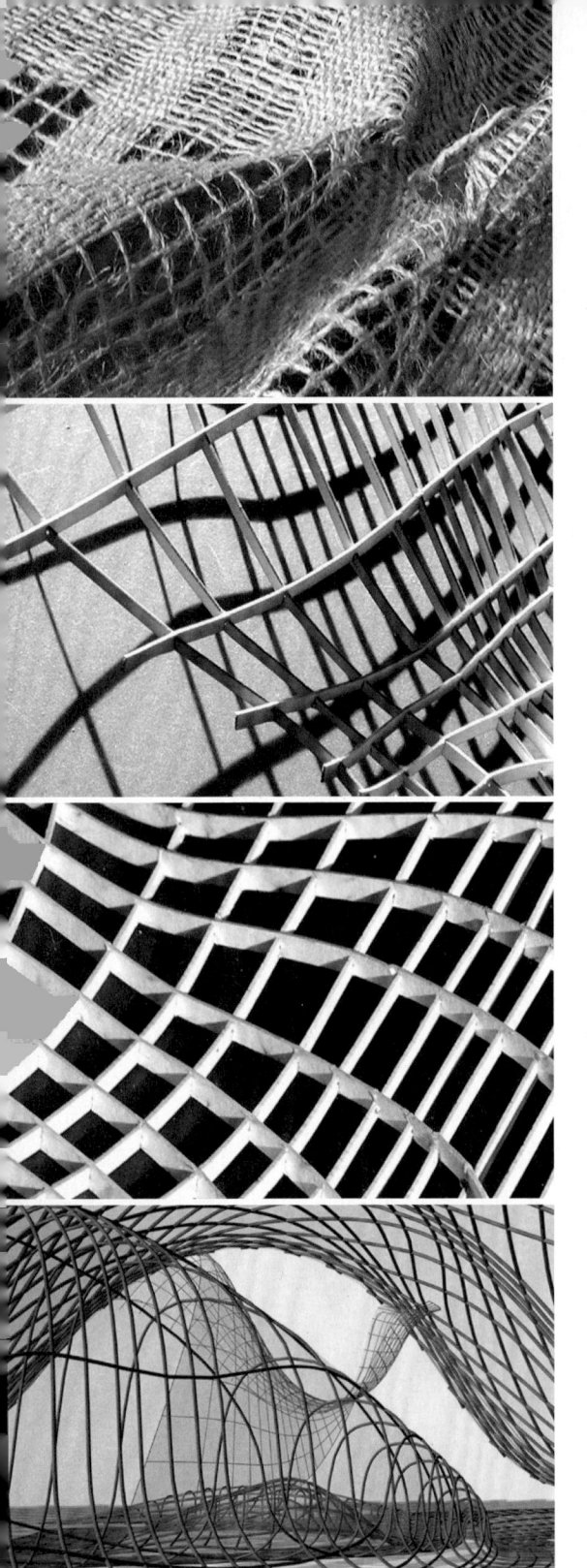

LUDO GROOTEMAN

The fibrous character of the material sample that accompanies the opening page of Cordula Stach's project is significant for the understanding of its potential. The image shows a folded piece of fabric with an irregular weaving pattern and roughness of texture. The individual strands of the fibre create a differentiated field of micro-connections across the surface. It is this fibrousnesses that catches the eye; every strand of rope is frayed and interlinked with others, so it is no longer a detached entity.

The piece of fabric displays various effects, whether geometric, tactile or structural. Both the roughness and the porosity seem to vary across the surface. The fabric's discrete components are still recognisable, but their relation to the whole is too complex to be perceived at once. The left side of the image shows how a strategically manipulated point causes the rest of the fabric to deform in a logical yet hardly predictable way. The same multi-scalar complexity applies to the structural principle. Whereas the weaving pattern provides an overall structural coherence, the roughness of the individual strands allows the individual fibres to be displaced while the overall surface is kept intact. These strands entangle with neighbouring strands, forming micro-structures across the surface and generating highly localised structural behaviour.

Due to the complexity of this material, its properties (though promising) are difficult to assess, either in terms of analysing the structural behaviour, or as an instrument for designing an architectural project. Local manipulations result in regional and global effects (across the entire surface) and vice-versa. Any simulation or interpretation is bound to be a reduction of the initial complexity of the behaviour and the diversity of architectural effects.

The effects are well worth the effort, as they are manifold and diverse; yet the very literal transfer of material properties seems to have far more potential. In translating the models to a building scale, Cordula Stach is therefore absolutely right to devise a material strategy rather than indulge in material effects. She designs, as it were, a pre-programmed skin that can be adapted in particular ways. Although the manipulation points and levels of flexibility are predetermined across the surface, the potential configurations are boundless.

The fabric is translated into a latticed surface model with fairly stiff sections that are connected with flexible or fixed joints (the latter play the same role as the resin-hardened regions of the fabric). The elasticity of the strut combined with the varying flexibility of the joints produces a complex behaviour similar to that of the piece of fabric, resulting in an architectural model with comparable possibilities for manipulation and multi-scalar effects.

However the translation of the fabric into a gridshell model, with reference to the Mannheim Multihalle, seems to eliminate some of the material's most fascinating properties along the way. One wishes that a more literal material translation were possible.

Both the erratic fibre organisation (described above) and the principle of weaving are worth maintaining. The individual strands are all similar and there are no significant differences within the fibre, yet no two parts of the fibre are exactly the same. The surface becomes lively and deep. This principle is accelerated by the differentiation of the weaving pattern.

Furthermore, large parts of the fibrous surface are structurally passive or only partially active. The homogeneity of the surface structure gives rise to an equal potential throughout. Significant differentiation occurs only after application, when large parts of the surface become partially or totally redundant. This level of redundancy does not matter, as the relatively low-tech nature of the material means that fabrication is simple and cheap: little energy is required for assembly or disassembly.

All these properties – the intrinsic multi-scalar differentiation of the fabric, the low-tech fabrication technique, and the redundancy principle – are worth translating to the building scale. One way of approaching this would be to take a strictly material route, selecting or developing materials that have comparable properties but are more appropriate to a building scale. Instead of sisal rope, one could look at steel wire, glass or carbon fibre, which have similar fibre structures. Or one could consider certain composites, combining a fibrous material with resin or plastics in order to control structural behaviour, as this project does on the model scale.

It would furthermore be useful to accelerate certain properties in respect of general building requirements, such as the need to create a waterproof shell and form an interior environment. The most obvious way to achieve this would be the development of a secondary skin attached to the lattice, which would allow the required adaptability.

But one could also imagine a material strategy more in line with the main fibrous organisation. The hairiness could become more extreme, inducing these properties in the skin without adding secondary components. The substructures would become denser and more layered, and the weave would thicken into something like a fur fabric made of different kinds and densities of fibrous material.

This project undertook a critical revision of conventional building envelopes made up of a large number of mono-functional elements, such as primary structure, secondary structure, rain cover, thermal insulation, shading systems and so on. It investigated whether much of the required functionality could instead be provided by the strategic use of a few elements and their specific orientation to environmental input. The starting-point for the project was the question: what would be the architectural equivalent to the environmental performance of hairy surfaces, such as seen in plants or animals, and what could be the related effect of a carefully orchestrated porosity of a surface?

A detailed study was made of varied strategies of shading and ventilating spaces in the Middle East, focusing in particular on the spectacular interlaced wooden window-screens known as mashrabiyya and the wind-towers of Yazd (Iran). A simple system was then devised that consists of two types of elements: a lattice-type surface as a connective element that delivers some level of structural capacity in conjunction with the second set of elements – 'sticks' that are intended to modulate luminous, thermal and airflow conditions.

The sticks are oriented perpendicular to the lattice surface and held in place by it. They are geometrically varied in length and cross-sectional profile and diameter. The length of the sticks and the stiffness of the lattice determine the degree to which the carrying lattice can be elastically deformed and, thus, the degree to which the surface of the envelope can be articulated. This is of fundamental importance since the orientation of the sticks in relation to thermal input and airflow direction directly influences the environmental performance of the system. Other crucial parameters in this respect are the stick density, materiality and reflectivity.

Once the geometric logic of the system was established, a series of physical and digital models were devised to test the performance of each configuration with regard to shadows cast and modulation of luminous flow (lumen) and illuminance (lux), gauging the amount of visible light and thermal energy filtered by the system. Direct light was studied, as well as light reflected or absorbed by the sticks, depending on their surface characteristics. The thermal mass of the sticks is determined by the choice of material and the thermal performance by the reflectivity of their surface. Different surface finishes were tested, some that reflect light specularly, that is with little spread, and some that reflect light diffusely, with the aim to establish the available performance range in the reflection of visible light and thermal energy into the spaces that are enveloped by the material system.

Another crucial parameter was the control of visibility across the porous material threshold of the system. With all sticks being normal to the lattice, the global curvature affects the visual permeability of the system through the alignment of the normal vector, which corresponds with the stick direction and the sight-line of a passer-by. For example if the orientation of a field of sticks matches the viewing direction, this region appears more transparent. The combined effects of user-movement with the varied curvature of the system allows for the organisation and modulation of complex fields of view ranging from relatively transparent to entirely opaque.

A first context study focused on the design of a teahouse for Shinjuku Park. The clearly defined activities to be housed by a tea pavilion provided the critical input for an instantiation of the system. The initial aim here was to establish required privacy ranges for related activities: the visual permeability of each boundary threshold was determined by the density of the sticks and their angle of inclination relative to the viewing direction. However, defining a space solely on this basis may deliver a configuration that is not necessarily the optimum one for the required environmental performance, i.e. while privacy levels are maintained, airflow and thermal flow may either be accelerated or decelerated causing a degree of discomfort. The second design phase therefore focused on the interrelation and negotiation of various system parameters and interdependent performative effects.

Once the scope of possible calibration was established, the system was further developed in the context of Tokyo's Shinjuku station, which is known to be an urban heat-island. Due to the immense thermal mass and sealed surfaces of the built environment, temperatures are up to 4° C higher than average, causing great discomfort for the users of the area. As a response to the particular environmental and programmatic context, the project proposed a partial enveloping of the station, so that thermal energy can be stored above the platform level and other inhabited surfaces. In this case the role of the sticks across most of the exposed surface was to take up the thermal energy, to accelerate airflow and to release and dispose of heat in a controlled manner. The system's enormous surface area relative to the overall size of the envelope and the enclosed volume allows for a rapid dispersal of heat, not unlike the behaviour of cooling fins on an engine.

Other regions of the material system modulated visual permeability with respect to way-finding within the large and complex station, so that the architecture could begin to incorporate signage and pictograms, so reducing visual clutter. Views along each trajectory of movement were carefully studied in order to provide orientation, exposing both large-scale landmarks and, on a smaller scale, relevant routes through the station and to and from platforms. Engaging the built environment in this way holds great potential and should thus be further researched.

Based on a material system consisting of relatively simple individual elements, the project developed a building envelope that integrates various performative aspects: structural capacity, thermal behaviour, light transmission and visual permeability can now be negotiated and modulated through the manipulation of a series of system-inherent parameters such as the local stick geometry and materiality, the relation between stick collectives and regional curvature, and the overall geometry and orientation of the system.

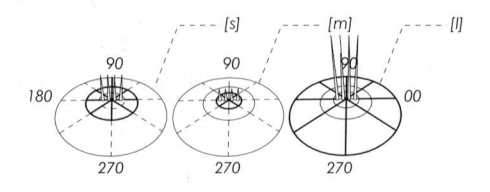

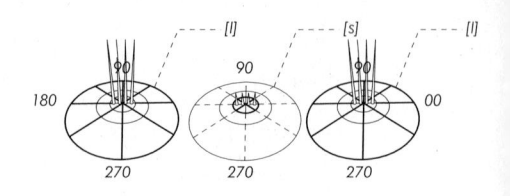

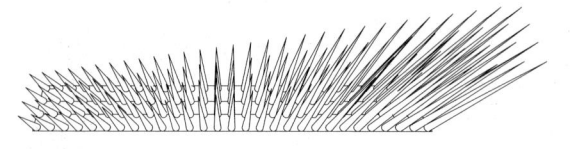

Stick Height = Full diameter [FD] >
half diameter [hd] >
twice diameter [td]

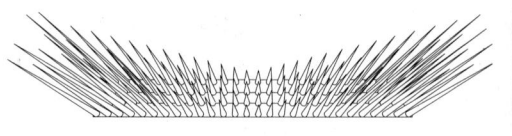

Stick height = Twice diameter of circle [td] >
half diameter of circle [hd] >
Twice diameter of circle [td]

Rolling sequence = 21

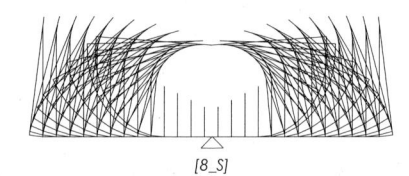

Rolling sequence = 17

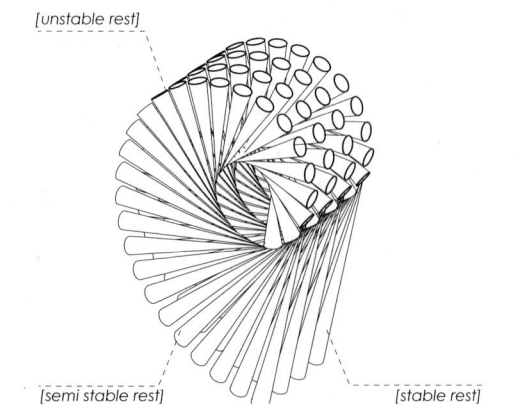

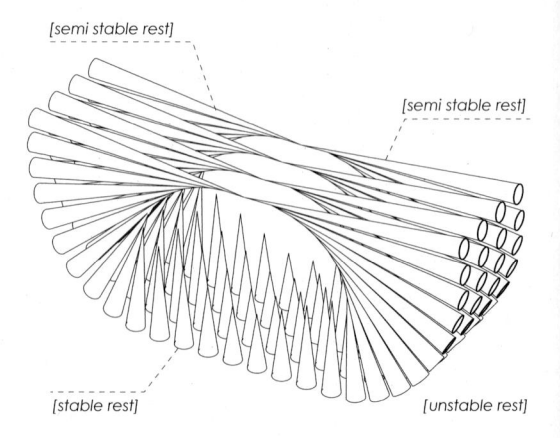

[unstable rest]
[semi stable rest]
[stable rest]

[semi stable rest]
[semi stable rest]
[stable rest]
[unstable rest]

134 The basic system consists of a lattice-type surface and a set of elements or 'sticks' that are oriented perpendicular to the lattice surface and that are held in place by it. Geometric differentiation of individual sticks changes the behaviour of the overall system.

Original Position | Rolling up Process | Finalized Stage

Rolling up over and over

Rolling up outwards

Rolling up outwards

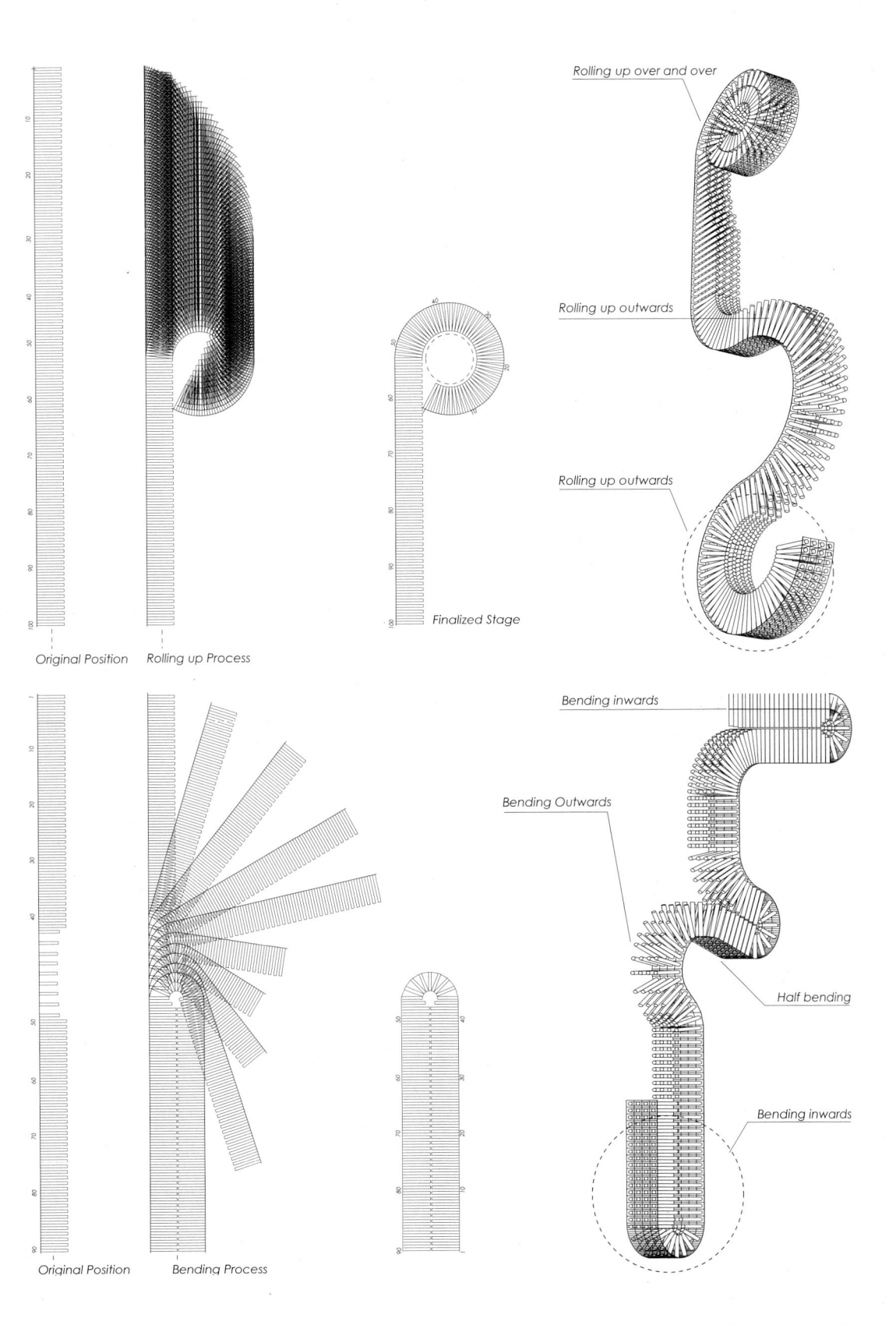

Original Position | Bending Process

Bending inwards

Bending Outwards

Half bending

Bending inwards

The lattice-type surface together with the stick elements can deliver different levels of structural capacity through rolling up (top) or bending (bottom) processes of the system.

135

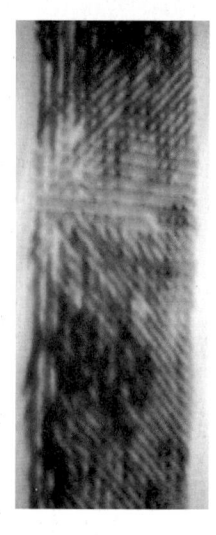

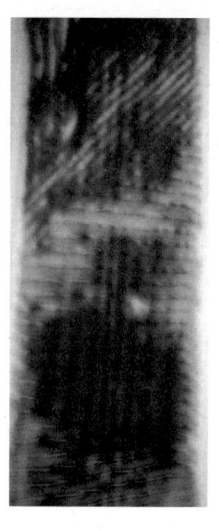

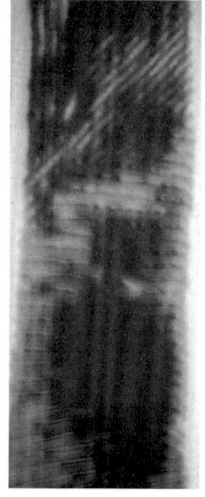

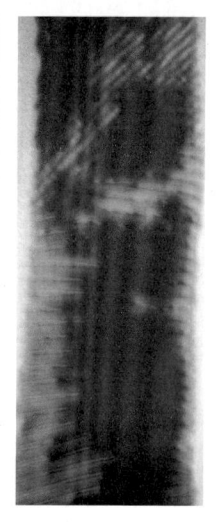

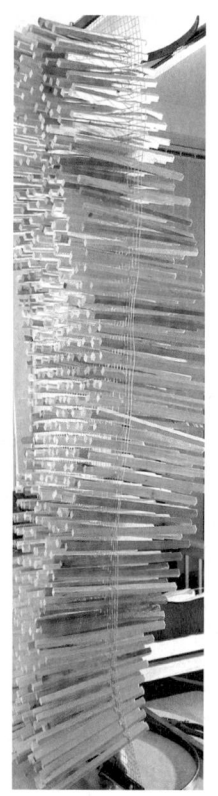

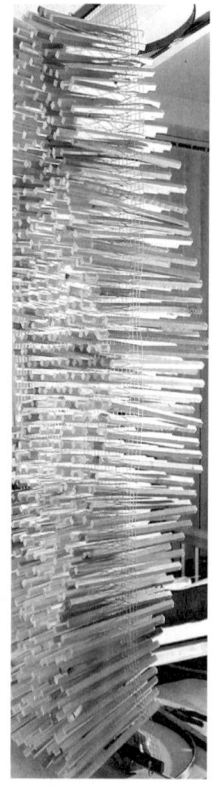

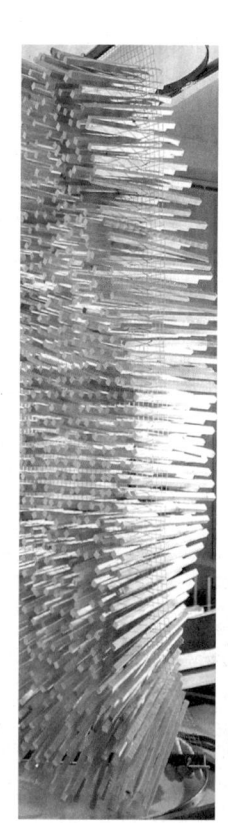

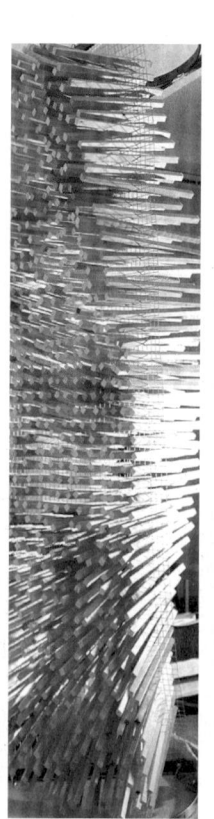

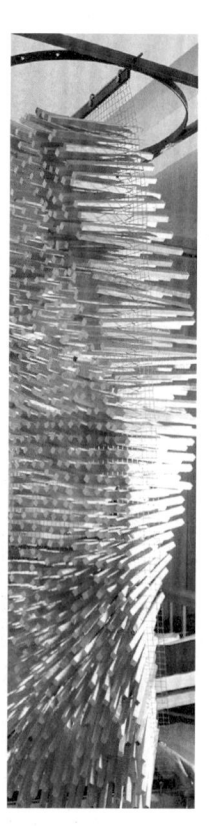

| moment 1 | moment 2 | moment 3 | moment 4 | moment 5 |
| 00 degree | 15 degree | 30 degree | 45 degree | 60 degree |

| moment 1 | moment 2 | moment 3 | moment 4 | moment 5 |
| 00 degree | 15 degree | 30 degree | 45 degree | 60 degree |

A series of physical tests indicate the performative capacity of different system configuration resulting from rotational movement with regards to shadow cast and modulation of luminous flow.

Different orientations of the stick elements resulting from an irregularly curved lattice surface create differentiated fields of luminous intensity and shadow.

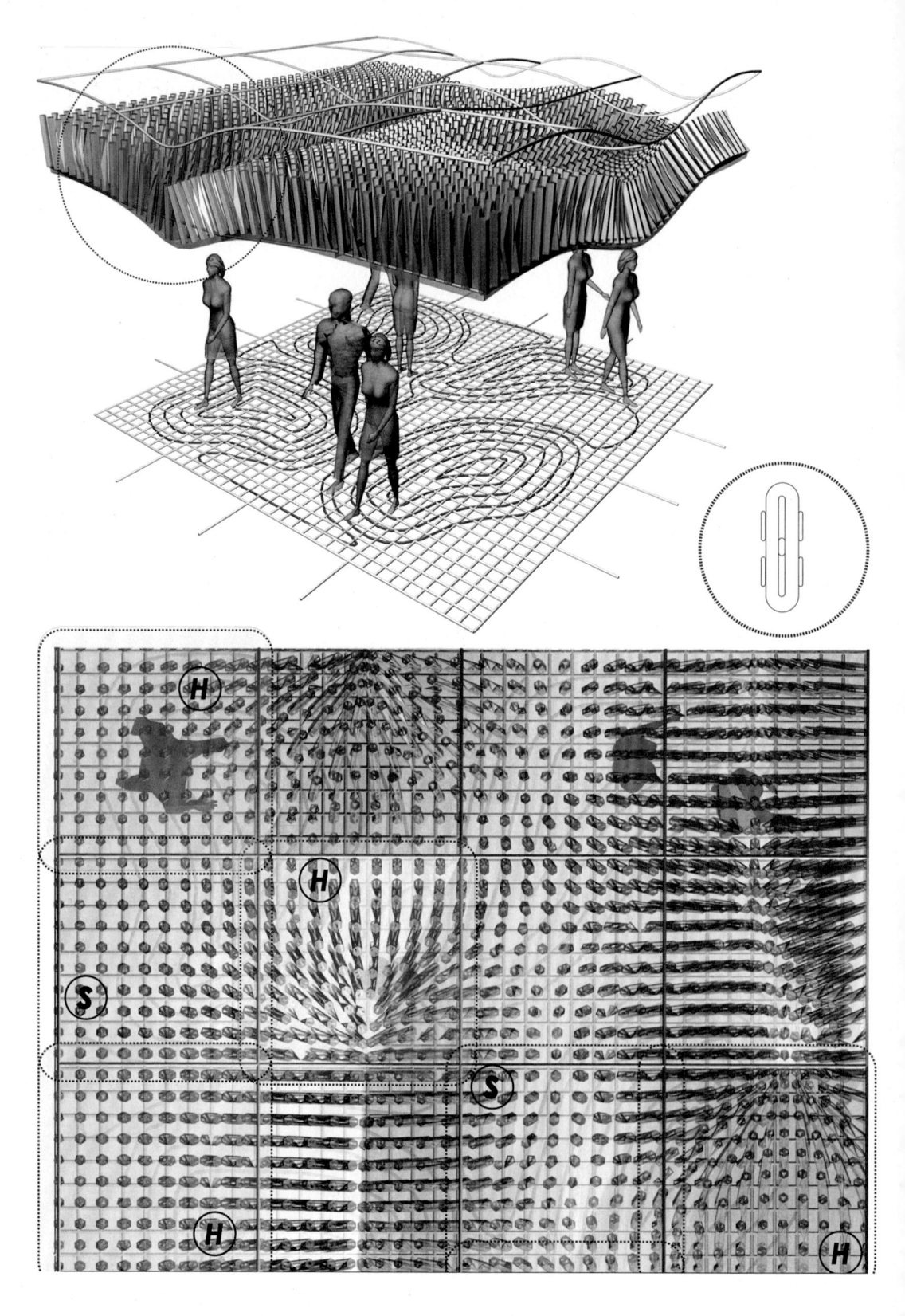

138   The geometric manipulation of the lattice surface allows for local adjustments of stick orientation and the related permeability of the system.

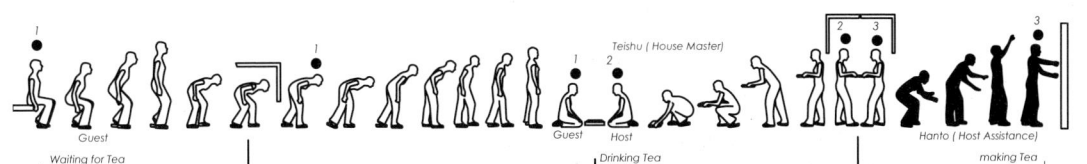

1		1	1 2 Teishu (House Master)	2 3 3
Guest		Guest Host		Hanto (Host Assistance)
Waiting for Tea		Drinking Tea		making Tea
Machiati Room Waiting Room	(Door : 36 inches Height) Crawl in Entrance	Chashitsu Room Main room of the ceremony		Mizuya room Preparation room
Koshikake machiai (Waiting Bench)				

Rolling inwards
three internal circles

Bending inwards
Sitting zone

Interlocking zone
Connection to room 2

Supporting Zone
Bending Outwards
Maximum stick height: 48cm

Side Grid

3.00 m

Bending Outwards
Maximum stick height: 20cm
Light control zone

Bending inwards

Floor Grid
3.00 m

Bending Outwards
Supporting Zone
Maximum stick height: 38cm

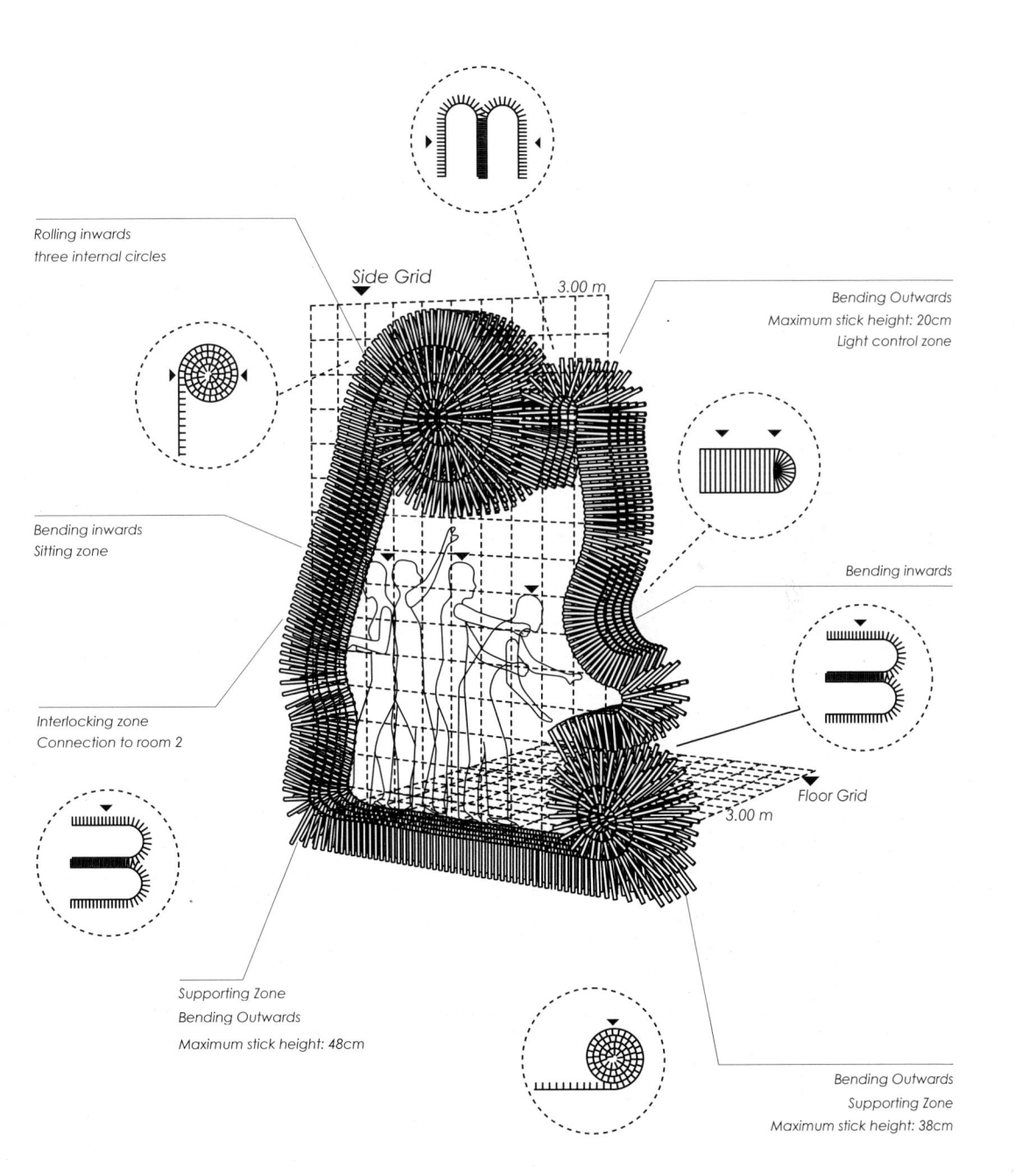

The specific lattice and stick configuration is derived in response to environmental and spatial criteria.

COMMENTS

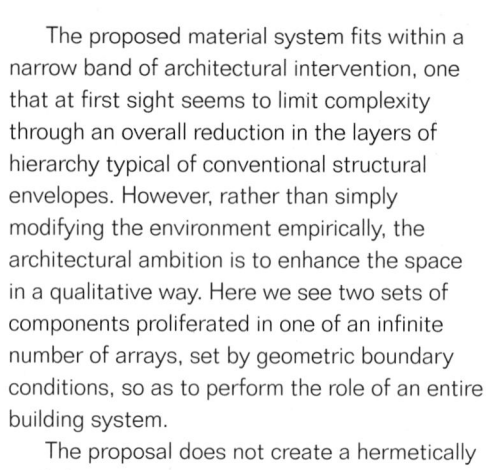

SIMON BEAMES

The proposed material system fits within a narrow band of architectural intervention, one that at first sight seems to limit complexity through an overall reduction in the layers of hierarchy typical of conventional structural envelopes. However, rather than simply modifying the environment empirically, the architectural ambition is to enhance the space in a qualitative way. Here we see two sets of components proliferated in one of an infinite number of arrays, set by geometric boundary conditions, so as to perform the role of an entire building system.

The proposal does not create a hermetically sealed environment. It is a built form organised in such a way as to avoid mechanical intervention and the consequent energy requirements. The structural components can perform specific environmental functions: light filtration, humidity control, heat sink and distribution network.

This material system can be easily related to a common biomimetic analogy: the hair and skin of mammals adapted to their local environment. The individual strands designed to transfer heat away from the body, wick sweat, provide evaporative cooling, absorb the UV thermal potential and form an environmental barrier, work in collaboration with the skin that may be coloured, rough, smooth, or porous to increase the performance of the strands and the overall envelope system. The effect is cool in response to airflow, hot in response to UV, cool in response to UV, hydrophobic, hydrophilic, and so on.

If these systems were to be applied to an inanimate structure, how could that structure be adapted to ameliorate effects of the local environment? Apart from creating a spatial arrangement, the same structural component exposed to the ambient environment would need to be functionally adaptable, with effective environmental performance such as shading daylight, reducing or collecting rain, dispersing and controlling or dampening the wind effect. To modulate humidity control, for instance, the system would need to operate in a similar way to a Sorption wheel: wicking and drying to control humidity within a space, with ambient moisture collected on the inside surface of the mat, close to the base of the sticks. The porous sticks can then act like fabric wicks, and generate an asymmetric flow away from the interior. As the water rises in the sticks it comes into contact with accelerated airflow and evaporates. The geometric distribution of the sticks is critical to the efficiency of the humidity collection; a local environment must be formed to encourage air-circulation not stratification, and the spines must then spread to the external air to encourage flow and consequent contact with the moist surfaces. The system could operate a little like a fleece fabric.

The visible and habitable structure that is seen in the proposal may form only part of a system. We can speculate that the system could perform more effectively if above-ground ambient components were considered together with the local below-ground geological components. A development of this project could therefore be based on a speculation as to the performance criteria of the foundations, considered as a direct extension of the stick and mat.

The potential subterranean intervention, penetrating the ground to form a network distribution of sticks, could form part of a ground heat source or cool the reclamation system. The ground temperature at Tokyo Shinjuku station is a uniform $10°$ C, from 2 m down. A normal distribution of mini bore holes with a diameter of 100 mm requires spacing of up to 6 m to ensure maximum efficiency in mobilising the ground's thermal capacity. The overall performance is directly related to the length of material that can be submerged in contact with the thermally constant ground. In order to provide an effective system, to thermally control an environment of 500 m^2, say, it may be necessary to have a field of 40 bore holes to a depth of 100 m. In the proposal the densely spaced cylindrical stick system has a great deal of length and effective surface area. Does clustering the sticks in greater numbers as fields provide equal or greater potential to mobilise the latent ground heat, compared to a traditional system? And can this complement the part exposed above ground to create a closed circuit environmental control material system?

With a two-'strand' parallel system of rejection and reclamation connecting the sticks via the mat surface to sticks that connect to the above-ground environment, this may be effective. Synthesising the logic of substructure and superstructure with an environmental system limits the number of construction components, gives all components multifunctionality and, rather than touching the ground lightly, embeds the intervention into the environment.

It is worth speculating as to the material logic of the individual components now the potential functionality is understood. The system of structural components may be capable of adapting to the boundary conditions of the surface, rolling, bending, interlocking, creating friction and internally carrying a liquid while externally directing air flow. The component should be manufactured from a porous material, capable of mass production; the surface quality of the sticks is critical, are they shiny or matt? Curved or flat? Should the surface have a micro-profile of riblets? What is the porosity of the mat? The outlined performance requires a hybrid: we can speculate that a solid, thermally conductive material is required: foamed aluminium, for instance, could meet these criteria.

Physical characteristics include the potential extrusion manufacture and therefore control of length and cross-sectional area, mass and a predictable connection interface. While the material is porous, certain tests need to be undertaken to establish the absorption properties; an asymmetric flow is important to avoid surface water from being soaked into the structure. Critical to this is the interconnectivity of cells within the foamed volume, orientation of the cells, availability of air to be replaced by the water, ability to sustain a capillary action and so on. The external surface of the foamed aluminium can be polished to promote internal reflections, dark or light, to achieve UV absorption. The key is to design an extrusion that can transport the liquid internally as a closed circuit.

Further research for this incredible project needs to focus on the detail design of the cross-section through the stick, and the connection detail of these sticks to the mat and to each other, as well as to the ground.

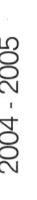

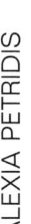

The 'photolepidote' project [from the Greek Φως/phos, 'light', and Λεπια/lepia, 'scales'] pursues spatial arrangement and light modulation through a structural tiling system that is parametrically defined by two sub-systems: the tiles and their distribution on the attachment surface.

The tiles are geometrically varied and related to relevant manufacturing strategies. Their particular performance capacity is dependent on their geometric articulation, on the angle to an input source that results from a specific layering of the tiles, and on their materiality and surface finishing. These last two criteria define the thermal mass and reflectivity of the tile surface.

Made in an associative modelling environment, the tile can be geometrically varied in its size, thickness and outline. Tiles can be laser-cut from sheet material if they have a uniform thickness and 90° cutting edge, but varying sizes and outlines. Tiles with varying thickness and angle of cutting edge can either be manufactured through CNC-milling and cutting, or through injection moulding, depending on the required characteristics of the tile material.

The determinant factors for tile assemblies also lie within the parametric model of the individual tile, with the variables set as tile width, length, thickness, outline of top and bottom surface, top and bottom profile and, most importantly, location of the attachment point.

The second sub-system is the attachment surface onto which the tiles are fixed. Its purpose is to keep the tiles in place while allowing surface curvature to emerge from the articulation of each tile and the way it touches neighbouring tiles. The attachment surface is therefore made from a relatively elastic material – a flat surface formed of strips – that accommodates the emergent surface curvature as the system is assembled tile by tile. The length of the strips and their assembly template are informed by the desired tile distribution patterns and resultant surface curvature. Orthogonal and diagonal lattice layouts were tested. Diagonal layouts require less material but are prone to shearing, whereas the orthogonal configuration is more resistant to shear forces but requires more material. As the lattice is made from simple strips it can be manufactured by conventional means. The overlapping of tiles results in angle changes from tile to tile, due to tile thickness and positioning.

Since the articulation and distribution of the tiles determines the surface curvature of an overall assembly, different distribution strategies were tested. With the attachment point being normal to the attachment surface, and the tiles overlapping, bending is induced into the lattice und curvature is achieved across the surface. In other words, it is the articulation and layering of the tiles that induces curvature in the lattice through bending and torsion, instead of pre-shaping the lattice. Tiles are therefore always placed on the outside of the curved surface: when a transition between convex and concave curvature is required the tiles shift from one side of the attachment surface to the other at the point of inflection.

The orientation of each tile and the gaps between the tiles determine the range of effect of direct, indirect or diffuse light. Calibrating the overall effect for spatial regions within the envelope, for instance the finely nuanced pattern of direct light or shadow cast within the space of the project was one of the primary tasks in the development of the system and its environmental performance analysis; calibrating the thermal mass of each tile in relation to its exposure was another. For this purpose it was important to establish a parametric logic in an associative modelling environment that adjusts geometric variables in relation to orientation and exposure. Further research might examine, for instance, the thickness of the tile in relation to its material characteristics and exposure to thermal input, so as to achieve the desired thermal performance.

Since the focus of inquiry was the luminous environment and, more specifically, exposure to the thermal and visible part of daylight, the pilot project was set in a location near the Arctic Circle that allowed a great variety of exposure angles to be tested over the course of the different seasons – at summer and winter solstice as well as autumn and spring equinox.

Set in a public square and park in Stockholm, the pilot project needed to provide for circulation routes across the site while accommodating defined and ad-hoc activities and the chosen environmental performance range. In doing so, the curvature of the envelope of the pilot project needed to be articulated in such a way as to negotiate potentially conflicting requirements.

Given the great diversity of spatial, structural, programmatic and environmental performance requirements, it was important to consider just how deterministic the project could or should hope to be.

The project developed by means of strategically selecting locations for which it was necessary to fulfil given requirements, for instance a minimum sectional height and width in pedestrian circulation areas, together with certain light conditions. The surface curvature of the entire envelope was then interpolated between the perimeter and the strategic control locations, resulting in areas of lesser control. These could then enable a more free appropriation in terms of use, in affiliation with ranges and gradients of exposure to environmental conditions akin to those found in parks.

As long as requirements are met in crucial locations, these in-between spaces can provide for as yet unknown conditions that will emerge along with the opportunities for inhabitation provided by them.

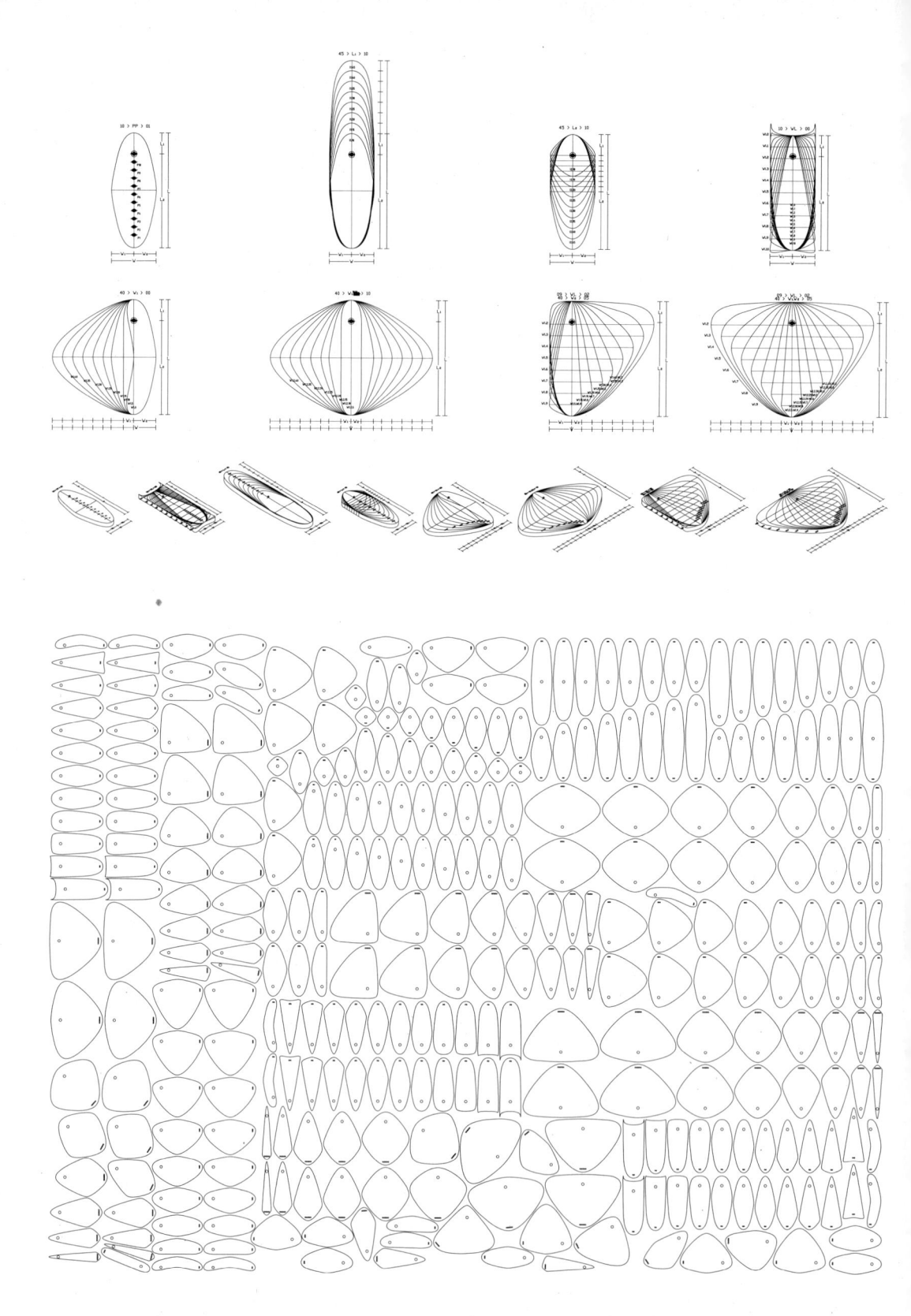

144 In order to facilitate the construction of self-supporting tile surfaces with non-uniform curvature, a parametric tile component is defined as an envelope of possible geometric alterations within a particular range (top). Each individual tile placed on a surface is directly linked to a manufacturing protocol for laser cutting from sheet material (bottom).

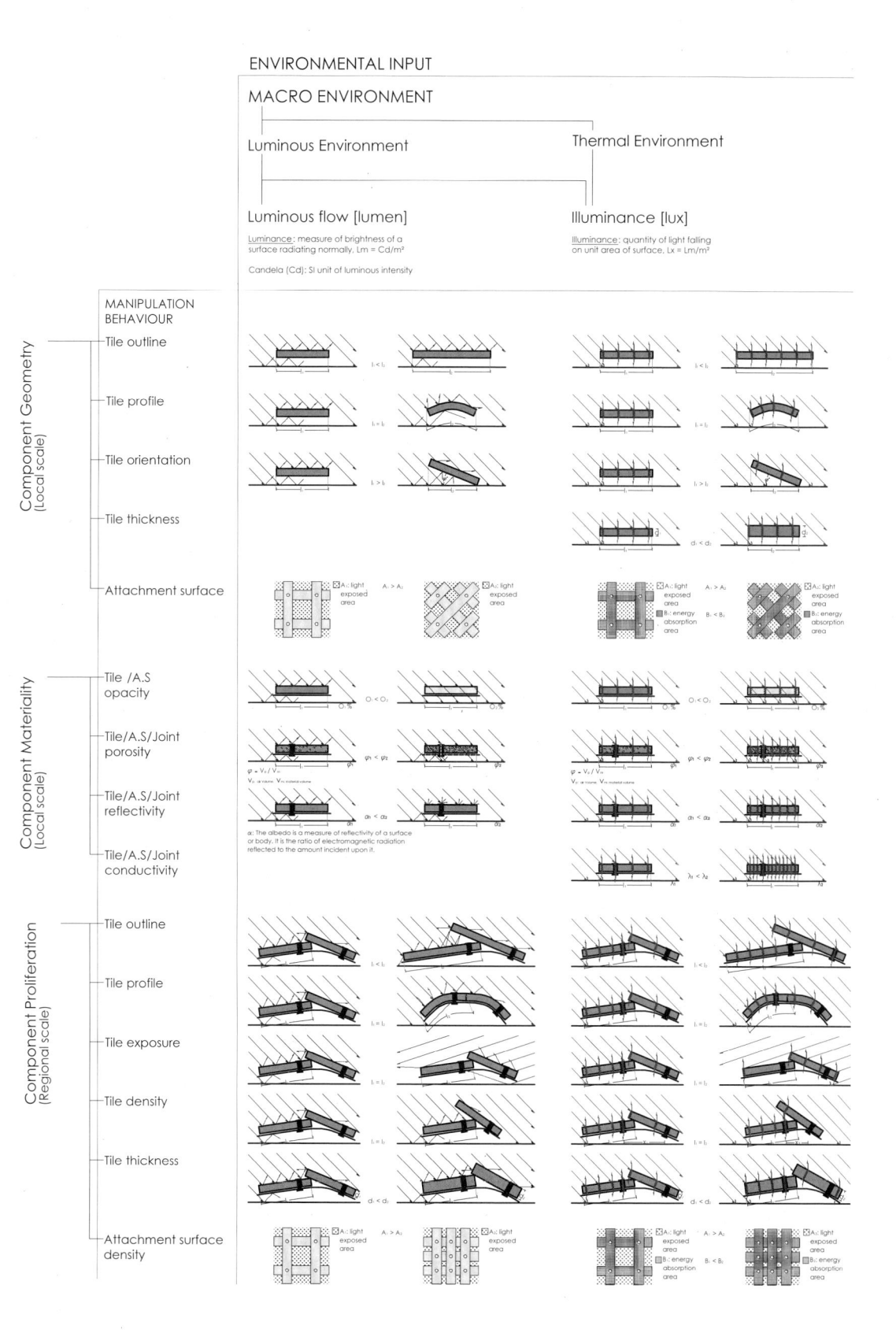

The assembly of parametrically varied components (bottom) on an initially flat substructure leads to a double-curved system morphology resulting from the local interactions of adjacent tiles (top).

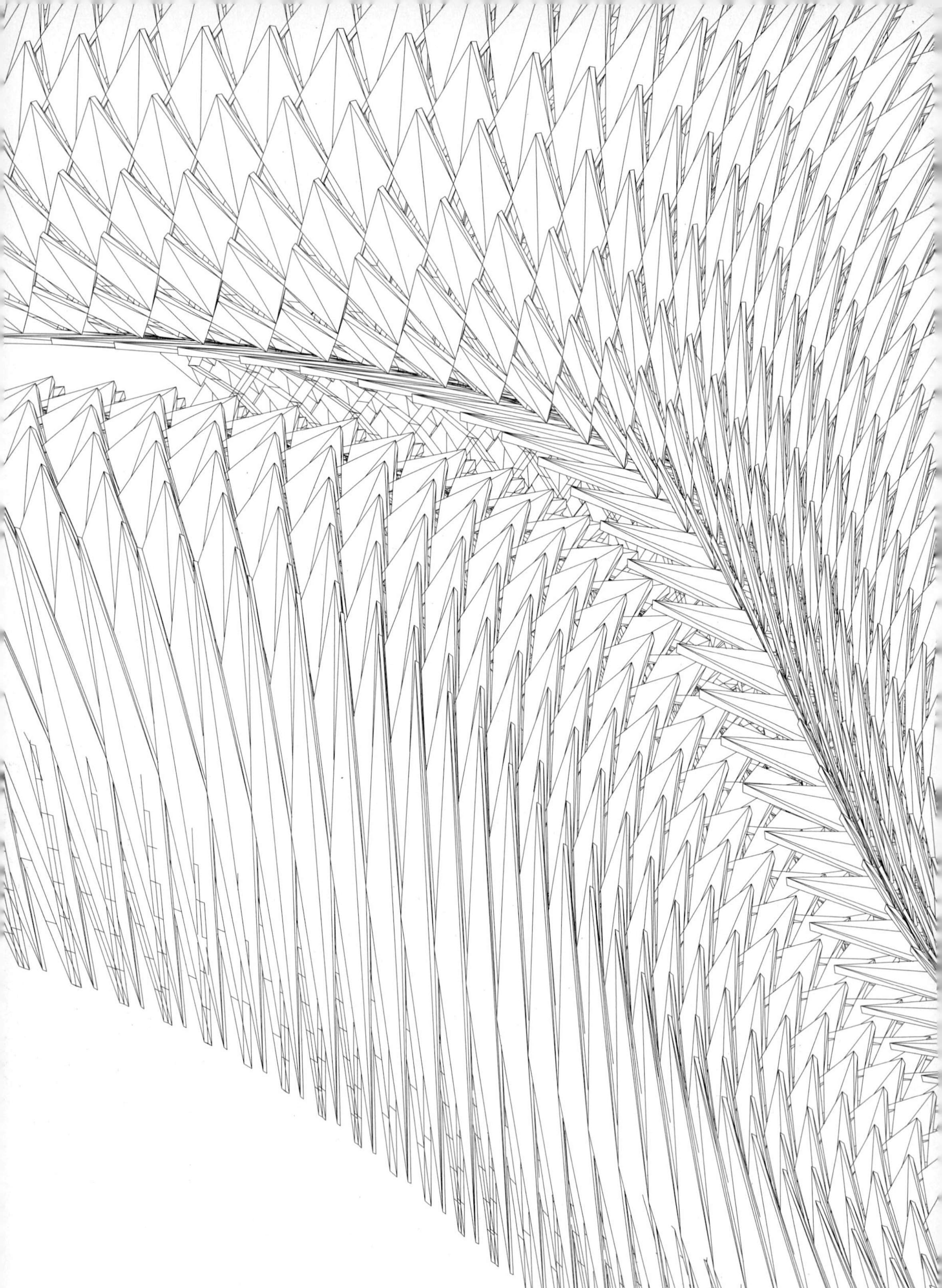

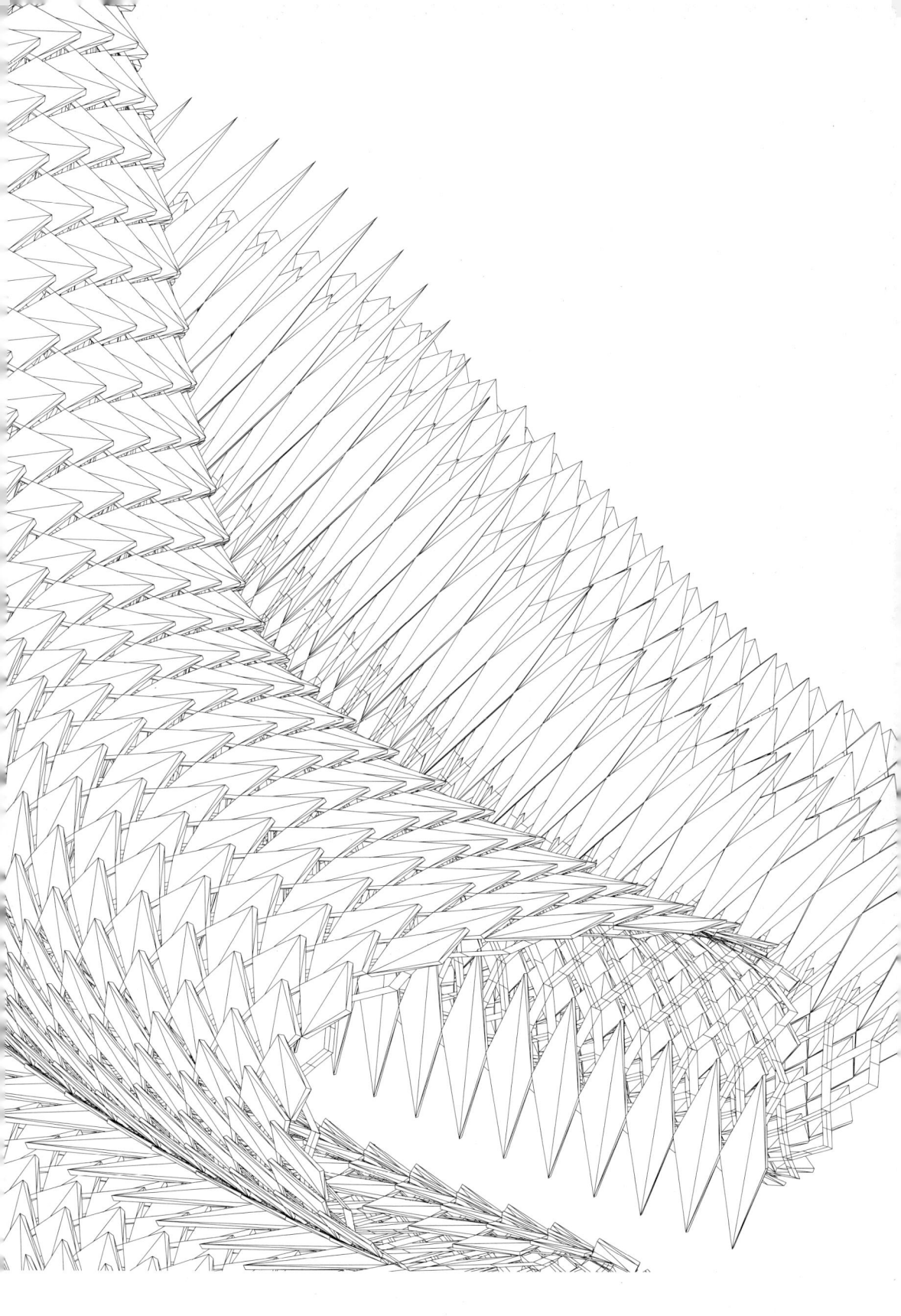

A second generation of parametrically defined diamond-shaped tiles enables the generation of complex morphologies in which the structural tiles are defined in relation to local surface curvature and strategic tile overlap.

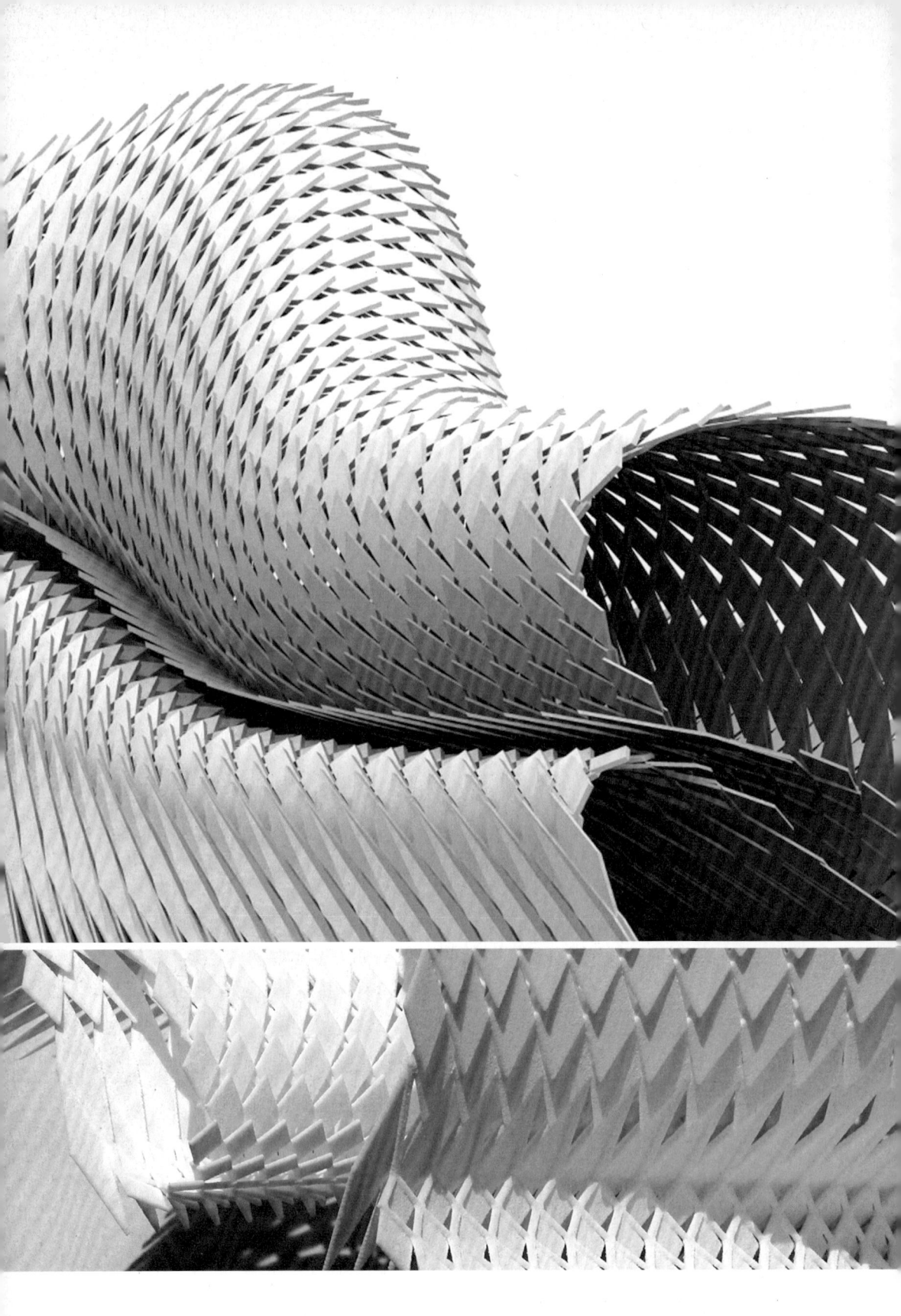

148 The digital models of differentiated tile morphologies developed in an associative modelling application (top) provide the data for rapid prototyping using selective laser-sintering technology (bottom). Both the digital and physical models suggest the performative capacity of the system to interact with the luminous and thermal environment.

In addition to rapid prototype modelling a full-scale prototype structure was built to corroborate the structural and environmental performance capacity of the system.

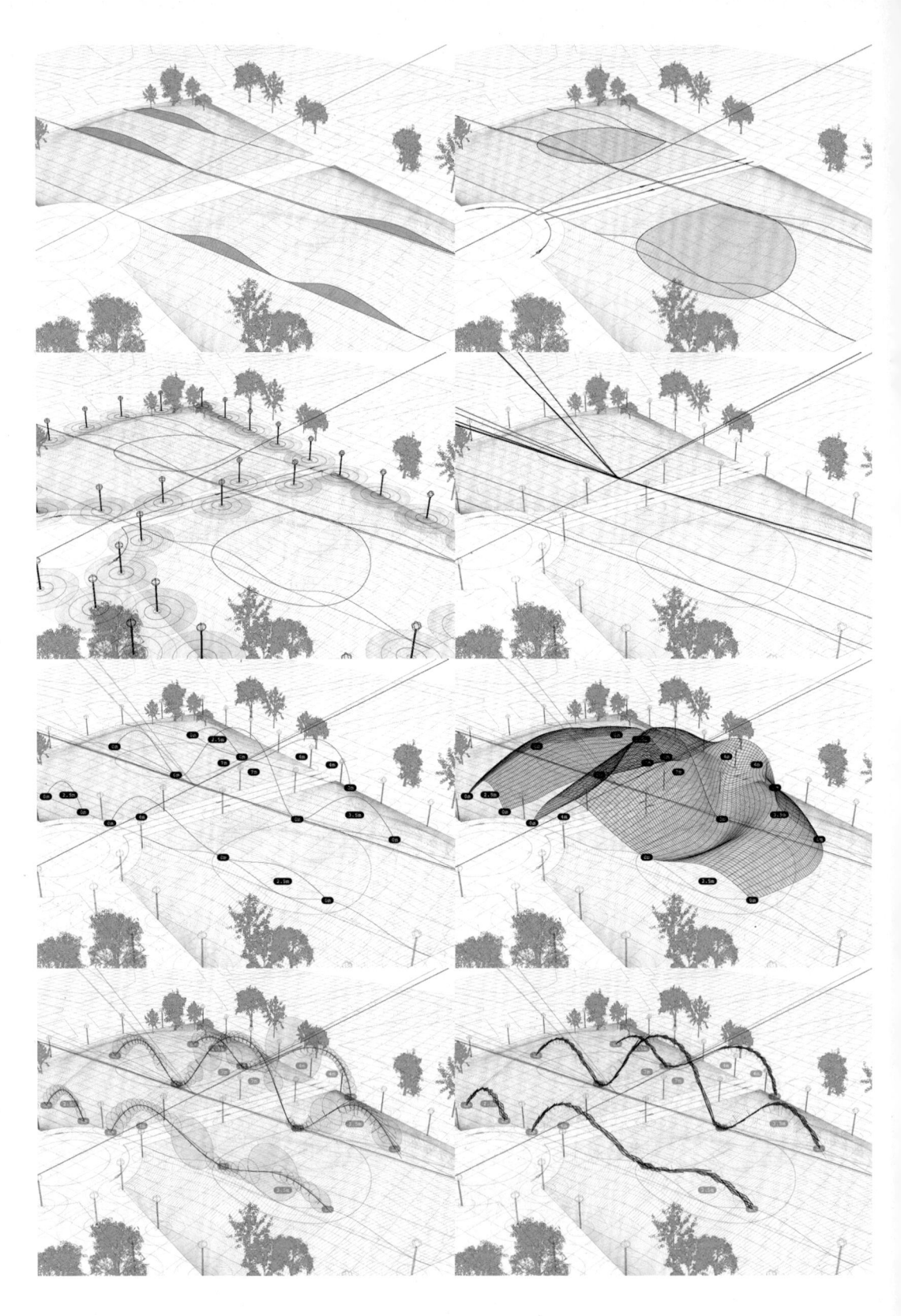

150 A pilot project for a site in Stockholm is developed through strategic locations for which it was necessary to fulfil given requirements as for example a minimum sectional height and width in pedestrian circulation areas and specific light conditions. The surface curvature of the entire envelope was then interpolated between the perimeter and the strategic control locations.

A rapid prototype model shows a part of the context-specific configuration of the tile system (top). Digital light simulations and analysis show the distribution of shifting zones of luminous intensity resulting from daily as well as seasonal changes (bottom).

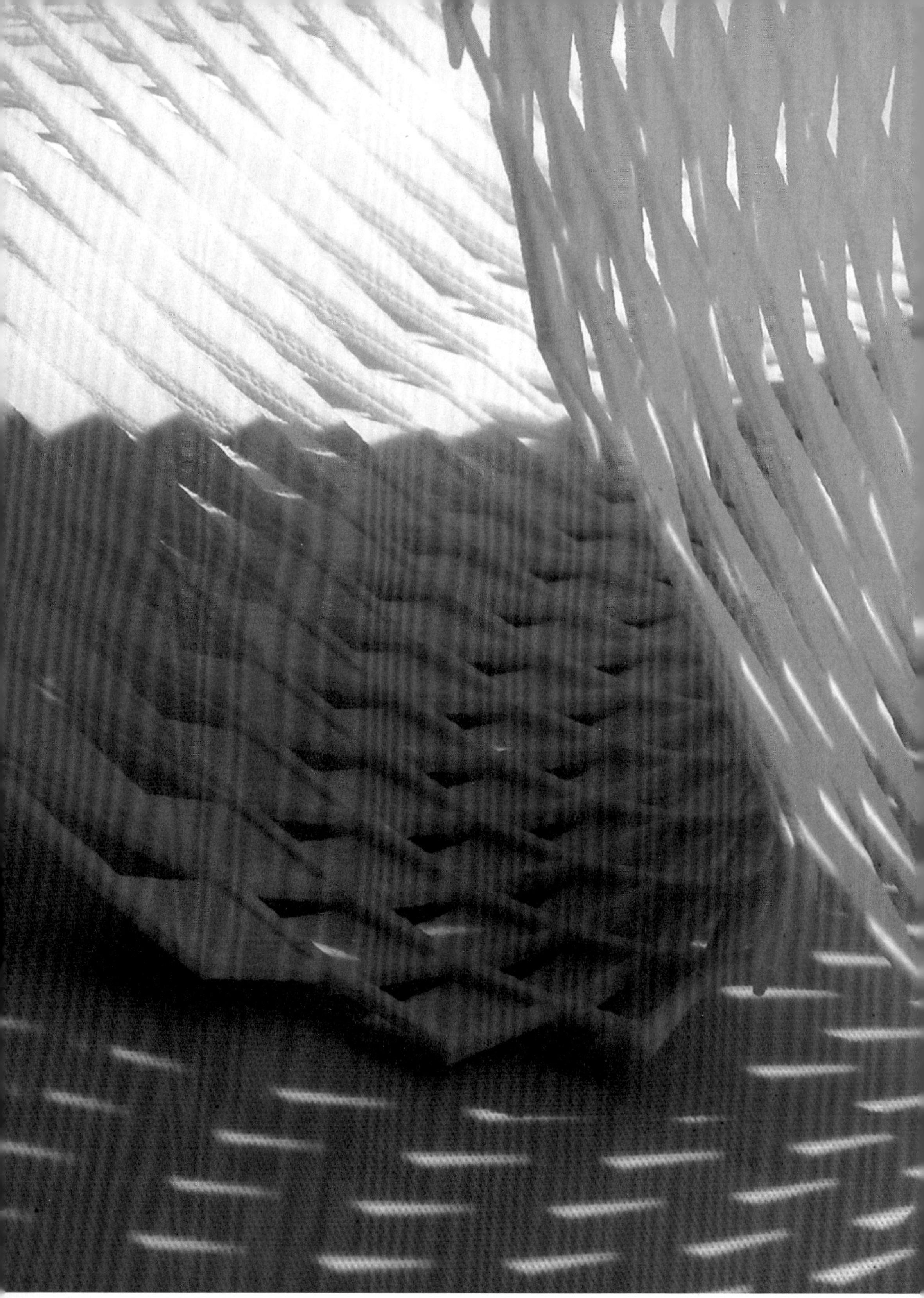

Close-up view of a rapid prototype model fabricated with selective laser-sintering technology shows the differentiated morphology of the developed material system.

COMMENTS

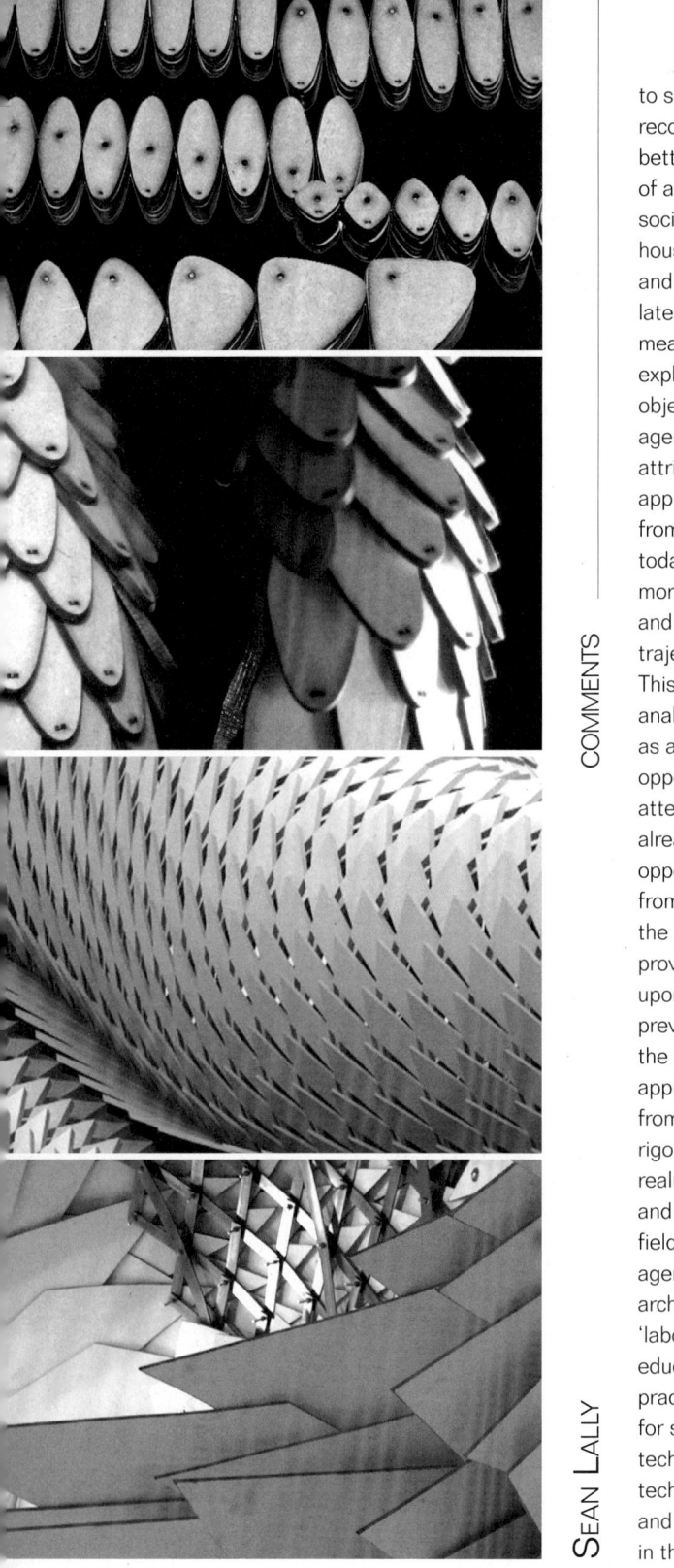

SEAN LALLY

As architects, we often find it necessary to state lofty goals in order to be immediately recognised as serving the advancement and betterment of society through the practice of architecture. These goals range from the socially conscious – such as those pertaining to housing, energy conservation, urban growth, and revitalisation – to those investigating the latest theories in universal orders and the means by which they can inform architectural explorations. These are often impressive objectives that produce easily marketable agendas for the general public to engage and attribute to the architectural profession. This approach however differs rather substantially from an emerging avenue of research occurring today in architecture, one that takes its cues more from the realms of the physical sciences and engineering and less from the traditional trajectories associated with the profession. This approach focuses more on the testing and analysis of certain tool sets and technologies as an avenue of architectural progression and opportunity. Often, these investigations are attempting to produce difference within an already existing set of parameters; one in which opportunities and innovation come not so much from the introduction of 'new' polemics but from the testing and application of techniques that provide abilities for visualising and operating upon a set of existing variables that were previously intangible as they pertained to the architect's toolset. The result of such an approach is a freedom of design that comes not from the technology itself, but from scientific rigour. Architects have migrated further into the realm of the sciences, adopting the practices and methodologies associated with these fields in order to execute their own research agendas. These methodologies are prevalent in architecture today and range from the adopted 'laboratory' strategy of a traditional studio education, to the organisation of architectural practices that seek similar grant-type funding for support and research, to the software technologies that often have very focused and technique-specific choreographies. As architects and educators today, we find ourselves in the position of questioning, testing and reevaluating the tools and techniques available. The exploitation of available tools through the production of difference – that is, the creation of variable and multiple conditions through the execution of controlled and limited variables – can be understood as a design freedom for the broader profession in understanding potentials and limitations for future systems. These tools and techniques will never act as neutral translators of information into built form, but will always act upon and inform such intentions through the implementation of the tools themselves.

Photolepidote introduces us to one of the more fruitful investigations occurring today. It does so from an area of investigation that often has been entangled in (and therefore obscured by) the banner of 'sustainable design', but that in actuality has roots as far back as Yves Klein's work in the early 1950s. In this project, materials including light, heat, and air velocity move beyond the poetics of mood, effect and atmosphere and become materials that can be quantified and instrumentalised as systematically and effectively as the force of gravity onto material. As with many of the advancements that occur in visualisation software, the objectives are generally to depict and work within preconceived intentions – that is, to visually represent that which we know to exist. In the case of spatial qualities including temperature and light, the intentions are usually to achieve and represent preconceived notions of interior comfort including temperature and exposure to sunlight. Materials and variables that are often dismissed as qualitative and secondary to the design process have the potential to do more than just accentuate and manage preconceived interior configurations; instead, they can be used to question and re-inform what constitutes boundary and edge in architecture other than that of surface geometry. Investigations like Photolepidote, demonstrate the potentials of available technologies to go beyond simply optimising preconceived spatial qualities and conditions, instead acting as generators and facilitators for questioning and innovating architectural design.

In the case of Photolepidote, geometry and form are prominent facilitators of the design investigation; but both materiality and luminosity play more than a supportive role in the project. This is immediately evident in Alexia Petridis's decision to question what constitutes a geographic site for placing and investigating a project. The project identifies site not as a dimensionally defined boundary of adjacency and context, but a longitudinal and climatic context. Photolepidote's focus on performance as it pertains to instrumentalising and orchestrating existing environmental light through geometric curvature and material luminosity is climatically and environmentally highly specific. By locating the project near the Arctic Circle, Petridis further emphasises the role of materiality – in this case light – in articulating and generating architectural design. The use of light and its range of intensities, which can be amplified and muted as well as focused for the generation of heat, reflection and shadows, demonstrate its appropriation as a generator for spatial organisation and programmatic allocations. 'Programmatic' manipulation as a means for design innovation is overshadowed by a more elementary approach to spatial organisation that questions the primary frameworks and operational techniques that architects work with in how we define and control boundaries in architecture. Photolepidote demonstrates the use of environmental gradients and microclimates (provided from a limited number of variables including existing environmental light, curvature and luminosity of panelisation) can provide the architect with other options for organising and interpreting programmatic and organisational configurations.

Architectural investigations that question issues as fundamental as what constitutes boundary and edge for the organisation and definition of space and activity are going to do so not with broad brushstrokes, but through smaller controlled experiments focused on producing difference within an existing framework of technologies and materials. Investigations that test and subvert preconceived and elementary notions of design through rigorous, controlled laboratory-like settings will provide design freedoms that begin from experiments that build upon cumulative discoveries referenced and applied over time.

2004 - 2005

DANIEL COLL I CAPDEVILA

The surfaces that delimit the spaces of this project perform multiple tasks, defining a material assembly that can accommodate a range of spatial and environmental conditions for healing environments within a densely built urban fabric.

Healing spaces are commonly homogeneous and unresponsive to the individual needs of convalescing patients, including their varying requirements for privacy and their changing sensitivity to light, sound, temperature and airflow. The widespread recognition that such conditions are detrimental to the recovery process has led to the establishment of a new UK National Health Service plan that emphasises the wellbeing of patients and sets the framework for more heterogeneous healing spaces. This project is a response to that ambition.

Alvar Aalto's Tuberculosis Sanatorium in Paimo, Finland was analysed as a case study. While the modernist building consists of standardised spaces, these are carefully orientated with respect to chosen views, ventilation and daylight exposure. Internal conditions are further modulated over the course of a day and the seasons by the conifer trees that are planted around the hospital or in containers on the roof terrace. The trees provide oxygen and filter sunlight and airflow. Such a strategy is evidently not possible in a built-up urban context. Here instead, the envelope of healing spaces must be able to modulate conditions and provide for choice, ideally without resorting to an unsustainable plethora of technical devices. In this respect the project constitutes a critique of the missed opportunities since Le Corbusier's project for the Venice Hospital, in which the exterior canopy formed the only climatically exposed space of a scheme otherwise entirely subdivided into cellular units that, in their utter isolation and homogeneity, were strangely akin to prison cells cut off from the outside world.

The basic building element of this project is a simple strip cut from sheet steel. The variables of the strip are its length, width, thickness and consequently its edge definition, together with its material properties such as bending and torsional stiffness. Simple physical form-finding experiments in bending and twisting the strips led to a systematic account of geometric behaviour under these actions: the informed displacement of an edge of a strip and its resultant surface curvature.

The curvature of the strip elements resulting from bending and twisting was then considered in the make-up of a component, assembled from three strips. A parametric interrelation and hierarchy was established involving the basic element of a single strip; the component made up from three strips; a neighbourhood of interrelated components at a regional scale; multiple organisations of components at the scale of the entire material system; and a feedback setup between extrinsic influences and the material system.

The strip element is defined through a series of geometrical relationships that are always maintained. The three strips that make up the component are tangentially aligned at their edges. Each region of components is assigned a minimum of one control point, and all components within that region are aligned tangentially with their edges normal to the control point's location. This defines the components' degree of inclination relative to the input vector of a climatic condition, whether luminous, sonic or eolic. By controlling the input angle it is possible to determine the output angle and, in doing so, achieve the desired ranges of environmental modulation.

In order to also attain a spatial variety the overall arrangement is organised as a deep section consisting of multiple layers of components that can be split or joined together to provide enclosure.

The necessity for the assembly to be structurally self-supporting led to an exploration of multiple objective optimisation strategies. For example, structural performance may require a particular surface curvature and environmental performance another. A balance is achieved by adjusting the various levels of the hierarchical articulation of the system, by selecting a different definition of the strip surface inclination – regional, component, or element level – depending on the given input and desired output vectors and ranges. Likewise, the thickness of the strip can be varied to compensate locally for required rotations of the strip relative to environmental performance. Taking this into account, the project related the structural and the manufacturing approach by assigning a specific material thickness to the strips that are laser-cut from sheets.

The context for a design study was the Rochford Hospital in Essex, where a recent redesign has actually reduced the amount of green outdoor spaces available to patients. The environmental input was provided by a detailed mapping of the spatial arrangement of a particular location, incorporating time-based visual exposure, circulation and luminous and sonic impact. This informed the parametric setup of the system as described above. The architectural aims of the project were then related to a series of locations in which specified conditions needed to be achieved. The transition between these locations offers spatial and environmental ranges that evolve without deterministic control, providing a rich palette of choices beyond the one conceived by the designer.

AA Diploma Honours 2005

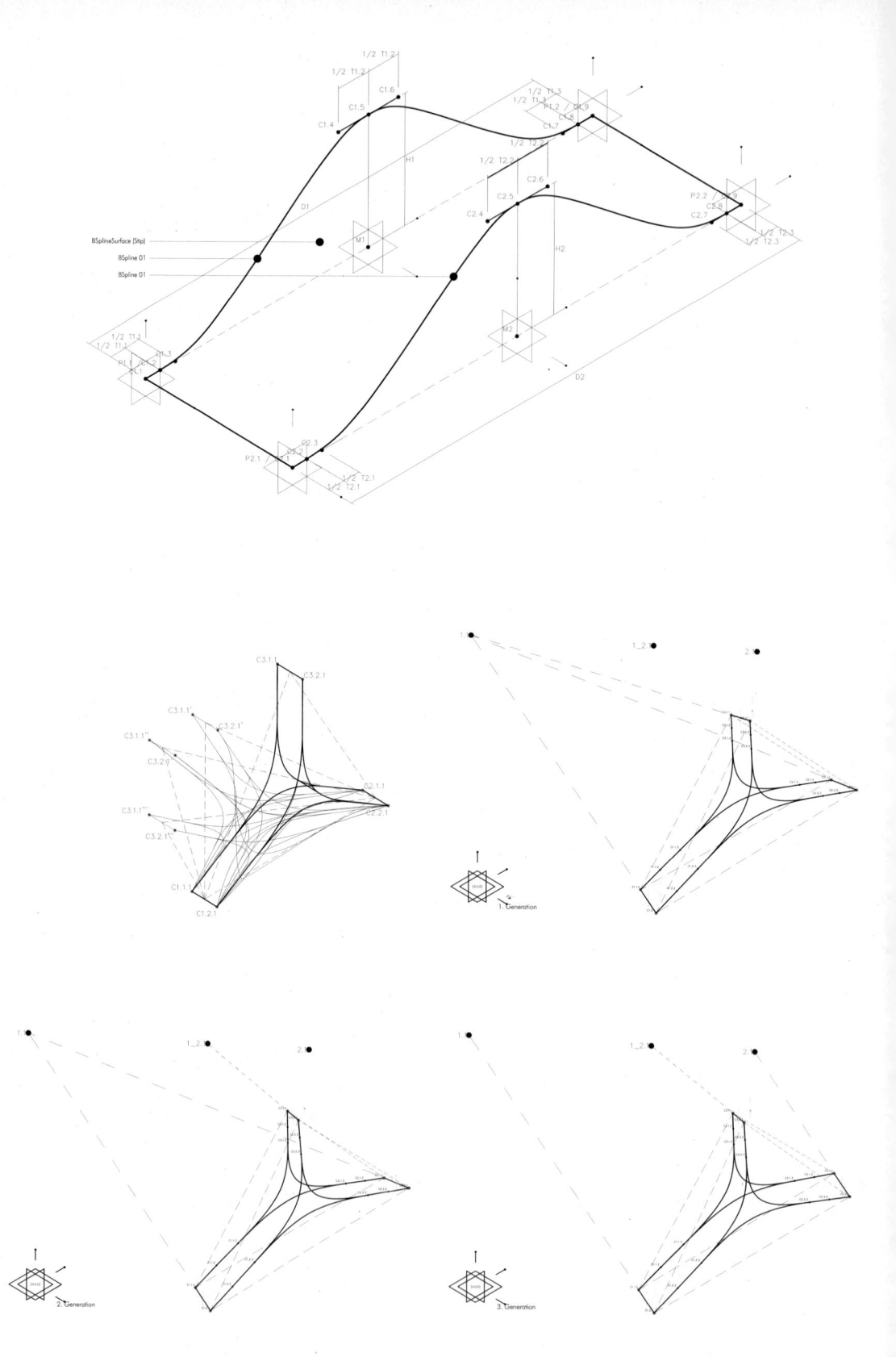

158   The digital definition of generic strip elements in an associative modelling application defines the relevant parameters such as length, width and thickness and embeds the fabrication and assembly constraints in a series of geometric relationships (top). Three parametric strip elements constitute a digital component that can be linked to one, two or three external control points (bottom).

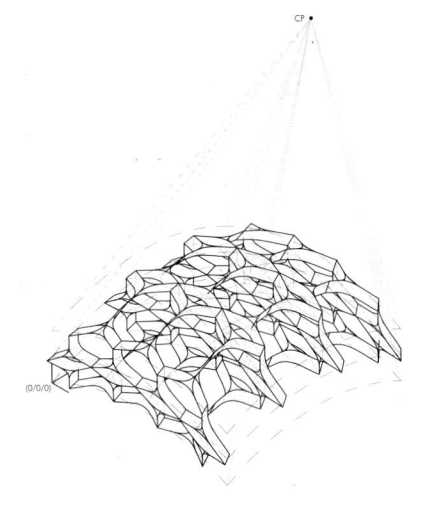

1. Location of control point
-Reference Control Point: 20,60,40

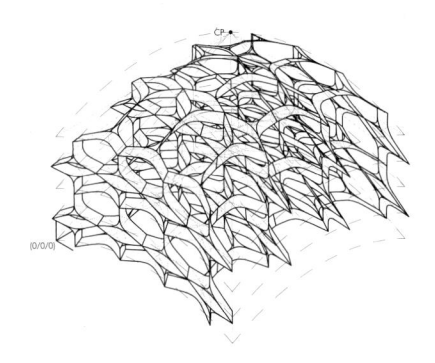

2. Number of Offsets
-Offset Surface: 5

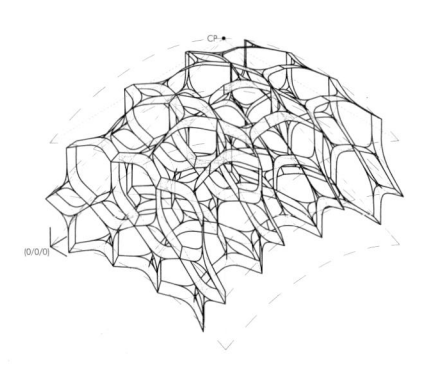

3. Offset Distance
-Offset Of Control Surface: 10 Units

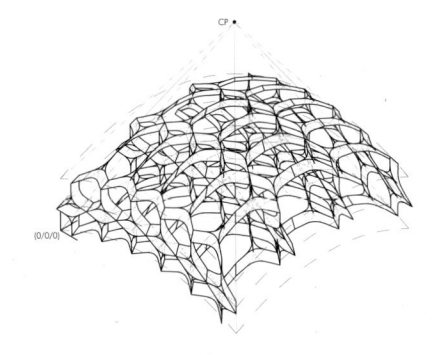

4. Number of Components in U-Direction
-Comp. in U-Direction: 6

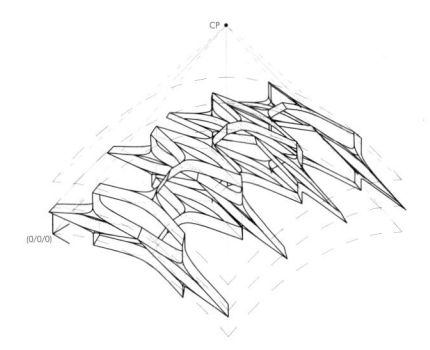

5. Number of Components in V-Direction
-Components in V-Direction: 2

6. Edge Width
-Edge Width of Components: 5 Units

Regional sub-location of a larger component system shows the geometric behaviour resulting from changes to the variables of the following parameters: 1. Position of external control point 2. Number of offset control surfaces 3. Surface offset distance 4. Number of components in U-direction 5. Number of components in V-direction 6. Edge width of component.

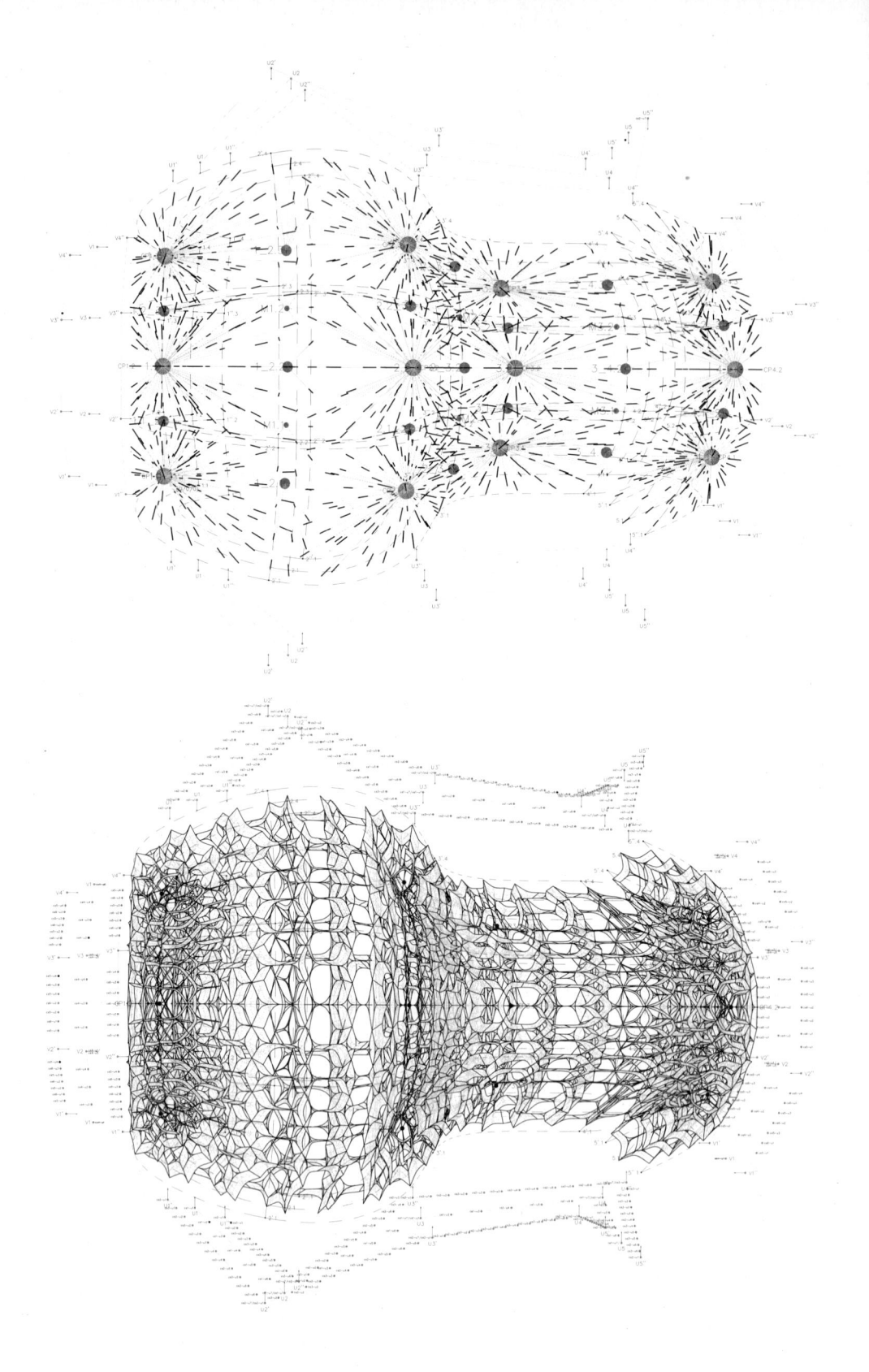

160　In response to a geometric control framework defined by global system variables such as number and offset distance of host surfaces, global curvature in U- and V-direction and the position of external control points (top) a specific component population is generated. Each component is geometrically different yet remains coherent with the underlying production and construction logics (bottom).

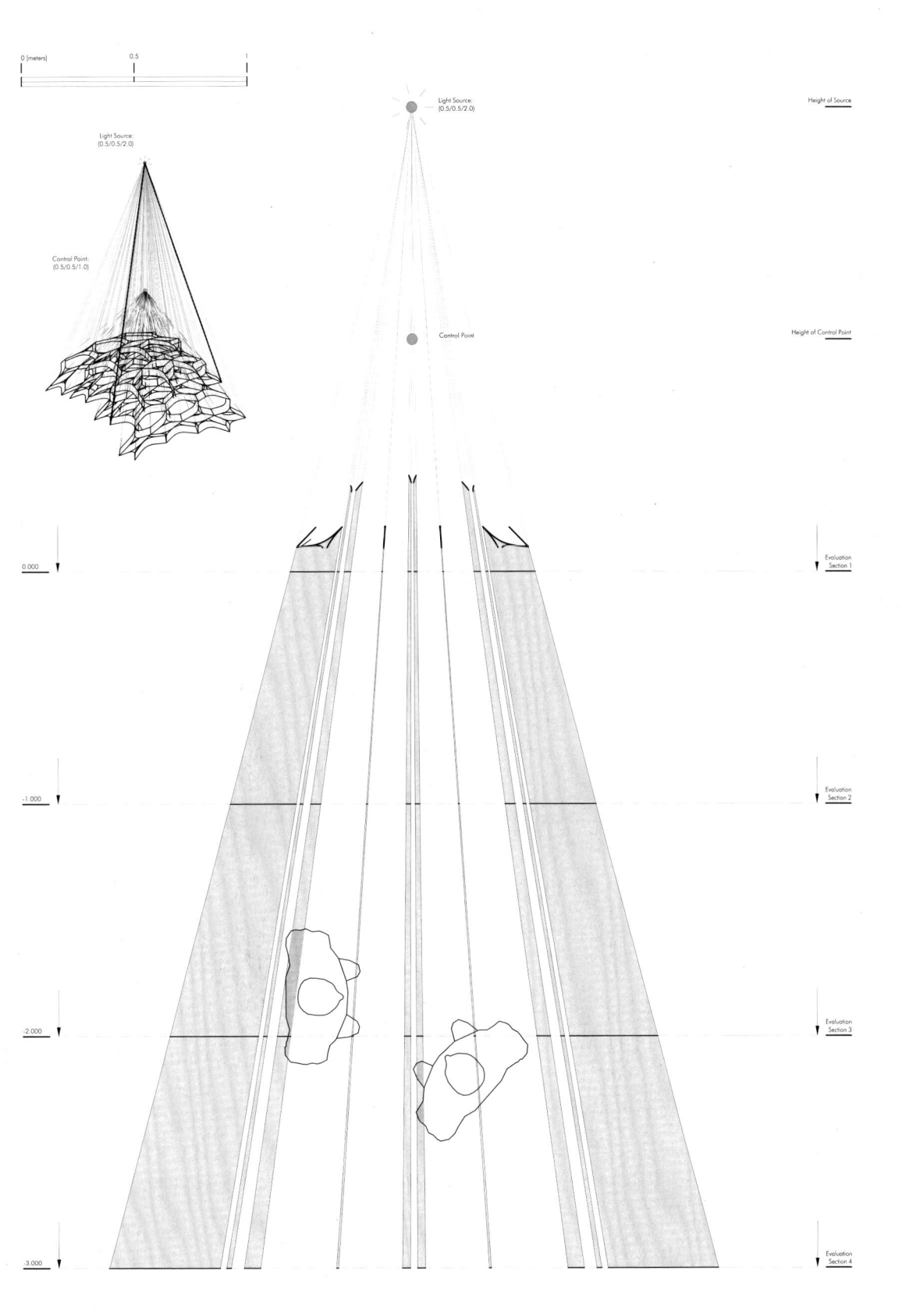

The manipulation of local, regional and global system variables becomes instrumental in unfolding the performative capacity of the system. The example shows the modulation of direct light radially emitted from an artificial light source transmitted through and interacting with the system.

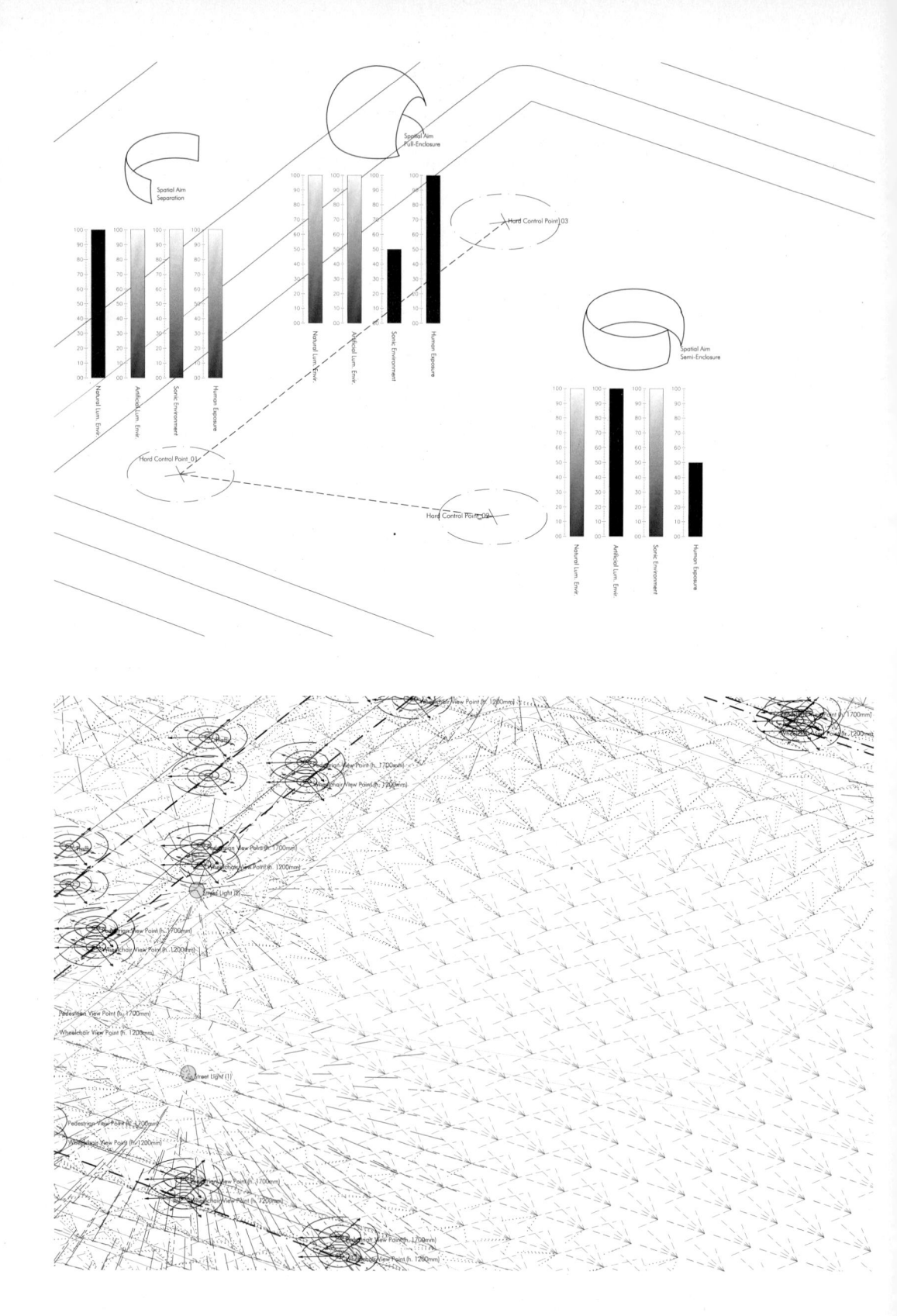

162   A non-medical healing and relaxation context (Rockford Hospital in Essex) is used for a pilot design intervention. The environmental input is provided by a detailed mapping of the spatial arrangement of a particular location, incorporating time-based visual exposure and enclosure (top), circulation, sonic impact and vectors of direct luminous flow (bottom).

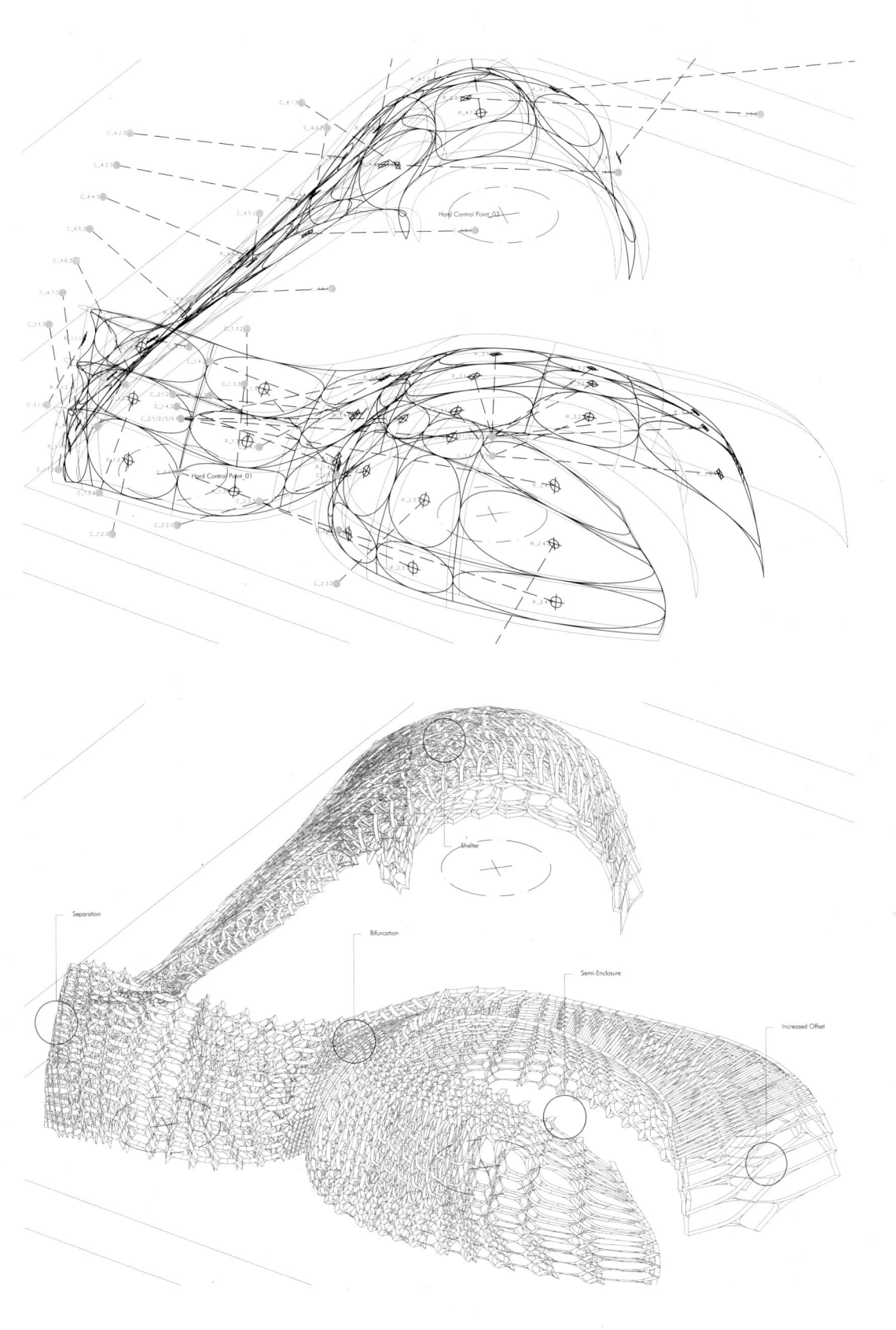

Based on the mapping of relevant spatial and environmental data a context specific parametric framework is established (top) and populated with strip components. The resulting system provides a heterogeneous healing environment of situations environmentally controlled by the designer and emergent conditions of gradient exposure, sonic and luminous intensity (bottom).

Fabrication process: 84 strip elements are laser cut from flat steel sheets of three different thicknesses chosen as a response to different structural requirements across the system. Through the alignment of edges related elements are shaped and spot-welded to create a component. The resulting 28 components are assembled into a full-scale prototype.

The construction of a partial full-scale prototype fabricated from laser-cut, mild steel strips corroborates the coherence of the parametric design technique with logics of manufacturing, assembly and construction.

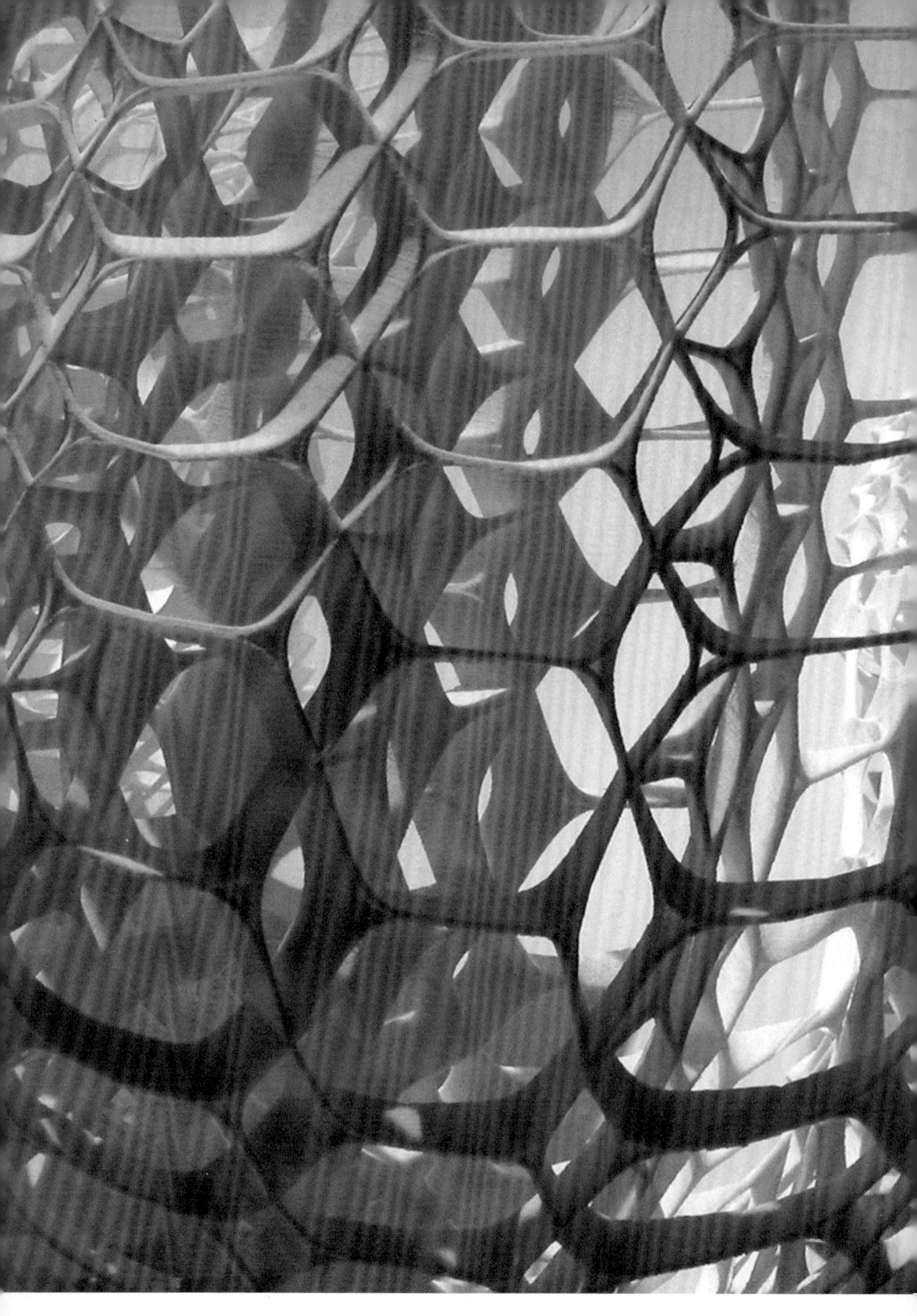

View of a rapid prototype model [selective laser-sintering] showing one instance of a global configuration of the strip system, together with its specific modulation of light penetration and shadow casting.

COMMENTS

WOLF MANGELSDORF

The project explores the use of a geometrically defined component system that fulfils a number of requirements for the design of effective healing environments. This multiple performance idea, based on the modulation, design adaptation and assembly of one component type, is what makes the project all at once simple and highly complex. In this context the most interesting aspect is how the component is developed and later assembled into larger systems.

At its core is a piece of sheet metal whose structural performance is extremely limited and, in relation to the usually more complex environmental performance criteria, at best undefined. Through a series of clever transformations – cutting, twisting and interconnection – a simple component is created as the basis for the assembly of a macro-arrangement that fulfils the ambitious design brief.

As a first step, structurally stable elements are formed out of flat steel sheets by using the elastic flexibility of the material: the sheets are laser-cut to a predefined pattern. They are then twisted and bent into a geometrically self-stabilising form and permanently fixed together by spot-welding them at their ends. This method is simple, easily controlled and effective.

Through the bending process, which remains within the elastic limits of the material, a pre-stress is introduced into the components. This elastic bending deformation determines the component geometry through a balance of forces in the three metal sheets that together constitute the base component. To achieve this, their cutting patterns have to be precisely defined.

As the geometry of the components is based on the equilibrium of forces and stresses within a system of bent plates, their structural performance is characterised by a certain flexibility and elasticity in their reaction to external forces. At the same time, however, the components, like springs, will always have the tendency to return to their given original form, locked in through the manufacturing process.

The clever thing about the design and assembly of the component is that structural stability can be achieved within a bandwidth of similar geometries, which in turn allows the geometrical adaptation of the elements to environmental criteria, which are of great importance for defining the healing spaces. Modulation of the steel plate thickness further widens that range of geometrical freedom.

This allows the design to concentrate equally on all of the desired performance criteria: those that define the space in volumetric and hence primarily structural terms, as well as those that generate the necessary environmental conditions, either as a reaction to specific circumstances or by actively creating and influencing the environment through the space-defining elements.

This multitude of performances is achieved through the hierarchy of the component assembly: the geometry of the individual plate element, the interrelations between neighbouring components, the macro-geometry of the assembly, and the addition of layers with offset parameters that are defined in the design.

Herein lies the real value of the system. Rather than a conventional separation of different design parameters, with individual but independent components, it proposes an integrated multifunctional surface system built from simple elements. The beauty of this system is that the elements in themselves are not multifunctional. They are simply structured and have no apparent function. It is their intelligent modulation, adaptation and combination which achieves the multi-functionality.

The big advantage of this low-tech approach is that not much can go wrong with its mechanics or systems. It is the designer who controls the performance and, once this is set up, it should remain usable and active for the lifespan of the system. That is, of course, as long as the basic parameters do not change.

This last point could be seen as a weakness, as the system in its present form is static and the interrelations between the components – and hence their individual geometries – are set out by the designer from the beginning. Any changes to areas of the macro-structure have repercussions on the whole of the system, which limits adjustment and adaptability to some extent.

Underlying this project is a desire to give an everyday material a novel life: to go beyond the conventional framework of use through an investigation of its micro-scale material properties and its macro-scale behaviour and context-modulation capacity. The work unfolds as a resonance between the intrinsic properties of wood veneer and the extrinsic organisational and performative desires introduced in the course of the research process. As such, it is a project triggered by contingencies rather than a linear development of a solution to a problem.

In addition, the project lays down a specific challenge to the idea of a passive conservation of protected and environmentally sensitive areas of coastline. It proposes to modulate its hosting terrain in a finely nuanced way by involving the shifting sand dunes, and is designed to gradually decompose without leaving permanent traces. This suggests that the duration of an intervention goes beyond the durability of its materials: the architectural artifact can become an instrument for acting on different time-scales both during and beyond its own existence.

At the basis of this research is the anisotropy of wood, with its specific fibre-directionality and related response-range to environmental stimuli tested against the specific requirements of the context. Initially the basic elements were finite length strips made from layers of laminated veneer; rotating layers against one another allowed an investigation of different fibre-layouts. In existing approaches to making laminated structures, individual components are laminated in pre-designed moulds and then joined using plates or other connection systems. Most of the time only single curvature can be achieved; for double curvature, pre-bent components must be cut to final shape or else the system will store energy. In this research, however, shifting the layers of veneer made possible a continuous lamination process able to produce a large assembly without construction gaps.

A correlated manufacturing strategy was developed, incorporating the possibility of rotating selected sub-locations along their long axis. Replacing the moulds with a nodal support system allowed the laminated components to be clamped at the end points and so made self-organising, that is, able to find their form within the given constraints during the fabrication process. This manufacturing process enables double-curvature to be achieved from sub-locations and the overall system. Most importantly, this implies an exploration of a continuous sequence of fabrication in which primary laminated components are joined through successive laminations – a process referred to as continuous lamination. Thus, while the overall assembly consists of finite lengths of veneer strip, the continuous laminae arrangement does not yield a division into elements. The overall assembly becomes a single element, in which each local dimensional change produced by environmental stimuli affects the system at large.

Achieving a laminar flow by maintaining curvature continuity between the individual elements results in a continuous multiple load-path system that, together with the anisotropic characteristics of timber, helps to maintain the flexibility and integrity of the overall assembly.

Changing the fibre orientation between the veneer layers, so as to adapt it to the changing geometry of the sub-locations and the required curvature of the overall system, helps to induce the particular material behaviour required for the process of lamination. Allowing the individual components to self-organise during the process of fabrication helps achieve the most natural form relative to strategically defined and placed constraints. Achieving flexibility across individual paths and accommodating local deformations helps to absorb stresses caused by shrinkage and swelling due to changes in temperature and humidity.

Differential material deterioration caused by different levels of sand abrasion can be strategised by locally adapted geometry such as an increase or decrease of cross-section in the exposed areas. More material will last longer then less material under the same condition of orientation and exposure. Local articulation in relation to abrasion thus also includes rotation of sub-locations, as much as their cross-sectional articulation.

The multiple and redundant load-paths help to reduce risks of failure associated with local material deterioration due to sand and salt abrasion.

With the continuity of the system maintained on the geometric level as well as in the process of lamination, the structural forces are continuously distributed along the multiple load-paths, reducing stresses normally concentrated around point connections.

Relating the systematic use of manufacturing-enabled form-finding to extrinsic influences affects the articulation of the sub-locations and the overall system and their orientation to the sun-path and prevailing wind direction. The resulting surface curvatures and varied levels of system porosity can then be used to modulate airflow and related ranges of sand-deposition, as well as exposure to sunlight. The overall flexibility of the system – a product of its material elasticity – enables a higher responsiveness to the fluctuations of the wind loads. Several dynamics are thus interrelated: airflow, system deflection and local terrain formation through modulated aggregation, as well as velocity of airflow, air-borne sand and abrasion of the material assembly. Ultimately the main concern of this project is the strategic entwining of these time-cycles.

This investigation of timber veneer suggests a follow-up research of a system based on the full freedom offered by fibre-layouts in composite materials.

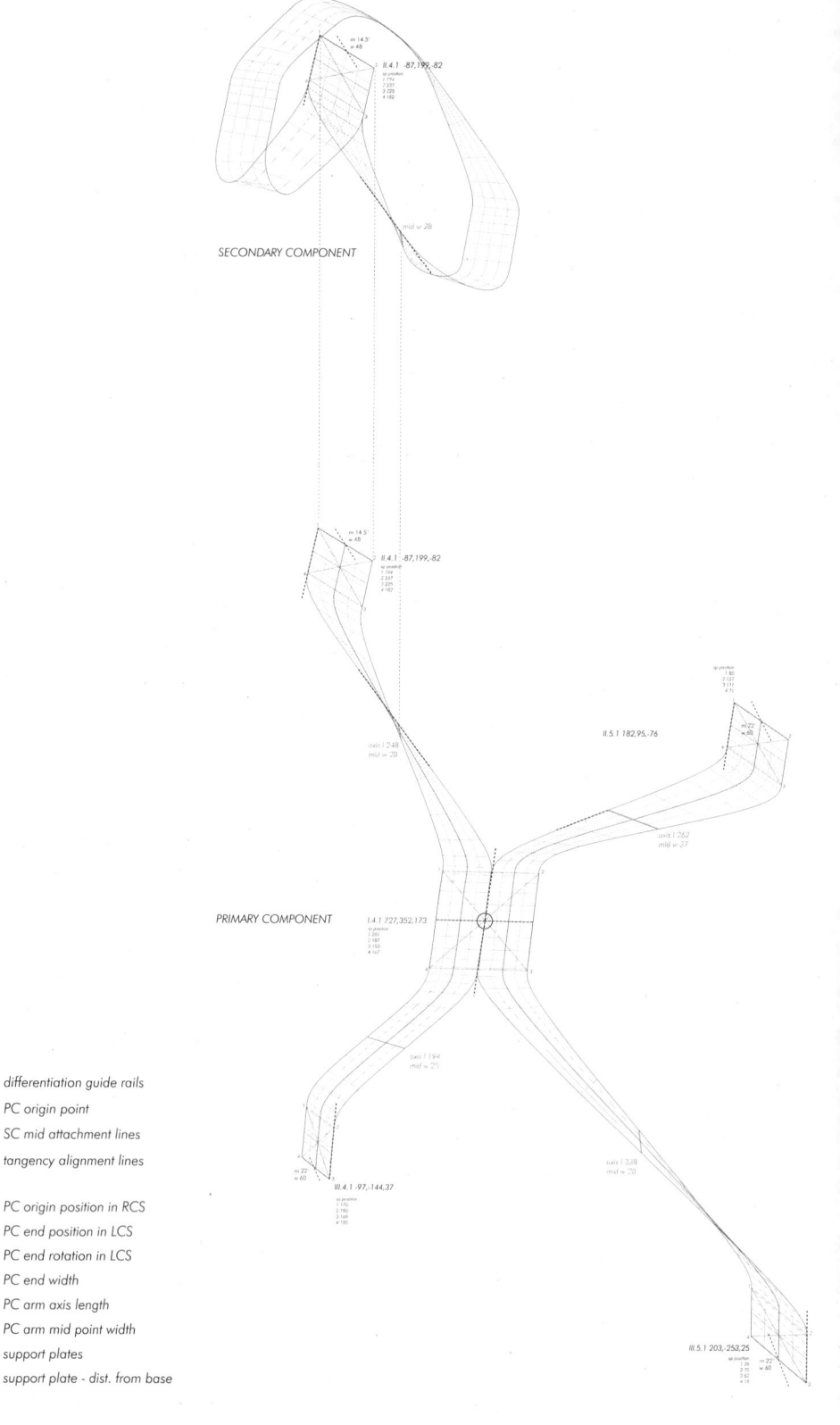

SECONDARY COMPONENT

PRIMARY COMPONENT

·······○·······	differentiation guide rails
———	PC origin point
	SC mid attachment lines
············	tangency alignment lines
I.1.1 175,261,400	PC origin position in RCS
III.1.1 -172,-146,45	PC end position in LCS
rn 00°	PC end rotation in LCS
w 30	PC end width
axis l 248	PC arm axis length
mid w 28	PC arm mid point width
⊠	support plates
sp position	support plate - dist. from base

172 The form of the primary cross-shaped local components is determined by the location of insertion points used in the process of lamination and by the inclination and rotation of its ends. The secondary components join the elements and establish the overall geometric and material continuity following a pre-established path.

In a larger assembly the insertion points of lamination geometrically vary for each local component. Due to the definition of the component that recognises and embeds the self-forming tendency of the veneer before lamination, a wide range of different geometric insertion point relationships can be produced.

174

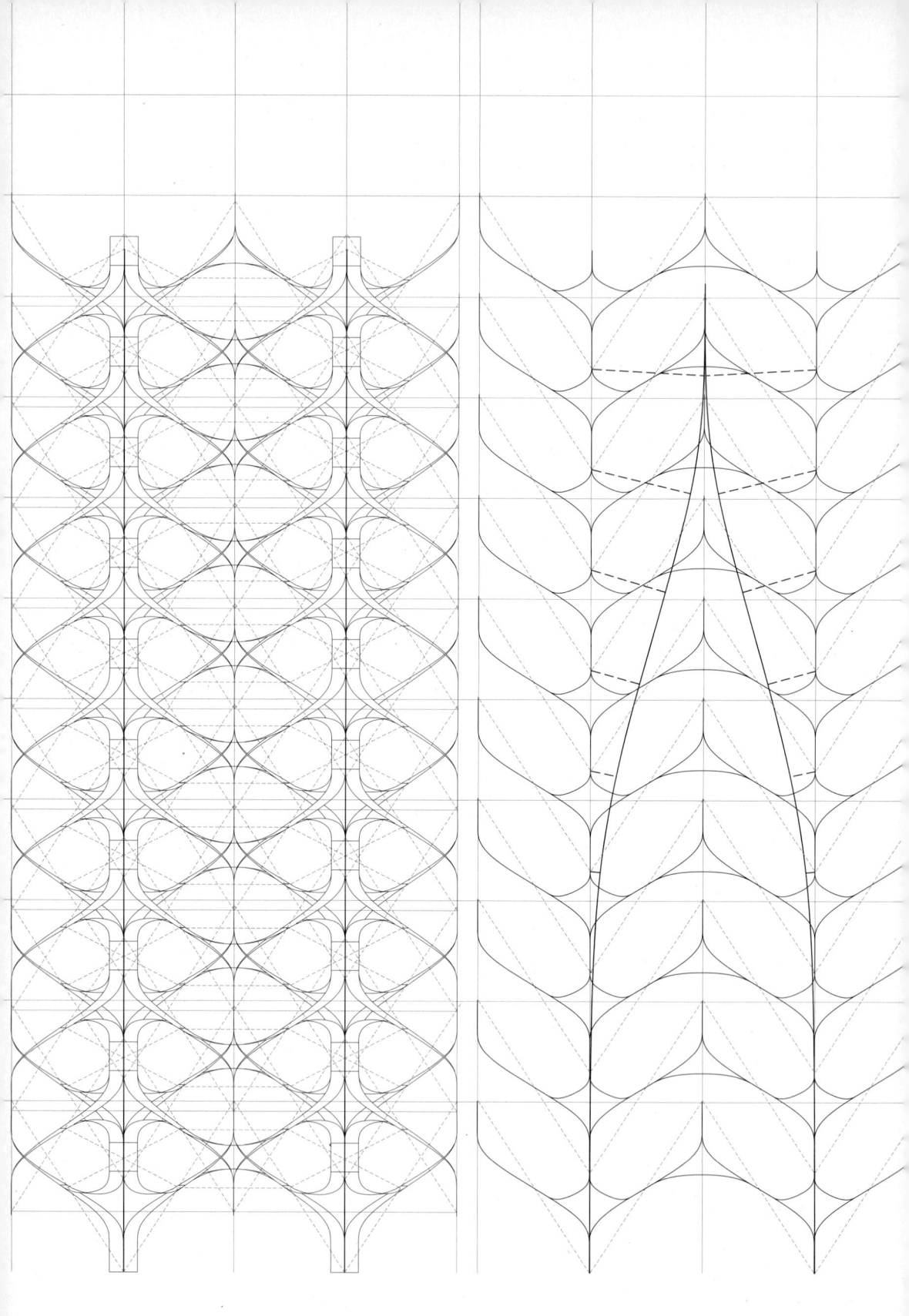

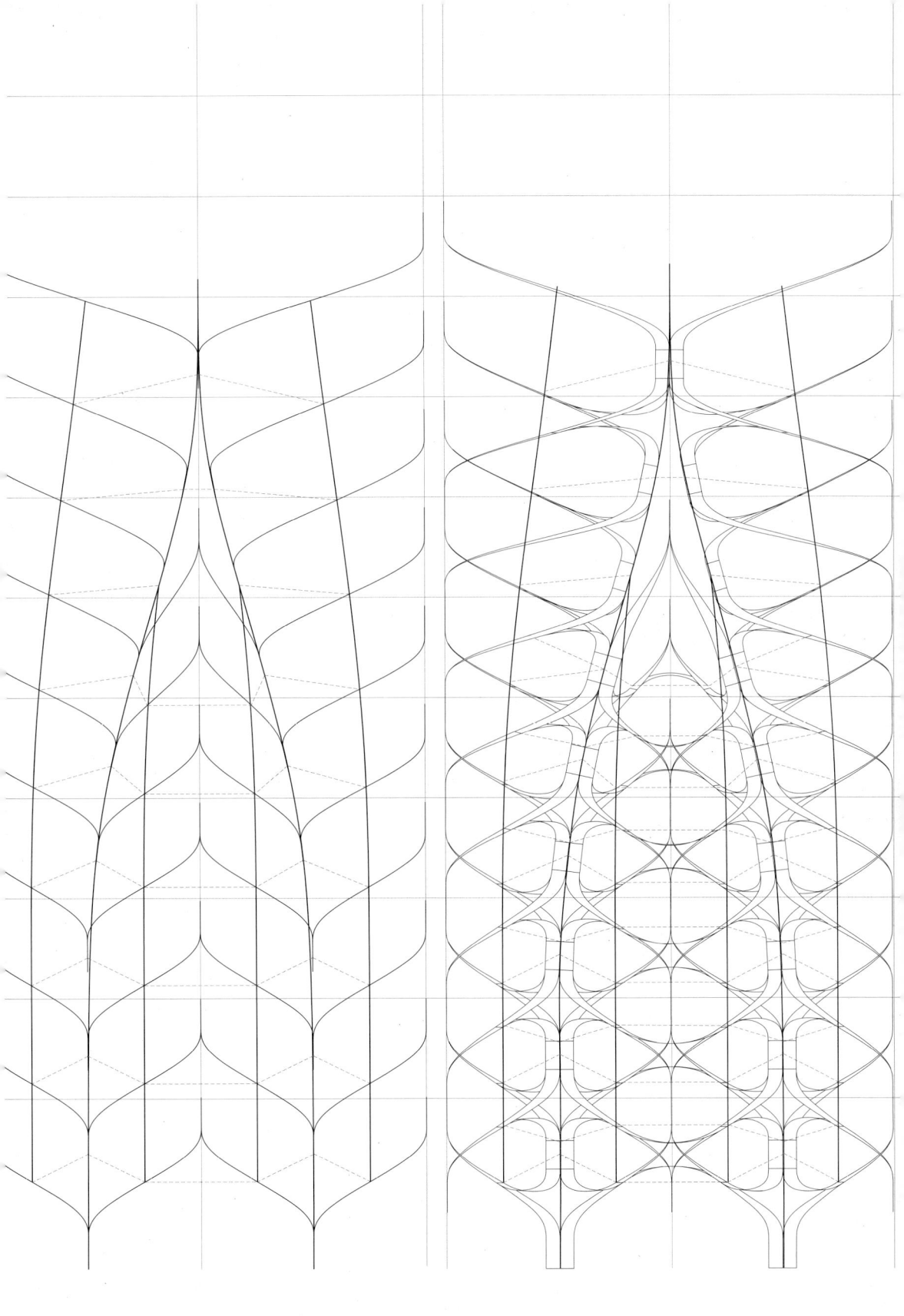

Differentiation within larger component systems is achieved through varying layouts of guide rails that control the position of insertion points and thus the number, size and orientation of individual components. Different types of guide rail layouts include linear configurations (opposite page) and bifurcations (this page).

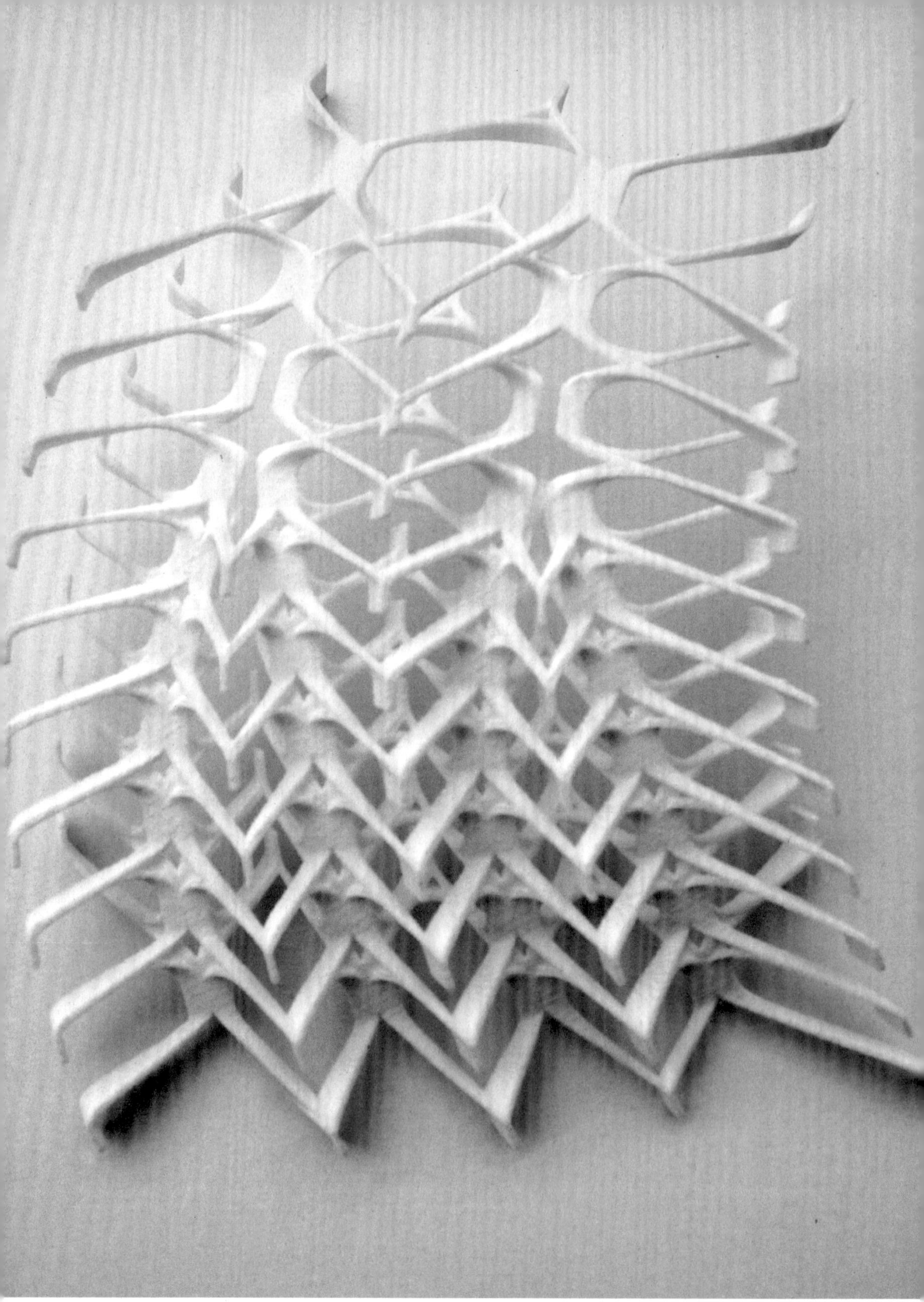

Two different rapid prototype models produced through selective laser-sintering that show the geometric adaptation of a multi-component system to two specific geometric frameworks. Each component adjusts to the particular location of its defining insertion point.

178 Lamination process (from left to right and top to bottom): 1-2. Support plates. 3. Positioning of patterns in relation to fibre orientation. 4. Cutting. 5-7. Labelled primary and secondary component patterns. 8. Vacuum pressing of the disconnected primary cross-shaped components. 9-11. Positioning on the support plates. 12. Continuous lamination of secondary components.

The pre-laminated (vacuum-pressed) secondary components are gradually laminated onto the cross-shaped primary components and form local loops that each time join four individual elements introducing material continuity and adding structural rigidity to the overall system.

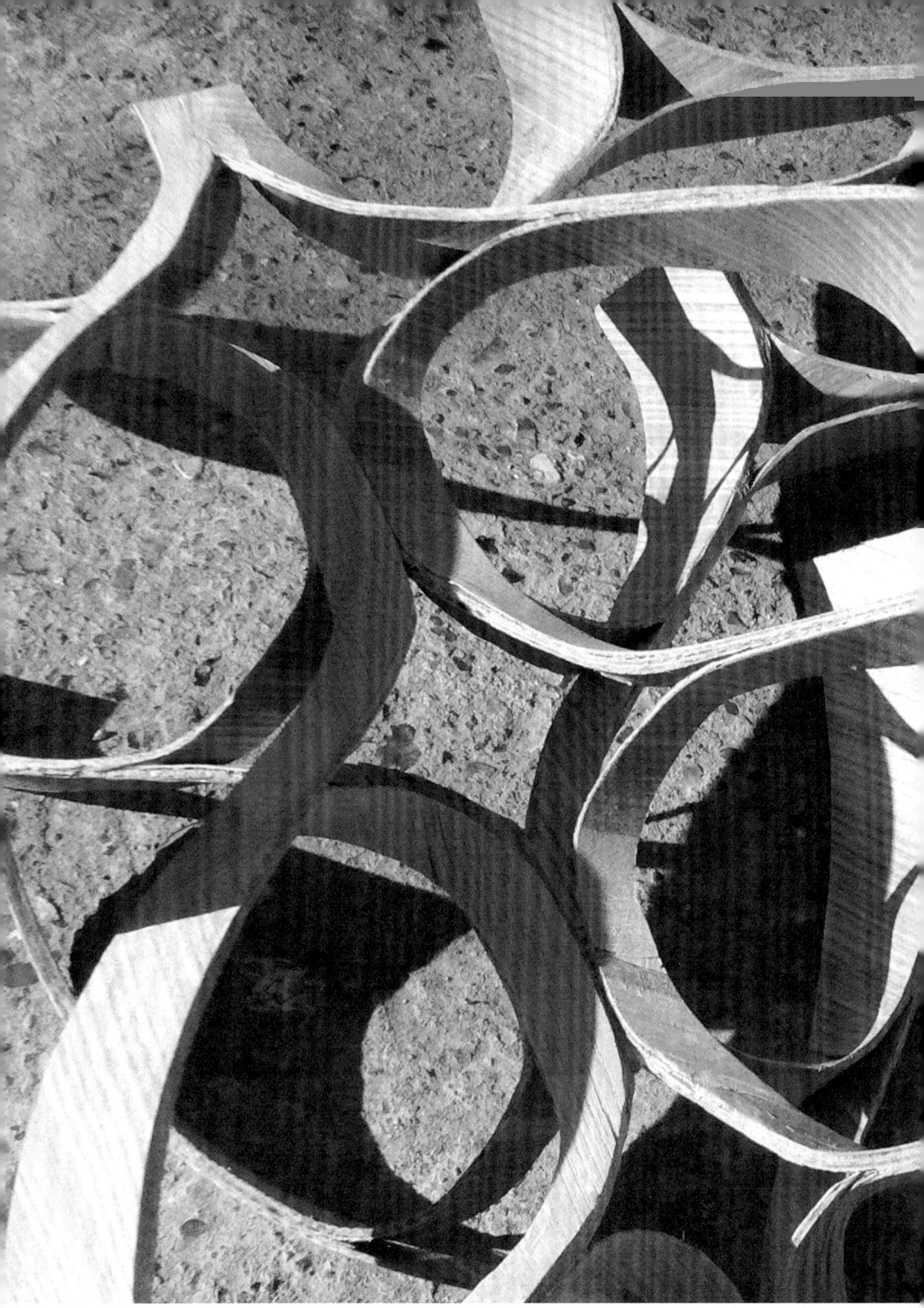

Full-scale prototype manufactured from multiple layers of veneer through processes of continuous lamination.

COMMENTS

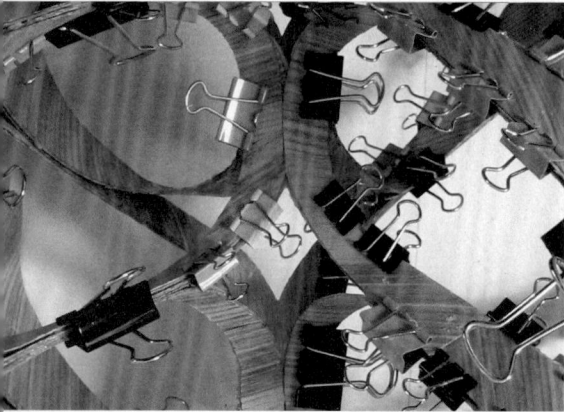

EVA SCHEFFLER

We know that architecture cannot be reduced to the mere act of building. However, it is striking and fascinating in how far the project Continuous Laminae rethinks multifarious preconceptions deeply rooted in the profession through the act of constructing. Probably most indicative for its challenging character is the project's attitude towards these processes of construction from which a whole cascade of novel strategies for architecture unravels.

Architects most often do not construct buildings but rather create buildings by providing the necessary data and instructions for construction. Whereas dramatic changes to the underlying concepts and methods of developing the organisation and gestalt of a building can be delineated in architectural history it is most often taken for granted that the format enabling the transfer from plan notation to tectonic articulation is one of scalar representation. Architects' obsession with drawings and models as appropriate directives for subsequent 'realisation' are ultimately based on the desire for geometric control. Ever since the separation of designing and making from one into many hands, the profession has developed representational formats, standards and regulations based on and expressed through measurable dimensions. Consequently any project to be constructed is conceived and communicated as metric quantities expressed through coordinate points that define the exact location and shape of all tectonic elements; may this be as an elaborate set of drawings or, more recently, as a comprehensive computer model. While this way of working seems to be deeply entrenched as the appropriate modus operandi in the profession, one of the most basic yet conspicuous aspects of Aleksandra Jaeschke's work is the liberation from these conventions and the exploration of an alternative strategy. Here the physical gestalt of what she calls a system is not defined through a representational model or drawing but through processes of formation and procedures of assembly. Rather then translating a predetermined shape she deploys the rich morphological repertoire innate in the material, in this case wood veneer, through the careful choreography of manipulative actions. The fascinating fact that characteristic bending and twisting, alignment and overlap can be induced in simple veneer strips through defined manipulative procedures becomes the generative driver of the project. Clearly this poses a major challenge to the inventory of architectural notational formats as self-forming tendencies and elastic behaviour, which is of critical importance for her project, cannot simply be drawn or modelled in the established representational manner.

With the implicit aim of dissolving the typical distinction between representational plan or model and construction system, the project initially resorts to a process of designing by making. The preparation of the specific pieces to be assembled in terms of cutting-pattern specification is developed hand in hand with the lamination process and the build up of a system that is much larger than the individual strips may initially suggest. This assembly of strips is defined through the specific location of points of strip-overlaps relative to each other from which the characteristic and instrumental continuity of the system arises. The nexus of different lines of enquiry into the system's behaviour and morphology resulting from manipulative procedures becomes an operative, parametrically described framework that defines the wood veneer system through processes of making. Although never explicitly mentioned in her descriptions but implicitly the core of the project this procedural protocol or notational framework promises a multitude of opportunities of establishing a more immediately 'material' understanding of design. Probably closer to notational systems in dance or choreography this framework provides an envelope of possibilities formed by material constraints that is capable of transforming external input into a series of sequential fabrication and assembly actions from which a specific articulation with particular effects unfolds. The versatility of such an approach seems then to depend on three factors: First, the initial definition and set-up of a combined computational and material notational framework that links manipulative procedure, processes of making and possible gestalt-instances of the wood veneer assembly;

second, the external information that triggers a specific morphological response as for example particular vectors of light rays may inform changes in porosity due to changes in strip width and third, the ability of this feedback system to undergo major changes in kind or even to transform itself in response to radical changes outside the anticipated performance range. While the project establishes a resourceful strategy addressing the first two aspects, the third still leaves a series of question for future research and provides interesting inroads for further speculations. For example, in order to enable the 'material system' to undergo major developmental changes and to differentiate into different types the notational framework would have to incorporate procedures that create disturbances in the build up of larger arrangements, or in other words that allow for topological variance in strip connection and assembly, as well as looped procedures acting on themselves producing a system with different levels of hierarchy in articulation. Beyond homologies and shape variation, the predominant ways of altering the system as of yet, the proposition of shifting towards a different, manipulative procedure and material behaviour-based notational system for architectural design will come to full fruition once the system's intricacy and robustness propagates across a wide range of scales driven by conflicting input. Especially in the context of the overarching research agenda of exploring architectural opportunities from the material and performance effects of differentiated assemblies, rather then inflicting predetermined functions on tectonic arrangements, it seems to be of critical importance to embed in the operative notational framework the ability for changes in kind and thus continuous reinvention.

Meta-patch consists of uniformly sized plywood surface elements which are mounted onto larger sheets of the same material which are in turn connected to form a large surface. The linear arrays of small rectangular surface elements are each connected to a larger patch. Each rectangular element is attached by four bolts, one in each corner. Two of the bolts are permanently fixed in opposite corners, thereby defining the length of the diagonal line between them. The other two bolts remain adjustable. Tightening these bolts increases the distance between the element's corners and causes the patch to bend. As the small elements are incrementally actuated, the larger patch acquires curvature too. As all the larger patches become curved, so does the overall surface. The global form is achieved through a vast array of local actuations in a true 'bottom-up' manner.

In order to identify and utilise the collective effect of this vast array of distributed force inductions it was necessary to develop a specific design strategy. In most form-finding processes operations focus on an exertion of force on strategic system-points that leads to a 'global' manipulation of the overall system. Here 'global' refers to the entirety of a system while 'local' describes a sub-location. One of the key realisations in the project has been that the self-organising capacity of material systems is not limited to 'global' form-finding processes but can also be deployed in a 'local' manner.

A series of test models with varying patch geometries and material specifications provided the basis for a detailed chart that notates the correlation of element and patch variables such as size, thickness and fibre orientation, actuator locations and torque settings and resulting system behaviour. This data enabled the scripting of the parametric definition, assembly sequence and actuation protocols for a prototype construction in which the possibility of providing a larger opening (a proto-door or window, so to speak) was investigated by means of a certain length of unconnected patches that curve in opposite directions, without jeopardising the capacity of the overall system to be self-supporting.

In accordance with the particular distribution

of actuator positions, the elements are connected to the patches and the patches are assembled into a larger structure with different orientations of the element-clad sides. The resulting material system consists of 48 identical patches, 1,920 uniform elements and 7,680 bolts. After assembly the over eight-metre-long structure is initially entirely flat. Through the subsequent incremental actuation of fastening delineated bolts, the structure acquires curvature and a stable, self-supporting form with alternating convex and concave curvature. Alteration of actuation states makes it possible to change curvature and to examine the system's inherent performative capacities.

The patches onto which the elements are mounted are perforated with holes in a variety of sizes and patterns. In this way modulation of porosity and adjustment of structural capacity through curvature are correlated with the manipulation of the system's material and geometric behaviour. As the actuation of the elements (and patch curvature) increases, the openings in the surface are increasingly exposed. If the surface region is oriented strategically with respect to the sun-path, for instance, it becomes possible to determine the amount of direct light exposure areas behind the surface. Light also gets reflected by the reverse side of the actuated elements, painted white. The curvature of the elements at each point determines the output angle.

Modulation of airflow needs to be understood in relation to the Bernoulli principle, which states that velocity and pressure of a moving fluid are reverse proportional. As air moves from a wider to a narrower constraint, for instance, a corresponding volume must move a greater distance forward in the narrower constraint and thus must move at greater speed. The degree of curvature of the local element in relation to the larger area it is embedded within, together with the orientation and therefore exposure of the hole, will in each case determine whether there is greater velocity or greater pressure of airflow.

The tough (yet-to-be-cracked) nut is how to correlate the different performance criteria in an instrumental manner. A specific amount of curvature across the entire system is necessary for it to hold itself up. This curvature might not, however, correspond with the spatial requirements or the local surface curvature for light and airflow modulation. In other words, if no airflow or light is required across a large region of the system, the single elements should be flat and the holes closed, but this might undermine the structural performance of the system. Here further research is needed.

Another area of further research would focus on how to set several thousand actuators to the required degree. Here the anisotropic makeup of the material might be of great use. Given the correct fibre layout, the actuation work might be performed by the material itself in response to changing environmental conditions. With timber, for instance, this might be related to relative humidity, as an increase in humidity can amplify system curvature.

It is also conceivable that a composite material would be designed to specifications that match relevant environmental stimuli with a corresponding system response. Two lines of inquiry arise from this realisation: first, experiments with fibre-layout are crucial in order to induce the required curvature ranges; second, the choice of environmental stimulus or stimuli that are to induce the shape-changes of the system are crucial as they will determine the exact make-up of the material composite.

Margaret Everson Fossey Fellowship 2004-05

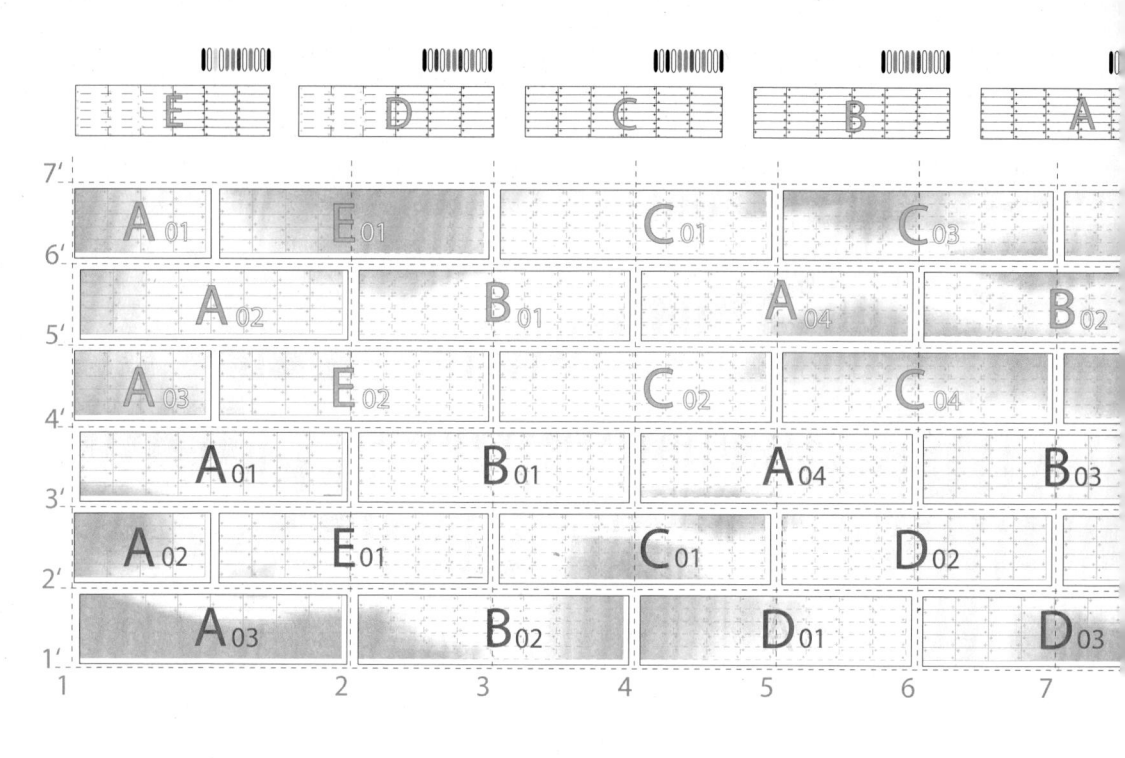

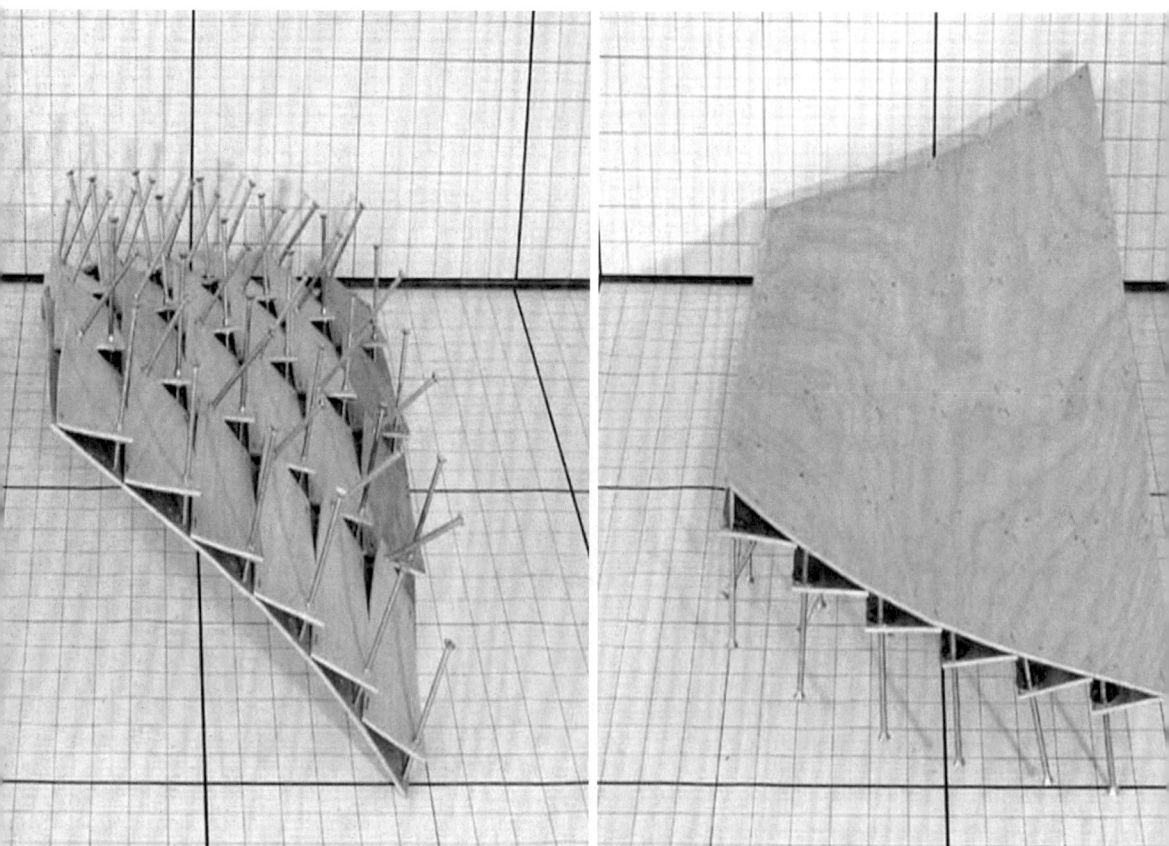

186   The scripted actuation protocol for a full scale prototype structure provides all information for the manufacturing, assembly and actuation of the local actuator elements and timber patches. It becomes instrumental in defining and manipulating the relation between differential actuation of distributed local elements and the resulting global curvature (top).

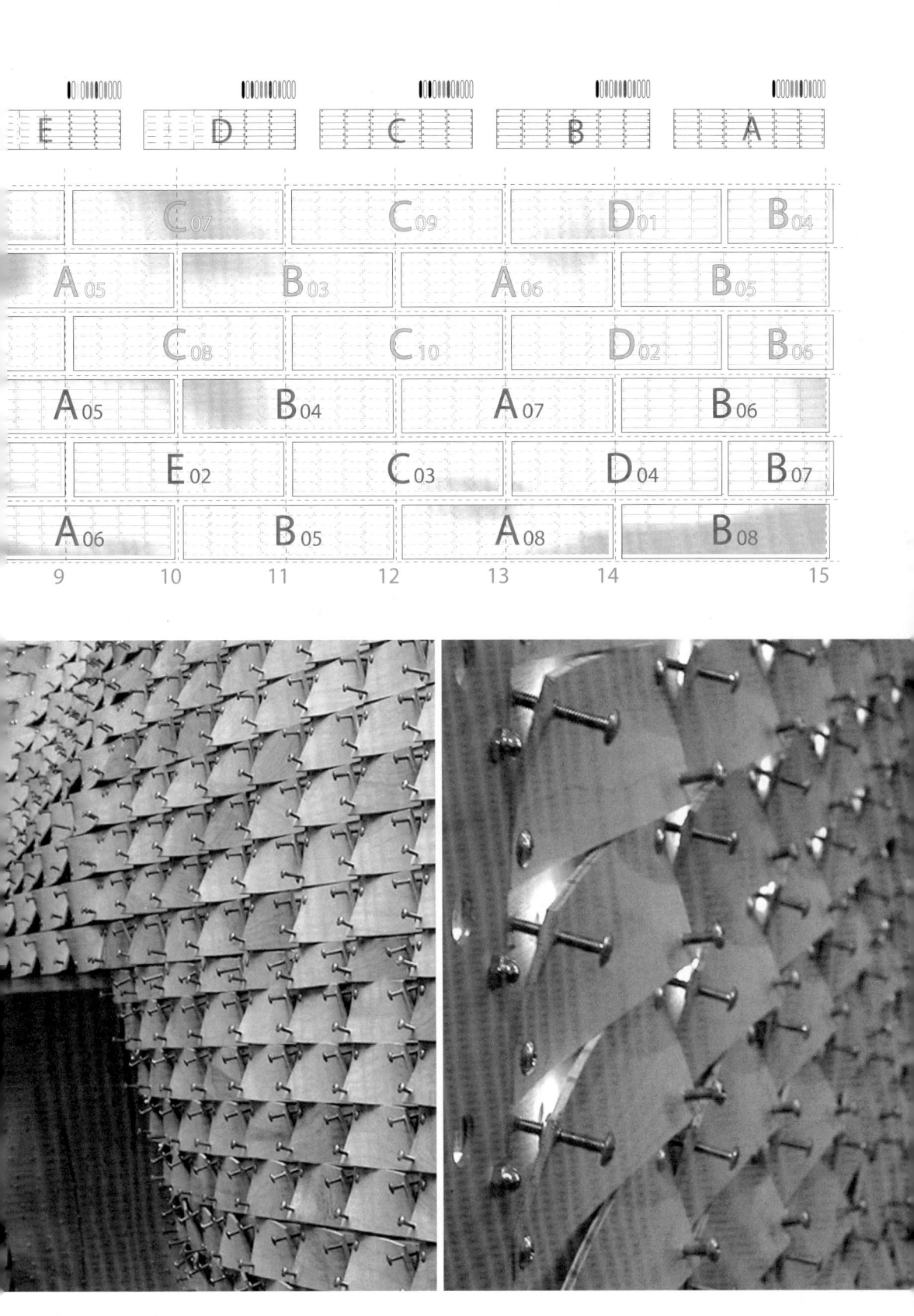

An initial test model shows the curvature of a larger, initially entirely flat timber sheet induced by the fastening of local actuator bolts attached at opposite corners of uniform timber elements (bottom p.186). A close-up view of actuation elements and patches (bottom left) indicates the performative capacity of the actuated system to modulate transmission of light. (bottom right)

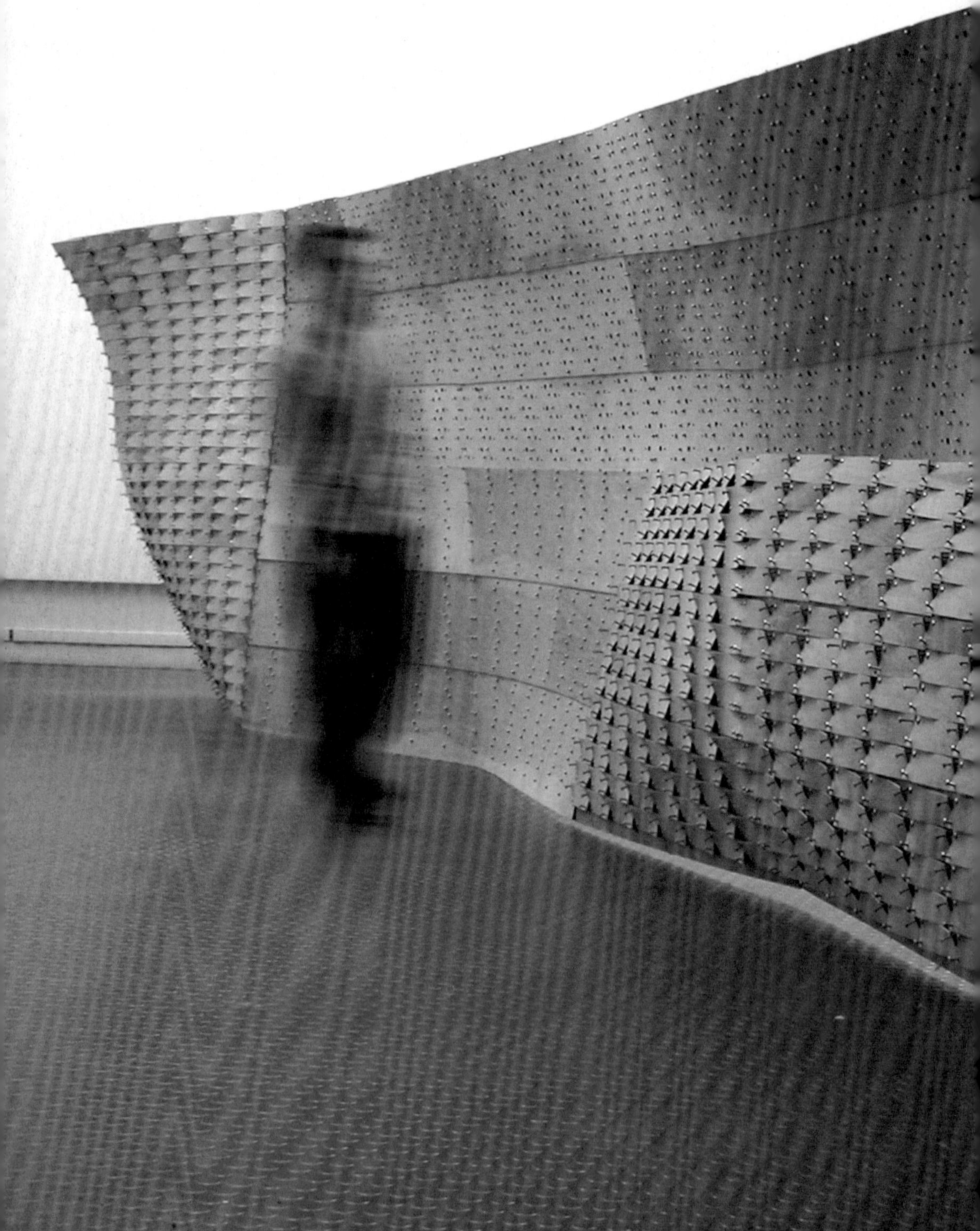

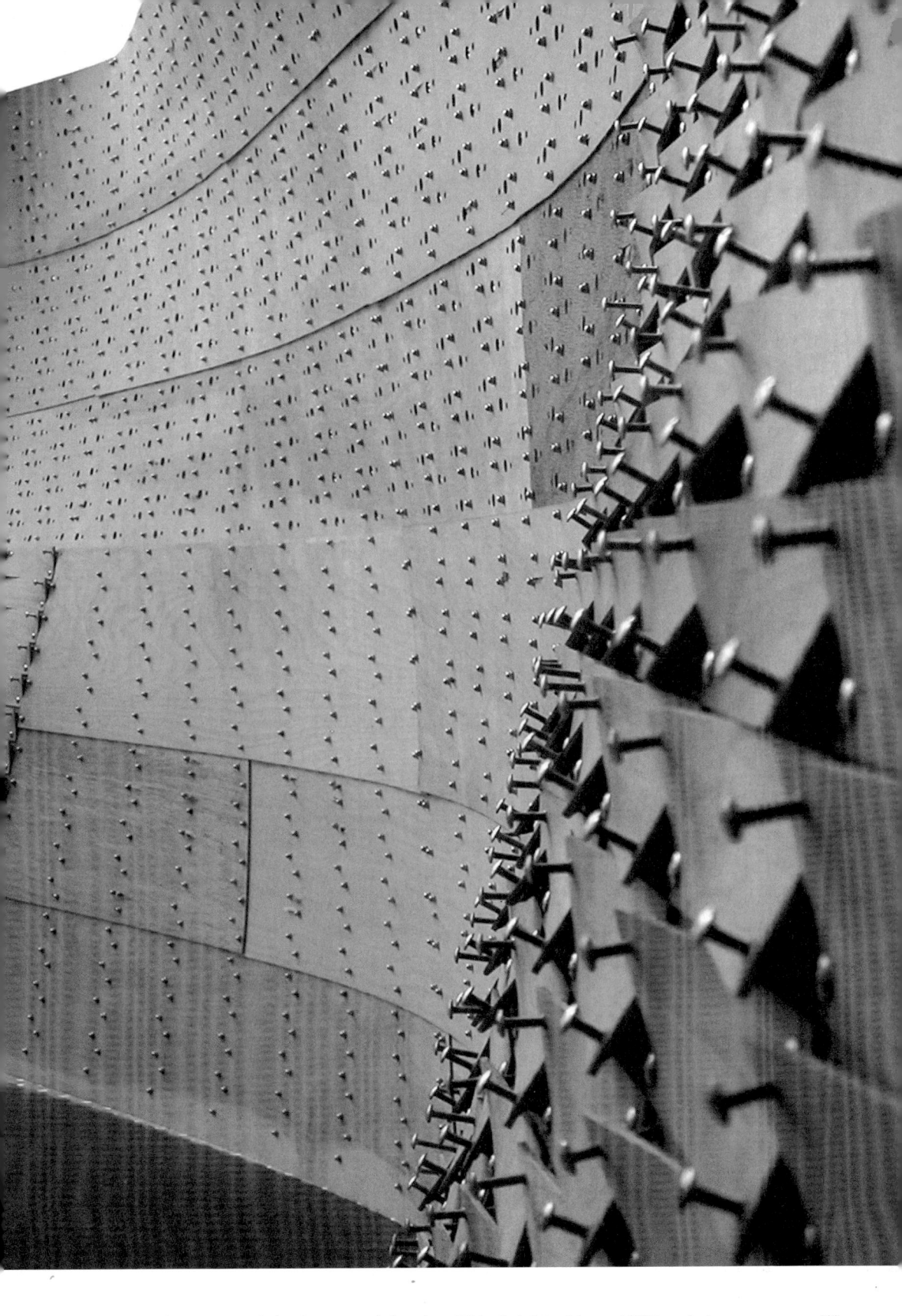

After the adjustment of 7,680 actuator bolts, the system – built up from 48 identical, flat patches and 1920 equal, planar elements – takes on the defined global curvature which greatly enhances the structural capacity of the system.

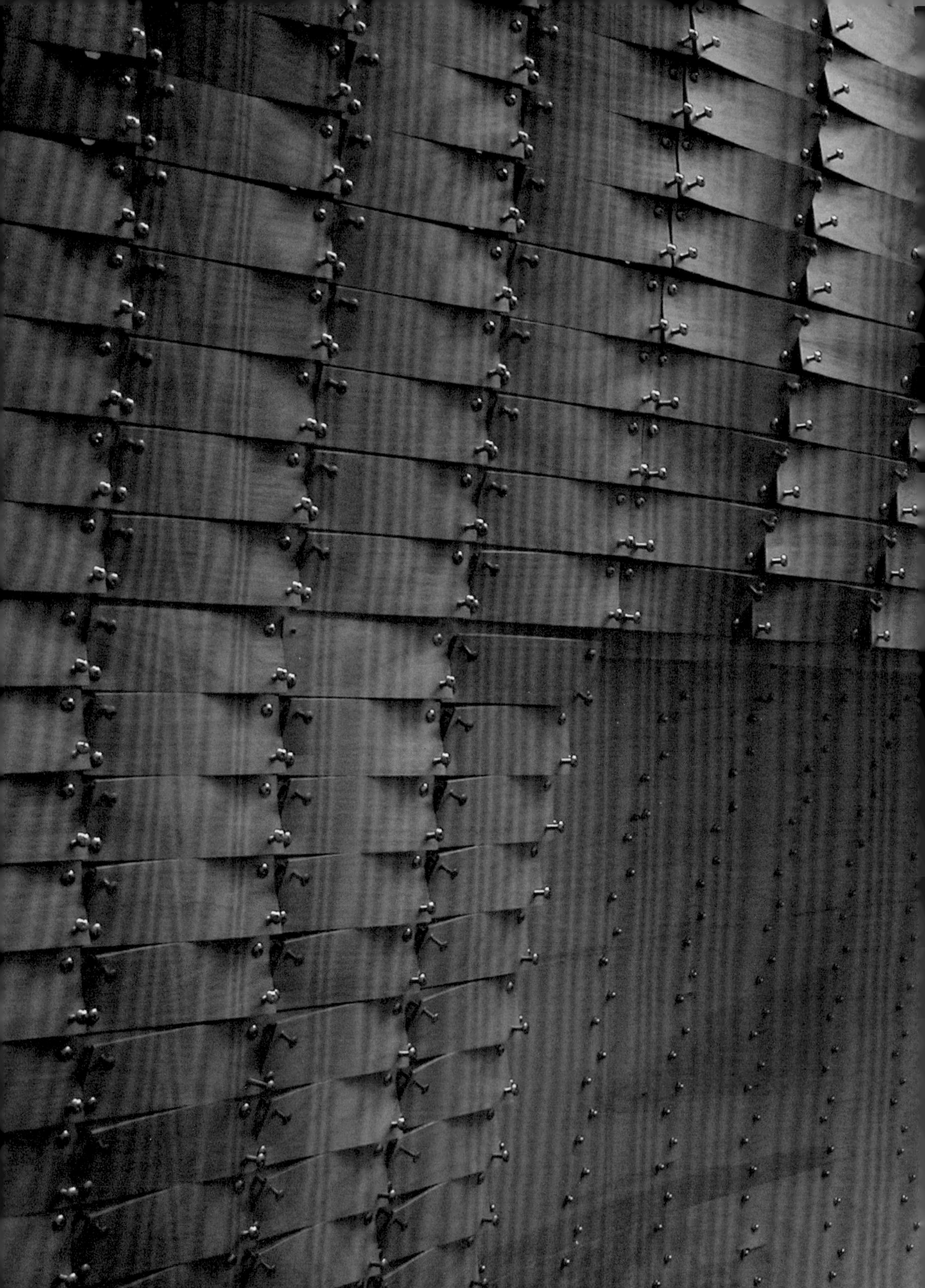

Full-scale metapatch prototype structure on display at the 'Modulations' exhibition at Rice School of Architecture, Houston.

Joseph Kellner and Dave Newton have designed and built an emergent wall. That is, it emerges as the sum total of nearly 2,000 rectangles of sheet plywood mounted, in groups of 40, onto larger rectangles of plywood which are then joined edge to edge to make the wall. But not just pinned, or glued, but bolted. Adjustably. Each of the rectangles can be pushed away from or pulled towards the main mounting sheet by turning the bolts one way or the other. And because the larger and the smaller sheets of plywood are of similar thickness and stiffness, this pushing and pulling affects the shape of both smaller and larger elements. The small, adjustable ones warp and form the larger, passive ones so that the overall shape of the wall is driven by individual elements which can't 'see' the overall shape which they are producing. The curvature of the assembly emerges from the concerted activity of many small blind actuators. Just like an ant nest might be built by the activities of many tiny insects. It's hierarchical and emergent. Except it isn't. Who knows if ants have a God which oversees the shape of the nest and sees that it is good? Probably they don't. Probably the shape of the nest is entirely derived from the activities of animals which can never conceive of the major outcome of their activities. But to the wall, Joseph and Dave are Gods. They can push, pull, twist and turn until the bolts are prestraining the structure to produce just the shape they want. They even do it to a plan. In this way they can alter its surface shape and the flow patterns around it to produce a desired outcome. It's a willing wall, which will do as its Gods will. But wouldn't it be more fun if the wall had a will of its own? Where there's a will there's a way!

First, each bolt must be replaced by a separate actuator, one that can transmit force from a more convenient central source. They could be electrical – a little motor driving a screw thread – or pneumatic or hydraulic – a piston working in a tube controlled by a valve. Then we need sensors. What will we sense? Joseph and Dave point out that wood warps when wet, so we already have hygrosensing built in. We could also sense airflow, light, heat.

COMMENTS

JULIAN VINCENT

Let's say we want the wall to give shade. Then where it's warm the actuators actuate, and where it's cool they are passive. And they go on moving until the temperature on the shady side of the wall is lower than on the sunny side, over as wide an area as possible. But what's the plan? Who has the Big Idea. Exit Joseph and Dave. The days of Gods are over. The wall rules. The wall has rules. It moves and shakes until the temperature criterion is met and then relaxes, satisfied in the knowledge of a wall's job well done. Give it a memory so that the next time it is asked to provide shade it can work out where the heat is coming from and use its experience to give a better, quicker, service. How about having another wall, or three? And a roof? We have a self-adjusting house.

The small rectangles – the actuators – are the drivers. If they each have sensors they can be more or less independent. They may need to know what's going on up to three or four rectangles away in any direction, but that's all. They are cells. The wall is a leaf, driven, directed, pointed, by the cells from which it is made. What independence shall we give to each cell, to each wooden rectangle? At present the rectangles can bend and buckle so that they not only change the shape of the wall but can strengthen it and stiffen it in particular directions. The wall can adjust itself to a variety of loads. As the wind loads change, or as the loads inside the house change, the walls change their load-bearing ability. The rectangles provide both skeleton and muscles. Can we ask the house to streamline itself, so that the windspeed over all parts of the walls is the same, and there is no resistance to flow and no down-wind vorticity? As Buckminster Fuller was well aware, such a house will lose far less heat to the passing winds. And if the rectangles can open up to allow air to flow through, we have adaptive ventilation as well.

Let's imagine that we can give the rectangles a range of properties. What if each rectangle can make itself transparent when the sun is shining on it? When the sun is out, the individual rectangles on the irradiated area of the wall let the light in. This functional window travels around the house as the sun moves, always letting light and heat into the living space. And because you know the time from the direction of the sun, you find yourself living in a house-sized sundial. Activities are spread around the room according to their appointed time. When the light hits a photoreceptor on the kettle heater – at 5 o'clock, of course – the kettle switches itself on and it's time for tea.

We don't want an intelligent building; we want intelligent bricks.

COMMENTS 2

MICHAEL WEINSTOCK

The form of the 'Metapatch' resembles a standing wave. The curvature is not fixed, but can be changed by adjusting the curvature of the small patches, which in turn act on the larger surface. The global form is able to change from a flat surface to an articulated sine wave, and can be stabilised at any state in between. It needs curvature for structural stability – stand a flat sheet on edge and it will topple to one side or the other; introduce a curve and it will stand. There are many different curvatures that will give this structural capacity to a flat sheet, particularly when two or more opposed curves are formed to be continuous. The Metapatch is a material construct that has an active form, one that is capable of being adjusted to multiple curvatures in a smooth and continuous manner. This makes it quite different to the traditional architectural understanding of a form as a static tectonic geometry, the outermost surface of a structure or artefact. The Metapatch is closer to the biological understanding of form – as something never quite static, subject to change but persistent over time, and generated by internal processes. In this domain form is not a finished thing so much as a persistent three-dimensional pattern of material that emerges from the processes of complex systems, and is constantly renewed. Form, in this way of thinking, is something like the wave that appears downstream of the pier of a bridge in a fast flowing river, consistent in the sense that it remains in approximately the same place with approximately the same geometry, though it is also constantly subject to small changes as the velocity and volume of the river fluctuate.

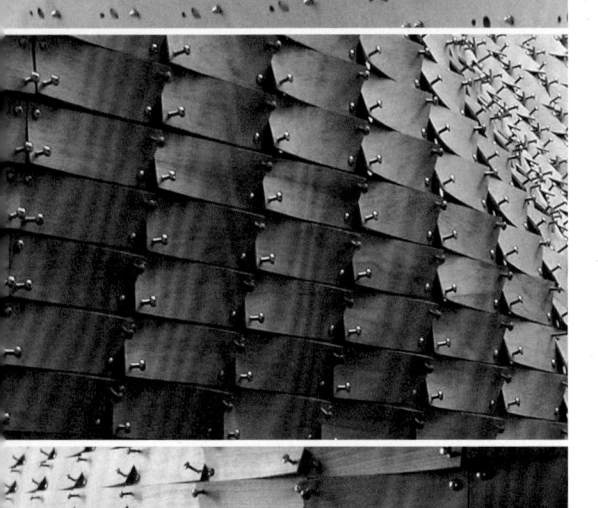

Working with physical material is attractive to architects, and is part of the atelier tradition of experimentation with arrangements of materials that are stressed to produce stable organisations. The Metapatch is the result of a new and intensely interesting experimental process that follows in the tradition of the short history of architectural and engineering form-finding, which may have begun with Gaudí's hanging-chain models and the systematic body of experiments seen in the work that Frei Otto carried out over three decades. These techniques include, amongst others, catenary chain models and hanging models of cloth stabilised with plaster under the stress of gravity, elasticated and non-elasticated fabrics stressed by tensile forces, wood stressed by torsion forces and membranes differentially stressed by air pressure. A different but related system for physical form-finding is the branching thread structure stressed by water and shrinkage. In all these systems, physical stress produces the self-organisation of material.

Form-finding experiments tend to produce forms that are consistent with some of the characteristics of natural self-organising systems, offering the possibilities of forms emerging from experiments with an 'inbuilt' material arrangement that tends towards structural stability. The Metapatch experiment, carried out by Newton and Kellner under the guidance of Michael Hensel and Achim Menges, has produced a new insight into form-finding processes, one that is not evident in the body of inherited work from Gaudí, Otto and Isler. What has been discovered in the studio is that physical stresses need not be applied in one singular process to the whole material system, but that stress can be applied in an incremental process at a local level. What is profoundly impressive about this experiment is that the found form is not a singular static configuration of stability, as it is for example with hanging chains or branched threads, but rather a dynamical material system that has more than one stable form.

The surface substrate to which the patches are attached has another physical characteristic that produces an interesting performance, in that it has multiple openings. Although the material (thin plywood) is not porous in itself, porosity has been achieved by arrays of holes, differentiated by size and by patterns, and as the curvature of the Metapatch is changed, so the openings are concealed or exposed. Curvature changes at a local level produce increased structural capacity as well as increases or decreases in the flow of light and air through the system.

Natural self-organising systems are dynamic, subject to fluctuation over time, and to reorganisation. The Metapatch experiment establishes a means of producing an emergent morphology that is strongly correlated to biological material organisations that have achieved their form and performance characteristics through stress-driven self-organisation. The Metapatch as an active surface structure can negotiate between form, structure and behaviour, and it does so by a large number of very simple interactions between element, patch and surface. The development of an active and environmentally responsive 'architectural skin' has been much discussed in theoretical discourse over the last decade, and this experiment offers a new approach and a new model for that development. The Metapatch is an exemplary work, carried out with the persistence, rigour and ingenuity that is the signature of the Hensel Menges studio.

This project explored ways to incrementally change an assembly from a vector-active to a surface-active structural system, so as to instrumentalise the gradient porosity of the system relative to environmental performance.

The investigation of the behaviour of vector-active surface structures initially focused on cylindrical bodies with thin walls that display a characteristic buckling pattern when exposed to loads beyond a critical threshold. A first set of experiments revealed a tetrahedral local buckling pattern, which suggested a possibility for translation into a surface system with triangulated faces or a triangular frame structure. The related tetrahedral space-frame and tetrahedral surface morphology were constructed in separate models and then fused in one configuration suggesting a gradient transition between the two structural systems. This system was investigated further in the next series of physical and digital models, which explored different strategies for achieving a smooth transition from space-frame to surface morphology by incrementally increasing or decreasing the aperture in the triangular faces of the tetrahedra.

As the morphology developed, the initial associative modelling set-up was progressively modified in order to achieve a gradient structural condition, from vector-active space frame to surface-active folded structural system. As the associative model quickly became very complex, scripting was required to handle the amount of data to be processed.

Alongside the development of the digital modelling method a number of rapid prototype models were made throughout the design process to examine whether the geometry was correctly modelled. Tests on physical models showed that an additional strategy was required to fix the corners of the tetrahedra in space in order to prevent the system from buckling out of plane under loading. One approach to preventing buckling involved a connective layer of hexagons, while another focused on the multiplication of element layers. Both strategies increase the connectivity within the system. Where they differ, however, is in the depth of structure required: if the depth of structure is limited, then there is a decrease of element sizes in the layered option, which in turn affects the environmental performance of the system. At this stage the system has four distinct characteristics: [i] triangular faces of tetrahedra varied with respect to their porosity, [ii] tetrahedral elements varied in size, and [iii] hexagonal elements varied in cross-sectional profile thickness relative to structural necessity, or alternatively [iv] the multiplication of element layers.

The next step was to investigate how different performance requirements would affect the degree of porosity of the faces of the tetrahedrons and their size. Here, the transition from space-frame to surface morphology offers a range of performative capacities through related changes of porosity. Thus the system cannot only be manipulated in response to different structural requirements, but can also be informed by critical environmental parameters so as to modulate airflow and interact with luminous flow.

Digital Finite Element analysis and Computer Fluid Dynamics analysis were used in order to establish the complex interrelation between the morphology of the system and its structural behaviour and environmental modulation. This process began with basic digital studies that simulated airflow around differently articulated single elements, varying the angles of the faces of the tetrahedrons and the size of aperture in each face, as well as the range of sizes within each element. Configurations consisting of a greater number of differentiated elements were then analysed and the performative capacity of the system was documented and notated in a digital protocol. This directly informed subsequent generations of the system in response to a specific climatic and luminous context.

The investigation of geometric-topological articulation and performative capacity was paralleled by an investigation of manufacturing options. Various approaches to unfolding assemblies into flat-sheet patterns for laser-cutting were examined and tested in a series of scaled physical models. As a specific cutting technique, an industrial origami method was chosen that allows the flat sheets to be scored from one side only, while folding is possible in both directions. The associative modelling set-up was developed so that each assembly was automatically unfolded and laid out for laser- or CNC-cutting. With this manufacturing approach each profile is hollow unless another material is cast into it in order to increase the self-weight or thermal mass of the element or change sub-assemblies differentially across the entire system.

Once the issue of cutting and folding had been resolved the project pursued a second complementary manufacturing strategy, in which space-frame-like slender profiles that make up a tetrahedron can be cut as three pieces for each face. This was done to achieve increased self-weight and thermal mass in one production step. Initially elements were cut from styrofoam and assembled to ensure that the correct cutting angles were defined. Subsequently elements were cut from MDF to produce models for load-testing. Physical load tests went hand in hand with digital tests based on finite element method.

The design was informed by extensive measuring and mapping of thermal, luminous and aeolic conditions across a selected test site. Environmental measurements were listed and updated on a data spreadsheet set up to automatically re-interpolate all 20,000 measurement values across the site. This spreadsheet data was linked directly to a map generated within an associative modelling environment. Once the sizes, distribution and orientation of all elements of the material system were established according to the set spatial arrangements, the associative model of the material system could be linked to the mapping set-up. This established an instrumental link and a rigorous feedback between material system and environmental conditions. New environmental conditions can now update the design and, in the same way, the environmental impact of the intervention can be visualised, analysed, evaluated and fed back into the design process. This sophisticated set-up enables an expedient interrelational modulation of material system and environmental conditions.

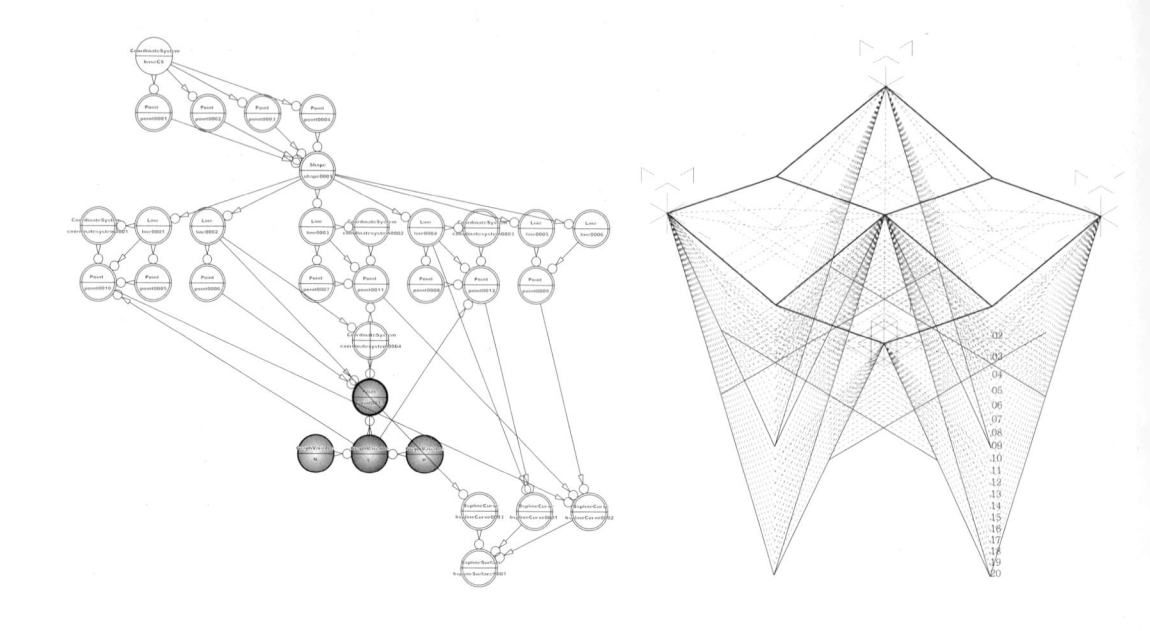

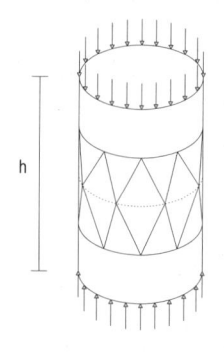

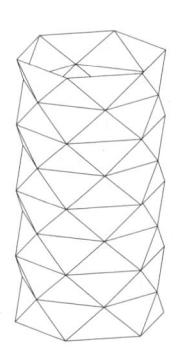

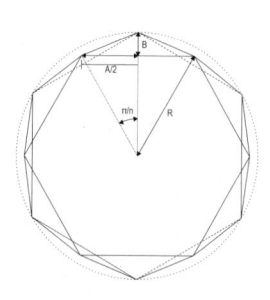

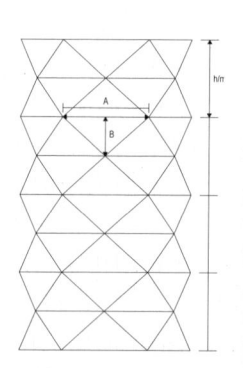

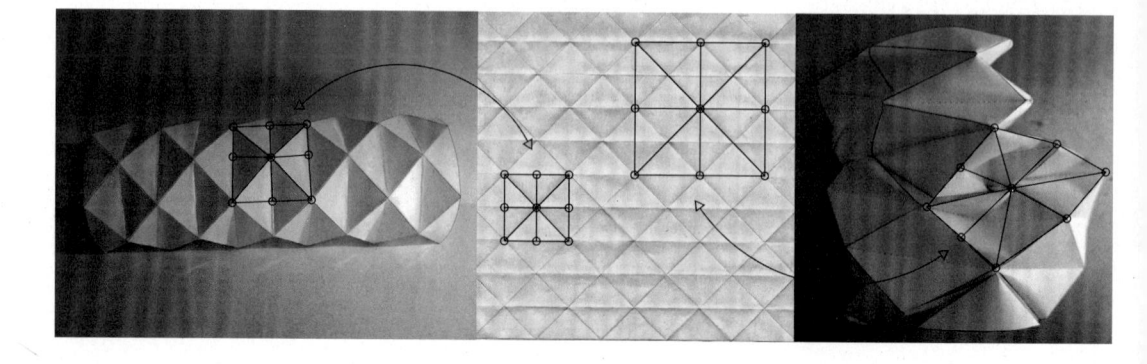

198 The tetrahedral buckling patterns displayed by cylindrical bodies with thin walls when exposed to loads beyond a critical threshold informed the development of an initial geometric component (bottom). In an associative modelling application this component is defined as a number of variable and fixed geometric relations (top left) generating varied, individual instances. (top right)

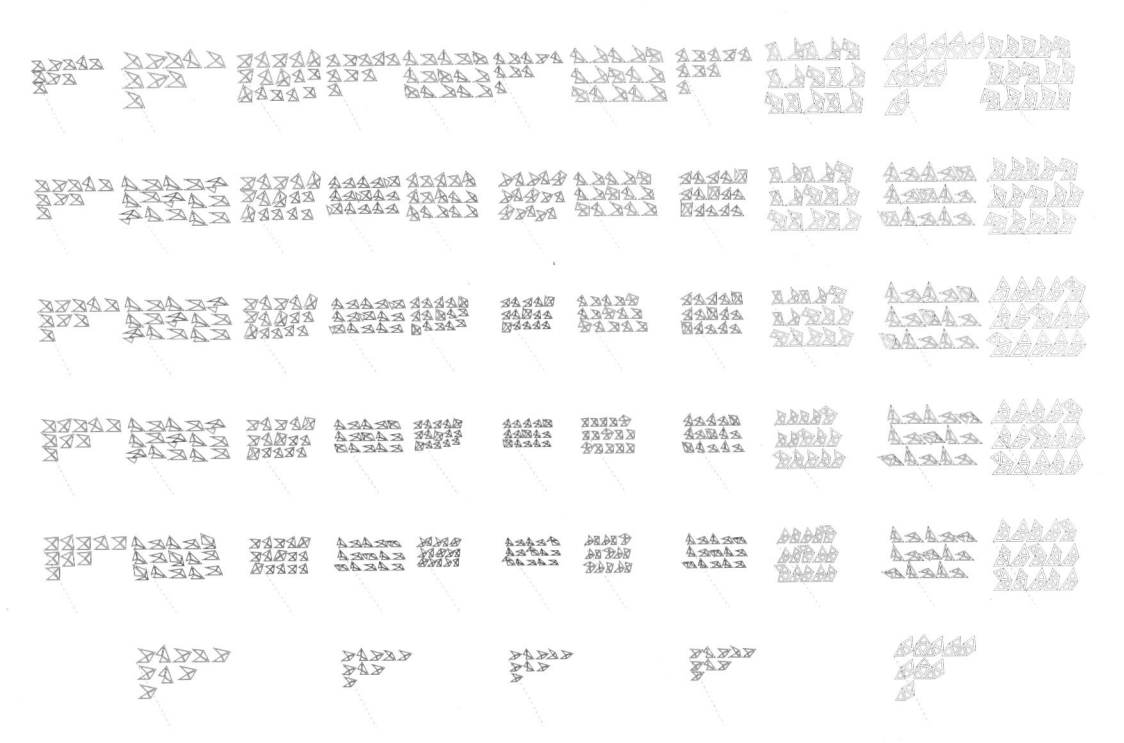

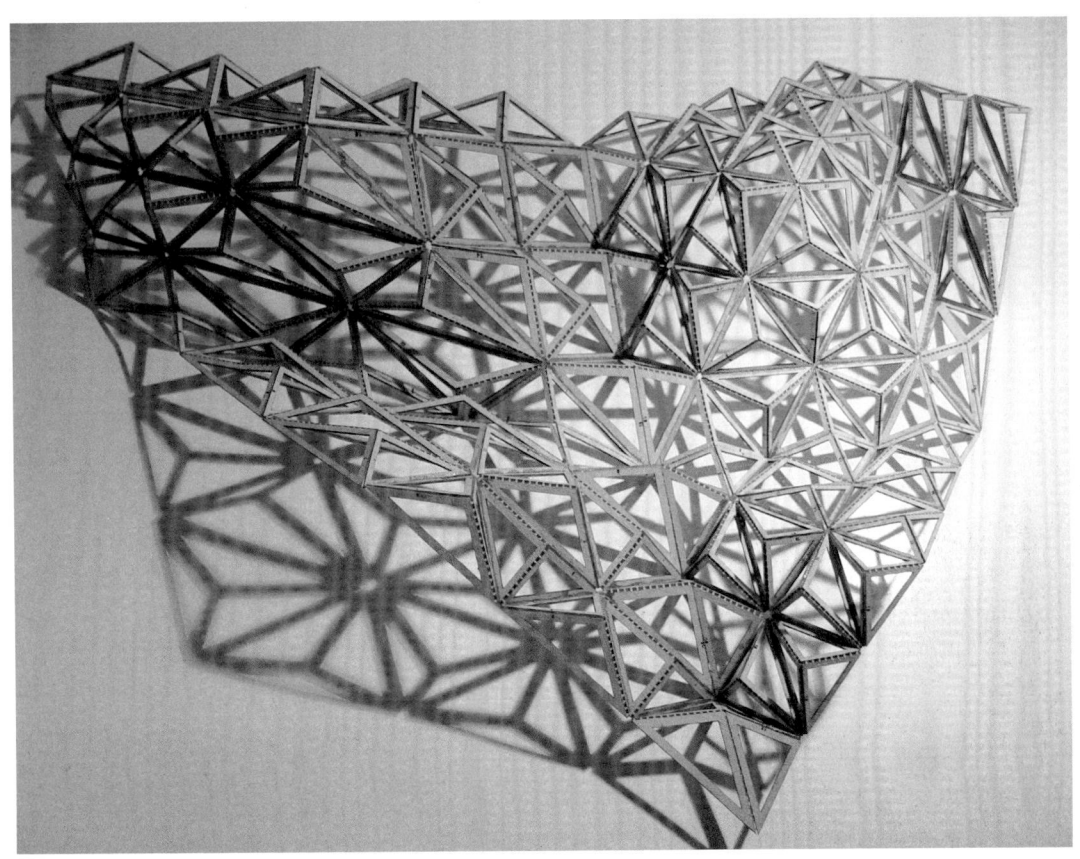

Each component placed within the parametric model automatically generates an associated flat sheet cutting-pattern for laser-cutting processes (top). For the fabrication and assembly of a scaled prototype the specific cutting technique of industrial origami allows for flat sheets to be scored from one side only, while making folding possible in both directions (bottom).

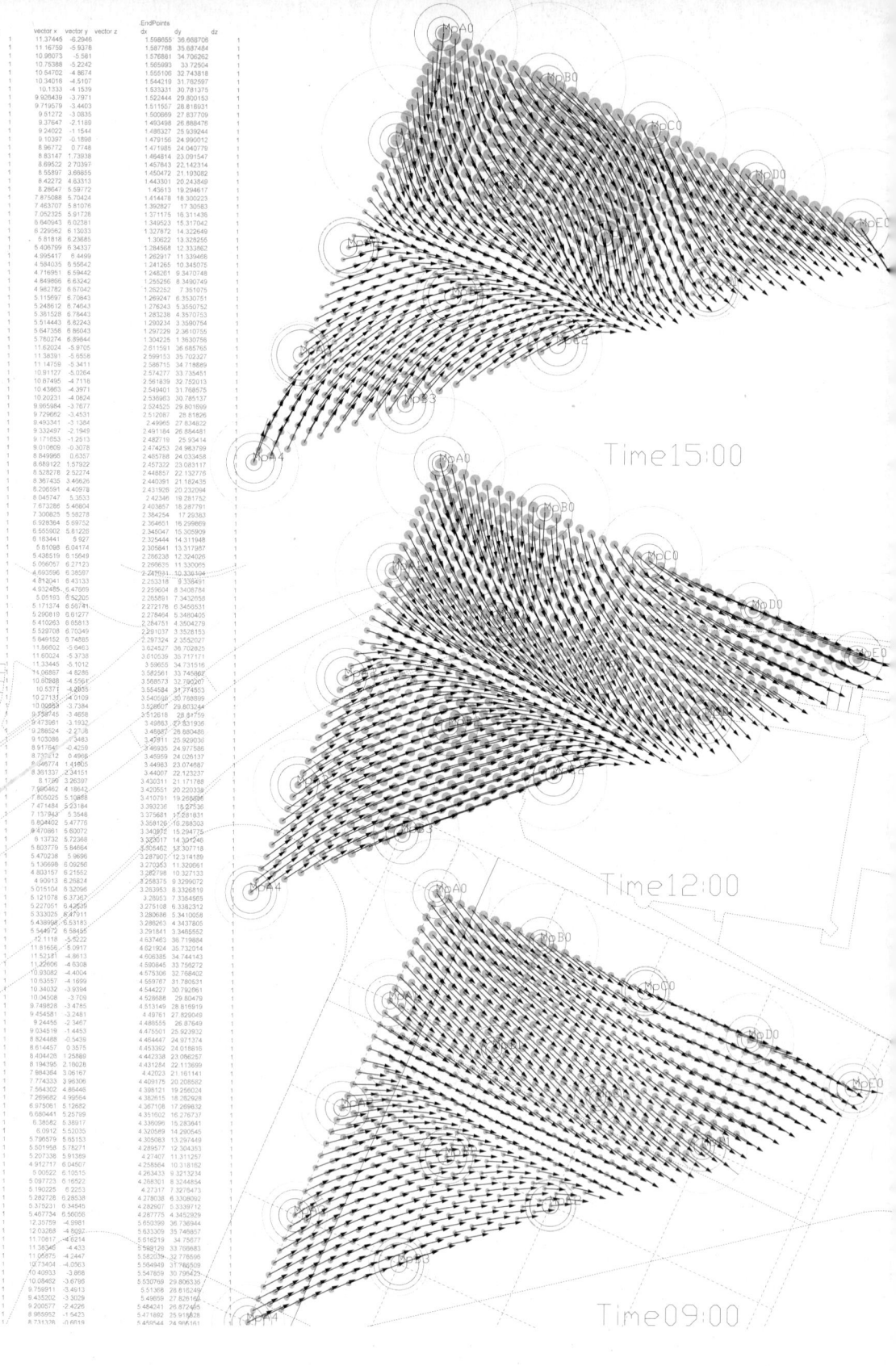

The particular parametric specification of the system is informed by extensive measuring and mapping of thermal, luminous and aeolic conditions across the specific test site. Environmental measurements taken for different times of the day were listed on a data spreadsheet.

Close-up view of a digital system prototype in which each component carries the potential for geometric changes informed by an external database.

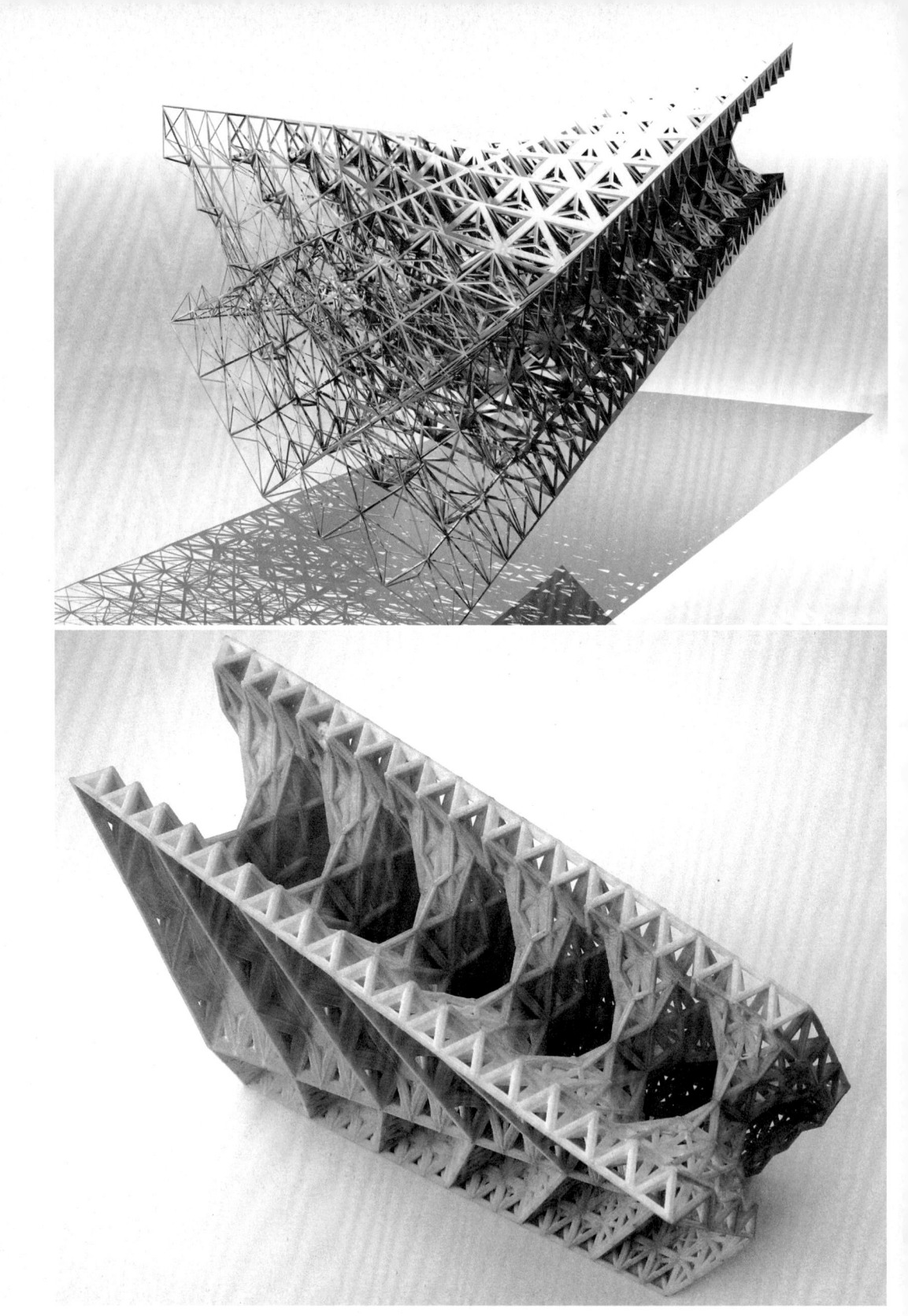

202   The digital system (top) and a related rapid prototype model (bottom) show the ability of the system to incrementally change from vector active space frame structure to surface-active structural folded system within one assembly. This enables gradient porosity of the system which can be instrumentalized relative to environmental performance.

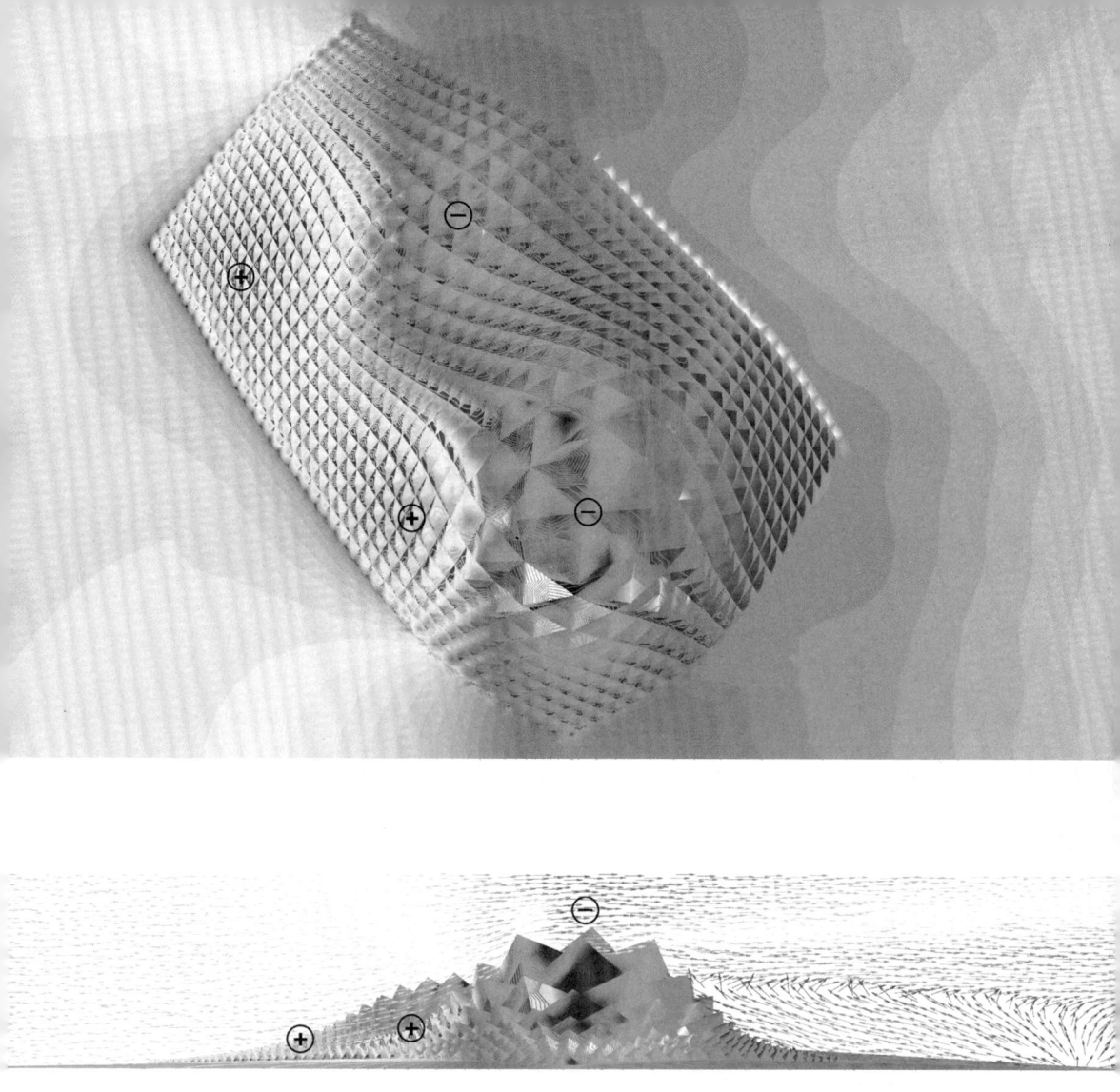

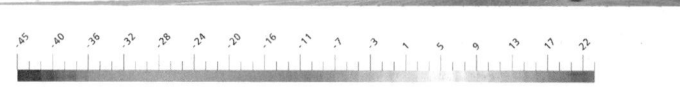

The regional and global articulation is derived through the aerodynamic behaviour of the system (top) tested in computer fluid dynamics. According to the particular modulation of high and low pressure zones in relation to prevailing wind directions the overall shape (bottom) is based on the project specific natural ventilation strategy.

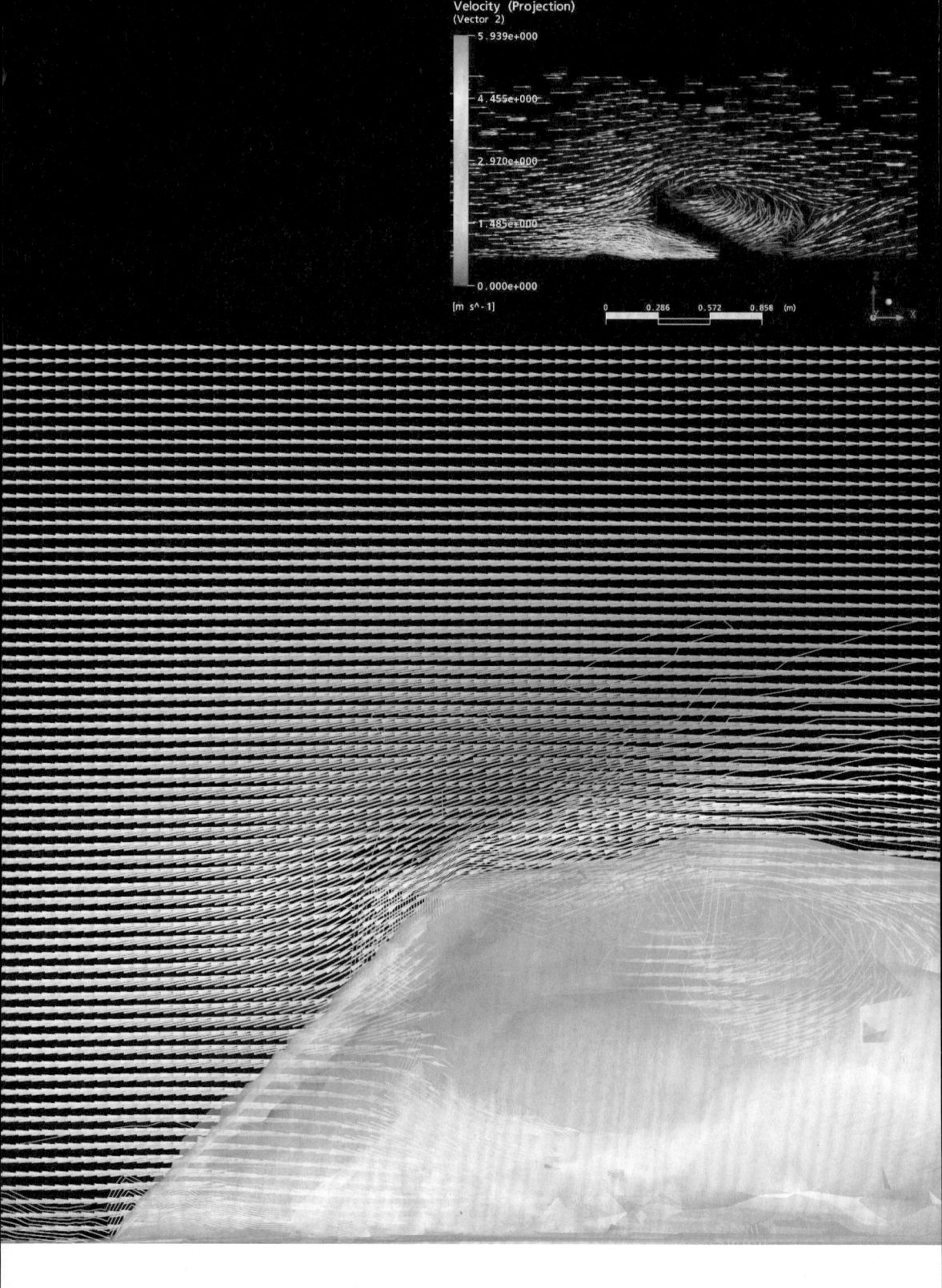

204 Through CFD (Computer Fluid Dynamics) modelling the performative capacity of the digital system prototype to modulate airflow was investigated (big image). Through the parametric differentiation of system porosity the strategic acceleration and deceleration of airflow can be achieved.

Tetrahedron_Porosity : Pressure

In combination with the analysis of the local component in terms of airflow velocity (small image left) and differential distribution of pressure zones (small image right) a comprehensive dataset for further evolutionary steps of the system can be established.

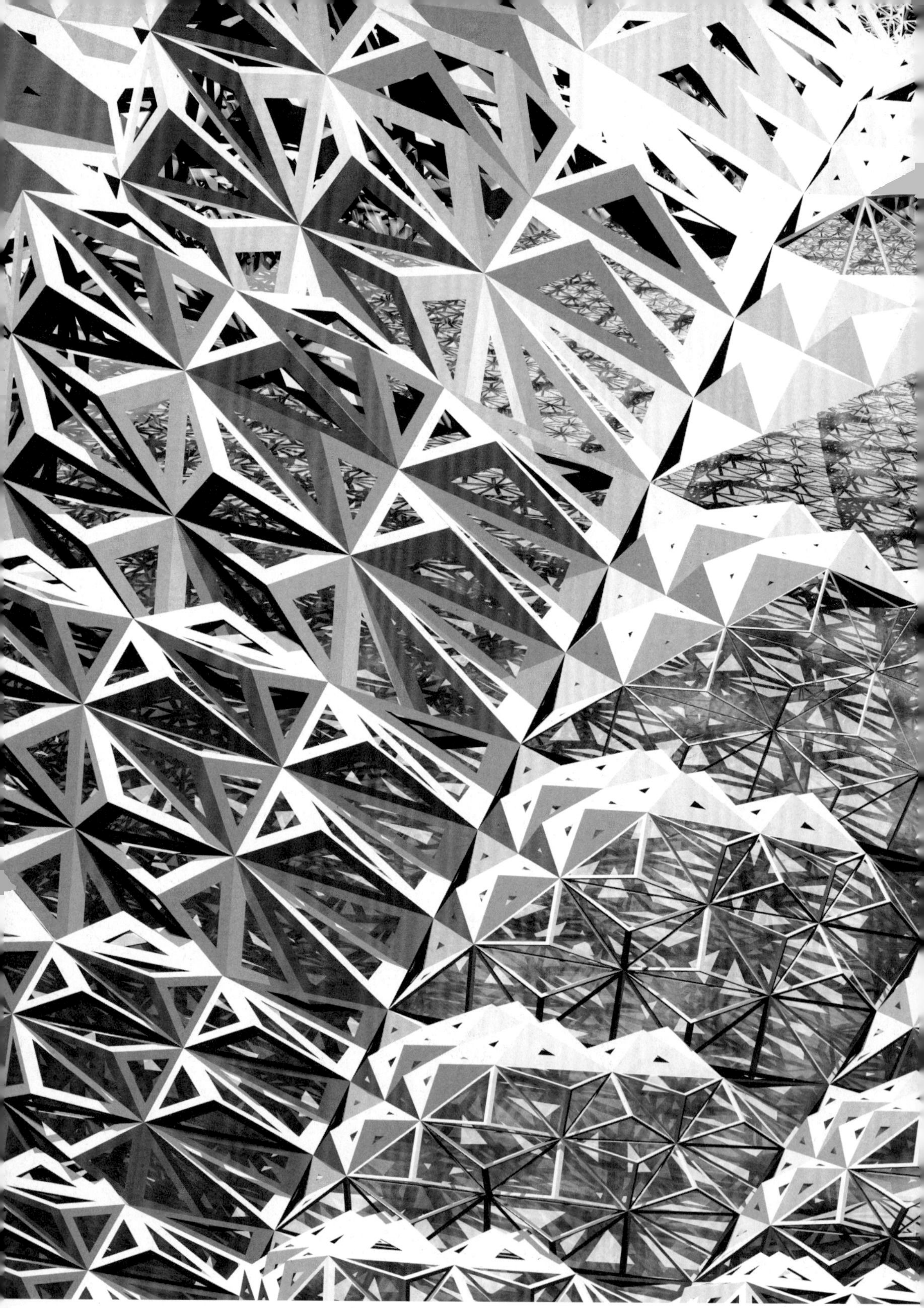

The development of a system specific to a particular performance context was defined through scripting an associative modelling setup informed by critical performative criteria. The resultant morphology responds to structural and environmental criteria through a gradient transition from a space frame to a folded system with different degrees of porosity.

In architecture the relation between surface and water is often considered as conflicting. One is fixed, the other fluid and dynamic; one provides protection, the other is something we need protecting from. This perhaps explains why the strategic use of water as a mediator of luminous and climatic conditions remains largely unexplored, despite its natural abundance. As a counterbalance, this research aims to explore the intricate relationship between these two material systems, and their interrelated behaviour.

Water has a fluid and temporal character, and its tendency to flow or to stagnate is informed by the geometry of its host surface – in this instance a second material system defined as strategically manipulated fabrics. The internal arrangement of the fabrics, as woven assemblies of fibres, means that they are able to self-organise as particular fold formations in relation to local manipulations with a high capacity for geometrical and topological differentiation.

A fold on a piece of fabric can be defined as a set of parameters of displacement in relation to geometric features such as height, length and orientation. Specific results are achieved by displacing strategic points on the surface, creating folds as a result of the self-organising tendencies of the fabric. Furthermore, the treatment of the fold itself produces two categories of formal effects: one where it remains standing, the projected fold, and another flat fold where the fabric is forced back onto itself. A first set of experiments focused on the manipulation of these different types of systematic folding. Physical models were made to study the geometry of the different smock, tuck and pleat types in order to devise digital models. Eventually pleating was chosen for further development. Pleats are measured folds that are formed at the perimeter of a sheet of fabric. They are usually fixed by means of stitching. Pleat folds are either flat or projected. They can either be unconfined, running continuously all the way through a sheet of fabric, or they can be bound between two or more stitches.

Physical and digital modelling was used to

establish the geometric logic and parametric set-up of modelling pleats. Associative modelling then made it possible to populate complex double-curved surfaces with flat and projected pleats. Establishing a parametrically controlled set of manipulations of woven systems not only provided a design tool for a wide range of fold morphologies but also modified the structural properties of fabric surfaces. For example, as a surface is repeatedly folded it develops three-dimensional curvature which can be interpreted as an increase in its depth and therefore an enhancement of its load-bearing capacity. At this stage a structural and an environmental hypothesis was formulated in order to direct the research.

The structural hypothesis was two-fold: [i] when the pleated fabric is hardened through the application of a binding matrix, the increased cross-sectional height of the pleat will act as the equivalent of the structurally active height of a beam; [ii] due to the presence of the pleats the fabric sheet does not require 100% surface contact with a mould during the application of resin; the mould can therefore be reduced to a much lesser degree of support.

The environmental hypothesis stated that the combination of surface curvature and pleats makes it possible to collect, channel and store water strategically on the surface. This provides differential thermal mass and, in combination with airflow, a natural means of cooling that can operate without additional mechanical ventilation and cooling devices, much like traditional methods.

The structural hypothesis was corroborated through physical models and digital Finite Element method, which established the required pleat configuration and structural depth of the surface in each region relative to the load applied. This included the relationship of self-weight and span as well as additional loading through stored water. The structural logic had to be complemented with a strategy to run off excess water, so as not to stretch the system beyond its load-bearing limit or desired environmental performance range.

The manufacturing approach focused on the reduction of the mould relative to the pleating of fibreglass mats, as well as the application of resin to derive a structurally sound composite. Loading tests were executed on the physical models to establish the relation between layering of fibreglass and pleat density and depth.

Subsequently regional surface curvature and local pleat distribution and articulation were examined for their capacity to distribute and store water, acting as a thermal mass depending on parameters such as depth, volume and flow, which regulate the absorption and release of heat over a specified time. Together with the overall surface curvature, the pleat depth is instrumental in this process. Water is collected in areas exposed to airflow both for cooling purposes and to provide a heat sink. Water is also used as a resource and collected or flushed out to define areas of either dry or wet ground. Furthermore water is considered as a modulator of other environmental dynamics. For example, it can interact with light either as reflective or absorbent surface depending on a series of parameters such as depth and speed of flow, producing a range of performative effects from direct and reflected to diffused lighting conditions.

The capacity for using water in this way is particularly useful in areas that are generally arid but subject to short torrential downpours. In such instances the water might not always be fully exposed, but could flow between layers of pleated composite, or change between interior and exterior in order to achieve the desired environmental performance.

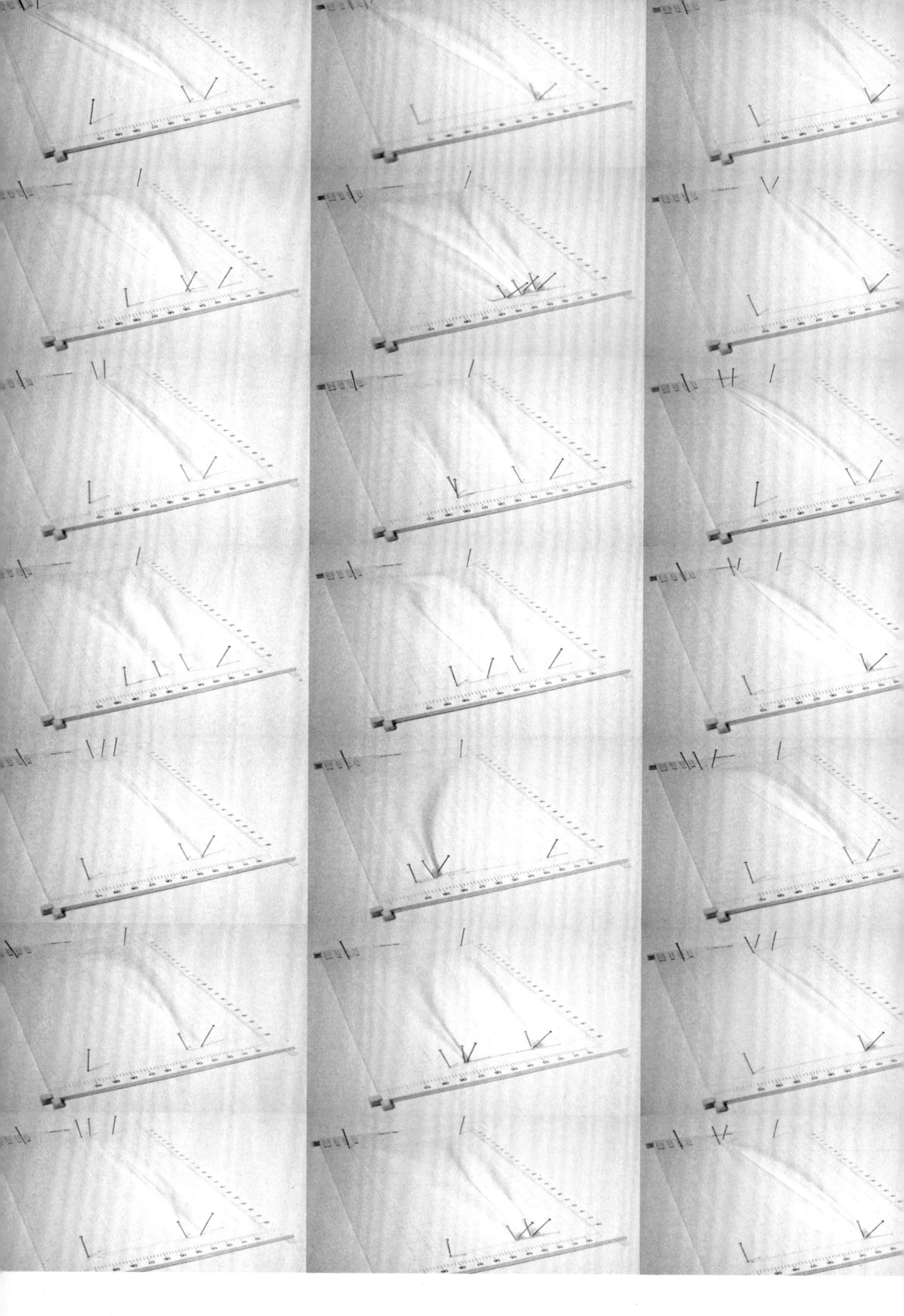

210 Axonometric (left) and planar view (right) show initial physical experiments conducted with a patch of cotton fabric supported on a solid independent flat plane. The strategic displacement of points is always introduced on the periphery of the surface and recorded in an x y coordinate system. On the base of a larger number of tests the characteristic three-dimensional geometries

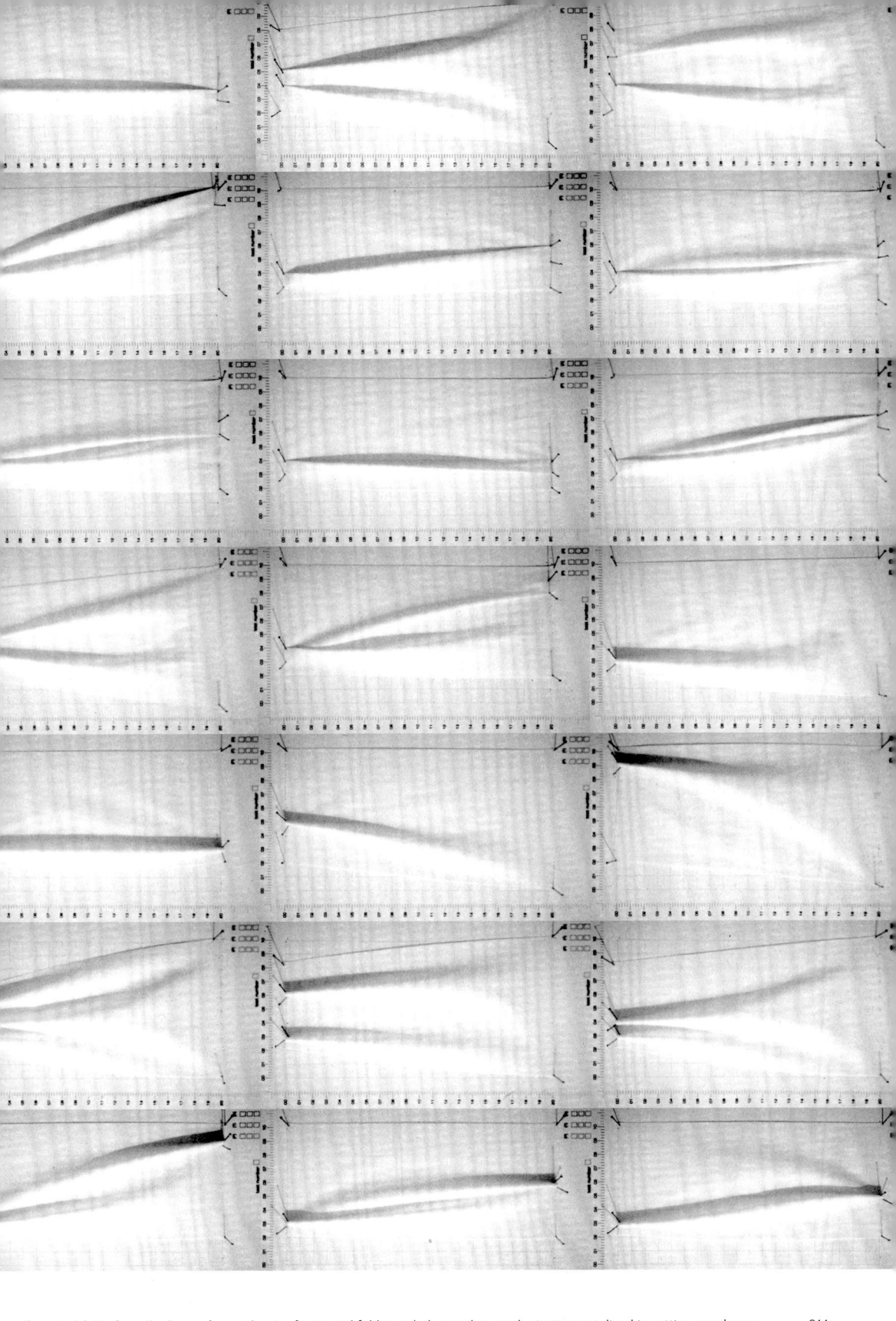

of created folds form the base of a catalogue of potential fold morphologies that can be instrumentalised in setting up a larger system. The experiments aim at recording formal tendencies and patterns of the self-organising capacity of fabric rather than precise metric data.

Projected Fold

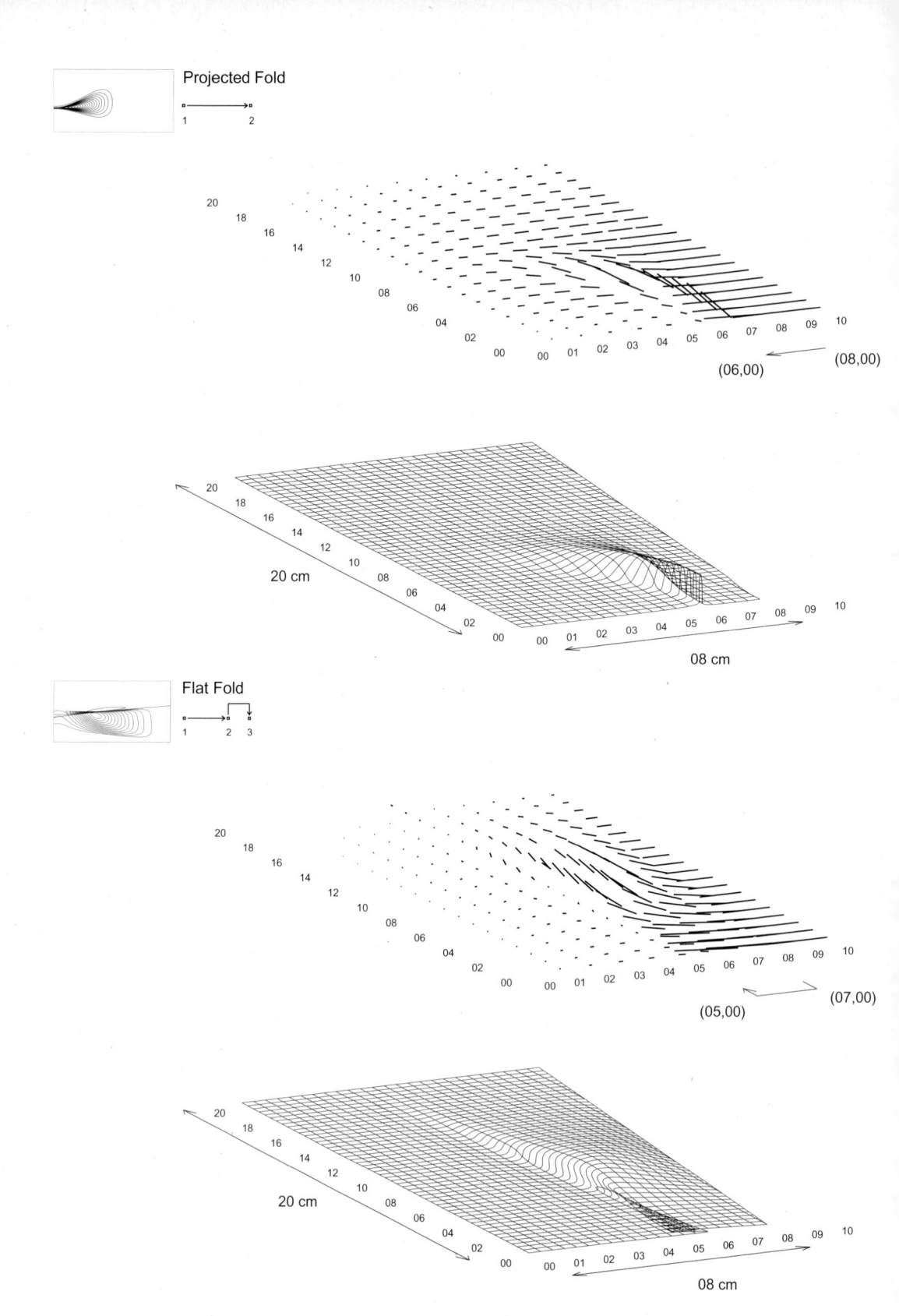

Flat Fold

212　　In order to establish a base for a parametric tool, two types of folds are generated through the fabric displacement and subsequently digitised. They are defined as the projected fold, consisting of two stitched together and the flat fold if the profile is stitched flat back on the fabric.

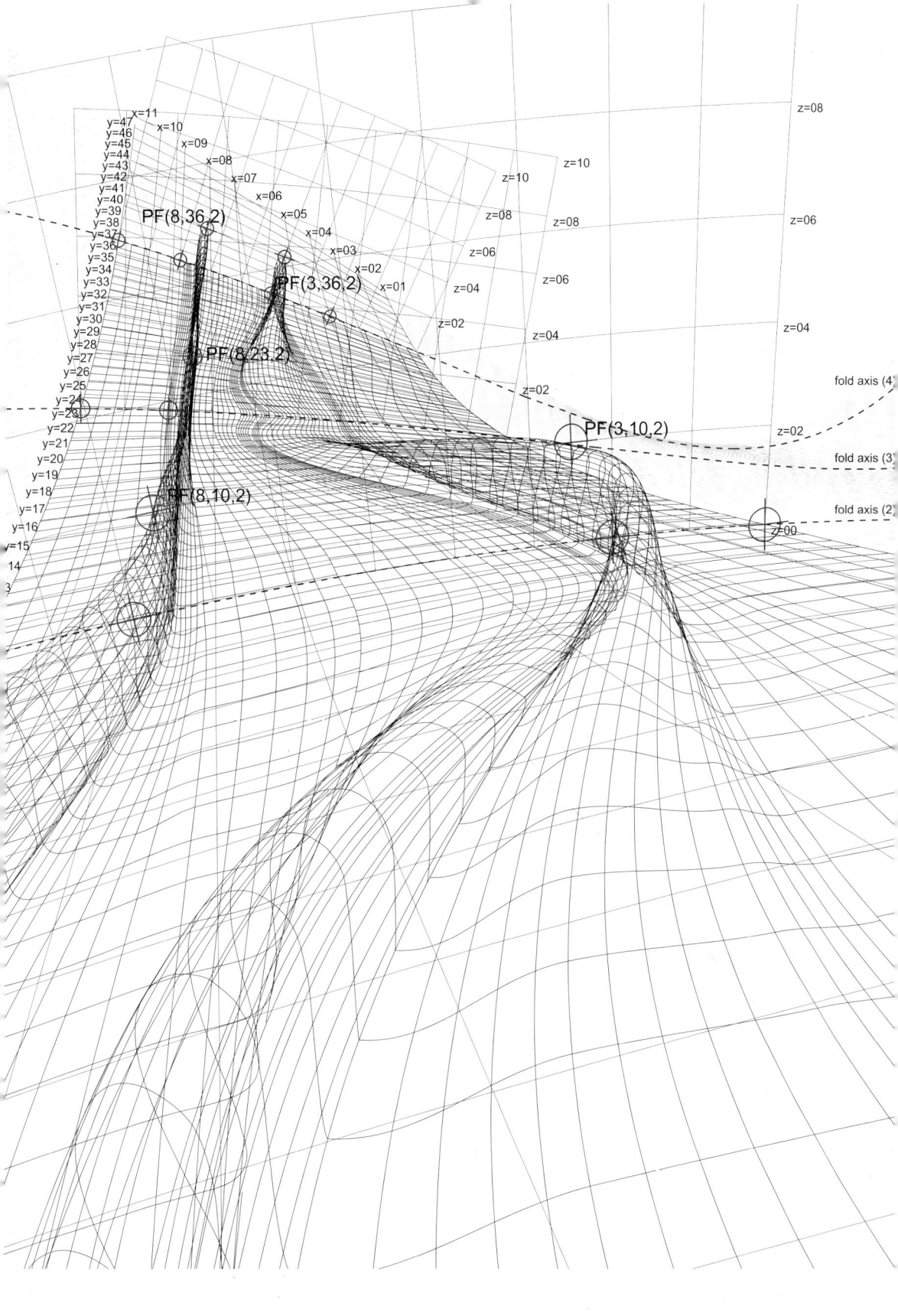

A parametric tool is developed that enables the local, regional and global manipulations of a folded system. This allows for generating continuous folds defined by a host surface from which the critical local coordinate systems for strategic fabric displacements are derived.

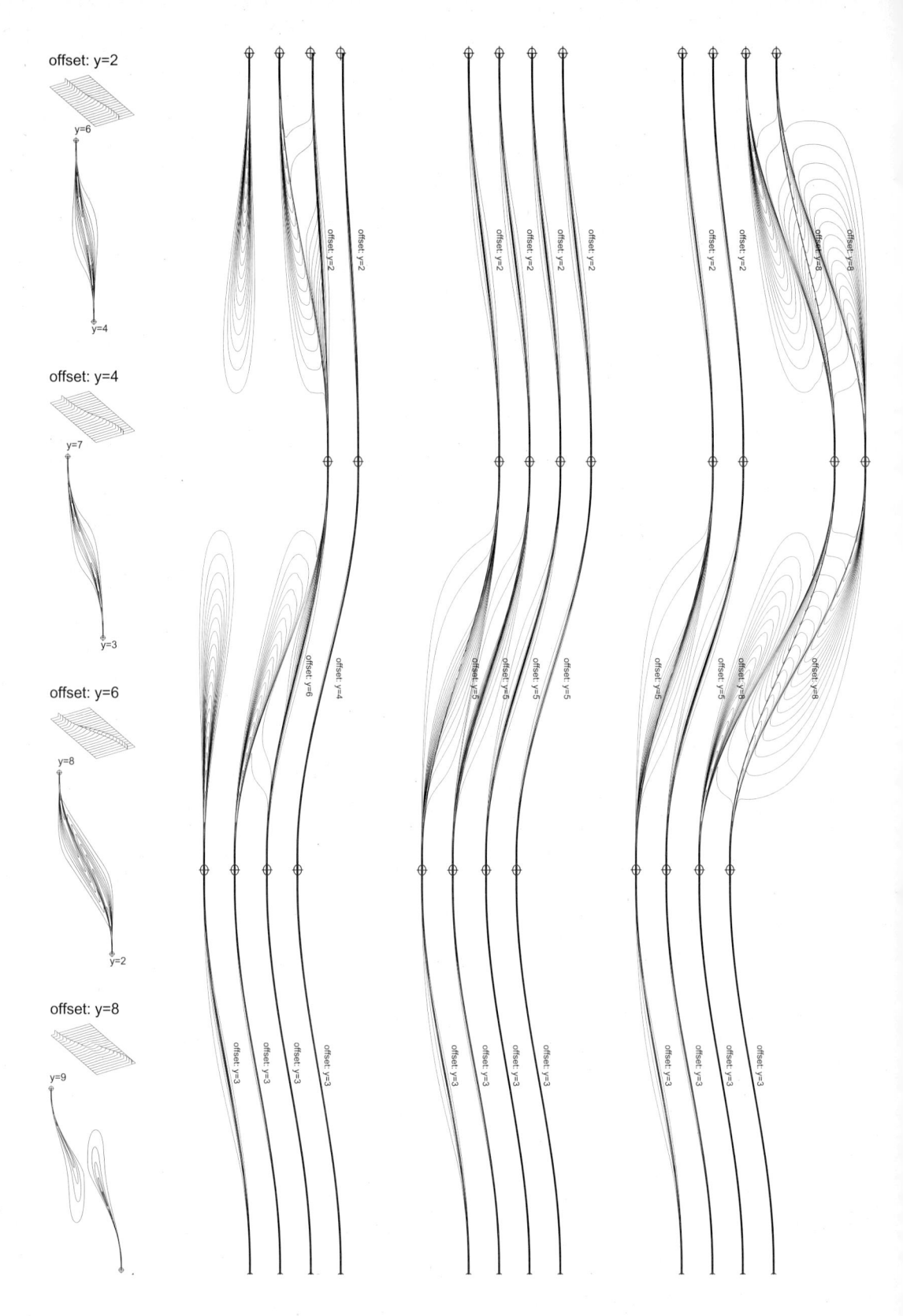

214　　　The self-organisation capacities of the fabric suggest different levels of potential continuity of the folds depending on the lateral offset between the displacement points. These morphological effects can be instrumentalised to create channel bifurcations and divisions for a water management system on the folded surface.

Strip formation

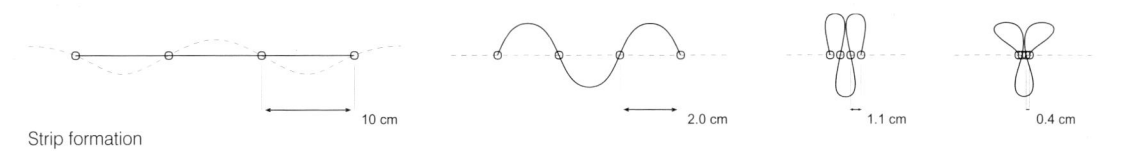

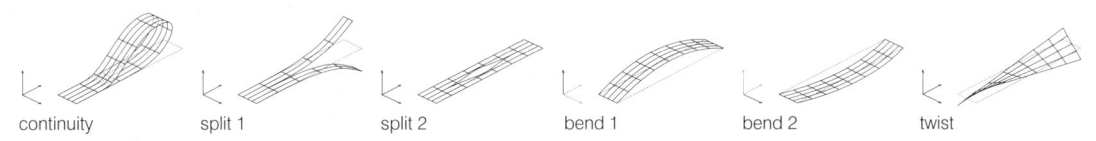

10 cm 2.0 cm 1.1 cm 0.4 cm

continuity split 1 split 2 bend 1 bend 2 twist

Topological and geometrical manipulations

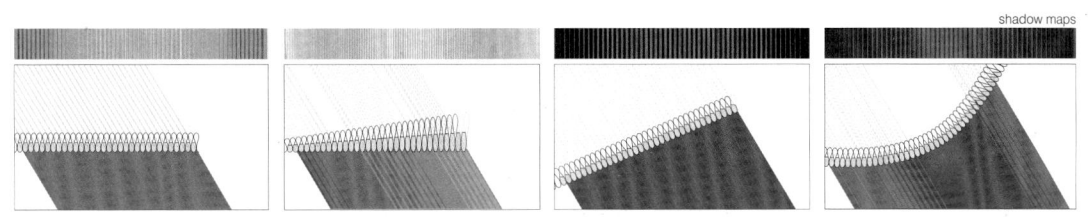

shadow maps

Effects of global geometrical transformation on water collection and light modulation

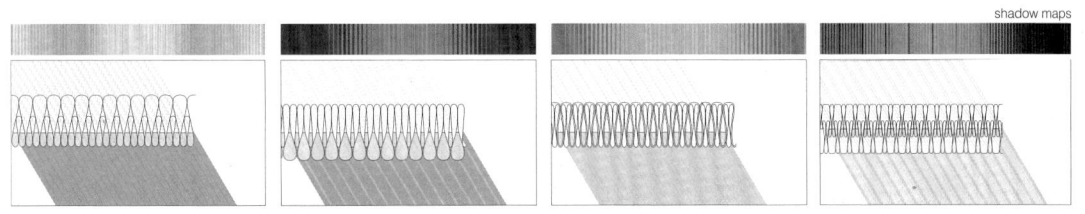

shadow maps

Effects of local geometrical transformation on water collection and light modulation

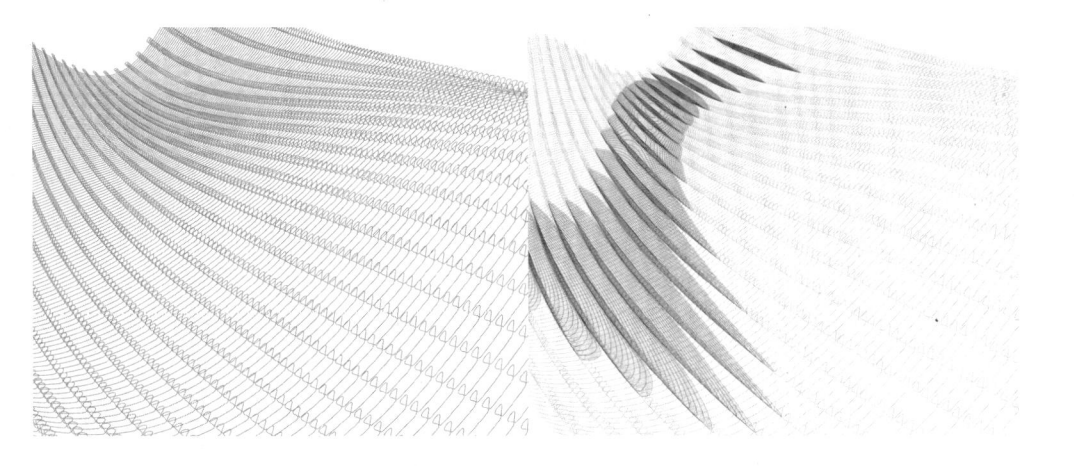

The possible manipulation of fold morphologies enables the integration of the control of rainwater along the surface. Water flows can be accelerated, decelerated or collected, and therefore serve as an environmental modulator to control light and thermal conditions through the strategic distribution of thermal mass and different degrees of light reflection and refraction.

216   The development of a parametric technique enables the transfer of digital geometric data onto a larger physical fabric system through the notation of strategic displacement and connection points. Here the folds do not result from individual displacements but from a collective displacement induced through a continuous string.

Instead of relying on a mould, the manufacturing of the system employs the self-organisational capacity of glass-fibre fabric to form a system of a series of projected folds (top) that can be arranged on a larger formwork and subsequently hardened through the application of resin in order to form a structurally stable system (bottom).

Three main geometries can be identified within all membrane structures: the hyperbolic paraboloid, an anticlastic surface geometry also known as a hypar; the barrel; and the conoid. The research began by investigating these basic membrane morphologies through physical and digital form-finding experiments, as the first step in establishing a complex and vast assembly from an articulated membrane component.

Membranes are form-active tension systems. Their form relates directly to the distribution of tension relative to the location and displacement of boundary points or edges. The displacement of two boundary points on a four-sided elastic membrane may create a hypar, for example. In initial experiments the investigation focused on establishing three-dimensional arrays of hypars as a starting point for developing ways of proliferating a simple membrane component. These experiments indicated that when hypars were organised and interconnected in several layers, the centre layer of hypars tended to flatten out due to the related flow of forces. Consequently the articulation of the membrane component was altered through the introduction of a fifth control point at the centre of the membrane patch, resulting in a hybrid of hypar and cone. This fifth control point serves to maintain sufficient curvature in a larger assembly of membrane elements.

One of the primary aims was to achieve an independent membrane assembly that does not rely on an external framework providing anchor points for pre-tensioning. Instead of a rigid external framework, a strategy of embedding elements with compressive strength in the multi-component membrane array was developed. Initial tests investigated the possibility of selectively applying resin on connected membrane components, so that these elements could begin to bear compressive forces. However, the compressive strength of the resultant embedded framework proved difficult to calibrate with the tension forces of the remaining elastic components.

After a further set of experiments a new strategy was devised, based on an initially tensile macro-structure of a wire mesh fabricated from tubular elements with compressive loading capacity; the tubes could be fixed in particular form-found configurations to provide the framework for a population of elastic membrane components.

An additional strategy for stabilising the system utilised two interacting elastic membrane components offset through the introduction of distributed compression masts followed by a partial application of resin. Through this, a two-fold strategy for the treatment of elastic membranes within the macro-net could be established. The membranes can remain elastic if the larger framework is set in a specific configuration through fixed joints between mesh members: maintaining the elasticity in the secondary membrane components allows for subsequent reconfigurations of the resulting space. Another possibility is to apply to the elastic membrane a hardening matrix into which tertiary, reconfigurable elements are integrated.

The final approach was to switch the structural performance of the membranes and the net locally. The membrane assembly can either be in tension or in compression when hardened with resin, while the net can change from bearing tension forces to compression forces when the joints are fixed. By adapting the distribution and articulation of elements locally, structural performance can be varied across the system in response to changing spatial requirements or environmental conditions.

To facilitate the digital modelling in an associative modelling environment a dynamic relaxation function was embedded in the software – a process made possible thanks to the collaboration of Chris Williams and Lisa Matthews at Bath University.

As a result, it was no longer necessary to switch between software packages and much more complex assemblies could be achieved in a much shorter time.

The key features of a larger assembly include the layering of membrane elements and the overall porosity of the system. Any opportunistic utilisation of the system for spatial arrangements and environmental performance must be based on these characteristics. The environmental performance of the system was initially investigated on the basis of the three basic geometries: hypar, conoid and barrel. Two criteria were chosen: airflow and light modulation. Airflow tests were mainly conducted on physical models, as digital software packages are presently limited in their ability to import such highly differentiated and complex geometries. The studies could therefore only focus on smaller regions of the overall assembly. Here the development of appropriate methods and tools must go hand in hand with further studies of the system.

Light modulation, by contrast, was much more easily studied. Physical tests could be conducted to analyse elements and smaller regions of an assembly, while digital analysis could reveal the capacity of an overall assembly to cast shadow, to modulate illuminance and luminous flow. The repercussions of such modulation in a specific context are highlighted by the Inclusive Edge project in the Favela do Pilar in Bairro do Recife, in which the author of this research collaborated.

While membranes ultimately constitute the most reduced material threshold in living nature they nevertheless succinctly divide an inside from an outside, as can be seen with cell walls. In doing so, biological membranes perform intelligent filtering of substances and information across their threshold. The developed membrane assembly is in some respects different, as it does not clearly divide an inside from an outside, but rather provides for a smooth spatial transition between degrees of enclosure and exposure. Compared to the hard threshold, this offers more choice in the arrangement of spaces and ways of communicating between them. In addition, due to its modulated porosity the membrane assembly can perform an intelligent filtering and modulation of environmental conditions. In doing so, this system synthesises material and environmental threshold conditions and enables their interrelated variability.

AA Diploma Honours 2006

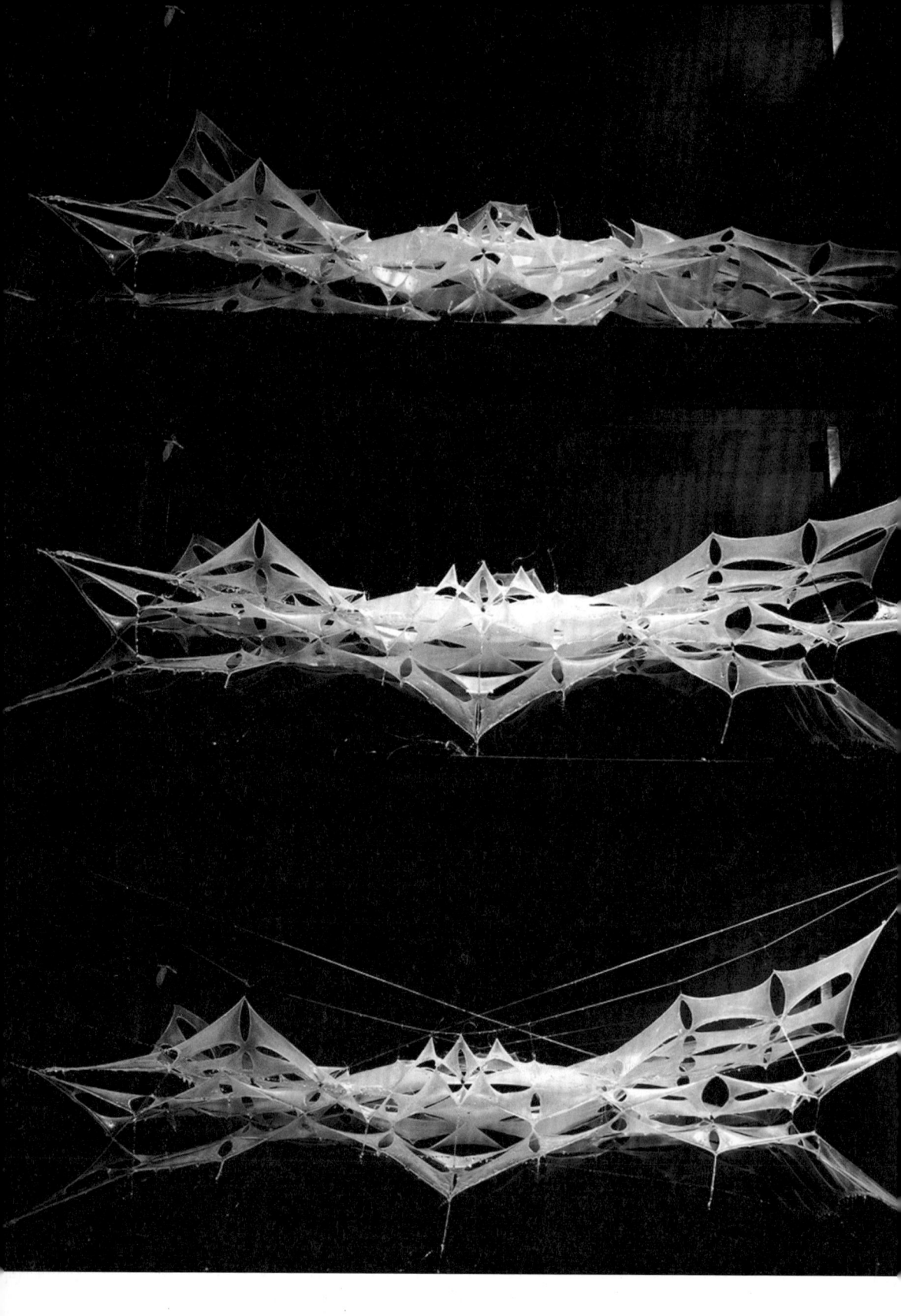

220 In order to develop a strategy of embedding elements with compressive strength in three-dimensional arrays of hypars (bottom) initial tests investigated the possibility of applying resin on connected membrane components (centre). However, the compressive strength proved difficult to calibrate with the remaining tension and gravitational forces leading to the collapse of the model (top).

Hypars organised and interconnected in several layers tend to flatten in the centre layers due to the related tensional forces. Consequently the articulation of the membrane component was altered through the introduction of a fifth control point at the centre of the membrane patch, resulting in local hybrids of hypar and cone morphology.

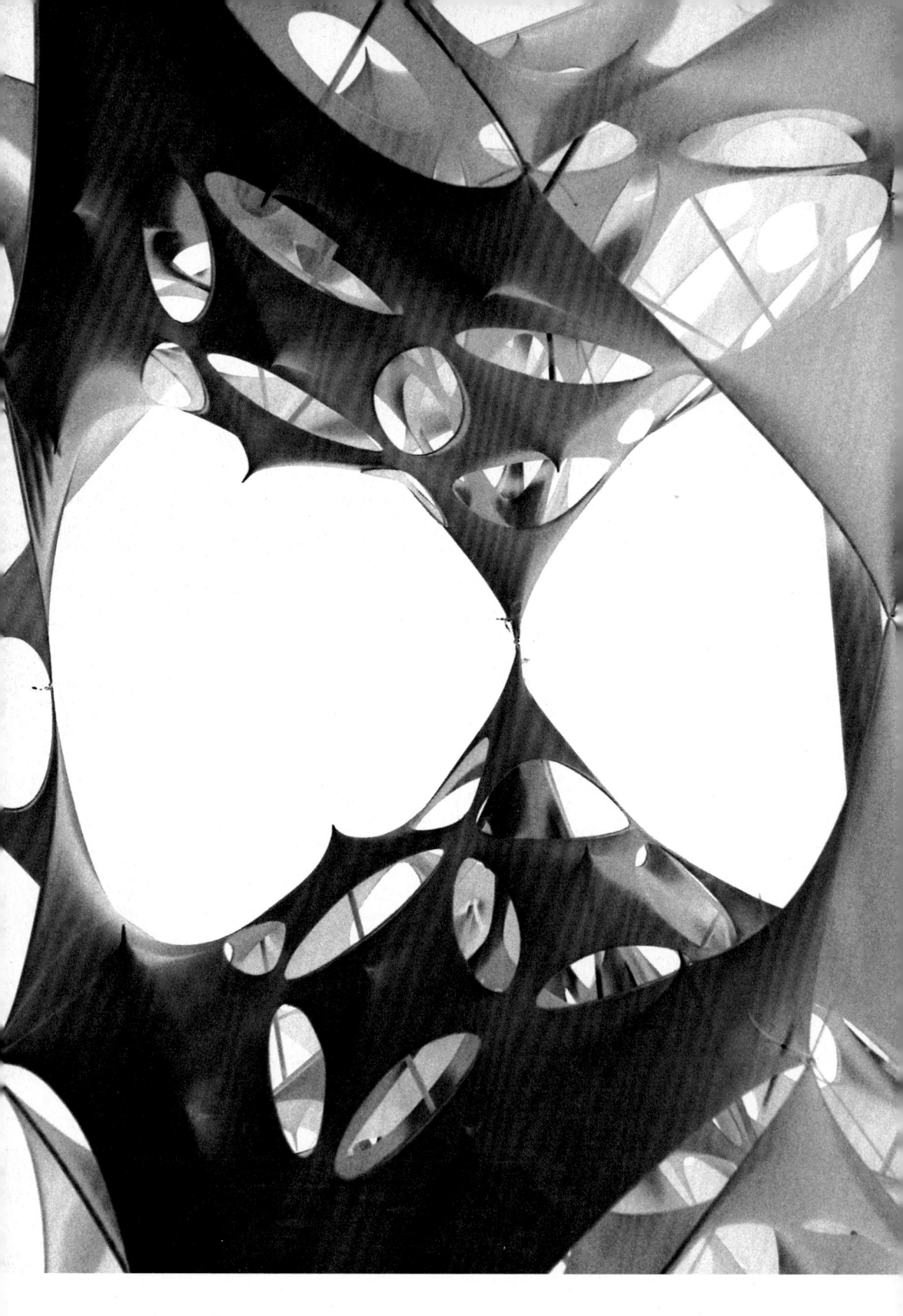

222 Further manipulations aimed at locally stabilising the proliferated membrane system included the introduction of local compressive elements.

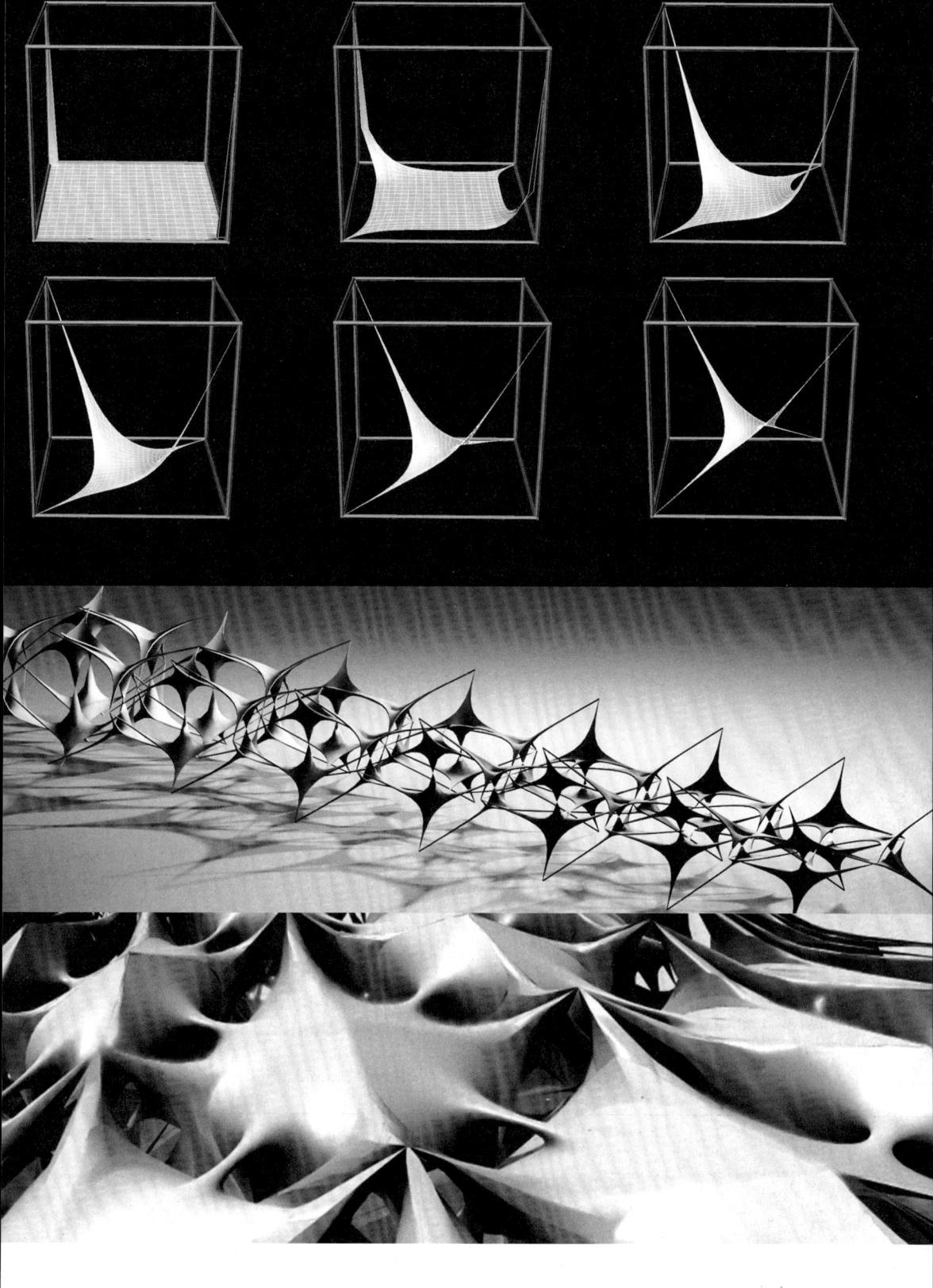

The digital development of membrane morphologies is based on processes of computational form finding. Digitally defined meshes settle into an equilibrium state through iterative re-calculations (top: illustrated in 6 steps). Digital form-finding processes embedded in a parametric design tool enable the simulation of material behaviour for complex membrane morphologies (bottom).

An initial proliferation test indicates the adaption of each dynamically relaxed component within a larger parametric framework defined in an associative modelling application.

226 The parametric framework enables the rapid generation and evaluation of various local (bottom) and overall (top) system configurations exploring varying degrees of porosity and enclosure.

The macro-structure providing for subsequent processes of component proliferation is based on an initially tensile net of a wire mesh fabricated from tubular elements with compressive loading capacity. The macro-structural tubes were fixed in particular form-found configurations to provide the framework for a population of elastic membrane components.

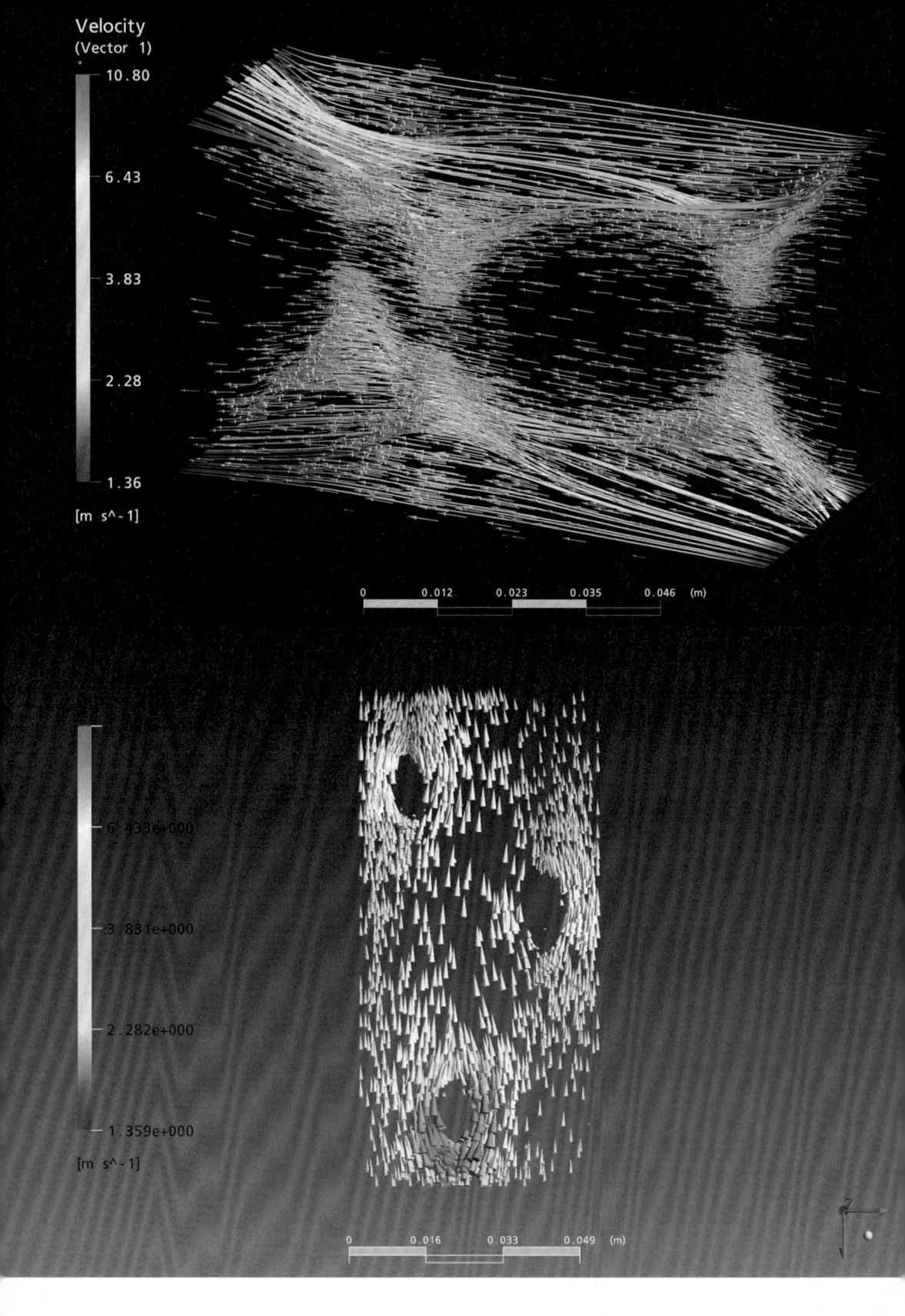

228 Computer Fluid Dynamics were used to analyse the performative effects of local and regional membrane morphologies on airflow. The system's capacity to accelerate/decelerate flow and to distribute differential pressure could be instrumentalised for the context-specific articulation.

A full-scale prototype was constructed in order to test the integral design strategy of negotiating structural and environmental performances through the parametric definition of the membrane system.

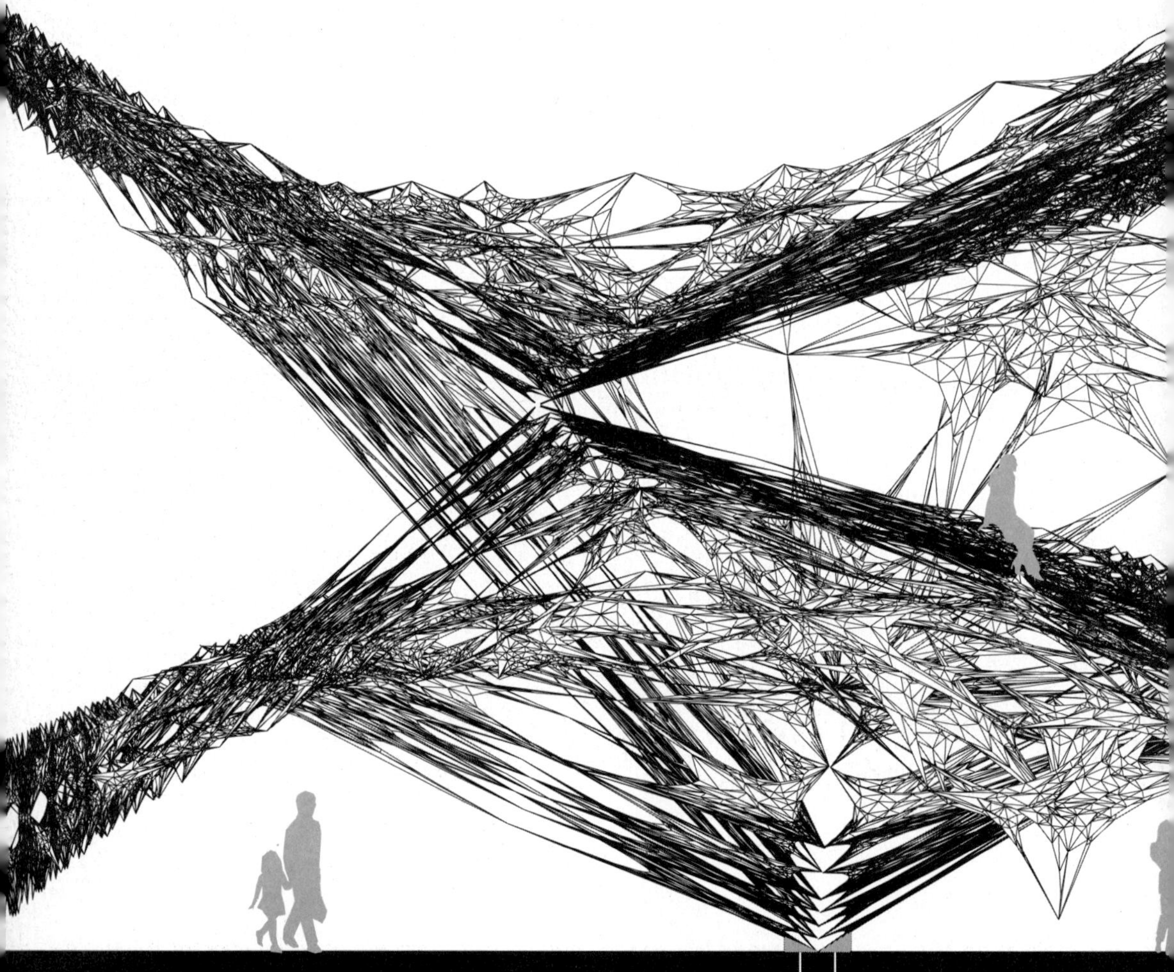

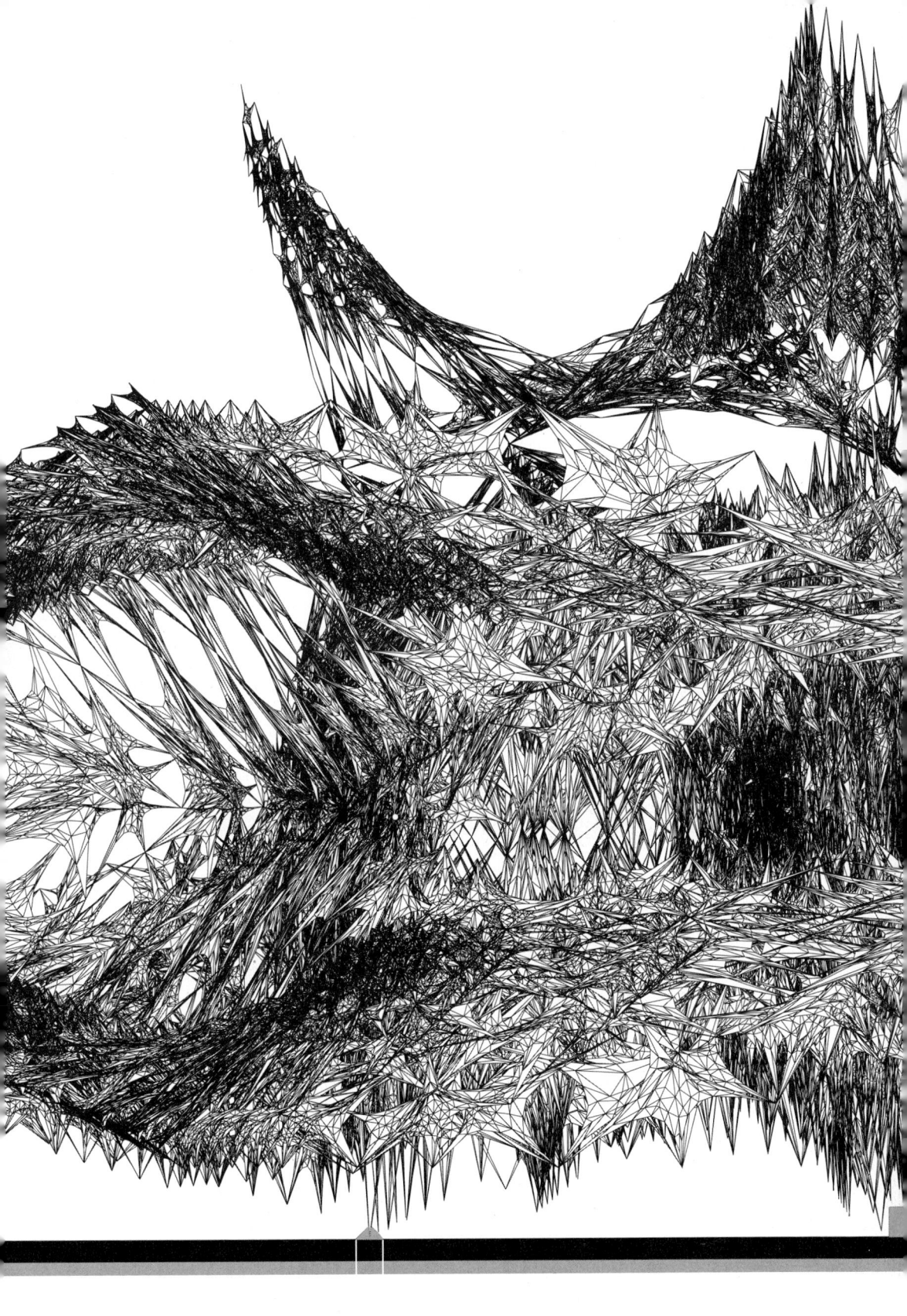

The context specific articulation of the membrane system is based on a parametric model that drives the digital form finding processes of all local membrane patches. The particular membrane configuration shown here without the supporting macro mesh resulted from the local regional and global negotiation of spatial criteria and structural as well as environmental performance.

HANI FALLAHA 2003 - 2004

The focus of this project is the creation of rapidly deployable refugee shelters for the Middle East, where political, social and religious conflicts frequently result in the displacement and forced migration of large numbers of people. The shelter types typically provided by aid organisations take little account of the often extreme weather conditions in the region. Nor do they meet the basic demographic and cultural requirements of those being housed. The average family size in the Middle East exceeds six; the standard shelter has a maximum capacity of four to five, and its design ignores the fact that tradition dictates a clear separation between male and female living spaces. Valuable resources are thus routinely wasted, with camps being inefficiently occupied.

The project tackles these problems by means of a low-tech pneumatic shelter system that makes use of the natural abundance of sand in the region. An exploration of various strategies for deploying specific characteristics of pneumatic membranes in relation to the climatic context was informed by issues of environmental control, privacy and the often-overlooked fact that short-term emergency shelters tend to become permanent. Camp organisation was investigated in terms of shelter size, distribution and orientation.

Because of their non-linear properties, differential material capacities and multiple states of stability, pneumatic systems are well suited to the construction of highly articulated structures that are transparent, lightweight and rapidly deployable. To develop a design that would suit the shelter typology, the project explored pneumatic systems on three scales: single cushion, group of cushions, and overall assembly of a shelter unit. A range of structurally self-supporting surfaces is created by three different cushion types: elongation cushion, angle-change cushion, and adjustable bifurcated cushion. Each of these components is also informed by the way its shape changes according to its level of inflation, in terms of length and angle and degree of curvature. Larger assemblies examined how cushions needed to be positioned, rotated and then connected in order to create a surface curvature that provides for structural capacity.

A strategy was devised to utilise sand – the sole readily available local building material – to deliver additional performance capacity to the system. The sectional differentiation of the pneumatic shelters is based on aerodynamics, modulating airflow and creating zones of pressure differential to remove sand from or deliver it to specified areas of the system, so as to stabilise it and modulate the light and temperature conditions of the interior. Small pockets welded into the leading edges of cushions face the direction of airflow and collect sand to increase the overall weight of the structure and the thermal mass of the shelter. The distribution pattern of the sand-collectors on these cushions contributes to the modulation of solar penetration and visual exposure. Angle-change cushions can be deployed at regular intervals to enable the users to control ventilation and access.

Inflation and repair strategies were examined, too. The pneumatic surface was designed to contain overall and local inflation points. A one-way valve connects each cushion to the next, starting from a given section's overall inflation point. The placement of valves throughout the surface minimises the impact of damage to any single cushion by limiting deflation to the directly affected area.

The shelter's incorporation into a settlement strategy is a vital aspect of successfully resettling refugees. After careful analysis of common camp layout strategies, the project outlined five basic criteria for assessing and defining a specific camp layout: unit orientation, distance between units, access to services, social and cultural requirements, and degree of permanence of the settlement. Each parameter is investigated as part of the overall development of the shelter typology. For example, distance between units takes into account factors such as sand saltation (the properties of sand movement) and secondary surface overflow (how far windblown sand will carry past an obstacle), to arrive at an optimum shelter distance equal to one half the height of the shelter.

A crucial aspect of the system was to allow for shelter extension or subdivision, a reflection of the reality that camp populations vary, sometimes dramatically, over time. The shelter unit allows for subdivision into various separate spaces while maintaining the minimum required space for a family to live in. Thus, if the camp's occupancy is below its maximum capacity, the extra space can be allocated to and divided among inhabitants within each unit, instead of spreading families over several units.

One of the concerns for refugee accommodation relates to the intended or emergent degree of permanence of a given shelter or encampment. There are many examples where canvas tents have over time been replaced by reinforced concrete structures. In response, the design directly incorporates the possibility to acquire a more solid material articulation if desired.

In certain parts of the structure pneumatic cushions can serve as ready-made forms for filling in sand or pouring in concrete. The initial geometric investigation resulted in the creation of a three-dimensional, structurally capable pneumatic system, and further testing revealed cushion forms that would not deform when filled with sand or concrete, allowing for the possibility of applications in roofs, facades and other structural components.

RIBA Silver Medal 2004
AA Diploma Honours 2004

Inflated Cushion

Structural Analysis

total length of seams : 149.7 cm
total surface area : 882.6 cm^2
total volume : 1302.0 cm^3

Structural Behavior:
bending resistance x axis:
bending Resistance y axis:
bending Resistance z axis:

length of member a: 30.0 cm
length Of member b: 30.0 cm
length of member c: 11.25 cm
length of member d: 14.0 cm

Cutting Pattern

13.25 cm
60.00 cm
30.81 cm
14.00 cm

Side view
(Inflated cushion)

Elongation

Angle change

Bifurcation

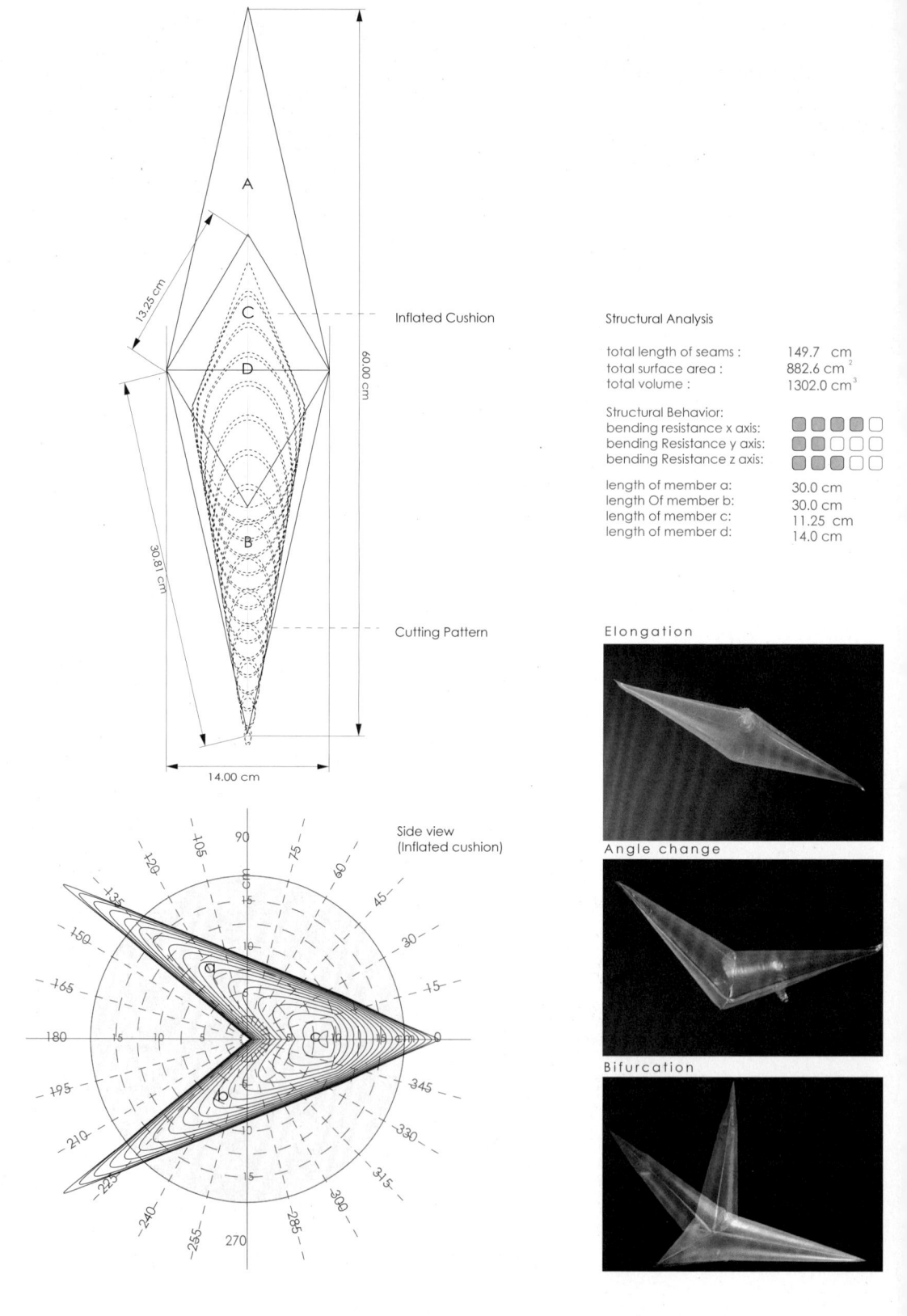

234   The project is based on three basic types of pneumatic cushion components: elongation, angle change and bifurcation components. Each cushion component is parametrically defined by a number of geometric relationships that embed critical pneu characteristics and derive the related cut pattern for each parametric instance.

secondary surface

secondary surface
connection points

primary chamber
diameter

primary chamber seams

primary and secondary
surfaces

diameter gradient of chambers

sectional exploded front view

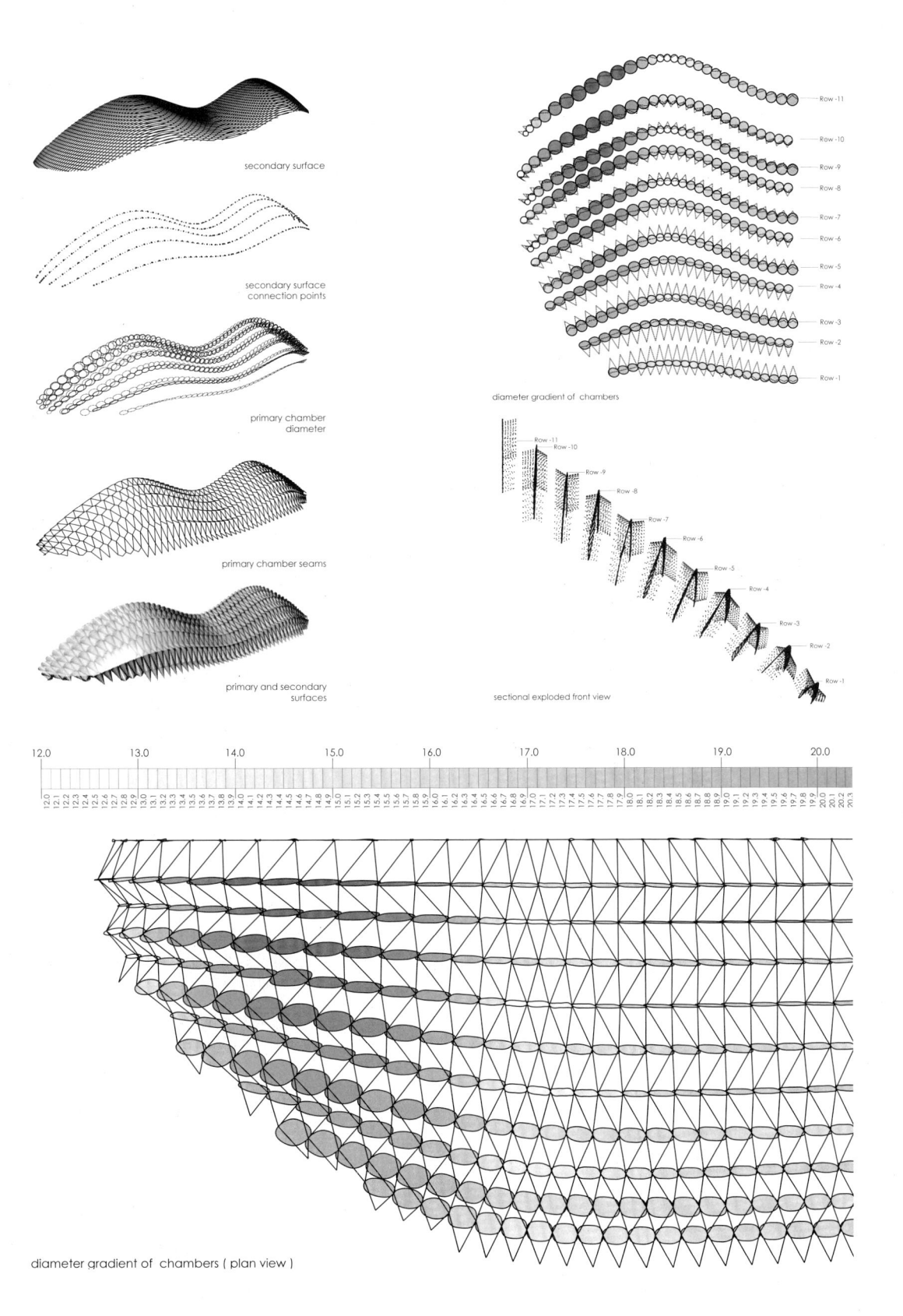

diameter gradient of chambers (plan view)

The overall system is articulated through a series of connected and parametrically defined primary chambers with varying diameter and volume and a secondary foil surface. The diameter of the pneumatic cushions defines the overall geometry of the system after inflation.

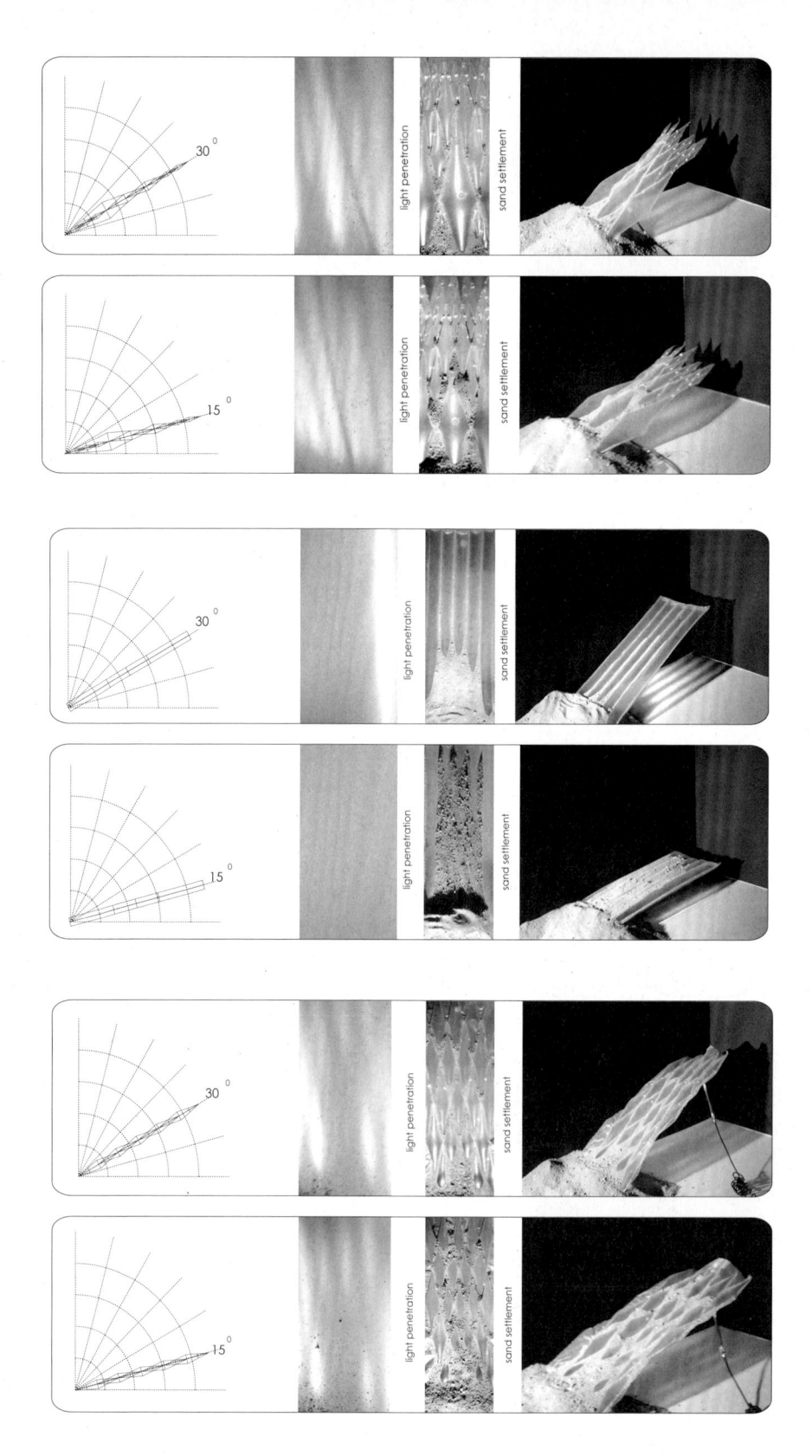

236 The system is designed to exploit the harsh conditions of arid deserts. Different cushion articulations allow for strategically exploiting sand settlement to stabilise the lightweight structure and to control the light and climatic conditions in the space below.

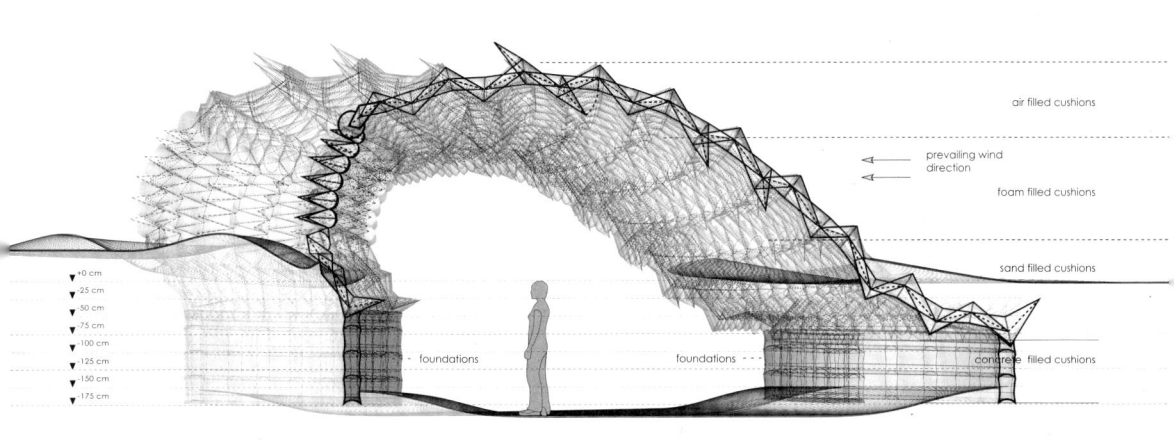

The section of the shelter considers the aerodynamic behaviour of the shelter in relation to prevailing wind directions. Furthermore the sectional articulation allows for increasing clear height of interior spaces during the transformation process from a temporary refugee camp to a more permanent settlement.

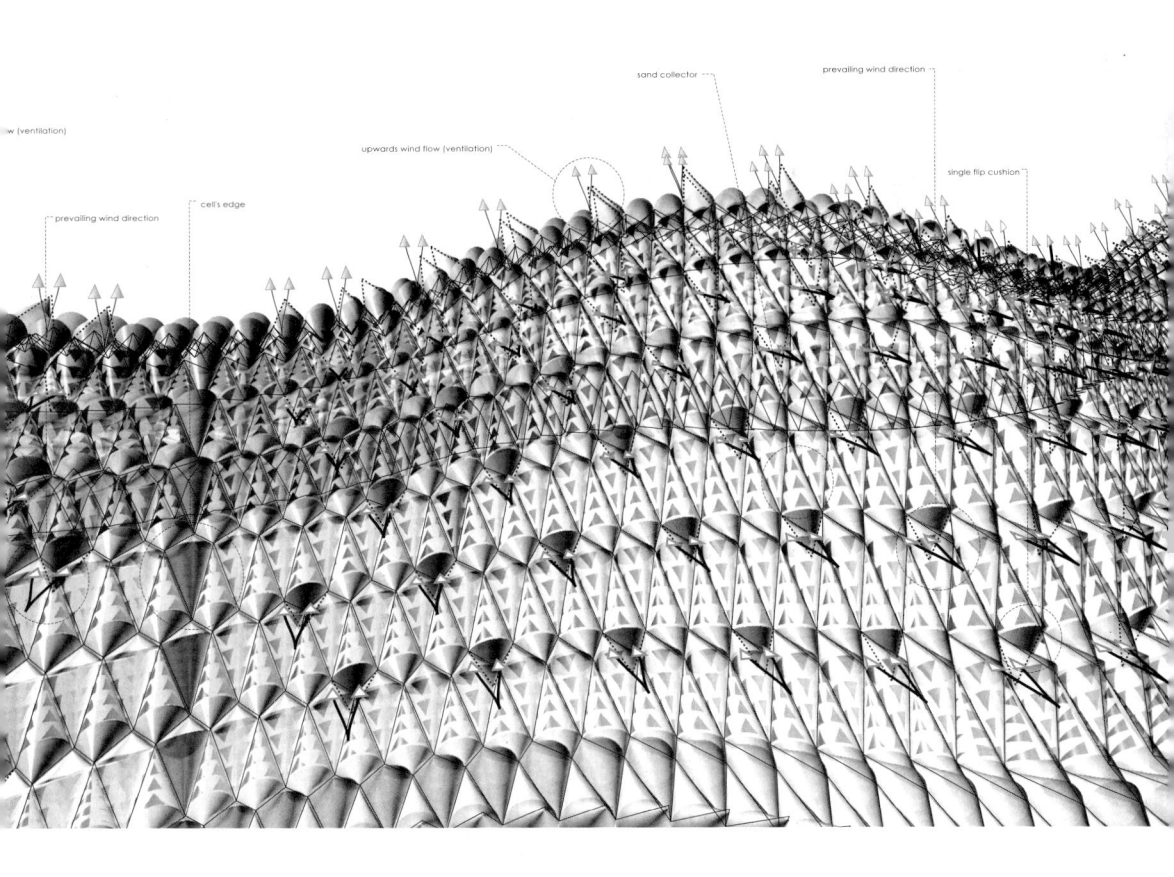

Triangular sand collectors welded on the outer cushion layers enhance the environmental performance and provide extra stability by increasing the overall weight and thermal mass of the shelter. The collector patterns allow for modulating solar penetration and degree of privacy as well as protecting the skin from sand storms.

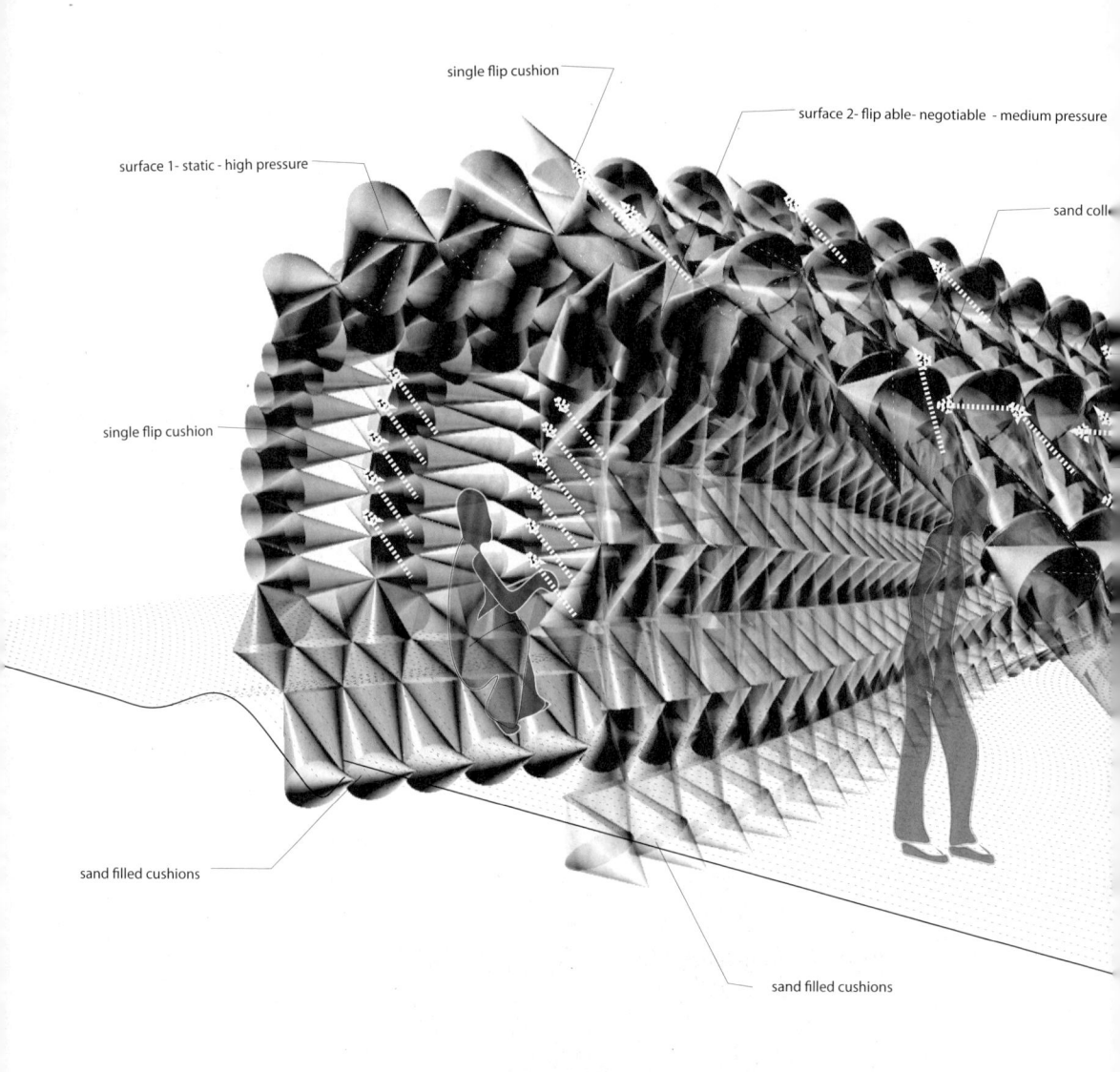

- surface 1 - static - high pressure
- single flip cushion
- surface 2 - flip able - negotiable - medium pressure
- sand coll[ection]
- single flip cushion
- sand filled cushions
- sand filled cushions

predominant wind direction

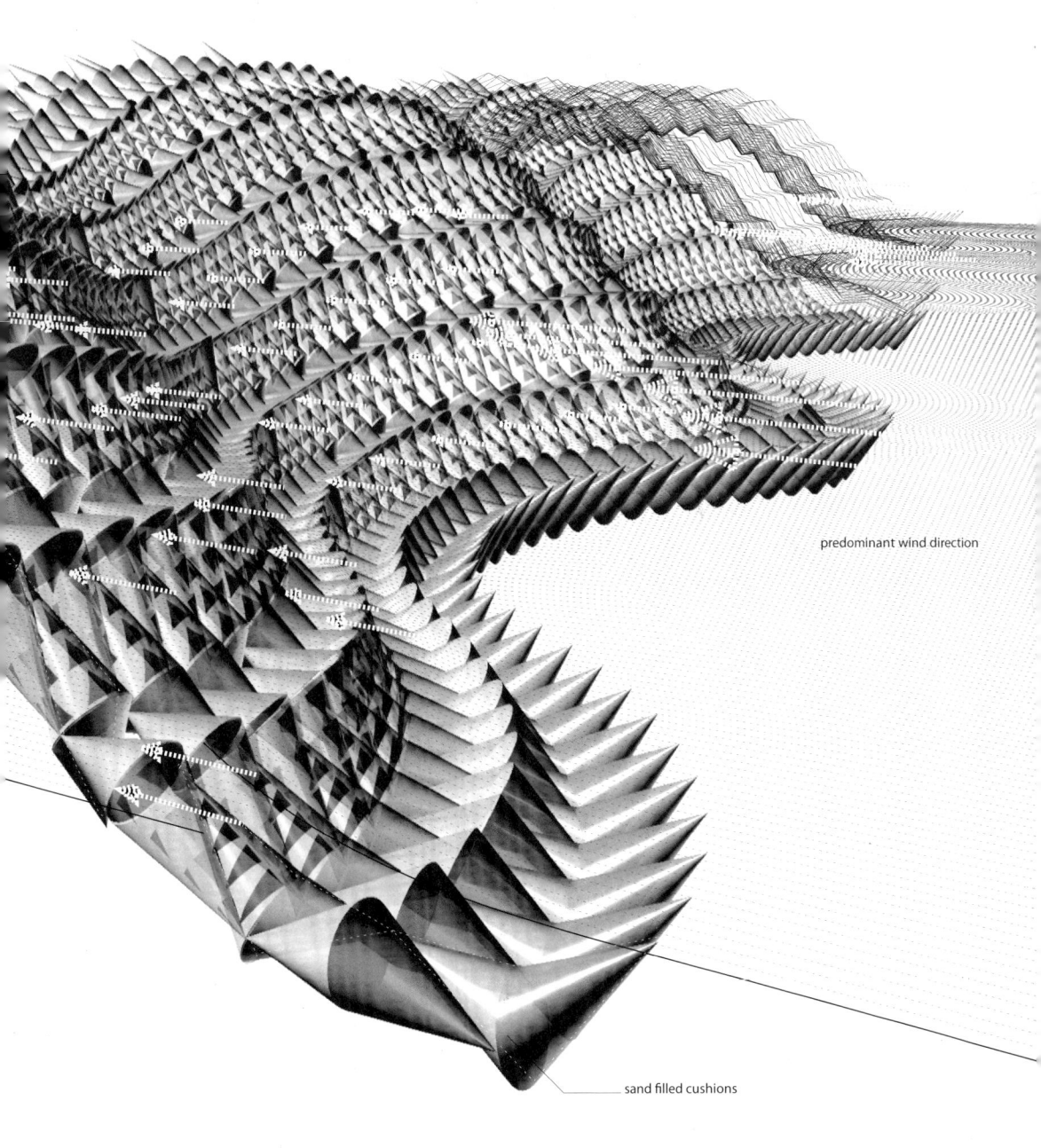

sand filled cushions

The sectional differentiation of the pneumatic shelters is based on aerodynamics, modulating airflow and creating zones of pressure differential to remove sand from or deliver it to specified areas of the system, so as to stabilise it and modulate the light and temperature conditions of the interior.

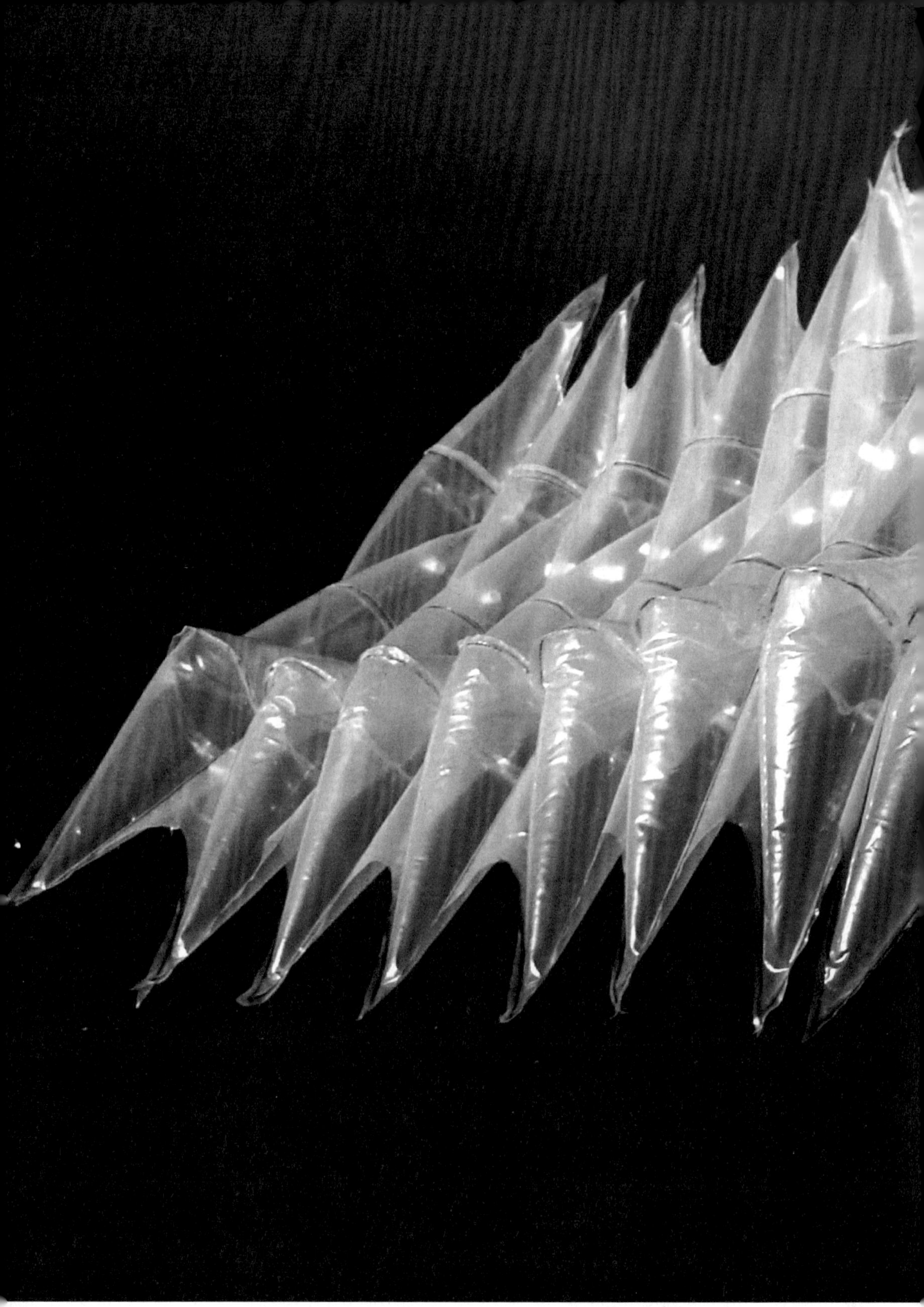

A sectional pneumatic prototype indicates the possibility of constructing highly articulated systems that are transparent, lightweight and rapidly deployable.

COMMENTS

This project presents a convincing, holistic response to a complex problem: the design of a shelter system for refugees in the Middle East. A very broad understanding of the parameters and requirements for such shelters informed the development of a simple system based on the application and overlay of a number of intelligent design strategies. This involved a detailed study of the climatic parameters that affect the performance of the proposed shelter system as well as the cultural background and the living conditions in the region.

At first glance it struck me that the choice of a transparent pneumatic system for rapid deployment seemed to be at odds with the climatic conditions of the Middle East. However, the lightweight, flat and easily transported material is able to produce a highly adaptive and highly appropriate shelter structure when used in conjunction with sand, which is naturally available and can be found, as it were, for free on the building sites.

At the basis of the proposal are three different types of inflatable structural cushions, which have been developed in great detail. Geometrical and structural tests were carried out both physically and digitally, to assess the properties of the cushions individually, in groups and in larger arrangements. From this assembly strategies were developed for the rapid deployment of shelter structures, taking into account the performance of the individual cushion – in relation to its type, rotation, and level of inflation – and its placement within the global structural arrangement.

The selected global geometry utilises the individual cushion elements in the most efficient way. The shelter structures are all based on doubly curved surfaces. This allows the air pressure in the cushions to make them stand up, without the need for any assisting framing or ancillary structures. Structure and enclosure are one – there are no redundant parts, so transport requirements are kept to a minimum. Moreover, the structures gain their stability gradually as they are inflated from the base material, which is flat, lightweight and at the same time easy to transport and place. The assembly process as well as the maintenance of the structures

WOLF MANGELSDORF

has been thought out to the level of valve placement, inflation and repair strategy.

But the inflated covers are only part of the story, and this is what makes this project so interesting. It is their use in conjunction with the sand which gives them their full spatial and environmental qualities. More than that: the sand accumulates by itself on the inflated structure through a combination of the intelligent placement of the shelter in the prevailing winds and the application of sand pockets within the surface.

Again, the placing of the structure in the wind plays a dual role. On the one hand it creates the necessary protection from the wind and the sand that is carried with it. On the other hand, this sand is used to complete the structure in a number of ways: its increased weight provides greater stability and the sand-filled pockets form the enclosure, thermal mass and opacity that generate the protection on the inside of the shelter.

This rather complex strategy is based on a brave approach: rather than designing against the burning sun, sand and wind, the proposed structure utilises these generally hostile and adverse conditions and turns them to its advantage. This is not the easy way, as it requires a deep understanding of these conditions – probably a greater understanding than if an attempt had been made to design against them in a less responsive and inclusive way.

The shelter structures were tested rigorously in a series of model experiments in the wind tunnel. These tests investigated the accumulation of the sand, the behaviour of the structure under changing conditions and, eventually, the lighting conditions within the shelter. It is evident that analysis of the tests informed the development of the project from the placement of the sand pockets to the overall orientation of the shelter structure in the prevailing wind.

All this has led to a fully integrated and inspiring proposal that goes far beyond the most common conventions in architectural and engineering design: it not only manages to combine a variety of parameters in a simple deployable system in a truly holistic approach but also (and this is its truly innovative element) employs an actively reactive design strategy that utilises the hostile site conditions to great effect by incorporating them into the shelter deployment and the design itself.

This research commenced from a detailed study of Winfried Wurm's work in the 60s in the field of pneumatic structures, which focused on double-cone cushions made from two layers of foil. Wurm found that it was possible to achieve double-curved pneumatic surfaces through the geometric definition of these elements and the way they are made. In taking his work further, this research investigates the possibility of integrating selectively cast reinforcement between two layers of pneumatic cushions so as to increase the structural capacity of the system along particular cross-sections or across selected regions.

The project aims at establishing a combined digital and physical form-finding process for the development of a double-layered pneumatic structure, in which the air-filled cushions provide the formwork for such an interstitial, cast support structure. While they are initially a self-supporting formwork for the casting process, the pneus become the building skin supported by the internal frame once it has hardened. Through this interrelation between pneu geometry and arrangement and the resultant combined cushion and frame system, a performative envelope can be developed.

An extensive physical modelling phase was conducted in parallel with developing the parametric definition of the system in a digital associative modelling environment, enabling a rapid check of the possibilities and limits of possible geometric and topological alterations of the system. The critical aspect of this development phase was the embedding of the pneu characteristics and manufacturing logics in a generic digital component. A pneumatic cushion consists of a flexible envelope that separates the internal air from the surrounding medium and is tensioned by differential air pressure between the inside and the outside. This produces a pre-tensioned envelope whose structural capacity is defined by the basic geometric principles of enclosing the maximum volume with a minimal surface area. In self-forming processes this form has an equal tension at any point and in all directions during inflation. These interdependent structural and morphological aspects, combined with a related method of developing a cutting pattern for the cushion envelope, are captured in a digital, parametric component that allows for proliferations into larger pneumatic systems. The careful definition of the initial component ensures that any instance derived from a differentiated multi-component system remains coherent with the morphological and manufacturing logics of a pneumatic cushion.

Subsequently two physical modelling tasks were pursued in order to cross-check the digital and physical system behaviour as well as inform the definition of the parametric set-up with additional fabrication constraints. First, the size of models was increased incrementally to investigate and determine relevant manufacturing techniques. Each pneumatic surface is made from two membrane layers that are cut to shape and welded together. The related cut pattern is derived digitally as part of the component population. A variety of different strategies of flat patterning and related assembly processes were investigated. A process of unrolling the double cone as four envelope parts with four linear and two curvilinear seams was established, whereby the single PVC membrane patches were connected by a high-frequency welding machine.

Secondly, the casting procedure was developed to establish greater control over the distribution of the cast material between two layers of pneumatic surfaces. Initial tests focused on basic parameters such as the calibration of the weight of the cast material in relation to the required air pressure and different methods of gravity, as well as pressure-driven casting. A further series of tests then engaged with the critical parameters for manipulating the system's structural and environmental performance. By altering the geometry and volume of the interstitial space between the two pneumatic layers, the articulation of the cast internal framework can be strategically modified. For example, a geometric differentiation of the interstitial space for casting can be achieved through a strategic offsetting of the two central axes of the upper and lower layers of the cushions, combined with adjustments to layer distance and air pressure.

This enables the designer to define specific shapes and cross-sections of the cast frame for each sub-location of the system. Manipulating the pneu morphology allows for a vast variety of possible frame characteristics ranging from delicate member structures to entirely closed parts that transform into opaque plates. In this process of differentiating the system the articulation of the pneus and related frame articulation are always directly linked to the manipulation of structural and environmental performance. Change of volume, shape and section becomes instrumental in modulating the structural capacity, transparency and thermal mass of the systems and its related behaviour of interacting with external forces and environmental influences.

Through this differential distribution of reinforcement and the additional introduction of reconfigurable elements, the system can provide for a broad scope of hardness, softness, bounciness and changeability.

The aim of the pilot project was to design a rapidly deployable children's playscape, beyond the superficial scope of a bouncy castle, that could be put up in areas without any provision for children to play, whether in the commercialised centre of cities, in suburban areas without collective spaces or even in places that have experienced a disaster and lost any such provisions.

An investigation of types of spatial organisation, spatial transitions and environmental modulation was undertaken to provide a richly articulated context for play and discovery. Deploying matrixes of interconnected rooms and box-in-box sections, the project offers children the kind of spatial experience that our built environment too often lacks. Its spaces are not yet coded by pre-determined programmatic utilitarianism; in other words, there is no clear sense of how they are to be used. The material articulation of the boundary threshold and the environment modulated by it is varied, with spatial transitions and sectional interstices. In this way the project invites the imaginative individual and collective appropriation of the spaces by children.

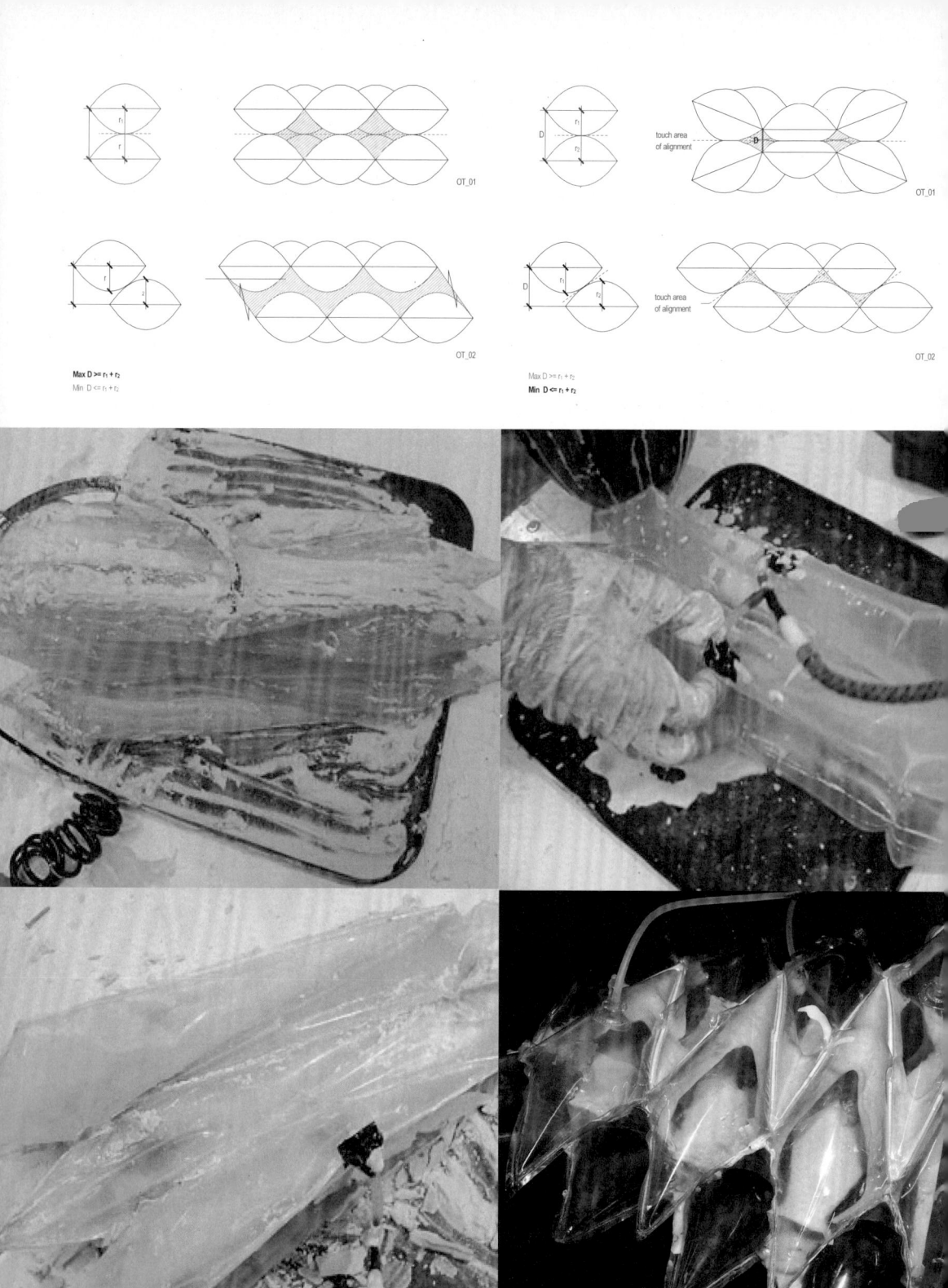

246 Following the definition of the pneumatic component system a series of experiments investigated the possibility of integrating local cast reinforcement between the air-filled cushions. While the pneus are initially a self-supporting formwork for the casting process, they transform into the building skin supported by the internal frame once it has hardened.

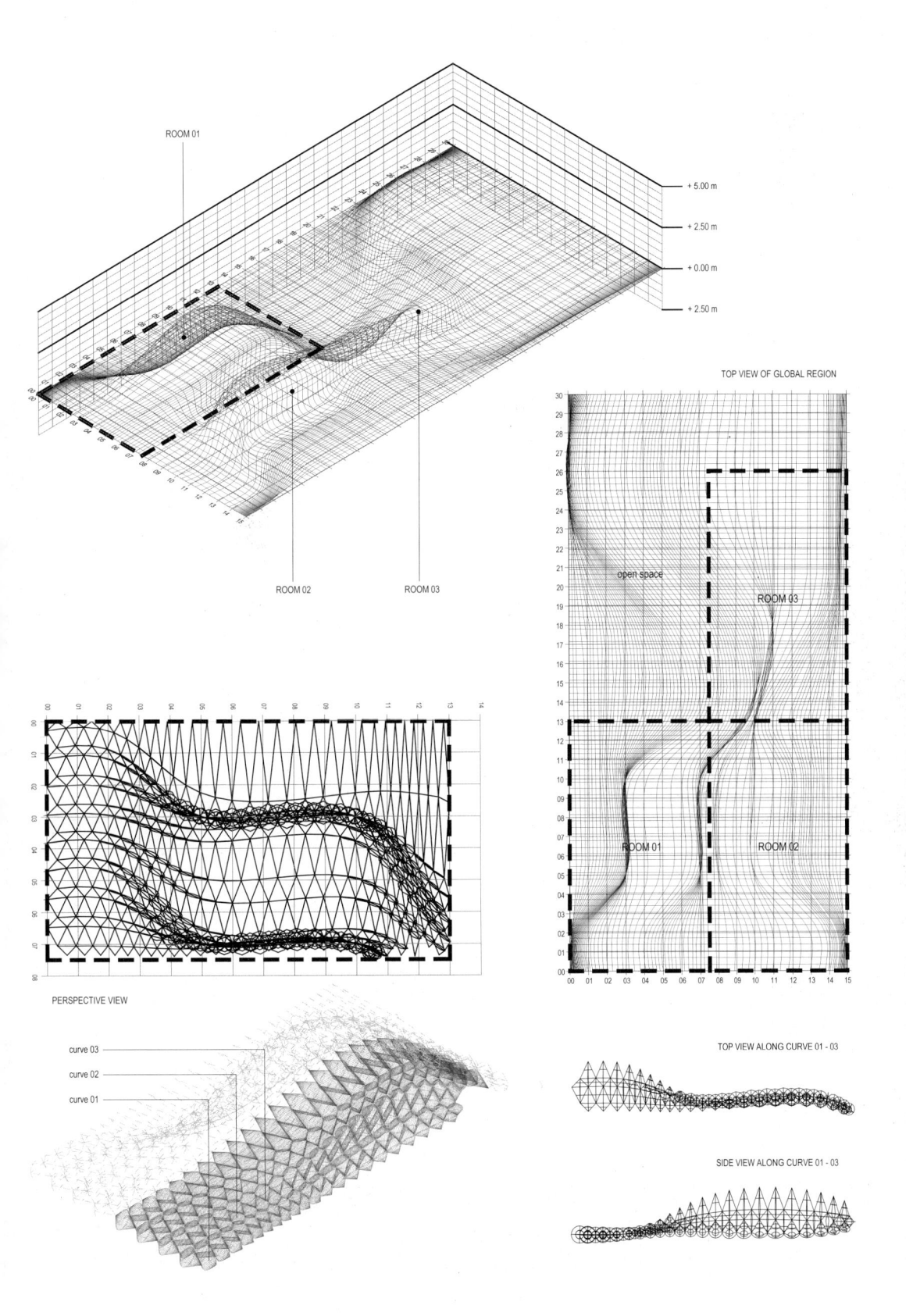

Manipulating the pneu morphology allows for a vast variety of possible frame characteristics ranging from entirely closed parts transforming into opaque plates to delicate member structures. In this process of differentiating the system the articulation of the pneus and related frame articulation are always directly linked to the manipulation of structural and environmental performance.

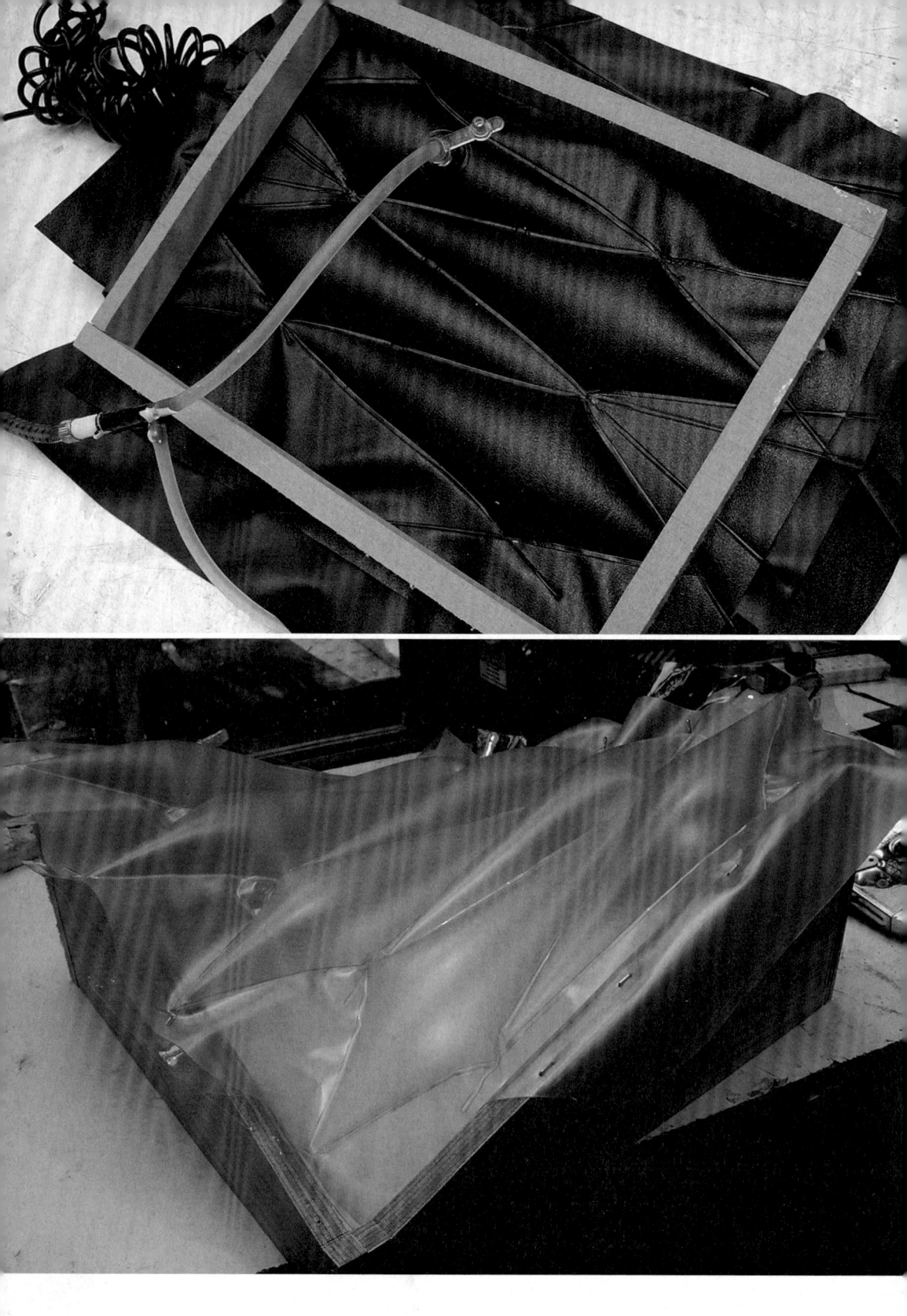

Each pneumatic cushion is made from two membrane layers that are cut to shape and welded together (top). The related cut pattern is derived digitally as part of the component population. A variety of different strategies of flat patterning and related assembly processes were investigated in order to achieve double-curved surface articulations (bottom).

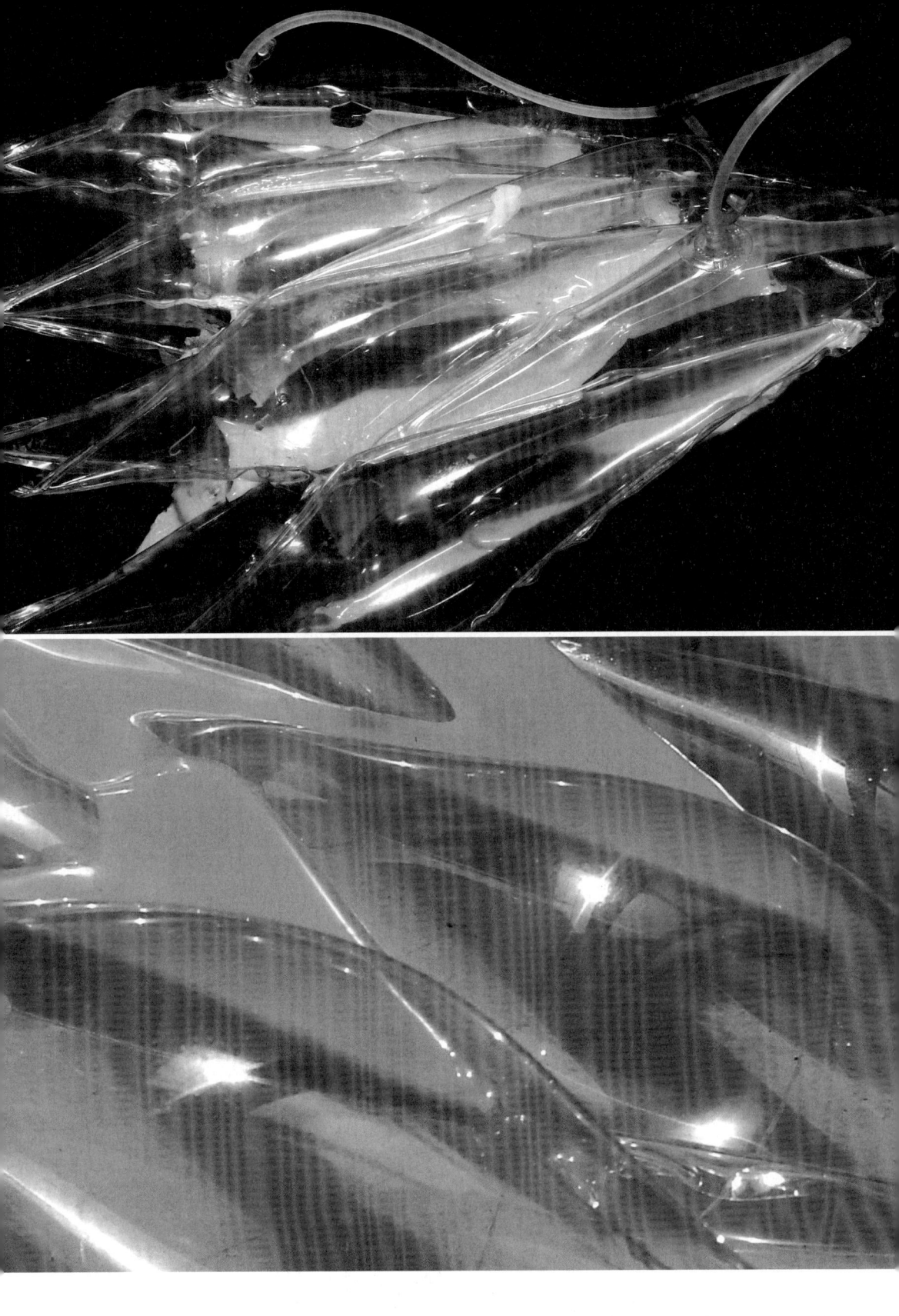

The fabrication and connection of PVC membrane cushions through high-frequency welding allowed for the testing of a range of casting strategies for the interstitial support structure (top). The specific volume, shape and section of each pneumatic element becomes instrumental in modulating the cast framework (bottom).

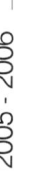

This research was triggered by an interest in the formation process of diatoms and radiolaria. Diatomes or diatomophycea are unicellular or colonial algae. The cell is encased by a characteristic and highly differentiated cell wall, which is impregnated by silica, the uptake and deposition of which requires generally less energy than the formation of an organic cell wall. The silica cell wall often features elements such as resting spores, which usually occur in response to stress. Radiolaria belong to the order of marine planktonic protozoans and feature a central protoplasm comprising chitinous capsule and siliceous spicules that are perforated by pores.

The initial phase of the material system development focused on producing a skeletal framework articulated through the interstitial spaces left between pressurised containers, so-called pneus. Thus the first series of physical experiments explored ways of casting plaster between air-filled cushions to achieve the typical shape of the mineralised skeletons between pneus that occur in nature. Based on different cushion arrangements four-, five- and six-armed configurations were produced this way, and they became the basic elements of the material system. Each of these elements is parametrically defined as the relation between pneu organisations and internal pressure by which aspects such as the volume, shape and thickness of each element can be varied. Based on this parametric set-up, a series of digital multi-element systems were derived from variable inputs. While the system demonstrated the ability for morphological differentiation it was clear at the same time that this process would only deliver articulation on one scale of hierarchy. Consequently secondary and tertiary levels of articulation were developed by a design strategy using a series of meso- and micro-pneus to further subdivide the interstitial space between macro-pneumatic cushions. Yet another series of experiments focused on how it might be possible to gain porosity in the cast form itself. Finally the structure comprises a parametrically defined, open capillary system articulated across various scales of hierarchy ranging from macro- to micro-material organisation.

Once the system hierarchies were established it was important to understand the environmental performance capacity of the material system. Through literature study a list of casting materials that feature different thermal characteristics was established. Physical experiments and digital analysis served to establish the possible range of light and airflow modulation relative to morphological features such as the size and density of pores and other characteristics of the material system. A careful evaluation of these tests served to further develop the parametric definition and related performative capacities of the material system in such a manner that each sub-location and hierarchy can be articulated in particular response to a number of performance requirements.

The next step was to embed the fabrication and construction logics into this operative digital model of the system. A range of manufacturing approaches were considered and tested, resulting in the production of a full-scale prototypical portion of the material system that integrated computer-aided manufacturing processes and pneumatic form-finding as a construction method. A cast form was milled on a 5-axis CNC-machine from high-density polystyrene blocks, from which first a fibreglass form and later a cast form from plaster were produced. Air-pressured cushions were distributed into the form and inflated to the defined pressure for each location, and then concrete and other materials were cast into the interstitial spaces between the pneumatic units and the mould.

The modelling experiments were paralleled by an analysis of mat-buildings. This typology emerged from Team X's interest in Middle Eastern settlement forms characterised by low-rise and high-density buildings that are capable of providing environmental comfort in hot climates. The critique of contemporary mat-buildings condemns both the excessive amount of circulation space required, as well as the failure to deliver sufficient environmental exchange between interior and exterior. This is down to wrong proportional scaling of courtyards, as well as the hard threshold that strictly divides interior from exterior.

In order to overcome these problems alternative spatial and environmental strategies are needed. The former may be addressed by a decisive move away from the exclusive use of the corridor and cellular room arrangements in mat-buildings, and by introducing spatial arrangements based on greater communication between space, such as matrices of interconnected rooms and raumplan arrangements with sectional communication of spaces. The latter can be addressed by a material threshold characterised by a tailored porosity that enables environmental exchange to take place between spaces with varying degrees of interiority or exteriority.

It is obvious that a rigorous implementation of the environmental strategy is far more difficult or potentially inappropriate in cold climates. Nevertheless, the pilot project was located in a warm climate, in Bairro do Recife, Brazil, so that its potential for environmental modulation could be verified. The aim of the project was to provide a transition from public to private space in plan as well as in section, such that locals and the transient population of tourists who arrive by cruise liner have spaces for both interaction and privacy. The design was informed by extensive mapping of vehicular and pedestrian movement and of thermal, luminous and aeolic conditions across the site. Environmental measurements were listed on an Excel spreadsheet set up in such a way that the insertion of new measurement values automatically re-interpolates all values. The spreadsheet was linked with a map generated within an associative modelling environment that gets updates through the Excel sheet. Once the sizes of all elements of the material system and their distribution according to the set spatial arrangements were established, the associative model of the material system could be linked to the mapping. With this a rigorous instrumental link and feedback between material system and environmental conditions was established. New environmental conditions can update the design and, likewise, the environmental impact of the projected intervention within the selected context can be visualised and analysed.

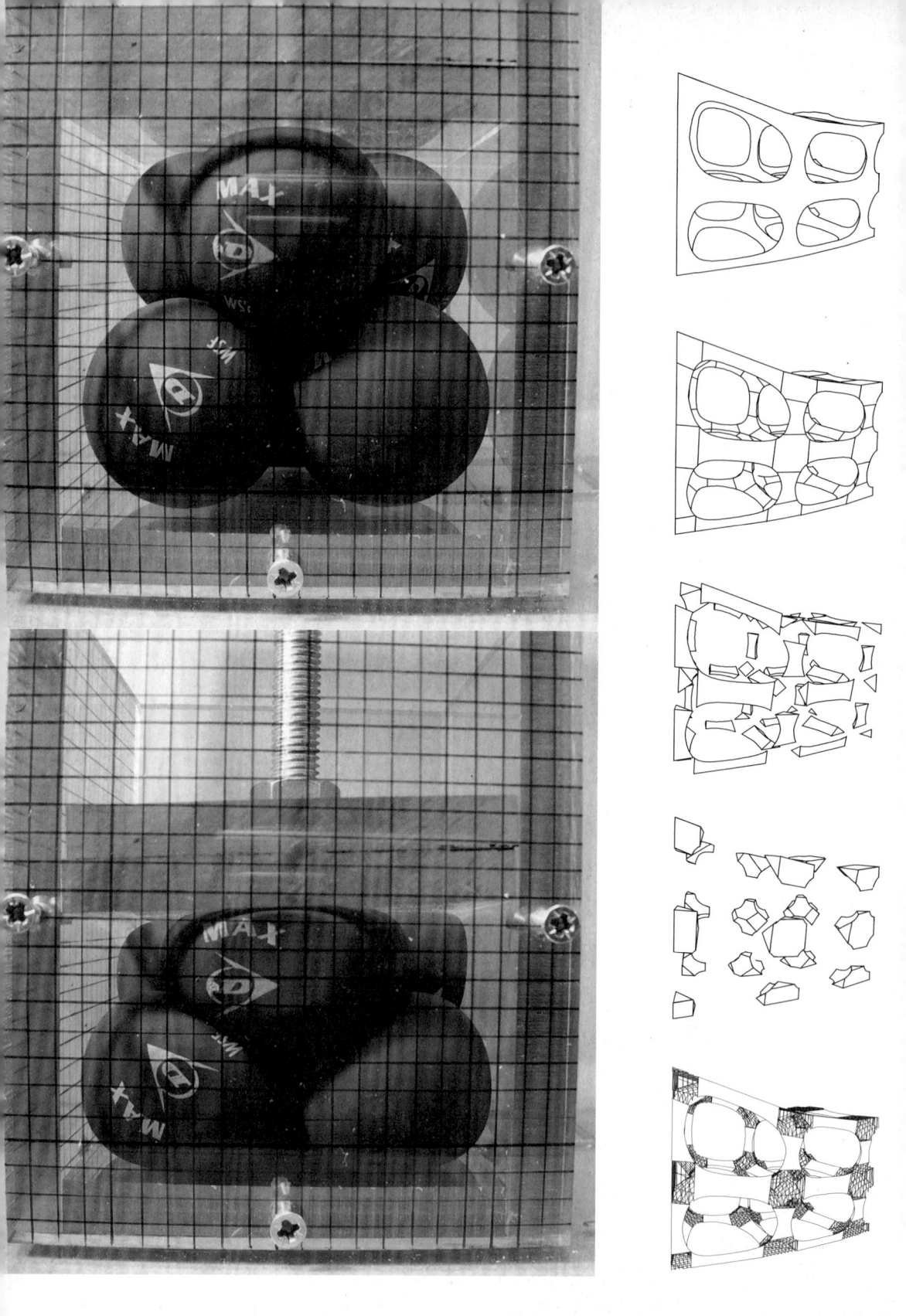

252 The initial phase of the material system development focused on producing a skeletal framework (left) articulated through the interstitial spaces left between compressed, spherical containers (right).

The interstitial space between two CNC-milled styrofoam blocks filled with pneumatic containers served as a variable mould for casting a system with different degrees of porosity.

5 Arm Component

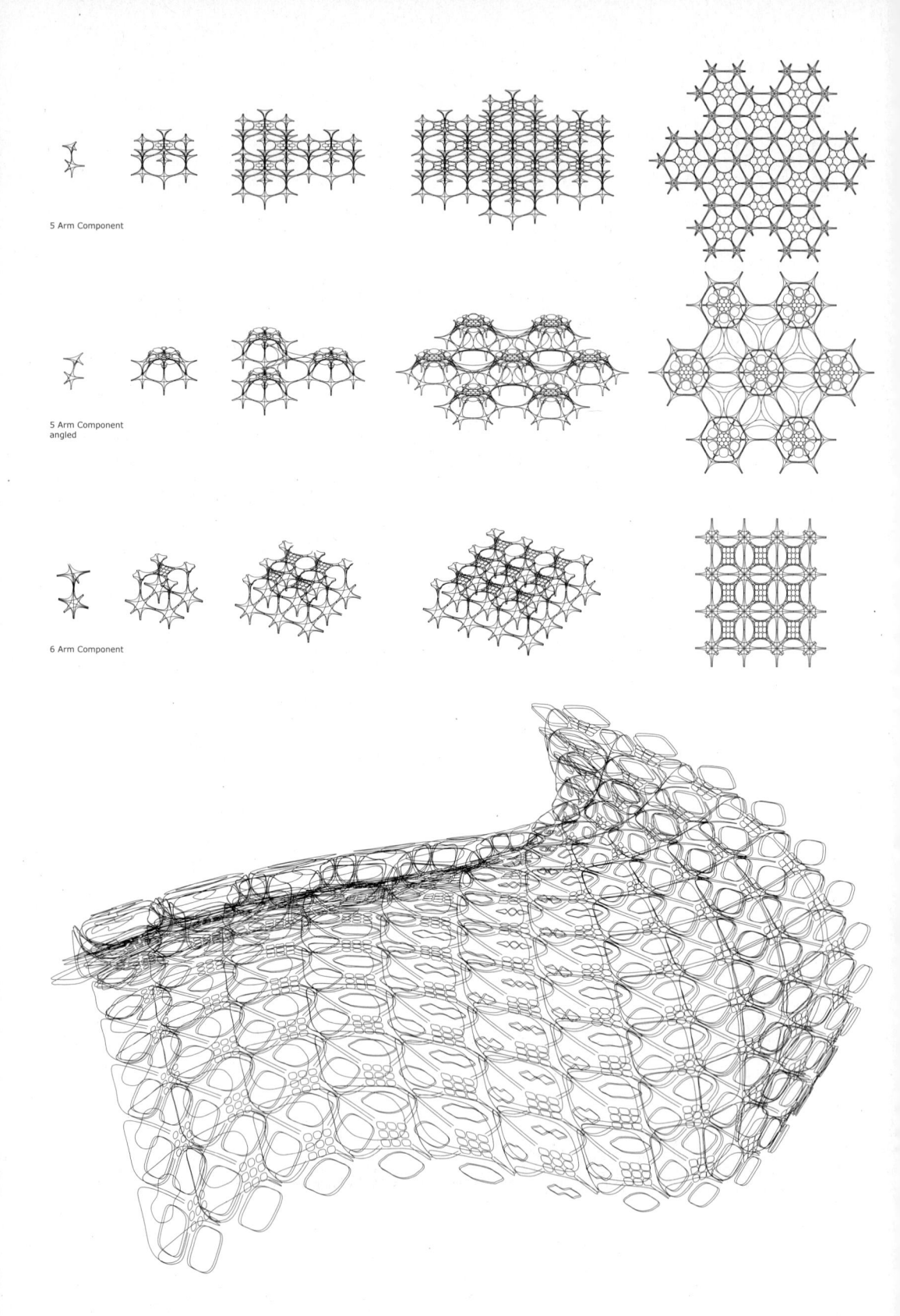

5 Arm Component
angled

6 Arm Component

254 Different component types were parametrically defined as the relation between pneu organisation and internal pressure by which aspects such as shape, volume and thickness of each element can be varied (top). Based on this parametric set-up multi-element systems can be derived from variable inputs (bottom).

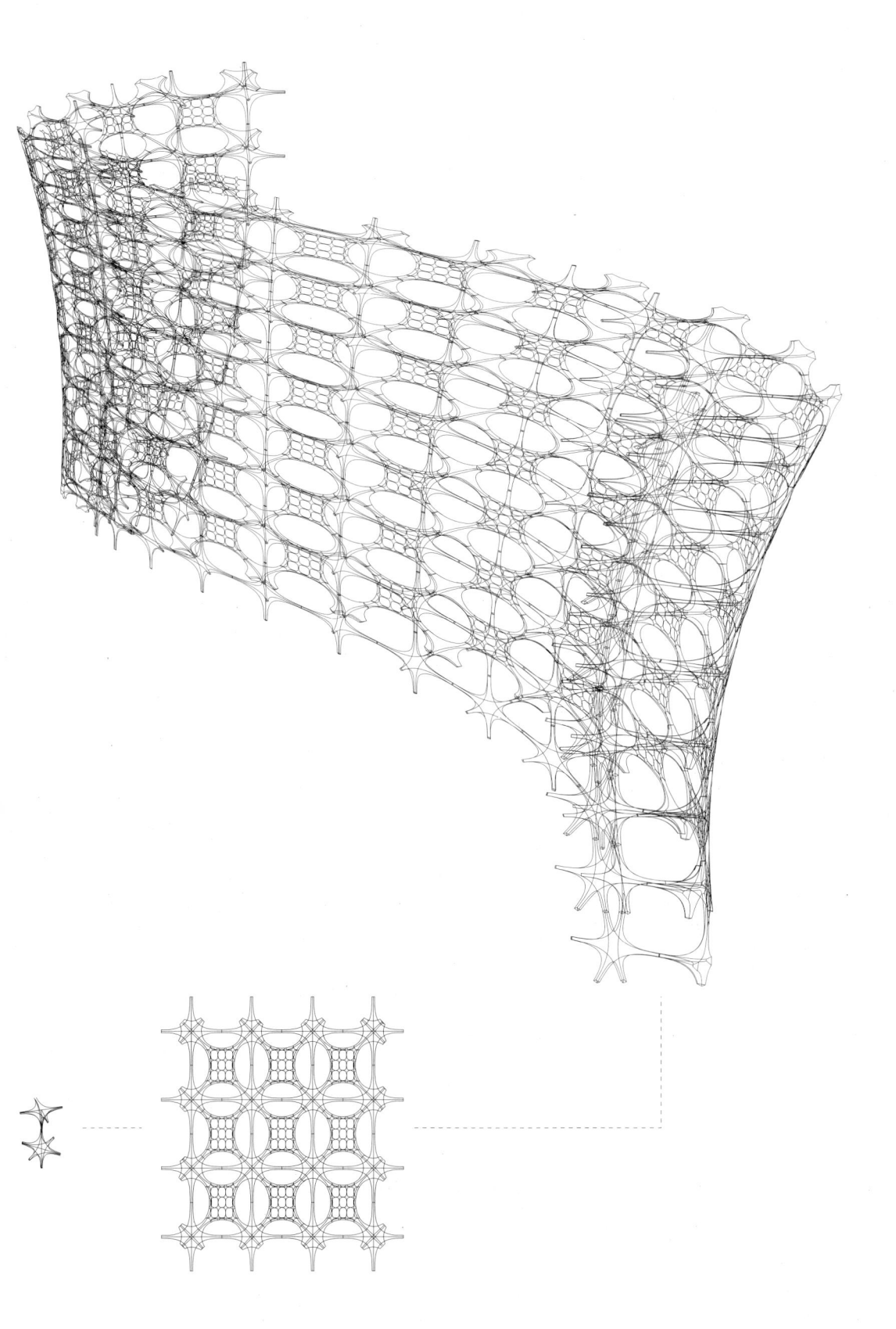

The proliferation of the system is based on a single component. Through the multiplication into component collective and the associative adaptation to an overall geometry, a system morphology with varying degrees of porosity can be achieved.

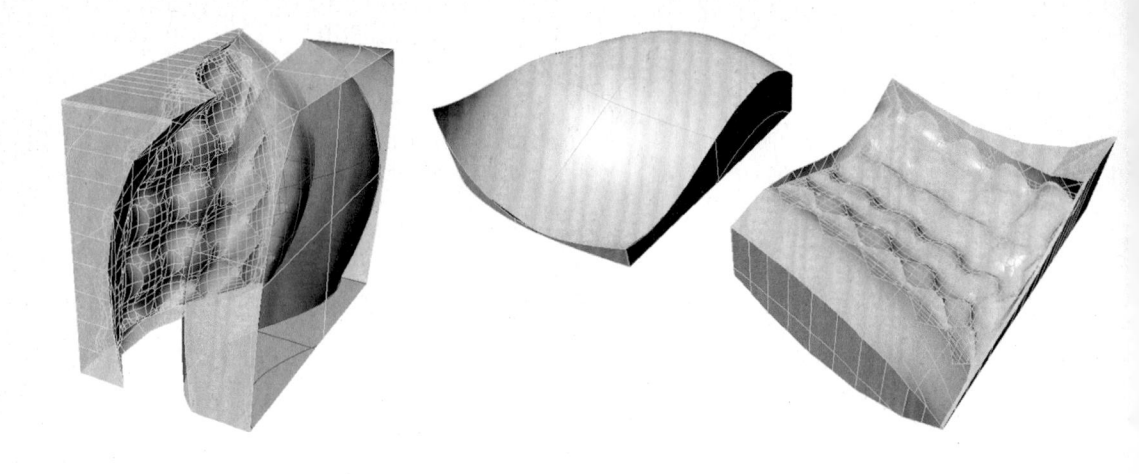

[A] Position: [0,0.166,0.166]	[B] Position: [0.166,0.33,0.166]	[C] Position: [0.33,0.499,0.166]	[D] Position: [0.499,0.666,0.166]	[E] Position: [066,0.833,0.166]	[F] Position: [0833,1,0.166]
Value HE: [50]	Value HE: [250]	Value HE: [450]	Value HE: [600]	Value HE: [650]	Value HE: [700]
Value LE: [20]	Value LE: [20]	Value LE: [20]	Value LE: [20]	Value LE: [20]	Value LE: [20]
Value LC: [100]	Value LC: [70]	Value LC: [50]	Value LC: [30]	Value LC: [10]	Value LC: [5]
Value LL: [100]	Value LL: [70]	Value LL: [50]	Value LL: [30]	Value LL: [10]	Value LL: [5]
Value LR: [100]	Value LR: [70]	Value LR: [70]	Value LR: [50]	Value LR: [30]	Value LR: [10]
Value LS: [6]	Value LS: [15]	Value LS: [17]	Value LS: [19]	Value LS: [20]	Value LS: [20]
Value BS: [30]	Value BS: [25]	Value BS: [20]	Value BS: [15]	Value BS: [10]	Value BS: [5]

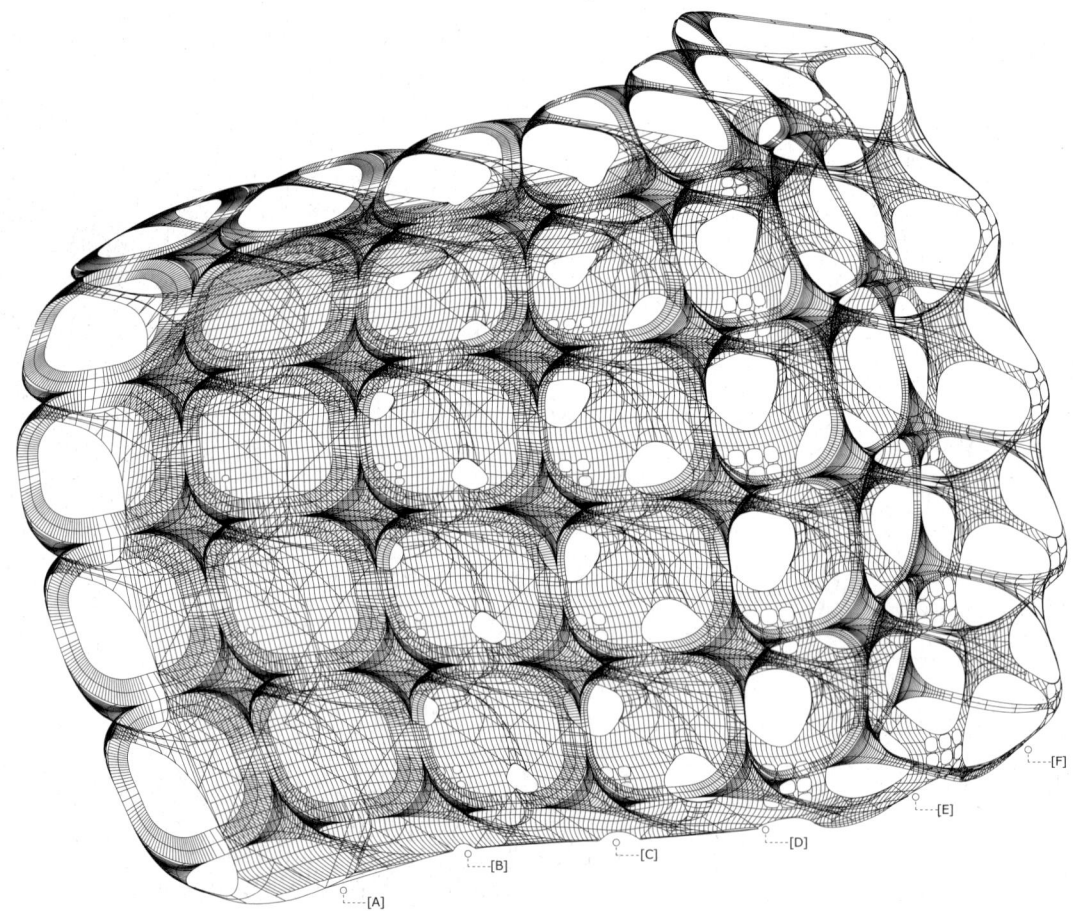

256   In order to facilitate the casting of a full-scale prototype, a sandwich formwork to be filled with pneumatic containers (top) was prepared for digital fabrication by extracting the relevant data directly from the parametric model (bottom).

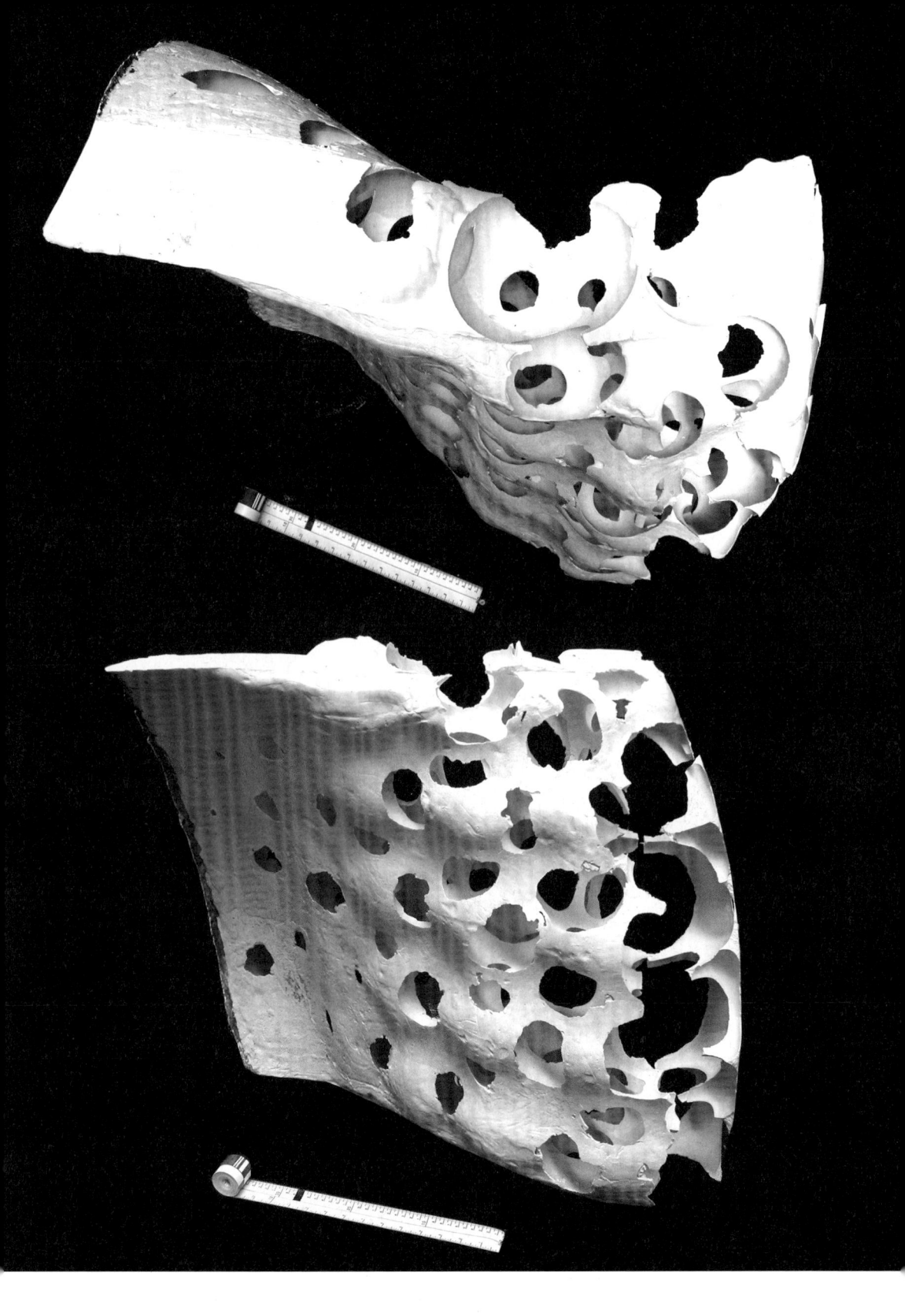

The macro formwork for casting a prototype structure was milled from a solid high-density styrofoam block with a 5-axis CNC machine and then filled with pneumatic cells. The remaining interstitial space was cast with plaster.

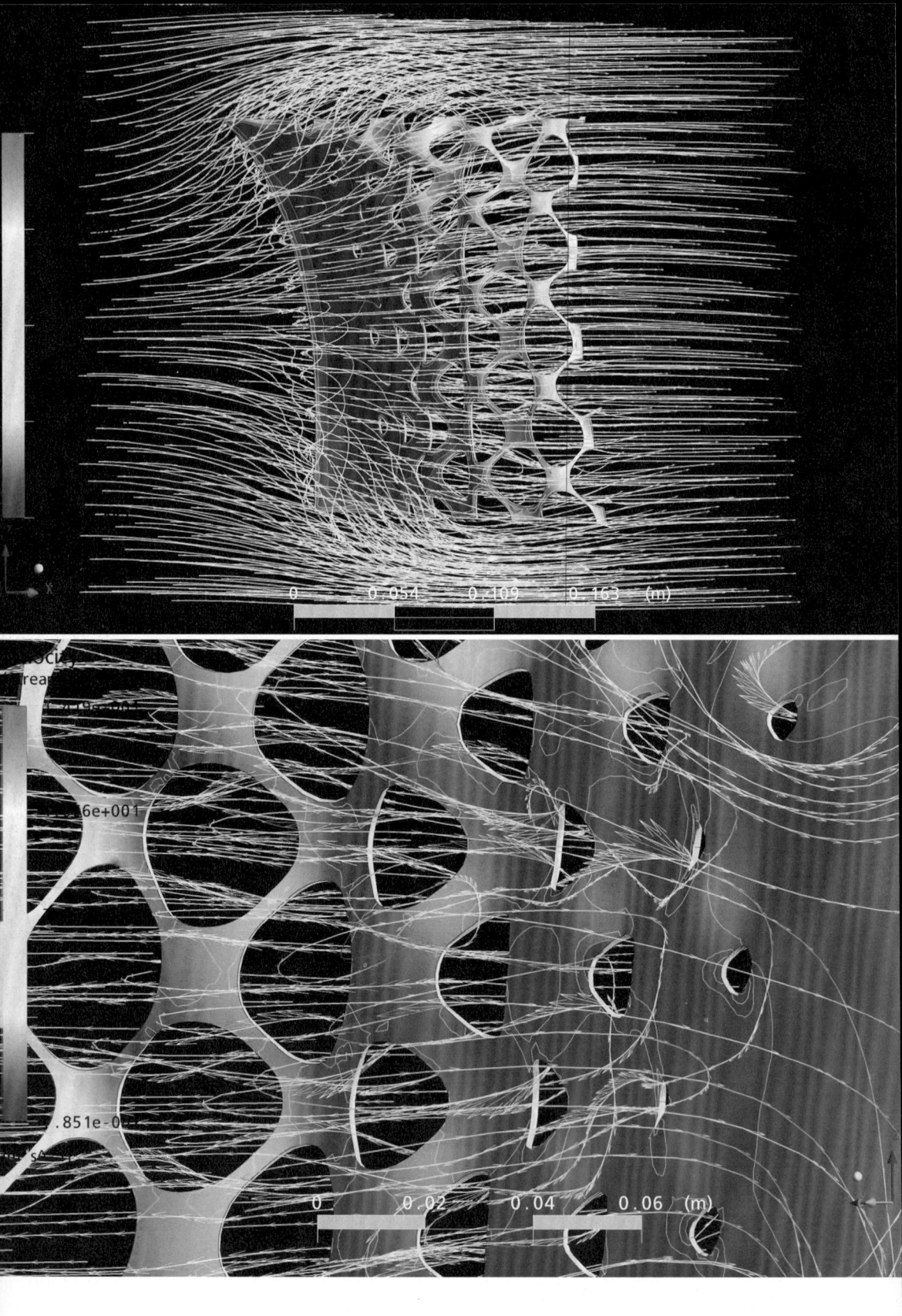

258 The system's performative capacity to modulate airflow through local and regional porosity gradation was analysed through CFD (Computer Fluid Dynamics) modelling.

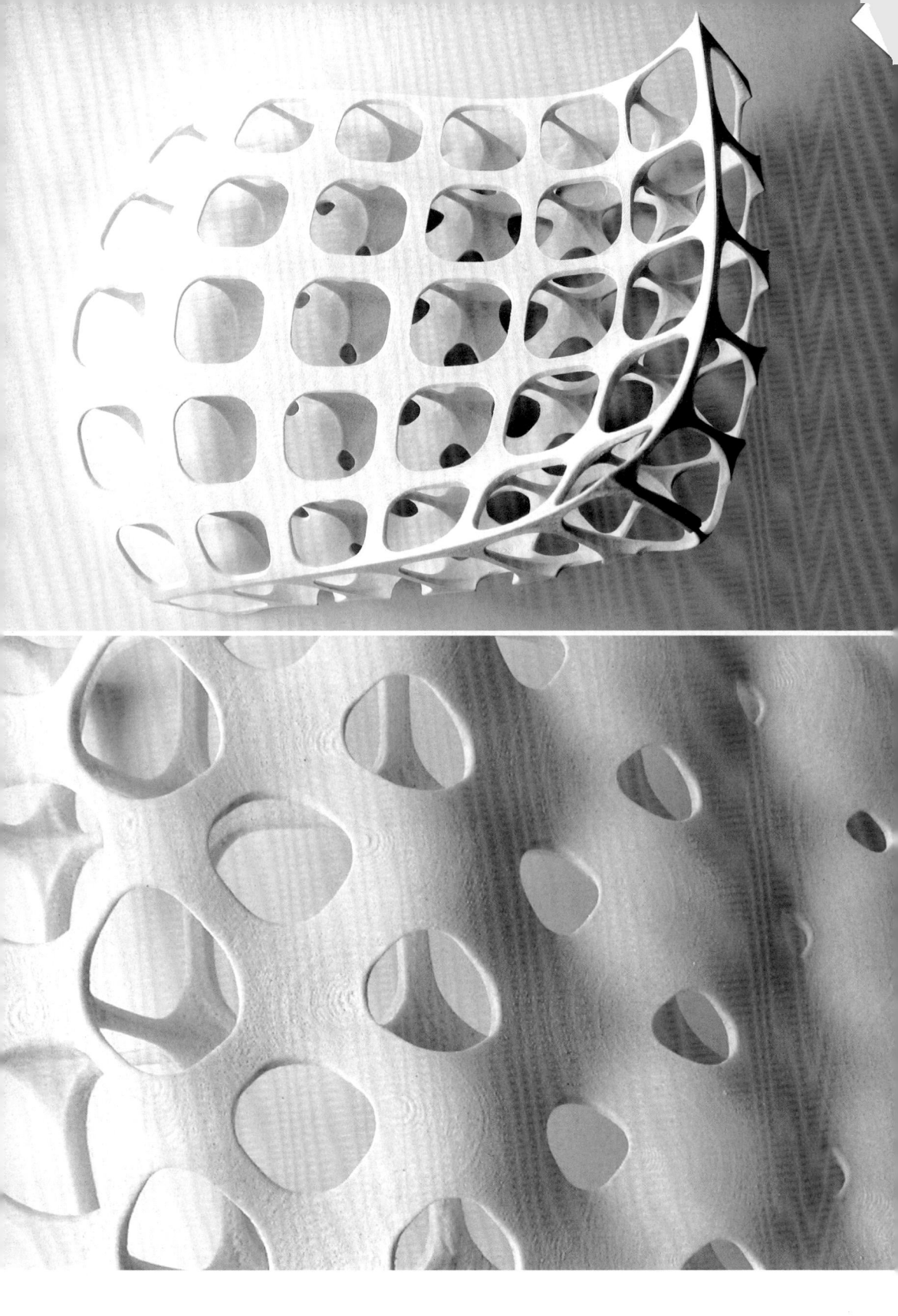

The interstitial spaces and resulting porous structure were digitally parameterised. This enabled rapid prototyping of a series of geometric models for further analysis of the morphology and related environmnetal performances.

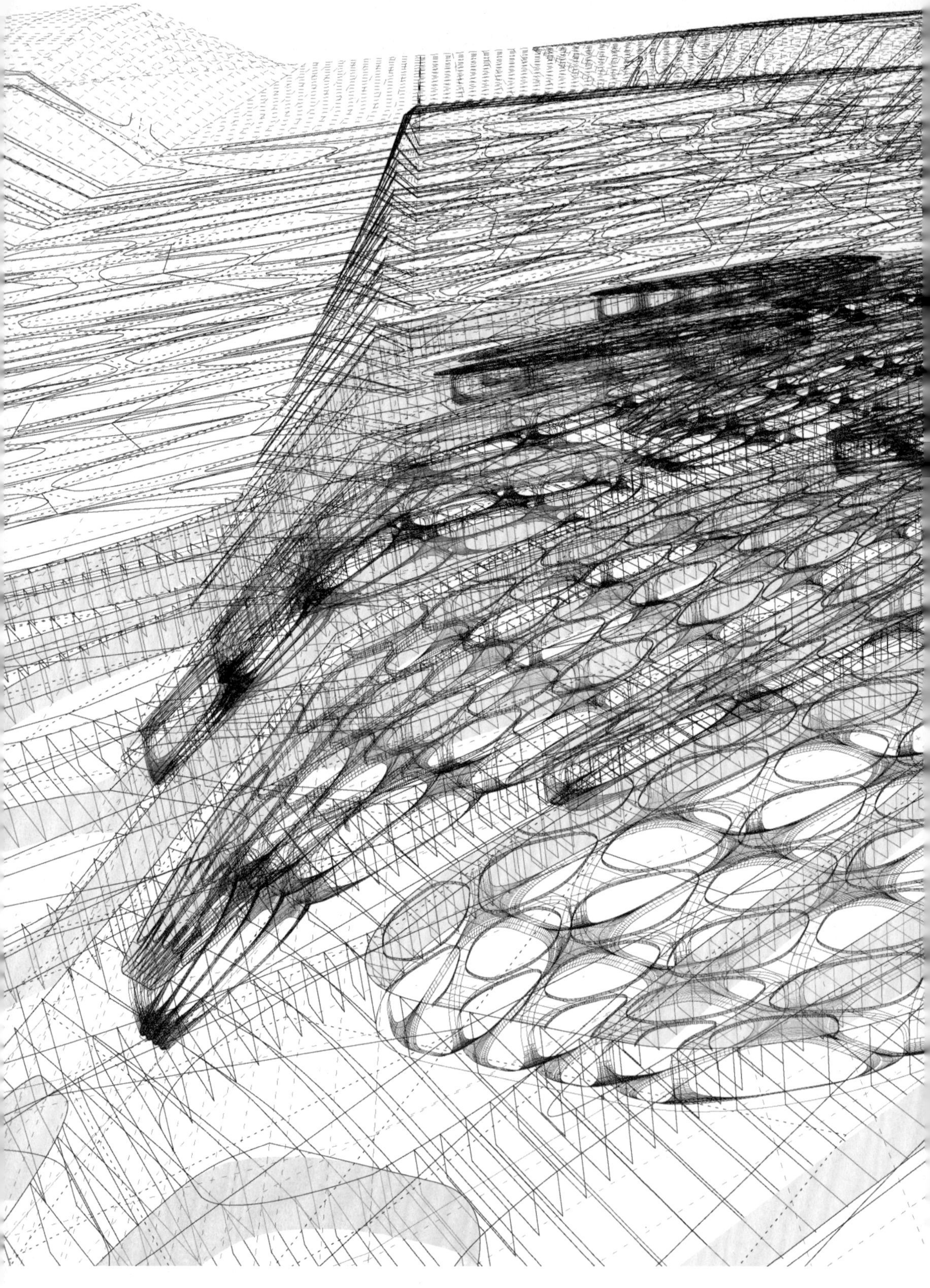

Driven by context specific information the parametric definition of the system enables an integral set up of the context specific articulation responding to a range of performance criteria. The specific implementation of the system within a performative context results from negotiation of a series structural, environmental and spatial parameters.

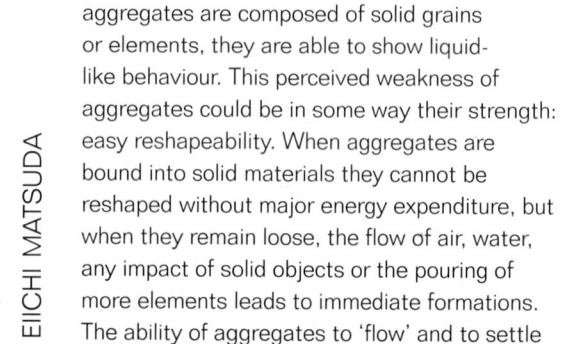

Aggregates are defined as materials formed from a loosely compacted mass of fragments or particles. Granular substances exist in great abundance in nature, as for instance in sand dunes that are shaped by wind and water. The building industry makes use of aggregates as granular material for construction, commonly bound with cement to form concrete or bitumen. Among composite materials aggregate filling is equally common as fibre reinforcement. What if, however, these materials are not bound? Can they be of use in their loose form for constructing architectures?

In architectural history there have been a few instances of utilising natural, as found materials for man-made conglomerations, but a rigorous design approach that strategises the specific design of both the single elements and the aggregation process remains largely unexplored. In fact an investigation into what one may call aggregate systems is a radical departure from most architectural design approaches which are predominantly based on assembly processes and systems. Contrary to assembly and composite systems, aggregates are formed not through the connection of elements by joints or a binding matrix, but through the loose combination of many separate elements. Under the influence of external forces, as for example gravity and wind, elements aggregate into heaps which develop as a state of equilibrium between the dead weight and the internal friction resistances. In other words: elements rest upon one another without being connected in any way.

Liquefaction, the transmission from solid to liquid matter is one particularly interesting property of aggregate systems. While aggregates are composed of solid grains or elements, they are able to show liquid-like behaviour. This perceived weakness of aggregates could be in some way their strength: easy reshapeability. When aggregates are bound into solid materials they cannot be reshaped without major energy expenditure, but when they remain loose, the flow of air, water, any impact of solid objects or the pouring of more elements leads to immediate formations. The ability of aggregates to 'flow' and to settle into self-stabilising formations that can support themselves and external loads and resist shearing stresses is of particular interest for the development of an alternative design and construction approach in architecture.

Frei Otto's team at the Institute for Lightweight Structures at the University in Stuttgart undertook an extensive amount of basic research on natural aggregation patterns, mostly with sand, pouring it into piles or draining it through funnels, creating crater-like formations. The careful design of the granular elements themselves, however, has not been undertaken anywhere with great rigour and still requires a great deal of research.

So this particular research started with the consideration of the basic element and the possibility of fabricating it easily in great numbers to conduct a multitude of experiments. In this case the basic element was made from three matchsticks forming a three-axial configuration. A number of variations of this geometry were strategised in order to increase or decrease the extent to which the elements can hook into one another and have more surface contact and thus friction between them. Ten thousand elements were made and colour-coded at the tips of each axis in order to be able to discern aggregation pattern and rotation upon pouring with greater ease.

Once the elements were made the experiments could begin. Initially the aggregation experiments were only constrained by a horizontal surface. Crucial variables were the number of elements per experiment, element geometry, pouring speed, pouring height, and the roughness and thus degree of friction provided by the horizontal surface. The critical mass of each element geometry and constraining surface was established in the form of maximum pile height before collapse, angle of inclination and maximum horizontal distribution of elements. Of central importance also was the density of elements in each pile. The variation in density and porosity across different sub-locations of the poured system and across different pouring instances was mapped for each experiment, as this was one of the crucial environmental modulation parameters.

For the next few hundred experiments the constraining surface arrangements were changed, by adding vertical and inclined surfaces to the horizontal one. Further constraints that were tested included vertical poles, as well as cables spanned between them. These constraints are seen as part of a given context in which the system might be applied, such as existing landscape or building surfaces against which the aggregate might be poured.

The third generation of experiments introduced non-permanent constraints that could be easily removed after the aggregation process. The most successful experiments focused on inflated formwork set within a series of permanent constraints. The aggregates are poured with the formwork inflated. Once the aggregate has settled, the formwork is deflated and the aggregate undergoes another cycle of liquefaction while it resettles into another fragile stable state. During this process a few redundant elements fall off the system and can be removed, but the remaining elements stabilise in a configuration which reveals cavernous spaces that carry their own self-weight, much like vaults.

The system is characterised by a delicate and fragile stability based on numerous friction points and multiple load-paths, which also show other interesting characteristics: at a specific density water sprayed from above is collected by the elements and runs from element to element down to the ground datum instead of dropping off into the cavernous spaces. Defining different size ranges of aggregates and their pouring sequence can enhance this effect and contribute to a fine modulation of the luminous environment within the cavernous spaces. Once the relationship between these modulations and the behavioural patterns of the aggregate influenced by the above-mentioned critical parameters has been established the designer can instrumentalise the performative capacity of the system and exploit its ability for rapid deployment, perpetual reconfiguration and self-stabilisation.

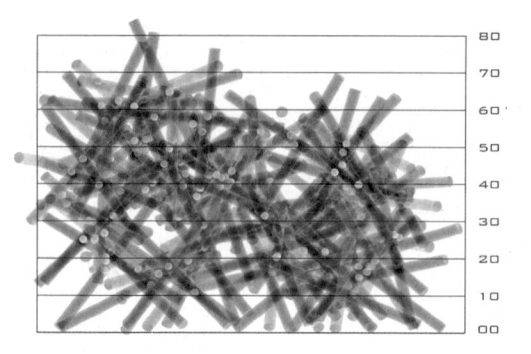

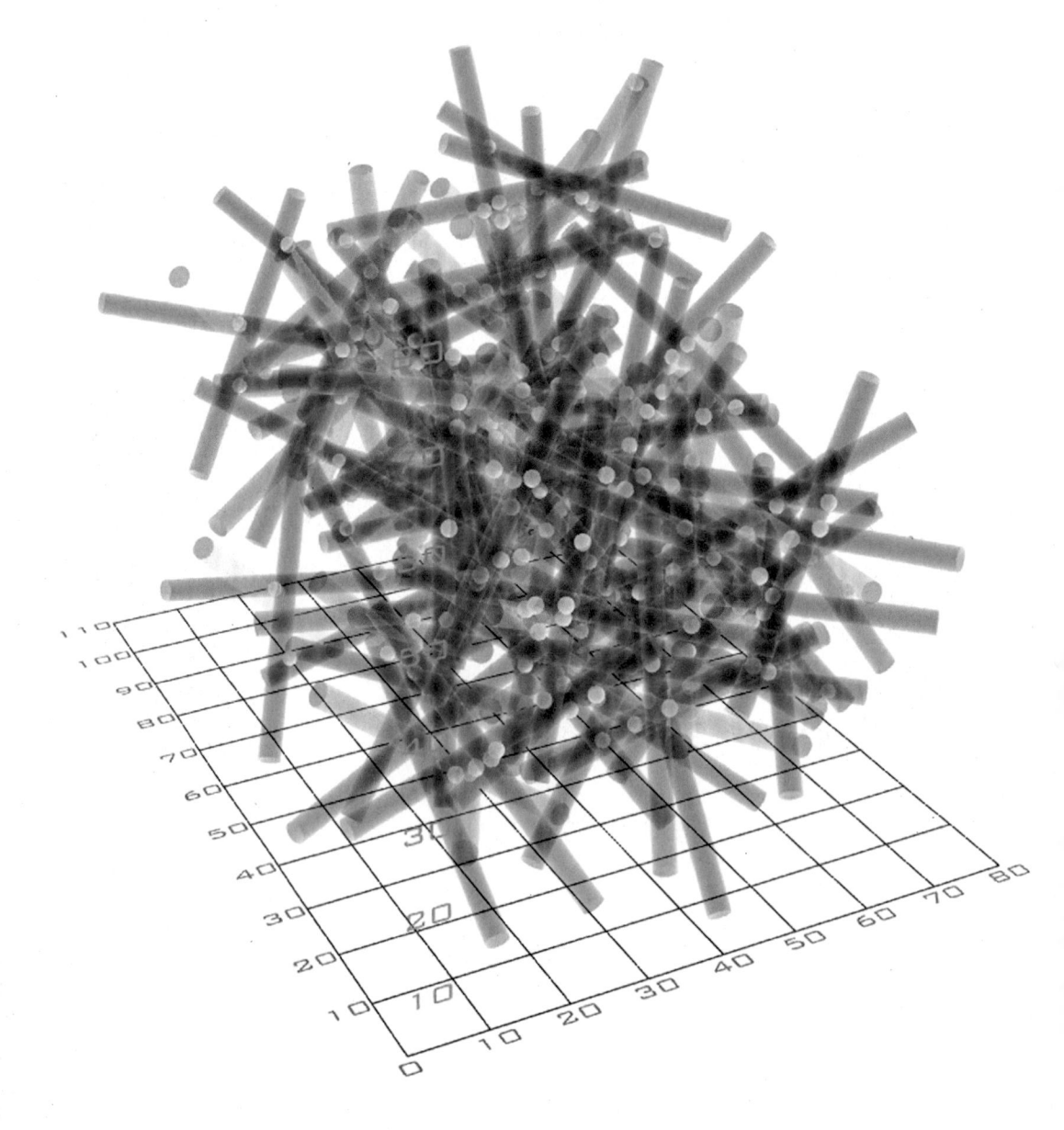

264 Digital experiments conducted in a physics simulation environment indicate the distribution of aggregates under the influence of gravity. This digital technique allows us to trace the contact points between the individual aggregate elements.

section 01

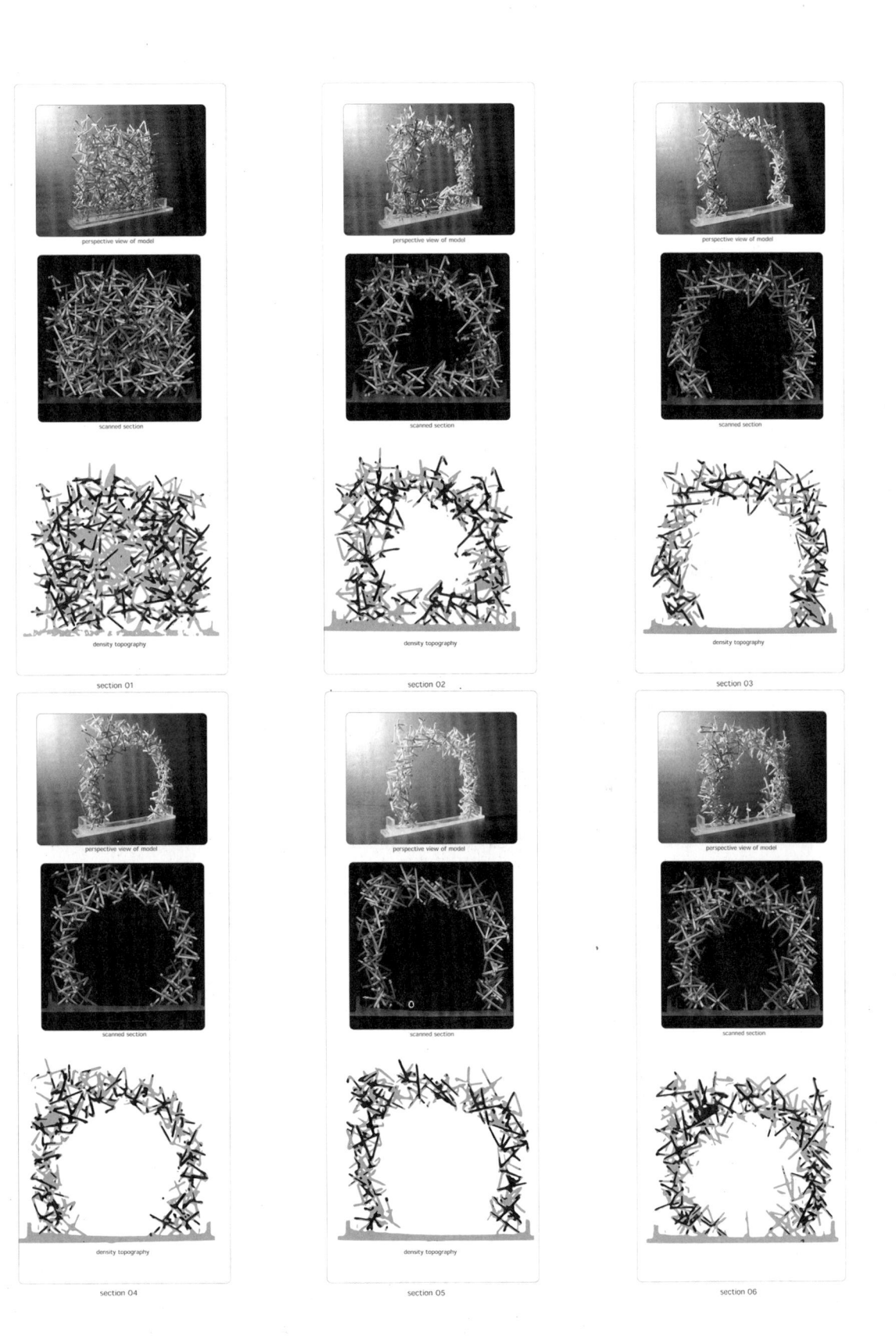

section 02

section 03

section 04

section 05

section 06

A physical model of an aggregate system, poured into a box filled with an inflated balloon, was stabilised by the application of resin. After deflating the balloon, the solidified model was cut into sections. The resulting slices were scanned on a flatbed scanner in order to trace areas of different densities and the location of element contact points.

Density 01   Density 02   Density 03

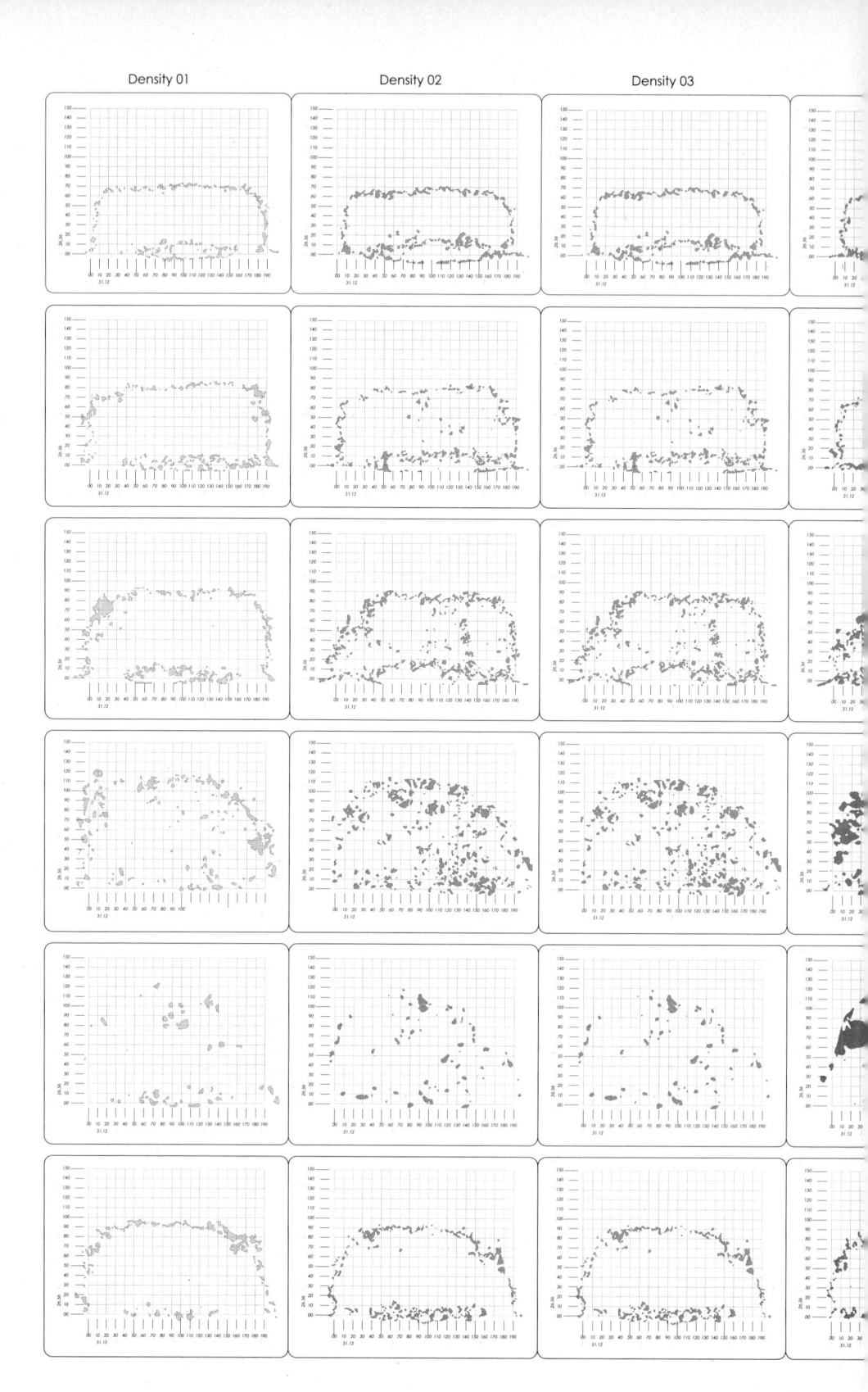

266

Density 05 Density 06 Density 07

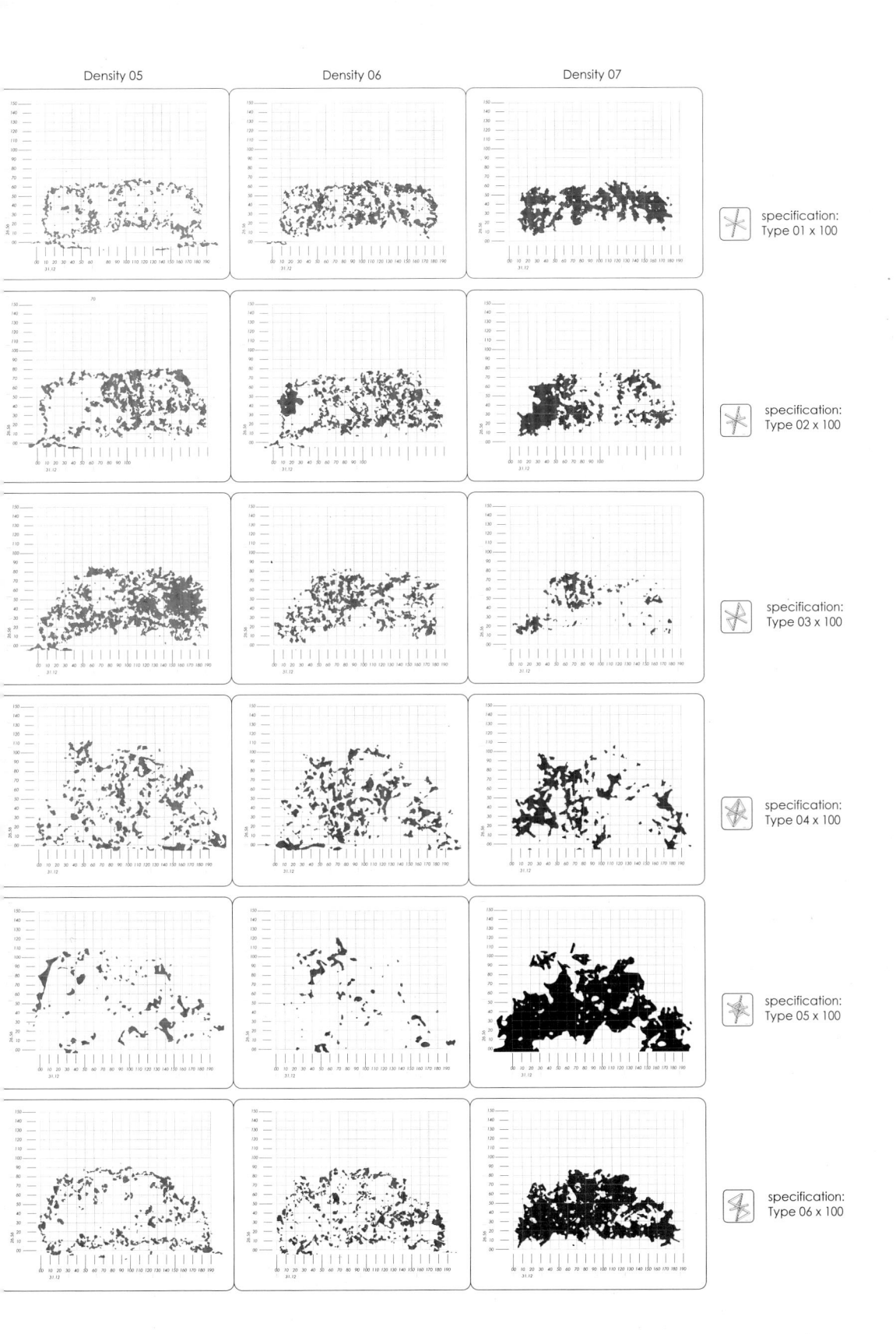

specification:
Type 01 x 100

specification:
Type 02 x 100

specification:
Type 03 x 100

specification:
Type 04 x 100

specification:
Type 05 x 100

specification:
Type 06 x 100

In order to investigate the tendency of each geometric element-type to aggregate with different densities, a large number of aggregation tests were conducted. The table shows the identification of resulting zones of densities (from left to right) for different element types (from top to bottom).

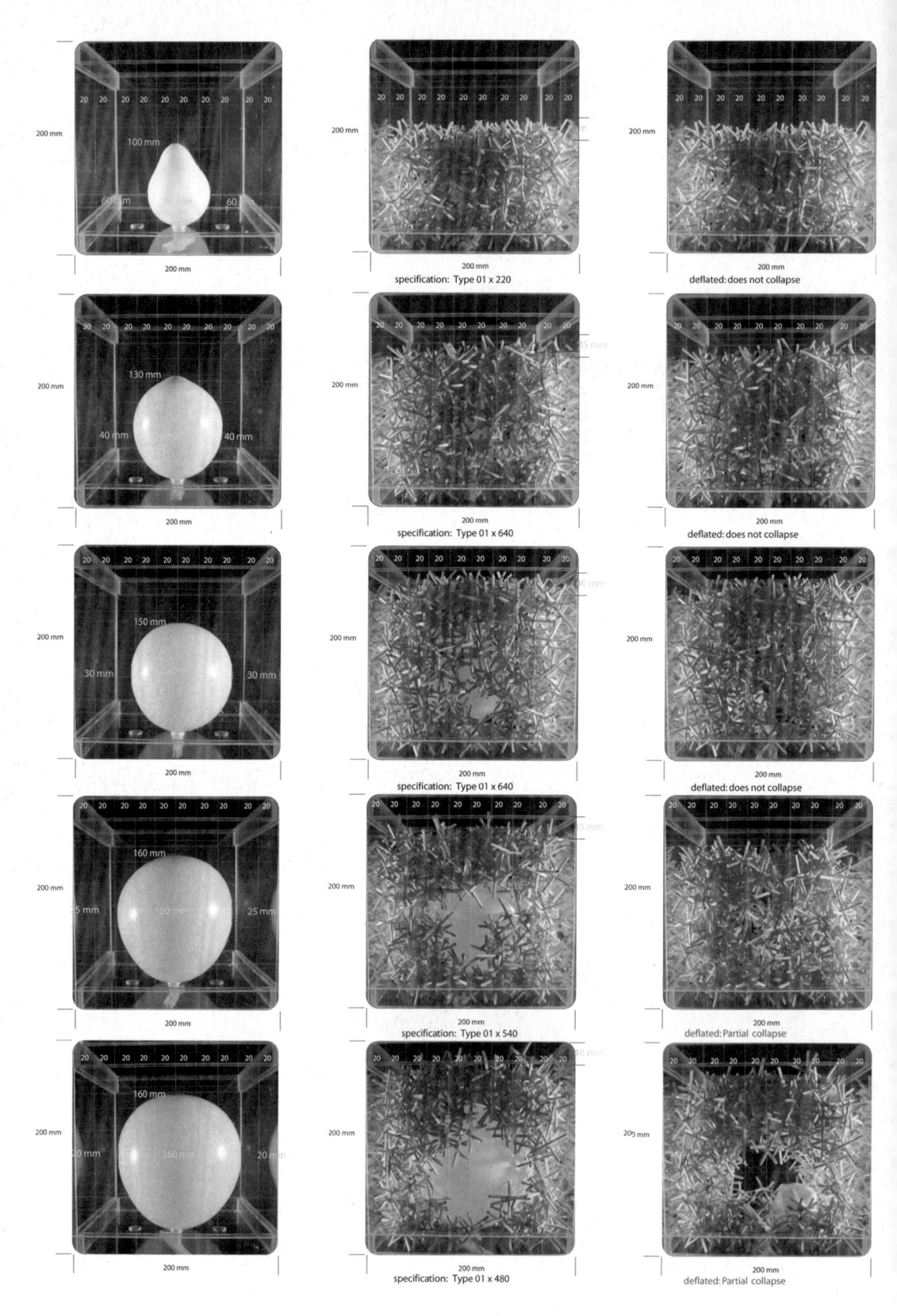

specification: Type 01 x 220 — deflated: does not collapse

specification: Type 01 x 640 — deflated: does not collapse

specification: Type 01 x 640 — deflated: does not collapse

specification: Type 01 x 540 — deflated: Partial collapse

specification: Type 01 x 480 — deflated: Partial collapse

The aggregate has the ability to form a self-supporting structure over a cavity produced by an inflated formwork. This was tested in a series of experiments by pouring aggregate elements into a cubic test container filled with a balloon (centre) and deflating the balloon for the self-stabilising process to take place.

In order to investigate formation patterns resulting from varied support conditions of the temporal formwork, a larger experiment set-up features different boundary conditions and the placement of centred and peripheral inflatable formwork.

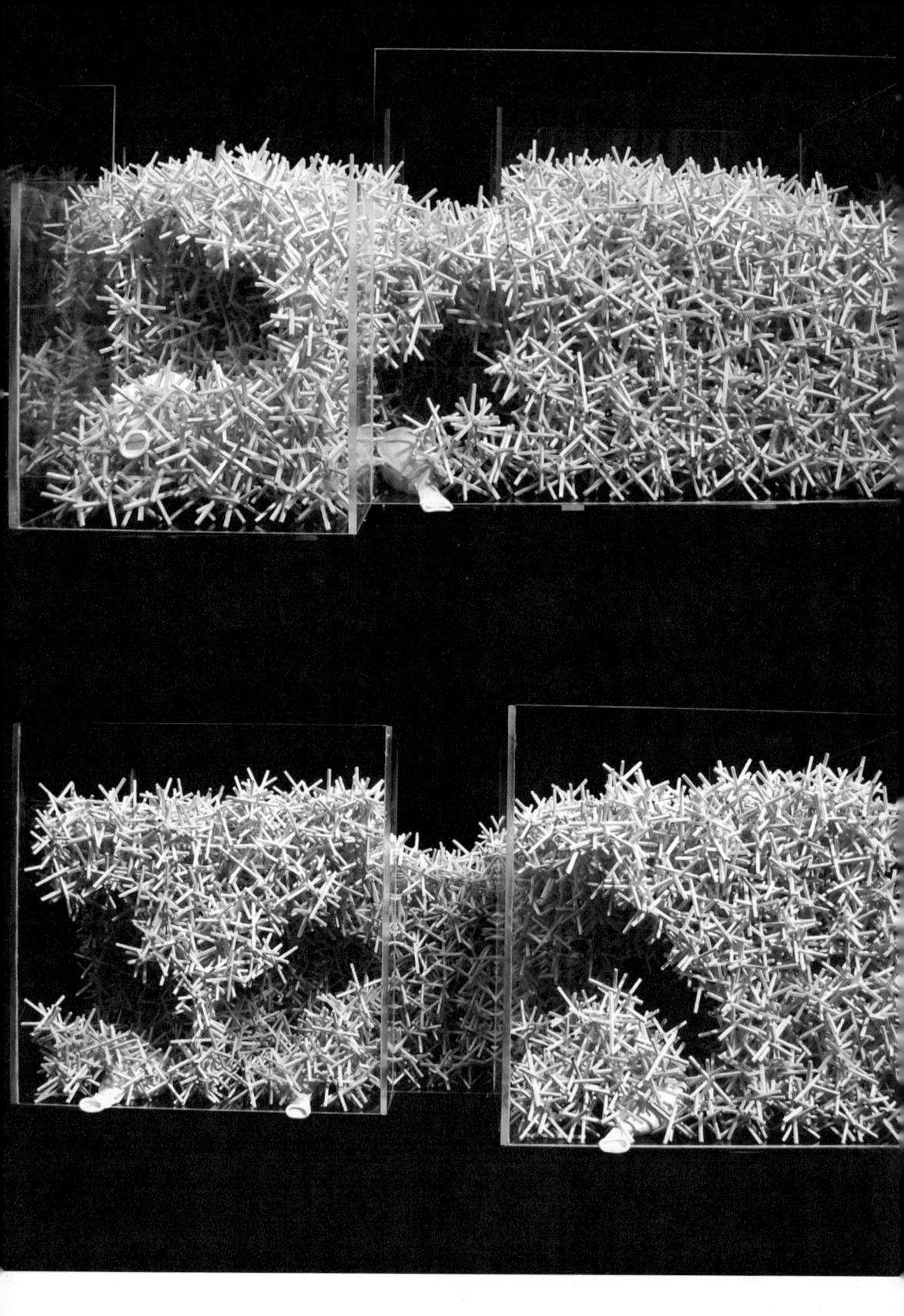

270　　A series of test conducted using the larger experiment set-up corroborate the system's ability to form a self-supporting structure with open, closed and connected cavities. Through this spaces with varied degrees of enclosure can be created.

Environmental modulation of the emerging spaces takes place through additional aggregates of varying size ranges that allow for regulating the density and porosity of the enclosure.

Eiichi Matsuda's project seems to have had several lives and to have gone through several reincarnations since it was originally designed. Some have been similar permutations, others showed interesting developments of form and behaviour. Together, they have delivered a new typology to the research of material systems.

The design in itself consists of a single element repeated thousands of times. The individual object gains its attributes from two interdependent yet contradictory requirements of the overall system. Whilst it has the ability to become structural – a fixed, aggregated form – it retains its fluidity. The higher the degree of fluidity, the sooner critical states emerge in which a sudden collapse can relaunch the aggregation process in its typical formation. The attribute negotiating this condition is the 'stickiness' between the elements. In Eiichi's project, the individual element consists of a simple three-axis cross that gains its stickiness through mechanical interlocking in relation to its weight. This does not allow, however, for a high level of human-to-object influence (one of its main qualities as a model) once applied at the real scale. The pouring of the aggregate, its reconfiguration and disassembly all require mechanical aids. If we shift the relation between weight and interlocking we will have two possible outcomes. If more weight is added with a lower level of mechanical linkages occurring, the result will be much like a pile of bricks. If, however, the weight and size of the element are reduced and the mechanical linkages increased through the addition of hooks, the result might be a lighter element with a bur-like stickiness. The increase in mechanical linkages shifts the basic principles of the project in a number of ways: disaggregation becomes very difficult, and formations of the elements no longer create a true aggregate as the elements begin to hang from each other, forming a loose net. Although the strengthened interlocking allows for more differentiation in the resulting form, the fluidity of the aggregate is compromised.

The potential solutions to these problems might be found within the relation of the individual element to external factors throughout the construction, that is, the aggregation

THEO LORENZ COMMENTS

process. The question is whether we could change the element's characteristics and thus its aggregation behaviour, for instance the phase change of water to gas or ice under the influence of temperature. The element's aggregation patterns as well as its structural behaviour would then begin to respond to specific environmental conditions such as wind, water and temperature and, on a larger scale, to the context-specific topography and atmosphere. In addition to such external factors, the morphology of the element could respond to human interaction through the aggregation and reconfiguration sequence. With this, the project would develop the possibility to accumulate a different knowledge of 'Morpho-Ecologies'. The design of the single element would therefore have to combine knowledge of material behaviour with knowledge of atmospheric conditioning as well as construction logics, ergonomics and human intervention.

From the former discussion, four lines of inquiry can be distilled, which can be followed separately or in combination.

The first is geometry-based, in which Eiichi Matsuda's project can be seen as a starting point. Is there a geometry that can be a precise negotiation of the different behavioural criteria within the construction process? A form that retains its fluidity when poured and sticks when at rest and yet continues to allow for manual separation and disassembly? Aside from its own geometry, additional factors of influence are context-specific geometric constraints, the pouring device, the cast, and the topography onto which the aggregate settles.

The second line of research might be material-based. Here, the material form and characteristics change during the process, in order to seek the appropriate geometry according to atmospheric influences such as temperature and humidity.

The third line of research might focus on disaggregation: the forces required to close and open a link or hook through gravity or pull. The objects close their links like a trap once they hit each other with enough force, but can still be pulled apart manually.

The fourth line of inquiry might focus on communication between elements. Like smart dust, each aggregate has an embedded intelligence that can sense its position within the overall aggregation, reacting and adapting accordingly.

Each of the four strands would be worth exploring, and would require a high level of engineering and testing. In combination, their possibilities seem infinite.

In conclusion, construction through aggregation is only at the dawn of its evolution. Every element or particle, even one as simple as a grain of sand, might be understood, deployed or designed as part of an overall system taking into account material, spatial and atmospheric conditions, as well as the impact of such a system on its progression. The latter is of particular interest with a built environment that can easily be aggregated and disaggregated. This would yield a profound revision of deeply entrenched forms of practice in architecture.

I am looking forward to seeing how this typology of aggregate will develop.

Aggregates are fast to work with. Once the specific aims and constraints for a series of experiments are outlined, it is possible to carry out many experiments in a relatively short time. With this realisation another question arises: if an aggregate system was designed on a human scale, making the system easy to manipulate and aggregations swift to produce, would the passer-by then begin to engage with it and manipulate it? Would time-specific usefulness of the aggregate emanate from this interaction? These questions arose from this work in parallel with other research interests and related experiments discussed below.

Initial tests utilised off-the-shelf mass-produced elements from a DIY store to establish a first taxonomy of the relationship between the aggregation behaviour under the influence of gravity and the particular geometric characteristics of the different aggregate elements. Key features such as the tendency and capacity for interlocking were extracted from these tests and informed the set-up of a specific geometric articulation of a purpose-made aggregate element. Other key features in the search for the element geometry were ease of fabrication and weight and price of the material. If aggregation was to be easy, the size and weight of each element would have to be calibrated for use by a single passer-by of any age.

As aggregate systems depend on a large number of elements, the production time and cost per element were also of critical importance. Different strategies for fabrication were explored ranging from automated laser-cutting to manual production with a band saw. Finally, a fabrication strategy of cutting the aggregate elements with a mitre saw from plywood panels was chosen as this allowed the number of cuts through a specific nesting pattern to be minimised and five sheets to be cut at the same time, resulting in an average cost of US$ 0.19 per aggregate element. This initial element consisted of two equal parts that can be assembled in two configurations – an A type and an X type – which differ in terms of overall size and ability to interlock.

Once the specific geometry of the

aggregate unit types A and X had been defined a series of aggregation tests were conducted.

The investigation focused on specific characteristics that can be deduced from the aggregation patterns over several hundred tests, such as the angle of inclination or the resultant density of each aggregate. This implies that every time a relevant parameter in the formation process is altered, a whole series of new aggregation tests have to be analysed in order to discern recurrent aggregation patterns.

Three categories of variables can be identified:

The first category takes the geometric articulation and material characteristics of the individual aggregate element into account. As the aggregate element was defined as a constant in this project, the main variables were the two geometric types A and X.

The second manipulation category defines the aggregation process or pouring conditions through the variables of aggregate element emission path, pouring speed and time.

The third category comprises the particular boundary conditions that constrain the pouring area and aggregation process.

For each parameter defined as a variable in the three manipulation categories a series of tests were conducted and documented in a chart. For example, different boundary surfaces and formwork configurations, as well as different pouring conditions were tested, notated and analysed across 26 sets of experiments. From these experiments the density or porosity of different system instances and also sub-locations of each aggregate were measured and mapped.

The ability to manipulate the aggregation process and thus influence performative characteristics of the resultant system was further explored in a large-scale aggregation. In order to test the system's performative capacity to modulate luminous flow, the aggregate was poured into formwork consisting of removable panels and a tall windowpane. The density and porosity variations resulting from specific manipulations of the aggregation process were then analysed in relation to the transmission of daylight over several days. The resulting light conditions were photographed every 15 minutes in order to map the specific luminosity modulation.

To test the structural capacity of the system various formworks were made for wall, arch, half-vault and vault configurations. Each aggregate was checked for its capacity to carry its self-weight, by removing the formwork incrementally. In addition, each aggregate was carefully loaded with additional point-loads. Other experiments focused on the removal of elements to the point of collapse of each aggregate, to begin to be able to assess the redundancy of load-paths.

Curious spectators were asked to assist in the experiments, which were undertaken over several weeks, in order to provoke an interest in the system. During the last few weeks, while the environmental modulation experiments were taking place, other aggregates from earlier experiments were left in place, together with piles of elements and posters that invited the free use of these elements. Ad hoc experiments and aggregates began to emerge in different parts of the building over a period of several weeks, conducted by unknown contributors. This suggested that the ease of manipulation of the system invites curiosity, specifically as the system does not indicate any particular use. Each new instance of the system only emerges from direct interaction, in much the same way as the aggregates might be used. Most importantly, a new sensibility arises from this interaction, based on the realisation that some part of the built environment can be changed with great ease and direct effect.

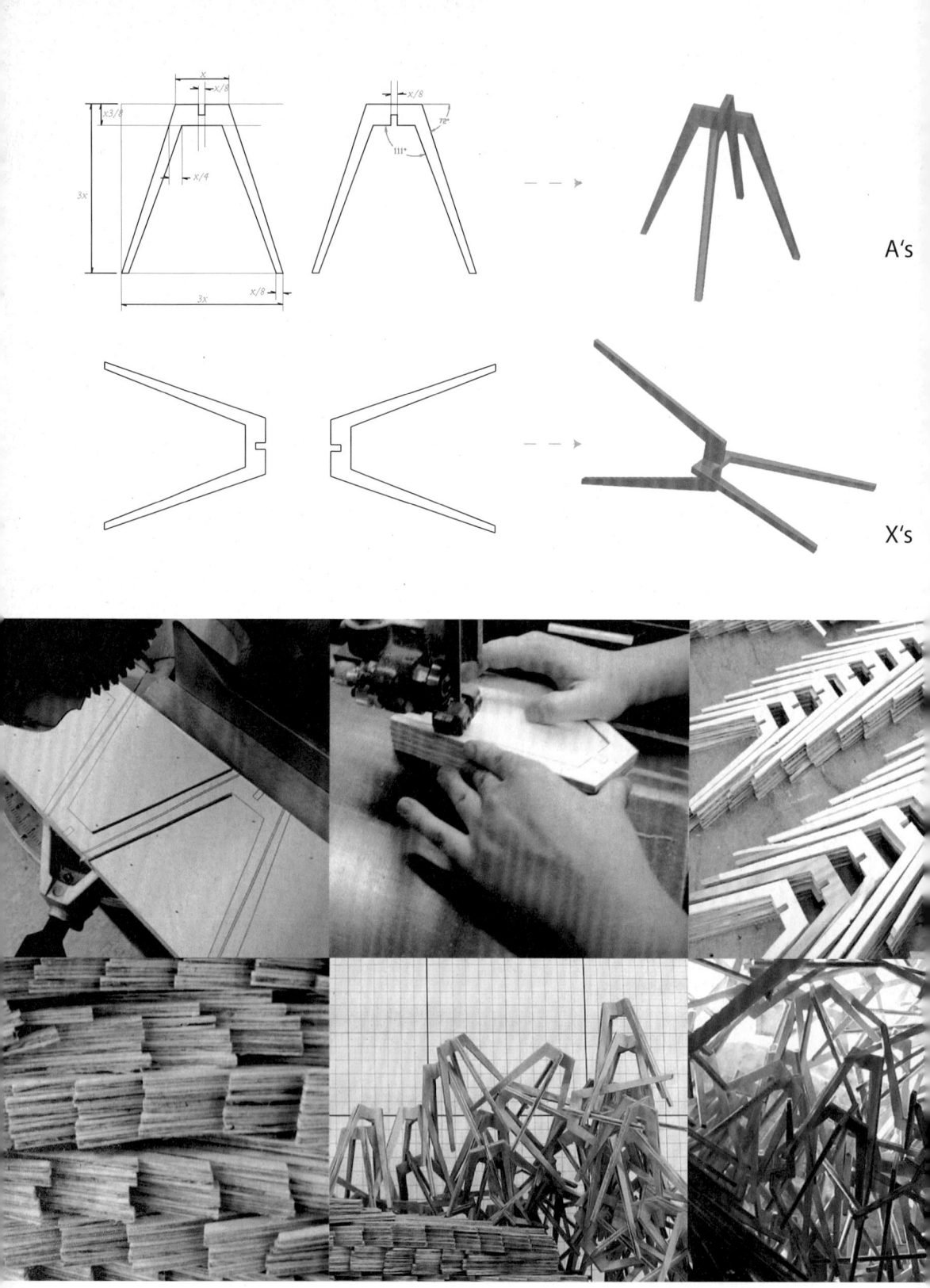

276   The basic aggregate element can be assembled from one element shape in two ways: an A and X configuration (top). The geometric definition of the basic aggregate shape is optimised for ease of manual production and assembly.

Various aggregation processes were tested in series of experiments to explore, notate and understand the interrelated influences of the element type, the pouring conditions and the articulation or use of existing external constraints.

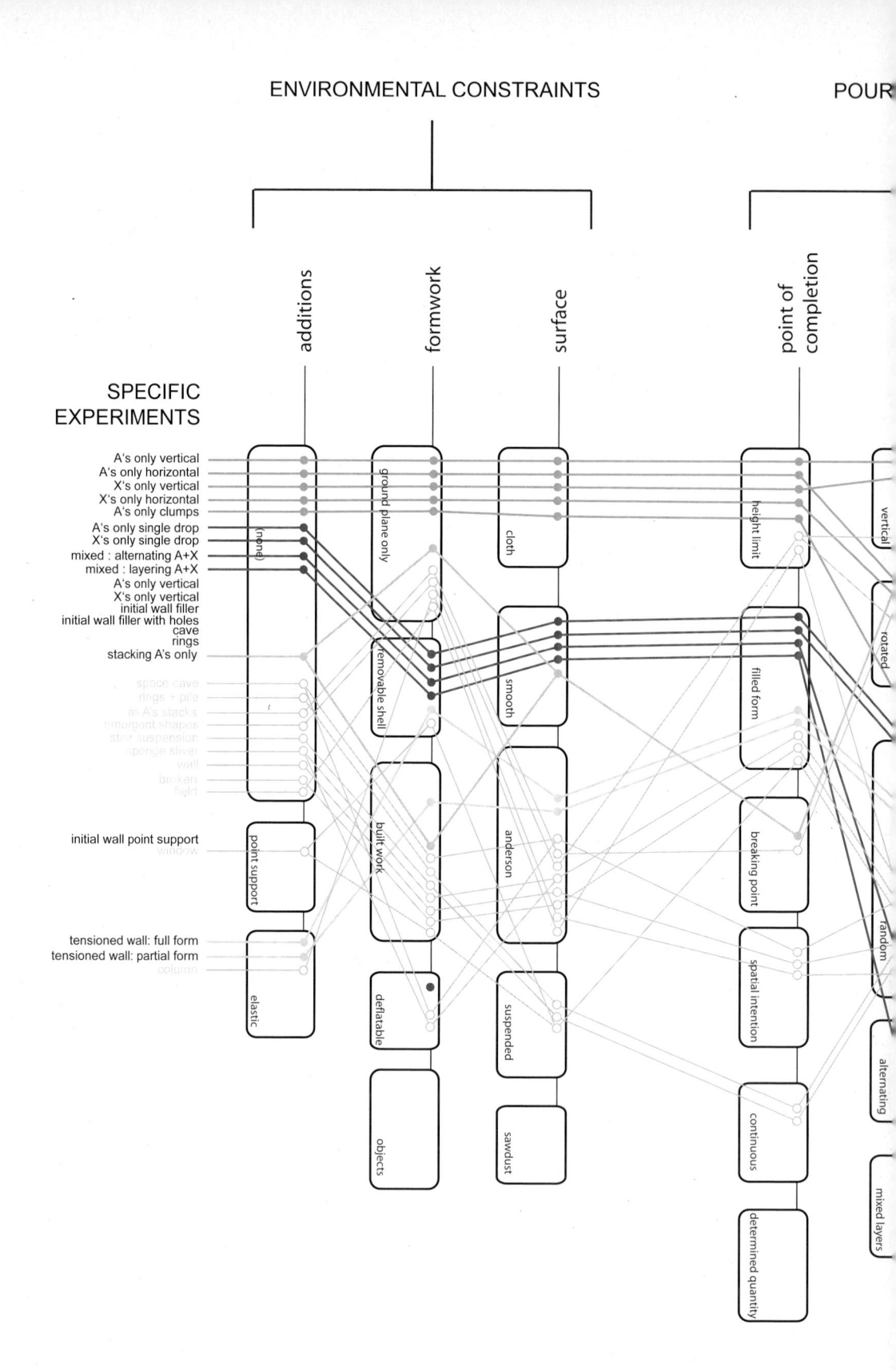

ENVIRONMENTAL CONSTRAINTS

POUR

- additions
- formwork
- surface
- point of completion

SPECIFIC EXPERIMENTS

- A's only vertical
- A's only horizontal
- X's only vertical
- X's only horizontal
- A's only clumps
- A's only single drop
- X's only single drop
- mixed : alternating A+X
- mixed : layering A+X
- A's only vertical
- X's only vertical
- initial wall filler
- initial wall filler with holes
- cave
- rings
- stacking A's only
- space cave
- rings + pile
- all A's stacks
- emergent shapes
- stair suspension
- sponge sliver
- wall
- broken
- field
- initial wall point support
- window
- tensioned wall: full form
- tensioned wall: partial form
- column

Categories:
- (none)
- point support
- elastic
- ground plane only
- removable shell
- built work
- deflatable
- objects
- cloth
- smooth
- anderson
- suspended
- sawdust
- height limit
- filled form
- breaking point
- spatial intention
- continuous
- determined quantity
- vertical
- rotated
- random
- alternating
- mixed layers

278

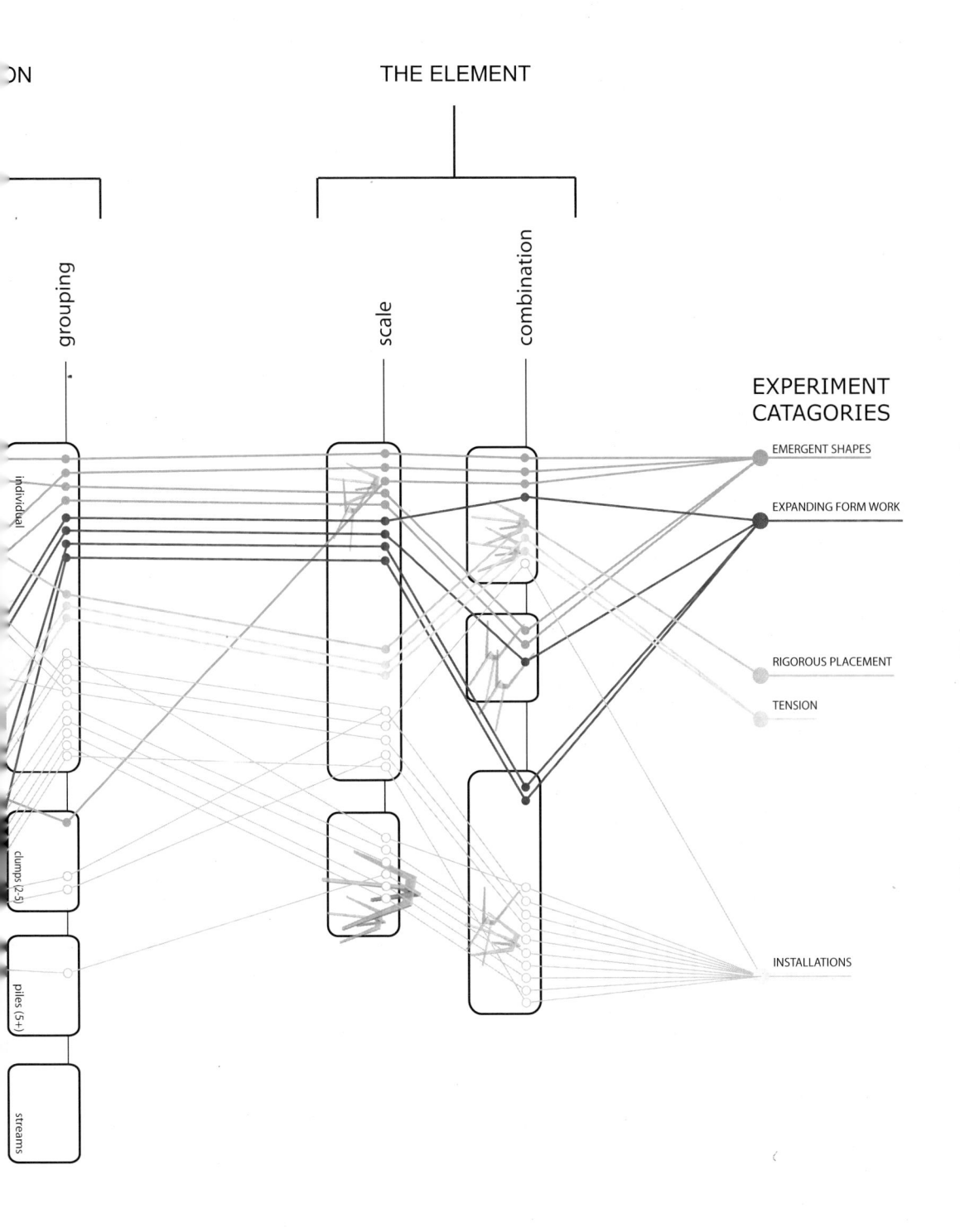

THE ELEMENT

grouping | scale | combination

individual
clumps (2-5)
piles (5+)
streams

EXPERIMENT CATAGORIES

EMERGENT SHAPES

EXPANDING FORM WORK

RIGOROUS PLACEMENT

TENSION

INSTALLATIONS

Twenty-six experiments of five experiment categories were defined in an aggregate manipulation chart. The chart indicates the three main categories for possible manipulations of the system (the aggregate element, the pouring conditions and the environmental constraints) in relation to critical design parameters and the conducted tests.

280 The aggregate's performative capacity to modulate luminous flow was investigated through a larger system constructed by pouring the aggregate into formwork consisting of removable panels and a tall windowpane.

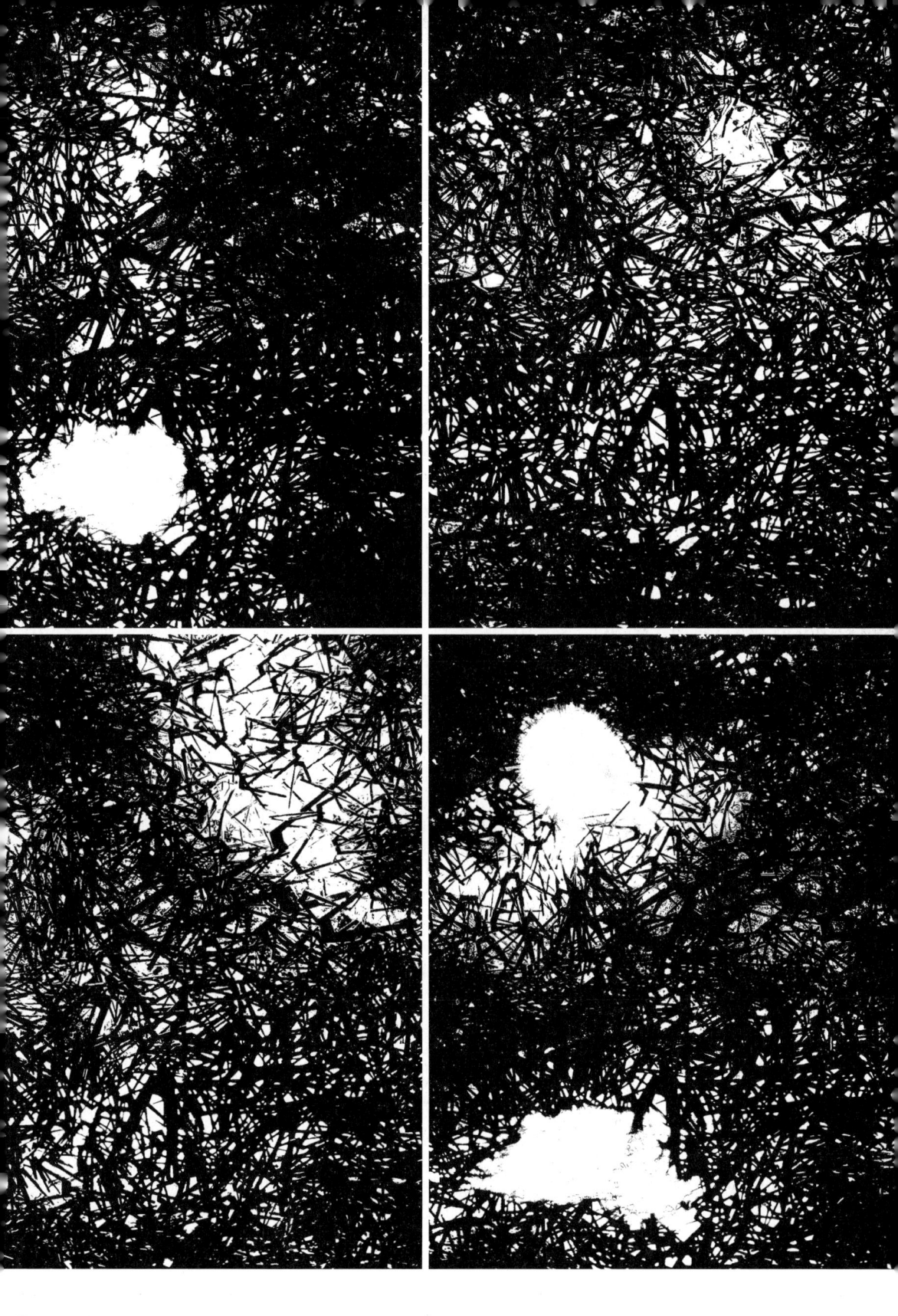

The system's density and porosity variations were analysed in relation to the transmission of daylight over several days. The resulting light conditions were photographed at regular intervals in order to subsequently map the specific luminosity modulation.

282 Different degrees of porosity resulting from specific manipulations of the aggregation process enable differential modulation of light transmission across various sub-locations of the system.

Aggregate System exhibited in the 'Modulations' Exhibition at Rice School of Architecture, Houston, 2004.

We know that architects love gravity. Friction, they're not so sure about. As a result, we have often sought to fix the ordering of architecture in two predominate and typically polar locations: in geometry and in details. The former, whether Vitruvian or topological, is treated as something that operates on the architectural whole at a level of abstraction if not ideality. The latter situates material as the condition of an architectural order that is always already concrete. For geometricians, 'architecture' resides in abstract concepts that need to be translated into material in a way that preserves the precision of the transcendent mathematical order; for the detailers architecture is the representational ordering of material conjunctions in such a way as to create effects and, ultimately, a gestalt. Both require extreme precision and determination. Of course this duality rarely appears in its pure form; the classical Greek Temple combined the two in a way that would later constitute a total canon. In the nexus of complex geometry and mass-customised component systems, the merging of geometry and material detail to create a totally integrated architecture is the goal of architectural knowledge. In this respect, the architectures of morphogenesis and emergence are Vitruvian insofar as they attempt to seamlessly incorporate the part into a greater whole. Architecture's orthography, or normativity, lies not in 90 degrees per se, but at this intersection of the geometric and material vectors that resolve gravitational force as architectural form.

In this context, granular or aggregate approaches to ordering and material are a ubiquitous but dangerously wild topic of architectural knowledge. The discovery of the performative emergence that occurs with aggregates plays a central, if often implicit, role in the plasticity of form and space enabled by the development of concrete. This is often accompanied by an anxiety that such architectures are less serious, or at least less rational, relying a bit too much on sensation and pleasure, whether we are talking of the vaults of Roman baths or Saarinen; the isomorphism of geometry with material detail seems effaced as a problem of rational solution, becoming instead the expression of a hand or a will. In poured concrete, the detail and the geometry merge in a way that no longer allows them to be represented as such, moving literally to a molecular level that does not operate at the scale of the visual and thus needs to be tamed by the re-appearance of geometry via the expressive use of construction artefacts, such as Kahn's tie-holes and form joinery.

While the adhesive alchemy of concrete can be recuperated into the detail to create a geometric whole, cohesive aggregates such as sand are even more disturbing in that their form, by relying solely on friction (a dynamic force rather than static equilibrium), is not monumental but rather an index of energy as pure potential, which may be released slowly or catastrophically. Aggregate Modulations occupies this precarious location as the architectural equivalent of sand dunes. Made up of two variants of the same component, differentiated only by the location of a connective slot that locks two elements together via friction, the entire system coheres via friction on two scales. First there is the scale of the two different forked units, or grains, that loosely nest into each other; one has direction to its roughness because its tines are oriented the same way, the other is bi-directional. The second scale is the roughness of the plywood from which they are cut, replete with splinters that catch each other like an ad-hoc Velcro. These units can literally be thrown together – and there seems an art of throwing rather than joinery here – into surprisingly supple forms. Rather than a joint or a geometry, the order of this architecture is pure friction. Like concrete, this system needs a frame or formwork to take its shape, whether simply a floor datum, a window frame or a filigree of wire upon which it can grow like a crystal advancing along a frothy edge. But rather than use these as temporary scaffolds for a monumental permanence, the friction-held systems destabilise the architectural frame into which they are installed. The resultant likelihood of the components being reconfigured, like shifting and shimmering sand dunes, uncannily reminds us that all matter is constantly undergoing dynamic processes of transformation. Forms are merely momentarily stored energy. In our age of nanotechnology and smart dust, researching the architectural potential of aggregates is crucial in developing a new understanding of architectural space and form that literally team with life and transformation. The decidedly 'low-tech' approach of Aggregate Modulations demonstrates that such potential to radically alter the built environment depends not on technological gizmos but on shifting concepts and modes of operation towards a different, aggregate, understanding of the relationship between geometry and material.

Thus perhaps the real potential of Aggregate Modulations lies not in its status as proto-architecture but in its promise as projective urbanism, an infrastructural diagram of the sorts of orders that would need to be researched to chart and facilitate a metropolis for the electronic multitude. This also suggests the need to reverse the knowledge transfer from science to architecture that is so common. Geometricians and scientists, including Frei Otto, have long echoed architects' monumental will to geometry and detail at an urban scale by trying to find singular patterns, typically fractal, that determine settlement patterns and urban growth at the micro- and macro-scales. They argue that order is located in the bottom-up operations that produce a global, even universal order at the level of geometry, regardless of its material growth medium (that is the social and economic, which are presented as merely epiphenomena). This strangely monumentalises the growth patterns themselves and reduces the true slurry complexity of urbanism into simplistic discourse of, at best, nature. At worst it suggests a Pythagorean reification of geometry as cause and effect. The challenge of Aggregate Modulations to such discourses is to open a trajectory of further research in which aggregates can be approached as a society of granular infrastructure that creates not a material gestalt but rather a swarming multiplicity of self-organised multiplicity ordered by local cohesions rather than geometric monumentality.

Designing with aggregates may commence either from the design of the elements that will make up the aggregate or from the utilisation of natural grains with designed and natural constraints to the aggregation process. This project commenced from the latter, choosing sand as the material. Sand is interesting, as it is observable in nature in dune and ripple formations, in which the dunes are modulated by airflow and water which are in turn modulated by the dunes and ripples. This establishes an interesting feedback of mutual modulation that brings about formations that follow clearly discernible rules. The initial task was to establish these rules through experiments and research.

The first set of experiments focused on pouring and draining sand in order to verify the geometric rules that underlie the formation of sand-piles and holes with respect to the perimeter angle of the formation. Variables included the amount of sand to be used, pouring speed, funnel size and the angle of the receiving surface. A sand pile is a dynamically stable shape as it retains the inclination of its slope during the process of pouring. Such systems are non-equilibrium dissipative structures, in which, as Philip Ball describes it 'the spatial scale of the pattern formation bears no relation to the size of its constituents', displaying robustness throughout perturbations. Transient disturbances can disrupt dissipative structures momentarily, with sand-piles collapsing when a critical threshold is reached, but eventually the same pattern formation as before will continue and the piles build up again.

The second set of experiments focused on blowing sand horizontally in order to observe formations resulting from the interaction of airflow and sand.

The experiments were then repeated introducing a number of obstacles and constraints to the pouring, draining and blowing processes in order to study the impact on formation pattern. A series of geometrically differentiated lattice structures were introduced in order to observe formation patterns in relation to the inclination, orientation and distance between lattice members and different distribution and size of holes. Wind-blown sand aggregation together with draining through the multilayered, differentiated lattices results in pile formations in lower layers and below the lattice datum. Sand gets captured, drained in specific ways and formed against a series of constraints on top, within and below the lattice datum.

A further set of experiments focused on local hardening of the aggregate by mixing a binding agent into thin layers of sand that are strategically poured over current formations, using them as formwork, to achieve selectively more permanent formations. These hardened surfaces can then become more permanent constraints for further sand formation processes or just remain in the shape they have attained. Through this process of selective hardening in combination with continual shifts in sand aggregation, the system can be calibrated to achieve a structurally capable and geometrically variable basic system as well as reconfigurable zones. Both remain coherent with the underlying logics of sand aggregations.

As the size and articulation of specific formations and features, from piles to ripples, is crucial in relation to use, the amount of sand, pouring time and selective hardening of surfaces needs to be well calibrated. This involves a careful study of ergonomics in relation to formation and feature sizes on the one hand, and the required duration and malleability of the formations on the other hand. Here the inherent ability of sand aggregations to be very malleable and adaptable, for example in responding to the shape and weight of a human body, and its constancy of settling back into recurrent formation patterns once a particular impact ceases to exist and sand is redistributed, become of strategic importance for the design process. Different degrees of stability and constancy can be devised and organised in different sub-locations and across various size ranges of the sand aggregate system.

The largest size range relates to a landscape scale and involves the distribution of ridges and troughs and the angles of inclination of surfaces. Through the modulation of terrains of changing geometric character and topography, different degrees of connectivity and exposure can be strategised. This size range also has the largest impact on the thermal environment, given the considerable thermal mass of large sand-piles. The orientation of non-symmetrical sand-formation relative to the sun-path is of crucial importance with regard to the exposure of surfaces. With regard to the formative process the relation between prevailing winds and sun-path will determine the placement of obstacles.

In order to achieve some level of enclosure the lattices and the hardened aggregate areas were utilised, since they provide permanent elements necessary for the structural capacity. Thus in the medium range, cavities with varying degrees of enclosure and spatial connectivity are established. Here the perforation patterns and sizes allow for modulating micro-environmental zones through the interaction of medium-size sand heaps with air flow and sunlight. The closure of lattice areas can be achieved locally through small pneumatic cushions that close off single lattice fields to prevent sand passing through. Over time, the resultant solar gain and ventilation influences, and in return is also influenced by, the formation process of the system on a larger and smaller size range. On the human scale, the sand articulation provides multiple ergonomic opportunities that respond to the user's body and can be adjusted by the individual inhabitant.

Exploiting the natural tendency of sand to accumulate and aggregate in particular patterns, the project developed a range of micro to medium landscapes with varying ergonomic, environmental and spatial characteristics and opportunities for a site in the harbour of Recife in Brazil. This area of the harbour served the temporary storage and transport of other granular material, such as sugar, weed and pet coke. The newly introduced dynamically stable landscape traces this history. It is proposed to occupy not only the open areas as a public landscape typical for Brazil, the urban beach, but also some of the vast structures that served the storage of sugar, thus providing for a new type of indoor public landscape.

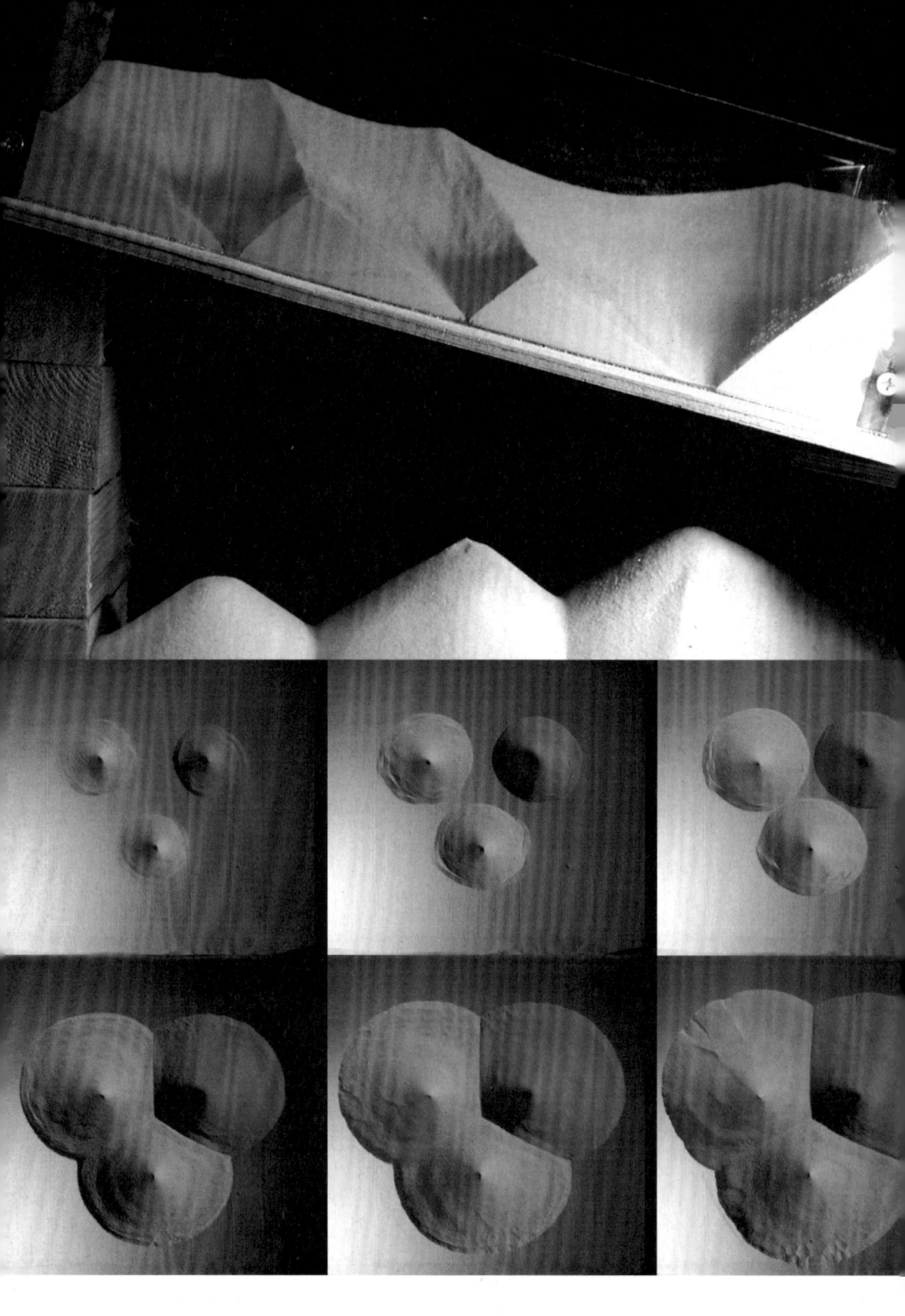

288   The initial sets of experiments investigated the relationship between pouring or draining sand and geometric rules that underlie the formation of sand-piles and holes. Variables included the angle of the base surface (top), the amount of sand, pouring speed, and funnel size and configuration. During the process of pouring or draining different sand formations emerge (bottom).

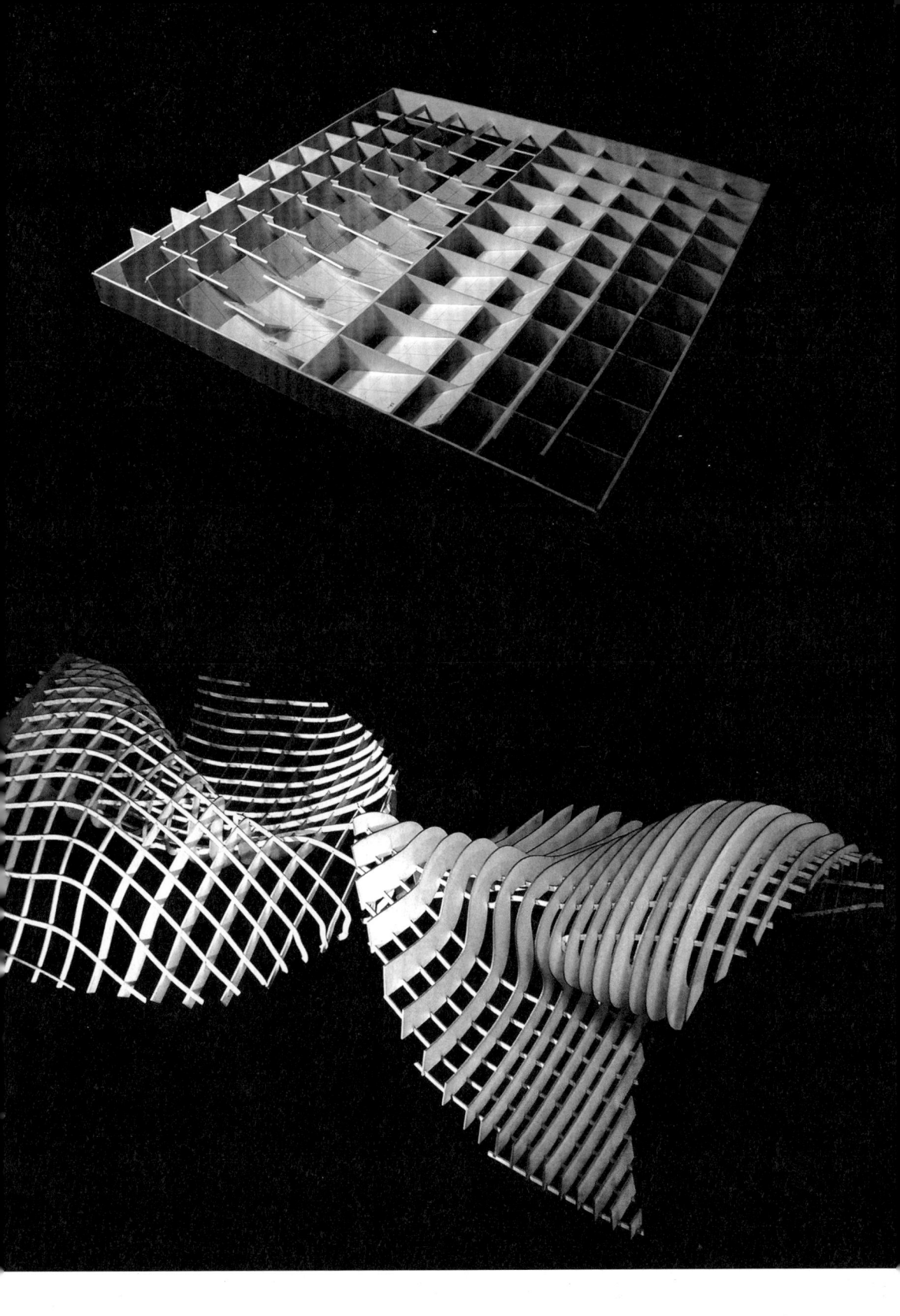

In order to investigate more complex sand formation patterns a series of parametrically varied planar (top) and double-curved base surfaces (bottom) were defined.

SURFACE CONDITION

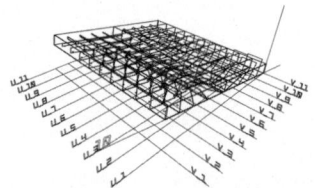

V_11AXIS : 10DEGREE

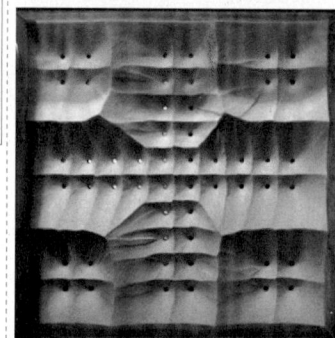

PATTERN_03

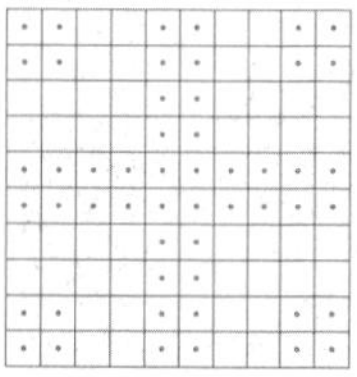

PATTERN_04

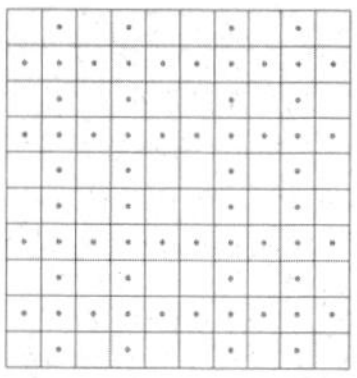

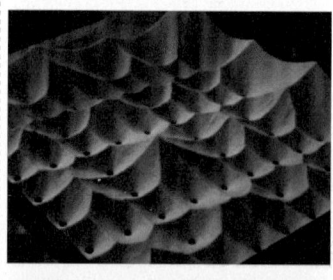

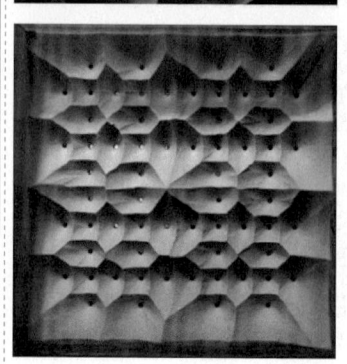

290

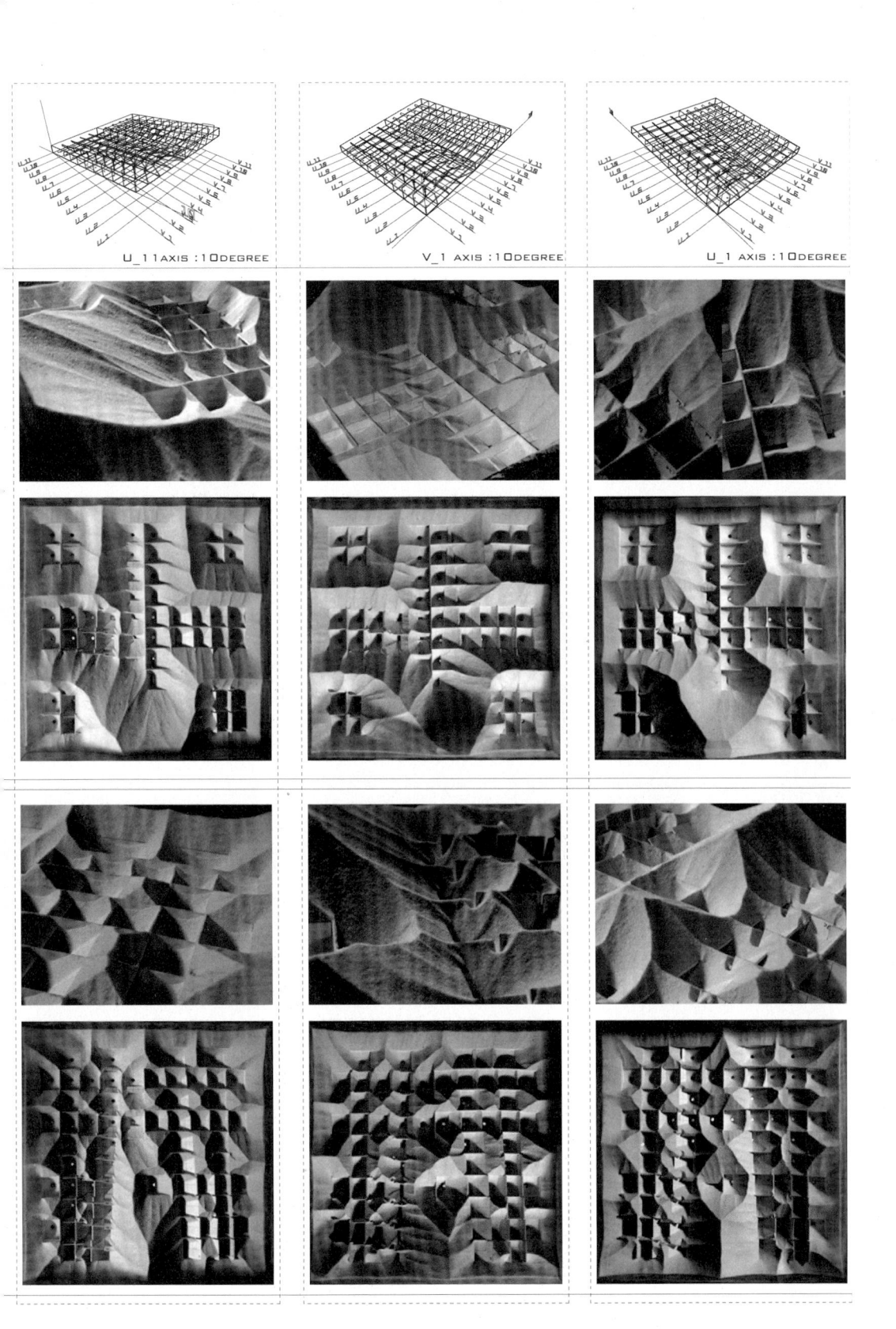

The interrelation between local geometric variance of the base surface and its overall inclination enables the strategic manipulation of the resulting sand formations. Further variables include the configuration of different hole patterns.

Another series of basic experiments focused on blowing sand horizontally across a surface with variable inclination in a wind tunnel in order to observe formations resulting from the interaction of airflow, surface and the granular sand substance.

Using the wind tunnel to expose a double-curved lattice system to horizontally blown sand indicates the possibility of strategically exploiting the geometric surface definition to channel the formation of sand heaps on top, below and adjacent to the system.

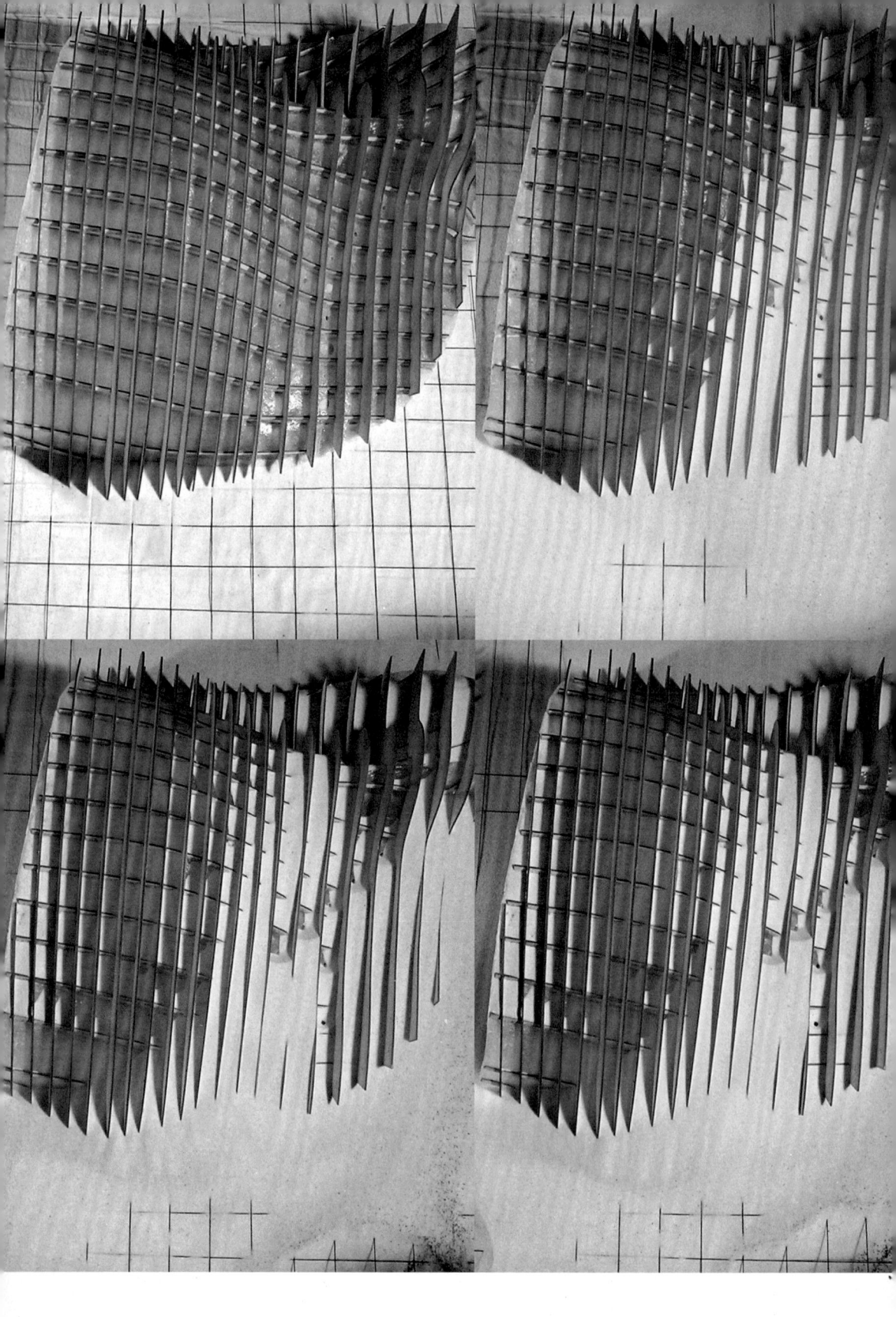

294 Instrumentalising the natural tendency of sand to accumulate and aggregate in particular patterns, the specific surface articulation enables the strategic capturing, overflow and release of sand over time.

This set of experiments suggests a combination of wind-blown sand aggregation together with draining the sand through multilayered, differentiated lattices, which in turn results in pile formations in lower layers and below the lattice datum. Sand thus gets captured, drained in specific ways and formed against a series of constraints on top, within and below the lattice datum.

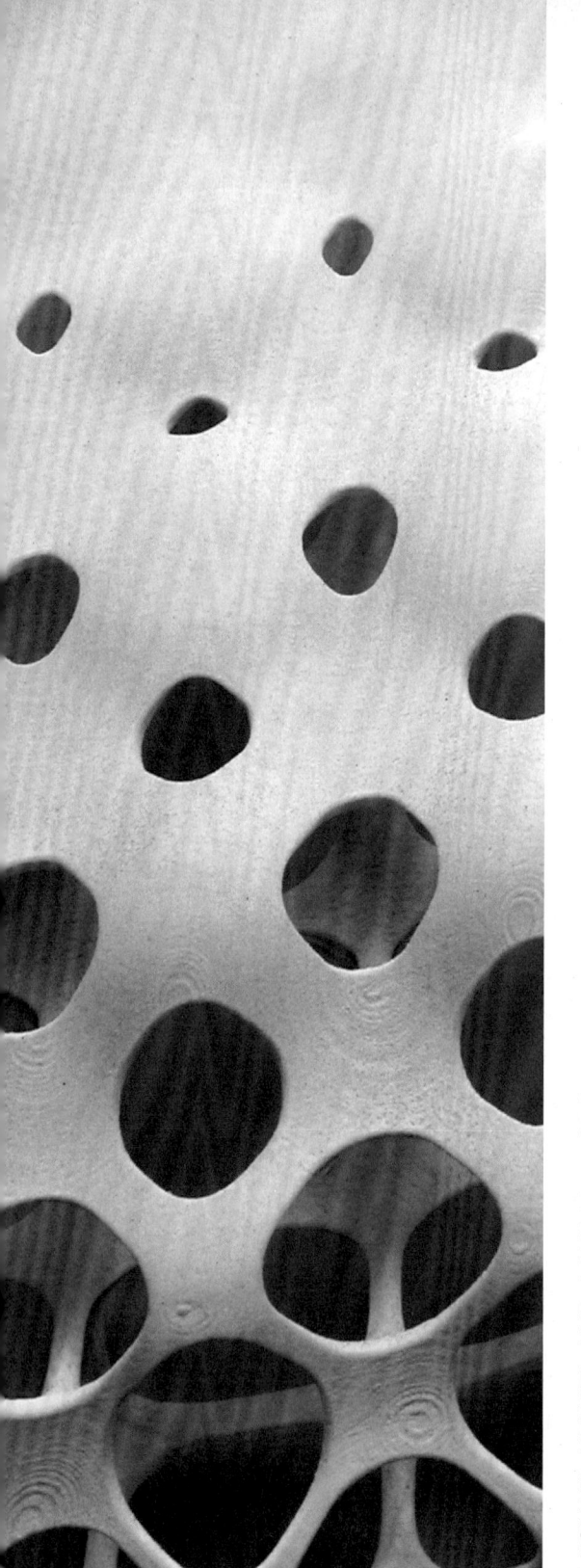

MICHAEL HENSEL AND ACHIM MENGES

6 ESSAYS

Most of the papers in this chapter were presented as part of the Differentiation in Nature and Design Symposium held at the Architectural Association in March 2006. Some additional papers have been contributed by friends and colleagues with whom the notion of differentiation resonated.

The Morpho-Ecological approach introduced in this book is rooted in a biological paradigm and draws its operative and instrumental notions from the discipline of biology. In biology, differentiation is a process whereby cells develop specialised functional biochemistries and morphologies that were previously not present. As a by-product of evolution, specialised multi-cellularity implies the division of labour. In plants, for instance, unspecialised cells differentiate into vascular, supportive and storage tissue. The changes in cells and tissues that result in their specialisation also enable the emergence of a greater variety of organisms.

This principle – of simple elements that acquire different functionality depending on their location within a larger system relative to context-specific exposure to environmental stimuli – points to an alternative approach to architectural design. It suggests a decisive shift from building systems to the notion of differentiated material systems, with self-organisational capacities that can be utilised across numerous scales, from the material make-up to the performance of elements within the larger functional economy of an overall system.

The symposium aimed at discussing potential instrumental relations between biology, engineering and architectural design. The first session began by establishing links between biology, engineering and design. Michael Weinstock and Julian Vincent discussed such relations, drawing eventual links to the discipline of biomimetic engineering.

The second session focused on the repercussions on engineering. Wolf Mangelsdorf from Buro Happold discussed applications of differentiation in structural engineering.

The third session focused on the theoretical and methodological implications for the discipline of architecture. Mark Burry reported on his ongoing work on the Sagrada Familia and the morphological differentiation present in Gaudí's work. Peter Trummer contributed a paper that examined the ramifications of population thinking for design.

Christopher Hight discussed various iterations of the emergence of differentiation in architectural design.

This collection of papers only scratches the surface of the powerful notion of differentiation, but hopefully it will suffice to arouse the reader's curiosity about a new approach to architectural design – an approach which aims to leave behind heterogeneous space with higher-level functionality for the sake of a more human-friendly environment.

Differentiation is a feature of all natural systems. It occurs between cells within biological tissues, between tissues, organs and structures within individual phenotypes or organisms, between individuals in populations, and between communities and species. Systems of energy-flow control differentiation in each level of hierarchy. Living systems interact with the non-living world to form the ecosystem, the highest level of biological organisation. This interaction is critical to the understanding of differentiation in the biota, as without environment there is no organism, and without organisms there is no environment. Relationships between living organisms and the environment are vectored by energy and material flows, organised by trophic levels in a co-evolutionary process between living things and their physical and chemical environments. Analysis of energy flows and morphological differentiation, co-evolution, and speciation in ecological systems[1] offers a metabolic strategy for buildings and cities that recognises the dynamics of critical changes in the global environment.

MONSTERS AND MUTATIONS

The mythical monsters of the classical world were imaginary creatures, composed of parts of known animal and human forms. The sphinx, for example, had the head of a woman and the body of a lion, the centaur was a horse that had a human torso and head, and the chimera was a fire-breathing monster that had the head of a lion, the body of a goat and the tail of a serpent. These were beings that combined mankind and animals, but it is not their cultural significance that I want to refer to, rather the fact that through these combinations they could achieve more than mere mortals. Monsters were aggregations of differences, and the union of these differences produced a higher functionality.

We describe a system as complex if it is made up of several parts that are so thoroughly connected that the system cannot be broken down into elements or components without destroying it. As with the monsters of antiquity, the parts are distinct or different from each other, and at the same time they are connected. A system has more complexity the more parts it has, and the more connections between them. An increase of differences is differentiation, an increase in the number or strength of connections between them is integration. For a system to be complex, both differentiation and integration are necessary. Complexity[2] theory focuses on the effects produced by the collective behaviour of many simple units that interact with each other, such as atoms, molecules or cells. The complex is heterogeneous, with many varied parts that have multiple connections between them, and the different parts behave differently, although they are not independent. Recent developments in the mathematics of evolutionary biology extend the concept of a biological form or individual organism from an autonomous self-organised individual system, to a more complex meta-system with multiple hierarchies. The origin of the concept of a self-organising system lies in the intersection of biology and mathematics in the 1920s[3], but the recent focus on relations between multiple hierarchies stems from the recognition of the fact that individual organisms are not completely autonomous, but exist within higher-level systems, which in turn are multiple and varied parallel systems that interact within populations, environments and ecologies.

The term differentiation has a specific meaning in biology, describing the process that takes place during the development of the embryo and leads to the formation of specialised cells, tissues, and organs. The mathematician and philosopher Whitehead[4] argued that process rather than substance is the fundamental constituent of the world, and that nature consists of patterns of activity interacting with each other. Natural systems are processes, and it is process that produces, elaborates and maintains the form or structure of all living and non-living things.

It might be thought that genetics and embryology take quite different approaches to differentiation, as they appear to have fundamentally different arguments. What is common to both systems of thought is differentiation. Genetics argues that all living things are the product of natural selection, operating on inherited small changes over many generations. It is these small changes (to the genome) that produce differentiation within populations, and drive evolution. Every reproductive cycle requires the organism to replicate its genetic material, and this process is susceptible to small copying errors, so that offspring are produced that are a little bit different from the parents. In the most extreme account, organisms are described[5] as a kind of temporary host for the genes, a mechanism for their perpetuation.

Darwin argued that just as humans breed livestock and vegetables by 'unnatural' selection, organising systematic changes in them, so wild organisms themselves are changed by natural selection.[6] The mathematics of more recent evolutionary models developed by Heylighen[7] and Stewart[8] are based on differentiation or the distributed variation of different individuals within populations. Both individual organisms and the ecologies in which they exist are evolved by multiple parallel systems that interact with each other, and it is this interaction that produces the self-organisation of the ecology as a whole. In this argument the morphogenetic differentiation of any single individual occurs at a relatively low hierarchical level in the meta-system of nature. What is considered significant is the differentiation of the population, how many individuals exhibit differences from the norm. This can be plotted by a curve. One common, even notorious, example is the Bell curve, which shows that an axis drawn through the highest part of the curve corresponds to the norm of the population, and the horizontal distance from that axis measures the deviation from that norm. Changes in the percentile differentiation of the population will produce different curves.

Differentiation during the development of an individual is controlled by the Homeobox genes (originally discovered in the fruitfly *Drosophila*) that turn other genes on or off during development, controlling the order of morphogenesis and the position of different parts in relation to the body plan. Differentiation in all species is controlled by the Homeobox genes.[9] Mutations of a single gene, called *Antennapedia*, produce changes to the morphology and function of the fly's antennae, so that it develops a leg rather than an antenna. This is possible because all cells in the fly have all of the information necessary to become legs or antennae. Every cell in an organism carries a complete genome, all of the information necessary for the development of the complete organism. *Antennapaedia* and its homologues control limb development in all vertebrates, so that the forelimbs

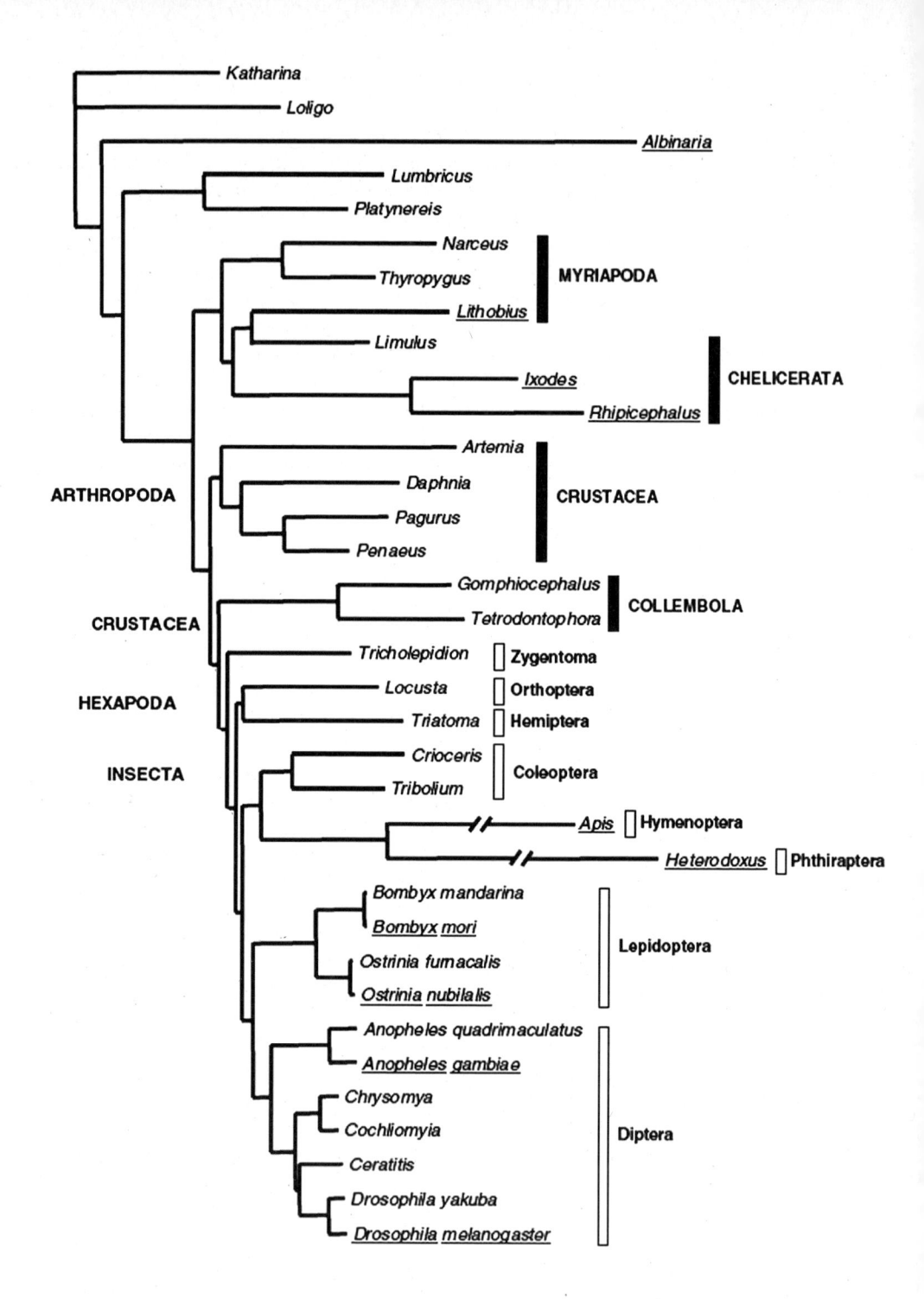

Differentiation of insects and crustaceans. This is a small section of the total phylogram of Arthropoda. It is constructed from genetic molecular analysis rather than the traditional morphological analysis. It plots the result of the genetic analysis that demonstrates that Hexapoda (insects) are most closely related to the crustaceans Branchiopoda (fairy shrimp, water fleas) and Cephalocarida (Horseshoe shrimps), thereby defining all insects as terrestrial crustaceans. The multiple differentiations in Arthropoda are all evolved from a simple tubular ancestor. This can only be understood and visualised as a series of cascading hierarchies that proceed through species differentiation from a single morphology to over a million morphologies.

of birds develop as wings, and the extremities of the forelimbs develop as hands in humans or flippers in seals. Homeobox DNA sequences have been conserved throughout evolution and are controlling factors to the development of even distantly related organisms.

Changes to the Homeobox genes have substantial effects on the morphology of individuals, and when these changed individuals survive the rigours of natural selection, new descendant species are formed. If individual mutations offer the advantage of superior functionality in some capacity, then the mutant organism will have an enhanced reproductive fitness. If its progeny inherit the changed genome, then evolutionary change will occur. Differentiation by speciation, new species arising from a common ancestor, is normally described in phylograms, or tree-like charts. The underlying logic is to plot the sequence of morphological differentiations that lead from the 'form' of a common ancestor to the multiple differentiated forms of the whole group or taxon.[10] For example, *arthropoda* includes crustaceans, centipedes, spiders and scorpions, insects and worms, which are all descended from a simple tube-like worm. This group has over one million species alive today, with a fossil record that starts in the early Cambrian era, and it accounts for over 80 per cent of all known organisms. The sequence of morphological differentiation produced segmented bodies, exoskeletons, and jointed legs.

BODY PLANS

Embryology treats organisms as whole beings that evolve not only by the small incremental changes of genetic mutation and natural selection, but through transformations. D'Arcy Thompson[11] argued that natural selection is efficient at removing the 'unfit', but that the significant differentiations of new structures are a product of the mathematical and physical properties of living matter, just like the shape of non-living things in the natural world. Transformations between major groups do not happen in the completed adult, but may occur in embryos. The embryos of highly differentiated adults are strikingly similar. Genetic information does not need to fully specify the adult form, as the action of the natural forces in the environment and consequent mathematical principles determine the scales, bounding limits and informing geometries of the development of adult forms. In more contemporary expressions organisms are described as members of a class of complex dynamic systems with distinctive properties of order and form, and it is these characteristics of organisms that are the drivers of evolution.[12] The differentiated morphology of living organisms is determined not only by the genome, but also by the combination of the internal forces such as chemical activities and pressure in their cells, and of external environmental forces such as gravity; the effect of these natural forces is expressed in different ways depending on the size of the organism.

Embryological development of an individual organism is a process of differentiation. The sequence of differentiation commences when the fertilised egg divides to produce a cluster of cells, and as numbers increase, organises itself into a hollow sphere. A thickened flat plate forms on the surface of the sphere and the edges curl up and meet at the dorsal midline to form a hollow tube. The next step in differentiation is when one end of the tube grows and becomes convoluted, and subsequently develops into the brain. The other parts of the tube follow a similar process and subsequently become the spine and lower limbs. A fully recognisable version of the final adult body plan is achieved very early in embryological differentiation. This process is identical in fish, birds, mice and men. The duration of the process of differentiation does depend on the final body size, so that a full body plan is evident in mice by day 14 of gestation, and a similar point is reached in the gestation period of humans by day 60; but it is clear that there is a commonality, a fundamental unity to the processes of morphenogenetic differentiation across species and phyla.

Plants have a different process of differentiation. The body plan of the adult plant is controlled by the Homeobox genes, as in animals, but the body plan is not evident in the 'embryo' or young

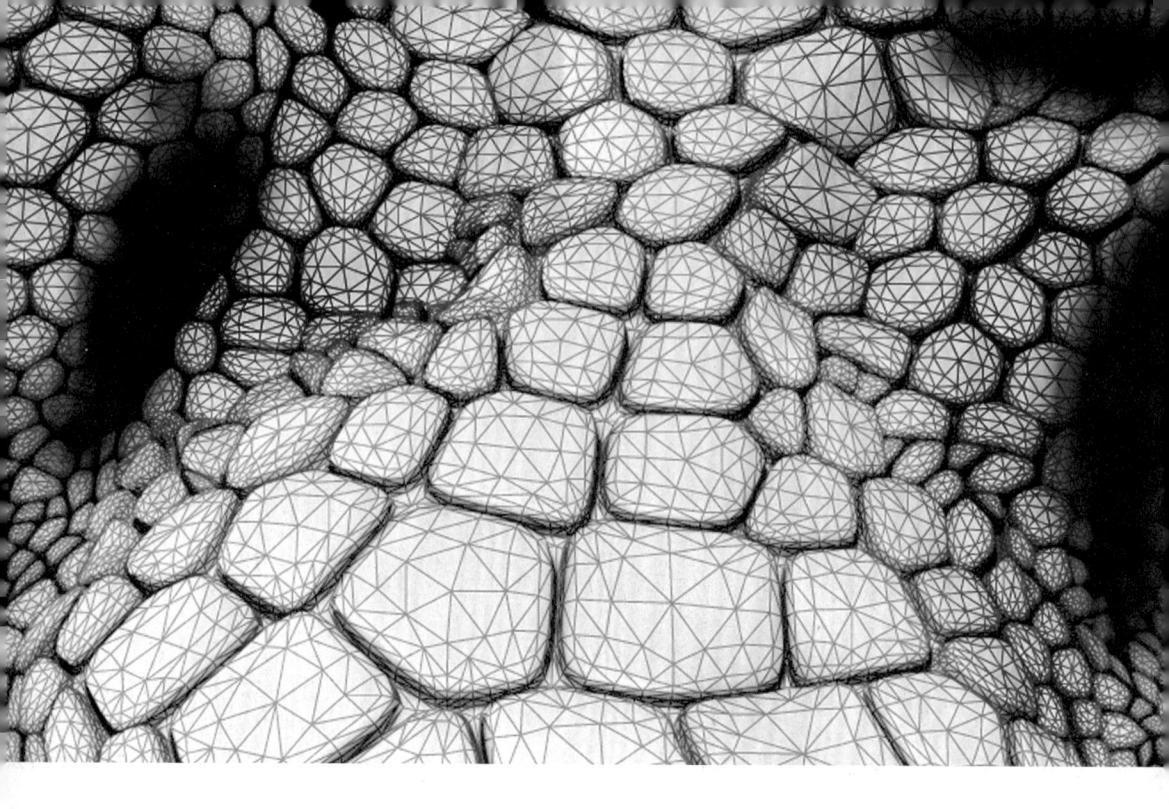

Digital model of the surface differentiation of crocodile skin. This patch of the digital model demonstrates a single hierarchy of differentiations. All the skin 'plates' are topologically identical but are geometrically variant, and distributed over curved surfaces. The smaller plates are distributed in areas of higher and more complex curvature, which is also the area where maximum flexibility is required by the movement of the crocodile. Larger 'plates' tend to be distributed in areas of lower curvature and where there is a lower requirement for flexibility. Geometrical variation and scalar differentiation are integrated to produce higher functionality. Digital model and rendering by Nikolaos Stathopoulos and Pavel Hladik.

shoot when the first growth begins from the seed. They differ from animals too in that the stem is capable of developing branches, leaves and the cones or flowers of its reproductive system throughout the life of the plant. The body plan is adaptable to environmental conditions, developing morphologically and functionally according to sunlight, temperature and nutrients. There are only four basic body plans for plants; the unicellular, the colonial, the syphonous and the multicellular; and each has its own method of growth. Unicellular plants such as the green algae *Chlamydomonas* are the most ancient, and the significant differentiation between unicellular and colonial plants is that unicellulars remain independent and do not aggregate. Unicellular organisms are typically very small, which has the advantage of a large surface area relative to the contained volume, making the metabolic process very efficient. Because of this ratio of surface area to volume, smaller organisms rapidly absorb nutrients through passive diffusion,[13] process them efficiently, and grow and reproduce speedily. This makes them able to respond to favourable environmental conditions which may be brief or seasonal to complete their life-cycle, and remain dormant in unfavourable conditions.

Most of those advantages are maintained when single cells are aggregated together. Siphonous plants typically have a cylindrical geometry as the module to be iterated in the construction of the body. A cylinder of any size always has the same ratio of surface area to volume. In aggregation each cell retains its individual capacity for rapid growth and reproduction, and in appropriate geometrical arrangements, metabolic activities can be coordinated. Syphonous and Colonial plant systems achieve greater overall size by aggregating cells that are not strongly differentiated or specialised in themselves. An interesting colonial plant is the alga Water Net (*Hydrodictyon*)

Digital model of the surface differentiation of Maize Coral. This patch of the digital model demonstrates two hierarchy levels of differentiation, in the linear arrays of the 'maize' elements, and the articulated surface material that connects and supports them. The individual elements are geometrically variant, but the scalar differentiation does not need to be very diverse. The connective tissue is topologically distinct. Digital model and rendering by Nikolaos Stathopoulos and Pavel Hladik.

that has an ordered morphology like a hollow sack, made up of a 'mesh' of cylindrical cells lying against each other. Each cell has to be morphologically similar, and contribute to the global colonial morphology.

Large land-based multicellular plants require differentiated tissues that are specialised for the vertical movement of nutrients, as leaves and branches became more and more elevated from the ground supplies of nutrients and water. Vascular tissues are typically located in the central axis, where they will experience the lowest tensile, compression or torsional shear stresses, but in this position they are less effective structurally. Other tissues surround the vascular bundles that are differentiated with higher structural capacity to respond and adapt to environmental stresses and dynamic loadings[14] of gravity and wind pressure. The differentiated distribution of cells, fibres and bundles, according to height and slenderness, produces variable stiffness and elasticity within multicellular plants. Variations in the section produce anisotropic properties, and a gradation of values between stiffness and elasticity along the length of the stem that is particularly useful for resisting dynamic and unpredictable loadings.[15]

It is clear that body plans in very different plant lineages have converged on very similar anatomies and morphologies, and similar structural solutions, even though they use different ways of organising growth. The relationship between the surface area of the plant body, through which plants acquire nutrients and energy, and the living body volume determines the metabolic rate. The differentiation of cells, tissues and organs produces physiological domains within the plant body.

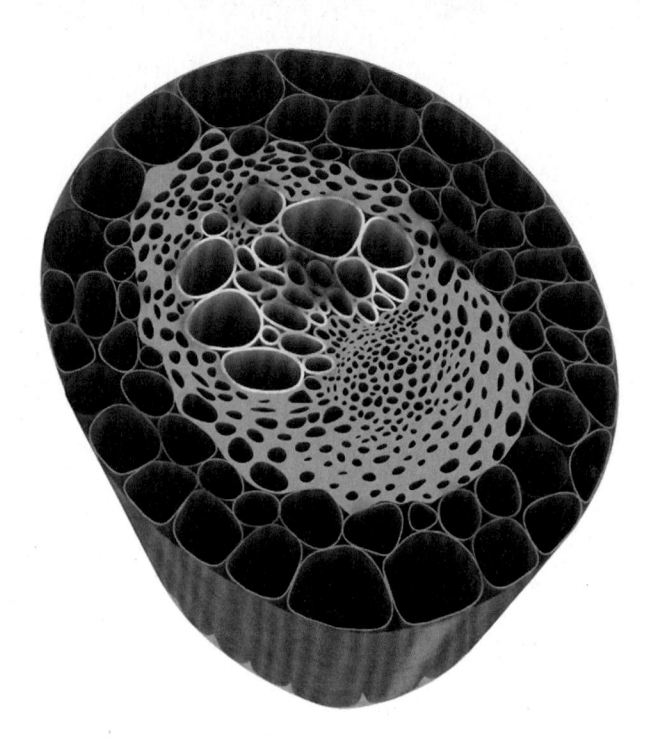

Digital model of a differentiated cell bundle in a plant stem. The section of this digital model shows the linear bundling and differentiation of cells in a typical plant stem. The large tubes at the centre are the vascular bundle, consisting of Xylem and Phloem tubes that move nutrients and distribute carbohydrates and hormones, and contribute to structural support. Parenchyma cells that maintain and exchange materials with the elements, and contribute to the stiffening of the stem by taking up or losing water to change their internal pressure, surround the vascular bundle. The outer skin is the dermal layer. Differentiation of cells within the plant tissue produces structural and metabolic functions that are integrated. Digital model and rendering by Nikolaos Stathopoulos and Pavel Hladik.

ENERGY AND ECOLOGY

When severe climate changes have occurred they have caused extinction events. There have been five major mass extinction events, each causing extensive glaciations and a retreat of living organisms to a narrow zone around the equator. The biota and the environment recovered after each event, but it took evolution tens of millions of years in each case for the full recovery of biodiverse ecosystems.[16] Innumerable lesser dips have occurred, either at local or global levels, and it is clear that the environment plays a significant role in differentiation by speciation. New species arise from a common ancestor species, acquiring new adaptations to a changed environment, expanding their geographical range and further differentiating into multiple descendant species. These in turn will fall from dominance when a different climatic change occurs, making way in time for the rise of a new, better adapted species. This process of differentiation, known as adaptive radiation, has been replayed in endless iterations, and some species may be stable for millions of years before disappearing rapidly when the ecosystem is disrupted. There is a gradient, from pole to equator, in the number of taxa, so that the largest number of species occurs in the equatorial zones, and it is evident that the more solar energy is available, the more life flourishes. Furthermore, the more stable the climate is, from season to season and from year to year, the greater the differentiation or diversity of species.[17]

Energy is a critical factor in ecological differentiation. Prigogine[18] is credited with the mathematical foundation of a new branch of studies focused on the role of energy in biological studies. He set up a rigorous and well-grounded study of pattern formation and self-organisation that is still of use in the experimental study and theoretical analysis of biological and non-biological systems. Prigogine argued that all biological organisms and many natural non-living systems are maintained by the flow of energy through the system. Furthermore, energy systems tend towards a hierarchical evolution of ever greater complexity. The pattern of energy flow is subject to many small variations, which is adjusted by 'feedback' from the environment to maintain equilibrium, but occasionally there is such an amplification that the system must reorganise or collapse. A new order emerges from the chaos of the system at the point of collapse. The reorganisation creates a more complex structure, with a higher flow of energy through it, and is in turn more susceptible to fluctuations and subsequent collapse or reorganisation. The tendency of biological systems to ever increasing complexity, and of each reorganisation to be produced at the moment of collapse in the equilibrium of a system extends beyond the energy relations of an individual organism and its environment. Evolutionary development in general emerges from energy flows in dynamic systems.[19]

Sunlight and the oxygen and carbon dioxide cycle are essential to the energy processes of all forms of life. The chloroplasts and mitochondria needed for the energy production and processing systems have similar genetic sequences in all multi-cellular species. Differentiation by the incorporation of the genome of 'pre-adapted' parts is known as symbiogenesis. Mitochondria and chloroplasts in cells are thought to have once been independent unicellular organisms that invaded the cells of larger organisms and subsequently co-evolved with their host organisms into the energy-production system in plants and animals. The evolutionary differentiation from unicellular organisms to more complex organisms may not have been possible without the incorporation of energy-producing systems into the larger organisms. There are other common features, in addition to the genetic sequence, of organic energy systems. All organisms must not only produce energy, they must also transport it. The morphology of branching networks is found in all organisms of all species. It can be geometrically defined as a space-filling, fractal-like branching pattern[20] that reaches all parts of the organism, and the final unit of this branching pattern is always an identical size.

There is a relationship between energy, lifespan and body mass: small organisms are typically more metabolically active than larger organisms, and the larger the organism, the slower the metabolism. Bigger organisms live longer and expend more energy than small organisms. Metabolic relationships to mass and lifespan are complex, but a gram of living tissue consumes approximately the same amount of energy in its life-span independently of the organism or species of which it is part. Within any specific taxon, such as mammals or plants, the metabolic rate of activity will vary from species to species, and the rate of energy consumption per unit body mass declines as the body size increases. A gram of tissue in a mouse uses up 25 times more energy than a gram of tissue in an elephant. The mouse must eat much more frequently, and much larger quantities in relation to its body mass than the elephant. But when unrelated taxa are compared that differ greatly in size, such as a comparison between bacteria and mammals, the metabolic activity per unit body mass is approximately the same for bacteria and elephants. What varies is the life-span, by many orders of magnitude. Energy is the critical factor in biological differentiations of morphological and temporal scale.

Within animal taxa, metabolisms are differentiated by the regime of internal thermoregulation and by the relation of internal body temperature to the external temperature, that is to say some organisms maintain a constant body temperature and others allow their internal temperature to vary. Constant body temperature is a demanding energy regime for an organism – it must generate its own heat when the external temperature is colder. In this regime, typically of birds and mammals, very little food is converted into body mass, the majority of food must be converted into fuel to maintain a constant body temperature. Food consumption is up to 10 times more than for a comparable size animal with variable temperature, and elaborate morphological and system adaptations are necessary, which in turn presents difficulties when the external temperature rises through seasonal variation. These animals have the advantage of remaining active in very cold climates, but need to do so to acquire food to maintain their energy regime. Few can survive in very hot environments.

Variable temperature regimes, such as the metabolisms of amphibians and reptiles, are less energy demanding, and most food can be converted into body mass. Metabolic activity does not regulate body temperature, which tends to be the same as or close to the environmental temperature, as solar energy is absorbed as heat to raise internal temperatures. They are less active as the temperature drops, but do not need to be so active to acquire food; in fact they can survive long periods without food, and some reduce their metabolic rate when food is scarce. They cannot survive in very cold climates.

CODA

Many models for architecture are offered by differentiation in natural systems: by differentiation between cell morphologies within biological tissue, between tissue organisations, between organs and structures within individual organisms, between individuals in populations, and between species and body plans. I have presented a brief outline of the major tropes of differentiation, from small incremental and random genetic mutations to the genetic sequence of morphological differentiation in speciation; and from the morphogenetic differentiation of embryological development of an individual organism to the environmentally driven morphological response of plant body plans. I have argued that energy plays a critical role in differentiation at all biological scales, from the cell to the ecosystem. The architectural consequences of this study have yet to be fully worked out, but I suggest that the study of differentiation and energy offers a new model for architecture. This model relates pattern and process, form and behaviour, design and construction, and so has a symbiotic relationship with the natural world. Architecture must make a positive contribution to the environment, and can do so by developing a metabolism for buildings and cities that extends far beyond the minimising environmental strategies of 'sustainability'. In the natural sciences, metabolism refers to all energy transformations, the sum of the complex chemical and physical changes that take place within an organism and promote growth, sustain life, and enable the processes of living organisms. A model abstracted from complex natural systems must incorporate individual and groups of environmentally intelligent buildings, with interlinked systems of material and energy flows, organised to generate oxygen, sequester carbon, fix nitrogen, collect and purify water, acquire solar energy, and respond intelligently to impending climatic changes.

FOOTNOTES

[1] This text is an outline of a larger study to be published by Wiley-Academy in 2007, Michael Weinstock, *The Architecture of Emergence – Algorithms, Energy and the Evolution of Form in Nature and Architecture.*

[2] Warren Weaver, 'Science and Complexity', *American Scientist*, 36: 536 (1948).

[3] I have traced the conceptual origins to the intersection of ideas and techniques in the work of D'Arcy Thompson and Whitehead. Michael Weinstock, 'Morphogenesis and The Mathematics of Emergence', in *AD Emergence: Morphogenetic Design Strategies*, ed. Hensel, Menges and Weinstock (London: Wiley-Academy, 2004).

[4] Alfred North Whitehead, *The Concept of Nature* (Cambridge University Press, 1920).

[5] Richard Dawkins, *The Selfish Gene, The Extended Phenotype,* and *The Blind Watchmaker* (Oxford University Press,

1976/89, 1982, 1986).

[6] Charles Darwin, *On the Origin of Species by Means of Natural Selection, or the Preservation of Favoured Races in the Struggle for Life* (London: John Murray, 1859).

[7] Francis Heylighen, 'Self-Organisation, Emergence and the Architecture of Complexity', *Proceedings of 1st European Conference on System Science*, 1989

[8] H.A. Simon, 'The Architecture of Complexity', Proceedings of the American Philosophical Society 106, reprinted in *The Sciences of the Artificial*, 3rd ed (Cambridge, Mass.: MIT Press, 1996).

[9] S.B. Carroll, 'Homeotic Genes and the Evolution of Arthropods and Chordates', 1995 *Nature* 376: 479/485.

[10] Known as Phylogenetic Systematics, first formalised by W. Hennig in *Grundzüge einer Theorie der Phylogentischen Systematik* (Berlin: Aufbau Verlag, 1950) and *Phylogenetic Systematics* (Urbana: University of Illinois Press, 1966).

[11] D'Arcy Wentworth Thompson, *On Growth and Form* (Cambridge University Press, first pub. 1917).

[12] Stuart Kauffman, *The Origins of Order – Self Organisation and Selection in Evolution* (Oxford University Press, 1993).

[13] P. S. Nobel, *Biophysical Plant Physiology and Ecology* (New York: Freeman, 1983).

[14] An introduction to some aspects of dynamics in biological systems is presented by Professor George Jeronimidis in 'Biodynamics', in *AD Emergence: Morphogenetic Design Strategies*, ed. Hensel, Menges and Weinstock (London: Wiley-Academy, 2004).

[15] Weinstock, Michael, 'Self Organisation and the Structural Dynamics of Plants', in *AD Morphogenetic Design: Techniques and Technologies*, ed. Hensel, Menges and Weinstock (London: Wiley-Academy 2006). In this article I have traced how evolutionary biology has utilised redundancy or excess capacities in order to adapt to environmental instability and how, with the assistance of George Jeronimidis and Nikolaos Stathopoulos, the Emtech Masters programme at the Architectural Association has explored the integrated morphologies of plants with a digital modelling and analysis of bamboos and palms.

[16] Edward O. Wilson, *The Diversity of Life* (Norton/Harvard University Press, 1993).

[17] This is known as the Energy-Stability-Area Theory of Biodiversity.

[18] Ilya Prigogine, Introduction to *Thermodynamics of Irreversible Processes* (first ed. pub. 1955, third and last ed. pub 1968)

[19] Any physical system that can be described by mathematical tools or heuristic rules is regarded as a dynamic system. Dynamic System theory classifies systems by the mathematical tool rather the visible form of a system.

[20] K. J. Niklas, *Plant Allometry: The Scaling of Form and Process* (University of Chicago Press, 1994).

Although recognised as 'beautiful', biological structures are often also stigmatised as 'imperfect', by which it is usually meant that they are asymmetric or irregular and of a complex shape whose functioning is not immediately apparent. Examples are curved bones, an asymmetric leaf, a gnarled branch. Maybe they appear to break easily, or even to encourage fracture, or take loads to one side. I shall show that these are characteristics not of 'imperfection' but of design for durability, and suggest that in an uncertain world, survival is more beautiful than symmetry.

VENUS FLYTRAP

I shall start with an example of perfection, to act as a foil for what follows. The Venus fly trap is a leaf which flips from one shape (open) to another (closed) in 40 ms or so. This fast shape change is characteristic (though not diagnostic) of a 'perfect' system. The leaf consists of two laminae on either side of a thick midrib (fig. 1). Various mechanisms for the movement have been proposed, but any mechanism which requires a physiological change (e.g. the uptake of water, resulting in turgor) will be too slow (Hodick and Sievers, 1989). It is obvious that the only type of mechanism which can provide the speed is elastic, using the strain energy provided by turgor pressure, which can reach 1 MPa or more inside the cells. This has the advantage that the turgor and the mechanical properties of the cells and tissues do not need to change during the fast phase of closure, though such changes do occur in both earlier and later phases (Fagerberg and Allain, 1991). A recent model explored an elastic mechanism, although the leaf was modelled as a plate with zero thickness, which is clearly inadequate (Forterre et al., 2005). This still leaves in question the nature of the trigger for the instability. The disturbance of one of the three large hairs that stick out of the upper surface of each half of the leaf initiates the action. But how is the signal transmitted? Surprisingly, it is still considered to be an (undetectable!) electrical signal of the sort one finds in the nerves of animals. How about an elastic instability?

It is easily possible for a real plate of finite thickness to change shape from one curvature to another (equivalent to the fly trap leaf being open or closed) without any change having taken place in the elastic properties (e.g. stiffness) of that plate (Jeronimidis and Parkyn, 1988). With the model system the shape change is elastic and reversible; often it is symmetrical, requiring the same forces and displacements to flip it from one curvature to

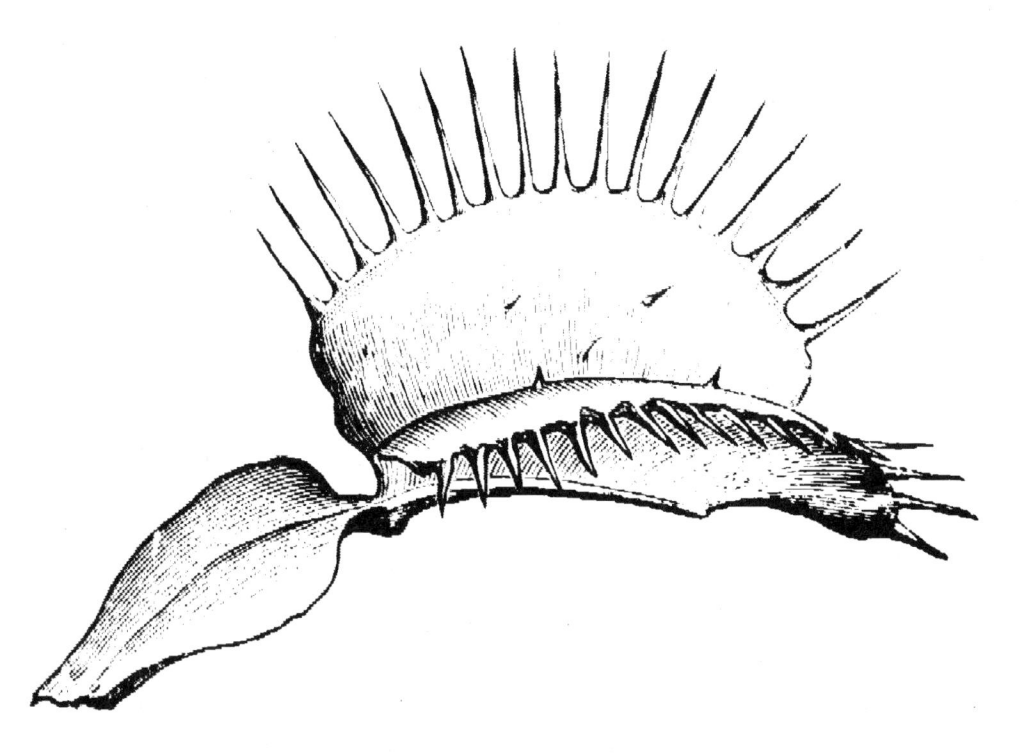

FIGURE 1 Leaf of the Venus fly trap in the open position, showing complex curvature and sensory hairs.

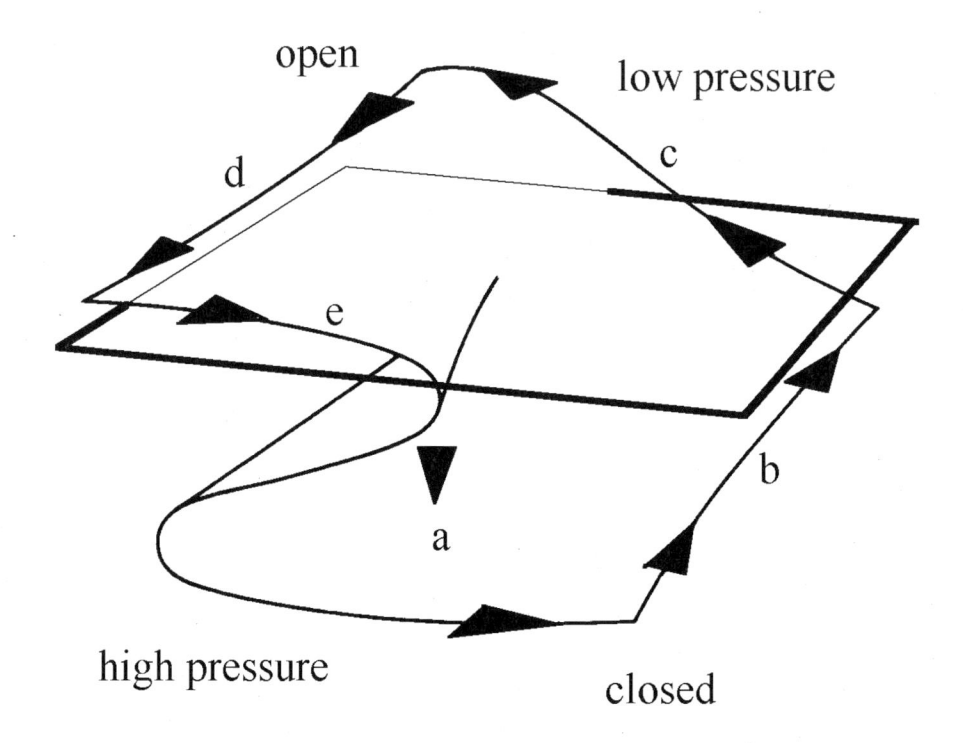

FIGURE 2 Cusp catastrophe curve. The shape changes of the fly trap leaf follow the arrows around the surface; the superimposed plane indicates when the leaf is more or less flat.

the other. It is also possible to construct a plate in which the behaviour is not symmetrical and the plate is stable in one configuration but only just stable in the other. This would be equivalent to the closed and open positions of the leaf, respectively. Thus it is possible for the fly trap leaf to go from a quasi-stable open position to a stable closed position without any change of its elastic properties, nor any need of turgor changes. High-speed video shows that the shape change starts near the thin free edge of the leaf and travels towards the main central vein. The triggering shape change could be quite local and – since there is no presumption of where the instability should be triggered – perhaps even confined to the region around a single sensory hair. This removes the necessity for a global signalling mechanism within the entire leaf.

The sudden action of the Venus fly trap can be modelled as a catastrophe surface. Catastrophe theory derives from the mathematics of topology (Thom, 1975) and is to do with instability. The simplest is the cusp catastrophe (fig. 2). Along the left edge (d) the fly trap leaf is open, and along the right edge (b) it is closed. The vertical axis tells you, therefore, whether the leaf is open or closed, which could also be related to the curvature of the leaf. When the leaf is open it is curved outwards; when closed it is curved inwards. The plane surface superimposed on the curved catastrophe surface indicates zero curvature – the leaf is flat. But when the leaf is under high turgor pressure it is impossible for it to maintain a flat surface – it is unstable. As the leaf closes the curvature reduces slowly, moving from left to right along path e, then comes to the cliff edge and reverses suddenly (a) and the leaf closes. If all is well, it closes around the small insect which has just been disturbing the trigger hairs. The mechanism of opening along path c is less obvious, but seems to be associated with a drop in pressure inside the cells, due to softening of the cell walls: as the cells expand under turgor, the pressure drops and so does the amount of stored elastic strain energy. Thus the leaf can now open, but does not have to go through a catastrophe jump since there just isn't the strain energy available.

What has this to do with safe design? It's all about avoiding the build-up of elastic energy to a level at which it can't be controlled, or keeping the mechanism away from the cliff edge. Since that elastic energy can be easily converted into fracture energy, or can lead to unpredictable shape change, such control is very important. The Venus fly trap conforms to our safety rules (but certainly isn't safe from the fly's point of view!), because although it has a relatively large amount of strain energy which it releases suddenly, it somehow manages to keep well away from the point at which change in curvature is inevitable. A very similar example is given by the end-on loading of a strut (fig. 3). The load can be increased until at some point even a slight asymmetry in loading will cause the strut to bend to one side or the other. But the more symmetrical the loading, the higher the load at which the strut will bend, and the more catastrophic the subsequent behaviour. Clearly we are looking for ways in which strain energy can be dissipated, or loaded and unloaded, relatively slowly and therefore controllably. It looks as if biological systems accept that overloads will occur, and that fracture is always likely, but that the overload will be applied slowly and the fracture will be progressive. This gives the organism time to move away from the potentially damaging load and allows the damage to be absorbed by a greater portion of the material structure, so making it easier to repair successfully.

EULER BUCKLING

When a column or strut is loaded on end with perfect symmetry, it will support the load until it fails in compression, until it reaches a certain aspect ratio (depending to some degree on the material being used) and then bends out of the way in an elastic manner unless overloaded. The transition between a compressed column and bending strut can be very sudden. However, if the eccentricity of loading is high, the column will bend more gradually but at a lower load, so the safety is high although the maximum loads may be much lower. This type of response might explain why

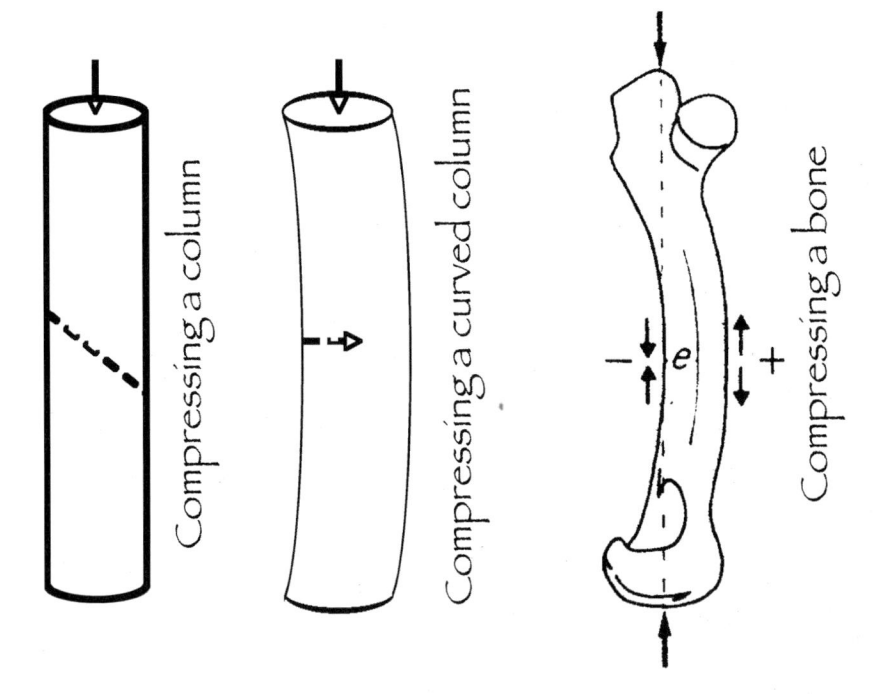

FIGURE 3 A symmetrically loaded column; a symmetrically loaded bent column (more or less equivalent to an asymmetrically loaded straight column); a typical bone under end loading.

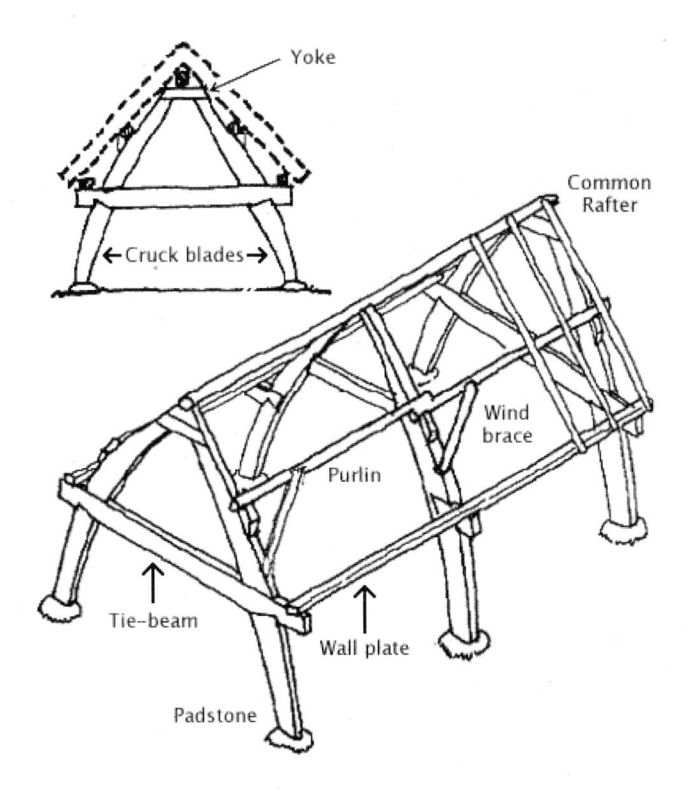

FIGURE 4 A cruck framework for a building.

long bones in vertebrates are not straight, so they can always fail in bending and thus absorb higher deformation and more strain energy, acting as a shock absorber (fig. 3). Although the maximum force that can be resisted is far less, the energy is far greater.

Could this be why the main members of the cruck frame (fig. 4) are nearly always bent? The trees from which the cruck frames were derived were commonly restrained in a bent position so that they would grow in the right shape. There are relatively few cruck-framed buildings with straight crucks. One can imagine that in a timber building, in which the components will deform more than in a brick or stone building, the structure will be steadier if the timbers can deform and bed in during construction. However, it seems that nobody knows why crucks are nearly always bent. It would be worth looking at those buildings in which the deformation of the crucks in the end walls (and perhaps some of the dividing walls) has been blocked by infilling with brick or stone, rather than the more compliant wattle and daub of traditional walls. Are the strains of time less evenly spread? Are they in more danger of collapse?

There are other natural structures which make use of Euler buckling. Palm trees are an obvious example, but a less obvious one is the hedgehog, whose prickles (spines), of constant length over the entire body, are slightly curved with the base inserted off-centre. Thus, although they are only 20 mm long and 1 mm in diameter – placing them as long columns on the Euler buckling diagram – they never fail in compression across the entire section since they always buckle out of the way. These factors render the spines ideal for shock absorption: the hedgehog (well known for having a 'three-dimensional environment') can climb trees in search of food, then curl up and drop to the ground relying on the spines to bend and spread the high loads at impact. The spines thus have to be able to store large amounts of elastic strain energy. In order to help them deform to the extreme which their material properties will allow, they are internally reinforced in two ways (fig. 5): there are longitudinal stringers which brace the wall of the spine against local buckling, and there are numerous septa or bulkheads which hold the section in the round shape, resisting the ovalisation which heralds bending failure in the midsection of an overloaded spine. Viewed as tubes with an infill of cellular material, the spines of Erinaceus europeae (one of the phylogenetically most advanced hedgehogs) are extremely efficient at storing strain energy.

HOLES IN WOOD, PAPER AND BONE

While man's approach is commonly to make structures stronger, nature adopts a different strategy. Indeed it is arguable, as J.E. Gordon said, that not only do you understand a material or structure most completely if you understand its fracture behaviour, but that most biological materials are designed to resist fracture, which is why biologists on the whole do not regard failure as an important phenomenon (Vincent, 1994). It just doesn't occur often enough in biological materials or organisms, and if it does, not only can the organism retire to lick its wounds, it can let them heal and return to normal living. For instance, hardwoods (from broad-leaved trees) are mostly more durable than softwoods (from conifers). This is due to a number of factors, one of which is the presence of large holes in the structure. Whereas all the wood (xylem tissue) in a softwood tree is made up of water-conducting tubes about 50 μm in diameter, in hardwood trees there are more specialised water conductors – tracheids – which are 10 times larger. These are distributed in two main patterns reflecting the time of year at which they are laid down: diffuse (throughout the year) and ring (a single time in the year – usually spring). Oak is a ring-porous wood, and the distinct layers of tracheids give it its strong 'grain' patterns. Hickory is a diffuse-porous wood with the tracheids spaced more or less at random, so sometimes they are close together, sometimes far apart. Beech is also diffuse-porous but the tracheids are spaced more evenly. It is this spacing which seems to account for the different behaviour of these woods on impact across the grain (Hepworth et al., 2002). Oak is relatively brittle, breaking at the tracheid rings where there is significantly

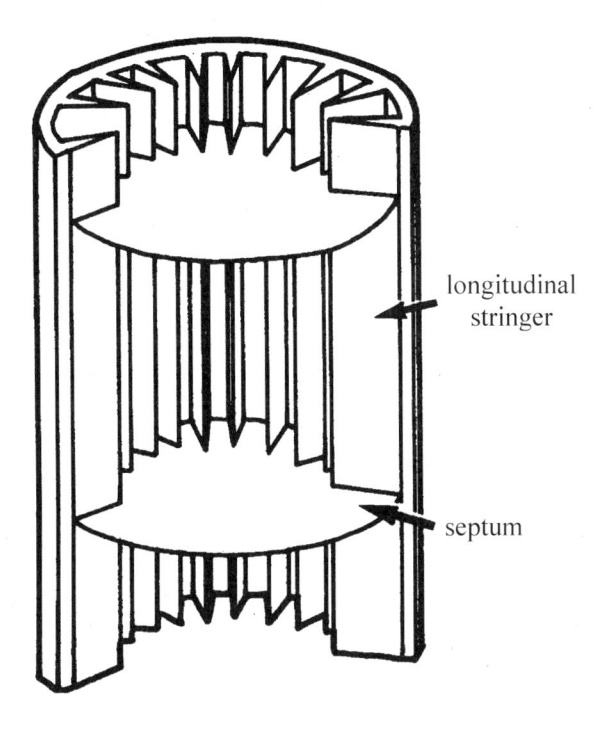

FIGURE 5 A part section of part of a hedgehog spine. In reality the joins between the different elements are more complex and there are more septa per unit length.

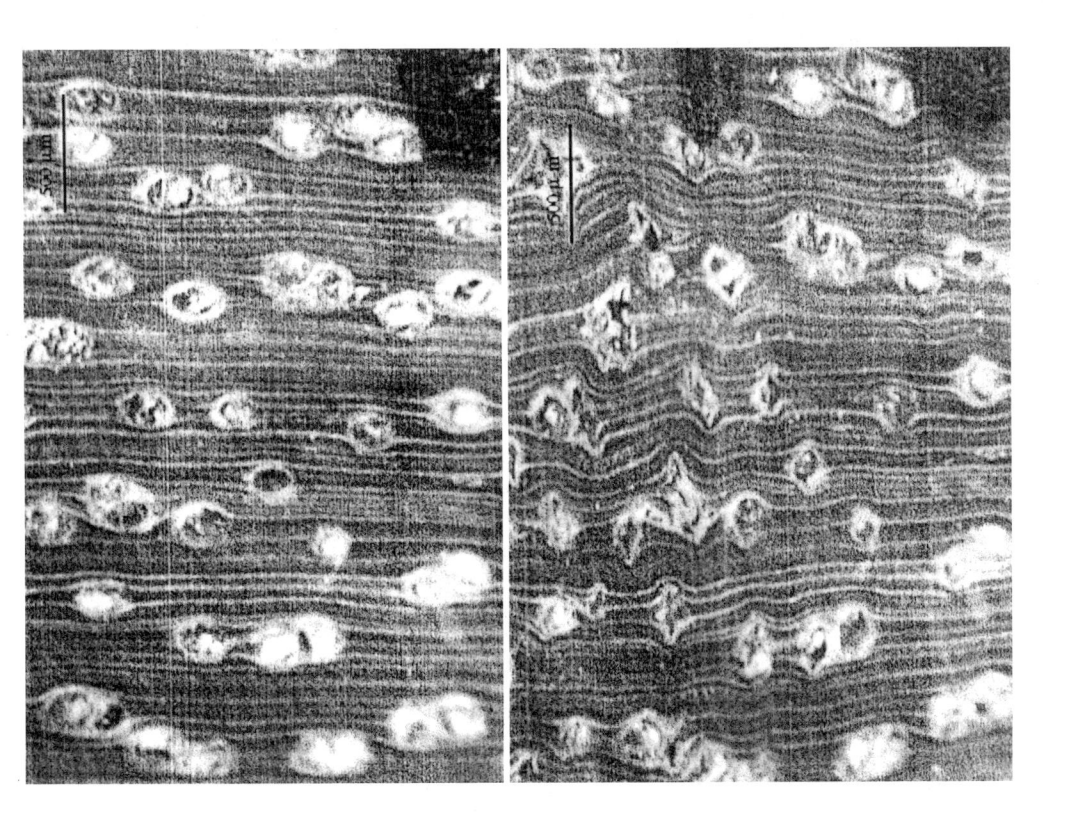

FIGURE 6 A polished section of beech wood showing large water-conducting vessels; before compression (left) and after compression (right). Note how the damage is concentrated around the vessels.

less material. Hickory is much tougher since the tracheids, by introducing local compliance, allow the more solid wood around them to collapse, so absorbing impact energy. However, the random spacing leaves areas of wood undeformed. Beech absorbs yet more energy since the even spacing of the tracheids ensures that a greater proportion of the wood is deformed (fig. 6). Thus the careful placing of areas of weakness in a structure can ensure that important parts of the structure are protected (a strategy rather like autotomy in reptiles and arthropods, which can lose a tail or a leg to an attacker but escape otherwise intact), and also that any damage is evenly spread throughout the structure, so ensuring the maximum absorption of energy. Confirmation of the importance of holes comes from experiment and analysis. We can drill small holes into softwood, mimicking the tracheids. Although there is a lot of scatter in the results, the increase in impact resistance is definite (fig. 7).

We can also punch holes in paper and see what effect this has on the energy of failure in tension. Since we are introducing compliance by removing material, it is likely that the greatest effect is going to be obtained with the stiffest and most brittle paper. Tracing paper, although strong, tears easily, because it is made from cellulose fibres (separated plant cells) that are beaten for a long time in order to break open the structure and soften them so that they will stick together in the final material. This ensures that there are few light-reflecting air gaps, so the paper is translucent. This also makes it easier to see where damage has occurred since the paper appears whiter in reflected light in those places where the fibres have pulled apart.

The holes were punched in a regular diamond pattern, evenly spaced, so that the maximum distance could be maintained between them, allowing for a larger amount of damage before the paper tore. The tendency of damaged zones to join up was modelled using finite elements (fig. 8). There are three ways the paper can absorb strain energy. The first and most obvious is by breaking; the second is by damage around the holes; the third is by plastic deformation in the bulk of the paper, remote from the holes and the crack, which is less easily noticed because it doesn't occur in specific areas. The introduction of a small number of holes reduced the energy absorption of the paper, but with more holes energy absorption increased, then decreased again. This was due to an increase in the strain at failure, since stress decreased linearly as loss of material reduced the effective width of the specimen. When these factors were taken into account, theory produced a curve much like that produced by the experiments. It appears that the localised zones of plastic deformation around the holes dissipate some of the energy which would cause plastic deformation in material away from the holes, diminishing the benefits. But presumably because this local-global balance is non-linear, the energy increases, suggesting that if one wants to put holes into a structure, there is an optimum number, irrespective of what the holes are doing. The problem remains that the rough edges of the holes (which are punched with a sharpened ball-point pen, ball removed) tend to start cracks, so the holes need to be made more carefully to realise the full energy-absorbing potential of this approach.

A third example showing the importance of holes and cellular material is given by antler bone (Hansen, 1999). Antlers have to be very tough because they transmit heavy shock loads into the neck muscles, when the rutting stag fights. But they also represent a drain on the stag's store of calcium, so they have to be made of the minimum amount of material. They are replaced annually, so they can afford to sustain a certain amount of damage – in fact about one-third of antlers are broken in any one season (Kitchener, 1991). Antlers cannot be repaired in service since they are technically dead, at least on the outside. The skin covering is sloughed off as the velvet.

The antler is a tube of solid bone (cortex) filled with a more cellular bone (medulla) extending about half the radius from the middle (fig. 9). The interface between the two areas is graded so that there is no step change in density. From the point of view of bending stiffness, the medulla is irrelevant. It has a small second moment of area and it is of low density. However, if the antler is loaded from the side in compression rather than bending, it has a very marked effect. Without

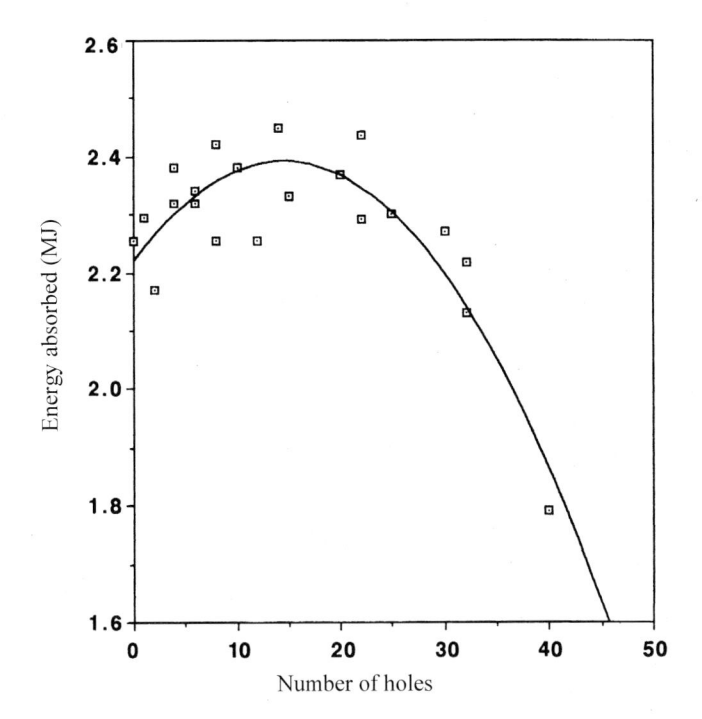

FIGURE 7 Increase in energy absorption by pine wood, which mostly has vessels only 50 μm in diameter, when holes 0.6 mm in diameter are drilled parallel to the grain.

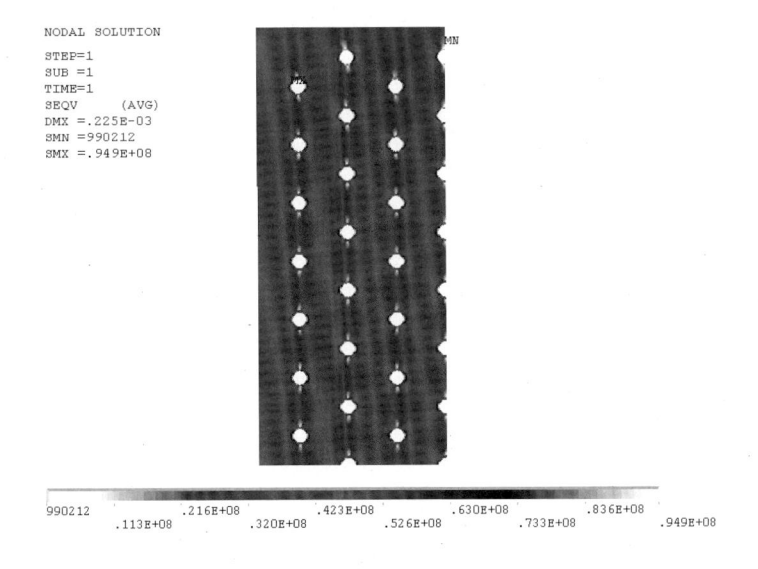

FIGURE 8 Finite element model showing strain concentration distribution in a piece of material, stretched vertically, into which a number of small holes have been punched.

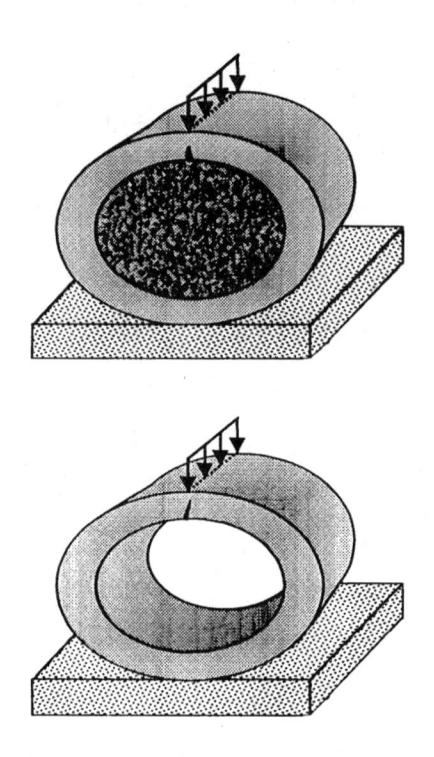

FIGURE 9 Sections of antler bone with (top) and without (bottom) the central (medullary) bone, a cellular material.

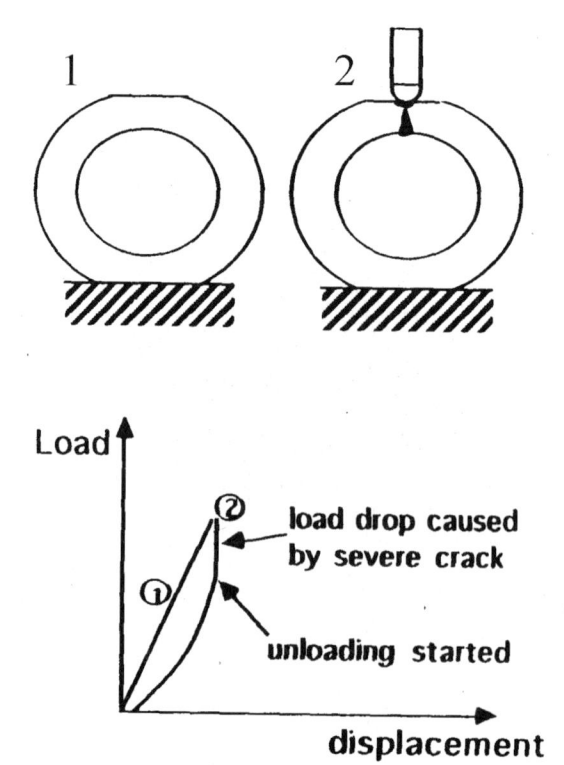

FIGURE 10 Compressive behaviour of antler with the medullary bone removed.

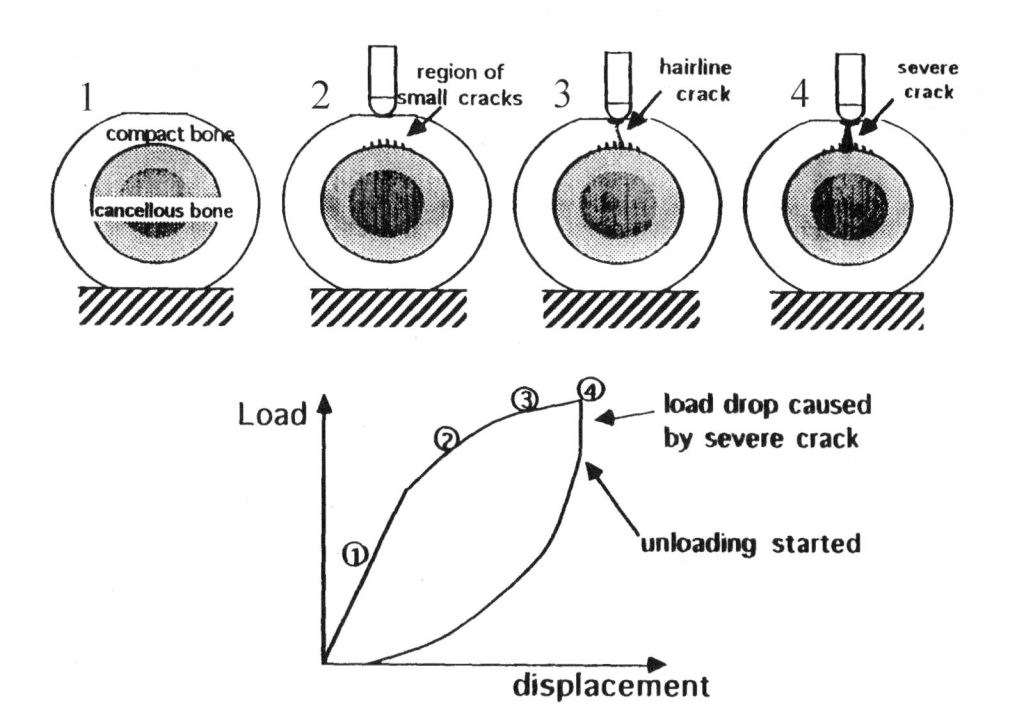

FIGURE 11 Compressive behaviour of antler with medullary bone retained.

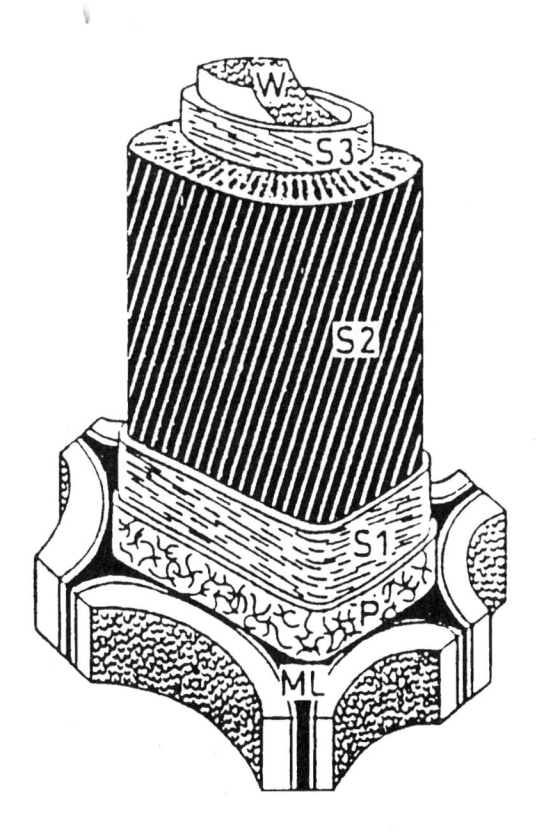

FIGURE 12 A typical wood (xylem) cell showing the orientation of cellulose microfibrils in the layers of the cell wall.

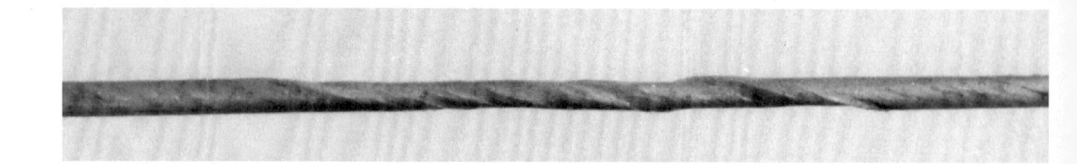

FIGURE 13 A straw made from glass-fibre/resin composite showing failure when it is stretched.

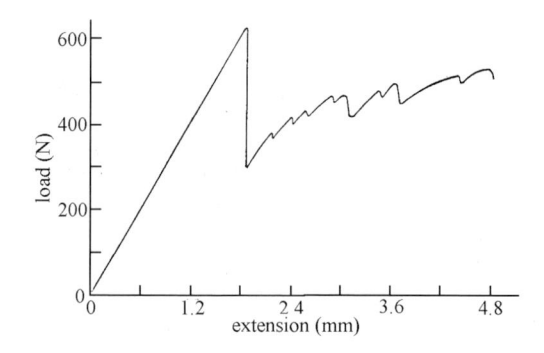

FIGURE 14 Force-deflection curve derived from a straw like that in fig 13 when stretched.

FIGURE 15 What happens when spruce wood is stretched.

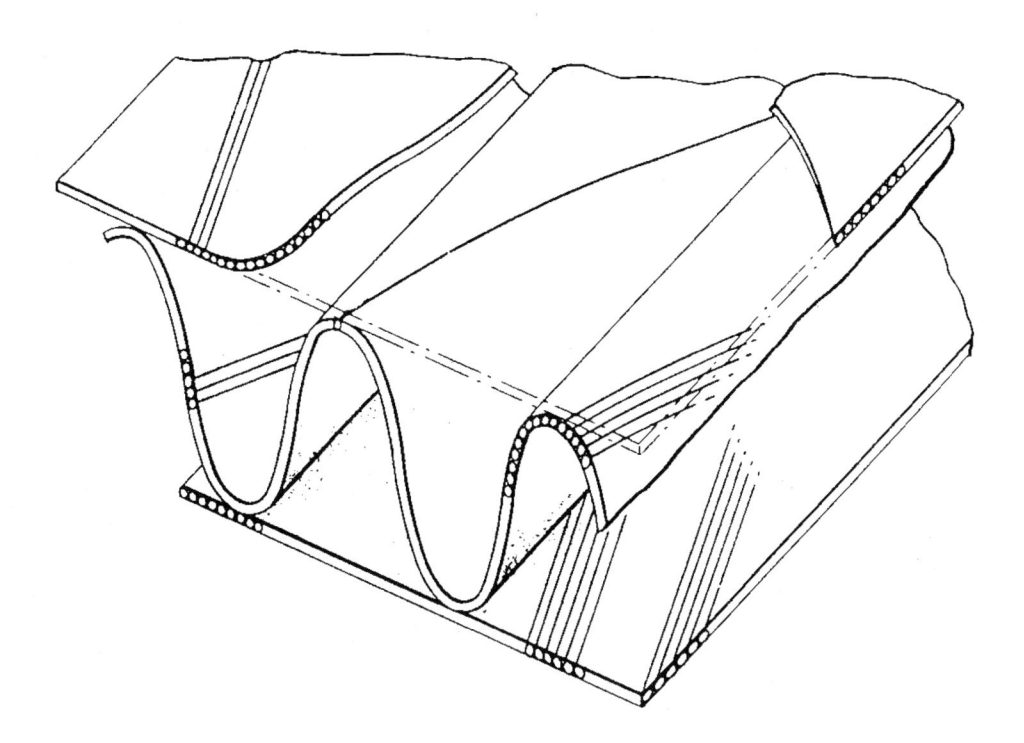

FIGURE 16 A biomimetic material based on the mechanism of failure of wood.

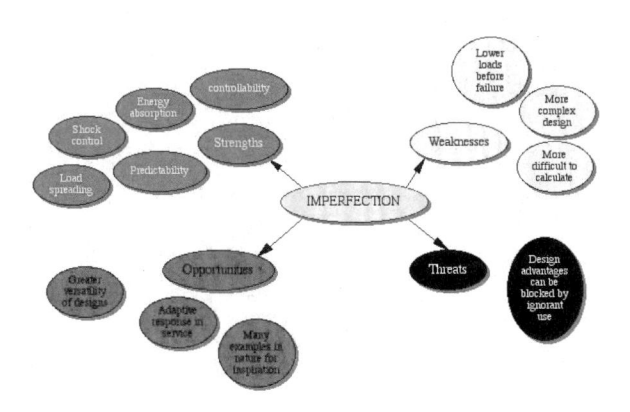

FIGURE 17 Advantages and disadvantages of imperfection.

the medulla the tube of cortical bone breaks very easily (fig. 10). With the medulla in place, small cracks start on the inner surface of the cortex but are bridged and reinforced by elements of the medulla. A new crack starts adjacent, and in turn is bridged (fig. 11). Eventually one of the cracks is propagated through the cortex, but by now the small cracks have allowed the bone to absorb a large amount of strain energy through controlled cracking, allowing the antler to absorb three times more strain energy before failure.

Finally, perfection is associated with symmetry. There are many studies which show that beauty in a face is associated with bilateral symmetry. The same is true of trees, at least at the macro level. But down at the cellular level there is no such symmetry. The cellulose microfibrils in the walls of the xylem, or wood cells, wind around the tubes in a single direction, making an angle averaging at 15 degrees to the longitudinal axis (fig. 12). The direction of winding is always the same throughout the tree. This winding angle induces an unusual form of failure in tension. The mechanism can be seen in a spirally wound paper art straw (preferably at least 10 cm long and 3-5 mm diameter) loaded in tension. When the straw breaks it does so partly by buckling inwards and partly by the development of a spiral fracture running some distance along it (fig. 13). This not only gives toughness due to the length of the crack but also gives force-deflection behaviour like that of a metal with a distinct yield point and a post-yield region where the material, although having failed, is still capable of supporting a load (fig. 14). In bulk wood, the individual cells additionally pull apart laterally as they buckle inwards, absorbing even more energy (fig. 15). The spiral organisation of the cellulose fibres increases toughness at the expense of the axial stiffness, which is reduced, but by relatively little.

This mechanism led to the design and production of a biomimetic material (Gordon and Jeronimidis, 1980). Early forms were assemblages of straws of spirally wound glass fibres stuck together with resin. But these are not very easy to wind and glue together, although weight-for-weight the biomimetic wood is 50 times tougher than any other man-made material. There is a cheaper and easier way using sheets of parallel fibres of glass in an uncured resin matrix which are folded and glued in a mould to produce a corrugated structure looking like corrugated cardboard. The fibres are arranged at an angle (about 15 degrees) to the long gaps between the corrugations (fig. 16), so producing something like the spiral windings in the wood cell wall (Chaplin et al., 1983). This material is being developed for protection against explosives and against knives and bullets. It is particularly suited for use in clothing since it is so light, being a cellular material.

It is instructive to do a SWAT analysis of imperfection (fig. 17), which shows that it might be difficult to manage, and we may be less inclined to do so due to our predilection for 'beauty' and 'perfect' structures. It is easy to see why symmetry and perfection are regarded as 'good'; but imperfection, despite the disapprobation the name implies, can produce structures which are far more durable.

REFERENCES

Chaplin, R. C., Gordon, J. E. and Jeronimidis, G. (1983), *Development of a novel fibrous composite material*, USA.

Fagerberg, W. R. and Allain, D. (1991). 'A quantitative study of tissue dynamics during closure in the traps of Venus's flytrap Dionaea muscipula Ellis', *American Journal of Botany* 78, 647-57.

Forterre, Y., Skotheim, J. M., Dumais, J. and Mahadevan, L. (2005), 'How the Venus flytrap snaps', *Nature* 433, 421-5.

Gordon, J. E. and Jeronimidis, G. (1980), 'Composites with high work of fracture', *Philosophical Transactions of the Royal Society* A 294, 545-50.

Hansen, U. N. (1999), 'Modeling of bone microcracking', in *NAFEMS World Congress*.

Hepworth, D. G., Vincent, J. F. V., Stringer, G. and Jeronimidis, G. (2002), 'Variations in the morphology of wood structure can explain why hardwood species of similar density have very different resistances to impact and compressive loading', *Philosophical Transactions of the Royal Society* A 360, 255-72.

Hodick, D. and Sievers, A. (1989), 'On the mechanism of trap closure of venus flytrap Dionaea muscipula Ellis', *Planta* 179, 32-42.

Jeronimidis, G. and Parkyn, A. T. (1988), 'Residual stresses in carbon fibre-thermoplastic matrix laminates', *Journal of Composite Materials* 22, 401-15.

Kitchener, A. C. (1991), 'The evolution and mechanical design of horns and antlers' in *Biomechanics in Evolution*, eds. R. J. M. V and W. R. J), Cambridge University Press.

Thom, R. (1975), *Structural stability and morphogenesis, an outline of a general theory of models*. Reading, Mass.: WA Benjamin Inc.

Vincent, J. F. V. (1994), 'The mute dogs of nature', *Science & Public Affairs*, Autumn, 41-3.

INTRODUCTION

Structures using curvature (e.g. shells, cable nets, and gridshells) provide the most efficient way to form large-scale, lightweight enclosures. Utilising predominantly axial forces to perform their structural action, this type of structure is defined by geometry and boundary conditions, their loading and forces acting on them. These lock their form into their characteristic shape, giving them static equilibrium.

Looking at the principles of lattice shells in combination with bending stiffness and geometrical manipulation, this paper explores the introduction of multiple states of equilibrium as a means of creating adaptable structures that can be actively deformed or made to react to different boundary and load configurations through geometrical reconfiguration and adaptation.

It relates to design work carried out at the Architectural Association, both in the MA/MArch course in Emergent Technologies and in Diploma Unit 4, where model tests have been used to study aspects of deformability of structures as part of changing performance criteria.

The paper advocates a new way of approaching geometry in the design of structures and looks in depth at the techniques that can be applied during the design of such structures to control their adaptable deformation.

GEOMETRY AND STRUCTURAL BEHAVIOUR

At the basis of the approach lie a few fundamental ideas on how forces can be carried within a structure, particularly the differences between direct axial forces and bending and in this context the role played by geometry and curvature in a structure.

We start with a comparison between bending and direct axial forces. Two simple structures, a triangulated system and a cantilever, both of which fulfil the same purpose, demonstrate how strength and stiffness are distributed entirely differently according to their structural system. Whilst the former can resolve forces into pure tension and pure compression, the latter relies on splitting them into tension and compression within the same member, which has direct implications for stiffness, stresses and deflection of this structure.

It becomes clear that a structure carrying forces in bending will require more material than one where loads are taken in axial forces only, assuming that deformations

Japan Pavilion by Buro Happold and Shigeru Ban – erection sequence.

are to be comparably limited. However, it also shows that arrangement of the system that uses only axial forces has to be designed for the force combination it is supposed to carry. In other words, reversing the direction of force would cause its collapse, whilst in the cantilever ,internal forces would be able to adjust to the new load.

The principle of using geometry to carry loads in axial forces only is best utilised in curved structures, where the curvature follows the thrust lines that relate to the forces applied. These structures receive their strength through the use of geometry which dictates that they act in axial forces only.

The superimposition of bending and axial action creates an interaction and influences stiffness and deformation as stresses and resulting strains are added. This becomes interesting in surface structures, where curvature and in-plane action are utilised as the primary structural action. Bending stiffness is usually provided on a secondary level where the curvature is not compatible with out-of-balance loads or point-loads. At the same time, utilising bending stiffness within curved structures can also provide flexibility in the design approach in cases where the pure in-plane action of a shell or lattice-shell structure with its stringent requirements on curvature and boundary conditions cannot be realised efficiently.

On the other hand, where bending stiffness is kept to the minimum, high bending flexibility of the structural members of a surface structure can be utilised in the construction process. The lack of bending resistance of individual members permits deformations without locking in detrimental stresses or creating a reduction in member capacity through the superimposition of bending and axial stresses. Flexible structural members therefore facilitate the creation of surface curvature, which in turn allows the in-plane action of doubly curved lattice shells to be activated.

These principles have been successfully employed in a number of structures such as the Mannheim Multihalle gridshell or, more recently, the Weald and Downland Museum or the cardboard tube structure of the Japan Pavilion at the Hanover Expo, the example shown here. The individual members of the lattice shell structures could be laid out flat, with gravity bending them into their final position by manipulation of the support structures. Transferring the member arrangement, which requires propping the flat condition, with its lack of bending resistance, into a stiff surface structure, takes advantage of the axial capacity and axial stiffness of the members once they are locked into the restraints at the boundaries.[1]

The new roof design of the British Museum exemplifies the concept of providing bending stiffness where geometry and boundary conditions cannot be rigorously implemented to provide pure shell action. Bending stiffness contributes to the overall structural performance in this shell without lateral support at the external perimeter. To achieve this, bending stiffness is allocated where required and changes along the length of structural lines are made using fabricated structural sections, which are adapted to the conditions of their position within the structure. This concept produces a structure that predominantly utilises curvature in a self-contained geometry and supplements this with bending stiffness, whose distribution is predetermined through the analysis of the structure. The structural solution minimises section sizes and produces an elegant integration of structure and skin.[2]

ELASTICITY AND STRENGTH

The elastic behaviour of a structure is dependent on both the material and the profiles, that is, cross-sectional area, torsion resistance and moment of inertia, of its members. In general the rule *the bigger the stiffer* applies a crude but simple and easily controlled way to design static structures. There are, however, other ways to generate and distribute the necessary stiffness. An additive arrangement of small members can equally provide stiffness by combining their individual section properties and, if local stability issues are considered in the design, they can obviate the need for large structural members. Connections between members control their interactions and theoretically allow stiffness as well as strength to be added where necessary or when required. Larger-scale triangulation and arrangements of multi-layer structures, and in particular surfaces, can allow the possibility of locally increasing axial and bending stiffness and providing a macro-stiffness on a larger scale. This approach, which could be compared to weaving techniques, allows in turn the reduction of individual member stiffness in the macro-arrangement, adopting a concept used in the design of fibre-reinforced structures to allocate stiffness where required.

This can be combined with the adaptation of the cross-section of members, similar to the stiffness allocation in the structure of the British Museum roof. Utilising the breadth-to-depth ratio, varying thickness or varying section geometry, stiffness can also be mobilised differently in different directions.

ADAPTABLE EQUILIBRIUM

Based on these considerations, a new way of looking at structural adaptability, deformation and flexibility can be explored, without contradicting elastic stiffness and, more importantly, without limiting the deformation under primary loading conditions, the key serviceability criterion for the design of structures.

Obviously, aspects of structural stability, both local and global, will need careful consideration if such design concepts are being followed. This becomes particularly interesting when using highly flexible members, which by their nature provide a lower resistance against buckling and other instabilities that depend on bending or torsional stiffness. However, where the single element stiffness is reduced, again the interconnection and defined allocation of members in the larger system can be designed and utilised to guarantee that stability criteria do not become the governing design aspect.

As much as stiffness and strength are required to withstand outer forces, global equilibrium is needed for the overall stability of a structure and its capacity to safely carry its loads into its foundations. Where outer forces are not directly resisted by reaction, potential, energy will be transformed into kinetic energy with resulting movements to satisfy Newton's laws of motion. In general these movements are undesirable in structures, with the result that one objective of the design is to avoid them.

However, movements could be treated as transitions between static positions for which a stable static equilibrium state can be provided. Controlling this transition, through the manipulation of boundary conditions and active change, can be difficult. The necessity of controlled energy input into the structure becomes evident and is probably the most interesting aspect of the research into adaptable, flexible and movable structures.

With the transition stage itself being part of the use of the structure, the concept of movement is not that of moving elements within a stable framework, but the integration of the adaptable elements and motion parts within the structure itself, acting in the context of a larger reorganisation of structural elements.

MOVEMENT AND CONTROL

Integrating the movement into the entire structure makes it necessary to consider the global interdependence of all structural elements. The movement and transition thus influence the entire structure, and local effects will have repercussions on the global structural system.

In this context there are a number of simple possibilities for the control of the interaction of structural parts which are interrelated and in combination allow the adaptation of the global structural system:

British Museum roof – distributed stiffness.

$A_1 = \frac{D_1^2}{4}\pi$

$I_1 = \frac{D_1^4}{32}\pi$

$D_2 = \frac{1}{2}D_1$

$A_2 = \frac{D_2^2}{4}\pi = \frac{D_1^2}{16}\pi = \frac{1}{4}A_1$

$I_2 = \frac{D_2^4}{32}\pi = \frac{D_1^4}{512}\pi = \frac{1}{16}I_1$

$D_2 = \frac{D_1}{2}$

$A_3 = 4A_2 = A_1$

$I_3 = 4\frac{A_1}{4}(\frac{D_1}{4})^2 + 4\frac{I_1}{16} = \frac{1}{2}I_1 + \frac{1}{4}I_1 = \frac{3}{4}I_1$

$2D_2 = D_1$

$A_4 = 4A_2 = A_1$

$I_4 = 4\frac{A_1}{4}(\frac{D_1}{2})^2 + 4\frac{I_1}{16} = 2I_1 + \frac{1}{4}I_1 = \frac{9}{4}I_1$

Stiffness and size, stiffness and bundling.

— The Control of the Joints

Here the mechanisms that provide and manipulate the connection of structural members and thus, in the wider sense, the possibility to have individual members act in a larger context are of greatest importance. Where joints are usually designed to be of a static nature, their change of geometry, rotation capacity or stiffness is of interest.

Change of geometry can in this case be active by generating the movement either within the joint or the areas directly adjacent to the joint, or passive by allowing rotation and movement induced by applied forces that act on a larger area and thus on a number of joints.

The allocation of a predefined stiffness to a joint will then set any movements or rotations in relation to the applied forces, providing a base resistance to deformations within a specified limit.

Friction equally provides a possibility for movement control and resistance to deformation. However, due to a variety of factors such as material quality, manufacturing tolerances as well as wear and tear, it is considered less predictable and therefore difficult to handle:

— The Exploration of Different Geometrical Arrangements

In order to utilise axial forces as the primary structural action, the geometry of a surface structure has to maximise the benefits that can be gained from curvature. Different geometrical arrangements will generate varying efficiency in the use of curvature and thus in the possibility to use axial forces as primary load-bearing action. Regions with insufficient curvature will have to act in bending, with consequences for the structure.

On the other hand this provides an advantage: where the use of curvature becomes an encumbrance, axial capacity can be supplemented with bending stiffness in order to facilitate flexible arrangement with varying geometrical parameters.

— The Adaptation of Boundary Conditions

A number of characteristics and parameters can be summarised as boundary conditions.

Besides the actual edge and support conditions, these also comprise geometric envelopes including maximum and minimum pitches and curvature and imposed forces, which have a direct effect on the geometrical and load-bearing requirements.

Edges and support conditions are not always easily changed. However, the concept of adaptable structures would assume that these could be part of the transition, at least in defined, distinct areas, creating openings or closures which redefine the relationship of building and environment.

When looking at the adaptation of boundary conditions, emphasis will also be on the application of forces that could generate geometrical changes. These could be systems of forces that act against supports as well as forces that act within the structure, causing controlled deformation in conjunction with an adjustment of joint geometry.

The changes and transitions generated can be of a local or a global nature, depending on the application of the movement-generating force within the structure.

Whilst it seems possible that any of these three forms of manipulation could be looked at in isolation, only their combination offers sensible possibilities for the adaptation and transformation of structural systems. The interaction of the various changes within the system will need to be designed and predictable in order to fulfil the postulated criteria of safe control of any kinetic transition process.

Multihalle Mannheim under construction.

The example of the Hybgrid project by Sylvia Felipe and Jordi Truco[3] exemplifies some of the deformations and adaptations that have been discussed. The project, prepared as a design thesis in Emergent Technologies in 2002/2003, utilises the elasticity of its members and local adjustments in the joints in order to change the overall geometry of the structure. The adaptation is possible in a predefined geometrical range. The multi-layer structure, which is composed of simple straight members, provides a limited bending strength to adapt to areas of low curvature.

In addition to the abovementioned stress, deflection and stability criteria, careful consideration has to be given to the movement-induced changes of stresses and strains. Fatigue issues which are not of great concern in the design of static structures become one of the key design criteria.

Although outside the scope of this paper, the influence of a designed movement on a structure will produce a different approach to any cladding and non-structural elements, that will be affected by the movement on a secondary level. Such elements will have to be able to act in a variety of static states as well as in the geometrical transition a structure might undergo. As such, they must be part of the discussion about flexible adaptable architectural spaces.

STRUCTURAL DESIGN

The necessity to control the transition stages in the life of the structure therefore has to be reflected in the possibility to exercise this control in the design stages as well. As a consequence, where movements become an integral part first of the structural design and then of the arrangement and interaction of the structural members, the design has to treat movement as key.

The movement at any stage has to be stable within given parameters, designed after an exploration of limitations and potential unstable conditions. This creates the need for interactive design tools that allow the simulation of any of the transition stages and give the engineer the

Weald and Downland Grid Shell – joint detail.

Japan Pavilion – tied joints and paper tubes.

means to correct the behaviour of the structure by exploring its limits. These limits refer not only to the stress and deflection that structural analysis investigates, but also to the range of stable equilibrium states and the stability of all transitions, which will enable the designer to define safety factors for both the static and the dynamic conditions of the structure.

At this point traditional structural engineering software that uses a top-down matrix analysis approach (Finite Elements Method) will most likely fail – such software requires the engineer to predict the equilibrium state before the analysis is carried out. Any deviation from the stable configuration of the structure will lead to an abortion of the calculation process. Even iterative processes require starting near a stable equilibrium towards which the iteration converges (if at all); they cannot deal with the complex transition states produced by the designed movement of structures.

The failings of traditional design software have led, so far, to a reliance on physical modelling approaches in the design of structures that use this kind of adaptability. This, however, entails other severe limitations: even if the same material can be used at different sizes (which often proves to be extremely difficult), the scaling of structures remains problematic.

Both bending stiffness and axial stiffness do not scale linearly, and both scale differently. Any manipulation of structures that relies on a superimposition of bending and axial stresses as well as the activation of bending stiffness to compensate for incompatibilities in the geometrical arrangement thus depends heavily on the scale of model employed. This shortcoming can partly be overcome by a systematic step-by-step scaling of models, with a rigorous analysis of applied forces, changes to boundary conditions and resulting deformations with an extrapolation of the recorded data – an approach that was utilised in the design of the large-scale model of Hybgrid.

However, even if this process is carried out with extreme care, a number of secondary effects remain problematic, such as friction in joints, model building tolerances and material differences. More importantly, however, the force dependence of the geometry greatly limits digital modelling, as physical aspects of the form definition, which are of highest importance for the design approach, are not considered.

New analysis concepts, whose principles have first been developed in the computer animation industry, are currently being explored[4] and are now being researched in the framework of the Emergent Technologies programme at the AA. They utilise object-oriented programming ideas for the simulation of structural behaviour. With their help, associative modelling and time-step analysis together seem achievable, which would allow the interactive study of the behaviour of a structural system necessary to determine the transitory equilibrium states required for this approach to adaptable structures.

Such a bottom-up structural design tool looks at the properties of the individual member and its interaction with other members to which it is connecte. It should allow the control and design of the transition stages: the analysis becomes a time-step operation where forces and their effects are calculated according to the physical and geometrical properties of all elements. As Newton's laws of motion apply for every step of the analysis, acceleration and movement become part of the equilibrium consideration. As such, movements can be captured in the same way as static conditions.

Since local and global stability are key aspects during all dynamic stages of the structural system, an interactive design tool must take P-□ second-order effects into consideration and incorporate these into the parameters of the structural model.

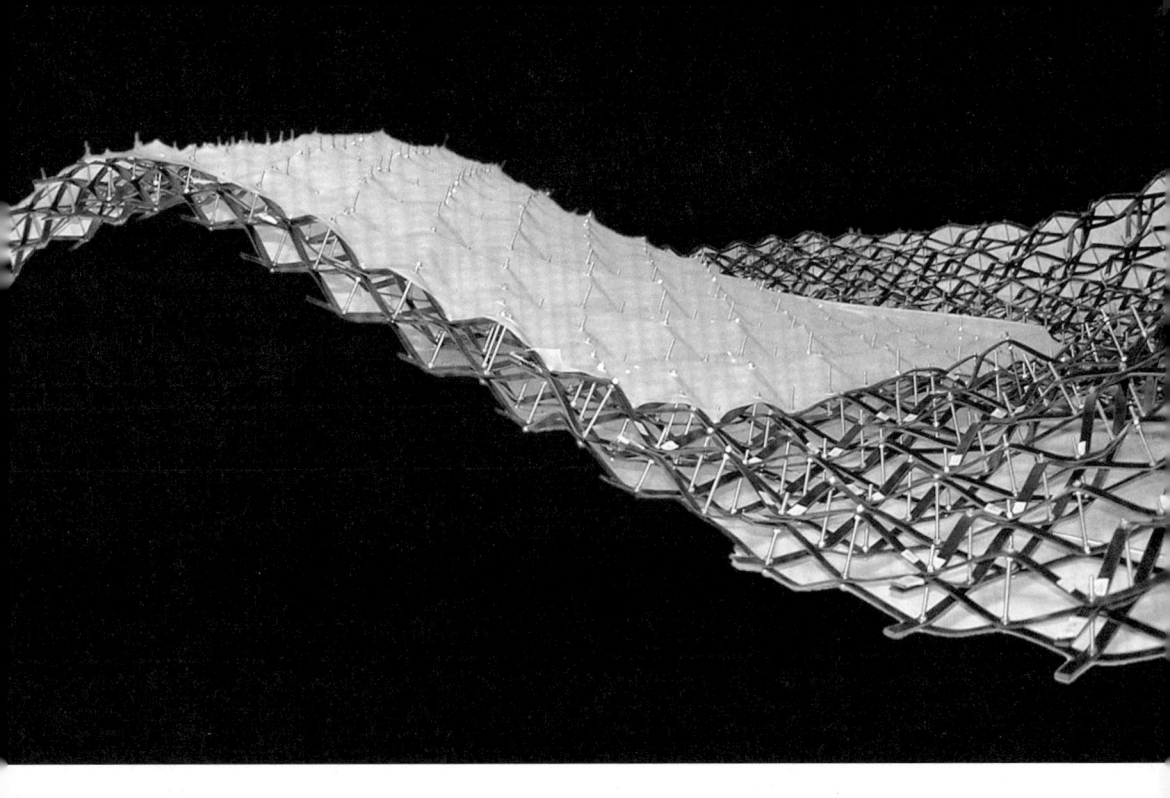

Hybgrid – model arrangement.

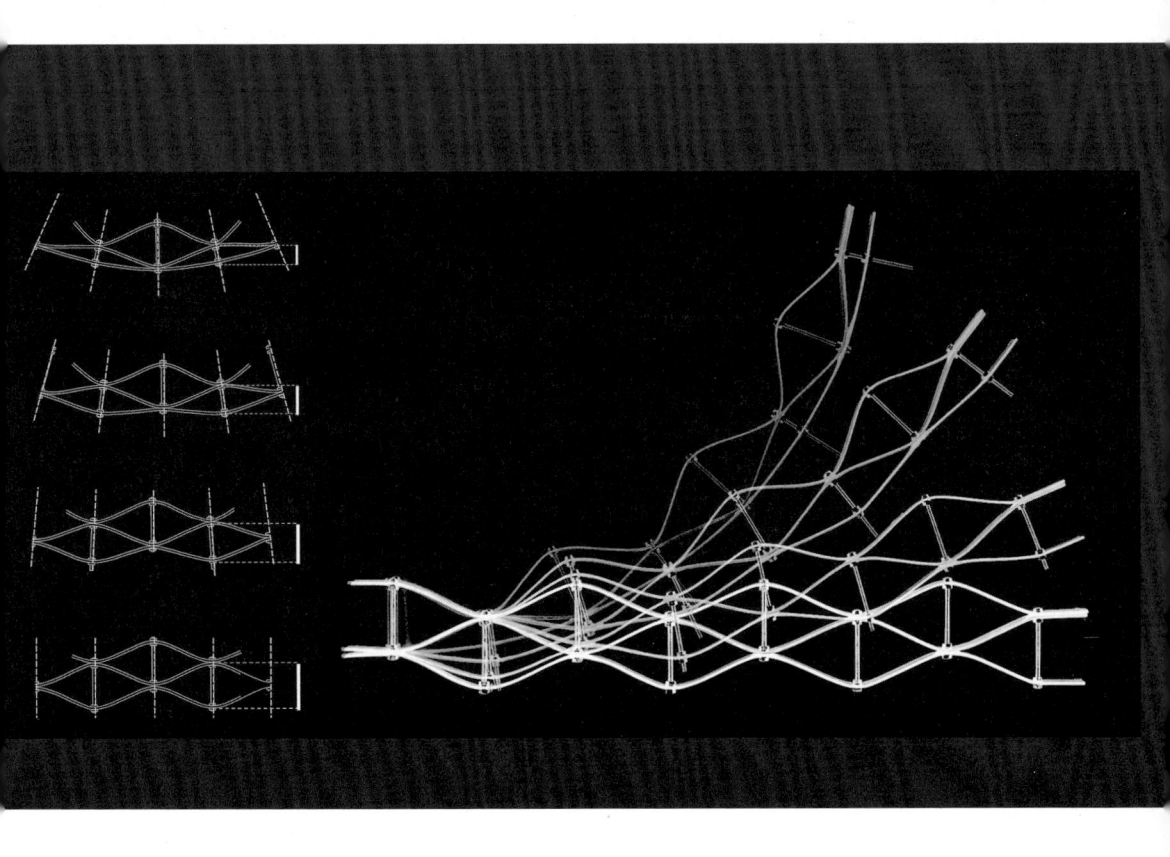

Hybgrid – geometric transformations.

331

OUTLOOK AND CONCLUSION

The arrangement of members and material in a structure can allow us to manipulate stiffness as well as strength. This can happen on various levels, be it by member orientation, by fibre addition on a micro- or a macro-level, or by the control of the interaction of members. However, it is always to be seen in the context of the global structural behaviour. The intelligent combination and distribution of bending and axial action will allow us to utilise the much higher axial stiffness while we can design the member arrangements so that bending flexibility can enable adaptability and controlled movements. The geometry of the structure will play a most important role in this allocation of forces and stiffness, creating the need for surfaces to be structurally designed and integrated into the combination load-paths.

With sufficient built-in redundancy, which could be exploited as a characteristic of structurally designed geometry, safe load redistribution and the provision of a multitude of load-paths can assist the transition stages of dynamic adaptation. These can be forced onto the structure or allowed to occur by the designed application of external forces, mechanical devices or the simple adjustment of the boundary conditions.

The further exploration of these principles in the design will only be possible if the current design possibilities are expanded. The proposed route forward is an analysis approach, incorporating physical properties and their repercussions on the formation of the structure and its geometry into the digital modelling, which is at present limited to geometrical aspects only. This virtual physical modelling must continue in parallel with real physical modelling, which, taking into consideration the scale effects, provides the most direct way to explore complex structural behaviour.

FOOTNOTES

[1] McQuaid, M; *Japan Pavilion, Expo 2000, Shigeru Ban*, Phaidon Press, London, 2003.

[2] Schischka, J. and Brown, S; 'The Engineering Design and Construction of the British Museum Great Court Roof', *Proc. International Symposium on Widespan Enclosures*, 26-28 April 2000, University of Bath, 2000.

[3] Hensel, M., Menges, A. and Weinstock, M; *Emergence – Morphogenetic Design Strategies*; 62-3; AD Wiley, London, 2004.

[4] Jankovic, L., Jankovic, S., Chan, A. H. C., and Little, G. H.; 'Emergent Modelling for Structural Design, International Conference on Complexity and Complex Systems', September 2000, University of Warwick, 2000.
and Jankovic, L., Jankovic, S., Chan, A. H. C., and Little; 'Bottom-up Structure Processors, International Conference on Computational Engineering & Sciences', ICES'01, August 2001, Puerto Vallarta, Mexico, 2001.

Seeking the *optimum solution* in architectural design is a highly motivating proposition, and a quest that can be a significant driver in the design process. Looking at the Parthenon's peristyle from a structural point of view, there has to be a presumption that each individual column is supporting a similar load, that each is doing its share of the work. Similarly, if we take a Gothic masterpiece such as the Cathedral of Saint Pierre, Beauvais, we might conclude that the immense forces exerted by gravity are directed axially to the ground through the columns, and that the columns are aligned axially to the forces being exerted. As the columns are vertical this would imply that the forces, too, are vertical, whereas we know that this is not the case.[1] Static inefficacy is not an issue as both examples have stood the test of time. We accept that they might be overstructured in order to conform to a set of priorities that do not include either striving for equal load distribution or accomplishing a lean fitness tied to task.

When the quest for the optimum solution is structurally motivated, however, it comes across as a more contemporary challenge, and necessarily computationally oriented since it is on the face of it highly technical in nature. It cannot be argued that the historical examples I cite are optimal structures in their choice of materials alone or in their actual disposition. The columns might appear to be doing their assigned task well enough, but efficiency cannot be assumed. Indeed in the case of the Gothic masters, we applaud the invention of decorated pinnacles as a means to provide vertical mass to offset the effects of lateral loads, much as we admire the flying buttresses designed to transfer inconvenient loads – if that is really what they were designed to do. Flying buttresses can be seen as precursors to differentiated structure, and their invention was one of the key historical moments in the structural enrichment of our architectural repertoire. Nonetheless, even in contemporary practice, innovation has but a shadow of the sophistication found in the evolution of natural structures, from which architecture can strive to draw inspiration.

Historically, any optimisation of architectural design was most likely to have been based on pragmatic and readily solvable priorities such as 'comfort performance', 'programme', 'environmental responsiveness' and 'built value over construction cost'. However an emphasis on efficiency and practicality would typically be overridden by the architect's skill in judging an appropriate 'stopping point' in the design from an aesthetic point of view. The artistic intervention appears paramount in the architect's

Colònia Güell Crypt – exterior view. (left) Colònia Güell Crypt – entrance porch to the crypt. (right)

modus operandi, yet emphasising beauty over function is not a priority in the natural world.

Whether practically or aesthetically motivated, the *optimum* does have a greater hold over the way we design today. This may be attributed to a number of pressures, ranging from economics to environmental consideration, or even a search to mirror the beauty of natural forms, which are nearly always optimised in evolutionary terms. The methodology for doing this seems increasingly to rely on mathematical algorithms and the use of recursive computational procedures that home in on the 'ideal' solution.[2] But it is crucial to bear in mind that, far from representing the complete suite of opportunities, applying algorithms in this way may only be part of a more complex design process. If one fails to do this, and accepts the application of one or more algorithms as the automatic recourse for optimising design performance computationally, there is a risk that all other concerns and influences become secondary – if not actual slaves to a numerically assertive imperative that is difficult to argue with. This paper makes a case for the extensive and fertile ground that still lies beyond algorithmic design space. It points to ways of growing optimised design solutions that are conceptually beyond the reach of the application of algorithms on their own. In these processes the algorithmic contribution is seen as a useful adjunct, not the prime driver. Looking to nature as a conceptual rather than a literal sponsor of optimised solutions, we need to ask whether we can retain an enquiring interest in the analogue equivalent to digitally assisted optimisation. Might we consider the value of acquiring usable 'data' through empirical research and physical experiment as being at least equal to relying on the presumed foresight of software engineers working as our proxies? History again helps us, but via the exception rather than the rule.

The Catalan architect Antoni Gaudí (1852-1926) provides clues to the use of natural (rather than machinic) computational approaches to optimising structural design. He relied on natural forces applied to physical rather than digital models. His hanging model for the Colònia Güell crypt, which I shall discuss in more detail below, is a highly original vehicle with which to gauge alternative

336 Colònia Güell Crypt – interior central view.

Colònia Güell Crypt – interior oblique view.

Colònia Güell Crypt – interior ceiling vaults. (left) Colònia Güell Crypt – Gaudí hanging model. (right)

338　　Colònia Güell Crypt – 'restored' hanging model, built from photographs and currently located in the Sagrada Familia museum. Model made by Jos Tomlow et al (refer to endnotes)

Colònia Güell Crypt – detail of restored hanging model.

strategies for optimisation: in my view it is a better benchmark than anything that has emerged from the digital design world, including parametric design, Evolutionary Structural Evolution (ESO), animation and mathematical borrowing, which I would argue are digital adjuncts to design based on observations of natural systems, and not replacements for them. Looking at experimental physical models from this perspective helps to lift the debate, moving it from a discussion about which natural systems we should draw from (often presumed to be at the microscopic level, leading to nanotechnology, etc.), to an attempt to determine appropriate scale and degree of scientific observation as an overlay to intuition.

Physical models afford haptic experimentation with the actual forces that structures are designed both to counteract and interact with. Their use, regardless of digital fashionability, is not necessarily predisposed to a strictly analytical approach, and can enrich any argument that otherwise relies on a literal interpretation of natural systems at a microscopic scale for the purposes of deriving algorithmic input. By taking into account the simple and straightforward macroscopic analysis of the natural world around us, we can help to ensure that, when it comes to selecting differentiated structural design options, a conceptual engagement with issues such as *division of labour* takes precedence over a reliance on computational rigour *per se* – or indeed a deferral to the wonderful natural world as revealed by the microscope, as opposed to something we can touch with our hands. The intention of this paper is to help sustain the value of observation of the natural world around us. Taking its cue from the methods of Gaudí, it proposes that observation can be combined with more intuitively driven design sensibilities, providing a real alternative to the exclusive acceptance of the seductive powers of the digitally engaged algorithm.

ORGANIC ROOTS

The sensibilities of others reaffirm our own. My interest in the relationship between architectural statics and natural structures probably came to the fore with my first tree-house construction. I remember being acutely interested in the way the trunk of the apple tree bifurcated into branches, the relationship between little branches and big branches being revealed as I attempted to impose my own artifice on the tree using minimal intervention methods such as rope and twine rather than the handier hammer and nail. This meant exploring available branching as a construct, and committing to some kind of relatively benign host relationship rather than parasitism. I wanted to harmlessly construct a new space for myself while ensuring that the apple tree could continue to provide a leafy canopy for itself.

This early practical engagement with trees developed into a more scientific and aesthetic interest in nature later on during my final years at high school, when atypically (for that time in the UK), I was able to combine three science A levels with a fourth in fine art, while undertaking a first year in pure and applied mathematics. After art, biology was my next preferred subject, and it was with genuine fascination that I stepped into the world of botanical and marine macro- and micro-structures. Perhaps in line with a predilection of my biology teacher, a significant proportion of the curriculum seemed to be dedicated to observing and then formally recording our observations, principally through accurate drawings of what we could see, either through the microscope or via the internal arrangements of dead creatures revealed by the bizarre tool-set kept in a canvas roll bearing the sinister name of 'dissection kit'.

I found the whole business extraordinarily aesthetic. The visual and haptic experimental appeal definitely came ahead of any more scholarly engagement in scientific enquiry, but nonetheless was intimately associated with it: that is to say, for me the observations led to wider ranging scholarship, as opposed to expertise gained by drilling down in the search for proof in the laboratory. New concepts such as 'division of labour' and 'differentiation' were introduced to us by our teacher who, despite his advancing years, retained an infectious enthusiasm for ideas that at first appeared trivial to us. As our investigations proceeded, these concepts began to acquire real meaning, beginning with the smallest sub-organisms offered up by drops of water from what had previously seemed to be an inert pond. Even at the age of seventeen, I still experienced a childlike wonder at encountering this complex hidden world – a feeling that I am sure can be appreciated by anyone who can recall looking down the microscope for the first time and seeing the secret life maintained in such innocuous-seeming soups.

Slowly moving up the food chain, diatoms and radiolarians were the first complex organisms we dealt with, having messed around with amoeba and their vacuoles, then successfully hunted down green and brown hydra. How cells divided, why they took on particular roles, and how organisms stopped growing were perplexing issues that were never fully resolved, because upon leaving school and taking up the study of architecture in the mid-1970s, I found that none of these personal interests held any discernable appeal for my late-modernist educators. The science stopped, but my enquiry continued down less formal tracks, and for me an untutored interest in the 'organic' within 'organic architecture' and the role of observation remains a highly motivating factor in any design process.

Although in those days of architectural apprenticeship there was always an insistence on the vertical and horizontal straight line – invariably constrained by the right angle – I was very much aware of the iconoclasts who had railed against such restrictions, using associations with nature to inform their work. What interested me in particular were the processes of experimentation that were being invoked, and investigations of natural physical phenomena through haptic engagement, as opposed to purely mathematical, geometrical, or computational expeditions. Thus, for the purposes of my argument here, I do not need to draw on the work of Häring, Otto, Spuybroek, et al, however valid their claims might be, since Gaudí engaged with the core 'organic' issues.

ORGANIC DESIGN

'Organic architecture' defies straightforward definition. Whether a literal link is made back to Frank Lloyd Wright, who is credited with having coined the term in 1908,[3] or to the sensibilities of organicists such as Hugo Häring (1882-1958), or to the voluptuous twirls and tendrils of the Art Nouveau protagonists, a clear and unequivocal reading remains elusive. Organic architecture certainly cannot be reduced to the extrapolation of the systems found in nature as the useful models for equivalent functions in architecture, where the dermis becomes semi-permeable surface and the articulated skeleton the reconfigurable armature. Nonetheless, there are some common attributes shared by those who promote an extension of natural systems, processes and artefacts into architecture. First, there is a vital resonance that ranges from visual connections with natural forms (if not systems) to a less superficial and humanist association between form and habitation. Then there is the fundamental appeal of natural materials at a tectonic as well as systematic level. Deepest of all, there is a fundamental intellectual engagement with nature that combines the immediateness of the senses with both structural and philosophical considerations. A cultural engagement is another matter altogether, beyond the range of issues explored here.

Antoni Gaudí is the most conspicuous proponent of this combination of sensuality and fundamental intellectual engagement with nature. He grew up in a region south of Barcelona, near the town of Reus, and from early on exhibited an interest in his natural surroundings. The rugged landscape of Reus is famed for the intensity of the Mediterranean sunlight: Gaudí said that its favourable angle of incidence was the hallmark of his region and others on a similar latitude.

Gaudí claimed that 'originality is the return to the source',[4] that is, a return to nature. His own work during the whole of his extensive career reflected this belief. Early on, for example in the townhouse Casa Vicens (from 1883), this was expressed as an appliqué of natural motif over a historicist framework. Later, during the years he was aligned to *modernismo* (approximately 1890-1910), this 'returning to the source' became a more engrained refrain. The almost submarine aspects of Casa Batlló (1905-7), or the more terrestrial features of the quarry-like sculpted undulations for Casa Milà (1906-1910) could serve as sufficient evidence of Gaudí's passionate invocation of the natural world around him, but then the chapel at Colònia Güell (1898-1916) takes the debate on to an entirely different level – one that has surely not been surpassed since. For the chapel Gaudí decided to harness the same forces that the structure would ultimately confront in terms of static resistance, as the means to describe the building form itself. Much is made of the resulting hanging 1:10 model that was set up in a tin shed adjacent to the proposed site for the church. This showed that gravity would exert in tension forces that inform the shape in 3D as much as in 2D; on the upside-down model a hanging chain adopts the catenary curve which mirrors so closely the parabolic thrust arch, the optimum shape for an arch accommodating load in compression. The logic held that a cohesive network of articulated nodes and connections with accurately scaled representations of loading applied to the nodes would pull the resulting mesh into a self-determining gravity-respecting shape. To accentuate the form in any particular zone, more mass would be applied to that zone, thereby influencing the shape at that point. At the scale of the model, such loading was achieved by applying additional bags of birdshot, whereas at the scale of the building, this eccentric loading would most likely be manifest as an additional tower or pinnacle, for example.[5]

This is an utterly haptic process. As the accompanying illustrations show, the scale of the model gives it a height of several metres, allowing the designer to actually walk among the myriad strings, bags of birdshot and connections. This process of refining the design took around eight years, and the project was a consuming interest for Gaudí. Once the design was finally settled, construction began and proceeded at an intense pace for six years, before petering out over a couple of years. The client had become unwell, and his family was less disposed than he was to

Sagrada Familia – central nave columns and vaults.

Sagrada Familia – detail of clerestory and central nave vaults.

Sagrada Familia – central nave vaults.

344 Sagrada Familia – Gaudí's quest for the ideal column (centre and right hand) using double helix. Earlier experiment using single helix on left-hand side. (left) Gaudí's method for testing the bearing capacity of stone. (right)
source: Arxiu del Temple de la Sagrada Familia

Sagrada Familia – central nave 'columns of 8', showing the captured growth sequence in the column sections.

support what must have seemed a magnificent debacle. The project is great, in that it represents an architectural intention given voice in a 4D design process – a conversation between man and the forces of gravity, an accommodation of practical exigencies within a wholly poetic construct. The project was a personal disaster for Gaudí as it was abandoned sixteen years after its inception, with only the basement crypt (more or less) completed. While this relatively modest built portion still serves well as a chapel, the stalling of so ambitious a design for the church interior proved a bitter disappointment. Today the project as a whole remains the highpoint of an organic architectural endeavour where natural exertions, forces, materials and systems are in perfect harmony with their architectural complement.

The discussion so far has focused on the qualities of the design as a process. This is fascinating in its own right, but as the accompanying images show, the part of the building that was actually realised has a distinctive merit beyond representing a building experiment where the structure is seemingly more sympathetic to the forces accommodated than resistive to the forces applied. With the exception of a small proportion of good bricks applied with consummate panache, the building fabric is extremely modest. The central columns are naturally occurring basalt prisms, much of the walls are made from over-fired kiln bricks, and even the window grills recycle discarded corduroy loom needles from the associated textile factory. Apparently Gaudí regarded this building as a prototype for the completion of the Sagrada Família (1882-), long underway by this time, and still so far from completion. In the porch ceiling and to a lesser extent the interior ceiling (both illustrated), we can see the introduction of the first of the ruled-surfaces that Gaudí extracted from nature as the guiding principles for all the surfaces in Sagrada Familia. In this instance they are hyperbolic paraboloids. As the following quote reveals, he saw the need for improvement in articulations between conjoined structural elements:

> *He used these ruled-surfaces because he believed them to be the most perfect. 'To conceal the imperfect union between the stiles and lintel of an opening', he would say, 'we use capitals, imposts, etc. Nature produces none of these features to resolve the continuity'.*[6]

The reason why I believe that the Colònia Güell Chapel has such a prominent position in the history of architecture, beyond its obvious status as an aesthetic and cultural tour de force, is that it is the best example of a project bridging pre- and post-digital design priorities. For many years Gaudí made several visits a week to a site way beyond the city boundaries – a scenario that would be anathema to any twenty-first-century project manager, as it hardly conforms to the contemporary values of just-in-time delivery and lean construction. For the thinker researching the connection between trapping the forces that architectural structure must address and turning them around as a positive feature, the project is a gift. It could almost be said to legitimise current interests in employing a variety of 4D software originally designed for the animation film industry, except for the fact that it has the potential to belittle such efforts: we end up comparing a conceptual leap of faith in the pre-digital era with mere acts of cleverness in digital domains.

With respect to the extrapolation of his learning to the Sagrada Familia church – and we should note that the main leaps in his thinking there came at least a decade after the design phase of the Colònia Güell Chapel – Gaudí is paraphrased as follows:

> *When building the Sagrada Familia and studying other churches he was deeply critical of the Gothic style – a style that had inspired such eulogies from the literati and engineers of his youth. Of the Gothic he said that it was an imperfect style, as yet unresolved; an industrial style, a mere mechanical system; the decoration was always artificial, and could be eliminated entirely without it losing any particular quality. He would say sarcastically that the Gothic was at its best in ruins and in moonlight. In answer to those who objected to this criticism with, 'But you are building the Sagrada Familia in the Gothic style', his, reply was: 'No, Sir. The Sagrada Familia is Greek.' This seemingly paradoxical statement has a basis of truth: the Gothic of the Sagrada Familia is more apparent than real, for its structure goes beyond it, and in the positioning of*

volumes and the resolution of details the church has never been orthodox Gothic. Its original design was Gothic with touches of Baroque – which is the same as saying that it was not Gothic.[7]

I may have painted myself into a corner here by implying that analysis of natural systems with a view to interpreting them in architecture is more suited to a visceral than a scientific sensibility – that we must look to Gaudí principally for the formal, decorative, tectonic and artistic enrichment he brought to our craft, rather than the physics of materials and mathematics. This is not my intention. Someone recently accused me of trying to kill these attributes of Gaudí's work with my 'silly' proposition about his use of geometry, which he claimed was at the expense of the bigger and far more tactile qualities. Mindful of this critic, I shall refrain from a long discussion about my final illustration, an array of sections through one of the series of columns that provide the supports throughout Sagrada Familia. If my critic is reading this, and can decipher the game of life that underlies the composition of all of Gaudí's columns for the church, can he really deny the value of understanding the whole of Gaudí's repertoire, not just the pretty bits? Not only did Gaudí reflect profoundly on the natural world, and engage his architecture directly with it, he also turned to the sciences for that essential translation of concept to building, as we can see from the elaborate efforts he took to calibrate the compressive resistance of stone, from the way he experimented with the helical qualities of trees for his columns (he regarded the nave of his great church as a forest canopy), and ultimately from the growth algorithm from which the form of his columns are derived. But I believe that this algorithm came second to the conceptual feat he undertook in this regard, and that this is probably the more appropriate line of enquiry for architects seeking to differentiate structure by drawing from nature. Gaudí certainly never assumed that the whole culture of architecture, born from millennia of development leading to change upon change, could be subverted by computational regimes, or that homing in on the ideal solution could only occur through the literal and scientific rather than the philosophical emulation of natural systems.

ACKNOWLEDGEMENTS   I acknowledge the support of the Australian Research Council in part-funding the research from which this piece is drawn.

FOOTNOTES

[1] Robert Mark, *Experiments in Gothic Structure* (MIT Press, 1982).

[2] An algorithm is taken to be a procedure working within an absolute set of conditions will form a task working from an initial point to some defined point of termination.

[3] Frank Lloyd Wright, *An Organic Architecture*, 1939, in Bruce Pfeiffer (ed.), *Frank Lloyd Wright Collected Writings* Vol. 3 (Rizzoli, 1993).

[4] I. Puig-Boada, *El pensament de Gaudí* (Editorial La Gaya Ciència, 1981), 98.

[5] See Jos Tomlow, *Das Modell*, IL 34, Stuttgart, 1989 for the definitive account of the reconstruction of Gaudí's original model.

[6] I. Puig-Boada, T*he Church of the Sagrada Família* (Ediciones de Nuevo Arte Thor, first edition 1929, rep. 1988), 132.

[7] ibid. 131.

The populationist stresses the uniqueness of everything in the organic world. What is true for the human species – that no two individuals are alike – is equally true for all other species of animals and plants. Indeed, even the same individual changes continuously throughout its lifetime and when placed into different environments. All organisms and organic phenomena are composed of unique features and can be described collectively only in statistical terms. Individuals, or any kind of organic entities, form populations of which we can determine the arithmetic mean and the statistics of variation. Averages are merely statistical abstractions, only the individuals of which the populations are composed have reality. The ultimate conclusions of the population thinker and of the typologist are precisely the opposite. For the typologist, the type (eidos) is real and the variation an illusion, while for the populationist the type (average) is an abstraction and only the variation is real. No two ways of looking at nature could be more different.'(Ernst Mayr)[1]

At the time Ernst Mayr wrote this statement, in 1959,[2] his work was focused on defining the difference between biological and physical sciences. He predicted a shift from the centuries-old way of understanding the world, through the eyes of the physicist, towards a new biological understanding of our environment. What did Ernst Mayr mean by such a shift, and what lessons can be drawn from this debate in biology for our own discipline, namely architecture?

If we look at the architecture of the last decade of the twentieth century, we can identify one reiterated theme: how to liberate the profession from its history of styles and aestheticism. The debate focused on the idea of architecture as a material practice, with its own production of effects and its own relation to the history of practices.[3]

It was Michel Foucault who suggested what such practices could mean when he said 'I can't exactly say that this distinction between sciences that are certain and those that are uncertain is of no interest ... but I must say that what interests me more [in regard to architecture, PT] is to focus on what the Greeks called the "techne", that is to say a practical rationality governed by a conscious goal.'[4] Not surprisingly, Foucault interprets the Greek word 'techne' as being directly related to the word 'technique', which indicates a clear relation between what we do and how we do it.

In the mid-1990s a new generation of architects

and theorists claimed that representational techniques were inadequate to deal with 'the new'. In particular, the interpretation of the diagram as a tool for contemporary architectural practice caused a polarisation of the debate. ANY Magazine 23,[5] titled 'diagram work', makes clear the opposing viewpoints. On the one hand, there is Peter Eisenman's definition of the diagram as a form of representation, something that works as a generative device but is never free of value and meaning. The opposition, personified by Sanford Kwinter, argued that the role of the diagram is to attempt to theorise the material reality of the late twentieth century. For Kwinter, the diagram is 'a genetic interpretation of form, fundamentally geometric in nature, [that] emits formative and organisational influences and is the engine of novelty'.[6]

The implications were clear. All current practices, with their preoccupation with techniques of representation and image-production, seemed inadequate to the task of dealing with the new. The conception of architecture as a material practice resulted in a general call for a return to 'the real'.[7]

Looking back, a similar paradigmatic shift from the academic world to the reality of practice could be witnessed in the United States in the early 1920s. The Beaux-Arts system, up to then the universal model for teaching design, came into question because it had no direct bearing on the world of reality. Architects were now having to confront the effects of capitalism. New industrial building typologies were forcing them to present themselves as construction experts, with a knowledge of efficiency and production, while at the same time aggressive business organisations were assuming control of the market for architectural services. Architecture had to make a move from a 'discipline of aesthetics' to a 'discipline on organisations'. For example, a commission for a new type of building such as the factory required a knowledge of production processes, of factory management and production control, and of the equipment and facilities for the workers. Such subjects were beyond the reach of the traditional training of the architect.

These tendencies gave rise to new educational principles and new kinds of architectural practice, known as rationalism. Rationalist practices continue to govern most types of architectural production, even today. Their proponents compensate for their lack of novelty by publishing books of their 'knowledge' as standardised recipes or types.[8]

TYPOLOGICAL THINKING IN ARCHITECTURE

To accommodate this shift, the discipline of architecture developed knowledge through forms of abstraction – tools that separate the essential from the concrete. The architectural tool that had been used historically to deal with such paradigmatic transformation was instrumentalised by one form of essentialism: 'The concept of type thus became the basis of architecture, a fact attested to both by practice and by theory'.[9]

Throughout the history of architecture, different kinds of type definitions emerged through the application of typological or essentialist thinking. One of the first concepts of typology was Jeremy Bentham's plan of the Panopticon – a 'diagram of a mechanism of power reduced to its ideal form'[10] – which became, by the end of the eighteenth century, the ideal model for institutional buildings including prisons, hospitals, military quarters and schools. The nineteenth century produced Durand's idea of classification as a form of typological thinking. Durand categorised buildings on the basis of their common functions and drew them in the same scale for the purposes of comparison. In the same century we find Quatremère de Quincy's definition of the type: 'A type presents less the image of a thing to copy or imitate completely, than the idea of an element which must itself serve as a rule for a model.'[11] By the beginning of the 20th century, the modern movement used the idea of types as models for the standardisation of norms, functions and manufacturing techniques. Le Corbusier searched for the essence of building typologies with the aim of developing a contemporary architectural expression for his time. In the 1970s Gianfranco Caniggia, following in the footsteps of Muratori, defined type as a mental map: the concept of a house, for example, was 'a product of past and present spontaneous consciousness'.[12] Aldo Rossi defined typology in a similar vein, as a summing up of all repeatable and interpretable forms to argue the city as a 'whole'.[13] We can even find kinds of typological thinking today. Rem Koolhaas, for example, describes the diversity of contemporary cities as being generic and therefore typological.[14]

All typologies describe the essence of the object in order to explain its identity. Without these fundamental features, an object would not be what it is. The problem of typological thinking is that it denies any morphogenetic process. It rather defines timeless categories.

POPULATION THINKING

Other disciplines developed within their discourse an alternative to essentialism, generally known as 'multiplicities'. From geometry to mathematics, from biology to philosophy, the concept of multiplicity is not a new thing: it is simply a different way of looking at the same reality. The definition of multiplicity is in absolute opposition to what has been defined above as essentialist thinking. In the words of Deleuze, 'Multiplicity must not designate a combination of the many and the one, but is rather an organisation belonging to the many as such, which has no need whatsoever of unity in order to form a system.'[15] Multiplicity is not just an opposition to categorisation or to the idea of types; it is also fundamentally related to the processes that drive the appearance of the variety of forms within our world.

The first documented record of the concept of multiplicities is the 'manifold' defined by Bernhard Riemann and Friedrich Gauss. Riemann formulated two different kinds of multiplicities: 'discrete' and 'continuous'. Gauss developed the idea of geometrical surfaces based on the properties of curvature itself. This enabled him to describe surfaces as a multiplicity, overcoming the Cartesian method in which a surface is embedded in a three-dimensional space. Additionally, both Riemann and Gauss used differential and integral calculus as a new problem-solving resource.[16] Another multiplicity crucial to the development of geometry was 'Group Theory', which allows objects to be analysed in ways which reveal the properties that stay invariant in transformation. In 1872, Felix Klein rewrote all different types of geometry as variations of Euclidean geometry, by applying Group Theory to his argument.[17]

Another form of multiplicity emerged in the field of biology in the nineteenth century, as one of the fundamental concepts describing the theory of evolution. Charles Darwin questioned all theories promoted by essentialist thinkers, such as the creationists, who claimed, and still do,[18] that all variations of life are descended from static archetypes. The most extreme form of essentialism at that time was 'transmutationism', a belief that new types can only originate through the instantaneous mutation or 'saltation' of existing ones. For a transmutationist, the world is full of discontinuities. A second form of essentialism is 'transformationism', which holds that types could gradually be transformed over time, although the type was still essentially invariable at any given moment.[19]

Darwin's book *The Origin of Species* argued that all new species either emerge through the reproductive isolation of sub-populations or through mutations. What we find among living organisms, he said, are not constant classes (types), but variable populations. This approach – now referred to as population thinking – was congenial to most naturalists. Their systematic studies had revealed that animals and plants showed as much variation and uniqueness as did human species. An individual changes continuously throughout its lifetime, even within a living environment.[20] The relationship between individual organisms and individual species, in terms of population thinking, is one between the 'whole' and its parts; it is not, as the essentialists would have it, the relation between a member and its natural kind. This relationship between the whole and its parts can be called a multiplicity; the organisational principle that defines it, a 'many'.

Today, thanks to people like Ernst Mayr, we know not only that we cannot find any individual that is identical to another, we also understand how evolution works. After Mendelson introduced the terms 'genotype' and 'phenotype' in the early 1880s, and Avery demonstrated that genetic material consists of nucleic acids in 1944, biologists began to understand how nature produces variations. Today biologists know the source of variability and the means by which it is maintained from generation to generation: the genetic material is the genome (haploid) or the genotype (diploid) which controls the production of the body of an organism and its entire attribute, the phenotype. This phenotype is the result of the interaction of the genotype with the environment during its development.

This applies to all species, to animals as well as to plants. Population thinking shows how endless variation of different genetic types emerges within a specific environment as a result of morphogenetic processes. As Ernst Mayr's research indicates, we no longer can deal with reality by considering the type as real and the variation as an illusion; instead we have to consider the type as an abstraction and the variation as real.[21]

ARCHITECTURE OF THE MANY

By 'architecture of the many' I do not mean the translation of a biological discourse into the discipline of architecture; nor do I mean an evolutionary architecture such as existed in the 1970s. The term refers to the necessity of understanding the driving forces that create architectural variation and the organisational principles that construct these variations as a multiplicity.

As I mentioned above, it seems misguided for our contemporary design processes to follow a hylomorphic model in which matter is represented through form. Such a model is based on the idea that form is fixed and matter is homogenous; it assumes the coherence of the model through the deduction of matter from form. (In a material practice governed by typologies, a fixed form guarantees the identical reproduction of the object itself.) A second critique, as important as the first, is the critique on the hylomorphic model itself. Deleuze writes that 'between form and matter might be a zone of energetic and molecular dimension, a space on itself that deplores its materiality through matter and propels its traits through form'.[22]

In my view the challenge for architecture is to develop architectural products that are formulated through the interrelationship of the two main properties which drive variations in architecture, throughout history and today. These properties may be termed 'extensive' and 'intensive'.[23] Extensive properties are metrical, e.g. length, width or volume. They belong to the field of geometry and define mainly quantitative dimensions of the architectural object itself. Intensive properties are non-metrical, e.g. temperature, structural forces, pressure, tension, energy and density. In terms of architecture, they describe physical qualities of objects and belong not to the object itself but mainly to the environment that generates its existence.

Such an approach has nothing to do with the design of pre-given forms like typologies. It is concerned, rather, with the expression of material or materialised organisation through form. Some sections of the contemporary discourse of architecture call this an architecture of performance, or more precisely a means to search for new affects through research on material properties.[24]

Over the last couple of years I have attempted to focus my own teaching and practice not so much on the material effects of our profession, as on an exploration of a territory that I believe is equally relevant to the discipline of architecture and its understanding of itself as material practice: the embedded organisation behind the object itself, the so-called territory of regimes. More precisely, I have focused on those 'regimes that organise, ally, and distribute bodies, materials, movements, and techniques in space while simultaneously controlling and developing the temporal relationships between them.'[25] The challenge posed by these regimes is to understand architectural objects in terms of the practices that perform on them, rather than reduce architecture to solely its material and geometric volumes.

Now what is so interesting about these regimes? Architectural tasks have to be negotiated within a reality that is in itself messy and inconsistent. The practice of architecture has become more and more affected by late capitalism, or what Scott Lash and John Urry most convincingly describe as the shift from organised to disorganised capitalism. Any architectural process is confronted with new forms of politics (Ulrich Beck, 1991), with new forms of economy (Scott Lash and John Urry, 1994) and new forms of multitudes (Michael Hardt and Antonio Negri, 2004). All are governed by new forms of bureaucracies better known by the name of 'expert systems' (Giddens, 1996), which produce the knowledge of all regimes that relate to the production of buildings, their use and their influence on the design. Expert systems are mostly represented by institutions that define rules and regulations for the profession of architecture and therefore directly affect daily practice. The effect of this trend can be seen by the increase of regulations within the European Union, which has simultaneously defined standardised codes for practice in all member states, regardless of the historical differences in the evolution of their architectural professions.

The projects that I developed under this umbrella of 'Spatial Regimes'[26] focused on the study of office buildings, dealing mainly with legislative, administrative and institutional regimes and their embedded codes, regulations and protocols. A particular concern was the regimes of economic feasibilities, rent policies, accessibility devices, evacuation strategies and cost performances which have an effect on the material organisation of office building in the Netherlands. Each of the projects unfolded the geometrical (extensive) and the non-metrical (intensive) properties that guarantee the performance of these policies. Each developed geometrical notations between the two different sort of properties, to understand a policy not as a fixed entity but as a gradual iteration of differences. In projects 1 and 2 new architectural prototypes emerged out of the interrelation of various regimes. Project 3, an investigation of cost performance for institutional office buildings in the Netherlands, yielded variations of building concepts that constitute a 'many', meaning they have in common the same cost performance but are differentiated in size and kind.

At first sight, population thinking seems to be of no use to our discipline, since architecture is genderless. What we can learn from it, however, is a means to overcome typological thinking by understanding the organisational principle that constructs a 'many' or 'multiplicity', rather than a type and its variation. Only by thinking in terms of the 'many' can we practise within the messiness and diversity of reality. Only then can we throw overboard the concept of types and any principles that once made us believe we could control life.

FOOTNOTES

[1] Ernst Mayr, *Evolution und die Vielfalt des Lebens* (Heidelberg: Springer Verlag 1978) 37; published in English as *Evolution and the Diversity of Life* (Cambridge, Mass.: Harvard University Press, 1976).

[2] The date is mentioned by Elliot Sober in his essay 'Evolution, Population Thinking, and Essentialism' in *Conceptual Issues in Evolutionary Biology* (Cambridge, Mass.: MIT Press, 1998), 161.

[3] I would like to refer here to the text by Stan Allen in *Practice, architecture, technique and representation* (G+B Arts international, 2000), XVIII, in which he overcomes the classic theory/practice distinction by stating that both are practices, one primarily hermeneutic, devoted to interpretation and the analysis of representation, the other material, producing new objects or new organisation of matter.

[4] 'Space, Knowledge and Power', interview with Paul Rabinov, *Skyline*, March 1982, reprinted in Michael K. Hays, *Architecture Theory Since 1968* (Cambridge, Mass.: MIT Press, 1998), 428-39.

[5] Cynthia C. Davidson (editor), *ANY magazine 23 – diagram work* (New York: Anyone Corporation, 1998).

[6] ibid. Peter Eisenman's definition of the diagram is taken from 'Diagram: An Original Scene of Writing', Sanford Kwinter's from 'The Genealogy of Models: The Hammer and the Song'.

[7] ibid., 'The Diagrams of Matter', by R.E. Somol.

[8] For example, the 'Building Type Basics' series, including A. Eugene Kohn and Paul Katz, *Kohn Pederson Fox* (New York: John Wiley & Sons, 2002).

[9] In the original text Aldo Rossi used the word 'treatises' instead of theory. I want to emphasise here that not all concepts of types are necessarily scientific. Aldo Rossi, *The Architecture of the City* (American edition, Cambridge, Mass.: MIT Press, 1984), 40.

[10] Michel Foucault, *Discipline and Punish – The Birth of the Prison* (UK: Penguin, 1991), 205

[11] In S. Younés, *The True, The Fictive, and The Real: The Historical Dictionary of Architecture of Quatremère de Quincy* (London: Andreas Papadakis, 1999), 254 ff.

[12] Gianfranco Caniggia and Gian Luigi Maffei, *Architectural Composition and Building Typology – Interpreting Basic Building*, (Florence: Alinea, 2001, translated by Susan Jane Frazer), 43-56.

[13] I refer here to a draft by Pier Vittorio Aureli, 'The Difficult Whole, Typology and Individuality of the urban fact in Aldo Rossi's early theoretical work. 1953-1964.'

[14] 'The Generic City', by Rem Koolhaas, in *S,M,L,XL* (Cologne: Taschen, 1997), 1238.

[15] Gilles Deleuze, *Difference & Repetition* (London: Athlone Press, 1994), 182.

[16] This describing and their explanations are borrowed by Manuel DeLanda, *Intensive Science & Virtual Philosophy* (New York: Continuum, 2002), 11-12.

[17] Felix Klein, *Das Erlanger Programm – Vergleichende Betrachtungen über neuere geometrische Forschungen*, 1872.

[18] I refer here to contemporary voices from parts of the US in the time of Bush's administration.

[19] Ernst Mayr, *What Evolution is* (BasicBooks, 2001), 84-90.

[20] ibid. 91-126.

[21] ibid. 92.

[22] Gilles Deleuze, Félix Guattari, *A Thousand Plateaus* (New York: Continuum, 2003), 409.

[23] Gilles Deleuze, *Difference & Repetition*, op. cit. 223, and Manuel DeLanda, *Intensive Science*, op. cit. 45.

[24] I refer to the disciplinary contribution on the topic of material affects developed by Jeffrey Kipnis.

[25] Sanford Kwinter, 'The Complex and the Singular', in his book Architectures of Time (Cambridge, Mass.: MIT Press, 2001), 14.

[26] 'Spatial Regimes' is the title of a series of design projects I taught at Rotterdam Academy of Architecture. More recently I have developed a similar research with more focus on design techniques, which runs under the name 'Associative Design' at the Berlage Institute in Rotterdam.

ITERATION 1_THE ORDER OF EFFECTS

What is this wavy pattern? Is it an illustration of an early Bridget Riley painting of vibrating lines or an image from a book on optical illusions? Or is it perhaps an image of a natural formation: the deposition of bacteria upon a growth medium or a satellite photo of sand dunes and their self-organised patterning?

This image is neither a documentation of a natural phenomenon nor an illustration of a cultural artefact. It is rather a reproduction of a moiré effect, something that cannot easily be bracketed into nature or culture.

Observed since ancient times, the moiré effect is created by overlaying two or more relatively simple patterns; in this case one is a field of horizontal lines and the other a grid of tightly spaced dots. The alignment, overlap and differences between the component fields cause secondary patterns to appear. That is to say, the emergent organisation of wavy areas, curved lines and complex patterning of the moiré effect is the interference that occurs between two relatively simple and repetitive fields of units.[1] If one shifts the component fields, the moiré pattern will shimmer, disappear and different ones will appear. The experience is quite magical and enjoyable.

Like all such things, moiré can be described with mathematical precision; and as with so many of these mathematical phenomena the term 'moiré', though French, appears to derive from the Arabic-Persian word 'mukhayyar', meaning mohair, the wool from the belly of the Angora goat, which has an intensely wavy pattern. Indeed, moiré effects often feature in weaving and textiles since the discrete patterning of warp and woof systems can be strategised to produce complex interference patterns. Such moiré effects can also be induced in non-visual ways, for example in sound – the music of Steve Reich, with its pulsing and phase-shifting, uses the same principles of interference between discrete fields, in this case overlapping pulses of tone rather than inked spots, to produce an emergent sonic effect. Thus moiré can serve as a general model for any ordering effect of variation produced by the difference, or interference, between heterogeneous discrete and repetitive components.

In addition, the moiré effect can be an instrument. Today it is often used to measure microscopic strains in materials through a process called interferometrics. A pattern is imposed upon a material, the material is subjected to a stress, and then the original pattern is projected again on the deformed substrate. The moiré

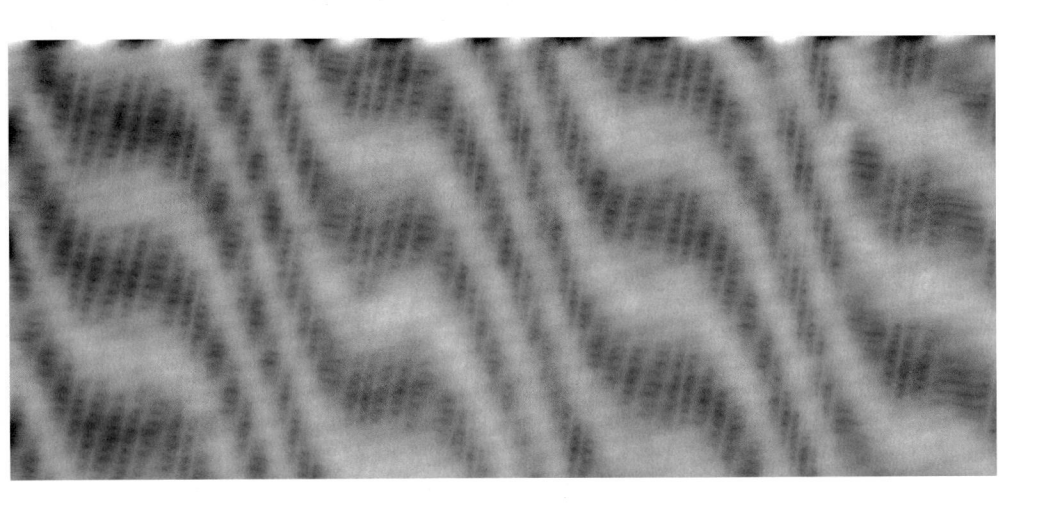

What is this wavy pattern? Cropped and enlarged detail of image shown on p. 356

effect that is produced is a measurement of the deformation, a means to map the movement of force through complex material formations. Here the difference and interference between two discrete integer fields can be used to model the continuous flow of forces and transformation.

In interferometrics, moiré is an effect used to measure the physical organisation of matter. In weaving or music or graphics, the moiré is an aesthetic ordering as an effect produced by technological and material processes. Hence, moiré refers at once to the material organisation found in nature, to a measure of order, and to a subjective affect. And yet, moiré is not simply a representation of order, but a phenomenon in itself. Indeed, in so far as it is a measure and an ordering, it is one that is both immanent and emergent to that which it measures or orders.

This is what seems to be at stake in any architectural discussion of differentiated component systems managed by morphogenetic design processes, wherein a unit is subjected to a process of repetition and transformation and then assembled, or perhaps we should say populated, into a complex, continually differentiated field. The emergent order of such architecture is not known from the outset of the design process but appears through painstaking operations and parametric variation, just as the moiré pattern can be produced and changed through systematic variations of its components. Moreover, it is necessary in such architecture that this process is rendered both as an order and an effect. It is not that components are repeated or that they are varied, but that the interval of variation becomes a smoothly differentiated pattern. Local variations of the components work at an entirely different scale from the global pattern which emerges. In other words, the global form of the architecture makes its forces of formation apparent. The measure of order is thus neither the unit nor the whole, static or animated, nor even an external reference, but is rather the interference between repetition of a unit and its interval of differentiation.

This interference pattern between components supplants the traditional role of the detail and the joint found in classical and high-tech architectural approaches. This signals a shift in these architectures from an organic model of order, where the joints between parts are carriers of meaning because of their essential role in articulating a static ordering of parts to wholes and of hierarchical relation. The differentiated component instead indexes forces and time as informatic variation; they are not meaningful nor signifying; they are quanta of information in a series of feedback loops, in which, as Gregory Bateson declared, information is merely the difference that makes a difference. Renzo Piano's architecture of the 'piece' belongs to a different, mechanistic, world than that of the modulated component.

Moiré pattern produced by the overlay of a screen of dots and lines.
source: Le Corbusier, *Modulor 2*, page 152 [cropped and enlarged], copyright FLC/ADAGP, Paris and DACS, London 2006

ITERATION 2_THE SIDE-EFFECTS OF ORDERING

This brings us back to my original question. I have said that this image is of a moiré effect and I have discussed the immanent measure of order it refers to. But I have not yet said how this particular moiré effect is technically produced. And the answer to this reveals the other side of moiré's relationship to order: its status as a side-effect of technologies of reproduction – an accident, an error, detritus.

Our world is littered with moiré effects. You can see them on television when someone wears a bad suit or striped shirt that begins to ooze and dance and shimmer before your eyes. Digital photography is similarly plagued, as is the scanning of images from books or other half-tone documents. The very technology used to create this book is liable to produce moiré. In all these examples, moiré arises whenever the pattern being imaged approaches the sampling frequency or resolution of the imaging plane; suit stripes interfere with the scan-lines of a television, the brickwork of a building interferes with the grid of the digital camera's CCD, the dots of offset printing interact with the resolution of the scanner, and so on. In all these cases, the moiré is an unwanted side-effect, an artefact of the technologies of transmission and electronic reproduction.

But the particular moiré pattern with which we are concerned is the unintentional artefact of a more low-tech procedure familiar now only to an ageing generation of architects: Zip-A-Tone™. For those too young to recall the Paleolithic period of mechanical reproduction a brief history might be in order. Zip-A-Tone was the brand name for vast arrays of clear sticky-backed plastic sheets, on which were printed various standard Pantone colours or patterns including 'grey scales' and dot-screens at various densities. These would be cut out and adhered to ink drawings to produce a variety of rendering and shading effects. Invariably, slivers of dotted plastic film would end up all over your clothes, hands and the drafting table, one scrap would get stuck on top of another and, abracadabra, a moiré pattern appeared in the margins of the drawing. Such happy accidents are how I think every architect of a certain age 'discovered' moiré and part of me remains convinced that it was the first step of architecture's fascination with emergence, complexity and the like. For myself, the discovery was at once compulsive and frustrating. I wanted to know how to make such orders appear on purpose and with some sort of instrumentality. To do so required shifting from hard-control architectures of representation, signification and composition to soft-control paradigms, something well beyond the capabilities of a medium based on sticky plastic. In any case, I remember thinking these fragments of patterns that appeared on these marginal scraps were far more compelling than the drawing I was sticking the Zip-A-Tone onto and the hylemorphism it seemed to represent.

But then I never worked for Wes Jones, Neil Denari, or Peter Eisenman, who turned the use of Zip-A-Tone into an art form. What all these architects shared was a Benjaminian interest in architecture in the age of mechanical and proto-electronic reproduction, and specifically in how the technologies of reproduction dissipate the aura of the original into a simulacral proliferation of copies. An attempt was made to displace the economy of the original and the copy itself by developing processes that would 'automatically' generate architectural form by performing algorithmic operations upon repetitive elements. For Eisenman, this was an attempt to displace the architect as author and reposition him as the operator of machinic diagrammatic processes, often using proto-morphogenetic operations of architectural ordering. Eisenman's renderings in the late 1980s attempted to appear as if they were digitally produced just as the architecture depicted therein was the result of computational processes: always already a reproduction rather than an original 'drawing', Zip-A-Tone was used to produce this effect, to make his laboriously hand-produced drawings appear as if they were made by a machine. The drawings were like the dots on the Zip-A-Tone screens themselves, merely an instance of an infinite mechanical series.

This is similar to the effect Wes Jones produced with his intensely laboured dot-screened renderings of his International Harvester Style architecture. The Zip-A-Tone dot-screens mimicked the dot patterns of offset printing and, secondarily, Pop-Art's mobilisation of printing to subvert the aura of painting. Ironically, this produced artefacts so singular that they sold for thousands of dollars. When one got up close to Jones's drawings, the layers of Zip-A-Tone revealed the collage ethic of the work itself, their palimpsest layering becaming evident due to peeling corners and edges caught by the light. Nevertheless, this was an architectural order of repetition and processes that began to question the traditions of representation, typology and authorship, with Zip-A-Tone offering a representational effect of autonomy of the artefacts and creating a problematic status for the architect as author of the original work of architecture itself.

Of course all this is at stake in today's architectures of differentiated components and morphogenetic fields – but we might say that the economy of the original-copy has been turned inside out. Like the moiré's startling appearance at the margins of architectural representation, at the edge of the drawing table, on the border between order and effects, discourses of emergence attempt to conjure aura through precisely calibrated interactions of repetitive units. Here mechanical, or at least parametric, repetition produces unexpected and irreducible effects. Rather than dissolve the presence of the architecture through mechanical reproduction, singularity is located and unfolded as the spontaneous rise of higher levels of order via electronic processes of re-production. For one does not make orders like the moiré; instead, one modulates the conditions in which it might arise by altering assorted variables (angles, density, scaling) that are familiar to parametric design processes of digital simulation.

In their relationship to order and representation, simulation and modelling softwares are fundamentally different from the hylemorphically drawn contour line filled in with a field (such as the drawings of Eisenman and Jones, which were dependent on pen-and-ink technologies). When the fields of repetitive component systems are generated using computational algorithms or other information processes of variation and recombination, a visual effect is produced by operating on the very material variables of the component themselves; this turns them from representations, that is copies, of an order that originates elsewhere into a manifestation of the integration of information embedded in the material performance itself.

This reverses Walter Benjamin's argument that the processes of mechanical reproduction drain the work of art of its aura, displace the authentic, and dissolve its singular presence into processes of repetition. Here it is the origination of aura, the singularity of form that is produced via highly mediated processes of modulated repetition. The author or architect, no longer having any recourse to authenticity, dissolves into one of many factors within a quasi-natural process of evolution of form. There is no original to be copied, only variations to be coaxed and modulated by informatic processes or recombination. Thus, moiré stands at technical, historical and representational margin – between an architecture that circulates within a logic of the model, or original, and the copy in the age of mechanical reproduction on the one hand; and the ordering of simulacra, variations without original model, that are made possible by electronic infrastructures of information on the other. The accidental has become the emergent and relocated itself at the centre of our field of vision.

Moiré pattern produced by the overlay of two Zip-A-Tone sheets.
source: Le Corbusier, *Modulor 2*, page 152, copyright FLC/ADAGP, Paris and DACS, London 2006

ITERATION 3_HISTORICAL INTERFERENCE

I have situated moiré as an instrument for investigating what might be at stake in differentiated component systems; I have examined its historicity and relationship to technologies of architectural representation, in terms of ideas of the original, or model, and the copy. Yet, I have still not answered what this particular image of a moiré effect is as an image. That is, what is this scan, this copy, that I have made a reproduction of exactly? I have said it is made by Zip-A-Tone, but I did not cut it out and stick it together.

It is time I came clean: the source of this image is, perhaps, both unexpected and significant in suggesting a genealogy that today's interests in emergent order and repetitive components extends and convolutes. This curious image, along with a few others, will be found amid the various diagrams, computations, sketches and miscellanea that make up Le Corbusier's 1955 sequel, *Modulor 2: Let the User Speak Next*. Given all that I have said about the moiré effect, its appearance here would seem a non-sequitur on the part of Le Corbusier (perhaps an example of the surrealist montage of content he so often used within his texts, and wilfully perverse on my part). After all, as we all (supposedly) know, the Modulor was concerned with an attempted revival of Vitruvian humanist and Platonic proportioning systems. Le Corbusier proposed a new measuring system designed to govern every mode of cultural and technological production. The measure was derived from the supposed – some might say, fantasised – correspondence between the height of an idealised human body and the Golden Section ratios or Fibonacci series found in natural forms such as seashells. Adapting his prewar technique of trace regulators to this new measure, Le Corbusier employed the Modulor as a compositional device that privileged the repetition of mass-produced units, such as in its most infamous deployment, the *Unité d'Habitation*. The conceit lay in the proposition that it would enable industrial products to be manufactured in a way that would be harmonious to the human subject. Understood in these terms as a retrograde classicism, the Modulor seems to represent the exact opposite of anything we might be interested in discussing in reference to emergence and complexity.

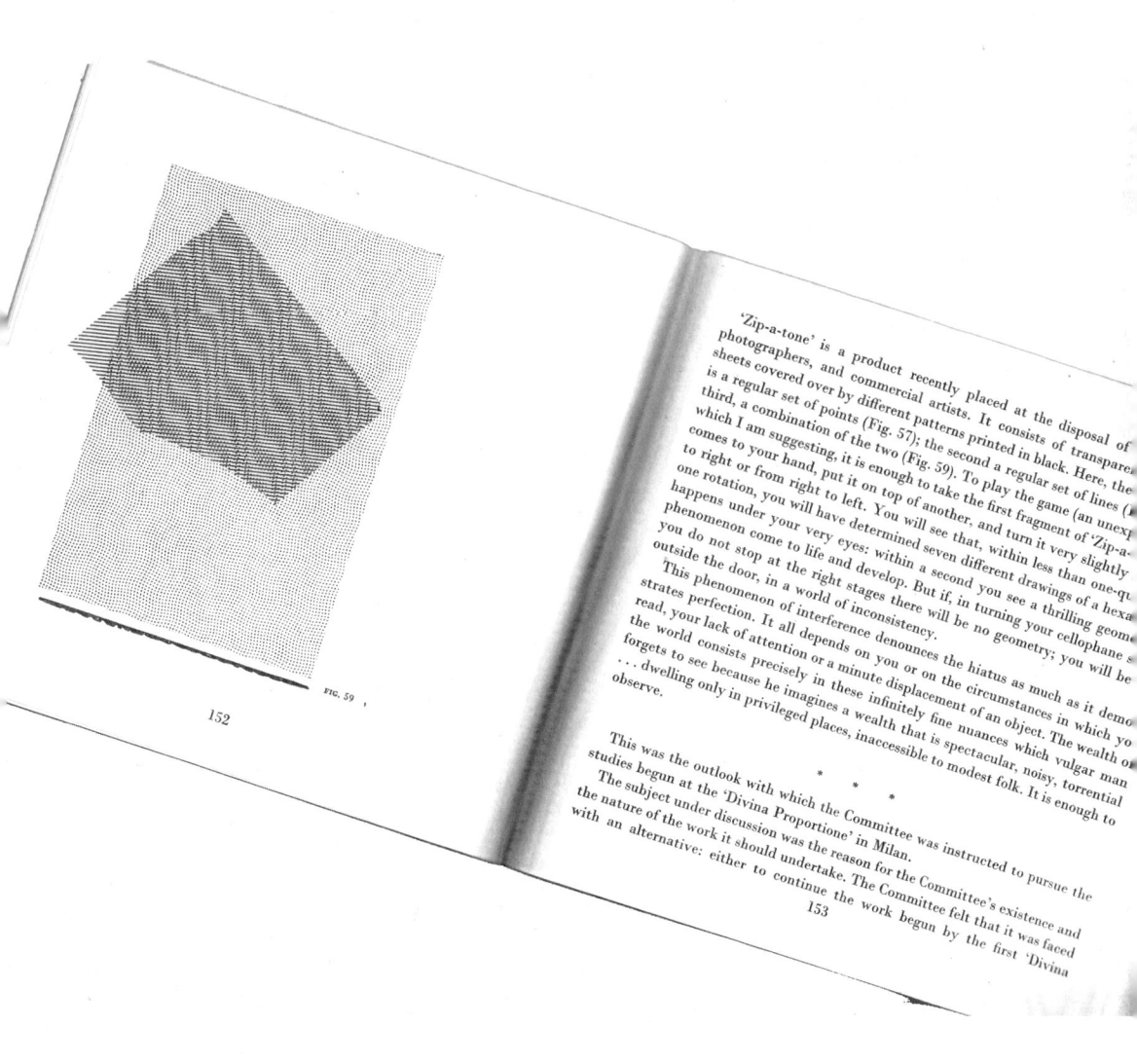

Moiré pattern reproduced by Le Corbusier in *Modulor 2*, 1952.
source: Le Corbusier, *Modulor 2*, pages 152-153, ccopyright FLC/ADAGP, Paris and DACS, London 2006

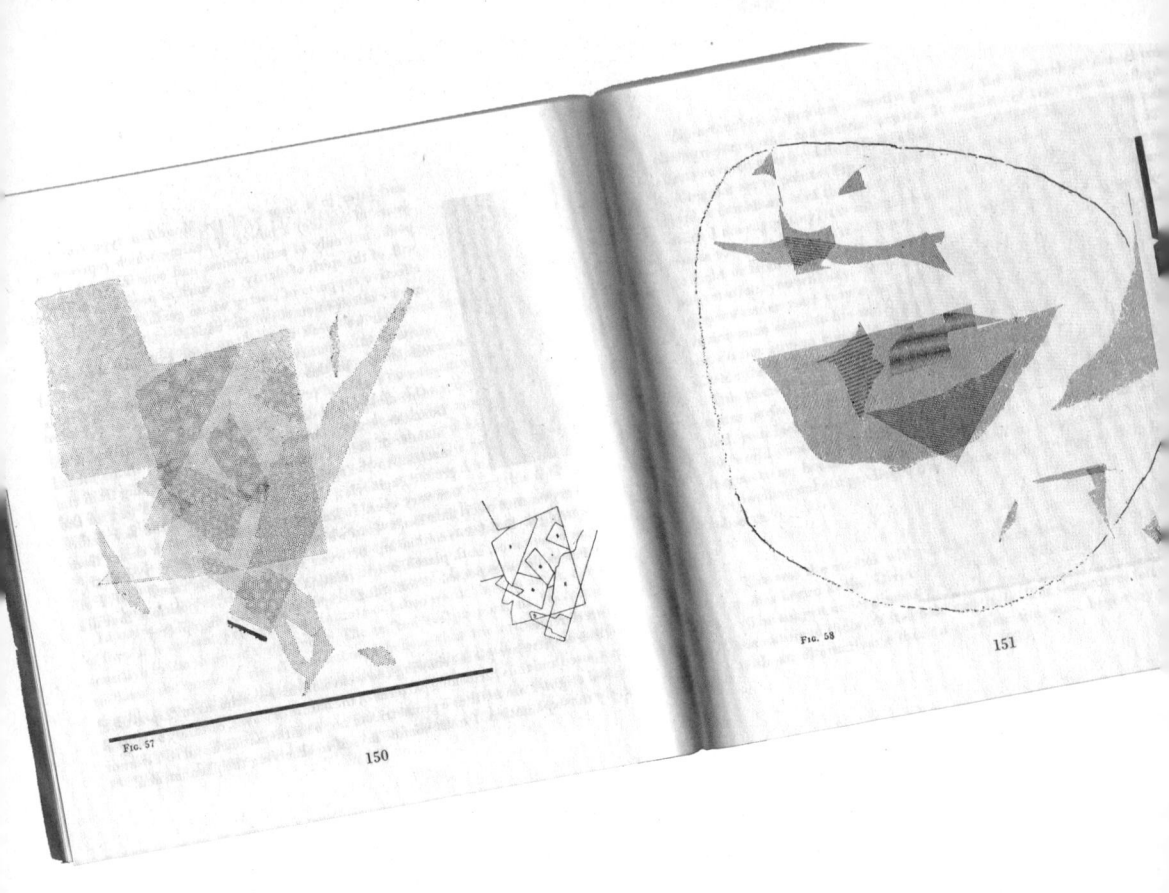

Pages of moiré patterns created by accidental overlay of Zip-A-Tone sheets, reproduced by Le Corbusier in *Modulor 2*, 1952.
source: Le Corbusier, *Modulor 2*, pages 150-151, copyright FLC/ADAGP, Paris and DACS, London 2006

    Yet here is evidence from the archive of Le Corbusier giving three full-page spreads to reproductions of moiré patterns. The only other content that receives such treatment in *Modulor 2* is either the Modulor itself or images of Le Corbusier's architecture. In a book about proportion, this seems disproportionate. But it is in these images that a different understanding of the Modulor can begin; or rather it is here that the grids of architecture's past can begin to interfere with the ordering of the present. The *Modulor 2* moirés were produced by Le Corbusier's assistants' use of Zip-A-Tone, side-effects scraps that Le Corbusier 'discovered' left on the drawing table. Le Corbusier described these moiré effects as state-of-the-art inventions of mechanistic society, discoveries of the same significance as the Fibonacci series within natural forms. Moreover, he presents them as if they were laboratory slides. Here, he says, are:
    three specimens of 'Zip-a-tone' superimposed and thus furnishing patterns of the nature of waves, certainly of mathematical origin. I am neither a geometrician nor a mathematician and so I cannot explain; I must confine myself to observing the phenomena [of] 'interference'[2]
    In these 'specimens', Le Corbusier reveals the Modulor as only superficially a discourse about the recovery of a Vitruvian proportioning system. The Modulor, in fact, needs to be understood within the genealogy of aesthetic and architectural attempts to develop an empirically based theory of effects for the modern subject of sciences. Is this not ultimately what I have described as what is at stake in today's discourses of morphogenetic architectural order?

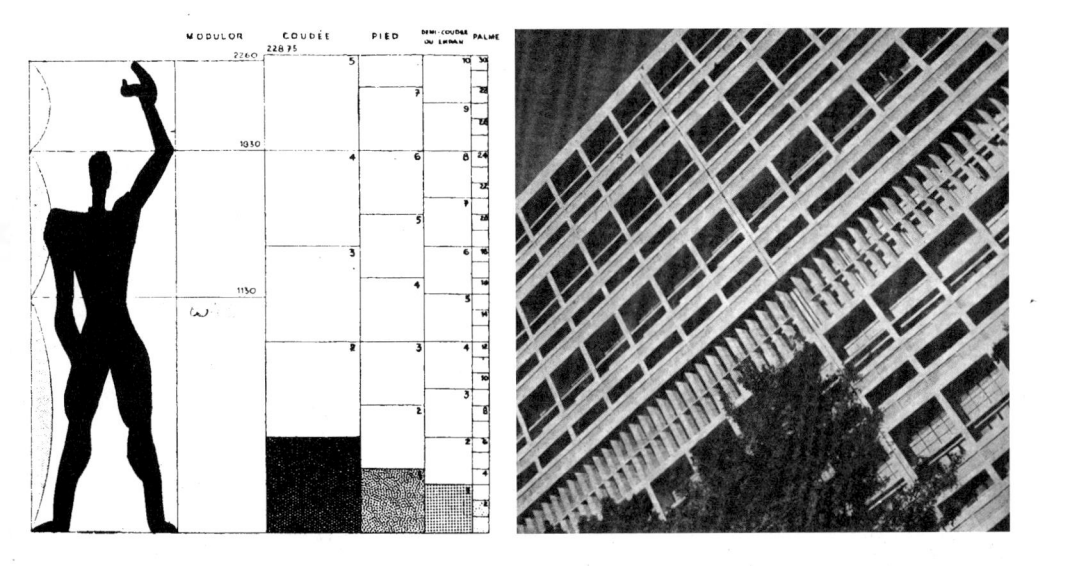

Le Corbusier, Modulor with figure (left) and photograph of Modulor grid embodied as bris-soleil at the Unité d'Habitation (right).
source: Le Corbusier, *Modulor 2*, copyright FLC/ADAGP, Paris and DACS, London 2006

ITERATION 4: MEASURED ORDER

Indeed, this need to formulate a theory of effects derived from empirical measure is always at stake when architects discuss repetitive organisations of the visual, structural and spatial measure of order. Perhaps, then, it is useful to linger over the historical discourse about the non-differentiated component system in architecture, which became a crucial problem for postwar architecture. The Japanese Metabolists, Buckminster Fuller, Archigram, Le Corbusier, to name but a few, all placed modularisation and repetitive component systems at the centre of their work. In these projects, the module was an attempt to displace the aesthetic limitations of the dominant International Style and to reclaim architecture's potential for revolutionary reconfigurations of social order, but it was also about giving an apparent order to the seeming chaos of industrial production and its endless repetitions of mass-produced products. For Le Corbusier, the Modulor was necessitated by the de-territorialisation of the world due to international trade of common mass-production. The problem was not standardisation, but that the standards had no basis: the metre for example, was abstract, pure exchange value. The world had become radically abstract and torrential. What was needed for this radically interlinked and fluid world was not simply a measure, but a measure aligned at once with the subject, technology and nature. The use of a repetitive module transformed this condition of repetition by attempting to employ the unit of repetition as a signifying measure of architectural – and thus, social – order.

Now as then, a measure is not really about quantification but about bringing otherwise diverse things and phenomena into relation via an identity. It is analogous, a ratio between two items, often independent of either, or an arbitrary interval. Thomas Kuhn and Ian Hacking argued that measurement itself gained a new status during the nineteenth century, when the empirical edict that to know of and about something it must be measurable, became a common feature of scientific discourse for the first time.[3]

However, for a measure to be more than instrumental and to take on explanatory power as it did in the late 1800s, there must exist some threshold beyond which exchange and identification becomes a problem. As Ernst Cassier noted, since the late nineteenth century, 'the process of measuring is recognised more and more clearly as a problem, and a logical and epistemological one'.[4] In other words, the commensurability of objects to subjects became an issue because, since the Kantian revolution of the late eighteenth century, knowledge was conditioned upon a subject Foucault called a 'transcendental Empirical doublet', a subject at once the object of measure but also the agent of that measurement. Measurement was not simply descriptive; it was a diagrammatic technique that mediated between the phenomena known to the subject and the objective world of things (noumena); objects of empirical knowledge were constructed as such through measure, which in turn, operated as a schematic ordering of the subject and its world of representations.

Thus architecture searched for a measure that could ground its ordering according to the world made empirically available to that subject. In this way, the history of modern architecture is a search for a measure that would operate within a theory of architectural effects that would bridge the order of things and the order of the subject.

For example, in one of the first attempts to construct a modern theory of architectural form for the post-Kantian subject (*Einfühlung*, or empathy theory), Robert Vischer argued that the perception of space and form was judged via the reciprocal return of empathic projection back onto the bodily schema:

> in rooms with low ceilings our whole body feels the sensation of weight and pressure. Walls that have become crooked with age offend our basic sense of physical stability. The perception of exterior limits to a form can combine in some obscure way with my sensation of my own physical boundaries, which I feel on, or rather with my own skin...
>
> I project my own life into the lifeless form...I am mysteriously transplanted and magically transformed into the Other'.[5]

For such a projection to occur correctly there needed to be a fundamental 'similarity' between the 'object and the subject in question'.[6] Otherwise the reflection of the subject in the world would be distorted, preventing the identification and at best producing trauma. To ensure this alignment, Vischer advocated the use of the Golden Section as a 'law of proportion' determined by 'nothing other than the subjective laws of the normal human body.'[7] That is to say, the Golden Section offered a ratio, a measure, through which the world of objects could be aligned with the subject, ensuring a commensurability between the subject's perception and the composition of objects, a precondition of the possibility of aesthetic judgment. This was not an objective law of nature, but a subjective law.

In 1876 Gustav Fechner attempted to transform Vischer's magical projections into scientific phenomena. Fechner performed three different empirical experiments: firstly, he showed non-expert test subjects rectangles of various proportions; secondly, he asked the subjects to measure various abstract shapes and everyday objects and state which they preferred; thirdly, he asked that they complete partially drawn figures in the way they most preferred. In every case, the Golden Section emerged as a statistical attractor. For Fechner the results suggested that the Golden Section, like Durkheim's suicides of Galton's mean regressions, was an average based on equilibrium. He argued that 'People tolerate most often and for the longest time a certain medium degree of arousal, which makes them feel neither over stimulated nor dissatisfied.'[8] A square was too static, an elongated rectangle too off balance; the Golden Section, often called the Golden Mean, was selected because it maintained the normative equilibrium of the subject's sensation. Fechner called this 'tendency towards stability' the 'principle of the aesthetic middle' to which a subject would naturally gravitate. Thus, the Golden Section was preferable not because it spoke to an ideal, nor even because it was the most pleasurable or beautiful, but simply because it maintained equilibrium of the subject in relation to its world of sense. In these theories of effects for the subject of the human sciences, proportioning systems serve as measures that mediate between the subject and the empirical world available to that subject.

Now we are in a position to understand Le Corbusier's interest in moiré. He argued that the order of moiré was elusive; like Vischer's empathic projections, the conditions must be right, the alignment crucial. Le Corbusier declared that moiré emerges:

under your very eyes: within a second you see a thrilling geometrical phenomenon come to life and develop. But…if you do not stop at the right stages there will be no geometry; you will be left outside the door, in a world of inconsistency.[9]

That is, unless one knows where to stop, how to align the two fields, no pattern will appear, only a seemingly random assortment of elements. Moreover, he argued that it takes a specialist skill to recognise the value of the moiré over the 'noisy' and 'torrential' random patterns.[10] Genius becomes a connoisseurship of measured effects.

It is through this idea of the subject's alignment with an elusive but immanent order that the Modulor can be understood. Because the Modulor was supposedly derived from the height of the average Frenchman (later American) and the Golden Section, that which was governed by the Modulor would be aligned with the embodied perception of the human subject. The world of cultural and industrial production would also be grounded and made meaningful by replicating its geometries. The Modulor would ensure the proper alignment of the subject with the world of objects, technology would be disciplined by the patterns of nature; the emergent order would then ensue and be unconsciously felt by untrained subjects. In turn, these subjects would be orthopedically integrated into the smooth flow of things. The Modulor, like Fechner's Golden Section experiments, would ensure equilibrium between technical, social, subjective and natural domains.

One might recall here today's alignment of natural processes or growth with the economies of mass-customisation and post-Fordism. Is there not now a similar attempt to find in architecture a measure that would traverse natural processes and cultural production – a mobilisation of nature and its doppelgänger, structure, as a source for regrounding architectural order as a legitimating function, as well as an explicit demand for highly specialised knowledge of these ordering systems? In other words, the idea of a differentiated component architecture is to make an architecture that is a 'measure' operating simultaneously as: a generative technique; the ordering of that which is produced; and the production of the effects of that measure on the subject or the distribution of programme – that, a social order. The idea of an emergent architectural order produced by an interval attempts to mediate the social, cultural, technical and natural by rendering visual architectural order as a measuring measure.

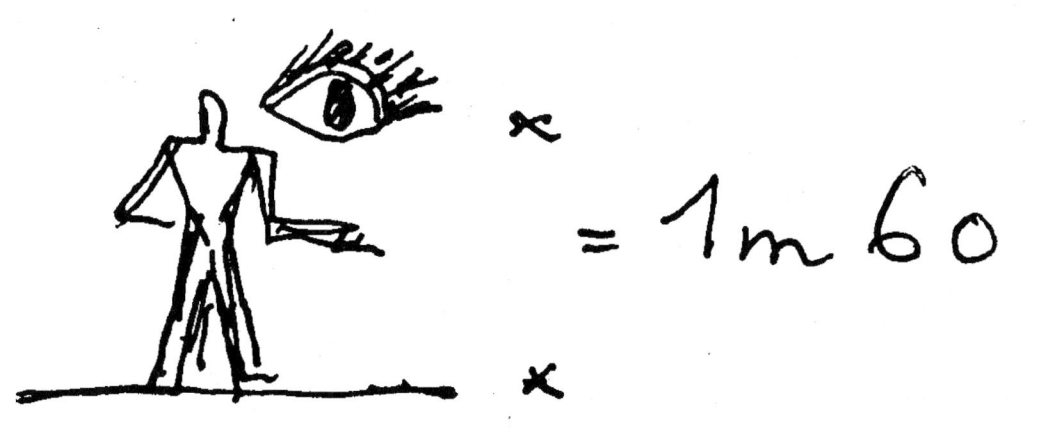

Le Corbusier's drawings of the Modulor as an optical ordering aligned with perspectival perception.
source: Le Corbusier, *Le Modulor*, page 79, copyright FLC/ADAGP, Paris and DACS, London 2006

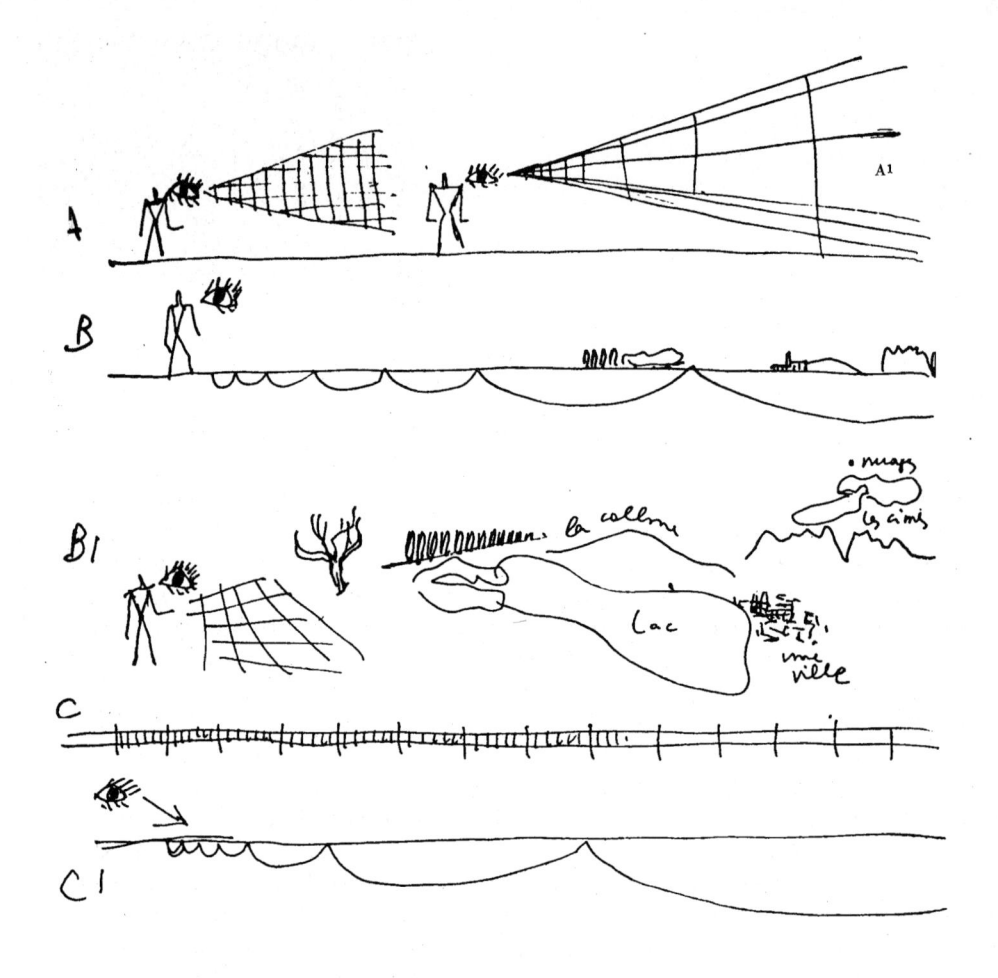

Le Corbusier's drawing of the 'Modulor Man' with height given in reference to the position of the eye.
source: Le Corbusier, Le Modulor, page 76, copyright FLC/ADAGP, Paris and DACS, London 2006

ITERATION 5: OPTICAL MACHINES OF DIFFERENTIATION AND IDENTIFICATION

Le Corbusier, of course, used the body as the mediating measure between the world of sense and the orders of nature. Yet, Le Corbusier, like Vischer and Fechner, was more interested in the position of the eye to the world than any other bodily measure; the ratios of the Modulor are almost solely justified according to the position of the eye in a standing figure, and the argument for the Modulor as opposed to the Vitruvian figure is based on its relationship to the embodied perception of the human point of view in the world. Like moiré fields, the works of Vischer and Fechner, as well as Le Corbusier's Modulor, were optical machines. Their measures were to produce proper visual representations through which the subject could form proper identification via projection, reflection and cones of vision.

This identification was based on a model of the body given by concepts of the organic and whole. The task was to develop a theory of architectural reflection that would ensure resemblance to this model, of which everything in the world, including the human mind, was a more or less correct copy. An improperly proportioned room would produce a distorted reflection, a simulacrum, and thus cause interference between the human world and the objective earth.

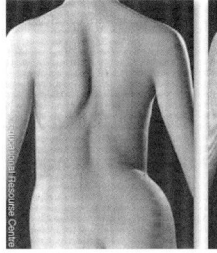

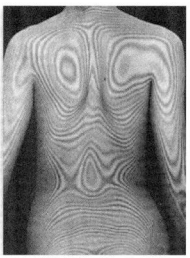

Medical photograph of interferometry using the moiré pattern to measure deviation of the spine from the normal of 90-degrees, suggesting the relationship between the interference pattern effect of the moiré and the normative discourses of orthography and the body at the core of Le Corbusier's Modulor.
source: http://www.rch.org.au/erc/photo/index.cfm?doc_id=141, copyright Gigi Williams

In retrospect, however, we can see that rather than ensuring a harmonious reflection of an *a priori* model, what was at stake was the construction of anthropogenic machines that themselves generated the conditions of resemblance. As Deleuze's diagrammatic ontology attempted to install, as Foucault's archaeologies demonstrated, and as Latour's hybrid epistemologies argue, we do not measure things to reveal order: we calibrate our world of sense to produce orderings in which 'things' and subjects are possible to know in their relation to each other. Latour argues not only that humans are measures *par excellence*, but that it is these measures which produce us. And thus Le Corbusier's fascination with moiré finally reveals a truth stranger than his fictions: the subject is nothing other than a field of effects produced by technologies of empirical measure machines.

Thus, while it is true that the architecture of morphogenesis and differentiated structures often looks to nature and the natural sciences as a model of its ordering, invoking its theories, its scientists and its phenomena, fields like biomimetics, and so on, as the basis for architectural form-making, ultimately neither nature, the subject, nor an intermediary body, can serve as a model of order that we should attempt to copy. Rather, all such models can offer are protocols for the production of order itself, but orders without models, pure simulations. As I have argued, rather than dissolve manmade originals by repetition, these intensely iterative evolutionary processes forge specificity and singularity. For us, the body's anatomy – no longer a model as such – can instead serve as a phenotype that results from the transferal and recombination of informational codices, its forms the result of the chemical gradients and processes these codes trigger. Bodies are constructed and informed by their interactions as populations, which are parametrically differentiated according to performance criteria defined by genetic fitness. Mutation, or interferences, are not deviations of order but are instead the motor for the evolution of greater order, innovation and transformation. In this informatic framework, as in the electronic reproductions I described previously, there is no resemblance to a model, but only processes of differentiation and specification. The entire world, the subject itself, is nothing less or more than interference patterns. Rather than Modulor Men, we are Moiré Manifolds.

The architectures of morphogenesis and differentiated repetition seek to convey to the subject not extrinsic orders, but to embed a simulation of informational life processes in architecture. That is to say, this ordering is a measure of the intelligence installed in architecture through the laborious operations of the architect and of this architecture's similarity to the natural forms and processes to which this architectural discourse so closely allies itself. The effects of differentiation and variation are signatures of these evolutionary processes, evidence of the spontaneous rise of order.

Indeed, rather than understand this sort of design process as a scientific method, we can see it as a conjuring of order, an alchemy wherein base material, or simple elements, undergo a transmutation into complex alloys of geometry, forms and forces. Instead of ensuring harmonious alignment of the subject with the world, as Le Corbusier dreamt through the Modulor, today's modulation machines produce order that neither resembles an abstract system that transcends architecture (such as Platonic forms, the body, nature), nor is reducible to constituent parts (such as Durand's modules). This differentiation must be legible as an effect because it is the measure of the architectural order itself, an order that is wholly immanent to the process of transformation and repetition that produced it. The work of architecture is here a quasi-natural object produced by wholly technical means. In other words, the attempt is to produce architecture as if it were a form of life, or a life-form.

INFINITE LOOP: THE INTERFERENCES OF HISTORY

Lastly, in so far as the evolutionary processes of nature can be said to be historical, or as Collingwood once argued, vice versa, then Le Corbusier's moiré raises issues about historical discourse's relationship to contemporary design. In attempting to refer current interests to broader historical issues of architecture in modernity, I do not mean to say that the historicity of the present should be defined by the past. I am not saying that it has all been done before, nor am I attempting to legitimise current work or past objects, or even attempting to establish a continuity or transcendent rupture point between our present and the past. All these belong to ideas of history and knowledge that operate according to logics of the model and the copy, none of which we should be content to mobilise since they would all amount to a retreat from a real understanding of difference and repetition and lapse back into a logic of the Same, where the past and present are assessed according to their identity to a model, either of an essentialist definition of architecture as discipline, a model of the past such as the Classical, or an essentialism of the present, such as the Zeitgeist. This makes it impossible to ever really understand the transformations of knowledge and of practices since any such change is subjected to judgement based on its resemblance to an extrinsic model. It would be bizarre to argue for architectural orders based on the differential and to historically situate this polemic via its resemblance or even lack of resemblance to a historical model.

To understand the possibility of a different sort of use of history and the relationship of current debates to architecture's histories, moiré might be useful one more time. All I hope to have accomplished is to have set up interference patterns between historical constructions and contemporary interests. Perhaps each iteration of the moiré has set up a vibration in thought, a pulse that traverses our understandings of architectural history and the relationship of the present, a wave that informs the future transformations of our topographies of thought and practice. The discipline is neither closed nor static nor definable as a set of knowledges and skills; nor is it linearly moving in time like the clichéd Klee's *Angelus Novalis*. Like moiré itself, the discipline is an effect of the interaction between present and historical constructions and our operations upon this surface of becoming. The past and present are filled with facts, with objects, with statements; these are real and non-relative and incomplete, but their importance lies in the virtual connections that can be continually reworked, rediscovered, re-modulated into different constellations. Their historical development, or movement, is not that of translation, but of vibratory waves.

Our discipline is the interference patterns that we produce between our present mobilisation of concepts and knowledges and their overlay onto the objects of our past as a way of measuring transformation. This gives a role for historical and theoretical practices beyond the logics and judgements offered by critical theory. New organisations and patterns appear which traverse the past and the present, destabilising their co-ordinates and mobilising their performance as a continuous surface of evolutionary transformation. Our present condition of possibility is a moiré effect on top of moiré effects, a thousand sheets deep, that we can twist and torque and delight in their shimmering.

FOOTNOTES

[1] The moiré effect had a brief but significant appearance as an alternative ordering technique to collage in Stan Allen, 'Field Conditions', *Points + Lines: Diagrams and projects for the city* (New York: Princeton Architectural Press, 1999), 97-8.

[2] Le Corbusier, *Modulor 2: Let the User Speak Next* (London: Faber and Faber, 1958), 152-3.

[3] A view most forcefully promulgated by Lord Kelvin, who importantly established a different sort of constant by proposing a new scale of temperature at which zero marks not freezing of water but 'heat death', the complete cessation of molecular motion and thus the breakdown of all matter in an entropic finality. T. S. Kuhn, 'The Function of Measurement in Modern Physical Science', *The Essential Tension* (Chicago: University of Chicago Press, 1977); originally published in 1961.

[4] Cassier, *The Problem of Knowledge: Philosophy, science, and history since Hegel* (New Haven: Yale University Press, 1950), 50.

[5] Robert Vischer, 'On the Optical Sense of Form: A Contribution to Aesthetics', *Empathy, Form, Space* (Santa Monica: Getty Center, 1994), 104.

[6] ibid 95.

[7] ibid 98.

[8] Gustav Fechner, *Vorschule der Aesthetik* (Leipzig: Breitkopf and Hartel, 1976), 260.

[9] Le Corbusier, *Modulor 2*, 153.

[10] ibid.

AGGREGATES
Bagnold, R. A.; The Physics of Blown Sand and Desert Dunes; Methuen, London, 1954

BIONICS – BIOMIMETIC ENGINEERING
Nachtigall, Werner; Bionik – Grundlagen und Beispiele für Ingenieure und Naturwissenschaftler; 2nd Edition; Springer, Berlin, Heidelberg, New York, 2002
Nachtigall, Werner; Bau-Bionik – Natur < Analogien > Technik; Springer, Berlin, Heidelberg, New York, 2003
Mattheck, Claus; Design in Nature – Learning from Trees; Springer, New York, 1998

BIOMECHANICS
Nachtigall, Werner; Biomechanik; 2nd Edition; Vieweg, Wiesbaden, 2001
Vogel, Steven; Comparative Biomechanics – Life's Physical World; Princeton University Press; Princeton and Oxford, 2003

COMPLEXITY
Cowan, George A.; Pines, David and Meltzer, David, eds.; Complexity – Metaphors, Models and Reality; Proceedings Volume XIX, Santa Fe Institute – Studies in the Science of Complexity; Addison-Wesley, Reading, MA, 1994
Pullman, Bernard, ed.; The Emergence of Complexity in Mathematics, Physics, Chemistry and Biology; Proceedings – Plenary Session of the Pontifical Academy of Sciences October 1992; Pontificia Academia Scientiarum, Vatican City, 1996

COMPUTER-AIDED MANUFACTURING
Chang, Tien-Chien; Wysk, Richard A. And Wang, Hsu-pin; Computer-aided Manufacturing; 3rd Edition; Prentice Hall International Series in Industrial and Systems Engineering; Pearson-Prentice Hall, Upper Saddle River, NJ, 2006
Kamrami, Ali K. and Sferro, Peter R., eds; Direct Engineering – Toward Intelligent Manufacturing; Kluwer Academic Publishers, Boston, Dordrecht, London, 1999
Stacey, Michael; Digital Fabricators; University of Waterloo Press, Cambridge, 2004

ENVIRONMENTAL DESIGN
Daniels, Klaus; Low-tech High-Tech: Building in the Information Age; Birkhäuser, Basel, Boston, Berlin, 1998
Hausladen, Gerhard; de Saldanha, Michael; Liedl, Petra and Sager, Christina; Climate Design – Solutions for Buildings that can do more with less Technology; Birkhäuser, Basel, 2005
Roaf, Sue; Crichton, David and Nicol, Fergus; Adapting Buildings and Cities for Climate Change; Architectural Press, Elsevier, London, 2005
Szokolay, Steven V.; Introduction to Architectural Science; Architectural Press, Elsevier, London, 2003

ELASTIC STRUCTURES
Villagio, Piero; Mathematical Models for Elastic Structures; Cambridge University Press, Cambridge, 1997
IL 31 Bamboo; Klaus Dunkelberg; Institute for Lightweight Structures, Karl Krämer Verlag, Stuttgart, 1985

FORM-FINDING
Nerdinger, Winfried; Frei Otto: Lightweight Construction – Natural Design; Birkhäuser, Basel, 2005
Otto, Frei and Rasch, Bodo; Finding Form; Edition Axel Menges, 1995
Otto, Frei and Rasch, Bodo; Natürliche Konstruktionen; DVA, Stuttgart, 1982
IL 21 Experiments Form-Force-Mass 1 – Basics; Institute for Lightweight Structures, Stuttgart, 1979
IL 22 Experiments Form-Force-Mass 2 – Form; Institute for Lightweight Structures, Stuttgart, 1988
IL 25 Experiments Form-Force-Mass 5; ed. Siegfried Gass; Institute for Lightweight Structures, Stuttgart, 1990
Arch+ Vol. 159-160; Form-findung von Biomorph bis Technoform; Arch+ Verlag, Aachen, May 2002

GEOMETRY
Evans, Robin; The Projective Cast – Architecture and its Three Geometries; MIT Press, Cambridge, MA, 1995
Gabriel, J. François, ed.; Beyond the Cube – The Architetcure of Space Frames & Polyhedra; John Wiley & Sons, New York, 1997
Henderson, David W. and Taimia, Daina; Experiencing Geometry – Euclidian and Non-Euclidian; 3rd edition; Pearson-Prentice Hall, Upper Saddle River, NJ, 2005

MEMBRANES
Höller, Ralf; Form-findung – Architektonische Grundlagen für den Entwurf von mechanisch vorgespannten Membranen und Seilnetzen; Verlag Dr. Thomas Balister – Architektonas 1, Mähringen, 1999
Koch, Klaus-Michael; Bauen mit Membranen; Prestel, München, 2004

MATERIALS
Addington, Michelle and Schodek, Daniel; Smart Materials and Technologies; Elsevier-Architectural Press, Oxford, 2005
Ball, Philip; Made to Measure – New Materials for the 21st Century; Princeton University Press, Princeton, NJ, 1997
Beylerian, George M. and Dent, Andrew; Material Connection, Thames & Hudson, London, 2005
Stattmann, Nicola; Ultra Light – Super Strong, Edition Form Birkhäuser, Basel, 2003
Arch+ vol. 172 – Material; Aachen, December 2004

MORPHOLOGY AND MORPHOGENESIS

Aubin, Jean-Pierre; Mutational and Morphological Analysis – Tools for Shape Evolution and Morphological Analysis; Birkhäuser, Boston, Basel, Berlin, 1999
Chaplain, M. A. J., Singh, G. D. and McLachlan, J. C., eds.; On Growth and Form – Spatio-temporal Pattern Formation in Biology; Wiley Series in Mathematical and Computational Biology, John Wiley & Sons, Chichester, 1999
Goethe, Johann Wolfgang; Schriften zur Morphologie; Goethe Sämtliche Werke, Deutscher Klassiker Verlag, Frankfurt am Main, 1987
Hensel, Michael, Menges, Achim and Weinstock, Michael; Techniques and Technologies in Morphogenetic Design; AD Wiley, London, 2006
Jean, Roger V.; Phyllotaxis – A Systemic Study in Plant Morphogenesis; Cambridge University Press; Cambridge, 1994
Thom, Rene; Structural Stability and Morphogenesis; Addison-Wesley, Redwood City, CA, 1989
Thompson, D'Arcy Wentworth; On Growth and Form; Cambridge University Press, Cambridge, 1942

NATURAL PATTERN / NATURAL STRUCTURES
Ball, Philip; The Self-made Tapestry – Pattern Formation in Nature; Oxford University Press; Oxford, 1999
Hildebrandt, Stefan and Tromba, Anthony; The Parsimonious Universe – Shape and Form in the Natural World; Springer, New York, 1996
Jenny, Hans; Cymatics – A Study of Wave Phenomena and Vibration; Macromedia Publ., Newmarket NH USA, 2001
Stewart, Ian; What Shape is a Snowflake?; Weidenfeld & Nicolson, London, 2001
SFB 230 Natural Structures – Principles, Strategies and Models in Architecture and Nature parts 1–3; Sonderforschungsbereich 230 Natürliche Konstruktionen vols. 6–7; Stuttgart, 1991–92

PNEUMATICS
IL 15 Air Hall Handbook; Drüsedau, Heide and Otto, Frei, eds.; Institute for Lightweight Structures, Stuttgart, 1983
IL 18 Forming Bubbles; Bach, Klaus; Burkhardt, Berthold and Otto, Frei, eds.; Institute for Lightweight Structures, Stuttgart, 1988
IL 19 Growing and Dividing Pneus; Cornelius Thywissen, ed.; Institute for Lightweight Structures, Stuttgart, 1979
IL 25 Pneu and Bone; Otto, Frei, ed.; Institute for Lightweight Structures, Stuttgart, 1995

SPATIAL STRATEGIES
Evans, Robin; Figures, Doors and Passages; in Translations from Drawings to Buildings and other Essays; AA Documents 2, Architectural Association, London, 1997
Kipnis, Jeffrey; Towards a New Architecture; in Folding in Architecture; AD, London, 1993
Risselada, Max, Ed.; Raumplan versus Plan Libre; Delft University Press, Delft, 1991
Schroer, Markus; Räume, Orte, Grenzen – Auf dem Weg zu einer Soziologie des Raumes; Suhrkamp, Frankfurt am Main, 2006
Sloterdijk, Peter; Sphären I Blasen; Sphären II Globen; Sphären III Schäume; Suhrkamp, Frankfurt am Main, 2004
Sloterdijk, Peter; Atmospheric Politics; in Making Things Public – Atmospheres of Democracy; Latour, Bruno and Weibel, Peter, eds.; MIT Press, Cambridge, Mass, 2005
Virilio, Paul and Parent, Claude; Architecture Principe – 1966 and 1996; Les Éditions de L'Imprimeur, Besançon, 1997

STRUCTURES
Anderson, Stanford, ed.; Eladio Dieste – Innovation in Structural Art; Princeton Architectural Press, New York, 2004
Beukers, Adriaan and van Hinte, ed; Lightness; 010 Publishers, Rotterdam, 1999
Engel, Heino; Structure Systems; 2nd Edition; Verlag Gerd Hatje; Ostfildern-Ruit, 1999
Mann, Walther; Statik und Festigkeitslehre; B.G. Teubner Verlag, Stuttgart, 1986
Schlaich, Jörg and Bergermann, Rudolf; Leicht Weit – Light Structures; Prestel, München, Berlin, London, New York, and DAM - Deutsches Architektur Museum, Frankfurt, 2003

TOPOLOGY
Alexandroff, Paul; Elementary Concepts of Topology; Dover Publications, New York, 1961
Goodman, Sue E.; Beginning Topology; The Brooks / Cole Series in Advanced Mathematics, Thomson – Brooks / Cole, Belmont, CA, 2005
Vassiliev, V. A.; Introduction to Topology; AMS American Mathematical Society, Providence, RI, 2001

EDITORS

MICHAEL U. HENSEL
Dipl.Ing Grad Dipl Des AA Architect AKNW
Partner OCEAN NORTH
Partner Emergence and Design Group
Board Member BIONIS Management Committee
Director Emergent Technologies and Design, Architectural Association School of Architecture, London
Unit Master Diploma Unit 4, Architectural Association School of Architecture, London
Architectural Association School of Architecture

Michael U. Hensel is an architect, urban designer, researcher and writer. He is a partner in OCEAN NORTH and the Emergence and Design Group, as well as a board member of the BIONIS - the Biomimetics Network for Industrial Sustainability - management committee.

Michael Hensel has held visiting professorships, taught, lectured, exhibited and published in Europe, the Americas, and the Middle and Far East and teaches at the AA, where he is director of the Emergent Technologies and Design Master Program and Unit Master of Diploma Unit 4. In 2004 he received the tutor prize of the Royal Institute of Architects.

His research interests include a synthetic life approach to architecture, a biological paradigm for architectural design and sustainability of the built environment, based on differentiated and multiple-performative material systems, spatial arrangements, and social formations, as well as contributing to a critical discourse on politics of space. Forthcoming publications include Morpho-Ecologies with Achim Menges, AA Publications 2006. He will be on the Editorial Board of the Journal of Biomimetic Engineering (Elsevier Science Press) commencing from 2007.

PROFESSOR ACHIM MENGES
AA Dipl (Hons) RIBA II
Partner OCEAN NORTH
Partner Emergence and Design Group
Studio Master Emergent Technologies and Design, Architectural Association School of Architecture, London
Unit Master Diploma Unit 4, Architectural Association School of Architecture, London
Professor for Form Generation and Materialization, University of Art and Design HfG Offenbach, Germany

Achim Menges is an architect and partner in OCEAN NORTH and the Emergence and Design Group. He studied at the Technical University Darmstadt and graduated from the Architectural Association with Honours. He has taught at the AA since 2002 and is currently Unit Master of Diploma Unit 4 and Studio Master of the Emergent Technologies and Design Master Program. He has also been a visiting professor at Rice University School of Architecture, Houston. Since 2005 he is Professor for Form Generation and Materialization at the HfG Offenbach University for Art and Design in Germany.

Achim Menges research focuses on the development of integral design processes at the intersection of evolutionary computation, parametric design, biomimetic engineering and computer aided manufacturing that enable a highly articulated, performative built environment. His research projects have been published and exhibited in Europe, Asia and the United States. Achim Menges received the FEIDAD (Far Eastern International Digital Architectural Design) Outstanding Design Award in 2002, the FEIDAD Design Merit Award in 2003, the Archiprix International Award 2003, RIBA Tutor Price 2004 and the International Bentley Educator of the Year Award 2005.

For further information see:
www.achimmenges.net

The EMERGENCE AND DESIGN GROUP was formed in 2002 as a multi-disciplinary design and research practice based in London. The group undertakes design and research that combines architecture, industrial design, Biomimetic engineering, digital morphogenesis, as well as advanced CAD/CAE/CAM and explores design approaches based on evolutionary design, self-organisation and emergence. Michael Hensel, Achim Menges, Nikolaos Stathopoulos and Michael Weinstock lead the group, which collaborates extensively with Buro Happold in London, and the Centre of Biomimetic Engineering at the University of Reading. The group initiated the Emergence and Design Network that brings together eminent experts and researchers of the disciplines that are related or adjacent to the groups research activities. Recent publications include Emergence – Morphogenetic Design Strategies, AD Wiley, 2004 and Techniques and Technologies in Morphogenetic Design, AD Wiley, 2006.

For further information see:
www.emergence-and-design.org

OCEAN NORTH is an experimental and multidisciplinary design collective which undertakes design research, projects and consultancy in the intersection between urban design, architecture, industrial design and cultural production. Michael Hensel, Achim Menges and Birger Sevaldson organise the think-tank. OCEAN NORTH's work has been widely published and exhibited in Europe, Asia and the Americas. Recent projects include the World Center for Human Affairs, exhibited in the 'A New World Trade Center exhibition at the Max Protetch Gallery in New York, the Venice Architectural Biennale in 2002 and the 'Blobjects' exhibition at San Jose Museum of Art in 2005, as well as the Jyväskylä Music and Art Center, exhibited at the Venice Architectural Biennale in 2004.

For further information see:
www.ocean-north.net

GRAPHIC DESIGN / LAYOUT

ALEKSANDRA JAESCHKE
AA Dipl RIBA II BA Visual Communications

Aleksandra Jaeschke is an architect and graphic designer. Born in Poland, she graduated from the Architectural Association in London.
She is partner in AION, an architectural studio based in Italy. The work of AION focuses on the material organization of the living, understanding buildings as the emergence of a stable condition from instability of materials involved in the design process: matter, technique, function and organization, made malleable throughout the process, become fluctuant materials that, through negotiation, reach a solid state in the singularity of each project.

For further information see:
www.a-i-o-n.com

AUTHORS

SIMON BEAMES
Director YOUMEHESHE
Technical Studies Lecturer and Tutor
Architectural Association School of Architecture

Simon is a founder member of YOUMEHESHE, an architectural practice created to design built environments that aim to improve the lives of people who use them.

Simon graduated from the Bartlett School of Architecture, cut his teeth at Foster Associates then was a senior associate at Grimshaw Architects. He teaches technical studies at the Architectural Association, is a CABE Enabler focused on Kindergarten projects and works as Architect for the Non Government Organisation, Children-on-the-edge.

He has been involved at the inception of several major projects across the world including Chek Lap Kok airport Hong Kong, the Reichstag Berlin, The American Air Museum Duxford; lead the design team for Battersea Power Station London and currently leads the design for the conservation of Cutty Sark Greenwich. For Children-on-the-Edge he has completed several exemplar social projects including the Haluacesti Orphanage, Romania, conversion into Family Units and the Cabra Village School Kosova. He is currently researching the design of a 'child friendly Space' strategy for application in disaster relief.

PROFESSOR MARK BURRY
Professor of Innovation (Spatial Information Architecture) at RMIT University, Melbourne, Australia
Consultant Architect to the Temple Sagrada Família, Barcelona, Spain
Visiting Professor at Liverpool University, UK
Honorary Professor of Architecture at Deakin University, Geelong, Australia
Professorial Research Fellow, Victoria University Wellington, New Zealand
Member of the Advisory Board of Gehry Technologies, Los Angeles, USA
Member of Australian Research Council College of Experts
Member of Prime Minister's Science, Engineering and Innovation Working Party

Professor Mark Burry has published internationally on two main themes: the life and work of the architect Antoni Gaudí in Barcelona, and putting theory into practice with regard to 'challenging' architecture; he has also published widely on broader issues of design, construction and the use of computers in design theory and practice. As Consultant Architect to the Temple Sagrada Família since 1979, Mark Burry has been a key member within the small team, untangling the mysteries of Gaudí's compositional strategies for the Sagrada Família, especially those coming from his later years, the implications of which are only now becoming fully apparent as they are resolved for building purposes. On February 18 2004, in recognition of his contribution to this project, Professor Burry was given the prestigious award ... 'Diploma I la insignia a l'acadèmic correspondent' and the title Senyor II. Lustre by la Reial Acadèmia Catalana de Belles Arts de Sant Jordi.

Professor Burry is director of RMIT's state-of-the-art Spatial Information Architecture Laboratory, which has been established as a holistic interdisciplinary research environment dedicated to almost all aspects of contemporary design activity. The laboratory focuses on collocated design research and undergraduate and postgraduate teaching with associated advanced computer applications and the rapid prototyping of ideas. The laboratory has a design-practice emphasis and acts as a creative think-tank accessible to both local and international practices, including ARUP in Melbourne and London, dECOi in Paris and Gehry Partners in Los Angeles.

For further information see:
www.sial.rmit.edu.au/

LUDO GROOTEMAN
Blue Architects

Ludo Grooteman is partner of Blue Architects, an architectural firm based in Amsterdam and Zürich. Blue Architects has 15 employees and a wide variety of projects throughout the Netherlands and Switzerland. The firm focuses on building design, but also regularly undertakes urban projects and interiors. He is also program director of the architectural masters program at the Rotterdam Academy of Architecture and Urban Design. He has taught, lectured or has been guest professor at various institutions, amongst which the AA in London, UCLA in Los Angeles and the TU in Vienna.

For further information see:
www.bluearchitects.com

PROFESSOR CHRISTOPHER HIGHT
Rice School of Architecture

Christopher Hight is an assistant professor at the Rice School of Architecture, where he is pursuing design research on emerging nexus of electronic infrastructures and biopolicital landscapes. The editor of the Architecture at Rice publication series, he obtained a masters degree from the Architectural Association's Histories and Theories Program as a Fulbright Scholar and a Ph.D. from the London Consortium at the University of London. Previously he taught in the Architectural Association's Design Research Laboratory, and has worked for the Renzo Piano Building Workshop. He is currently writing a book (Routledge) on the cybernetics, form and the subject of post-world war two architectural design. He has published and lectured internationally, including China, Europe, the Middle East, Australia and the United States, is the organizer of the symposium and edited book, Modulations, and the coeditor with Chris Perry of the forthcoming AD on collective design knowledge practices.

For further information see:
http://mutlitude.rice.edu:8668

SEAN LALLY
Principle - WEATHERS
Caudill Visiting Assistant Professor
Rice School of Architecture

Sean Lally founded the office WEATHERS in 2004 with a focus of exploring the potentials and implications of our spatial and organizational constructs as architects continue to engage advancements in the tools and techniques available today. He received is Bachelors degree in Landscape Architecture from the University of Massachusetts in 1996. After receiving his Masters in Architecture from the University of California in Los Angeles he was appointed the Wortham Fellow at the Rice School of Architecture before becoming the Caudill Visiting Assistant Professor in 2005.

Recent projects including the 'S.I.V. House' 2004, 'SIM Residence' 2004 and 'Amplification' 2006, have been featured in exhibitions including 'SOFTSPACE' at Rice University and the University of Minnesota., Past / Present / Future Exhibition in Los Angeles, the 2003 Possible Futures Exhibition for the Bienal Miami and the Gen(h)ome Project at the MAK Center Los Angeles 2006. Sean is also the co-editor on the forthcoming book SOFTSPACE (Taylor & Francis) Sept 2006.

For further information see:
www.w-e-a-t-h-e-r-s.com

THEO LORENZ
AA Unit Master Diploma Unit 14/ Foundation
T2 spatialwork ltd

Theo Lorenz is an Architect, media and interactive Designer. He has spent several years practising Architecture in London, mostly in his own office as the director of T2 spatialwork ltd. and between 2000 and 2003 at Grimshaw Architects. He is also co-founder of n-o-m-a-d (network of mediated architectural design) and spatialworknet.

Theo Lorenz is teaching at the Architectural Association School of Architecture in London since 2000. He taught for two years in the Intermediate school and is since 2002 Unit Master in the Foundation Course and the Diploma School. His work and teaching focuses on the effect of transformative Networks on Architecture.

For further information see:
www.t-2.org
www.spatialwork.net
www.n-o-m-a-d.org
www.aaschool.ac.uk/dip14

WOLF MANGELSDORF
Buro Happold

Wolf Mangelsdorf was born and grew up in Germany near Würzburg. He studied Architecture and Civil Engineering at Karlsruhe University, where he also worked for an architectural practice after graduation.

After a research stay at Kyoto University he moved to Britain in 1997 and became a design engineer at Anthony Hunt Associates working in their Cirencester and London offices.

Since 2002 he has been with Buro Happold in London where he is an Associate Director and project leader for a number of projects including the Battersea Powerstation and the Museum of Transport in Glasgow.

For the past five years he has been lecturer and tutor for technical studies in the Diploma School as well as for Emergent Technologies at the Architectural Association in London.

For further information see:
www.burohappold.com

EVA SCHEFFLER
Scheffler + Partner

Eva Scheffler is an architect registered in Germany and the UK. She studied at the Technical University of Darmstadt, Germany and graduated from the Architectural Association, where she also taught in the Summer School programme. After graduating in 2002 Eva Scheffler worked for Nicholas Grimshaw & Partners architects on a number of renowned projects such as the Battersea Power Station Redevelopment Project and the Cutty Sark Enclosure in London. In 2005 she joined Scheffler + Partner Architects in Frankfurt, Germany where she is currently designing a sustainable housing development with more than 50 apartments in the city of Frankfurt.

For further information see:
www.scheffler-partner.de

BRETT STEELE
AA Director

Brett Steele is director of the Architectural Association School of Architecture. His bio, syllabuses, photos and writings are online at www.resarch.net.

PETER TRUMMER
Unit Master and PhD candidate at the Berlage Institute Rotterdam

Peter Trummer is an architect and researcher. Since 2004 he is Unit Master of the Associative Design research program a postgraduate laboratory for architecture at the Berlage Institute in Rotterdam. In the beginning of this year he became a PhD candidate at the institute. The PhD focuses on design research and the topic of population thinking in architecture.

He was born in Graz, Austria and obtained his University Diploma at the Technical University of Graz in 1994. In 1995 he moved to Amsterdam, where he finished his postgraduate studies at the Berlage institute in 1997. He worked as project architect at UN-Studio and co-founded Offshore Architects in 2001. Since 2004 he has is own practice. In 2005 he was guest professor at the Academy in Nürnberg, Germany. He lectures, teaches and publishes internationally, including the Berlage Institute and Academy of Architecture in Rotterdam, AA in London and Rice University in Houston.

For further information:
www.berlage-institute.nl

PROFESSOR JULIAN VINCENT
Professor of Biomimetics
Department of Mechanical Engineering
University of Bath

In October 2000, Julian Vincent took the newly-created Chair in Biomimetics in the Department of Mechanical Engineering. His MA (zoology) was from Cambridge; his PhD (insect hormones) and DSc (insect cuticle) were from Sheffield. He spent most of his research career in the Zoology Department at the University of Reading, studying the mechanical design of organisms and working out ways in which aspects of the design can be used in technology. He has published over 250 papers, articles and books and has been invited to give conference lectures (mostly plenary) and research seminars around the World. His interests are very wide, covering aspects of mechanical design of plants and animals, complex fracture mechanics, texture of food, design of composite materials, use of natural materials in technology, advanced textiles, deployable structures in architecture and robotics, smart systems and structures. In 1990 he won the Prince of Wales Environmental Innovation Award. In 1997 he gave the Trueman Wood lecture at the RSA.

His remit in the University of Bath is to introduce concepts from biology into engineering and design, thus making the adaptive design of organisms available to advanced engineering design and control. In pursuit of this he is expanding a Russian system for inventive problem solving (TRIZ) to make biological design available to engineers, and wants to extend this general approach to all human endeavours

He is a keen musician, having played the banjo, solo, around the UK (including the Purcell Room on London's South Bank), Ireland, Germany and The Netherlands, on BBC 2 "Horizon" and Radios 4 and 3. During his days of penury he taught himself practical engineering by stripping and rebuilding old cars and motorcycles, sometimes at the side of the road. He only once failed to get home.

For further information see:
www.bath.ac.uk/expertise/showperson.php?username=ensjfvv
www.extra.rdg.ac.uk/eng/BIONIS/

MICHAEL WEINSTOCK
Director Emergent Technologies and Design
Master of Technical Studies
Architectural Association School of Architecture

Michael Weinstock is an Architect. Born in Germany, lived as a child in the Far East and then West Africa, and attended an English public school. Ran away to sea at age 17 after reading Conrad. Years at sea in traditional sailing ships, with shipyard and shipbuilding experience. Studied Architecture at the Architectural Association and has taught at the AA School of Architecture since 1989 as Unit Master and Master of Technical Studies. Conducted Unit programs in Intermediate and Diploma School focused on urban space and architectural design in London, Manchester, Barcelona, Tokyo and Manhattan. He is co-founder and Co- director of the Emergent Technologies and Design Masters program, with Michael Hensel. He has been Visiting Professor to the Genetic Architecture graduate research programme at ESARQ, Barcelona since 2004, is currently lecturing at Yale School of Architecture on Evolutionary Design, and has published widely. Michael Weinstock's research interests lie in exploring the convergence of Biomimetic Engineering, Emergence and Material Sciences. The potential of the convergence for the materialization of intelligent materials, structures, buildings and ultimately, the organization of Cities, provides the motivation and suggests the long term goal.

For further information see:
www.emergence-and-design.org
www.aaschool.ac.uk/et